PHILOSOPHY OF RELIGION

PHILOSOPHY OF

edited by

GEORGE L. ABERNETHY

and

THOMAS A. LANGFORD

RELIGION A BOOK OF READINGS

New York — The Macmillan Company

First Printing

Library of Congress catalog card number 62-7056

The Macmillan Company, New York
Brett-Macmillan Ltd., Galt, Ontario

Printed in the United States of America

for
Helen
and
Ann Marie

Preface

We believe the serious study and discussion of philosophical issues in religion are on the rise. Among scholars in the fields of philosophy and theology there is more interest in the work being done in each other's discipline and more of an effort to take seriously each other's interests than at any time for several decades. Philosophers and theologians are beginning to talk to each other, even if hesitantly and intermittently. Among students also there appears to be increased interest, and even so superficial a criterion as the phenomenal sale in college communities of paperbacks in the fields of philosophy and religion seems to support this contention. Philosophy of religion should be the bridge discipline which facilitates this kind of communication. We hope our book of readings will sustain such a dialogue.

The contemporary focus of our volume is deliberate. We believe that much recent work in this area is significant and should be better known. The distinctive contributions and claims of both contemporary theologians and philosophers have moved far beyond the positions of the early nineteen hundreds. For instance, in Britain, philosophers trained in linguistic analysis have been seriously turning to the problems of religious language. Although it is still too early to predict the full significance of that development, thoughtful students should be made aware of this growing field. In Europe and America existentialism has become prominent. We believe that something of this orientation should also be presented to the student.

At the same time, we have included important historical and traditional material. These selections furnish indispensable background for the new developments and deserve to be carefully studied. However, we have omitted readings from Plato and Aristotle, in spite of their significant contributions to the origins of the philosophy of religion, because their writings are already easily obtainable. Rather we have included source material less likely to be found in the average college library or, if found, not available in multiple copies. The lists of suggested readings at the end of each section of our book include references to works of these two philosophers and of other writers whom we acknowledge are important. These lists should, therefore, be regarded as integral to each section and not merely adventitious.

Since philosophy of religion is a serious discipline that demands careful, purposeful study, students of the subject should be required to do systematic and rigorous work. Accordingly, we have avoided selections that "write down" to students and have attempted instead to provide selections with sufficient vitality to draw students into the lively experience of philosophizing. Further, we have chosen deliberately to confine the book to the western tradition of philosophy and theology. The soundness of a course in philosophy of religion depends in part upon a careful delimitation of objectives and materials. In addition, most of our American students come with some experience, however minimal, of Judaism and Christianity. A sound liberal education, it seems to us, ought to make them aware of the basic philosophical issues and positions prominent in that heritage.

Some teachers have suggested we include materials from eastern religions. We agree that materials from the eastern religious and philosophical tradition are interesting and unquestionably significant, but to evaluate them solely in western terms is to falsify them. The eastern tradition, too, deserves systematic and rigorous study if it is to be understood, and six or seven selections from that tradition included in our book would not have served to represent it adequately. The teacher who is competent to interpret the eastern literature and who is fortunate enough to have students with prior study of world religions will find the necessary materials already collected for him. Professor William Theodore de Bary and his associates have brilliantly assembled the central materials in a three volume *Introduction to Oriental Civilizations: Sources of Indian Tradition, Sources of the Japanese Tradition, Sources of Chinese Tradition.* S. Radhakrishnan and C. A. Moore have edited a useful book, *A Sourcebook in Indian Philosophy.* Heinrich R. Zimmer's *Philosophies of India,* a first rate work of scholarship, is available in paperback. Among older works Paul Deussen's *The Philosophy of the Vedanta* and *The Philosophy of the Upanishads* contain useful selections and commentary. In the Mentor series of paperbacks, the instructor will find Professor E. A. Burtt's anthology *The Teachings of the Compassionate Buddha,* as well as the Bhagavad Gita and the Upanishads (without commentary) in fresh translation. Students of the philosophy of religion who have first become familiar with their own tradition will be in a better position to study these important eastern materials.

Our object is to provide a useful collection of sources, without claim that we have been able to include all that a student should read in a semester. Individual teachers have different orientations and will prefer different materials. Although we too have our own perspectives, we have tried to be fair to various points of view and thus to philosophy of religion as a whole. If we have succeeded in this and in assembling writings that provoke the thought and interest of students, we shall be pleased.

This book has brought together a person from philosophy and one from theology in an effort of common concern. The experience has proven to be stimulating and rewarding. We covet such interdisciplinary opportunity for others. Our appreciation should be expressed to more people than we can name. We especially acknowledge the generous cooperation of many authors and publishers without which this volume would not have been possible. Many friends and colleagues have made suggestions to us; for their criticisms and encouragement we are indebted. The manuscript has been read, in whole or in part, by Professor Horace L. Friess of Columbia University, Professor John A. Hutchison of Claremont Graduate School, Professor Michael Wyschogrod of Hunter College, Mr. J. P. Fell, Professor Henry LeRoy Finch of Sarah Lawrence College and Professor William A. Gerhard of Brooklyn College. We are grateful for their searching criticism and friendly advice. Finally a word of thanks to Messrs. Roger Howley and John Dennis Moore, of Macmillan, for their competent help in the completion of this book.

Table of Contents

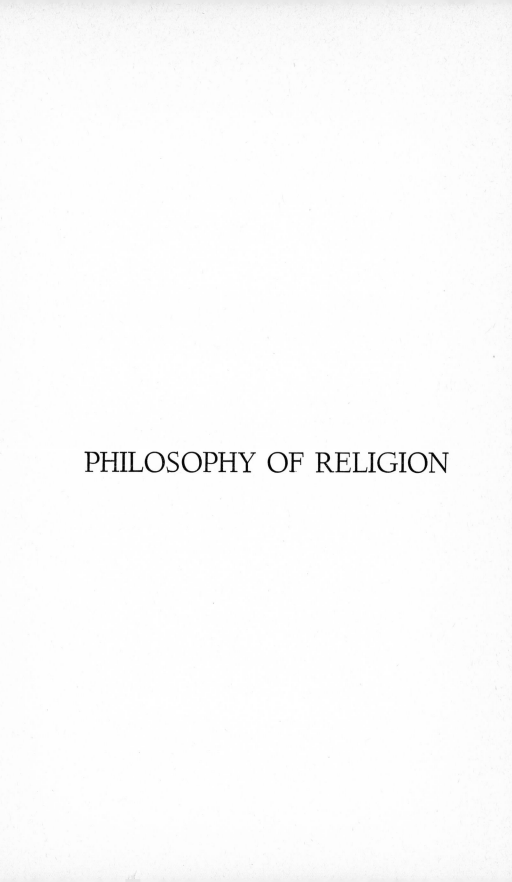

PHILOSOPHY OF RELIGION

I. Introduction

THE NATURE OF RELIGION

Religion is a pervasive and almost universal phenomenon in human societies. Yet one of the striking facts about the word *religion* is that, although we use it without hesitation, we have great difficulty in telling others what we mean by it. The most casual analysis of definitions of religion will often reveal that the authors treat some significant aspect of religion as though it were the whole or offer a definition so general as to be of little help in distinguishing religion from other phenomena. The lack of agreement among students of religion as to the nature of the subject is an inevitable consequence of wide differences in intellectual orientation and basic assumptions. Perhaps the most common orientations are rooted in the assumption that religion has a truly objective referent or else that it is merely a subjective experience. Theories of religion, then, often involve the working out or modification of one of these assumptions, or the attempt to combine them.

It may be debated whether any one religion is completely unique or whether all religions are basically the same with only trivial differences. But it is obvious that different religions do attempt, to some extent, to give different answers to human questions. Definitions and theories of religion reflect these differences. The philosophy of religion is, among other things, an attempt to think critically and comprehensively about these religious beliefs and claims. Clarity of statements, consistency of claims, adequacy of evidence, validity of argument and comprehensiveness of generalization are matters of primary concern for the philosophy of religion as it seeks to examine the definitions and theories of religion.

The selections which follow bring together representative thought from major western traditions on the understanding of the nature of religion. The selections form a series of contrasts ranging from mysticism, which claims direct intuitive awareness of ultimate reality and therefore considers itself supra-rational, to rationalism which includes the attempt to define

1

religion within the limits of reason alone. Definitions will be found which view religion primarily in terms of supra-naturalism, that is, in terms of a power beyond the visible, observable world, and those which eschew all supra-natural reference. There are also contrasts between views of religion as essentially a personal or subjective reality and of religion as primarily a social concern.

These selections are further representative of writers from different academic disciplines: e.g. philosophy, theology, psychoanalysis and sociology. While the types of interpretations included are not exhaustive, they should be adequate to provide significant background for the discussion of the nature of religion. The writings are arranged in what is generally a chronological order, but this should not be taken to imply that the positions they present are limited in their influence to specific historical eras; many of them have had lively champions in several centuries.

The first selection, from the writings of Plotinus, represents the mystical tradition. Plotinus is one of the major philosophical figures of the first centuries of the Christian era and his type of mystical religious experience has influenced the thinking of many subsequent thinkers. Standing in sharp contrast to Plotinus is Immanuel Kant. Kant's understanding of religion is cast against the background of its relation to ethics. Since the raising of the question of the relationship between ethics and religion represents another of the perennial attempts to understand religion, this selection constitutes an introduction to an important area of study.

Friedrich Schleiermacher and Søren Kierkegaard represent two different positions from within the Christian tradition. Schleiermacher found God and religion at the deepest level of every man's experience, in the natural and universal "feeling of absolute dependence." Kierkegaard, on the other hand, felt that every man in his natural experience is alien to God and separated from Him by an infinite gulf, so that every religion arising out of man's experience is necessarily false. True religion, he claims, comes into being only when the infinite gulf is bridged by a revelation which is appropriated in "a leap of faith" that defies the experience of alienation and affirms the encounter with the true God as revealed in Jesus Christ. A contemporary of these men who represents a position which is opposed to Christianity is Ludwig Feuerbach. Feuerbach, like his contemporaries, is concerned with the subjective basis of religion. But, unlike them, he pushes his analysis to the point of questioning the reality of the object of religious faith. Feuerbach insists that the gods are only the product of human imagination and thereby he reduces the religious realm to man and man's inner life. The psychological analyses of religion by these men constitute a fundamental contribution in the long line of investigations in this field.

Both John Dewey and William James, American philosophers in the first decades of this century, attempt to enlarge the province of religion: Dewey by broadening the social inclusiveness of religion and James by broadening the dimensions of the individual self. Dewey argues for the reality of a religious attitude which he finds compatible with a naturalistic and humanistic view of life. In other words, Dewey denies that reality has a supranatural significance although he insists that there is a basis for a strong sense of obligation to one's fellowman in a rational assessment of life. In Dewey's thought interest in the social implications of religion is central. William James concludes his famous study, *The Varieties of Religious Experience*, with his own interpretation of religion as the "subconscious continuation of the conscious life." James is one of the important figures responsible for our century's developing interest in man's subconscious life. Because of this dimension of life, James claims that man knows himself to be continuous with a wider, subconscious self in terms of which he can find a religious meaning.

Erich Fromm, a contemporary psychoanalyst, looks at religion from the perspective of psychoanalytical theory. Fromm argues that in humane religion, which he espouses, "God is the image of man's higher self, a symbol of what man potentially is or ought to become." Thus the problem of religion is not the problem of God, but the problem of man. It is the unique nature of man's religious experience which Fromm wants to delineate and assess. W. T. Stace represents a modern philosophical mysticism. In distinction from positions such as that of Fromm, Stace understands religion as the desire to break completely away from existence and to get beyond existence "into that nothingness where the great light is." God remains a mystery, but a mystery in which man can find his true being. Milton Yinger, a contemporary American sociologist, begins his study not with an attempt to define what religion *is* but with the desire to find out what religion *does*. The focus of Yinger's selection is upon the concrete behavior of religious votaries. Therefore this reading employs empirical description as well as tentative generalization. Our last selection is from a Jewish thinker. Martin Buber in his article attempts to point out the major characteristics of Jewish piety and to indicate something of its significance for those who have this religious commitment.

A critical examination of each of these points of view will lead one to an awareness of the varieties of religious experience and will form a background against which comparative judgments can be made.

PLOTINUS

PLOTINUS (204-270) a Neo-Platonic philosopher, taught at Rome and became one of the germinal influences in Western mysticism. His book, *The Enneads*, contains his most important philosophical and religious writings.

The Enneads*

7. Therefore we must ascend again towards the Good, the desired of every Soul. Anyone that has seen This, knows what I intend when I say that it is beautiful. Even the desire of it is to be desired as a Good. To attain it is for those that will take the upward path, who will set all their forces towards it, who will divest themselves of all that we have put on in our descent: so, to those that approach the Holy Celebrations of the Mysteries, there are appointed purifications and the laying aside of the garments worn before, and the entry in nakedness—until, passing, on the upward way, all that is other than the God, each in the solitude of himself shall behold that solitary-dwelling Existence, the Apart, the Unmingled, the Pure, that from Which all things depend, for Which all look and live and act and know, the Source of Life and of Intellection and of Being.

And one that shall know this vision—with what passion of love shall he not be seized, with what pang of desire, what longing to be molten into one with This, what wondering delight! If he that has never seen this Being must hunger for It as for all his welfare, he that has known must love and reverence It as the very Beauty; he will be flooded with awe and gladness, stricken by a salutary terror; he loves with a veritable love, with sharp desire; all other loves than this he must despise, and disdain all that once seemed fair.

This, indeed, is the mood even of those who, having witnessed the manifestation of Gods or Supernals, can never again feel the old delight in the comeliness of material forms: what then are we to think of one that contemplates Absolute Beauty in Its essential integrity, no accumulation of flesh and matter, no dweller on earth or in the heavens—so perfect Its purity—

---

* From Plotinus, *The Enneads*, trans. Stephen McKenna, revised by B. S. Page, pp. 61-64. Copyright, 1956, by Faber and Faber. Used by permission of Faber and Faber, Ltd., and Pantheon Books, Inc.

far above all such things in that they are non-essential, composite, not primal but descending from This?

Beholding this Being—the Choragus of all Existence, the Self-Intent that ever gives forth and never takes—resting, rapt, in the vision and possession of so lofty a loveliness, growing to Its likeness, what Beauty can the Soul yet lack? For This, the Beauty supreme, the absolute, and the primal, fashions Its lovers to Beauty and makes them also worthy of love.

And for This, the sternest and the uttermost combat is set before the Souls; all our labour is for This, lest we be left without part in this noblest vision, which to attain is to be blessed in the blissful sight, which to fail of is to fail utterly.

For not he that has failed of the joy that is in colour or in visible forms, not he that has failed of power or of honours or of kingdom has failed, but only he that has failed of only This, for Whose winning he should renounce kingdoms and command over earth and ocean and sky, if only, spurning the world of sense from beneath his feet, and straining to This, he may see.

8. But what must we do? How lies the path? How come to vision of the inaccessible Beauty, dwelling as if in consecrated precincts, apart from the common ways where all may see, even the profane?

He that has the strength, let him arise and withdraw into himself, foregoing all that is known by the eyes, turning away for ever from the material beauty that once made his joy. When he perceives those shapes of grace that show in body, let him not pursue: he must know them for copies, vestiges, shadows, and hasten away towards That they tell of. For if anyone follow what is like a beautiful shape playing over water—is there not a myth telling in symbol of such a dupe, how he sank into the depths of the current and was swept away to nothingness? So too, one that is held by material beauty and will not break free shall be precipitated, not in body but in Soul, down to the dark depths loathed of the Intellective-Being, where, blind even in the Lower-World, he shall have commerce only with shadows, there as here.

"Let us flee then to the beloved Fatherland": this is the soundest counsel. But what is this flight? How are we to gain the open sea? For Odysseus is surely a parable to us when he commands the flight from the sorceries of Circe or Calypso—not content to linger for all the pleasure offered to his eyes and all the delight of sense filling his days.

The Fatherland to us is There whence we have come, and There is The Father.

What then is our course, what the manner of our flight? This is not a journey for the feet; the feet bring us only from land to land; nor need you think of coach or ship to carry you away; all this order of things you must set aside and refuse to see: you must close the eyes and call instead upon another vision which is to be waked within you, a vision, the birth-right of all, which few turn to use.

9. And this inner vision, what is its operation?

Newly awakened it is all too feeble to bear the ultimate splendour. Therefore the Soul must be trained—to the habit of remarking, first, all noble pursuits, then the works of beauty produced not by the labour of the arts but by the virtue of men known for their goodness: lastly, you must search the souls of those that have shaped these beautiful forms.

But how are you to see into a virtuous Soul and know its loveliness?

Withdraw into yourself and look. And if you do not find yourself beautiful yet, act as does the creator of a statue that is to be made beautiful: he cuts away here, he smoothes there, he makes this line lighter, this other purer, until a lovely face has grown upon his work. So do you also: cut away all that is excessive, straighten all that is crooked, bring light to all that is overcast, labour to make all one glow of beauty and never cease chiselling your statue, until there shall shine out on you from it the godlike splendour of virtue, until you shall see the perfect goodness surely established in the stainless shrine.

When you know that you have become this perfect work, when you are self-gathered in the purity of your being, nothing now remaining that can shatter that inner unity, nothing from without clinging to the authentic man, when you find yourself wholly true to your essential nature, wholly that only veritable Light which is not measured by space, not narrowed to any circumscribed form nor again diffused as a thing void of term, but ever unmeasurable as something greater than all measure and more than all quantity—when you perceive that you have grown to this, you are now become very vision: now call up all your confidence, strike forward yet a step—you need a guide no longer—strain, and see.

This is the only eye that sees the mighty Beauty. If the eye that adventures the vision be dimmed by vice, impure, or weak, and unable in its cowardly blenching to see the uttermost brightness, then it sees nothing even though another point to what lies plain to sight before it. To any vision must be brought an eye adapted to what is to be seen, and having some likeness to it. Never did eye see the sun unless it had first become sunlike, and never can the Soul have vision of the First Beauty unless itself be beautiful.

Therefore, first let each become godlike and each beautiful who cares to see God and Beauty. So, mounting, the Soul will come first to the Intellectual-Principle and survey all the beautiful Ideas in the Supreme and will avow that this is Beauty, that the Ideas are Beauty. For by their efficacy comes all Beauty else, by the offspring and essence of the Intellectual-Being. What is beyond the Intellectual-Principle we affirm to be the nature of Good radiating Beauty before it. So that, treating the Intellectual-Cosmos as one, the first is the Beautiful: if we make distinction there, the Realm of Ideas constitutes the Beauty of the Intellectual Sphere; and The Good, which lies beyond, is the Fountain at once and Principle of Beauty: the Primal Good and the Primal Beauty have the one dwelling-place and, thus, always, Beauty's seat is There.

IMMANUEL KANT

IMMANUEL KANT (1726-1806) was professor at Koenigsberg, Germany, and one of the great philosophers. His writings stimulated much subsequent discussion of theory of knowledge, metaphysics, ethics and religion. The most significant among his many works are *The Critique of Pure Reason* and *The Critique of Practical Reason.*

Religion Within the Limits of Reason Alone*

Concerning the Service of God in Religion in General

Religion is (subjectively regarded) the recognition of all duties as divine commands.[1] That religion in which I must know in advance that something

* From Immanuel Kant, *Religion Within the Limits of Reason Alone,* trans. T. M. Greene and H. H. Hudson, pp. 142-151. Copyright, 1934, by Open Court Publishing Company. Used by permission of the Open Court Publishing Company.

[1] By means of this definition many an erroneous interpretation of the concept of a religion in general is obviated. *First,* in religion, as regards the theoretical apprehension and avowal of belief, no assertorial knowledge is required (even of God's existence), since, with our lack of insight into supersensible objects, such avowal might well be dissembled; rather is it merely a *problematical* assumption (hypothesis) regarding the highest cause of things that is presupposed speculatively, yet with an eye to the object toward which our morally legislative reason bids us strive—an *assertorial* faith, practical and therefore free, and giving promise of the realization of this its ultimate aim. This faith needs merely *the idea of God,* to which all morally earnest (and therefore confident) endeavor for the good must inevitably lead; it need not presume that it can certify the objective reality of this idea through theoretical apprehension. Indeed, the *minimum* of knowledge (it is possible that there may be a God) must suffice, subjectively, for

is a divine command in order to recognize it as my duty, is the *revealed* religion (or the one standing in need of a revelation); in contrast, that religion in which I must first know that something is my duty before I can accept it as a divine injunction is the *natural* religion. He who interprets the natural religion alone as morally necessary, *i.e.*, as duty, can be called the *rationalist* (in matters of belief); if he denies the reality of all supernatural divine revelation he is called a *naturalist*; if he recognizes revelation, but asserts that to know and accept it as real is not a necessary requisite to religion, he could be named a *pure rationalist*; but if he holds that belief in it is necessary to universal religion, he could be named the pure *supernaturalist* in matters of faith.

The rationalist, by virtue of his very title, must of his own accord restrict himself within the limits of human insight. Hence he will never, as a naturalist, dogmatize, and will never contest either the inner possibility of revelation in general or the necessity of a revelation as a divine means for the introduction of true religion; for these matters no man can determine through reason. Hence the question at issue can concern only the reciprocal claims of the pure rationalist and the supernaturalist in matters of faith, namely, what the one or the other holds as necessary and sufficient, or as merely incidental, to the unique true religion.

When religion is classified not with reference to its first origin and its inner possibility (here it is divided into natural and revealed religion) but with respect to its characteristics which makes it *capable of being shared widely with others*, it can be of two kinds: either the *natural* religion, of which (once it has arisen) everyone can be convinced through his own

---

whatever can be made the duty of every man. *Second,* this definition of a religion in general obviates the erroneous representation of religion as an aggregate of *special* duties having reference directly to God; thus it prevents our taking on (as men are otherwise very much inclined to do) *courtly obligations* over and above the ethico-civil duties of humanity (of man to man) and our seeking, perchance, even to make good the deficiency of the latter by means of the former. There are no special duties to God in a universal religion, for God can receive nothing from us; we cannot act for Him, nor yet upon Him. To wish to transform a guilty awe of Him into a duty of the sort described is to forget that awe is not a special act of religion but rather the religious temper in all our actions done in conformity with duty. And when it is said: "We ought to obey God rather than men," † this means only that when statutory commands, regarding which men can be legislators and judges, come into conflict with duties which reason prescribes unconditionally, concerning whose observance or transgression God alone can be the judge, the former must yield precedence to the latter. But were we willing to regard the statutory commands, which are given out by a church as coming from God, as constituting that wherein God must be obeyed more than man, such a principle might easily become the war-cry, often heard, of hypocritical and ambitious clerics in revolt against their civil superiors. For that which is permissible, *i.e.*, which the civil authorities command, is *certainly* duty; but whether something which is indeed permissible in itself, but cognizable by us only through divine revelation, is really commanded by God—that is (at least for the most part) highly uncertain.

  † *Cf.* Acts V, 29.

reason, or a *learned* religion, of which one can convince others only through the agency of learning (in and through which they must be guided). This distinction is very important: for no inference regarding a religion's qualification or disqualification to be the universal religion of mankind can be drawn merely from its origin, whereas such an inference is possible from its capacity or incapacity for general dissemination, and it is this capacity which constitutes the essential character of that religion which ought to be binding upon every man.

Such a religion, accordingly, can be *natural*, and at the same time *revealed*, when it is so constituted that men *could and ought to have discovered it* of themselves merely through the use of their reason, although they *would* not have come upon it so early, or over so wide an area, as is required. Hence a revelation thereof at a given time and in a given place might well be wise and very advantageous to the human race, in that, when once the religion thus introduced is here, and has been made known publicly, everyone can henceforth by himself and with his own reason convince himself of its truth. In this event the religion is *objectively* a natural religion, though *subjectively* one that has been revealed; hence it is really entitled to the former name. For, indeed, the occurrence of such a supernatural revelation might subsequently be entirely forgotten without the slightest loss to that religion either of comprehensibility, or of certainty, or of power over human hearts. It is different with that religion which, on account of its inner nature, can be regarded only as revealed. Were it not preserved in a completely secure tradition or in holy books, as records, it would disappear from the world, and there must needs transpire a supernatural revelation, either publicly repeated from time to time or else enduring continuously within each individual, for without it the spread and propagation of such a faith would be impossible.

Yet in part at least every religion, even if revealed, must contain certain principles of the natural religion. For only through reason can thought add revelation to the concept of a *religion*, since this very concept, as though deduced from an obligation to the will of a *moral* legislator, is a pure concept of reason. Therefore we shall be able to look upon even a revealed religion on the one hand as a *natural*, on the other as a *learned* religion, and thus to test it and decide what and how much has come to it from one or the other source.

If we intend to talk about a revealed religion (at least one so regarded) we cannot do so without selecting some specimen or other from history, for we must devise instances as examples in order to be intelligible, and unless we take these from history their possibility might be disputed. We cannot do better than to adopt, as the medium for the elucidation of our idea of revealed religion in general, some book or other which contains such examples, especially one which is closely interwoven with doctrines that are ethical and consequently related to reason. We can then examine it, as one of a variety of books which deal with religion and virtue on the credit of a revelation, thus exemplifying the procedure, useful in itself, of searching out whatever in it may be for us a pure and therefore a universal religion of reason. Yet we do not wish thereby to encroach upon the business of those to whom is entrusted the exegesis of this book, regarded as the summary of positive doctrines of revelation, or to contest their interpretation based upon scholarship. Rather is it advantageous to scholarship, since scholars and philosophers aim at one and the same goal, to wit, the morally good, to bring scholarship, through its own rational principles, to the very point which it already expects to reach by another road. Here the New Testament, considered as the source of the Christian doctrine, can be the book chosen. In accordance with our intention we shall now offer our demonstration in two sections, first, the Christian religion as a natural religion, and, second, as a learned religion, with reference to its content and to the principles which are found in it.

The Christian Religion as a Natural Religion

Natural religion, as morality (in its relation to the freedom of the agent) united with the concept of that which can make actual its final end (with the concept of God as moral Creator of the world), and referred to a continuance of man which is suited to this end in its completeness (to immortality), is a pure practical idea of reason which, despite its inexhaustible fruitfulness, presupposes so very little capacity for theoretical reason that one can convince every man of it sufficiently for practical purposes and can at least require of all men as a duty that which is its effect. This religion possesses the prime essential of the true church, namely, the qualification for unversality, so far as one understands by that a validity for everyone (*universitas vel omnitudo distributiva*), i.e. universal unanimity. To spread it, in this sense, as a world religion, and to maintain it, there is needed, no doubt, a body of servants (*ministerium*) of the invisible church, but not officials (*officiales*), in other words, teachers but not dignitaries, because in the rational religion of every individual there does not yet exist a church as a universal *union* (*omnitudo collectiva*), nor is this really contemplated in the above idea.

Yet such unanimity could not be maintained of itself and hence could not, unless it became a visible church, be propagated in its universality;

rather is this possible only when a collective unanimity, in other words a union of believers in a (visible) church under the principles of a pure religion of reason, is added; though this church does not automatically arise out of that unanimity nor, indeed, were it already established, would it be brought by its free adherents (as were shown above) to a permanent status as a *community* of the faithful (because in such a religion none of those who has seen the light believes himself to require, for his religious sentiments, fellowship with others). Therefore it follows that unless there are added to the natural laws, apprehensible through unassisted reason, certain statutory ordinances attended by legislative prestige (authority), that will still be lacking which constitutes a special duty of men, and a means to their highest end, namely, their enduring union into a universal visible church; and the authority mentioned above, in order to be a founder of such a church, presupposes a realm of fact [2] and not merely the pure concepts of reason.

Let us suppose there was a teacher of whom an historical record (or, at least, a widespread belief which is not basically disputable) reports that he was the first to expound publicly a pure and searching religion, comprehensible to the whole world (and thus natural). His teachings, as preserved to us, we can in this case test for ourselves. Suppose that all he did was done even in the face of a dominant ecclesiastical faith which was onerous and not conducive to moral ends (a faith whose perfunctory worship can serve as a type of all the other faiths, at bottom merely statutory, which were current in the world at the time). Suppose, further, we find that he had made this universal religion of reason the highest and indispensable condition of every religious faith whatsoever, and then had added to it certain statutes which provided forms and observances designed to serve as means of bringing into existence a church founded upon those principles. Now, in spite of the adventitiousness of his ordinances directed to this end, and the elements of arbitrariness in them, and though we can deny the name of true universal church to these, we cannot deny to him himself the prestige due the one who called men to union in this church; and this without further adding to this faith burdensome new ordinances or wishing to transform acts which he had initiated into peculiar holy practices, required in themselves as being constituent elements of religion.

After this description one will not fail to recognize the person who can be reverenced, not indeed as the *founder* of the *religion* which, free from every dogma, is engraved in all men's hearts (for it does not have its origin in an arbitrary will), but as the founder of the first true *church*. For attestation of his dignity as of divine mission we shall adduce several of his teach-

[2] [*ein Factum*]

ings as indubitable evidence of religion in general, let historical records be what they may (since in the idea itself is present adequate ground for its acceptance); these teachings, to be sure, can be no other than those of pure reason, for such alone carry their own proof, and hence upon them must chiefly depend the attestation of the others.

First, he claims that not the observance of outer civil or statutory churchly duties but the pure moral disposition of the heart alone can make man well-pleasing to God (Matthew V, 20-48); that sins in thought are regarded, in the eyes of God, as tantamount to action (V, 28) and that, in general, holiness is the goal toward which man should strive (V, 48); that, for example, to hate in one's heart is equivalent to killing (V, 22); that injury done one's neighbor can be repaired only through satisfaction rendered to the neighbor himself, not through acts of divine worship (V, 24), and that, on the point of truthfulness, the civil device for extorting it, by oath,[3] does violence to respect for truth itself (V, 34-37); that the natural evil but propensity of the human heart is to be completely reversed, that the sweet sense of revenge must be transformed into tolerance (V, 39, 40) and the hatred of one's enemies into charity (V, 44). Thus, he says, does he intend to do full justice to the Jewish law (V, 17); whence it is obvious that not scriptural scholarship but the pure religion of reason must be the law's interpreter, for taken according to the letter, it allowed the very opposite of all this. Furthermore, he does not leave unnoticed, in his designations of the strait gate and the narrow way, the misconstruction of the law which men allow themselves in order to evade their true moral duty and, holding themselves immune through having fulfilled their churchly duty (VII, 13).[4] He further requires of these pure dispositions that they manifest themselves also in *works* (VII,

---

[3] It is hard to understand why this clear prohibition against this method of forcing confession before a civil tribunal of religious teachers—a method based upon mere superstition, not upon conscientiousness—is held as so unimportant. For that it is superstition whose efficacy is here most relied on is evident from the fact that the man whom one does not trust to tell the truth in a solemn statement, on the truthfulness of which depends a decision concerning the rights of a human being (a holy thing, so far as this world goes), is yet expected to be persuaded to speak truly, by the use of a formula through which, over and above that statement, he simply calls down upon himself divine punishments (which, in any event, with such a lie, he cannot escape), just as though it rested with him whether or not to render account to this supreme tribunal. In the passage of Scripture cited above, the mode of confirmation by oath is represented as an *absurd* presumption, the attempt to make actual, as though with magical words, what is really not in our power. But it is clearly evident that the wise Teacher who here says that whatever goes beyond Yea, Yea, and Nay, Nay, in the asseveration of truth comes of evil, had in view the bad effect which oaths bring in their train—namely, that the greater importance attached to them almost lends a sanction to the common lie.

[4] The *strait gate* and the narrow way, which leads to life, is that of good life-conduct; the *wide gate* and the broad way, found by many, is the *church*. Not that the church and its doctrines are responsible for men being lost, but that the *entrance* into it and the knowledge of its statutes or celebration of its rites are regarded as the manner in which God really wishes to be served.

16) and, on the other hand, denies the insidious hope of those who imagine that, through invocation and praise of the Supreme Lawgiver in the person of His envoy, they will make up for their lack of good works and ingratiate themselves into favor (VII, 21). Regarding these works he declares that they ought to be performed publicly, as an example for imitation (V, 16); and in a cheerful mood, not as actions extorted from slaves (VI, 16); and that thus, from a small beginning in the sharing and spreading of such dispositions, religion, like a grain of seed in good soil, or a ferment of goodness, would gradually, through its inner power, grow into a kingdom of God (XIII, 31-33). Finally, he combines all duties (1) in one *universal* rule (which includes within itself both the inner and the outer moral relations of men), namely: Perform your duty for no motive [5] other than unconditioned esteem for duty itself, *i.e.* love God (the Legislator of all duties) above all else; and (2) in a *particular* rule that, namely, which concerns man's external relation to other men as universal duty: Love every one as yourself, *i.e.*, further his welfare from good-will that is immediate and not derived from motives of self-advantage. These commands are not mere laws of virtue but precepts of *holiness* which we ought to pursue, and the very pursuit of them is called *virtue*.

Accordingly he destroys the hope of all who intend to wait upon this moral goodness quite passively, with their hands in their laps, as though it were a heavenly gift which descends from on high. He who leaves unused the natural predisposition to goodness which lies in human nature (like a talent entrusted to him) in lazy confidence that a higher moral influence will no doubt supply the moral character and completeness which he lacks, is confronted with the threat that even the good which, by virtue of his natural predisposition, he may have done, will not be allowed to stand him in stead because of this neglect (XXV, 29).

As regards men's very natural expectation of an allotment of happiness proportional to a man's moral conduct, especially in view of the many sacrifices of the former which must be undergone for the sake of the latter, he promises (V, 11, 12) a reward for these sacrifices in a future world, but one in accordance with the differences of disposition in this conduct between those who did their duty *for the sake of the reward* (or for release from deserved punishment) and the better men who performed it merely for its own sake; the latter will be dealt with in a different manner. When the man governed by self-interest, the god of this world, does not renounce it but merely refines it by the use of reason and extends it beyond the constricting boundary of the present, he is represented (Luke XVI, 3-9) as

[5] [*Triebfeder*]

one who, in his very person [as servant], defrauds his master [self-interest] and wins from him sacrifices in behalf of "duty." For when he comes to realize that sometime, perhaps soon, the world must be forsaken, and that he can take along into the other world nothing of what he here possessed, he may well resolve to strike off from the account what he or his master, self-interest, has a legal right to exact from the indigent, and, as it were, thereby to acquire for himself bills of exchange, payable in another world. Herein he acts, no doubt, *cleverly* rather than *morally*, as regards the motives of such charitable actions, and yet in conformity with the moral law, at least according to the letter of that law; and he can hope that for this too he may not stand unrequited in the future.[6] Compare with this what is said of charity toward the needy from sheer motives of duty (Matthew XXV, 35-40), where those, who gave succor to the needy without the idea even entering their minds that such action was worthy of a reward or that they thereby obligated heaven, as it were, to recompense them, are, for this very reason, because they acted thus without attention to reward, declared by the Judge of the world to be those really chosen for His kingdom, and it becomes evident that when the Teacher of the Gospel spoke of rewards in the world to come he wished to make them thereby not an incentive to action but merely (as a soul-elevating representation of the consummation of the divine benevolence and wisdom in the guidance of the human race) an object of the purest respect and of the greatest moral approval when reason reviews human destiny in its entirety.

Here then is a complete religion, which can be presented to all men comprehensibly and convincingly through their own reason; while the possibility and even the necessity of its being an archetype for us to imitate (so far as men are capable of that imitation) have, be it noted, been made evident by means of an example without either the truth of those teachings nor the authority and the worth of the Teacher requiring any external certification (for which scholarship or miracles, which are not matters for everyone, would be required). When appeals are here made to older (Mosaic) legislation and prefiguration, as though these were to serve the Teacher as means of confirmation, they are presented not in support of the truth of his teach-

[6] We know nothing of the future, and we ought not to seek to know more than what is rationally bound up with the incentives of morality and their end. Here belongs the belief that there are no good actions which will not, in the next world, have their good consequences for him who performs them; that, therefore, however reprehensible a man may find himself at the end of his life, he must not on that account refrain from doing at least *one* more good deed which is in his power, and that, in so doing, he has reason to hope that, in proportion as he possesses in this action a purely good intent, the act will be of greater worth than those actionless absolutions which are supposed to compensate for the deficiency of good deeds without providing anything for the lessening of the guilt.

ings but merely for the introduction of these among people who clung wholly, and blindly, to the old. This introduction, among men whose heads, filled with statutory dogmas, have been almost entirely unfitted for the religion of reason, must always be more difficult than when this religion is to be brought to the reason of people uninstructed but also unspoiled. For this reason no one should be astonished to find an exposition, that adapted itself to the prejudices of those times, now puzzling and in need of pains-taking exegesis; though indeed it everywhere permits a religious doctrine to shine forth and, in addition, frequently points explicitly to that which must be comprehensible and, without any expenditure of learning, convincing to all men.

FRIEDRICH
SCHLEIERMACHER

FRIEDRICH SCHLEIERMACHER (1768-1834) was a German theologian who came out of Moravian pietism and German romanticism to become the systematizer of Protestant liberal theology. He was the most important Protestant theologian of the nineteenth century.

The Conception of the Church: Propositions Borrowed from Ethics*

The Piety Which Forms the Basis of All Ecclesiastical Communions Is, Considered Purely in Itself, Neither a Knowing nor a Doing, but a Modification of Feeling, or of Immediate Self-Consciousness.

1. That a Church is nothing but a communion or association relating to religion or piety, is beyond all doubt for us Evangelical (Protestant) Christians, since we regard it as equivalent to degeneration in a Church when it begins to occupy itself with other matters as well, whether the affairs of science or of outward organization; just as we also always oppose any attempt on the part of the leaders of State or of science, as such, to order

* From Friedrich Schleiermacher, *The Christian Faith*, ed. by H. R. Mackintosh and J. S. Stewart, propositions 3-4, pp. 5-18. Published, 1928, by T. & T. Clark. Reprinted by permission of publisher.

the affairs of religion. But, at the same time, we have no desire to keep the leaders of science from scrutinizing and passing judgment from their own point of view upon both piety itself and the communion relating to it, and determining their proper place in the total field of human life; since piety and Church, like other things, are material for scientific knowledge. Indeed, we ourselves are here entering upon such a scrutiny. And, similarly, we would not keep the leaders of State from fixing the outward relations of the religious communions according to the principles of civil organization— which, however, by no means implies that the religious communion is a product of the State or a component part of it.

However, not only we, but even those Churches which are not so clear about keeping apart Church and State, or ecclesiastical and scientific association, must assent to what we have laid down. For they cannot assign to the Church more than an indirect influence upon these other associations; and it is only the maintenance, regulation, and advancement of piety which they can regard as the essential business of the Church.

2. When Feeling and Self-consciousness are here put side by side as equivalent, it is by no means intended to introduce generally a manner of speech in which the two expressions would be simply synonymous. The term "feeling" has in the language of common life been long current in this religious connexion; but for scientific usage it needs to be more precisely defined; and it is to do this that the other word is added. So that if anyone takes the word "feeling" in a sense so wide as to include unconscious states, he will by the other word be reminded that such is not the usage we are here maintaining. Again, to the term 'self-consciousness' is added the determining epithet 'immediate,' lest anyone should think of a kind of self-consciousness which is not feeling at all; as, e.g., when the name of self-consciousness is given to that consciousness of self which is more like an objective consciousness, being a representation of oneself, and thus mediated by self-contemplation. Even when such a representation of ourselves, as we exist in a given portion of time, in thinking, e.g., or in willing, moves quite close to, or even interpenetrates, the individual moments of the mental state, this kind of self-consciousness does appear simply as an *accompaniment* of the state itself. But the real immediate self-consciousness, which is not representation but in the proper sense feeling, is by no means always simply an accompaniment. It may rather be presumed that in this respect everyone has a twofold experience. In the first place, it is everybody's experience that there are moments in which all thinking and willing retreat behind a self-consciousness of one form or another; but, in the second place, that at times this same form of self-consciousness persists unaltered during a series of diverse acts of thinking and willing, taking up no relation to these,

and thus not being in the proper sense even an accompaniment of them. Thus joy and sorrow—those mental phases which are always so important in the realm of religion—are genuine states of feeling, in the proper sense explained above; whereas self-approval and self-reproach, apart from their subsequently passing into joy and sorrow, belong in themselves rather to the objective consciousness of self, as results of an analytic contemplation. Nowhere, perhaps, do the two forms stand nearer to each other than here, but just for that reason this comparison puts the difference in the clearest light.

Note.—Steffen's account of feeling is closely akin to mine, and the passage from it to mine is easy (*Falsche Theologie*, pp. 99, 100). 'The immediate presence of whole undivided Being, etc.' On the other hand, the account given by Baumgarten-Crusius (*Einleitung in das Studium der Dogmatik*, p. 56), apart from its antithesis between feeling and self-consciousness, (a) does not comprehend the whole, but only the higher regions, of feeling, and (b) seems to transfer feeling into the realm of the objective consciousness by using the word 'perception' (*Wahrnehmung*). . . .

4. But now (these three, Feeling, Knowing, and Doing being granted) while we here set forth once more the oft-asserted view that, of the three, Feeling is the one to which piety belongs, it is not in any wise meant, as indeed the above discussion shows, that piety is excluded from all connexion with Knowing and Doing. For, indeed, it is the case in general that the immediate self-consciousness is always the mediating link in the transition between moments in which Knowing predominates and those in which Doing predominates, so that a different Doing may proceed from the same Knowing in different people according as a different determination of self-consciousness enters in. And thus it will fall to piety to stimulate Knowing and Doing, and every moment in which piety has a predominant place will contain within itself one or both of these in germ. But just this is the very truth represented by our proposition, and is in no wise an objection to it; for were it otherwise the religious moments could not combine with the others to form a single life, but piety would be something isolated and without any influence upon the other mental functions of our lives. However, in representing this truth, and thus securing to piety its own peculiar province in its connexion with all other provinces, our proposition is opposing the assertions from other quarters that piety is a Knowing, or a Doing, or both, or a state made up of Feeling, Knowing, and Doing; and in this polemical connexion our proposition must now be still more closely considered.

If, then, piety did consist in Knowing, it would have to be, above all, that knowledge, in its entirety or in its essence, which is here set up as the content of Dogmatics (*Glaubenslehre*): otherwise it must be a complete mistake for us here to investigate the nature of piety in the interests of our study of Dogmatics. But if piety is that knowledge, then the amount of such knowledge in a man must be the measure of his piety. For anything which, in its rise and fall, is not the measure of the perfection of a given object cannot constitute the essence of that object. Accordingly, on the hypothesis in question, the most perfect master of Christian Dogmatics would always be likewise the most pious Christian. And no one will admit this to be the case, even if we premise that the most perfect master is only he who keeps most to what is essential and does not forget it in accessories and side-issues; but all will agree rather that the same degree of perfection in that knowledge may be accompanied by very different degrees of piety, and the same degree of piety by very different degrees of knowledge. It may, however, be objected that the assertion that piety is a matter of Knowing refers not so much to the content of that knowledge as to the certainty which characterizes its representations; so that the knowledge of doctrines is piety only in virtue of the certainty attached to them, and thus only in virtue of the strength of the conviction, while a possession of the doctrines without conviction is not piety at all. Then the strength of the conviction would be the measure of the piety; and this is undoubtedly what those people have chiefly in mind who so love to paraphrase the word *Faith* as "fidelity to one's convictions." But in all other more typical fields of knowledge the only measure of conviction is the clearness and completeness of the thinking itself. Now if it is to be the same with *this* conviction, then we should simply be back at our old point, that he who thinks the religious propositions most clearly and completely, individually and in their connexions, must likewise be the most pious man. If, then, this conclusion is still to be rejected, but the hypothesis is to be retained (namely, that conviction is the measure of piety), the conviction in this case must be of a different kind and must have a different measure. However closely, then, piety may be connected with this conviction, it does not follow that it is connected in the same way with that knowledge. And if, nevertheless, the knowledge which forms Dogmatics has to relate itself to piety, the explanation of this is that while piety is, of course, the object of this knowledge, the knowledge can only be explicated in virtue of a certainty which inheres in the determinations of self-consciousness.

If, on the other hand, piety consists in Doing, it is manifest that the Doing which constitutes it cannot be defined by its content; for experience teaches that not only the most admirable but also the most abominable, not only the most useful but also the most inane and meaningless things, are done as pious and out of piety. Thus we are thrown back simply upon the form, upon the method and manner in which the thing comes to be done.

But this can only be understood from the two *termini*, the underlying motive as the starting-point, and the intended result as the goal. Now no one will pronounce an action more or less pious because of the greater or less degree of completeness with which the intended result is achieved. Suppose we then are thrown back upon the motive. It is manifest that underlying every motive there is a certain determination of self-consciousness, be it pleasure or pain, and that it is by these that one motive can most clearly be distinguished from another. Accordingly an action (a Doing) will be pious in so far as the determination of self-consciousness, the feeling which had become affective and had passed into a motive impulse, is a pious one.

Thus both hypotheses lead to the same point: that there are both a Knowing and a Doing which pertain to piety, but neither of these constitutes the essence of piety: they only pertain to it inasmuch as the stirred-up Feeling sometimes comes to rest in a thinking which fixes it, sometimes discharges itself in an action which expresses it.

Finally, no one will deny that there are states of Feeling, such as penitence, contrition, confidence, and joy in God, which we pronounce pious in themselves, without regard to any Knowing or Doing that proceeds from them, though, of course, we expect both that they will work themselves out in actions which are otherwise obligatory, and that the reflective impulse will turn its attention to them.

5. From what we have now said it is already clear how we must judge the assertion that piety is a state in which Knowing, Feeling, and Doing are combined. Of course we reject it if it means that the Feeling is derived from the Knowing and the Doing from the Feeling. But if no subordination is intended, then the assertion might just as well be the description of any other quite clear and living moment as of a religious one. For though the idea of the goal of an action precedes the action itself, at the same time it continues to accompany the action, and the relation between the two expresses itself simultaneously in the self-consciousness through a greater or less degree of satisfaction and assurance; so that even here all three elements are combined in the total content of the state. A similar situation exists in the case of Knowing. For the thinking activity, as a successfully accomplished operation, expresses itself in the self-consciousness as a confident certainty. But simultaneously it becomes also an endeavour to connect the apprehended truth with other truths or to seek out cases for its application, and thus there is always present simultaneously the commencement of a Doing, which develops fully when the opportunity offers; and so here also we find Knowing, Feeling, and Doing all together in the total state. But now, just as the first-described state remains, notwithstanding, essentially a Doing, and the second a Knowing, so piety in its diverse expressions remains essentially

a state of Feeling. This state is subsequently caught up into the region of thinking, but only in so far as each religious man is at the same time inclined towards thinking and exercised therein; and only in the same way and according to the same measure does this inner piety emerge in living movement and representative action. It also follows from this account of the matter that Feeling is not to be thought of as something either confused or inactive; since, on the one hand, it is strongest in our most vivid moments, and either directly or indirectly lies at the root of every expression of our wills, and, on the other hand, it can be grasped by thought and conceived of in its own nature.

But suppose there are other people who would exclude Feeling altogether from our field, and therefore describe piety simply as a Knowledge which begets action or as a Doing which proceeds from a Knowing: these people not only would have to settle first among themselves whether piety is a Knowing or a Doing, but would also have to show us how a Doing can arise from a Knowing except as mediated by a determination of self-consciousness. And if they have eventually to admit this point, then they will also be convinced by the above discussion that if such a complex does bear the character of piety, nevertheless the element of Knowing in it has not in itself got the length of being piety, and the element of Doing is in itself no longer piety, but the piety is just the determination of self-consciousness which comes in between the two. But that relationship can always hold in the reverse order also: the Doing has not got the length of being piety in those cases in which a determinate self-consciousness only results from an accomplished action; and the Knowing is in itself no longer piety when it has no other content than that determination of self-consciousness caught up into thought.

4. *The Common Element in All Howsoever Diverse Expressions of Piety, by Which These Are Conjointly Distinguished From All Other Feelings, or, in Other Words, the Self-Identical Essence of Piety, Is This: the Consciousness of Being Absolutely Dependent, or, Which Is the Same Thing, of Being in Relation With God.*

Note.—For the word *schlechthinig* [translated "absolute"], which occurs frequently in the following exposition, I am indebted to Professor Delbrück. I am unwilling to venture upon its use, and I am not aware that it has occurred anywhere else. But now that he has given it me, I find it very convenient to follow his lead in using it.

1. In any actual state of consciousness, no matter whether it merely accompanies a thought or action or occupies a moment for itself, we are never

simply conscious of our Selves in their unchanging identity, but are always at the same time conscious of a changing determination of them. The Ego in itself can be represented objectively; but every consciousness of self is at the same time the consciousness of a variable state of being. But in this distinction of the latter from the former, it is implied that the variable does not proceed purely from the self-identical, for in that case it could not be distinguished from it. Thus in every self-consciousness there are two elements, which we might call respectively a self-caused element *(ein Sich-selbstsetzen)* and a non-self-caused element *(ein Sichselbstnichtsogesetz-thaben)*; or a Being and a Having-by-some-means-come-to-be *(ein Sein und ein Irgendwiegewordensein)*. The latter of these presupposes for every self-consciousness another factor besides the Ego, a factor which is the source of the particular determination, and without which the self-consciousness would not be precisely what it is. But this Other is not objectively presented in the immediate self-consciousness with which alone we are here concerned. For though, of course, the double constitution of self-consciousness causes us always to look objectively for an Other to which we can trace the origin of our particular state, yet this search is a separate act with which we are not at present concerned. In self-consciousness there are only two elements: the one expresses the existence of the subject for itself, the other its co-existence with an Other.

Now to these two elements, as they exist together in the temporal self-consciousness, correspond in the subject its *Receptivity* and its (spontaneous) *Activity*. If we could think away the co-existence with an Other, but otherwise think ourselves as we are, then a self-consciousness which predominantly expressed an effective condition of receptivity would be impossible, and any self-consciousness could then express only activity—an activity, however, which, not being directed to any object, would be merely an urge outwards, an indefinite "agility" without form or colour. But as we never do exist except along with an Other, so even in every outward-tending self-consciousness the element of receptivity, in some way or other affected, is the primary one; and even the self-consciousness which accompanies an action (acts of knowing included), while it predominantly expresses spontaneous movement and activity, is always related (though the relation is often a quite indefinite one) to a prior moment of affective receptivity, through which the original "agility" received its direction. To these propositions assent can be unconditionally demanded; and no one will deny them who is capable of a little introspection and can find interest in the real subject of our present inquiries.

2. The common element in all those determinations of self-consciousness which predominantly express a receptivity affected from some outside quarter

is the *feeling of Dependence*. On the other hand, the common element in all those determinations which predominantly express spontaneous movement and activity is the *feeling of Freedom*. The former is the case not only because it is by an influence from some other quarter that we have come to such a state, but particularly because we *could* not so become except by means of an Other. The latter is the case because in these instances an Other is determined by us, and without our spontaneous activity could not be so determined. These two definitions may, indeed, seem to be still incomplete, inasmuch as there is also a mobility of the subject which is not connected with an Other at all, but which seems to be subject to the same antithesis as that just explained. But when we become such-and-such from within outwards, for ourselves, without any Other being involved, that is the simple situation of the temporal development of a being which remains essentially self-identical, and it is only very improperly that this can be referred to the concept "Freedom." And when we cannot ourselves, from within outwards, become such-and-such, this only indicates the limits which belong to the nature of the subject itself as regards spontaneous activity, and this could only very improperly be called "Dependence."

Further, this antithesis must on no account be confused with the antithesis between gloomy or depressing and elevating or joyful feelings, of which we shall speak later. For a feeling of dependence may be elevating, if the "having-become-such-and-such" which it expresses is complete; and similarly a feeling of freedom may be dejecting, if the moment of predominating receptivity to which the action can be traced was a dejecting nature, or again if the manner and method of the activity prove to be a disadvantageous combination.

Let us now think of the feeling of dependence and the feeling of freedom as *one*, in the sense that not only the subject but the corresponding Other is the same for both. Then the total self-consciousness made up of both together is one of *Reciprocity* between the subject and the corresponding Other. Now let us suppose the totality of all moments of feeling, of both kinds, as one whole: then the corresponding Other is also to be supposed as a totality or as one, and then that term "reciprocity" is the right one for our self-consciousness in general, inasmuch as it expresses our connexion with everything which either appeals to our receptivity or is subjected to our activity. And this is true not only when we particularize this Other and ascribe to each of its elements a different degree of relation to the twofold consciousness within us, but also when we think of the total "outside" as one, and moreover (since it contains other receptivities and activities to which we have a relation) as one together with ourselves, that is, as a World. Accordingly our self-consciousness, as a consciousness of our existence in the

world or of our co-existence with the world, is a series in which the feeling
of freedom and the feeling of dependence are divided. But neither an absolute feeling of dependence, *i.e.*, without any feeling of freedom in relation to
the co-determinant, nor an absolute feeling of freedom, *i.e.*, without any
feeling of dependence in relation to the co-determinant, is to be found in
this whole realm. If we consider our relations to Nature, or those which
exist in human society, there we shall find a large number of objects in regard to which freedom and dependence maintain very much of an equipoise:
these constitute the field of equal reciprocity. There are other objects which
exercise a far greater influence upon our receptivity than our activity exercises upon them, and also *vice versa*, so that one of the two may diminish
until it is imperceptible. But neither of the two members will ever completely disappear. The feeling of dependence predominates in the relation
of children to their parents, or of citizens to their fatherland; and yet individuals can, without losing their relationship, exercise upon their fatherland
not only a directive influence, but even a counter-influence. And the dependence of children on their parents, which very soon comes to be felt as
a gradually diminishing and fading quantity, is never from the start free from
the admixture of an element of spontaneous activity towards the parents:
just as even in the most absolute autocracy the ruler is not without some
slight feeling of dependence. It is the same in the case of Nature: towards
all the forces of Nature—even, we may say, towards the heavenly bodies—we
ourselves do, in the same sense in which they influence us, exercise a counter-
influence, however minute. So that our whole self-consciousness in relation
to the World or its individual parts remains enclosed within these limits.

3. There can, accordingly, be for us no such thing as a feeling of absolute freedom. He who asserts that he has such a feeling is either deceiving
himself or separating things which essentially belong together. For if the
feeling of freedom expresses a forthgoing activity, this activity must have an
object which has been somehow given to us, and this could not have taken
place without an influence of the object upon our receptivity. Therefore in
every such case there is involved a feeling of dependence which goes along
with the feeling of freedom, and thus limits it. The contrary could only be
possible if the object altogether came into existence through our activity,
which is never the case absolutely, but only relatively. But if, on the other
hand, the feeling of freedom expresses only an inward movement of activity, not only is every such individual movement bound up with the state
of our stimulated receptivity at the moment, but, further, the totality of
our free inward movements, considered as a unity, cannot be represented as
a feeling of absolute freedom, because our whole existence does not present
itself to our consciousness as having proceeded from our own spontaneous

activity. Therefore in any temporal existence a feeling of absolute freedom can have no place. As regards the feeling of absolute dependence which, on the other hand, our proposition does postulate: for just the same reason, this feeling cannot in any wise arise from the influence of an object which has in some way to be *given* to us; for upon such an object there would always be a counter-influence, and even a voluntary renunciation of this would always involve a feeling of freedom. Hence a feeling of absolute dependence, strictly speaking, cannot exist in a single moment as such, because such a moment is always determined, as regards its total content, by what is *given*, and thus by objects towards which we have a feeling of freedom. But the self-consciousness which accompanies all our activity, and therefore, since that is never zero, accompanies our whole existence, and negatives absolute freedom, is itself precisely a consciousness of absolute dependence; for it is the consciousness that the whole of our spontaneous activity comes from a source outside of us in just the same sense in which anything towards which we should have a feeling of absolute freedom must have proceeded entirely from ourselves. But without any feeling of freedom a feeling of absolute dependence would not be possible.

4. As regards the identification of absolute dependence with "relation to God" in our proposition: this is to be understood in the sense that the W*hence* of our receptive and active existence, as implied in this self-consciousness, is to be designated by the word "God," and that this is for us the really original signification of that word. In this connexion we have first of all to remind ourselves that, as we have seen in the foregoing discussion, this "Whence" is not the world, in the sense of the totality of temporal existence, and still less is it any single part of the world. For we have a feeling of freedom (though, indeed, a limited one) in relation to the world, since we are complementary parts of it, and also since we are continually exercising an influence on its individual parts; and, moreover, there is the possibility of our exercising influence on all its parts; and while this does permit a limited feeling of dependence, it excludes the absolute feeling. In the next place, we have to note that our proposition is intended to oppose the view that this feeling of dependence is itself conditioned by some previous knowledge about God. And this may indeed be the more necessary since many people claim to be in the sure possession of a concept of God, altogether a matter of conception and original, *i.e.*, independent of any feeling; and in the strength of this higher self-consciousness, which indeed may come pretty near to being a feeling of absolute freedom, they put far from them, as something almost infra-human, that very feeling which for us is the basic type of all piety. Now our proposition is in no wise intended to dispute the existence of such an original knowledge, but simply to set it aside as some-

thing with which, in a system of Christian doctrine, we could never have any concern, because plainly enough it has itself nothing to do directly with piety. If, however, word and idea are always originally one, and the term "God" therefore presupposes an idea, then we shall simply say that this idea, which is nothing more than the expression of the feeling of absolute dependence, is the most direct reflection upon it and the most original idea with which we are here concerned, and is quite independent of that original knowledge (properly so called), and conditioned only by our feeling of absolute dependence. So that in the first instance God signifies for us simply that which is the co-determinant in this feeling and to which we trace our being in such a state; and any further content of the idea must be evolved out of this fundamental import assigned to it. Now this is just what is principally meant by the formula which says that to feel oneself absolutely dependent and to be conscious of being in relation with God are one and the same thing; and the reason is that absolute dependence is the fundamental relation which must include all others in itself. This last expression includes the God-consciousness in the self-consciousness in such a way that, quite in accordance with the above analysis, the two cannot be separated from each other. The feeling of absolute dependence becomes a clear self-consciousness only as this idea comes simultaneously into being. In this sense it can indeed be said that God is given to us in feeling in an original way; and if we speak of an original revelation of God to man or in man, the meaning will always be just this, that, along with the absolute dependence which characterizes not only man but all temporal existence, there is given to man also the immediate self-consciousness of it, which becomes a consciousness of God. In whatever measure this actually takes place during the course of a personality through time, in just that measure do we ascribe piety to the individual. On the other hand, any possibility of God being in any way *given* is entirely excluded, because anything that is outwardly given must be given as an object exposed to our counter-influence, however slight this may be. The transference of the idea of God to any perceptible object, unless one is all the time conscious that it is a piece of purely arbitrary symbolism, is always a corruption, whether it be a temporary transference, *i.e.* a theophany, or a constitutive transference, in which God is represented as permanently a particular perceptible existence.

SØREN
KIERKEGAARD

SØREN KIERKEGAARD (1813-1855), Danish
Protestant lay-theologian, reacted against the
philosophy of Hegel. He was sharply critical
of the identification of Christianity and culture, demanded radical faith, and was the
key-figure in the development of modern religious existentialism.

What It Is to Become a Christian*

Objectively, What It Is to Become or to Be a Christian Is Defined in the Following Way:

1. A Christian is one who accepts the doctrine of Christianity. But if it is
the doctrine which is to decide in the last resort whether one is a Christian,
then instantly attention is directed outward, in order to learn to know in
the minutest detail what the doctrine of Christianity is, because this indeed
is to decide, not what Christianity is, but whether I am a Christian. That
same instant begins the erudite, the anxious, the timorous effort at approximation. Approximation can be protracted as long as you please, and in the
end the decision whereby one becomes a Christian is relegated to oblivion.

This incongruity has been remedied by the assumption that everyone in
Christendom is a Christian, we are all of us what one in a way calls Christians. With this assumption things go better with the objective theories.
We are all Christians. The Bible-theory has now to investigate quite objectively what Christianity is (and yet we are in fact Christians, and the objective information is assumed to make us Christians, the objective information which we who are Christians shall now for the first time learn to know—
for if we are not Christians, the road here taken will never lead us to become such). The Church theory assumes that we are Christians, but now
we have to be assured in a purely objective way what Christianity is, in
order that we may defend ourselves against the Turk and the Russian and
the Roman yoke, and gallantly fight out the battle of Christianity so that
we may make our age, as it were, a bridge to the peerless future which already is glimpsed. This is sheer aesthetics. Christianity is an existence-com-

* From Søren Kierkegaard, *Concluding Unscientific Postscript*, trans. David F. Swenson
and Walter Lowrie, pp. 537-544. Copyright, 1941, Princeton University Press. Reprinted
by permission of Princeton University Press. [Several footnotes omitted, Eds.]

26

munication, the task is to become a Christian and continue to be such, and the most dangerous of all illusions is to be so sure of being such that one has to defend the whole of Christendom against the Turk—instead of being alert to defend our own faith against the illusion about the Turk.

2. One says, No, not every acceptance of the Christian doctrine makes one a Christian; what it principally depends upon is appropriation, that one appropriates and holds fast this doctrine quite differently from anything else, that one is ready to live in it and to die in it, to venture one's life for it, etc.

This seems as if it were something. However, the category "quite differently" is a mediocre category, and the whole formula, which makes an attempt to define more subjectively what it is to be a Christian, is neither one thing nor the other, in a way it avoids the difficulty involved in the distraction and deceit of approximation, but it lacks categorical definition. The pathos of approximation which is talked of here is that of immanence; one can just as well say that an enthusiastic lover is so related to his love: he holds fast to it and appropriates it quite differently from anything else, he is ready to live in it and die in it, he will venture everything for it. To this extent there is no difference between a lover and a Christian with respect to inwardness, and one must again recur to the *what*, which is the doctrine—and with that we again come under No. 1.

The pathos of appropriation needs to be so defined that it cannot be confused with any other pathos. The more subjective interpretation is right in insisting that it is appropriation which decides the matter, but it is wrong in its definition of appropriation, which does not distinguish it from every other immediate pathos.

Neither is this distinction made when one defines appropriation as faith, but at once imparts to faith headway and direction towards reaching an understanding, so that faith becomes a provisional function whereby one holds what essentially is to be an object for understanding, a provisional function wherewith poor people and stupid men have to be content, whereas *Privatdocents* and clever heads go further. The mark of being a Christian (i.e. faith) is appropriated, but in such a way that it is not specifically different from other intellectual appropriation where a preliminary assumption serves as a provisional function looking forward to understanding. Faith is not in this case the specific mark of the relationship to Christianity, and again it will be the *what* of faith which decides whether one is a Christian or not. But therewith the thing is again brought back under No. 1.

That is to say, the appropriation by which a Christian is a Christian must be so specific that it cannot be confused with anything else.

3. One defines the thing of becoming and being a Christian, not objec-

tively by the *what* of the doctrine, nor subjectively by appropriation, not by what has gone on in the individual, but by what the individual has undergone: that he was baptized. Though one adjoins to baptism the assumption of a confession of faith, nothing decisive will be gained, but the definition will waver between accentuating the *what* (the path of approximation) and talking indefinitely about acceptance and acceptance and appropriation, etc., without any specific determination.

If being baptized is to be the definition, attention will instantly turn outward towards the reflection, whether I have really been baptized. Then begins the approximation with respect to a historical fact.

If, on the other hand, one were to say that he did indeed receive the Spirit in baptism and by the witness it bears together with his spirit, he knows that he was baptized—then the inference is inverted, he argues from the witness of the Spirit within him to the fact that he was baptized, not from the fact of being baptized to the possession of the Spirit. But if the inference is to be drawn in this way, baptism is quite rightly not regarded as the mark of the Christian, but inwardness is, and so here in turn there is needed a specific definition of inwardness and appropriation whereby the witness of the Spirit in the individual is distinguished from all other (universally defined) activity of spirit in man.

It is noteworthy moreover that the orthodoxy which especially has made baptism the decisive mark is continually complaining that among the baptized there are so few Christians, that almost all, except for an immortal little band, are spiritless baptized pagans—which seems to indicate that baptism cannot be the decisive factor with respect to becoming a Christian, not even according to the latter view of those who in the first form insist upon it as decisive with respect to becoming a Christian.

Subjectively, What It Is to Become a Christian Is Defined Thus:

The decision lies in the subject. The appropriation is the paradoxical inwardness which is specifically different from all other inwardness. The thing of being a Christian is not determined by the *what* of Christianity but by the *how* of the Christian. This *how* can only correspond with one thing, the absolute paradox. There is therefore no vague talk to the effect that being a Christian is to accept, and to accept, and to accept quite differently, to appropriate, to believe, to appropriate by faith quite differently (all of them purely rhetorical and fictitious definitions); but *to believe* is specifically different from all other appropriation and inwardness. Faith is the objective uncertainty due to the repulsion of the absurd held fast by the

THE NATURE OF RELIGION

passion of inwardness, which in this instance is intensified to the utmost degree. This formula fits only the believer, no one else, not a lover, not an enthusiast, not a thinker, but simply and solely the believer who is related to the absolute paradox.

Faith therefore cannot be any sort of provisional function. He who from the vantage point of a higher knowledge would know his faith as a factor resolved in a higher idea has *eo ipso* ceased to believe. Faith *must* not *rest content* with unintelligibility; for precisely the relation to or the repulsion from the unintelligible, the absurd, is the expression for the passion of faith.

This definition of what it is to be a Christian prevents the erudite or anxious deliberation of approximation from enticing the individual into byways so that he becomes erudite instead of becoming a Christian, and in most cases a smatterer instead of becoming a Christian; for the decision lies in the subject. But inwardness has again found its specific mark whereby it is differentiated from all other inwardness and is not disposed of by the chatty category "quite differently" which fits the case of every passion at the moment of passion.

The psychologist generally regards it as a sure sign that a man is beginning to give up a passion when he wishes to treat the object of it objectively. Passion and reflection are generally exclusive of one another. Becoming objective in this way is always retrogression, for passion is man's perdition, but it is his exaltation as well. In case dialectic and reflection are not used to intensify passion, it is a retrogression to become objective; and even he who is lost through passion has not lost so much as he who lost passion, for the former had the possibility.

Thus it is that people in our age have wanted to become objective with relation to Christianity; the passion by which every man is a Christian has become too small a thing for them, and by becoming objective we all of us have the prospect of becoming . . . *a Privatdocent.* . . .

Precisely because people in our age and in the Christendom of our time do not appear to be sufficiently aware of the dialectic of inward appropriation, or of the fact that the "how" of the individual is an expression just as precise and more decisive for what he has, than is the "what" to which he appeals—precisely for this reason there crop up the strangest and (if one is in the humor and has time for it) the most laughable confusions, more comic than even the confusions of paganism, because in them there was not so much at stake, and because the contradictions were not so strident. . . .

An orthodox champion fights in defense of Christianity with the most frightful passion, he protests with the sweat of his brow and with the most concerned demeanor that he accepts Christianity pure and simple, he will live and die in it—and he forgets that such acceptance is an all too general expression for the relation to Christianity. He does everything in Jesus' name and uses Christ's name on every occasion as a sure sign that he is a Christian and is called to fight in defense of Christendom in our age—and he has no inkling of the little ironical secret that a man merely by describing the "how" of his inwardness can show indirectly that he is a Christian without mentioning God's name.[1] A man becomes converted New Year's Eve precisely at six o'clock. With that he is fully prepared. Fantastically decked out with the fact of conversion, he now must run out and proclaim Christianity . . . in a Christian land. Well, of course, even though we are all baptized, every man may well need to become a Christian in another sense. But here is the distinction: there is no lack of information in a Christian land, something else is lacking, and this is a something which the one man cannot directly communicate to the other. And in such fantastic categories would a converted man work for Christianity; and yet he proves (just in proportion as he is the more busy in spreading and spreading) that he himself is not a Christian. For to be a Christian is something so deeply reflected that it does not admit of the aesthetical dialectic which allows one man to be for others something he is not for himself. On the other hand, a scoffer attacks Christianity and at the same time expounds it so reliably that it is a pleasure to read him, and one who is in perplexity about finding it distinctly set forth may almost have recourse to him.

All ironical observations depend upon paying attention to the "how," whereas the gentleman with whom the ironist has the honor to converse is attentive only to "what." A man protests loudly and solemnly, "This is my opinion." However, he does not confine himself to delivering this formula verbatim, he explains himself further, he ventures to vary the expressions. Yes, for it is not so easy to vary as one thinks it is. More than one student would have got *laudabilis* for style if he had not varied his expressions, and a great multitude of men possess the talent which Socrates so much admired in Polos: they never say the same thing—about the same. The ironist then is on the watch, he of course is not looking out for what is printed in large letters or for that which by the speaker's diction betrays itself as a formula (our gentleman's "what"), but he is looking out for a little subordinate

---

[1] In relation to love (by which I would illustrate again the same thing) it does not hold good in the same sense that a man merely by defining his "how" indicates what or whom it is he loves. All lovers have the "how" of love in common, the particular person must supply the name of his beloved. But with respect to believing (*sensu strictissimo*) it holds good that this "how" is appropriate only to one as its object. If anybody would say, "Yes, but then one can also learn the 'how' of faith by rote and patter"; to this one must reply that it cannot be done, for he who declares it directly contradicts himself, because the content of the assertion must constantly be reduplicated in the form of expression, and the isolation contained in the definition must reduplicate itself in the form.

clause which escapes the gentleman's haughty attention, a little beckoning predicate, etc., and now he beholds with astonishment (glad of the variation—*in variatione voluptas*) that the gentleman *has not* that opinion—not that he is a hypocrite, God forbid! that is too serious a matter for an ironist— but that the good man has concentrated his force in bawling it out instead of possessing it within him. To that extent the gentleman may be right in asserting that he has that opinion which with all his vital force he persuades himself he has, he may do everything for it in the quality of talebearer, he may risk his life for it, in very much troubled times he may carry the thing so far as to lose his life for this opinion—with that, how the deuce can I doubt that the man had this opinion; and yet there may have been living contemporaneously with him an ironist who even in the hour when the unfortunate gentleman is executed cannot resist laughing, because he knows by the circumstantial evidence he has gathered that the man had never been clear about the thing himself. Laughable it is, nor is it disheartening that such a thing can occur; for he who with quiet introspection is honest before God and concerned for himself, the Deity saves from being in error, though he be never so simple, him the Deity leads by the suffering of inwardness to the truth. But meddlesomeness and noise is the sign of error, the sign of an abnormal condition, like wind in the stomach, and this thing of stumbling by chance upon getting executed in a tumultous turn of affairs is not the sort of suffering which essentially characterizes inwardness.

It is said to have chanced in England that a man was attacked on the highway by a robber who had made himself unrecognizable by wearing a big wig. He falls upon the traveller, seizes him by the throat and shouts, "Your purse!" He gets the purse and keeps it, but the wig he throws away. A poor man comes along the same road, puts it on and arrives at the next town where the traveller had already denounced the crime, he is arrested, is recognized by the traveller, who takes his oath that he is the man. By chance, the robber is present in court-room, sees the misunderstanding, turns to the judge and says, "It seems to me that the traveller has regard rather to the wig than to the man," and he asks permission to make a trial. He puts on the wig, seizes the traveller by the throat, crying, "Your purse!"— and the traveller recognizes the robber and offers to swear to it—the only trouble is that already he has taken an oath. So it is, in one way or another, with every man who has a "what" and is not attentive to the "how": he swears, he takes his oath, he runs errands, he ventures life and blood, he is executed—all on account of the wig. . . .

LUDWIG · FEUERBACH

LUDWIG FEUERBACH (1804-1872) was a German philosopher who belonged to the left-wing Hegelian school. He taught that religion is a projection of human imagination and an expression of human need. His book, *The Essence of Christianity* has long been recognized as a provocative interpretation of religious belief.

The Essence of Religion*

Religion has its basis in the essential difference between man and the brute—the brutes have no religion. It is true that the old uncritical writers on natural history attributed to the elephant, among other laudable qualities, the virtue of religiousness; but the religion of elephants belongs to the realm of fable. Cuvier, one of the greatest authorities on the animal kingdom, assigns, on the strength of his personal observations, no higher grade of intelligence to the elephant than to the dog.

But what is this essential difference between man and the brute? The most simple, general, and also the most popular answer to this question is—consciousness:—but consciousness in the strict sense; for the consciousness implied in the feeling of self as an individual, in discrimination by the senses, in the perception and even judgment of outward things according to definite sensible signs, cannot be denied to the brutes. Consciousness in the strictest sense is present only in a being to whom his species, his essential nature, is an object of thought. The brute is indeed conscious of himself as an individual—and he has accordingly the feeling of self as the common centre of successive sensations—but not as a species: hence, he is without that consciousness which in its nature, as in its name, is akin to science. Where there is this higher consciousness there is a capability of science. Science is the cognisance of species. In practical life we have to do with individuals; in science, with species. But only a being to whom his own species, his own nature, is an object of thought, can make the essential nature of other things or beings an object of thought.

Hence the brute has only a simple, man a twofold life: in the brute, the

---

* From Ludwig Feuerbach, *The Essence of Christianity*, trans. George Eliot, pp. 1-3, 29-32. Published, 1957, Harper & Brothers (Torchbook Series). In the public domain. [Several footnotes omitted, Eds.]

inner life is one with the outer; man has both an inner and an outer life. The inner life of man is the life which has relation to his species, to his general, as distinguished from his individual, nature. Man thinks—that is, he converses with himself. The brute can exercise no function which has relation to its species without another individual external to itself; but man can perform the functions of thought and speech, which strictly imply such a relation, apart from another individual. Man is himself at once I and thou; he can put himself in the place of another, for this reason, that to him his species, his essential nature, and not merely his individuality, is an object of thought.

Religion, being identical with the distinctive characteristic of man, is then identical with self-consciousness—with the consciousness which man has of his nature. But religion, expressed generally, is consciousness of the infinite; thus it is and can be nothing else than the consciousness which man has of his own—not finite and limited, but infinite nature. A really finite being has not even the faintest adumbration, still less consciousness, of an infinite being, for the limit of the nature is also the limit of the consciousness. The consciousness of the caterpillar, whose life is confined to a particular species of plant, does not extend itself beyond this narrow domain. It does, indeed, discriminate between this plant and other plants, but more it knows not. A consciousness so limited, but on account of that very limitation so infallible, we do not call consciousness, but instinct. Consciousness, in the strict or proper sense, is identical with consciousness of the infinite; a limited conciousness is no consciousness; consciousness is essentially infinite in its nature. The consciousness of the infinite is nothing else than the consciousness of the infinity of the consciousness; or, in the consciousness of the infinite, the conscious subject has for his object the infinity of his own nature. . . .

Man—this is the mystery of religion—projects his being into objectivity, and then again makes himself an object to this projected image of himself thus converted into a subject; he thinks of himself as an object to himself, but as the object of an object, of another being than himself. Thus here. Man is an object to God. That man is good or evil is not indifferent to God; no! He has a lively, profound interest in man's being good; he wills that man should be good, happy—for without goodness there is no happiness. Thus the religious man virtually retracts the nothingness of human activity, by making his dispositions and actions an object to God, by making man the end of God—for that which is an object to the mind is an end in action; by making the divine activity a means of human salvation. God acts, that man may be good and happy. Thus man, while he is apparently humiliated to the lowest degree, is in truth exalted to the highest. Thus, in and through God, man has in view himself alone. It is true that man places the aim of his action in God, but God has no other aim of action than the moral and eternal salvation of man: thus man has in fact no other aim than himself. The divine activity is not distinct from the human.

How could the divine activity work on me as its object, nay, work in me, if it were essentially different from me; how could it have a human aim, the aim of ameliorating and blessing man, if it were not itself human? Does not the purpose determine the nature of the act? When man makes his moral improvement an aim to himself, he has divine resolutions, divine projects; but also, when God seeks the salvation of man, he has human ends and a human mode of activity corresponding to these ends. Thus in God man has only his own activity as an object. But for the very reason that he regards his own activity as objective, goodness only as an object, he necessarily receives the impulse, the motive not from himself, but from this object. He contemplates his nature as external to himself, and this nature as goodness; thus it is self-evident, it is mere tautology to say that the impulse to good comes only from thence where he places the good.

God is the highest subjectivity of man abstracted from himself; hence man can do nothing of himself, all goodness comes from God. The more subjective God is, the more completely does man divest himself of his subjectivity, because God is, *per se*, his relinquished self, the possession of which he however again vindicates to himself. As the action of the arteries drives the blood into the extremities, and the action of the veins brings it back again, as life in general consists in a perpetual systole and diastole; so is it in religion. In the religious systole man propels his own nature from himself, he throws himself outward; in the religious diastole he receives the rejected nature into his heart again. God alone is the being who acts of himself,—this is the force of repulsion in religion; God is the being who acts in me, with me, through me, upon me, for me, is the principle of my salvation, of my good dispositions and actions, consequently my own good principle and nature,—this is the force of attraction in religion.

The course of religious development which has been generally indicated consists specifically in this, that man abstracts more and more from God, and attributes more and more to himself. This is especially apparent in the belief in revelation. That which to a later age or a cultured people is given by nature or reason, is to an earlier age, or to a yet uncultured people, given by God. Every tendency of man, however natural—even the impulse to cleanliness, was conceived by the Israelites as a positive divine ordinance. From this example we again see that God is lowered, is conceived more entirely on the type of ordinary humanity, in proportion as man detracts from himself. How can the self-humiliation of man go further than when he disclaims the capability of fulfilling spontaneously the requirements of common decency? The Christian religion, on the other hand, distinguished the impulses and passions of man according to their quality, their character; it represented only good emotions, good dispositions, good thoughts, as revelations, operations—that is, as dispositions, feelings, thoughts,—of God; for what God reveals is a quality of God himself: that of which the heart is full overflows the lips; as is the effect such is the cause; as the revelation, such the being who reveals himself. A God who reveals himself in good dispositions is a God whose essential attribute is only moral perfection. The Christian religion distinguishes inward moral purity from external physical purity; the Israelites identified the two. In relation to the Israelitish religion, the Christian religion is one of criticism and freedom. The Israelite trusted himself to do nothing except what was commanded by God; he was without will even in external things; the authority of religion extended itself even to his food. The Christian religion, on the other hand, in all these external things made man dependent on himself, *i.e.*, placed in man what the Israelite placed out of himself in God. Israel is the most complete presentation of Positivism in religion. In relation to the Israelite, the Christian is an *esprit fort*, a free-thinker. Thus do things change. What yesterday was still religion is no longer such to-day; and what to-day is atheism, tomorrow will be religion.

JOHN DEWEY

JOHN DEWEY (1859-1952), longtime professor at Columbia University, was the most influential American philosopher of this century. His chief effort was to apply a form of pragmatism to all of the important areas of philosophy and to many political, social and educational problems in American life.

Religion Versus the Religious*

Never before in history has mankind been so much of two minds, so divided into two camps, as it is today. Religions have traditionally been allied with ideas of the supernatural, and often have been based upon explicit beliefs about it. Today there are many who hold that nothing worthy

* From John Dewey, *A Common Faith*, pp. 1-28. Copyright, 1934, by Yale University Press. Used by permission of Yale University Press.

of being called religious is possible apart from the supernatural. Those who hold this belief differ in many respects. They range from those who accept the dogmas and sacraments of the Greek and Roman Catholic church as the only sure means of access to the supernatural to the theist or mild deist. Between them are the many Protestant denominations who think the Scriptures, aided by a pure conscience, are adequate avenues to supernatural truth and power. But they agree in one point: the necessity for a Supernatural Being and for an immortality that is beyond the power of nature.

The opposed group consists of those who think the advance of culture and science has completely discredited the supernatural and with it all religions that were allied with belief in it. But they go beyond this point. The extremists in this group believe that with elimination of the supernatural not only must historic religions be dismissed but with them everything of a religious nature. When historical knowledge has discredited the claims made for the supernatural character of the persons said to have founded historic religions; when the supernatural inspiration attributed to literatures held sacred has been riddled, and when anthropological and psychological knowledge has disclosed the all-too-human source from which religious beliefs and practices have sprung, everything religious must, they say, also go.

There is one idea held in common by these two opposite groups: identification of the religious with the supernatural. The question I shall raise in these chapters concerns the ground for and the consequences of this identification: its reasons and its value. In the discussion I shall develop another conception of the nature of the religious phase of experience, one that separates it from the supernatural and the things that have grown up about it. I shall try to show that these derivations are encumbrances and that what is genuinely religious will undergo an emancipation when it is relieved from them; that then, for the first time, the religious aspect of experience will be free to develop freely on its own account.

This view is exposed to attack from both the other camps. It goes contrary to traditional religions, including those that have the greatest hold upon the religiously minded today. The view announced will seem to them to cut the vital nerve of the religious element itself in taking away the basis upon which traditional religions and institutions have been founded. From the other side, the position I am taking seems like a timid halfway position, a concession and compromise unworthy of thought that is thoroughgoing. It is regarded as a view entertained from mere tendermindedness, as an emotional hangover from childhood indoctrination, or even as a manifestation of a desire to avoid disapproval and curry favor.

The heart of my point, as far as I shall develop it in this first section, is that there is a difference between religion, *a* religion, and the religious;

between anything that may be denoted by a noun substantive and the quality of experience that is designated by an adjective. It is not easy to find a definition of religion in the substantive sense that wins general acceptance. However, in the *Oxford Dictionary* I find the following: "Recognition on the part of man of some unseen higher power as having control of his destiny and as being entitled to obedience, reverence and worship."

This particular definition is less explicit in assertion of the supernatural character of the higher unseen power than are others that might be cited. It is, however, surcharged with implications having their source in ideas connected with the belief in the supernatural, characteristic of historic religions. Let us suppose that one familiar with the history of religions, including those called primitive, compares the definition with the variety of known facts and by means of the comparison sets out to determine just what the definition means. I think he will be struck by three facts that reduce the terms of the definition to such a low common denominator that little meaning is left.

He will note that the "unseen powers" referred to have been conceived in a multitude of incompatible ways. Eliminating the differences, nothing is left beyond the bare reference to something unseen and powerful. This has been conceived as the vague and undefined Mana of the Melanesians; the Kami of primitive Shintoism; the fetish of the Africans; spirits, having some human properties, that pervade natural places and animate natural forces; the ultimate and impersonal principle of Buddhism; the unmoved mover of Greek thought; the gods and semi-divine heroes of the Greek and Roman Pantheons; the personal and loving Providence of Christianity, omnipotent, and limited by a corresponding evil power; the arbitrary Will of Moslemism; the supreme legislator and judge of deism. And these are but a few of the outstanding varieties of ways in which the invisible power has been conceived.

There is no greater similarity in the ways in which obedience and reverence have been expressed. There has been worship of animals, of ghosts, of ancestors, phallic worship, as well as of a Being of dread power and of love and wisdom. Reverence has been expressed in the human sacrifices of the Peruvians and Aztecs; the sexual orgies of some Oriental religions; exorcisms and ablutions; the offering of the humble and contrite mind of the Hebrew prophet, the elaborate rituals of the Greek and Roman Churches. Not even sacrifice has been uniform; it is highly sublimated in Protestant denominations and in Moslemism. Where it has existed it has taken all kinds of forms and been directed to a great variety of powers and spirits. It has been used for expiation, for propitiation and for buying special favors. There is no conceivable purpose for which rites have not been employed.

Finally, there is no discernible unity in the moral motivations appealed to and utilized. They have been as far apart as fear of lasting torture, hope of enduring bliss in which sexual enjoyment has sometimes been a conspicuous element; mortification of the flesh and extreme asceticism; prostitution and chastity; wars to extirpate the unbeliever; persecution to convert or punish the unbeliever, and philanthropic zeal; servile acceptance of imposed dogma, along with brotherly love and aspiration for a reign of justice among men.

I have, of course, mentioned only a sparse number of the facts which fill volumes in any well-stocked library. It may be asked by those who do not like to look upon the darker side of the history of religions why the darker facts should be brought up. We all know that civilized man has a background of bestiality and superstition and that these elements are still with us. Indeed, have not some religions, including the most influential forms of Christianity, taught that the heart of man is totally corrupt? How could the course of religion in its entire sweep not be marked by practices that are shameful in their cruelty and lustfulness, and by beliefs that are degraded and intellectually incredible? What else than what we find could be expected, in the case of people having little knowledge and no secure method of knowing; with primitive institutions, and with so little control of natural forces that they lived in a constant state of fear?

I gladly admit that historic religions have been relative to the conditions of social culture in which peoples lived. Indeed, what I am concerned with is to press home the logic of this method of disposal of outgrown traits of past religions. Beliefs and practices in a religion that now prevails are by this logic relative to the present state of culture. If so much flexibility has obtained in the past regarding an unseen power, the way it affects human destiny, and the attitudes we are to take toward it, why should it be assumed that change in conception and action has now come to an end? The logic involved in getting rid of inconvenient aspects of past religions compels us to inquire how much in religions now accepted are survivals from outgrown cultures. It compels us to ask what conception of unseen powers and our relations to them would be consonant with the best achievements and aspirations of the present. It demands that in imagination we wipe the slate clean and start afresh by asking what would be the idea of the unseen, of the manner of its control over us and the ways in which reverence and obedience would be manifested, if whatever is basically religious in experience had the opportunity to express itself free from all historic encumbrances.

So we return to the elements of the definition that has been given. What boots it to accept, in defense of the universality of religion, a definition that applies equally to the most savage and degraded beliefs and practices that have related to unseen powers and to noble ideals of a religion having the greatest share of moral content? There are two points involved. One of them is that there is nothing left worth preserving in the notions of unseen powers, controlling human destiny to which obedience, reverence and worship are due, if we glide silently over the nature that has been attributed to the powers, the radically diverse ways in which they have been supposed to control human destiny, and in which submission and awe have been manifested. The other point is that when we begin to select, to choose, and say that some present ways of thinking about the unseen powers are better than others; that the reverence shown by a free and self-respecting human being is better than the servile obedience rendered to an arbitrary power by frightened men; that we should believe that control of human destiny is exercised by a wise and loving spirit rather than by madcap ghosts or sheer force—when I say, we begin to choose, we have entered upon a road that has not yet come to an end. We have reached a point that invites us to proceed farther.

For we are forced to acknowledge that concretely there is no such thing as religion in the singular. There is only a multitude of religions. "Religion" is a strictly collective term and the collection it stands for is not even of the kind illustrated in textbooks of logic. It has not the unity of a regiment or assembly but that of any miscellaneous aggregate. Attempts to prove the universality prove too much or too little. It is probable that religions have been universal in the sense that all the peoples we know anything about have had a religion. But the differences among them are so great and so shocking that any common element that can be extracted is meaningless. The idea that religion is universal proves too little in that the older apologists for Christianity seem to have been better advised than some modern ones in condemning every religion but one as an imposter, as at bottom some kind of demon worship or at any rate a superstitious figment. Choice among religions is imperative, and the necessity for choice leaves nothing of any force in the argument from universality. Moreover, when once we enter upon the road of choice, there is at once presented a possibility not yet generally realized.

For the historic increase of the ethical and ideal content of religions suggests that the process of purification may be carried further. It indicates that further choice is imminent in which certain values and functions in experience may be selected. This possibility is what I had in mind in speaking of the difference between the religious and a religion. I am not proposing a religion, but rather the emancipation of elements and outlooks that may be called religious. For the moment we have a religion, whether that of the Sioux Indian or of Judaism or of Christianity, that moment the ideal factors in experience that may be called religious take on a load that is not inherent in them, a load of current beliefs and of institutional practices that are irrelevant to them.

I can illustrate what I mean by a common phenomenon in contemporary life. It is widely supposed that a person who does not accept any religion is thereby shown to be a non-religious person. Yet it is conceivable that the present depression in religion is closely connected with the fact that religions now prevent, because of their weight of historic encumbrances, the religious quality of experience from coming to consciousness and finding the expression that is appropriate to present conditions, intellectual and moral. I believe that such is the case. I believe that many persons are so repelled from what exists as a religion by its intellectual and moral implications, that they are not even aware of attitudes in themselves that if they came to fruition would be genuinely religious. I hope that this remark may help make clear what I mean by the distinction between "religion" as a noun substantive and "religious" as adjectival.

To be somewhat more explicit, a religion (and as I have just said there is no such thing as religion in general) always signifies a special body of beliefs and practices having some kind of institutional organization, loose or tight. In contrast, the adjective "religious" denotes nothing in the way of a specifiable entity, either institutional or as a system of beliefs. It does not denote anything to which one can specifically point as one can point to this and that historic religion or existing church. For it does not denote anything that can exist by itself or that can be organized into a particular and distinctive form of existence. It denotes attitudes that may be taken toward every object and every proposed end or ideal.

Before, however, I develop my suggestion that realization of the distinction just made would operate to emancipate the religious quality from encumbrances that now smother or limit it, I must refer to a position that in some respects is similar in words to the position I have taken, but that in fact is a whole world removed from it. I have several times used the phrase "religious elements of experience." Now at present there is much talk, especially in liberal circles, of religious experience as vouching for the authenticity of certain beliefs and the desirability of certain practices, such as particular forms of prayer and worship. It is even asserted that religious experience is the ultimate basis of religion itself. The gulf between this position and that which I have taken is what I am now concerned to point out.

Those who hold to the notion that there is a definite kind of experience which is itself religious, by that very fact make out of it something specific, as a kind of experience that is marked off from experience as aesthetic,

THE NATURE OF RELIGION

scientific, moral, political; from experience as companionship and friend-ship. But "religious" as a quality of experience signifies something that may belong to all these experiences. It is the polar opposite of some type of experience that can exist by itself. The distinction comes out clearly when it is noted that the concept of this distinct kind of experience is used to validate a belief in some special kind of object and also to justify some special kind of practice.

For there are many religionists who are now dissatisfied with the older "proofs" of the existence of God, those that go by the name of ontological, cosmological and teleological. The cause of the dissatisfaction is perhaps not so much the arguments that Kant used to show the insufficiency of these alleged proofs, as it is the growing feeling that they are too formal to offer any support to religion in action. Anyway, the dissatisfaction exists. Moreover, these religionists are moved by the rise of the experimental method in other fields. What is more natural and proper, accordingly, than that they should affirm they are just as good empiricists as anybody else—indeed, as good as the scientists themselves? As the latter rely upon certain kinds of experience to prove the existence of certain kinds of objects, so the religionists rely upon a certain kind of experience to prove the existence of the object of religion, especially the supreme object, God.

The discussion may be made more definite by introducing, at this point, a particular illustration of this type of reasoning. A writer says: "I broke down from overwork and soon came to the verge of nervous prostration. One morning after a long and sleepless night . . . I resolved to stop drawing upon myself so continuously and begin drawing upon God. I determined to set apart a quiet time every day in which I could relate my life to its ultimate source, regain the consciousness that in God I live, move and have my being. That was thirty years ago. Since then I have had literally not one hour of darkness or despair."

This is an impressive record. I do not doubt its authenticity nor that of the experience related. It illustrates a religious aspect of experience. But it illustrates also the use of that quality to carry a superimposed load of a particular religion. For having been brought up in the Christian religion, its subject interprets it in the terms of the personal God characteristic of that religion. Taoists, Buddhists, Moslems, persons of no religion including those who reject all supernatural influence and power, have had experiences sim-ilar in their effect. Yet another author commenting upon the passage says: "The religious expert can be more sure that this God exists than he can of either the cosmological God of speculative surmise or the Christlike God involved in the validity of moral optimism," and goes on to add that such experiences "mean that God the savior, the power that gives victory over sin on certain conditions that man can fulfill, is an existent, accessible and scientifically knowable reality." It should be clear that this inference is sound only if the conditions, of whatever sort, that produce the effect are called "God." But most readers will take the inference to mean that the existence of a particular Being, of the type called "God" in the Christian reliigon, is proved by a method akin to that of experimental science.

In reality, the only thing that can be said to be "proved" is the existence of some complex of conditions that have operated to effect an adjustment in life, an orientation, that brings with it a sense of security and peace. The particular interpretation given to this complex of conditions is not inherent in the experience itself. It is derived from the culture with which a particular person has been imbued. A fatalist will give one name to it; a Christian Scientist another, and the one who rejects all supernatural being still another. The determining factor in the interpretation of the experience is the particular doctrinal apparatus into which a person has been inducted. The emotional deposit connected with prior teaching floods the whole situation. It may readily confer upon the experience such a peculiarly sacred preciousness that all inquiry into its causation is barred. The stable outcome is so invaluable that the cause to which it is referred is usually nothing but a reduplication of the thing that has occurred, plus some name that has acquired a deeply emotional quality.

The intent of this discussion is not to deny the genuineness of the result nor its importance in life. It is not, save incidentally, to point out the possibility of a purely naturalistic explanation of the event. My purpose is to indicate what happens when religious experience is already set aside as something *sui generis*. The actual religious quality in the experience described is the *effect* produced, the better adjustment in life and its conditions, not the manner and cause of its production. The way in which the experience operated, its function, determines its religious value. If the reorientation actually occurs, it, and the sense of security and stability accompanying it, are forces on their own account. It takes place in different persons in a multitude of ways. It is sometimes brought about by devotion to a cause; sometimes by a passage of poetry that opens a new perspective; sometimes as was the case with Spinoza—deemed an atheist in his day—through philosophical reflection.

The difference between an experience having a religious force because of what it does in and to the processes of living and religious experience as a separate kind of thing gives me occasion to refer to a previous remark. If this function were rescued through emancipation from dependence upon specific types of beliefs and practices, from those elements that constitute a religion, many individuals would find that experiences having the force of bringing about a better, deeper and enduring adjustment in life are not so rare and infrequent as they are commonly supposed to be. They occur frequently in connection with many significant moments of living. The idea of invisible powers would take on the meaning of all the conditions of nature and human association that support and deepen the sense of values which carry one through periods of darkness and despair to such an extent that they lose their usual depressive character.

I do not suppose for many minds the dislocation of the religious from a religion is easy to effect. Tradition and custom, especially when emotionally charged, are a part of the habits that have become one with our very being. But the possibility of the transfer is demonstrated by its actuality. Let us then for the moment drop the term "religious," and ask what are the attitudes that lend deep and enduring support to the processes of living. I have, for example, used the words "adjustment" and "orientation." What do they signify?

While the words "accommodation," "adaptation," and "adjustment" are frequently employed as synonyms, attitudes exist that are so different that for the sake of clear thought they should be discriminated. There are conditions we meet that cannot be changed. If they are particular and limited, we modify our own particular attitudes in accordance with them. Thus we accommodate ourselves to changes in weather, to alterations in income when we have no other recourse. When the external conditions are lasting we become inured, habituated, or, as the process is now often called, conditioned. The two main traits of this attitude, which I should like to call accommodation, are that it affects *particular* modes of conduct, not the entire self, and that the process is mainly *passive*. It may, however, become general and then it becomes fatalistic resignation or submission. There are other attitudes toward the environment that are also particular but that are more active. We re-act against conditions and endeavor to change them to meet our wants and demands. Plays in a foreign language are "adapted" to meet the needs of an American audience. A house is rebuilt to suit changed conditions of the household; the telephone is invented to serve the demand for speedy communication at a distance; dry soils are irrigated so that they may bear abundant crops. Instead of accommodating ourselves to conditions, we modify conditions so that they will be accommodated to our wants and purposes. This process may be called adaptation.

Now both of these processes are often called by the more general name of adjustment. But there are also changes in ourselves in relation to the world in which we live that are much more inclusive and deep seated. They relate not to this and that want in relation to this and that condition of our surroundings, but pertain to our being in its entirety. Because of their scope, this modification of ourselves is enduring. It lasts through any amount of vicissitude of circumstances, internal and external. There is a composing and harmonizing of the various elements of our being such that, in spite of changes in the special conditions that surround us, these conditions are also arranged, settled, in relation to us. This attitude includes a note of submission. But it is voluntary, not externally imposed; and as voluntary it is something more than a mere Stoical resolution to endure unperturbed throughout the buffetings of fortune. It is more outgoing, more ready and glad, than the latter attitude, and it is more active than the former. And in calling it voluntary, it is not meant that it depends upon a particular re- solve or volition. It is a change *of* will conceived as the organic plenitude of our being, rather than any special change *in* will.

It is the claim of religions that they effect this generic and enduring change in attitude. I should like to turn the statement around and say that when- ever this change takes place there is a definitely religious attitude. It is not *a* religion that brings it about, but when it occurs, from whatever cause and by whatever means, there is a religious outlook and function. As I have said before, the doctrinal or intellectual apparatus and the institutional ac- cretions that grow up are, in a strict sense, adventitious to the intrinsic quality of such experiences. For they are affairs of the traditions of the culture with which individuals are inoculated. Mr. Santayana has connected the religious quality of experience with the imaginative, as that is expressed in poetry. "Religion and poetry," he says, "are identical in essence, and differ merely in the way in which they are attached to practical affairs. Poetry is called religion when it intervenes in life, and religion, when it merely supervenes upon life, is seen to be nothing but poetry." The differ- ence between intervening *in* and supervening *upon* is as important as is the identity set forth. Imagination may play upon life or it may enter profoundly into it. As Mr. Santayana puts it, "poetry has a universal and a moral func- tion," for "its highest power lies in its relevance to the ideals and purposes of life." Except as it intervenes, "all observation is observation of brute fact, all discipline is mere repression, until these facts digested and this discipline embodied in humane impulses become the starting point for a creative movement of the imagination, the firm basis for ideal constructions in society, religion, and art."

If I may make a comment upon this penetrating insight of Mr. Santayana, I would say that the difference between imagination that only supervenes and imagination that intervenes is the difference between one that com- pletely interpenetrates all the elements of our being and one that is inter- woven with only special and partial factors. There actually occurs extremely little observation of brute facts merely for the sake of the facts, just as there is little discipline that is repression and nothing but repression. Facts are usually observed with reference to some practical end and purpose, and that end is presented only imaginatively. The most repressive discipline has some end in view to which there is at least imputed an ideal quality; otherwise it is purely sadistic. But in such cases of observation and discipline imagination is limited and partial. It does not extend far; it does not permeate deeply and widely.

The connection between imagination and the harmonizing of the self is closer than is usually thought. The idea of a whole, whether of the whole personal being or of the world, is an imaginative, not a liberal, idea. The limited world of our observation and reflection becomes the Universe only through imaginative extension. It cannot be apprehended in knowledge nor realized in reflection. Neither observation, thought, nor practical activity can attain that complete unification of the self which is called a whole. The *whole* self is an ideal, an imaginative projection. Hence the idea of a thoroughgoing and deepseated harmonizing of the self with the Universe (as a name for the totality of conditions with which the self is connected) operates only through imagination—which is one reason why this composing of the self is not voluntary in the sense of an act of special volition or resolution. An "adjustment" possesses the will rather than is its express product. Religionists have been right in thinking of it as an influx from sources beyond conscious deliberation and purpose—a fact that helps explain, psychologically, why it has so generally been attributed to a supernatural source and that, perhaps, throws some light upon the reference of it by William James to unconscious factors. And it is pertinent to note that the unification of the self throughout the ceaseless flux of what it does, suffers, and achieves, cannot be attained in terms of itself. The self is always directed toward something beyond itself and so its own unification depends upon the idea of the integration of the shifting scenes of the world into the imaginative totality we call the Universe.

The intimate connection of imagination with ideal elements in experience is generally recognized. Such is not the case with respect to its connection with faith. The latter has been regarded as a substitute for knowledge, for sight. It is defined, in the Christian religion, as *evidence* of things not seen. The implication is that faith is a kind of anticipatory vision of things that are now invisible because of the limitations of our finite and erring nature. Because it is a substitute for knowledge, its material and object are intellectual in quality. As John Locke summed up the matter, faith is "assent to a proposition . . . on the credit of its proposer." Religious faith is then given to a body of propositions as true on the credit of their supernatural author, reason coming in to demonstrate the reasonableness of giving such credit. Of necessity there results the development of theologies, or bodies of systematic propositions, to make explicit in organized form the content of the propositions to which belief is attached and assent given. Given the point of view, those who hold that religion necessarily implies a theology are correct.

But belief or faith has also a moral and practical import. Even devils, according to the older theologians, believe—and tremble. A distinction was made, therefore, between "speculative" or intellectual belief and an act called "justifying" faith. Apart from any theological context, there is a difference between belief that is a conviction that some end should be supreme over conduct, and belief that some object or being exists as a truth for the intellect. Conviction in the moral sense signifies being conquered, vanquished, in our active nature by an ideal end; it signifies acknowledgment of its rightful claim over our desires and purposes. Such acknowledgment is practical, not primarily intellectual. It goes beyond evidence that can be presented to *any* possible observer. Reflection, often long and arduous, may be involved in arriving at the conviction, but the import of thought is not exhausted in discovery of evidence that can justify intellectual assent. The authority of an ideal over choice and conduct is the authority of an ideal, not of a fact, of a truth guaranteed to intellect, not of the status of the one who propounds the truth.

Such moral faith is not easy. It was questioned of old whether the Son of Man should find faith on the earth in his coming. Moral faith has been bolstered by all sorts of arguments intended to prove that its object is not ideal and that its claim upon us is not primarily moral or practical, since the ideal in question is already embedded in the existent frame of things. It is argued that the ideal is already the final reality at the heart of things that exist, and that only our senses or the corruption of our natures prevent us from apprehending its prior existential being. Starting, say, from such an idea as that justice is more than a moral ideal because it is embedded in the very make-up of the actually existent world, men have gone on to build up vast intellectual schemes, philosophies, and theologies, to prove that ideals are real not as ideals but as antecedently existing actualities. They have failed to see that in converting moral realities into matters of intellectual assent they have evinced lack of *moral* faith. Faith that something should be in existence as far as lies in our power is changed into the intellectual belief that it is already in existence. When physical existence does not bear out the assertion, the physical is subtly changed into the metaphysical. In this way, moral faith has been inextricably tied up with intellectual beliefs about the supernatural.

The tendency to convert ends of moral faith and action into articles of an intellectual creed has been furthered by a tendency of which psychologists are well aware. What we ardently desire to have thus and so, we tend to believe is already so. Desire has a powerful influence upon intellectual beliefs. Moreover, when conditions are adverse to realization of the objects of our desire—and in the case of significant ideals they are extremely adverse—it is an easy way out to assume that after all they are already embodied in the ultimate structure of what is, and that appearances to the contrary are *merely* appearances. Imagination then merely supervenes and is freed from the responsibility for intervening. Weak natures take to reverie as a refuge as strong ones do to fanaticism. Those who dissent are mourned over by the first class and converted through the use of force by the second.

What has been said does not imply that all moral faith in ideal ends is by virtue of that fact religious in quality. The religious is "morality touched by emotion" only when the ends of moral conviction arouse emotions that are not only intense but are actuated and supported by ends so inclusive that they unify the self. The inclusiveness of the end in relation to both self and the "universe" to which an inclusive self is related is indispensable. According to the best authorities, "religion" comes from a root that means being bound or tied. Originally, it meant being bound by vows to a particular way of life—as *les religieux* were monks and nuns who had assumed certain vows. The religious attitude signifies something that is bound through imagination to a *general* attitude. This comprehensive attitude, moreover, is much broader than anything indicated by "moral" in its usual sense. The quality of attitude is displayed in art, science and good citizenship.

If we apply the conception set forth to the terms of the definition earlier quoted, these terms take on a new significance. An unseen power controlling our destiny becomes the power of an ideal. All possibilities, as possibilities, are ideal in character. The artist, scientist, citizen, parent, as far as they are actuated by the spirit of their callings, are controlled by the unseen. For all endeavor for the better is moved by faith in what is possible, not by adherence to the actual. Nor does this faith depend for its moving power upon intellectual assurance or belief that the things worked for must surely prevail and come into embodied existence. For the authority of the object to determine our attitude and conduct, the right that is given it to claim our allegiance and devotion is based on the intrinsic nature of the ideal. The outcome, given our best endeavor, is not with us. The inherent vice of all intellectual schemes of idealism is that they convert the idealism of action into a system of beliefs about antecedent reality. The character assigned this reality is so different from that which observation and reflection lead to and support that these schemes inevitably glide into alliance with the supernatural.

All religions, marked by elevated ideal quality, have dwelt upon the power of religion to introduce perspective into the piecemeal and shifting episodes of existence. Here too we need to reverse the ordinary statement and say that whatever introduces genuine perspective is religious, not that religion is something that introduces it. There can be no doubt (referring to the second element of the definition) of our dependence upon forces beyond our control. Primitive man was so impotent in the face of these forces that, especially in an unfavorable natural environment, fear became a dominant attitude, and, as the old saying goes, fear created the gods.

With increase of mechanisms of control, the element of fear has, relatively speaking, subsided. Some optimistic souls have even concluded that the forces about us are on the whole essentially benign. But every crisis, whether of the individual or of the community, reminds man of the precarious and partial nature of the control he exercises. When man, individually and collectively, has done his uttermost, conditions that at different times and places have given rise to the ideas of Fate and Fortune, of Chance and Providence, remain. It is the part of manliness to insist upon the capacity of mankind to strive to direct natural and social forces to humane ends. But unqualified absolutistic statements about the omnipotence of such endeavors reflect egoism rather than intelligent courage.

The fact that human destiny is so interwoven with forces beyond human control renders it unnecessary to suppose that dependence and the humility that accompanies it have to find the particular channel that is prescribed by traditional doctrines. What is especially significant is rather the form which the sense of dependence takes. Fear never gave stable perspective in the life of anyone. It is dispersive and withdrawing. Most religions have in fact added rites of communion to those of expiation and propitiation. For our dependence is manifested in those relations to the environment that support our undertakings and aspirations as much as it is in the defeats inflicted upon us. The essentially unreligious attitude is that which attributes human achievement and purpose to man in isolation from the world of physical nature and his fellows. Our successes are dependent upon the coöperation of nature. The sense of the dignity of human nature is as religious as is the sense of awe and reverence when it rests upon a sense of human nature as a coöperating part of a larger whole. Natural piety is not of necessity either a fatalistic acquiescence in natural happenings or a romantic idealization of the world. It may rest upon a just sense of nature as the whole of which we are parts, while it also recognizes that we are parts that are marked by intelligence and purpose, having the capacity to strive by their aid to bring conditions into greater consonance with what is humanly desirable. Such piety is an inherent constituent of a just perspective in life.

Understanding and knowledge also enter into a perspective that is religious in quality. Faith in the continued disclosing of truth through directed cooperative human endeavor is more religious in quality than is any faith in a completed revelation. It is of course now usual to hold that revelation is not completed in the sense of being ended. But religions hold that the essential framework is settled in its significant moral features at least, and that new elements that are offered must be judged by conformity to this framework. Some fixed doctrinal apparatus is necessary for *a* religion. But faith in the possibilities of continued and rigorous inquiry does not limit access to truth to any channel or scheme of things. It does not first say that truth is universal and then add there is but one road to it. It does not depend for assurance upon subjection to any dogma or item of doctrine. It trusts that the natural interactions between man and his environment will breed more intelligence and generate more knowledge provided the scientific methods that define intelligence in operation are pushed further into the mysteries of the world, being themselves promoted and improved in the operation. There is such a thing as faith in intelligence becoming religious in quality—a fact that perhaps explains the efforts of some religionists to disparage the possibilities of intelligence as a force. They properly feel such faith to be a dangerous rival.

Lives that are consciously inspired by loyalty to such ideals as have been mentioned are still comparatively infrequent to the extent of that comprehensiveness and intensity which arouse an ardor religious in function. But before we infer the incompetency of such ideals and of the actions they inspire, we should at least ask ourselves how much of the existing situation is due to the fact that the religious factors of experience have been drafted into supernatural channels and thereby loaded with irrelevant encumbrances. A body of beliefs and practices that are apart from the common and natural relations of mankind must, in the degree in which it is influential, weaken and sap the force of the possibilities inherent in such relations. Here lies one aspect of the emancipation of the religious from religion.

Any activity pursued in behalf of an ideal end against obstacles and in spite of threats of personal loss because of conviction of its general and enduring value is religious in quality. Many a person, inquirer, artist, philanthropist, citizen, men and women in the humblest walks of life, have achieved, without presumption and without display, such unification of themselves and of their relations to the conditions of existence. It remains to extend their spirit and inspiration to ever wider numbers. If I have said anything about religions and religion that seems harsh, I have said those things because of a firm belief that the claim on the part of religions to possess a monopoly of ideals and of the supernatural means by which alone, it is alleged, they can be furthered, stands in the way of the realization of distinctively religious values inherent in natural experience. For that reason, if for no other, I should be sorry if any were misled by the frequency with which I have employed the adjective "religious" to conceive of what I have said as a disguised apology for what have passed as religions. The opposition between religious values as I conceive them and religions is not to be bridged. Just because the release of these values is so important, their identification with the creeds and cults of religions must be dissolved.

WILLIAM JAMES

WILLIAM JAMES (1842-1910) was professor at Harvard College and a distinguished American philosopher and psychologist. He attempted to use the pragmatic theory of truth to reconcile the basic claims of religion with an empiricist theory of knowledge. His book, *The Varieties of Religious Experience,* is a classic work.

*The Varieties of Religious Experience**

Conclusions

The material of our study of human nature is now spread before us; and in this parting hour, set free from the duty of description, we can draw our theoretical and practical conclusions. In my first lecture, defending the empirical method, I foretold that whatever conclusions we might come to could be reached by spiritual judgments only, appreciations of the significance for life of religion, taken "on the whole." Our conclusions cannot be as sharp as dogmatic conclusions would be, but I will formulate them, when the times comes, as sharply as I can.

Summing up in the broadest possible way the characteristics of the religious life, as we have found them, it includes the following beliefs:—

1. That the visible world is part of a more spiritual universe from which it draws its chief significance;

* From William James, *The Varieties of Religious Experience*, pp. 485-501, 512-515. Copyright, 1902. Longmans, Green and Co. In the public domain. [Footnotes omitted, Eds]

2. That union or harmonious relation with that higher universe is our true end;

3. That prayer or inner communion with the spirit thereof—be that spirit "God" or "law"—is a process wherein work is really done, and spiritual energy flows in and produces effects, psychological or material, within the phenomenal world.

Religion includes also the following psychological characteristics:—

4. A new zest which adds itself like a gift to life, and takes the form either of lyrical enchantment or of appeal to earnestness and heroism.

5. An assurance of safety and a temper of peace, and, in relation to others, a preponderance of loving affections.

In illustrating these characteristics by documents, we have been literally bathed in sentiment. In re-reading my manuscript, I am almost appalled at the amount of emotionality which I find in it. After so much of this, we can afford to be dryer and less sympathetic in the rest of the work that lies before us.

The sentimentality of many of my documents is a consequence of the fact that I sought them among the extravagances of the subject. If any of you are enemies of what our ancestors used to brand as enthusiasm, and are, nevertheless, still listening to me now, you have probably felt my selection to have been sometimes almost perverse, and have wished I might have stuck to soberer examples. I reply that I took these extremer examples as yielding the profounder information. To learn the secrets of any science, we go to expert specialists, even though they may be eccentric persons, and not to commonplace pupils. We combine what they tell us with the rest of our wisdom and form our final judgment independently. Even so with religion. We who have pursued such radical expressions of it may now be sure that we know its secrets as authentically as any one can know them who learns them from another; and we have next to answer, each of us for himself, the practical question: what are the dangers in this element of life? and in what proportion may it need to be restrained by other elements, to give the proper balance?

But this question suggests another one which I will answer immediately and get it out of the way, for it has more than once already vexed us. Ought it to be assumed that in all men the mixture of religion with other elements should be identical? Ought it, indeed, to be assumed that the lives of all men should show identical religious elements? In other words, is the existence of so many religious types and sects and creeds regrettable?

To these questions I answer "No" emphatically. And my reason is that I do not see how it is possible that creatures in such different positions and with such different powers as human individuals are, should have exactly the same functions and the same duties. No two of us have identical difficulties, nor should we be expected to work out identical solutions. Each, from his peculiar angle of observation, takes in a certain sphere of fact and trouble, which each must deal with in a unique manner. One of us must soften himself, another must harden himself; one must yield a point, another must stand firm,—in order the better to defend the position assigned him. If an Emerson were forced to be a Wesley, or a Moody forced to be a Whitman, the total human consciousness of the divine would suffer. The divine can mean no single quality, it must mean a group of qualities, by being champions of which in alternation, different men may all find worthy missions. Each attitude being a syllable in human nature's total message, it takes the whole of us to spell the meaning out completely. So a "god of battles" must be allowed to be the god for one kind of person, a god of peace and heaven and home, the god for another. We must frankly recognize the fact that we live in partial systems, and that parts are not interchangeable in the spiritual life. If we are peevish and jealous, destruction of the self must be an element of our religion; why need it be one if we are good and sympathetic from the outset? If we are sick souls, we require a religion of deliverance; but why think so much of deliverance, if we are healthy-minded? Unquestionably, some men have the completer experience and the higher vocation, here just as in the social world; but for each man to stay in his own experience, whate'er it be, and for others to tolerate him there, is surely best.

But, you may now ask, would not this one-sideness be cured if we should all espouse the science of religion as our own religion? In answering this question I must open again the general relations of the theoretic to the active life.

Knowledge about a thing is not the thing itself. You remember what Al-Ghazzali told us in the Lecture on Mysticism,—that to understand the causes of drunkenness, as a physician understands them, is not to be drunk. A science might come to understand everything about the causes and elements of religion, and might even decide which elements were qualified, by their general harmony with other branches of knowledge, to be considered true; and yet the best man at this science might be the man who found it hardest to be personally devout. *Tout savoir c'est tout pardonner.* The name of Renan would doubtless occur to many persons as an example of the way in which breadth of knowledge may make one only a dilettante in possibilities, and blunt the acuteness of one's living faith. If religion be a function by which either God's cause or man's cause is to be really advanced, then he who lives the life of it, however narrowly, is a better servant than he who merely knows about it, however much. Knowledge about life is one thing; effective occupation of a place in life, with its dynamic currents passing through your being, is another.

For this reason, the science of religions may not be an equivalent for living religion; and if we turn to the inner difficulties of such a science, we see that a point comes when she must drop the purely theoretic attitude, and either let her knots remain uncut, or have them cut by active faith. To see this, suppose that we have our science of religions constituted as a matter of fact. Suppose that she has assimilated all the necessary historical material and distilled out of it as its essence the same conclusions which I myself a few moments ago pronounced. Suppose that she agrees that religion, wherever it is an active thing, involves a belief in ideal presences, and a belief that in our prayerful communion with them, work is done, and something real comes to pass. She has now to exert her critical activity, and to decide how far, in the light of other sciences and in that of general philosophy, such beliefs can be considered *true*.

Dogmatically to decide this is an impossible task. Not only are the other sciences and the philosophy still far from being completed, but in their present state we find them full of conflicts. The sciences of nature know nothing of spiritual presences, and on the whole hold no practical commerce whatever with the idealistic conceptions towards which general philosophy inclines. The scientist, so-called, is, during his scientific hours at least, so materialistic that one may well say that on the whole the influence of science goes against the notion that religion should be recognized at all. And this antipathy to religion finds an echo within the very science of religions itself. The cultivator of this science has to become acquainted with so many groveling and horrible superstitions that a presumption easily arises in his mind that any belief that is religious probably is false. In the "prayerful communion" of savages with such mumbo-jumbos of deities as they acknowledge, it is hard for us to see what genuine spiritual work—even though it were work relative only to their dark savage obligations—can possibly be done.

The consequence is that the conclusions of the science of religions are as likely to be adverse as they are to be favorable to the claim that the essence of religion is true. There is a notion in the air about us that religion is probably only an anachronism, a case of "survival," an atavistic relapse into a mode of thought which humanity in its more enlightened examples has outgrown; and this notion our religious anthropologists at present do little to counteract.

This view is so widespread at the present day that I must consider it with some explicitness before I pass to my own conclusions. Let me call it the "Survival theory," for brevity's sake.

The pivot round which the religious life, as we have traced it, revolves, is the interest of the individual in his private personal destiny. Religion, in short, is a monumental chapter in the history of human egotism. The gods believed in—whether by crude savages or by men disciplined intellectually— agree with each other in recognizing personal calls. Religious thought is carried on in terms of personality, this being, in the world of religion, the one fundamental fact. To-day, quite as much as at any previous age, the religious individual tells you that the divine meets him on the basis of his personal concerns.

Science, on the other hand, has ended by utterly repudiating the personal point of view. She catalogues her elements and records her laws indifferent as to what purpose may be shown forth by them, and constructs her theories quite careless of their bearing on human anxieties and fates. Though the scientist may individually nourish a religion, and be a theist in his irresponsible hours, the days are over when it could be said that for Science herself the heavens declare the glory of God and the firmament showeth his handiwork. Our solar system, with its harmonies, is seen now as but one passing case of a certain sort of moving equilibrium in the heavens, realized by a local accident in an appalling wilderness of worlds where no life can exist. In a span of time which as a cosmic interval will count but as an hour, it will have ceased to be. The Darwinian notion of chance production, and subsequent destruction, speedy or deferred, applies to the largest as well as to the smallest facts. It is impossible, in the present temper of the scientific imagination, to find in the driftings of the cosmic atoms, whether they work on the universal or on the particular scale, anything but a kind of aimless weather, doing and undoing, achieving no proper history, and leaving no result. Nature has no one distinguishable ultimate tendency with which it is possible to feel a sympathy. In the vast rhythm of her processes, as the scientific mind now follows them, she appears to cancel herself. The books of natural theology which satisfied the intellects of our grandfathers seem to us quite grotesque, representing as they did, a God who conformed the largest things of nature to the paltriest of our private wants. The God whom science recognizes must be a God of universal laws exclusively, a God who does a wholesale, not a retail business. He cannot accommodate his processes to the convenience of individuals. The bubbles on the foam which coats a stormy sea are floating episodes, made and unmade by the forces of the wind and water. Our private selves are like those bubbles,—epiphenomena, as Clifford, I believe, ingeniously called them; their destinies weigh nothing and determine nothing in the world's irremediable currents of events.

You see how natural it is, from this point of view, to treat religion as a mere survival, for religion does in fact perpetuate the traditions of the most primeval thought. To coerce the spiritual powers, or to square them and get them on our side, was, during enormous tracts of time, the one great object in our dealings with the natural world. For our ancestors, dreams, hallucinations, revelations, and cock-and-bull stories were inextricably mixed with facts. Up to comparatively recent date such distinctions as those between what has been verified and what is only conjectured, between the impersonal and the personal aspects of existence, were hardly suspected or conceived. Whatever you imagined in a lively manner, whatever you thought fit to be true, you affirmed confidently; and whatever you affirmed, your comrades believed. Truth was what had not yet been contradicted, most things were taken into the mind from the point of view of their human suggestiveness, and the attention confined itself exclusively to the aesthetic and dramatic aspects of events.

How indeed could it be otherwise? The extraordinary value, for explanation and prevision, of those mathematical and mechanical modes of conception which science uses, was a result that could not possibly have been expected in advance. Weight, movement, velocity, direction, position, what thin, pallid, uninteresting ideas! How could the richer animistic aspects of Nature, the peculiarities and oddities that make phenomena picturesquely striking or expressive, fail to have been first singled out and followed by philosophy as the more promising avenue to the knowledge of Nature's life? Well, it is still in these richer animistic and dramatic aspects that religion delights to dwell. It is the terror and beauty of phenomena, the "promise" of the dawn and of the rainbow, the "voice" of the thunder, the "gentleness" of the summer rain, the "sublimity" of the stars, and not the physical laws which these things follow, by which the religious mind still continues to be most impressed; and just as of yore, the devout man tells you that in the solitude of his room or of the fields he still feels the divine presence, that inflowings of help come in reply to his prayers, and that sacrifices to this unseen reality fill him with security and peace.

Pure anachronism! says the survival-theory;—anachronism for which deanthropomorphization of the imagination is the remedy required. The less we mix the private with the cosmic, the more we dwell in universal and impersonal terms, the truer heirs of Science we become.

In spite of the appeal which this impersonality of the scientific attitude makes to a certain magnanimity of temper, I believe it to be shallow, and I can now state my reason in comparatively few words. That reason is that, so long as we deal with the cosmic and the general, we deal only with the symbols of reality, but *as soon as we deal with private and personal phe-*

nomena as such, we deal with realities in the completest sense of the term.
I think I can easily make clear what I mean by these words.

The world of our experience consists at all times of two parts, an objective and a subjective part, of which the former may be incalculably more extensive than the latter, yet the latter can never be omitted or suppressed. The objective part is the sum total of whatsoever at any given time we may be thinking of, the subjective part is the inner "state" in which the thinking comes to pass. What we think of may be enormous,—the cosmic times and spaces, for example,—whereas the inner state may be the most fugitive and paltry activity of mind. Yet the cosmic objects, so far as the experience yields them, are but ideal pictures of something whose existence we do not inwardly possess but only point at outwardly, while the inner state is our very experience itself; its reality and that of our experience are one. A conscious field *plus* its object as felt or thought of *plus* an attitude towards the object *plus* the sense of a self to whom the attitude belongs—such a concrete bit of personal experience may be a small bit, but it is a solid bit as long as it lasts; not hollow, not a mere abstract element of experience, such as the "object" is when taken all alone. It is a *full* fact, even though it be an insignificant fact; it is of the *kind* to which all realities whatsoever must belong; the motor currents of the world run through the like of it; it is on the line connecting real events with real events. That unsharable feeling which each of us has of the pinch of his individual destiny as he privately feels it rolling out on fortune's wheel may be disparaged for its egotism, may be sneered at as unscientific, but it is the one thing that fills up the measure of our concrete actuality, and any would-be existent that should lack such a feeling, or its analogue, would be a piece of reality only half made up.

If this be true, it is absurd for science to say that the egotistic elements of experience should be suppressed. The axis of reality runs solely through the egotistic places,—they are strung upon it like so many beads. To describe the world with all the various feelings of the individual pinch of destiny, all the various spiritual attitudes, left out from the description—they being as describable as anything else—would be something like offering a printed bill of fare as the equivalent for a solid meal. Religion makes no such blunder. The individual's religion may be egotistic, and those private realities which it keeps in touch with may be narrow enough; but at any rate it always remains infinitely less hollow and abstract, as far as it goes, than a science which prides itself on taking no account of anything private at all.

A bill of fare with one real raisin on it instead of the word "raisin," with one real egg instead of the word "egg," might be an inadequate meal, but it would at least be a commencement of reality. The contention of the survival-theory that we ought to stick to non-personal elements exclusively seems like saying that we ought to be satisfied forever with reading the naked bill of fare. I think, therefore, that however particular questions connected with our individual destinies may be answered, it is only by acknowledging them as genuine questions, and living in the sphere of thought which they open up, that we become profound. But to live thus is to be religious; so I unhesitatingly repudiate the survival-theory of religion, as being founded on an egregious mistake. It does not follow, because our ancestors made so many errors of fact and mixed them with their religion, that we should therefore leave off being religious at all. But being religious we establish ourselves in possession of ultimate reality at the only points at which reality is given us to guard. Our responsible concern is with our private destiny, after all.

.   .   .   .

Let me then propose, as an hypothesis, that whatever it may be on its *farther* side, the "more" with which in religious experience we feel ourselves connected is on its *hither* side the subconscious continuation of our conscious life. Starting thus with a recognized psychological fact as our basis, we seem to preserve a contact with "science" which the ordinary theologian lacks. At the same time the theologian's contention that the religious man is moved by an external power is vindicated, for it is one of the peculiarities of invasions from the subconscious region to take on objective appearances, and to suggest to the Subject an external control. In the religious life the control is felt as "higher"; but since on our hypothesis it is primarily the higher faculties of our own hidden mind which are controlling, the sense of union with the power beyond us is a sense of something, not merely apparently, but literally true.

This doorway into the subject seems to me the best one for a science of religions, for it mediates between a number of different points of view. Yet it is only a doorway, and difficulties present themselves as soon as we step through it, and ask how far our transmarginal consciousness carries us if we follow it on its remoter side. Here the over-beliefs begin: here mysticism and the conversion-rapture and Vedantism and transcendental idealism bring in their monistic interpretations and tell us that the finite self rejoins the absolute self, for it was always one with God and identical with the soul of the world. Here the prophets of all the different religions come with their visions, voices, raptures, and other openings, supposed by each to authenticate his own peculiar faith.

Those of us who are not personally favored with such specific revelations must stand outside of them altogether and, for the present at least, decide that, since they corroborate incompatible theological doctrines, they neutralize one another and leave no fixed result. If we follow any one of them, or if we follow philosophical theory and embrace monistic pantheism on non-mystical grounds, we do so in the exercise of our individual freedom, and build out our religion in the way most congruous with our personal susceptibilities. Among these susceptibilities intellectual ones play a decisive part. Although the religious question is primarily a question of life, of living or not living in the higher union which opens itself to us as a gift, yet the spiritual excitement in which the gift appears a real one will often fail to be aroused in an individual until certain particular intellectual beliefs or ideas which, as we say, come home to him, are touched. These ideas will thus be essential to that individual's religion;—which is as much as to say that over-beliefs in various directions are absolutely indispensable, and that we should treat them with tenderness and tolerance so long as they are not intolerant themselves. As I have elsewhere written, the most interesting and valuable things about a man are usually his over-beliefs.

Disregarding the over-beliefs, and confining ourselves to what is common and generic, we have in *the fact that the conscious person is continuous with a wider self through which saving experiences come*, a positive content of religious experience which, it seems to me, *is literally and objectively true as far as it goes.*

ERICH FROMM

ERICH FROMM (1900-   ), well-known psychoanalyst, has been interested in the phenomenon of religion in both individual and social life. He received his doctorate at the University of Heidelberg, came to America in 1934 and has taught at Columbia, Yale, Bennington and various psychiatric institutes.

What Is Humanistic Religion?*

It would far transcend the scope of this chapter to attempt a review of all types of religion. Even to discuss only those types which are relevant from the psychological standpoint cannot be undertaken here. I shall therefore deal with only one distinction, but one which in my opinion is the most

* From Erich Fromm, *Psychoanalysis and Religion*, pp. 34-38, 40-47, 48-55, 113-114. Copyright, 1950, by Erich Fromm. Reprinted by permission of Yale University Press.

important, and which cuts across nontheistic and theistic religions: that between *authoritarian* and *humanistic* religions.

What is the principle of authoritarian religion? The definition of religion given in the *Oxford Dictionary*, while attempting to define religion as such, is a rather accurate definition of authoritarian religion. It reads: "[Religion is] recognition on the part of man of some higher unseen power as having control of his destiny, and as being entitled to obedience, reverence, and worship."

Here the emphasis is on the recognition that man is controlled by a higher power outside of himself. But this alone does not constitute authoritarian religion. What makes it so is the idea that this power, because of the control it exercises, is *entitled* to "obedience, reverence and worship." I italicize the word "entitled" because it shows that the reason for worship, obedience, and reverence lies not in the moral qualities of the deity, not in love or justice, but in the fact that it has control, that is, has power over man. Furthermore it shows that the higher power has a right to force man to worship him and that lack of reverence and obedience constitutes sin.

The essential element in authoritarian religion and in the authoritarian religious experience is the surrender to a power transcending man. The main virtue of this type of religion is obedience, its cardinal sin is disobedience. Just as the deity is conceived as omnipotent or omniscient, man is conceived as being powerless and insignificant. Only as he can gain grace or help from the deity by complete surrender can he feel strength. Submission to a powerful authority is one of the avenues by which man escapes from his feeling of aloneness and limitation. In the act of surrender he loses his independence and integrity as an individual but he gains the feeling of being protected by an awe-inspiring power of which, as it were, he becomes a part.

In Calvin's theology we find a vivid picture of authoritarian, theistic thinking. "For I do not call it humility," says Calvin, "if you suppose that we have anything left. . . . We cannot think of ourselves as we ought to think without utterly despising everything that may be supposed an excellence in us. This humility is unfeigned submission of a mind overwhelmed with a weighty sense of its own misery and poverty; for such is the uniform description of it in the word of God." [1]

The experience which Calvin describes here, that of despising everything in oneself, of the submission of the mind overwhelmed by its own poverty, is the very essence of all authoritarian religions whether they are couched in secular or in theological language. [2] In authoritarian religion God is a

[1] Johannes Calvin, *Institutes of the Christian Religion* (Presbyterian Board of Christian Education, 1928), p. 681.

[2] See Erich Fromm, *Escape from Freedom* (Farrar & Rinehart, 1941), pp. 141ff. This attitude toward authority is described there in detail.

symbol of power and force, He is supreme because He has supreme power, and man in juxtaposition is utterly powerless.

Authoritarian secular religion follows the same principle. Here the Führer or the beloved "Father of His People" or the State or the Race or the Socialist Fatherland becomes the object of worship; the life of the individual becomes insignificant and man's worth consists in the very denial of his worth and strength. Frequently authoritarian religion postulates an ideal which is so abstract and so distant that it has hardly any connection with the real life of real people. To such ideals as "life after death" or "the future of mankind" the life and happiness of persons living here and now may be sacrificed; the alleged ends justify every means and become symbols in the names of which religious or secular "elites" control the lives of their fellow men.

Humanistic religion, on the contrary, is centered around man and his strength. Man must develop his power of reason in order to understand himself, his relationship to his fellow men and his position in the universe. He must recognize the truth, both with regard to his limitations and his potentialities. He must develop his powers of love for others as well as for himself and experience the solidarity of all living beings. He must have principles and norms to guide him in this aim. Religious experience in this kind of religion is the experience of oneness with the All, based on one's relatedness to the world as it is grasped with thought and with love. Man's aim in humanistic religion is to achieve the greatest strength, not the greatest powerlessness; virtue is self-realization, not obedience. Faith is certainty of conviction based on one's experience of thought and feeling, not assent to propositions on credit of the proposer. The prevailing mood is that of joy, while the prevailing mood in authoritarian religion is that of sorrow and of guilt.

Inasmuch as humanistic religions are theistic, God is a symbol of *man's own powers* which he tries to realize in his life, and is not a symbol of force and domination, having *power over man*.

Illustrations of humanistic religions are early Buddhism, Taoism, the teachings of Isaiah, Jesus, Socrates, Spinoza, certain trends in the Jewish and Christian religions (particularly mysticism), the religion of Reason of the French Revolution. It is evident from these that the distinction between authoritarian and humanistic religion cuts across the distinction between theistic and nontheistic, and between religions in the narrow sense of the word and philosophical systems of religious character. What matters in all such systems is not the thought system as such but the human attitude underlying their doctrines.

One of the best examples of humanistic religions is early Buddhism. The

Buddha is a great teacher, he is the "awakened one" who recognizes the truth about human existence. He does not speak in the name of a supernatural power but in the name of reason. He calls upon every man to make use of his own reason and to see the truth which he was only the first to find. Once man takes the first step in seeing the truth, he must apply his efforts to live in such a way that he develops his powers of reason and of love for all human creatures. Only to the degree to which he succeeds in this can he free himself from the bondage of irrational passions. While man must recognize his limitations according to Buddhistic teaching, he must also become aware of the powers in himself. The concept of Nirvana as the state of mind the fully awakened one can achieve is not one of man's helplessness and submission but on the contrary one of the development of the highest powers man possesses. . . .

Zen-Buddhism, a later sect within Buddhism, is expressive of an even more radical anti-authoritarian attitude. Zen proposes that no knowledge is of any value unless it grows out of ourselves; no authority, no teacher can really teach us anything except to arouse doubts in us; words and thought systems are dangerous because they easily turn into authorities whom we worship. Life itself must be grasped and experienced as it flows, and in this lies virtue. . . .

Another illustration of a humanistic religious system is to be found in Spinoza's religious thinking. While his language is that of medieval theology, his concept of God has no trace of authoritarianism. God could not have created the world different from what it is. He cannot change anything; in fact, God is identical with the totality of the universe. Man must see his own limitations and recognize that he is dependent on the totality of forces outside himself over which he has no control. Yet his are the powers of love and of reason. He can develop them and attain an optimum of freedom and of inner strength.

The distinction between authoritarian and humanistic religion not only cuts across various religions, it can exist within the same religion. Our own religious tradition is one of the best illustrations of this point. Since it is of fundamental importance to understand fully the distinction between authoritarian and humanistic religion I shall illustrate it further from a source with which every reader is more or less familiar, the Old Testament.

The beginning of the Old Testament [3] is written in the spirit of authoritarian religion. The picture of God is that of the absolute ruler of a patriarchal clan, who has created man at his pleasure and can destroy him at will.

---

[3] The historical fact that the beginning of the Bible may not be its oldest part does not need to be considered here since we use the text as an illustration of two principles and not to establish a historical sequence.

He has forbidden him to eat from the tree of knowledge of good and evil and has threatened him with death if he transgresses this order. But the serpent, "more clever than any animal," tells Eve, "Ye shall not surely die: For God doth know that in the day ye eat thereof, then your eyes shall be opened, and ye shall be as gods, knowing good and evil." [4] God proves the serpent to be right. When Adam and Eve have transgressed he punished them by proclaiming enmity between man and nature, between man and the soil and animals, and between men and women. But man is not to die. However, "the man has become as one of us, to know good and evil: and now, lest he put forth his hand, and take also of the tree of life, and eat, and live for ever," [5] God expels Adam and Eve from the garden of Eden and puts an angel with a flaming sword at the east "to keep the way of the tree of life."

The text makes very clear what man's sin is: it is rebellion against God's command; it is disobedience and not any inherent sinfulness in the act of eating from the tree of knowledge. On the contrary, further religious development has made the knowledge of good and evil the cardinal virtue to which man may aspire. The text also makes it plain what God's motive is: it is concern with his own superior role, the jealous fear of man's claim to become his equal.

A decisive turning point in the relationship between God and man is to be seen in the story of the Flood. When God saw "that the wickedness of man was great on the earth . . . it repented the Lord that he had made man and the earth, and it grieved him at his heart. And the Lord said, I will destroy man whom I have created from the face of the earth; both man, and beast, and the creeping thing, and the fowls of the air; for it repenteth me that I have made them." [6]

There is no question here but that God has the right to destroy his own creatures; he has created them and they are his property. The text defines their wickedness as "violence," but the decision to destroy not only man but animals and plants as well shows that we are not dealing here with a sentence commensurate with some specific crime but with God's angry regret over his own action which did not turn out well. "But Noah found grace in the eyes of the Lord," and he, together with his family and a representative of each animal species, is saved from the Flood. Thus far the destruction of man and the salvation of Noah are arbitrary acts of God. He could do as he pleased, as can any powerful tribal chief. But after the Flood the relationship between God and man changes fundamentally. A

[4] Genesis 3: 4-5.
[5] *Ibid.* 3: 22.
[6] *Ibid.* 6: 5 ff.

covenant is concluded between God and man in which God promises that "neither shall all flesh be cut off any more by the waters of a flood; neither shall there any more be a flood to destroy the earth." [7] God obligates himself never to destroy all life on earth, and man is bound to the first and most fundamental command of the Bible, not to kill: "At the hand of every man's brother will I require the life of man." [8] From this point on the relationship between God and man undergoes a profound change. God is no longer an absolute ruler who can act at his pleasure but is bound by a constitution to which both he and man must adhere; he is bound by a principle which he cannot violate, the principle of respect for life. God can punish man if he violates this principle, but man can also challenge God if he is guilty of its violation.

The new relationship between God and man appears clearly in Abraham's plea for Sodom and Gomorrah. When God considers destroying the cities because of their wickedness, Abraham criticizes God for violating his own principles. "That be far from thee to do after this manner, to slay the righteous with the wicked: and that the righteous should be as the wicked, that be far from thee. Shall not the Judge of all the earth do right?" [9]

The difference between the story of the Fall and this argument is great indeed. There man is forbidden to know good and evil and his position toward God is that of submission—or sinful disobedience. Here man uses his knowledge of good and evil, criticizes God in the name of justice, and God has to yield.

Even this brief analysis of the authoritarian element in the biblical story shows that at the root of the Judaeo-Christian religion both principles, the authoritarian and the humanistic, are present. In the development of Judaism as well as of Christianity both principles have been preserved and their respective preponderance marks different trends in the two religions.

The following story from the Talmud expresses the unauthoritarian, humanistic side of Judaism as we find it in the first centuries of the Christian era.

A number of other famous rabbinical scholars disagreed with Rabbi Eliezar's views in regard to a point of ritual law. "Rabbi Eliezar said to them: 'If the law is as I think it is then this tree shall let us know.' Whereupon the tree jumped from its place a hundred yards (others say four hundred yards). His colleagues said to him, 'One does not prove anything from a tree.' He said, 'If I am right then this brook shall let us know.' Whereupon the brook ran upstream. His colleagues said to him, 'One does not

[7] *Ibid.* 9: 11.
[8] *Ibid.* 9: 5.
[9] *Ibid.* 18: 25.

prove anything from a brook.' He continued and said, 'If the law is as I think then the walls of the house will tell.' Whereupon the walls began to fall. But Rabbi Joshua shouted at the walls and said, 'If scholars argue a point of law, what business have you to fall?' So the walls fell no further out of respect for Rabbi Joshua but out of respect for Rabbi Eliezar did not straighten up. And that is the way they still are. Rabbi Eliezar took up the argument again and said, 'If the law is as I think, they shall tell us from heaven.' Whereupon a voice from heaven said, 'What have you against Rabbi Eliezar, because the law is as he says.' Whereupon Rabbi Joshua got up and said, 'It is written in the Bible: The law is not in heaven. What does this mean? According to Rabbi Jirmijahu it means since the Torah has been given on Mount Sinai we no longer pay attention to voices from heaven because it is written: You make your decision according to the majority opinion.' It then happened that Rabbi Nathan [one of the participants in the discussion] met the Prophet Elijah [who had taken a stroll on earth] and he asked the Prophet, 'What did God himself say when we had this discussion?' The Prophet answered, 'God smiled and said, My children have won, my children have won.' " [10]

This story is hardly in need of comment. It emphasizes the autonomy of man's reason with which even the supernatural voices from heaven cannot interfere. God smiles, man has done what God wanted him to do, he has become his own master, capable and resolved to make his decisions by himself according to rational, democratic methods. . . .

That early Christianity is humanistic and not authoritarian is evident from the spirit and text of all Jesus' teachings. Jesus' precept that "the kingdom of God is within you" is the simple and clear expression of non-authoritarian thinking. But only a few hundred years later, after Christianity had ceased to be the religion of the poor and humble peasants, artisans, and slaves (the Am haarez) and had become the religion of those ruling the Roman Empire, the authoritarian trend in Christianity became dominant. Even so, the conflict between the authoritarian and humanistic principles in Christianity never ceased. It was the conflict between Augustine and Pelagius, between the Catholic Church and the many "heretic" groups and between various sects within Protestantism. The humanistic, democratic element was never subdued in Christian or in Jewish history, and this element found one of its most potent expressions in the mystic thinking within both religions. The mystics have been deeply imbued with the experience of man's strength, his likeness to God, and with the idea that God needs man as much as man needs God; they have understood the sentence that man is created

10 Talmud, Baba Meziah, 59, b. (My translation.)

in the image of God to mean the fundamental identity of God and man. Not fear and submission but love and the assertion of one's own powers are the basis of mystical experience. *God is not a symbol of power over man but of man's own powers.*

Thus far we have dealt with the distinctive features of authoritarian and humanistic religions mainly in descriptive terms. But the psychoanalyst must proceed from the description of attitudes to the analysis of their dynamics, and it is here that he can contribute to our discussion from an area not accessible to other fields of inquiry. The full understanding of an attitude requires an appreciation of those conscious and, in particular, unconscious processes occurring in the individual which provide the necessity for and the conditions of its development.

While in humanistic religion God is the image of man's higher self, a symbol of what man potentially is or ought to become, in authoritarian religion God becomes the sole possessor of what was originally man's: of his reason and his love. The more perfect God becomes, the more imperfect becomes man. He *projects* the best he has onto God and thus impoverishes himself. Now God has all love, all wisdom, all justice—and man is deprived of these qualities, he is empty and poor. He had begun with the feeling of smallness, but he now has become completely powerless and without strength; all his powers have been projected onto God. This mechanism of projection is the very same which can be observed in interpersonal relationships of a masochistic, submissive character, where one person is awed by another and attributes his own powers and aspirations to the other person. It is the same mechanism that makes people endow the leaders of even the most inhuman systems with qualities of superwisdom and kindness.[11]

When man has thus projected his own most valuable powers onto God, what of his relationship to his own powers? They have become separated from him and in this process he has become *alienated* from himself. Everything he has is now God's and nothing is left in him. *His only access to himself is through God.* In worshipping God he tries to get in touch with that part of himself which he has lost through projection. After having given God all he has, he begs God to return to him some of what originally was his own. But having lost his own he is completely at God's mercy. He necessarily feels like a "sinner" since he has deprived himself of everything that is good, and it is only through God's mercy or grace that he can regain that which alone makes him human. And in order to persuade God to give him some of his love, he must prove to him how utterly deprived he is of love; in order to

---

[11] Cf. the discussion about symbiotic relationship in *Escape from Freedom*, pp. 158 ff.

persuade God to guide him by his superior wisdom he must prove to him
how deprived he is of wisdom when he is left to himself.

But this alienation from his own powers not only makes man feel slavishly
dependent on God, it makes him bad too. He becomes a man without faith
in his fellow men or in himself, without the experience of his own love, of
his own power of reason. As a result the separation between the "holy" and
the "secular" occurs. In his worldly activities man acts without love, in that
sector of his life which is reserved to religion he feels himself to be a sinner
(which he actually is, since to live without love is to live in sin) and tries
to recover some of his lost humanity by being in touch with God. Simultaneously, he tries to win forgiveness by emphasizing his own helplessness
and worthlessness. Thus the attempt to obtain forgiveness results in the
activation of the very attitude from which his sins stem. He is caught in a
painful dilemma. The more he praises God, the emptier he becomes. The
emptier he becomes, the more sinful he feels. The more sinful he feels, the
more he praises his God—and the less able is he to regain himself.

Analysis of religion must not stop at uncovering those psychological processes within man which underly his religious experience; it must proceed to
discover the conditions which make for the development of authoritarian
and humanistic character structures, respectively, from which different kinds
of religious experience stem. Such a sociopsychological analysis goes far beyond the context of these chapters. However, the principal point can be
made briefly. What people think and feel is rooted in their character and
their character is molded by the total configuration of their practice of life—
more precisely, by the socio-economic and political structure of their society.
In societies ruled by a powerful minority which holds the masses in subjection, the individual will be so imbued with fear, so incapable of feeling
strong or independent, that his religious experience will be authoritarian.
Whether he worships a punishing, awesome God or a similarly conceived
leader makes little difference. On the other hand, where the individual feels
free and responsible for his own fate, or among minorities striving for freedom and independence, humanistic religious experience develops. The history
of religion gives ample evidence of this correlation between social structure
and kinds of religious experience. Early Christianity was a religion of the
poor and downtrodden; the history of religious sects fighting against authoritarian political pressure shows the same principle again and again.
Judaism, in which a strong anti-authoritarian tradition could grow up because secular authority never had much of a chance to govern and to build
up a legend of its wisdom, therefore developed the humanistic aspect of
religion to a remarkable degree. Whenever, on the other hand, religion allied
itself with secular power, the religion had by necessity to become authori-

tarian. The real fall of man is his alienation from himself, his submission to power, his turning against himself even though under the guise of his worship of God.

From the spirit of authoritarian religion stem two fallacies of reasoning which have been used again and again as arguments for theistic religion. One argument runs as follows: How can you criticize the emphasis on dependence on a power transcending man; is not man dependent on forces outside himself which he cannot understand, much less control?

Indeed, man is dependent; he remains subject to death, age, illness, and even if he were to control nature and to make it wholly serviceable to him, he and his earth remain tiny specks in the universe. But it is one thing to recognize one's dependence and limitations, and it is something entirely different to indulge in this dependence, to worship the forces on which one depends. To understand realistically and soberly how limited our power is is an essential part of wisdom and of maturity; to worship it is masochistic and self-destructive. The one is humility, the other self-humiliation.

We can study the difference between the realistic recognition of our limitations and the indulgence in the experience of submission and powerlessness in the clinical examination of masochistic character traits. We find people who have a tendency to incur sickness, accidents, humiliating situations, who belittle and weaken themselves. They believe that they get into such situations against their will and intention, but a study of their unconscious motives shows that actually they are driven by one of the most irrational tendencies to be found in man, namely, by an unconscious desire to be weak and powerless; they tend to shift the center of their life to powers over which they feel no control, thus escaping from freedom and from personal responsibility. We find furthermore that this masochistic tendency is usually accompanied by its very opposite, the tendency to rule and to dominate others, and that the masochistic and the dominating tendencies form the two sides of the authoritarian character structure.[12] Such masochistic tendencies are not always unconscious. We find them overtly in the sexual masochistic perversion where the fulfillment of the wish to be hurt or humiliated is the condition for sexual excitement and satisfaction. We find it also in the relationship to the leader and the state in all authoritarian secular religions. Here the explicit aim is to give up one's own will and to experience submission under the leader or the state as profoundly rewarding.

Another fallacy of theological thinking is closely related to the one concerning dependence. I mean here the argument that there must be a power

[12] See *Escape from Freedom*, pp. 141 ff.

or being outside of man because we find that man has an ineradicable longing to relate himself to something beyond himself. Indeed, any sane human
being has a need to relate himself to others; a person who has lost that
capacity completely is insane. No wonder that man has created figures outside of himself to which he relates himself, which he loves and cherishes
because they are not subject to the vacillations and inconsistencies of human
objects. That God is a symbol of man's need to love is simple enough to
understand. But does it follow from the existence and intensity of this
human need that there exists an outer being who corresponds to this need?
Obviously that follows as little as our strongest desire to love someone proves
that there is a person with whom we are in love. All it proves is our need
and perhaps our capacity. . . .

The underlying theme of the preceding chapters is the conviction that
the problem of religion is not the problem of God but the problem of man;
religious formulations and religious symbols are attempts to give expression
to certain kinds of human experience. What matters is the nature of these
experiences. The symbol system is only the cue from which we can infer
the underlying human reality. Unfortunately the discussion centered around
religion since the days of the Enlightenment has been largely concerned with
the affirmation or negation of a belief in God rather than with the affirmation or negation of certain human attitudes. "Do you believe in the existence
of God?" has been made the crucial question of religionists and the denial
of God has been the position chosen by those fighting the church. It is easy
to see that many who profess the belief in God are in their human attitude
idol worshipers or men without faith, while some of the most ardent
"atheists," devoting their lives to the betterment of mankind, to deeds of
brotherliness and love, have exhibited faith and a profoundly religious attitude. Centering the religious discussion on the acceptance or denial of the
symbol God blocks the understanding of the religious problem as a human
problem and prevents the development of that human attitude which can be
called religious in a humanistic sense.

Many attempts have been made to retain the symbol God but to give
it a meaning different from the one which it has in the monotheistic tradition. One of the outstanding illustrations is Spinoza's theology. Using
strictly theological language he gives a definition of God which amounts
to saying there is no God in the sense of the Judaeo-Christian tradition. He was still so close to the spiritual atmosphere in which the symbol
God seemed indispensable that he was not aware of the fact that he was
negating the existence of God in the terms of his new definition.

In the writings of a number of theologians and philosophers in the nineteenth century and at present one can detect similar attempts to retain the

word God but to give it a meaning fundamentally different from that which it had for the Prophets of the Bible or for the Christian and Jewish theologians of the Middle Ages. There need be no quarrel with those who retain the symbol God although it is questionable whether it is not a forced attempt to retain a symbol whose significance is essentially historical. However this may be, one thing is certain. The real conflict is not between belief in God and "atheism" but between a humanistic, religious attitude and an attitude which is equivalent to idolatry regardless of how this attitude is expressed—or disguised—in conscious thought.

WALTER T. STACE

WALTER T. STACE (1886-   ), emeritus professor of philosophy at Princeton, is a close student of mysticism and eastern religions. He calls himself an empiricist but is not closely associated with any particular school. He has written on Greek philosophy, Hegel, theory of knowledge, morals and religion.

What Religion Is*

"Religion," says Whitehead, "is the vision of something which stands beyond, behind, and within, the passing flux of immediate things; something which is real, and yet waiting to be realized; something which is a remote possibility, and yet the greatest of present facts; something which gives meaning to all that passes, and yet eludes apprehension; something whose possession is the final good, and yet is beyond all reach; something which is the ultimate ideal, and the hopeless quest." [1]

These words evidently express a direct intuition of the writer. They well up from his own personal religious experience and therefore stir the depths in us who read. What he says is not a faded copy of what someone else has felt or thought or seen, as the majority of pious utterances are—hackneyed and worn-out clichés, debased by parrot-like repetition, although they too, poor dead things, once issued fresh-minted from a living human soul. Here and there amid the arid hills of human experience are well-springs and foun-

* From Walter T. Stace, *Time and Eternity*, pp. 3-8. Copyright, 1952, by Princeton University Press. Reprinted by permission of Princeton University Press.
[1] A. N. Whitehead, *Science and the Modern World*, chapter 12.

tain-heads of religious intuition. They are the original sources of all religion. They need not always be of great grandeur. They may be humble rivulets of feeling. Or they may give rise to great rivers of refreshment flowing through the centuries. But always, great or small, they bear upon themselves the stamp of their own authenticity. They need no external proof or justification. Indeed they are incapable of any. We know them because the God in us cries out, hearing the voice of the God in the other, answering back. The deep calls to the deep.

Whitehead's words are of this kind.

Note first their paradoxical character. To the "something" of which they speak are attributed opposite characters which barely avoid, if they do avoid, the clash of flat contradiction. Each clause is a balance of such contradicting predicates. The meaning cannot be less than that paradox and contradiction are of the very essence of that "something" itself.

Note, too, the final words. That something which man seeks as his ultimate ideal is the "hopeless quest." This is not a careless expression, an exaggeration, a loose use of words. It is not rhetoric. If this phrase had come at the beginning of the passage, it might have been toned down in the succeeding sentences. But it strikes the final note. It is the last word.

And one can see why. For religion is the hunger of the soul for the impossible, the unattainable, the inconceivable. This is not something which it merely happens to be, an unfortunate accident or disaster which befalls it in the world. This is its essence, and this is its glory. This is what religion *means*. The religious impulse in men *is* the hunger for the impossible, the unattainable, the inconceivable—or at least for that which is these things in the world of time. And anything which is less than this is not religion— though it may be some very admirable thing such as morality. Let it not be said that this makes religion a foolish thing, fit only for madmen—although indeed from the world's point of view the religious man *is* a madman. For, mad or not, this impulse lies deep down in every human heart. It is of the essence of man, quite as much as is his reason.

Religion seeks the infinite. And the infinite by definition is impossible, unattainable. It is by definition that which can never be reached.

Religion seeks the light. But it is not a light which can be found at any place or time. It is not somewhere. It is the light which is nowhere. It is "the light which never was on sea or land." Never was. Never will be, even in the infinite stretches of future time. The light is non-existent, as the poet himself says. Yet it is the great light which lightens the world. And this, too, the poet implies.

Religion is the desire to break away from being and existence altogether, to get beyond existence into that nothingness where the great light is. It is

the desire to be utterly free from the fetters of being. For every being is a
fetter. Existence is a fetter. To be is to be tied to what you are. Religion is
the hunger for the non-being which yet is.

In music sometimes a man will feel that he comes to the edge of breaking
out from the prison bars of existence, breaking out from the universe altogether. There is a sense that the goal is at hand, that the boundary wall of
the universe is crumbling and will be breached at the next moment, when
the soul will pass out free into the infinite. But the goal is not reached. For
it is the unspeakable, the impossible, the inconceivable, the unattainable.
There is only the sense of falling backward into time. The goal is only
glimpsed, sensed, and then lost.

One thing is better than another thing. Gold is perhaps better than clay,
poetry than push-pin. One place is pleasanter than another place. One time
is happier than another time. In all being there is a scale of better and
worse. But just because of this relativity, no being, no time, no place, satisfies the ultimate hunger. For all beings are infected by the same disease,
the disease of existence. If owning a marble leaves your metaphysical and
religious thirst unquenched, so will owning all the planets. If living on the
earth for three-score years and ten leaves it unsatisfied, neither will living
in a fabled Heaven for endless ages satisfy it. For how do you attain your
end by making things bigger, or longer, or wider, or thicker, or more this or
more that? For they will still be *this* or *that*. And it is being this or that
which is the disease of things.

So long as there is light in your life, the light has not yet dawned. There
is in your life much darkness—that much you will admit. But you think that
though this thing, this place, this time, this experience is dark, yet that
thing, that place, that time, that experience is, or will be, bright. But this
is the great illusion. You must see that all things, all places, all times, all
experiences are equally dark. You must see that all stars are black. Only out
of the *total* darkness will the light dawn.

Religion is that hunger which no existence, past, present, or future, no
actual existence and no possible existence, in this world or in any other world,
on the earth or above the clouds and stars, material or mental or spiritual,
can ever satisfy. For whatever is or could be will have the curse on it of
thisness or thatness.

This is no new thought. It is only what religious men have always said.
To the saint Narada the Supreme Being offered whatsoever boon his heart
could imagine—abundance of life, riches, health, pleasure, heroic sons.
"That," said Narada "and precisely that is what I desire to be rid of and
pass beyond." It is true that the things here spoken of—health, riches, even
heroic sons—are what we call worldly, even material, things. But they are

symbolic only. They stand for all things of any kind, whether material or non-material—for all things, at least, which could have an existence in the order of time, whether in the time before death or in the time after.

It is true that simple-minded religious men have conceived their goal as a state of continued existence beyond the grave filled with all happy things and experiences. But plainly such happy things and experiences were no more than symbolic, and the happy heavens containing such things have the character of myth. To the human mind, fast fettered by the limits of its poor imagination, they stand for and represent the goal. One cannot conceive the inconceivable. So in place of it one puts whatever one can imagine of delight; wine and houris if one's imagination is limited to these; love, kindness, sweetness of spiritual living if one is of a less materialistic temper. But were these existences and delights, material or spiritual, to be actually found and enjoyed as present, they would be condemned by the saint along with all earthly joys. For they would have upon them the curse, the darkness, the disease, of all existent things, of all that is this or that. This is why we cannot conceive of any particular pleasure, happiness, joy, which would not *cloy*, which—to be quite frank—would not in the end be boring.

"In the Infinite only is bliss. In the finite there is no bliss" says the ancient Upanishad.[2] And we are apt to imagine that this is a piece of rhetoric, or at least an exaggeration. For surely it is not strictly speaking true that in the finite there is no happiness at all. No doubt the saint or the moralist is right to speak disparagingly of the mere pleasures of sense. But is there, then, no joy of living? What of the love of man and woman, of parent and child? What of the sweetness of flowers, the blue of the sky, the sunlight? Is it not quite false that there is no bliss in these? And yet they are finite. So we say. But we fail to see that the author of the verse is speaking of something quite different from what we have in mind, namely of that ultimate bliss in God which is the final satisfaction of the religious hunger. And we think that this ultimate blessedness differs only *in degree* from the happy and joyful experiences of our lives. Whereas the truth is that it differs *in kind*. The joys, not only of the earth, but of any conceivable heaven— which we can conceive only as some fortunate and happy prolongation of our lives in time—are not of the same order as that ultimate blessedness. We imagine any joyful, even ecstatic, experience we please. We suppose that the blessedness of salvation is something like this, only more joyful. Perhaps if it were multiplied a million times. . . . But all this is of no avail. Though we pile mountain of earthly joy upon mountain of earthly joy, we reach no nearer to the bliss which is the end. For these things belong to different orders; the one, however great, to the order of time; the other to the order

[2] Chandogya Upanishad.

of eternity. Therefore all the temporal joys which we pile upon one another to help our imaginations, are no more than symbolic, and the accounts of possible heavens mere myths.

Hence the religious soul must leave behind all things and beings, including itself. From being it must pass into Nothing. But in this nothing it must still be. Therefore also what it seeks is the being which is non-being. And God, who is the only food which will appease its hunger, is this Being which is Non-Being. Is this a contradiction? Yes. But men have always found that, in their search for the Ultimate, contradiction and paradox lie all around them. Did we not see that the words of Whitehead, with which we opened this chapter, must mean at least that contradiction and paradox lie at the heart of things? And is there any more contradiction here than we find—to give the most obvious example from traditional theology—in the doctrine of the Trinity? That, too, proclaims in unmistakable terms that there is contradiction in the Ultimate. The rationalizing intellect, of course, will not have it so. It will attempt to explain away the final Mystery, to logicize it, to reduce it to the categories of "this" and "that." At least it will attempt to water it down till it looks something like "common sense," and can be swallowed without too much discomfort! But the great theologians knew better. In the self-contradictory doctrine of the Trinity they threw the Mystery of God uncompromisingly in men's faces. And we shall see that all attempts to make religion a purely rational, logical, thing are not only shallow but would, if they could succeed, destroy religion. Either God is a Mystery or He is nothing at all.

J. MILTON YINGER

J. MILTON YINGER (1916-   ), professor of sociology at Oberlin College, has a major interest in sociology of religion. His book, *Religion, Society and the Individual*, is his most important publication in this field.

Religion, Society and the Individual*

Types of Definitions.   For our purposes, we need only to distinguish briefly three kinds of definitions of religion, and need not undertake a his-

* From J. Milton Yinger, *Religion, Society and the Individual*, pp. 6-17. © The Macmillan Company, 1957, and used with their permission.

tory or catalogue of definitions. (One can gather a hundred or more in a few hours time.) Many definitions are valuative; they describe what, in the given writer's judgment, religion *ought* to be, often expressed as what it "really" or "basically" *is*. Clearly such definitions are inappropriate for the tasks of science. Other definitions are descriptive or substantive. They designate certain kinds of beliefs and practices as religion, without, on the one hand, evaluating them, or, on the other, indicating their function or seeking to discover whether other beliefs and practices perform similar functions. Thus, in Tylor's words, religion is "belief in Spiritual Beings." This kind of definition has the advantage of being clear-cut and reasonably easy to apply. One can proceed from it to a classification of the kinds of Spiritual Beings and the kinds of practices and organizations that are found in various societies. By such a definition, attention is naturally drawn to the differences among religions as distinct historical entities. The emphasis is primarily on religions as *cultural* systems. Their doctrines, rites, sacred texts, typical group structures, and the like, are described, contrasted, and compared. This is what religion *is*, such definitions say, and these particular patterns indicate what Buddhism, Judaism, and the religion of the Arunta *are*.

Substantive definitions can be of great value, particularly for those who are concerned with religions as historical and cultural facts, not with religion as a pan-human phenomenon. They are of greater value in the study of stable societies, where distinctive and coherent religious systems are more likely to develop, than they are in the study of changing societies; for in the latter, religion itself also changes, continually complicating any effort to define what it is, but suggesting efforts to study what it does.

A Functional Definition

For many problems, it is the functional kind of definition suggested in the previous sentence that is most useful. One need not quarrel with those who prefer to define religion in terms of value or in terms of essence, but for analytic purposes the need is for a definition that focuses on process. A comparative science of religion, interested not only in the vast range of differences in belief and practice, but also in the similarities that justify the use of a common term to refer to the whole range, must be concerned with function. This is particularly true if the kinds of questions one is interested in refer not only to religion as a cultural fact, but to religion as a manifestation of personality and as one aspect of society. It is widely held today that for many purposes it is a mistake to separate the analysis of culture (the system of norms and usages designating "right" behavior to the members of a society) from the analysis of personality (the organized system of tendencies of an individual); and it is equally a mistake to separate these from the analysis of social systems ("networks of interactive relationships," as Parsons calls them). Special studies of culture, personality, and society are appropriate, of course; but their theories must remain on a highly abstract level. To come nearer to the understanding of concrete action we must study their mutual influence.

It is paradoxical that in order to focus attention more nearly on religion as concrete behavior, a definition must be more abstract. To define religion, for example, simply as "belief in God" (a definition that can be seen as either valuative or substantive or both) is to give it a fairly sharp referent; but such a definition suggests no question of the relationship between personal anxiety or concern for one's salvation, for example, and belief in God; and it poses no problems of the relationship between the efforts to maintain social order and religion as defined. The more abstract definition that we shall develop below carries implicit within it a concern for the analysis of actual behavior. It points to major questions of human action; and thus, in our judgment, is more fruitful for a science of human behavior. One does not say that it is more "true," but only that it will serve the needs of current scientific work more fully than valuative or substantive definitions. Those who think of definitions as attempts to capture the "essence" of something look with disfavor on this experimental approach; those who think of definitions as tools of analysis accept it.

The person who seeks to define religion in functional terms, to be sure, faces a number of difficulties. He must avoid a definition that is tied only to his own religious experience or to cultures similar to his own. He must recognize that the intense specialization of modern societies gives one a different perspective on religion than one gets in less highly differentiated societies, where the infusion of religious elements into all phases of life is more obvious. Perhaps the most serious difficulty is related to the ease with which one drifts into a valuative position in his definition without intending to. If religion is defined by what are thought to be its functions, then one should not be surprised to find it "functional." And this may lead, in turn, to a circularity of reasoning: If it can be shown that a given system of beliefs and practices that is generally thought to be a religion is not performing the functions by which religion has been defined, then one declares that such a system is not "really" religion at all. This error can be avoided by indicating that religion is an *effort* to perform certain functions for man. This does not imply the value position that it always succeeds, nor that systems which do not succeed are therefore not religions. And it does not necessarily imply that one desires those functions to be performed.

To solve or reduce this problem, however, may only serve to create another. Is every effort to perform certain functions, however wide the range of differences—in content of belief, in number of persons involved, in degree of historical continuity, etc.—to be called religion? Is there no place, in other words, for functional alternatives, because every possible "alternative" must, by definition, also be considered a religion? We shall deal with this question at several points in this essay, and need say here only that we shall define religion as a certain kind of effort to perform various functions. We shall identify it by the intensity or "ultimate" quality of the attempt, and by the interconnection of several related functions. Thus there is a great deal of room for functional alternatives. Since we are dealing with several continuous variables, the problem of more or less inevitably arises, and we shall be concerned to describe some systems of belief and action that are marginally religious, in our sense, to indicate that there is no sharp dividing line.

What, then, are the functions that distinguish religion as a human activity? To try to answer this question is essentially the task of this book; hence the highly condensed statement appropriate to a definition can only hint at problems that receive fuller treatment in later chapters. Paul Tillich has said that religion is that which concerns us ultimately. This can be a good starting point for a functional definition. While there are important disagreements concerning the "ultimate" problems for man, a great many would accept the following as among the fundamental concerns of human societies and individuals: How shall we respond to the fact of death? Does life have some central meaning despite the suffering, the succession of frustrations and tragedies? How can we deal with the forces that press in on us, endangering our livelihood, our health, the survival and smooth operation of the groups in which we live—forces that our empirical knowledge is inadequate to handle? How can we bring our capacity for hostility and our egocentricity sufficiently under control that the groups within which we live, without which, indeed, life would be impossible, can be kept together?

Put in this way, these questions appear to be self-conscious and rational. They are more appropriately seen as deep-seated emotional needs, springing from the very nature of man as an individual and as a member of society. The questions appear first of all because they are felt—the death of a loved one wrenches our emotions, the failure to achieve that for which we yearn saddens and bewilders us; the hostility between ourselves and those around us infuses our social contacts with tension and prevents the achievement of mutual values. Religion may develop an intellectual system to interpret and deal with these questions, but they express first of all an underlying emotional need, not a group of rationally conceived problems.

Religion, then, can be defined as a system of beliefs and practices by means of which a group of people struggles with these ultimate problems of human life. It is the refusal to capitulate to death, to give up in the face of frustration, to allow hostility to tear apart one's human associations.

All men experience these wrenching difficulties to some degree. For some persons, however, they stand out as the most significant experiences of life. These individuals are impelled to try to discover some meaning in what seems to be senseless suffering, some road to salvation through the obstacles of human life. The beliefs and rites that make up a religion are the expressions of those who have felt the problems most intensively, who have been most acutely sensitive to the tragedies of death, the burdens of frustration, the sense of failure, the disruptive effects of hostility. Powered by the strength of their feelings, such religious innovators have created "solutions" appropriate to the enormity of the problems—solutions that frequently have burst the bonds of man's senses and of nature, but have brought their adherents some relief. Thus religions are built to carry the "peak load" of human emotional need.

Defined in this way, religion is—and seems likely to remain—an inevitable part of human life. Although the ways of struggling with these ultimate problems are enormously diverse, and seem destined for continuous change, the problems themselves are universal. A society that did not furnish its members with beliefs and practices that sought to deal with these ultimate problems would struggle along with an enormous burden of tragedy unallayed and hostility unrestrained—if indeed it could survive at all. This is only to say that some effort to deal with these questions is essential to human life as we know it, and not to say that any given religious system adequately answers these questions.

Religion, of course, is not alone in attempting to deal with the ultimate problems of human life. Rational efforts are important in all societies. Moreover, there are many individual emotional responses to insecurity and the problem of evil in addition to religion. Even in the healthiest and wealthiest and most rational of societies, however, secular responses cannot eliminate the problems of suffering, evil, and hostility. Realizing the gap between their hopes and the realities of their existence, men everywhere seek *closure* by a leap of faith that says: this need not, this will not, be true. Some time, some place, some how, suffering and evil will be defeated. (The enormous variation in conceptions of time, place, and method measures the range of religious expressions.)

The Persistent Functions of Religion. In this sense, religion can be thought of as a kind of residual means of response and adjustment. It is an attempt to explain what cannot otherwise be explained; to achieve power, all other powers having failed us; to establish poise and serenity in the face of evil and suffering that other efforts have failed to eliminate. "When other helpers fail, when comforts flee," man can give himself over to despair, or he can seek relief by the leap of faith. Most people have chosen the latter, and have preferred, in Reinhold Niebuhr's words, "a citadel of hope built on the edge of despair," to acceptance of ultimate defeat.

Dunlap uses the concept of "residual" in his definition of religion which he describes as ". . . the institution, or feature of culture, which undertakes, in the service of mankind, those functions for which there is no other institution or for the undertaking of which no other institution is as yet adequately prepared." [1] This definition, although it is helpful, seems to the present writer to require further attention to the *persistent* functions of religion. Is there no core of functions that seems likely to be a continuing source of religious activity? Or are science, philosophy, art, government, medicine, and the like, chiseling steadily away at religion so that it is a "suicidal institution" as Dunlap calls it? The present writer finds it difficult to envisage a society in which major unresolved problems of the "ultimate" variety we have discussed do not remain. He suspects—and here he runs the danger of an attempt to prove by definition, a very unsatisfactory kind of proof—that the belief that man can devise secular processes for performing the functions now served by religion is in itself a "citadel of hope," and not an empirically validated proposition. It is an emotional and intellectual closure more congenial to the cultural training and personality tendencies of many people today, and thus serves at least a quasi-religion function for them.

The word "residual" need not carry the connotation of "unimportant final item" or "gradually disappearing." It might better be thought of as "that which always remains." Malinowski writes:

To us the most essential point about magic and religious ritual is that it steps in only where knowledge fails. Supernaturally founded ceremonial grows out of life, but it never stultifies the practical efforts of man. In his ritual of magic or religion, man attempts to enact miracles, not because he ignores the limitations of his mental powers, but, on the contrary, because he is fully cognizant of them. To go one step further, the recognition of this seems to me indispensable if we want once and for ever to establish the truth that religion has its own subject-matter, its own legitimate field of development; that this must never encroach on the domain where science, reason, and experience ought to remain supreme. [2]

[1] Knight Dunlap, *Religion: Its Function in Human Life*, p. 321.
[2] Bronislaw Malinowski, *The Foundations of Faith and Morals*, p. 34.

This is not a wholly satisfactory statement, from the point of view of science. It is subject to grave doubt that religion "never stultifies the practical efforts of man." Malinowski shifts easily into a value assertion when he declares that there is an area "where science, reason, and experience ought to remain supreme." But Malinowski implies, as opposed to Dunlap, that religion, as a residual mode of adjustment, is unlikely to disappear. This is an empirical question, for which we have only inadequate evidence. What evidence we have inclines the writer toward the view that religion as defined by the functionalist is a permanent aspect of human society, no more likely to disappear than "the family" (however much it may change) or "government" (despite the enormous range of variation).

William James, in one of his acute observations, notes that in those responses to life which "fall short of religion" we may come to accept the suffering and frustrations of life, but we regard them as impositions of necessity, and at best we accept them without complaint. In religious life, however, surrender and sacrifice are positively espoused; and in this attempt to conquer our problems, we may even add "unnecessary givings-up" in order to increase our happiness. "Religion thus makes easy and felicitous what in any case is necessary. . . ." [3] If we may tamper with James' statement a bit, to add that "religion is an *attempt* to . . .", we might be led to another definition of some value: Religion is an organized effort to make virtue of our ultimate necessities.

Are Individual Systems of Belief to Be Called Religion? A primary difficulty with a functional definition is that there is no obvious point at which one may draw a line and say: "Here religion ends and non-religion begins." In a religiously-heterogeneous and changing society, the question of "private" systems of belief and practice arises. Are they to be called religions? Are they not attempts to fulfill the same functions that shared and historically identified faiths seek to perform? In our view, one should answer this question in the negative. There is, to be sure, some truth in the statement that, "his work is his religion," or "he has dedicated himself to the discovery of a cure for cancer," with the implication that this is "his religion." There can be religious aspects of private systems of belief and action. A complete religion, however, is a social phenomenon; it is shared; it takes on many of its most significant aspects only in the interaction of the group. Both the feelings from which it springs and the "solutions" it offers are social, they arise from the fact that man is a group-living animal. The "ultimate questions" which we have identified as the center of the religious quest are ulti-

[3] William James, *The Varieties of Religious Experience*, p. 51.

mate primarily because of their impact on human association. Even death is not fundamentally an individual crisis, but a group crisis, threatening to tear the fabric of family and community.

Joachim Wach holds that all religions, despite their wide variations, are characterized by three universal expressions: the theoretical, or a system of beliefs, the practical, a system of worship, and the sociological, a system of social relationships. Until all of these are found, one may have religious tendencies, religious elements, but not a full religion, struggling with all the interrelated functions to which we have referred. Although the first of these expressions—the system of belief—is the one that modern man is most likely to think of as the heart of religion, both ethnological and etymological evidence suggests that religion as worship and religion as a system of social relationships may be the more basic aspects, belief coming in as an attempt to give coherence and meaning to worship and associations that have developed out of deeply felt needs. The word religion may have derived from the Latin *religare*, to bind together, or from *religere*, to rehearse, to execute painstakingly, suggesting both group identity and ritual. The testimony of most anthropologists gives support to the proposition that it is the acts of religion, and the associations, more than the beliefs, that give it a vital place in the life of preliterate societies. This may be less true in a literate society where the practice of seeking out explanations is more fully established and where religious specialists seek to relate religion to a complex and changing society.

The growing importance of the "belief" aspects of religion, however, should not lead us to misinterpret the nature of a religious intellectual system. It is a group of "mighty hypotheses," of "over-beliefs," of deductions that leap beyond those admissible by a calm appraisal of the facts. Man is not calm in face of the needs from which religion springs, As Durkheim says: "Science is fragmentary and incomplete; it advances but slowly and is never finished; but life cannot wait. The theories which are destined to make men live and act are therefore obliged to pass science and complete it prematurely." [4]

Are Non-theistic Systems of Belief to Be Called Religion?

If the functional approach to the definition and analysis of religion is taken, it is not the nature of the *belief*, but the nature of the *believing* that requires study. Even a quick glance over the vast range of phenomena that we call religion reveals an enormous variety. The only justification for referring to such diversity of belief, of worship, and of organization by one term is the assumption that the many forms represent different attempts to deal with the

[4] Emile Durkheim, *The Elementary Forms of the Religious Life*, p. 431.

same problems. In Paul Tillich's words: "We are all laboring under the yoke of religion; we all, sometimes, try to throw away old or new doctrines or dogmas, but after a little while we return, again enslaving ourselves and others in their servitude." [5] Many "non-religious" persons object to such a statement. They explicitly reject beliefs, forms of worship, and group associations that they identify as religious. It is unwise to argue this point, for from the perspective of the definition they use, they are correct in claiming to be "non-religious." The functionalist affirms simply that it is highly likely that such individuals, having left some traditional religion, will nevertheless affirm their faith in some "over-beliefs," will get emotional support from various symbols, acts, and ceremonies (worship), and will join with others in groups that seek to sustain and realize the shared beliefs. This point of view is seldom argued when it refers to some of the intense political movements of our time. Communism is now generally considered to have a religious quality.[6] Few deny the religious element in nationalism. In multireligious societies (in the traditional sense) or in societies where an established religion has lost much of its appeal, nationalism as a religious force is particularly likely to appear. Faith, symbols, worshipful acts, and organizations built around the nation all appear. This is not simply the nationalization of religion (*Gott mit uns*), but the religionization of nation (*Vaterland über alles*).

Many modern intellectuals, perhaps particularly among the writer's fellow social scientists, will agree that many modern political and other "secular" movements might appropriately be regarded as religions, but they see no parallel in their own lives. A supernatural view of the world has become meaningless to them, they are repelled by a boastful and worshipful nationalism; they feel comfortable with a quiet kind of scientific secularism, motivated by idle curiosity with perhaps a nudge from a desire to help solve some human problem. Certainly a functional definition of religion that attempts to include such phenomena strains our imaginations. Yet a term already includes, by common consent, the contemplations of a Buddhist monk and the ecstatic visions of a revivalist cult member, human sacrifice and ethical monotheism, may have room in it for science *as a way of life* (not as a method or as a group of tested propositions about nature). Not all scientists, in the methodological sense, accept science as a way of life. Many feel that the answers to man's ultimate problems are to be found in the traditional religions. But some turn to science even for this. If they do not

---

[5] Paul Tillich, *The Shaking of the Foundations*, p. 98.
[6] This view is expressed, for example, by Tillich, *ibid.*; by Erich Fromm, *Man for Himself*; by Reinhold Niebuhr, *Christianity and Power Politics*; by Jacques Maritain, *True Humanism. . . .*

require the ritualistic trappings and elaborate organization of a Comte, with his "positivistic religion," they certainly manifest many over-beliefs that, to repeat Durkheim's words, are "obliged to pass science and complete it prematurely." Few scientists doubt that the best way to grapple with human problems is to extend our knowledge of nature. Hydrogen bombs and the mass manipulation of people by propaganda may have given us pause, but they have not destroyed our "faith." That the gap between knowledge and action can be closed by knowledge itself is a mighty hypothesis that few of us would care to deny, but a careful reading of the story of man in the era of science would scarcely lead to the conclusion that the evidence is all in on that question. It is doubtless true that emotion-evoking symbols, rituals, elaborate group organizations for the purposes of reenforcing "science as a way of life" are rudimentary; but anyone who has attended a convention of scientists will hesitate to say that they are entirely lacking.

These sentences are not written to criticize science. Many of the author's own over-beliefs stem from science, and he finds them rich and satisfying. They are written rather to show that few men can avoid the problem of struggling with questions of "salvation" (how can man be saved from his most difficult problems), of the nature of reality, of evil (why do men suffer), and the like. Science as a way of life is an effort to deal with these questions.

Nor should this point of view be taken as a support for "religion in general." Some writers are happy about the recent trend toward a functionalist theory, as contrasted with earlier studies of religious origins, because they somehow find in this development support for a belief that *religion* is true, and often also a belief that the traditional religions have won scientific support. The problem is more complicated than they recognize.

Important problems of value inevitably arise from the functional approach. If almost any system of beliefs and actions can be religious, it is clear that one cannot regard religion in general as a "good thing." There are questions of choice. From the perspective of certain stated values, a given religion may be good, or it may be evil, or it may be a mixture of good and evil. The idea widely current in the United States that one ought "to be religious," with no reference to the nature or the consequences of various religions, is not a logical inference from the functionalist position.

We have looked at the problem of definition from several points of view. Perhaps our approach can be summed up in these words: The human individual, blessed (and sometimes cursed) with the power of language, capable, therefore, of anticipating the future, including a fore-knowledge of his own death, able to verbalize ideal states, to create standards, is continually threatened with failure, with frustration, with his conception of justice unfulfilled. These problems tend to loom up as overwhelming or "absolute evils." Religion is man's attempt to "relativize" them by interpreting them as part of some larger good, some conception of the absolute that puts the individual's problems into new perspective, thus to remove or reduce their crushing impact. At the same time, man's social relations, his societies, are threatened by these same problems. Fear and frustration can lead to disrupting hostilities, unless they can be reinterpreted as part of a shared experience. In addition to that, there is the tendency of each individual to think only of himself, to make his joys, his desires into "absolute goods," threatening the patterns of mutual adjustment that social life requires. Religion is the attempt to "relativize" the individual's desires, as well as his fears, by subordinating them to a conception of absolute good more in harmony with the shared and often mutually contradictory needs and desires of human groups.

Certain kinds of belief and action very commonly, if not universally, develop from this double root of religion—the fundamental individual and group needs. First, failure and frustration are symbolically reinterpreted: failure is only apparent, death is not what it seems. Second, religion brings one into a fellowship which emphasizes shared experiences. This has two aspects: it "spreads the burdens" of one's fears and frustrations, and thus is a kind of "psychic insurance policy"; and it lays emphasis on shared and universally available values—the scheme of salvation—rather than the scarce values, thus to make the inevitable failures with regard to the latter seem less important. This leads to a third element in religion. At least some of the values which it upholds are super-empirical. This does not necessarily mean that they are supernatural, but they are beyond the reach of constant refutation by the facts of immediate experience.[7] It is a likely hypothesis that the more punishing the actual experience of a society—the more uncertain the food supply, for example, and the heavier the hand of death—the greater is the likelihood that its religion will emphasize supernatural means and/or supernatural goals. Members of a society more favorably situated, or a group in such a society, may make their leap of faith by projecting the trends they see around them in the natural world. In either event, men believe "more than the facts would allow," in an effort to sustain life and hope and to give more meaning to existence.

Such a definition of religion is, of course, highly abstract. It is an attempt to isolate, by analysis, a common factor that is embedded in enormously diverse religious systems. A different point of view would isolate different common elements that we have overlooked and obscured. Moreover, an abstract definition must be seen as a starting point for the study of religion,

[7] See Kingsley Davis, *Human Society*, pp. 518-531.

a point from which religions, as concrete systems of belief and action, depart in varying degrees and in many directions. These departures, as we shall see, and the forces behind them, must be of vital concern to the student of religion.

MARTIN BUBER

MARTIN BUBER (1878-   ), Austrian-Jewish existentialist theologian, has made contributions in the fields of sociology, Old Testament studies and studies of Judaism as well as in theology. He is now Professor of Social Philosophy at Hebrew University in Jerusalem.

The Two Foci of the Jewish Soul*

I shall therefore speak to you about the Jewish soul by making a few references to its fundamental attitude; I shall regard it as being the concretion of this human element in a national form, and consider it as the nation-shaped instrument of such a fealty and rediscernment.

I see the soul of Judaism as elliptically turning round two centers.

One center of the Jewish soul is the primeval experience that God is wholly raised above man, that he is beyond the grasp of man, and yet that he is present in an immediate relationship with these human beings who are absolutely incommensurable with him, and that he faces them. To know both these things at the same time, so that they cannot be separated, constitutes the living core of every believing Jewish soul; to know both, "God in heaven," that is, in complete hiddenness, and man "on earth," that is, in the fragmentation of the world of his senses and his understanding; God in the perfection and incomprehensibility of his being, and man in the abysmal contradiction of this strange existence from birth to death—and between both, immediacy!

The pious Jews of pre-Christian times called their God "Father"; and when the naively pious Jew in Eastern Europe uses that name today, he does not repeat something which he has learned, but he expresses a realization which he has come upon himself of the fatherhood of God and the

* Reprinted by permission of Schocken Books Inc., New York, from *Israel and the World*, pp. 30-40, by Martin Buber, copyright 1948 by Schocken Books Inc.

sonship of man. It is not as though these men did not know that God is also utterly distant; it is rather that they know at the same time that however far away God is, he is never unrelated to them, and that even the man who is farthest away from God cannot cut himself off from the mutual relationship. In spite of the complete distance between God and man, they know that when God created man he set the mark of his image upon man's brow, and embedded it in man's nature, and that however faint God's mark may become, it can never be entirely wiped out.

According to hasidic legend, when the Baal Shem conjured up the demon Sammael, he showed him this mark on the forehead of his disciples, and when the master bade the conquered demon begone, the latter prayed, "Sons of the living God, permit me to remain a little while to look at the mark of the image of God on your faces." God's real commandment to men is to realize this image.

"Fear of God," accordingly, never means to the Jews that they ought to be afraid of God, but that, trembling, they ought to be aware of his incomprehensibility. The fear of God is the creaturely knowledge of the darkness to which none of our spiritual powers can reach, and out of which God reveals himself. Therefore, "the fear of God" is rightly called "the beginning of knowledge" (Ps. 111:10). It is the dark gate through which man must pass if he is to enter into the love of God. He who wishes to avoid passing through this gate, he who begins to provide himself with a comprehensible God, constructed thus and not otherwise, runs the risk of having to despair of God in view of the actualities of history and life, or of falling into inner falsehood. Only through the fear of God does man enter so deep into the love of God that he cannot again be cast out of it.

But fear of God is just a gate; it is not a house in which one can comfortably settle down—he who should want to live in it in adoration would neglect the performance of the essential commandment. God is incomprehensible, but he can be known through a bond of mutual relationship. God cannot be fathomed by knowledge, but he can be imitated. The life of man who is unlike God can yet be an *imitatio Dei*. "The likeness" is not closed to the "unlike." This is exactly what is meant when the Scripture instructs man to walk in God's way and in his footsteps. Man cannot by his own strength complete any way or any piece of the way, but he can enter on the path, he can take that first step, and again and again that first step. Man cannot "be like unto God," but with all the inadequacy of each of his days, he can follow God at all times, using the capacity he has on that particular day—and if he has used the capacity of that day to the full, he has done enough. This is not a mere act of faith; it is an entering into the life that has to be lived on that day with all the active fulness of a created person. This activity is within man's capacity: uncurtailed and not to be curtailed, the capacity is present through all the generations. God concedes the might to abridge this central property of decision to no primordial "Fall," however far-reaching in its effects, for the intention of God the Creator is mightier than the sin of man. The Jew knows from his knowledge of creation and of creatureliness that there may be burdens inherited from prehistoric and historic times, but that there is no over-powering original sin which could prevent the late-comer from deciding as freely as did Adam; as freely as Adam let God's hand go the late-comer can clasp it. We are dependent on grace; but we do not do God's will when we take it upon ourselves to begin with grace instead of beginning with ourselves. Only our beginning, our having begun, poor as it is, leads us to grace. God made no tools for himself, he needs none; he created for himself a partner in the dialogue of time and one who is capable of holding converse.

In this dialogue God speaks to every man through the life which he gives him again and again. Therefore man can only answer God with the whole of life—with the way in which he lives this given life. The Jewish teaching of the wholeness of life is the other side of the Jewish teaching of the unity of God. Because God bestows not only spirit on man, but the whole of his existence, from its "lowest" to its "highest" levels as well, man can fulfil the obligations of his partnership with God by no spiritual attitude, by no worship, on no sacred upper story; the whole of life is required, every one of its areas and every one of its circumstances. There is no true human share of holiness without the hallowing of the everyday. Whilst Judaism unfolds itself through the history of its faith, and so long as it does unfold itself through that history, it holds out against that "religion" which is an attempt to assign a circumscribed part to God, in order to satisfy him who bespeaks and lays claim to the whole. But this unfolding of Judaism is really an unfolding, and not a metamorphosis.

To clarify our meaning we take the sacrificial cultus as an example. One of the two fundamental elements in biblical animal sacrifice is the sacralization of the natural life: he who slaughters an animal consecrates a part of it to God, and so doing hallows his eating of it. The second fundamental element is the sacramentalization of the complete surrender of life; to this element belong those types of sacrifice in which the person who offers the sacrifice puts his hands on the head of the animal in order to identify himself with it; in doing so he gives physical expression to the thought that he is bringing himself to be sacrificed in the person of the animal. He who performs these sacrifices without having this intention in his soul makes the cult meaningless, yes, absurd; it was against him that the prophets directed their fight against the sacrificial service which had been emptied of its core.

In the Judaism of the Diaspora prayer takes the place of sacrifice; but prayer is also offered for the reinstatement of the cult, that is for the return of the holy unity of body and spirit. And in that consummation of Diaspora Judaism which we call hasidic piety, both fundamental elements unite into a new conception which fulfils the original meaning of the cult. When the purified and sanctified man in purity and holiness takes food into himself, eating becomes a sacrifice, the table an altar, and man consecrates himself to the Deity. At that point there is no longer a gulf between the natural and the sacral; at that point there is no longer the need for a substitute; at that point the natural event itself becomes a sacrament.

The Holy strives to include within itself the whole of life. The Law differentiates between the holy and the profane, but the Law desires to lead the way toward the messianic removal of the differentiation, to the all-sanctification. Hasidic piety no longer recognizes anything as simply and irreparably profane: "the profane" is for hasidism only a designation for the not yet sanctified, for that which is to be sanctified. Everything physical, all drives and urges and desires, everything creaturely, is material for sanctification. From the very same passionate powers which, undirected, give rise to evil, when they are turned toward God, the good arises. One does not serve God with the spirit only, but with the whole of his nature, without any subtractions. There is not one realm of the spirit and another of nature; there is only the growing realm of God. God is not spirit, but what we call spirit and what we call nature hail equally from the God who is beyond and equally conditioned by both, and whose kingdom reaches its fulness in the complete unity of spirit and nature.

The second focus of the Jewish soul is the basic consciousness that God's redeeming power is at work everywhere and at all times, but that a state of redemption exists nowhere and never. The Jew experiences as a person what every openhearted human being experiences as a person: the experience, in the hour when he is most utterly forsaken, of a breath from above, the nearness, the touch, the mysterious intimacy of light out of darkness; and the Jew, as part of the world, experiences, perhaps more intensely than any other part, the world's lack of redemption. He feels this lack of redemption against his skin, he tastes it on his tongue, the burden of the unredeemed world lies on him. Because of this almost physical knowledge of his, he *cannot* concede that the redemption has taken place; he knows that it has not. It is true that he can discover prefigurations of redemption in past history, but he always discovers only that mysterious intimacy of light out of darkness which is at work everywhere and at all times; no redemption which is different in kind, none which by its nature would be unique, which would be conclusive for future ages, and which had but to be consummated. Most of all, only through a denial of his own meaning and his own mission would it be possible for him to acknowledge that in a world which still remains unredeemed an anticipation of the redemption had been effected by which the human soul—or rather merely the souls of men who in a specific sense are believers—had been redeemed.

With a strength which original grace has given him, and which none of his historic trials has ever wrested from him, the Jew resists the radical division of soul and world which forms the basis of this conception; he resists the conception of a divine splitting of existence; he resists most passionately the awful notion of a *massa perditionis*. The God in whom he believes has not created the totality in order to let it split apart into one blessed and one damned half. God's eternity is not to be conceived by man; but—and this we Jews know until the moment of our death—there can be no eternity in which *everything* will not be accepted into God's atonement, when God has drawn time back into eternity. Should there however be a stage in the redemption of the world in which redemption is first fulfilled in one *part* of the world, we would derive no claim to redemption from our faith, much less from any other source. "If You do not yet wish to redeem Israel, at any rate redeem the goyim," the rabbi of Koznitz used to pray.

It is possible to argue against me, that there has been after all another eschatology in Judaism than that which I have indicated, that the apocalyptic stands beside the prophetic eschatology. It is actually important to make clear to oneself where the difference between the two lies. The prophetic belief about the end of time is in all essentials autochthonous; the apocalyptic belief is in all essentials built up of elements from Iranian dualism. Accordingly, the prophetic promises a consummation of creation, the apocalyptic its abrogation and supersession by another world, completely different in nature; the prophetic allows "the evil" to find the direction that leads toward God, and to enter into the good; the apocalyptic sees good and evil severed forever at the end of days, the good redeemed, the evil unredeemable for all eternity; the prophetic believes that the earth shall be hallowed, the apocalyptic despairs of an earth which it considers to be hopelessly doomed; the prophetic allows God's creative original will to be fulfilled completely; the apocalyptic allows the unfaithful creature power over the Creator, in that the creatures' actions force God to abandon nature. There was a time when it must have seemed uncertain whether the current apocalyptic teaching might not be victorious over the traditional prophetic messianism; if that had happened, it is to be assumed that Judaism would not have outlived its central faith—explicitly or imperceptibly it would have merged with Christianity, which is so strongly influenced by that dualism. During an epoch in which the prophetic was lacking, the Tannaites, early talmudic masters, helped prophetic messianism to triumph over the apocalyptic conception, and in doing so saved Judaism.

Still another important difference separates the two forms of Jewish belief about the end of days. The apocalyptists wished to predict an unalterable immovable future event; they were following Iranian conceptions in this point as well. For, according to the Iranians, history is divided into equal cycles of thousands of years, and the end of the world, the final victory of good over evil, can be predetermined with mathematical accuracy.

Not so the prophets of Israel: They prophesy "for the sake of those who turn." That is, they do not warn against something which will happen in any case, but against that which will happen if those who are called upon to turn do not.

The Book of Jonah is a clear example of what is meant by prophecy. After Jonah has tried in vain to flee from the task God has given him, he is sent to Nineveh to prophesy its downfall. But Nineveh turns—and God changes its destiny. Jonah is vexed that the word for whose sake the Lord had broken his resistance had been rendered void; if one is forced to prophesy, one's prophecy must stand. But God is of a different opinion; he will employ no soothsayers, but messengers to the souls of men—the souls that are able to decide which way to go, and whose decision is allowed to contribute to the forging of the world's fate. Those who turn co-operate in the redemption of the world.

Man's partnership in the great dialogue finds its highest form of reality at this point. It is not as though any definite act of man could draw grace down from heaven; yet grace answers deed in unpredictable ways, grace unattainable, yet not self-withholding. It is not as though man has to do this or that "to hasten" the redemption of the world—"he that believeth shall not make haste" (Isa. 28:16); yet those who turn cooperate in the redemption of the world. The extent and nature of the participation assigned to the creature remains secret. "Does that mean that God cannot redeem his world without the help of his creatures?" "It means that God does not will to be able to do it." "Has God need of man for his work?" "He wills to have need of man."

He who speaks of activism in this connection misunderstands the mystery. The act is no outward gesture. "The ram's horn," runs an haggadic saying, "which God will blow on that day will have been made from the right horn of the ram which once took Isaac's place as a sacrifice." The "servant" whom God made "a polished shaft" to hide apparently unused in his quiver (Isa. 49:2), the man who is condemned to live in hiding—or rather, not one man, but the type of men to whom this happens generation after generation— the man who is hidden in the shadow of God's hand, who does not "cause his voice to be heard in the street" (Isa. 42:2), he who in darkness suffers for God's sake (ibid.)—he it is who has been given as a light for the tribes of the world, that God's "salvation may be unto the end of the earth" (Isa. 49:6).

The mystery of the act, of the human part in preparing the redemption, passes through the darkness of the ages as a mystery of concealment, as a concealment within the person's relation to himself as well, until one day it will come into the open. To the question why according to tradition the Messiah was born on the anniversary of the day of the destruction of Jerusalem, a hasidic rabbi answered: "The power cannot rise, unless it has dwelt in the great concealment. . . . In the shell of oblivion grows the power of remembrance. That is the power of redemption. On the day of the Destruction the power will be lying at the bottom of the depths and growing. That is why on this day we sit on the ground; that is why on this day we visit the graves; that is why on this day was born the Messiah."

Though robbed of their real names, these two foci of the Jewish soul continue to exist for the "secularized" Jew too, insofar as he has not lost his soul. They are, first, the immediate relationship to the Existent One, and second, the power of atonement at work in an unatoned world. In other words, first, the *non-incarnation* of God who reveals himself to the "flesh" and is present to it in a mutual relationship, and second, the unbroken continuity of human history, which turns toward fulfillment and decision. These two centers constitute the ultimate division between Judaism and Christianity.

We "unify" God, when living and dying we profess his unity; we do not unite ourselves with him. The God in whom we believe, to whom we are pledged, does not unite with human substance on earth. But the very fact that we do not imagine that we can unite with him enables us the more ardently to demand "that the world shall be perfected under the kingship of the Mighty One."

We feel salvation happening; and we feel the unsaved world. No savior with whom a new redeemed history began has appeared to us at any definite point in history. Because we have not been stilled by anything which has happened, we are wholly directed toward the coming of that which is to come.

Thus, though divided from you, we have been attached to you. As Franz Rosenzweig wrote in the letter which I have already quoted: "You who live in an *ecclesia triumphans* need a silent servant to cry to you whenever you believe you *have partaken* of God in bread and wine, 'Lord, remember the last things.'"

What have you and we in common? If we take the question literally, a book and an expectation.

To you the book is a forecourt; to us it is the sanctuary. But in this place we can dwell together, and together listen to the voice that speaks here. That means that we can work together to evoke the buried speech of that voice; together we can redeem the imprisoned living world.

Your expectation is directed toward a second coming, ours to a coming which has not been anticipated by a first. To you the phrasing of world history is determined by one absolute mid-point, the year nought; to us it is an unbroken flow of tones following each other without a pause from their origin to their consummation. But we can wait for the advent of the One together, and there are moments when we may prepare the way before him together.

Pre-messianically our destinies are divided. Now to the Christian the Jew is the incomprehensibly obdurate man, who declines to see what has happened; and to the Jew the Christian is the incomprehensibly daring man, who affirms in an unredeemed world that its redemption has been accomplished. This is a gulf which no human power can bridge. But it does not prevent the common watch for a unity to come to us from God, which, soaring above all of your imagination and all of ours, affirms and denies, denies and affirms what you hold and what we hold, and which replaces all the creedal truths of earth by the ontological truth of heaven which is one.

It behooves both you and us to hold inviolably fast to our own true faith, that is to our own deepest relationship to truth. It behooves both of us to show a religious respect for the true faith of the other. This is not what is called "tolerance," our task is not to tolerate each other's waywardness but to acknowledge the real relationship in which both stand to the truth. Whenever we both, Christian and Jew, care more for God himself than for our images of God, we are united in the feeling that our Father's house is differently constructed than our human models take it to be.

SUGGESTED ADDITIONAL READINGS

The Nature of Religion

Bergson, Henri L. *The Two Sources of Morality and Religion*. Trans., R. Ashley Andra (and others). New York: Henry Holt and Company, 1935. (Also published in paperback by Doubleday and Co., Anchor Series.) A French philosopher contrasts static and dynamic religion and challenges the reader with his arguments for dynamic religion.

Bonaventura. *The Mind's Road to God*. Trans., George Boas. New York: Liberal Arts Press, 1953. (This is a paperback edition.) A medieval theologian of the Platonic tradition writes on the experience and knowledge of God.

Brightman, Edgar S. *A Philosophy of Religion*. New York: Prentice Hall, 1940. See especially pp. 16f. The nature of religion is explored by a twentieth century American philosopher who represents personal idealism.

Durkheim, Emil. *Elementary Forms of the Religious Life*. Trans., J. W. Swain. New York: The Macmillan Company, n.d. See especially Book I, chapter 1. Religion, in the most general sense, is analyzed by a noted French sociologist in terms of its origins and meaning.

Freud, Sigmund. *The Future of an Illusion*. Trans., W. D. Robson-Scott. New York: Liveright Publishing Corporation, 1949. (Also published in paperback by Doubleday and Co., Anchor Series.) A book in which Freud describes religion in terms of the projection of human needs and desires.

Hocking, William E. *The Meaning of God in Human Experience*. New Haven: Yale University Press, 1934. An American philosopher evaluates the place and importance in human life of belief in God.

Kierkegaard, Søren. *Fear and Trembling*. Trans., Walter Lowrie. Princeton: Princeton University Press, 1941. (Also published in paperback by Doubleday and Co., Anchor Series.) A matchless meditation on the philosophical, ethical and religious problems presented by the story of the temptation of Abraham to sacrifice Isaac.

Lessa, William A., and Evon Z. Vogt. *Reader in Comparative Religion*. Evanston, Illinois: Row, Peterson, 1958. A source book that brings together valuable anthropological materials.

Meister Eckhart. "The Aristocrat," *Meister Eckhardt*. Trans., Richard B. Blakney. New York and London: Harper and Brothers, 1941, pp. 74f. (Also published in paperback by Harper and Bros., Torchbook Series.) A representative selection from the works of a medieval German mystic whose writings are among the most philosophically oriented of those in the mystical tradition.

Oman, John. "The Sphere of Religion," *Science, Religion and Reality*. Edited by Joseph Needham. New York: The Macmillan Company, 1925. A helpful analysis of various interpretations of religion and their value by a recent British theologian.

Otto, Rudolf. *The Idea of The Holy*. Trans., John W. Harvey. London: Oxford University Press, 1923. (Also published in paperback by Oxford University Press, Galaxy Books.) A fundamental contribution to philosophy of religion. The author analyzes the meaning of religious concepts from the perspective of the liberal tradition in Christian thought.

Underhill, Evelyn. *Mysticism*. London: Methuen Publishing Company, 1949. (Published also in paperback by Meridian Books.) A basic study of the nature of mystical experience by an outstanding authority in the field.

Wach, Joachim. *The Sociology of Religion*. Chicago: The University of Chicago Press, 1944. (Also published in paperback by University of Chicago Press, Phoenix Books.) An important contribution in its field and valuable to anyone studying the nature of religion.

Whitehead, Alfred North. *Religion in the Making*. New York: The Macmillan Company, 1926. (Also published in paperback by Living Age Books.) A contemporary American philosopher discusses the nature and validity of religion.

II. Introduction

THE RELATION OF PHILOSOPHY OF
RELIGION TO THEOLOGY

Every discipline must attempt to make clear its place in the intellectual enterprise. The task is especially difficult when a discipline is a "border" or "bridge" discipline such as philosophy of religion, and it is rendered even more troublesome when those standing on each end of the bridge speak from a commitment to a "way of life." Nonetheless, the student of philosophy of religion needs to understand how adjudication of the claims of philosophy and of religion has been attempted and thus what are the major types of relationship between the two.

In the history of the reciprocal influence of theology and philosophy in the western tradition a number of views of the relationship between these two areas have been expressed. Some philosophers and theologians have tended to deny that any connection is possible, each claiming that the other's discipline is either irrelevant to his own or without any validity whatsoever. In such cases the possibility of philosophy of religion is denied.

At the other extreme there have been attempts to fuse the two disciplines completely. Here the view is that there exists no disparity between reason and revelation, for they are two sides of the same coin: reason seeks and can find what revelation would make evident. Proponents of this position feel that the best rational structuring of the universe is the best theology, for revelation is reason exercising its inherent power.

The majority of writers stand between these two polar positions and represent a number of alternative positions. One of these "middle" ways is to attempt to define a complementary relationship between theology and philosophy so that each discipline has a province of its own which completes the other. This approach finds its most important expression in the thought of Thomas Aquinas. Although theology was of primary importance for Thomas, he had, methodologically, a distinctive place for philosophy also. Another approach within this "middle ground" asserts that both phi-

93

losophy and theology have validity in their own realms, but each realm remains in tension and in an unsettled relation with the other. The theologian feels that theology is based on revelation which relates to the most essential dimensions of human life, such as man's capacity for finding ultimate value and meaning; whereas philosophy is primarily concerned with life at the level of sensory experience and logical analysis. Since man dwells in both realms, both are necessary and must be held together, even though such a correlation is tenuous. The philosopher who accepts this position may simply maintain that man lives in several dimensions, the religious and scientific for example, each of which represents one phase of an individual's manifold experience.

Another of the mediating ways may be characterized as theology's attempt to transform philosophy. In this approach the power of man's natural reason is taken to be of prime importance. Reason is not understood as being incompetent but rather as simply misguided. Theology does not impart "new" knowledge so much as it gives to reason light and new direction, a motive and goal by which it may actualize more fully its inherent power. It is also possible for philosophy to attempt to transform theology. Here the effort is to make theological ideas an integral part of the total philosophical system, and thereby to make evident the truth of the theological statements in light of the entire philosophical structure.

In the foregoing discussion a broad background is provided against which the following selections may be more easily approached and assessed. None of these tendencies is to be taken as a complete delimitation of any single thinker's approach nor as exhaustive of all of the possibilities, but they provide a framework within which individual selections may be evaluated.

In Wallace's essay on Hegel a position is depicted which represents the fusion of philosophy and theology. Hegel argues that the Absolute Mind or Spirit of the Universe becomes conscious of itself in human reason, and that therefore the laws of reason are the laws of the universe. In the exercise of reason the spirit of man participates in the Spirit of the Absolute, and thereby reveals the truth of the nature of the Absolute.

The articles by Thomas Aquinas and Samuel Thompson illustrate the attempt to bring theology and philosophy together in a complementary way. Both Aquinas, a medieval Roman Catholic theologian, and Thompson, a contemporary American Protestant philosopher, are concerned with the same task—that of showing how philosophy provides the fundamental groundwork upon which theology can build and add its own distinctive truth.

The selections from Emil Brunner and Karl Jaspers are representative of a theologian and a philosopher who look rather askance at each other's discipline. Brunner questions the validity of a positive relationship between philosophy and theology on the grounds that any such unity implies the bringing together of two disparate types of knowledge. For this reason Brunner disparages the possibility of finding common ground between the two disciplines. Jaspers, for his part, raises some questions about theologians, especially in regard to attitudes which he thinks lack flexibility, and as a result questions the possibility of genuine relationship.

The writings of Paul Tillich and William Temple, however, are two positive affirmations that connection between philosophy and theology is not only possible but necessary. From two different perspectives these philosophical-theologians attempt to make their case for a recognition of the co-involvement of the two disciplines. Temple acknowledges that both philosophy and theology have their proper spheres and that each is quite distinct from the other. Tension is inevitable when two disparate ways of reaching the same object—in this case God, or the spiritual realm—are employed. But the tension can be creative in the sense that the two disciplines can help each other to understand themselves more adequately, and even to find at some points common ground for agreement. Tillich argues that philosophy analyzes the structures of life and meaning, and by so doing raises questions about the purpose and significance of man's life. Theology, says Tillich, takes on its importance at this point. The task of theology is to explicate the answers which religion offers in response to these questions. In the case of each man, relation between philosophy and theology is understood as one of co-involvement and of mutual help.

In the assessment of these possibilities the student should come to a clearer understanding of what the province of philosophy of religion is and how the initial starting points of men who work in the area affect their methods and conclusions.

WILLIAM WALLACE

WILLIAM WALLACE (1844-1897) was Whyte
Professor of Moral Philosophy at Oxford and
translator of Hegel's *Logic* and *Philosophy of
Mind*. His discussion of Hegel's philosophy
of religion constitutes a part of his introduction to Hegel's *Philosophy of Mind*.

GEORGE W. F. HEGEL (1770-1831), nineteenth century German philosopher, is a
major representative of absolute idealism.

Hegel's Philosophy of Mind*

Religion and Philosophy

It may be well at this point to guard against a misconception of this
serial order of exposition. As stage is seen to follow stage, the historical
imagination, which governs our ordinary current of ideas, turns the logical
dependence into a time-sequence. But it is of course not meant that the
later stage follows the earlier in history. The later is the more real, and
therefore the more fundamental. But we can only understand by abstracting and then transcending our abstractions, or rather by showing how the
abstraction implies relations which force us to go further and beyond our
arbitrary arrest. Each stage therefore either stands to that preceding it as an
antithesis, which inevitably dogs its steps as an accusing spirit, or it is the
conjunction of the original thesis with the antithesis, in a union which
should not be called synthesis because it is a closer fusion and true marriage
of minds. A truth and reality, though fundamental, is only appreciated at
its true value and seen in all its force where it appears as the reconciliation
and reunion of partial and opposing points of view. Thus, e.g., the full
significance of the State does not emerge so long as we view it in isolation
as a supposed single state, but only as it is seen in the conflict of history, in
its actual "energy" as a world-power among powers, always pointing beyond
itself to a something universal which it fain would be, and yet cannot be.
Or, again, there never was a civil or economic society which existed save
under the wing of a state, or in one-sided assumption of state powers to

* From William Wallace, *Hegel's Philosophy of Mind*, Tr. from *The Encyclopaedia of
the Philosophical Sciences* by William Wallace, pp. xxxv-xlix. Published, 1894, by The
Clarendon Press. In the public domain.

itself: and a family is no isolated and independent unit belonging to a supposed patriarchal age, but was always mixed up with, and in manifold dependence upon, political and civil combinations. The true family, indeed,
far from preceding the state in time, presupposes the political power to give
it its precise sphere and its social stability: as is well illustrated by that
typical form of it presented in the Roman state.

So, again, religion does not supervene upon an already existing political
and moral system and invest it with an additional sanction. The true order
would be better described as the reverse. The real basis of social life, and
even of intelligence, is religion. As some thinkers quaintly put it, the known
rests and lives on the bosom of the Unknowable. But when we say that, we
must at once guard against a misconception. There are religions of all sorts;
and some of them which are most heard of in the modern world only exist
or survive in the shape of a traditional name and venerated creed which has
lost its power. Nor is a religion necessarily committed to a definite conception of a supernatural—of a personal power outside the order of Nature.
But in all cases, religion is a faith and a theory which gives unity to the
facts of life, and gives it, not because the unity is in detail proved or detected, but because life and experience in their deepest reality inexorably
demand and evince such a unity to the heart. The religion of a time is not
its nominal creed, but its dominant conviction of the meaning of reality,
the principle which animates all its being and all its striving, the faith it
has in the laws of nature and the purpose of life. Dimly or clearly felt and
perceived, religion has for its principle (one cannot well say, its object) not
the unknowable, but the inner unity of life and knowledge, of act and consciousness, a unity which is certified in its every knowledge, but is never
fully demonstrable by the summation of all its ascertained items. As such a
felt and believed synthesis of the world and life, religion is the unity which
gives stability and harmony to the social sphere; just as morality in its turn
gives a partial and practical realisation to the ideal of religion. But religion
does not merely establish and sanction morality; it also frees it from a
certain narrowness it always has, as of the earth. Or, otherwise put, morality
has to the keener inspection something in it which is more than the mere
moral injunction at first indicates. Beyond the moral, in its stricter sense, as
the obligatory duty and the obedience to law, rises and expands the beautiful
and the good: a beautiful which is disinterestedly loved, and a goodness
which has thrown off all utilitarian relativity, and become a free self-
enhancing joy. The true spirit of religion sees in the divine judgment not
a mere final sanction to human morality which has failed of its earthly close,
not the re-adjustment of social and political judgments in accordance with
our more conscientious inner standards, but a certain, though, for our part-

by-part vision, incalculable proportion between what is done and suffered. And in this liberation of the moral from its restrictions, Art renders no slight aid. Thus in different ways, religion presupposes morality to fill up its vacant form, and morality presupposes religion to give its laws an ultimate sanction, which at the same time points beyond their limitations.

But art, religion, and philosophy still rest on the national culture and on the individual mind. However much they rise in the heights of the ideal world, they never leave the reality of life and circumstance behind, and float in the free empyrean. Yet there are degrees of universality, degrees in which they reach what they promised. As the various psychical *nuclei* of an individual consciousness tend through the course of experience to gather round a central idea and by fusion and assimilation form a complete mental organisation; so, through the march of history, there grows up a complication and a fusion of national ideas and aspirations which, though still retaining the individuality and restriction of a concrete national life, ultimately present an organisation social, aesthetic, and religious which is a type of humanity in its universality and completeness. Always moving in the measure and on the lines of the real development of its social organisation, the art and religion of a nation tend to give expression to what social and political actuality at its best but imperfectly sets in existence. They come more and more to be, not mere competing fragments as set side by side with those of others, but comparatively equal and complete representations of the many-sided and many-voiced reality of man and the world. Yet always they live and flourish in reciprocity with the fullness of practical institutions and individual character. An abstractly universal art and religion is a delusion—until all diversities of geography and climate, of language and temperament, have been made to disappear. If these energies are in power and reality and not merely in name, they cannot be applied like a panacea or put on like a suit of ready-made clothes. If alive, they grow with individualised type out of the social situation: and they can only attain a vulgar and visible universality, so far as they attach themselves to some simple and uniform aspects,—a part tolerably identical everywhere—in human nature in all times and races.

Art, according to Hegel's account, is the first of the three expressions of Absolute Mind. But the key-note to the whole is to be found in Religion: or Religion is the generic description of that phase of mind which has found rest in the fullness of attainment and is no longer a struggle and a warfare, but a fruition. "It is the conviction of all nations," he says, "that in the religious consciousness they hold their truth; and they have always regarded religion as their dignity and as the Sunday of their life. Whatever excites our doubts and alarms, all grief and all anxiety, all that the petty fields of finitude can offer to attract us, we leave behind on the shoals of time: and as the traveller on the highest peak of a mountain range, removed from every distinct view of the earth's surface, quietly lets his vision neglect all the restrictions of the landscape and the world; so in this pure region of faith man, lifted above the hard and inflexible reality, sees it with his mind's eye reflected in the rays of the mental sun to an image where its discords, its lights and shades, are softened to eternal calm. In this region of mind flow the waters of forgetfulness, from which Psyche drinks, and in which she drowns all her pain: and the darknesses of this life are here softened to a dream-image, and transfigured into a mere setting for the splendours of the Eternal."

If we take Religion, in this extended sense, we find it is the sense, the vision, the faith, the certainty of the eternal in the changeable, of the infinite in the finite, of the reality in appearance, of the truth in error. It is freedom from the distractions and pre-occupations of the particular details of life; it is the sense of permanence, repose, certainty, rounding off, toning down and absorbing the vicissitude, the restlessness, the doubts of actual life. Such a victory over palpable reality has no doubt its origin—its embryology—in phrases of mind which have been already discussed in the first section. Religion will vary enormously according to the grade of national mood of mind and social development in which it emerges. But whatever be the peculiarities of its original swaddling-clothes, its cardinal note will be a sense of dependence on, and independence in, something more permanent, more august, more of a surety and stay than visible and variable nature and man,—something also which whether God or devil, or both in one, holds the keys of life and death, of weal and woe, and holds them from some safe vantage-ground above the lower realms of change. By this central being the outward and the inward, past and present and to come, are made one. And as already indicated, Religion, emerging, as it does, from social man, from mind ethical, will retain traces of the two *foci* in society: the individual subjectivity and the objective community. Retain them however only as traces, which still show in the actually envisaged reconciliation. For that is what religion does to morality. It carries a step higher the unity or rather combination gained in the State: it is the fuller harmony of the individual and the collectivity. The moral conscience rests in certainty and fixity on the religious.

But Religion (thus widely understood as the faith in sempiternal and all-explaining reality) at first appears under a guise of Art. The poem and the pyramid, the temple-image and the painting, the drama and the fairy legend, these are religion: but they are, perhaps, religion as Art. And that means that they present the eternal under sensible representations, the work of an artist, and in a perishable material of limited range. Yet even the carvers of a long-past day whose works have been disinterred from the plateaux of

Auvergne knew that they gave to the perishable life around them a quasi-immortality: and the myth-teller of a savage tribe elevated the incident of a season into a perennial power of love and fear. The cynic may remind us that from the finest picture of the artist, readily

"We turn
To yonder girl that fords the burn."

And yet it may be said in reply to the cynic that, had it not been for the deep-imprinted lesson of the artist, it would have been but a brutal instinct that would have drawn our eyes. The artist, the poet, the musician, reveal the meaning, the truth, the reality of the world: they teach us, they help us, backward younger brothers, to see, to hear, to feel what our rude senses had failed to detect. They enact the miracle of the loaves and fishes, again and again: out of the common limited things of every day they produce a bread of life in which the generations continue to find nourishment.

But if Art embodies for us the unseen and the eternal, it embodies it in the stone, the colour, the tone, and the word: and these are by themselves only dead matter. To the untutored eye and taste the finest picture-gallery is only a weariness: when the national life has drifted away, the sacred book and the image are but idols and enigmas. "The statues are now corpses from which the vivifying soul has fled, and the hymns are words whence faith has departed: the tables of the Gods are without spiritual meat and drink, and games and feasts no longer afford the mind its joyful union with the being of being. The works of the Muse lack that intellectual force which knew itself strong and real by crushing gods and men in its winepress. They are now (in this iron age) what they are for us,—fair fruits broken from the tree, and handed to us by a kindly destiny. But the gift is like the fruits which the girl in the picture presents: she does not give the real life of their existence, not the tree which bore them, not the earth and the elements which entered into their substance, nor the climate which formed their quality, nor the change of seasons which governed the process of their growth. Like her, Destiny in giving us the works of ancient art does not give us their world, not the spring and summer of the ethical life in which they blossomed and ripened, but solely a memory and a suggestion of this actuality. Our act in enjoying them, therefore, is not a Divine service: were it so, our mind would achieve its perfect and satisfying truth. All that we do is a mere externalism, which from these fruits wipes off some rain-drop, some speck of dust, and which, in place of the inward elements of moral actuality that created and inspired them, tries from the dead elements of their external reality, such as language and historical allusion, to set up a tedious mass of scaffolding, not in order to live ourselves into them, but only to form a picture of them in our minds. But as the girl who proffers the plucked fruits is more and nobler than the natural element with all its details of tree, air, light, etc. which first yielded them, because she gathers all this together, in a nobler way, into the glance of the conscious eye and the gesture which proffers them; so the spirit of destiny which offers us those works of art is more than the ethical life and actuality of the ancient people: for it is the inwardising of that mind which in them was still self-estranged and self-dispossessed:—it is the spirit of tragic destiny, the destiny which collects all those individualised gods and attributes of substance into the one Pantheon. And that temple of all the gods is Mind conscious of itself as mind."

Religion enters into its more adequate form when it ceases to appear in the guise of Art and realises that the kingdom of God is within, that the truth must be *felt*, the eternal *inwardly* revealed, the holy one apprehended by *faith*, not by outward vision. Eye hath not seen, nor ear heard, the things of God. They cannot be presented, or delineated: they come only in the witness of the spirit. The human soul itself is the only worthy temple of the Most High, whom heaven, and the heaven of heavens, cannot contain. Here in truth God has come down to dwell with men; and the Son of Man, caught up in the effusion of the Spirit, can in all assurance and all humility claim that he is divinified. Here apparently Absolute Mind is reached: the soul knows no limitation, no struggle: in time it is already eternal. Yet, there is, according to Hegel, a flaw,—not in the essence and the matter, but in the manner and mode in which the ordinary religious consciousness represents to itself, or pictures that unification which it feels and experiences.

"In religion then this unification of ultimate Being with the Self is implicitly reached. But the religious consciousness, if it has this symbolic idea of its reconciliation, still has it as a mere symbol or representation. It attains the satisfaction by tacking on to its pure negativity, and that externally, the positive signification of its unity with the ultimate Being: its satisfaction remains therefore tainted by the antithesis of another world. Its own reconciliation, therefore, is presented to its consciousness as something far away, something far away in the future: just as the reconciliation which the other Self accomplished appears as a far-away thing in the past. The one Divine Man had but an implicit father and only an actual mother; conversely the universal divine man, the community, has its own deed and knowledge for its father, but for its mother only the eternal Love, which it only *feels*, but does not *behold* in its consciousness as an actual immediate object. Its reconciliation therefore is in its heart, but still at variance with its consciousness, and its actuality still has a flaw. In its field of consciousness the place of implicit reality or side of pure mediation is taken by the reconciliation that lies far away behind: the place of the actually present, or the side of immediacy and existence, is filled by the world which has still to wait for its transfiguration to glory. Implicitly no doubt the world is reconciled with the eternal Being; and that Being, it is well known, no longer looks upon the object as alien to it, but in its love sees it as like itself. But for self-consciousness this immediate presence is not yet set in the full light of mind. In its immediate consciousness accordingly the spirit of the community is parted from its religious: for while the religious consciousness declares that they are implicitly not parted, this implicitness is not raised to reality and not yet grown to absolute self-certainty."

Religion therefore, which as it first appeared in art-worship had yet to realise its essential inwardness or spirituality, so has now to overcome the antithesis in which its (the religious) consciousness stands to the secular. For the peculiarly religious type of mind is distinguished by an indifference and even hostility, more or less veiled, to art, to morality and the civil state, to science and to nature. Strong in the certainty of faith, or of its implicit rest in God, it resents too curious inquiry into the central mystery of its union, and in its distincter consciousness sets the foundation of faith on the evidence of a fact, which, however, it in the same breath declares to be unique and miraculous, the central event of the ages, pointing back in its reference to the first days of humanity, and forward in the future to the winding-up of the business of terrestrial life. Philosophy, according to Hegel's conception of it, does but draw the conclusion supplied by the premises of religion: it supplements and rounds off into coherence the religious implications. The unique events in Judea nearly nineteen centuries ago are for it also the first step in a new revelation of man's relationship to God: but while it acknowledges the transcendent interest of that age, it lays main stress on the permanent truth then revealed, and it insists on the duty of carrying out the principle there awakened to all the depth and breadth of its explication. Its task—its supreme task—is to *explicate religion*. But to do so is to show that religion is no exotic, and no *mere* revelation from an external source. It is to show that religion is the truth, the complete reality, of the mind that lived in Art, that founded the state and sought to be dutiful and upright: the truth, the crowning fruit of all scientific knowledge, of all human affections, of all secular consciousness. Its lesson ultimately is that there is nothing essentially common or unclean: that the holy is not parted off from the true and the good and the beautiful.

Religion thus expanded descends from its abstract or "intelligible" world, to which it had retired from art and science, and the affairs of ordinary life. Its God—as a true God—is not of the dead alone, but also of the living: not a far-off supreme and ultimate Being, but also a man among men. Philosophy thus has to break down the middle partition-wall of life, the fence between secular and sacred. It is but religion come to its maturity, made at home in the world, and no longer a stranger and a wonder. Religion has pronounced in its inmost heart and faith of faith, that the earth is the Lord's, and that day unto day shows forth the divine handiwork. But the heart of unbelief, of little faith, has hardly uttered the word, than it forgets its assurance and leans to the conviction that the prince of this world is the Spirit of Evil. The mood of Théodicée is also—but with a difference—the mood of philosophy. It asserts the ways of Providence: but its providence is not the God of the Moralist, or the ideal of the Artist, or rather is not these only, but also the Law of Nature, and more than that. Its aim is the Unity of History. The words have sometimes been lightly used to mean that events run on in one continuous flow, and that there are no abrupt, no ultimate beginnings, parting age from age. But the Unity of History in its full sense is beyond history: it is history "reduced" from the expanses of time to the eternal present: its thousand years made one day,—made even the glance of a moment. The theme of the Unity of History—in the full depth of unity and the full expanse of history—is the theme of Hegelian philosophy. It traces the process in which Mind has to be all-inclusive, self-upholding, one with the Eternal reality.

"That process of the mind's self-realisation," says Hegel in the close of his *Phenomenology*, "exhibits a lingering movement and succession of minds, a gallery of images, each of which, equipped with the complete wealth of mind, only seems to linger because the Self has to penetrate and to digest this wealth of its Substance. As its perfection consists in coming completely to *know* what it *is* (its substance), this knowledge is its self-involution in which it deserts its outward existence and surrenders its shape to recollection. Thus self-involved, it is sunk in the night of its self-consciousness: but in that night its vanished being is preserved, and that being, thus in idea preserved,—old, but now new-born of the spirit,—is the new sphere of being, a new world, a new phase of mind. In this new phase it has again to begin afresh and from the beginning, and again nurture itself to maturity from its own resources, as if for it all that preceded were lost, and it had learned nothing from the experience of the earlier minds. Yet is that recollection a preservation of experience: it is the quintessence, and in fact a higher form, of the substance. If therefore this new mind appears only to count on its own resources, and to start quite fresh and blank, it is at the same time on a higher grade that it starts. The intellectual and spiritual realm, which is thus constructed in actuality, forms a succession in time, where one mind relieved another of its watch, and each took over the kingdom of the world from the preceding. The purpose of that succession is to reveal the depth, and that depth is the absolute comprehension of mind: this revelation is therefore to uplift its depth, to spread it out in breadth, so negativing this self-involved Ego, wherein it is self-dispossessed or reduced to substance. But it is also its time: the course of time shows this dispossession itself dispossessed, and thus in its extension it is no less in its depth, the self. The way to that goal,—absolute self-certainty—or the mind knowing itself as mind —is the inwardising of the minds, as they severally are in themselves, and as they accomplish the organisation of their realm. Their conservation,—regarded on the side of its free and apparently contingent succession of fact— is history: on the side of their comprehended organisation, again, it is the science of mental phenomenology: the two together, comprehended history, form at once the recollection and the grave-yard of the absolute Mind, the actuality, truth, and certitude of his throne, apart from which he were lifeless and alone."

Such in brief outline—lingering most on the points where Hegel has here been briefest—is the range of the Philosophy of Mind. Its aim is to comprehend, not to explain: to put together in intelligent unity, not to analyse into a series of elements. For it psychology is not an analysis or description of mental phenomena, of laws of association, of the growth of certain powers and ideas, but a "comprehended history" of the formation of subjective mind, of the intelligent, feeling, willing self or ego. For it Ethics is part and only part of the great scheme or system of self-development; but continuing into greater concreteness the normal endowment of the individual mind, and but preparing the ground on which religion may be most effectively cultivated. And finally Religion itself, released from its isolation and other world sacro-sanctity, is shown to be only the crown of life, the ripest growth of actuality, and shown to be so by philosophy, whilst it is made clear that religion is the basis of philosophy, or that a philosophy can only go as far as the religious stand-point allows. The hierarchy, if so it be called, of the spiritual forces is one where none can stand alone, or claim an abstract and independent supremacy. The truth of egoism is the truth of altruism: the truly moral is the truly religious: and each is not what it professes to be unless it anticipate the later, or include the earlier.

THOMAS
AQUINAS

THOMAS AQUINAS (c. 1226-1274), Dominican
Friar and the greatest of the medieval philosophers, produced a synthesis of Christian
faith and Aristotle's metaphysics which became the official theology of the Roman
Catholic Church. His chief works are *Summa
Theologica* and *Summa Contra Gentiles*.

The Summa Contra Gentiles*

Chapter VII

That the Truth of Reason Is Not in Opposition to the
Truth of the Christian Faith

Now though the aforesaid truth of the Christian faith surpasses the ability
of human reason, nevertheless those things which are naturally instilled in
human reason cannot be opposed to this truth. For it is clear that those
things which are implanted in reason by nature, are most true, so much so
that it is impossible to think them to be false. Nor is it lawful to deem false
that which is held by faith, since it is so evidently confirmed by God. Seeing
then that the false alone is opposed to the true, as evidently appears if we
examine their definitions, it is impossible for the aforesaid truth of faith to
be contrary to those principles which reason knows naturally.

Again. The same thing which the disciple's mind received from its teacher
is contained in the knowledge of the teacher, unless he teach insincerely,
which it were wicked to say of God. Now the knowledge of naturally known
principles is instilled into us by God, since God Himself is the author of
our nature. Therefore the divine Wisdom also contains these principles.
Consequently whatever is contrary to these principles, is contrary to the
divine Wisdom; wherefore it cannot be from God. Therefore those things
which are received by faith from divine revelation cannot be contrary to our
natural knowledge.

Moreover. Our intellect is stayed by contrary arguments, so that it cannot
advance to the knowledge of truth. Wherefore if conflicting knowledges

* From Thomas Aquinas, *The Summa Contra Gentiles*, trans. the English Dominican
Fathers, I, chapters VII-XII, pp. 14-23. Published, 1924, Burns Oates & Washbourne
Ltd. Used by permission of Burns & Oates Limited.

were instilled into us by God, our intellect would thereby be hindered from knowing the truth. And this cannot be ascribed to God.

Furthermore. Things that are natural are unchangeable so long as nature remains. Now contrary opinions cannot be together in the same subject. Therefore God does not instill into man any opinion or belief contrary to natural knowledge.

Hence the Apostle says (Rom. x. 8): *The word is nigh thee even in thy heart and in thy mouth. This is the word of faith which we preach.* Yet because it surpasses reason some look upon it as though it were contrary thereto; which is impossible.

This is confirmed also by the authority of Augustine who says (*Gen. ad lit.* ii): *That which truth shall make known can nowise be in opposition to the holy books whether of the Old or of the New Testament.*

From this we may evidently conclude that whatever arguments are alleged against the teachings of faith, they do not rightly proceed from the first self-evident principles instilled by nature. Wherefore they lack the force of demonstration, and are either probable or sophistical arguments, and consequently it is possible to solve them.

Chapter VIII

In What Relation Human Reason Stands To the Truth of Faith

It would also seem well to observe that sensible things from which human reason derives the source of its knowledge, retain a certain trace of likeness to God, but so imperfect that it proves altogether inadequate to manifest the substance itself of God. For effects resemble their causes according to their own mode, since like action proceeds from like agent; and yet the effect does not always reach to a perfect likeness to the agent. Accordingly human reason is adapted to the knowledge of the truth of faith, which can be known in the highest degree only by those who see the divine substance, in so far as it is able to put together certain probable arguments in support thereof, which nevertheless are insufficient to enable us to understand the aforesaid truth as though it were demonstrated to us or understood by us in itself. And yet however weak these arguments may be, it is useful for the human mind to be practised therein, so long as it does not pride itself on having comprehended or demonstrated: since although our view of the sublimest things is limited and weak, it is most pleasant to be able to catch but a glimpse of them, as appears from what has been said.

The authority of Hilary is in agreement with this statement: for he says

(*De Trin.*) while speaking of this same truth: *Begin by believing these things, advance and persevere; and though I know thou wilt not arrive, I shall rejoice at thy advance. For he who devoutly follows in pursuit of the infinite, though he never come up with it, will always advance by setting forth. Yet pry not into that secret, and meddle not in the mystery of the birth of the infinite, nor presume to grasp that which is the summit of under-standing: but understand that there are things thou canst not grasp.*

Chapter IX

Of the Order and Mode of Procedure In This Work

Accordingly, from what we have been saying it is evident that the intention of the wise man must be directed to the twofold truth of divine things and to the refutation of contrary errors: and that the research of reason is able to reach to one of these, while the other surpasses every effort of reason. And I speak of a twofold truth of divine things, not on the part of God Himself Who is Truth one and simple, but on the part of our knowledge, the relation of which to the knowledge of divine things varies.

Wherefore in order to deduce the first kind of truth we must proceed by demonstrative arguments whereby we can convince our adversaries. But since such arguments are not available in support of the second kind of truth, our intention must be not to convince our opponent by our arguments, but to solve the arguments which he brings against the truth, because, as shown above, natural reason cannot be opposed to the truth of faith. In a special way may the opponent of this kind of truth be convinced by the authority of Scripture confirmed by God with miracles: since we believe not what is above human reason save because God has revealed it. In support, however, of this kind of truth, certain probable arguments must be adduced for the practice and help of the faithful, but not for the conviction of our opponents, because the very insufficiency of these arguments would rather confirm them in their error, if they thought that we assented to the truth of faith on account of such weak reasonings.

With the intention then of proceeding in the manner laid down, we shall first of all endeavour to declare that truth which is the object of faith's confession and of reason's researches, by adducing arguments both demonstrative and probable, some of which we have gathered from the writings of the philosophers and of holy men, so as thereby to confirm the truth and convince our opponents. After this, so as to proceed from the more to the less manifest, we shall with God's help proceed to declare that truth which sur-

108

passes reason, by refuting the arguments of our opponents, and by setting forth the truth of faith by means of probable arguments and authority.

Seeing then that we intend by the way of reason to pursue those things about God which human reason is able to investigate, the first object that offers itself to our consideration consists in those things which pertain to God in Himself; the second will be the procession of creatures from Him; and the third the relation of creatures to Him as their end. Of those things which we need to consider about God in Himself, we must give the first place (this being the necessary foundation of the whole of this work), to the question of demonstrating that there is a God: for unless this be established, all questions about divine things are out of court.

Chapter X

Of the Opinion of Those Who Aver That It Cannot Be Demonstrated That There Is a God, Since This Is Self-evident

Possibly it will seem to some that it is useless to endeavour to show that there is a God: they say that it is self-evident that God is, so that it is impossible to think the contrary, and thus it cannot be demonstrated that there is a God. The reasons for this view are as follow. Those things are said to be self-evident which are known as soon as the terms are known: thus as soon as it is known what is a whole, and what is a part, it is known that the whole is greater than its part. Now such is the statement *God is*. For by this word *God* we understand a thing a greater than which cannot be thought of: this is what a man conceives in his mind when he hears and understands this word *God*: so that God must already be at least in his mind. Nor can He be in the mind alone, for that which is both in the mind and in reality is greater than that which is in the mind only. And the very signification of the word shows that nothing is greater than God. Wherefore it follows that it is self-evident that God is, since it is made clear from the very signification of the word.

Again. It is possible to think that there is a thing which cannot be thought not to exist: and such a thing is evidently greater than that which can be thought not to exist. Therefore if God can be thought not to exist, it follows that something can be thought greater than God: and this is contrary to the signification of the term. Therefore it remains that it is self-evident that God is.

Further. Those propositions are most evident in which the selfsame thing is predicated of itself, for instance: *Man is man*; or wherein the predicate is included in the definition of the subject, for instance: *Man is an animal*. Now, as we shall show further on, in God alone do we find that His being is His essence, as though the same were the answer to the question, *What is He?* as to the question, *Is He?* Accordingly when we say, *God is*, the predicate is either identified with the subject, or *at least* is included in the definition of the subject. And thus it will be self-evident that God is.

Moreover. Things that are known naturally are self-evident, for it is not by a process of research that they become evident. Now it is naturally known that God is, since man's desire tends naturally to God as his last end, as we shall show further on. Therefore it is self-evident that God is.

Again. That whereby all things are known must needs be self-evident. Now such is God. For just as the light of the sun is the principle of all visual perception, so the divine light is the principle of all intellectual knowledge, because it is therein that first and foremost intellectual light is to be found. Therefore it must needs be self-evident that God is.

On account of these and like arguments some are of opinion that it is so self-evident that God is, that it is impossible for the mind to think the contrary.

Chapter XI

Refutation of the Foregoing Opinion and Solution of the Aforesaid Arguments

The foregoing opinion arose from their being accustomed from the beginning to hear and call upon the name of God. Now custom, especially if it date from our childhood, acquires the force of nature, the result being that the mind holds those things with which it was imbued from childhood as firmly as though they were self-evident. It is also a result of failing to distinguish between what is self-evident simply, and that which is self-evident to us. For it is simply self-evident that God is, because the selfsame thing which God is, is His existence. But since we are unable to conceive mentally the selfsame thing which is God, that thing remains unknown in regard to us. Thus it is self-evident simply that every whole is greater than its part, but to one who fails to conceive mentally the meaning of a whole, it must needs be unknown. Hence it is that those things which are most evident of all are to the intellect what the sun is to the eye of an owl, as stated in *Metaph. ii.*

Nor does it follow, as the first argument alleged, that as soon as the meaning of the word *God* is understood, it is known that God is. First, because it is not known to all, even to those who grant that there is a God, that God is that thing than which no greater can be thought of, since many of the ancients asserted that this world is God. Nor can any such conclusion be gathered from the significations which Damascene assigns to this word *God*. Secondly because, granted that everyone understands this word *God* to signify something than which a greater cannot be thought of, it does not follow that something than which a greater cannot be thought of exists in reality. For we must needs allege a thing in the same way as we allege the signification of its name. Now from the fact that we conceive mentally that which the word *God* is intended to convey, it does not follow that God is otherwise than in the mind. Wherefore neither will it follow that the thing than which a greater cannot be thought of is otherwise than in the mind. And thence it does not follow that there exists in reality something than which a greater cannot be thought of. Hence this is no argument against those who assert that there is no God, since whatever be granted to exist, whether in reality or in the mind, there is nothing to prevent a person from thinking of something greater, unless he grants that there is in reality something than which a greater cannot be thought of.

Again it does not follow, as the second argument pretended, that if it is possible to think that God is not, it is possible to think of something greater than God. For that it be possible to think that He is not, is not on account of the imperfection of His being or the uncertainty thereof, since in itself His being is supremely manifest, but is the result of the weakness of our mind which is able to see Him, not in Himself but in His effects, so that it is led by reasoning to know that He is.

Wherefore the third argument also is solved. For just as it is self-evident to us that a whole is greater than its part, so is it most evident to those who see the very essence of God that God exists, since His essence is His existence. But because we are unable to see His essence, we come to know His existence not in Himself but in His effects.

The solution to the fourth argument is also clear. For man knows God naturally in the same way as he desires Him naturally. Now man desires Him naturally in so far as he naturally desires happiness, which is a likeness of the divine goodness. Hence it does not follow that God considered in Himself is naturally known to man, but that His likeness is. Wherefore man must needs come by reasoning to know God in the likenesses to Him which he discovers in God's effects.

It is also easy to reply to the fifth argument. For God is that in which all things are known, not so that other things be unknown except He be known, as happens in self-evident principles, but because all knowledge is caused in us by His outpouring.

Chapter XII

Of the Opinion of Those Who Say That the Existence of God Cannot be Proved, and That It Is Held by Faith Alone

The position that we have taken is also assailed by the opinion of certain others, whereby the efforts of those who endeavour to prove that there is a God would again be rendered futile. For they say that it is impossible by means of the reason to discover that God exists, and that this knowledge is acquired solely by means of faith and revelation.

In making this assertion some were moved by the weakness of the arguments which certain people employed to prove the existence of God.

Possibly, however, this error might falsely seek support from the statements of certain philosophers, who show that in God essence and existence are the same, namely that which answers to the question, *What is He?* and that which answers to the question, *Is He?* Now it is impossible by the process of reason to acquire the knowledge of what God is. Wherefore seemingly neither is it possible to prove by reason whether God is.

Again. If, as required by the system of the Philosopher, in order to prove whether a thing is we must take as principle the signification of its name, and since according to the Philosopher *(4 Metaph.) the signification of a name is its definition*: there will remain no means of proving the existence of God, seeing that we lack knowledge of the divine essence or quiddity.

Again. If the principles of demonstration become known to us originally through the senses, as is proved in the *Posterior Analytics*, those things which transcend all sense and sensible objects are seemingly indemonstrable. Now such is the existence of God. Therefore it cannot be demonstrated.

The falseness of this opinion is shown to us first by the art of demonstration, which teaches us to conclude causes from effects. Secondly, by the order itself of sciences: for if no substance above sensible substance can be an object of science, there will be no science above Physics, as stated in *4 Metaph.* Thirdly, by the efforts of the philosophers who have endeavoured to prove the existence of God. Fourthly, by the apostolic truth which asserts (Rom. i. 20) that the *invisible things of God are clearly seen, being understood by the things that are made.*

Nor should we be moved by the consideration that in God essence and existence are the same, as the first argument contended. For this is to be understood of the existence by which God subsists in Himself, of which we are ignorant as to what kind of a thing it is, even as we are ignorant of His essence. But it is not to be understood of that existence which is signified by the composition of the mind. For in this way it is possible to prove the existence of God, when our mind is led by demonstrative arguments to form a proposition stating that God is.

Moreover. In those arguments whereby we prove the existence of God, it is not necessary that the divine essence or quiddity be employed as the middle term, as the second argument supposed: but instead of the quiddity we take His effects as middle term, as in the case in *a posteriori* reasoning: and from these effects we take the signification of this word *God*. For all the divine names are taken either from the remoteness of God's effects from Himself, or from some relationship between God and His effects.

It is also evident from the fact that, although God transcends all sensibles and senses, His effects from which we take the proof that God exists, are sensible objects. Hence our knowledge, even of things which transcend the senses, originates from the senses.

SAMUEL M. THOMPSON

SAMUEL M. THOMPSON (1902-　　), Professor of Philosophy at Monmouth College, Illinois, is a Protestant who has attempted to restate some traditional emphases in contemporary terms. His book, A *Modern Philosophy of Religion*, develops these views.

The Philosophy of Religion*

Can Religion Establish Its Own Truth?

The question of whether a religion is true or false is not likely to arise directly from religious experience and practice. It is in our reflective moments, when we look back upon the religious attitudes and actions of ourselves and others, that the question comes. We discover that different people have different religious practices and ideas and that they seem as sincere and as sure they are right as we do ourselves.

Doubts of the truth of religion come also from the seeming conflicts between what we have been taught in the name of religion and what we learn from other sources about ourselves and our world. The whole range of

* From Samuel M. Thompson, A *Modern Philosophy of Religion*, pp. 24-40. Copyright, 1955, by Henry Regnery Company. Used by permission of the publishers.

modern culture in the western world has been marked in recent centuries by a persistent conflict between science and religion. There are conflicts also between religion and politics, religion and education, and between certain religious conceptions of man and the uses which modern industry makes of him. We could extend our catalogue to cover the whole range of modern life. For modern life, in those of its aspects which are distinctively modern, is fundamentally secular. Rather than something which permeates life and society and their institutions, religion in the modern world tends to be only one compartment among many. It is expected to keep its proper place and not to intrude beyond its established boundary lines. As Professor Allport says, some people "take over the ancestral religion much as they take over the family jewels. It would be awkward to bring it into too close a relationship with science, with suffering, and with criticism." [1]

It is quite possible that the question of the truth of religion, as it appears in modern thought, is not so much a question of truth in its specific philosophical or logical sense as it is an expression of conflicting loyalties. For where a life is divided into different compartments there is bound to be some degree of rivalry among the various interests involved. Each attempts to capture more of the self and, in so far as the self is a divided self, the more the self is taken by one interest the less is left for the others. We have carried this so far in modern life that we live by the clock and divide ourselves into parts which we measure by hours, minutes, and even by seconds.

If religion is, as we have suggested, an expression of basic evaluations and ultimate loyalties then to try to confine religion to a separate compartment of life as one activity among many is simply incompatible with its nature. As the human self is single and indivisible so the basic attitudes and values of a life must be all of one piece. A man cannot adopt one policy for one part of his activity and another and incompatible policy for another area of activity without destroying his own integrity. For when he is engaged in the one he must at times be aware of the other, and of the fact that the other is his; and so he must in some way or another be perplexed as to which man he is, whether he is one who follows now a policy of kindness and consideration or whether he is a man of ruthless selfishness and cruelty and disregard for the concerns of other people. He may think up excuses for his inconsistencies, or he may not permit himself to think of the matter at all; but he cannot remain in a condition of actual internal, or spiritual, disruption, whether it is conscious or unconscious, and find any real peace and satisfaction. For what brings peace to one part of him will be at odds with the

---

[1] *The Individual and His Religion* by Gordon W. Allport (New York: The Macmillan Company, 1930), p. 52. We shall consider this further in Chapter X, "Traditional and Modern Ideas of Man."

other part. So long as he is aware of himself as the same self which thinks and acts at different times he remains one single self, and he cannot act fully as a self unless the principles on which he acts are compatible with each other. This is the real conflict between the religious and secular aspects of modern life.

Although religious doubt may express a conflict of loyalties yet once it comes out into the open it is a challenge to religion's claim to be true. It makes little difference what is responsible for raising the question, once the truth of a religion is challenged that religion can meet the challenge only by justifying its claim to truth. I may be accused of lying or of dishonesty by someone whose only motive is malice or jealousy and who has no ground for his charge. But I cannot meet the charge by attacking his sincerity or his motives. To attempt to do so is to commit a logical fallacy, the fallacy of argument *ad hominem*. My only defense *against the charge*, if I feel it necessary to defend myself against it, is to show that it is false.

Charles A. Bennett insists that the

metaphysical pretensions of religion [by which he means its claim to be true] are the most important thing about it. We cannot reduce the drama of the religious life to a mere record of mental conflict, to so much natural history of the mind. Unless the issues of destiny are at stake, there is no genuine conflict and no drama. Thus I reject all attempts to hand over religion and its problems to anthropology or sociology or psychology, as though these sciences, separately or together, could provide us with a sufficient explanation or interpretation. The problems of religion are philosophical, and there is no substitute for a philosophy of religion.[2]

It is one thing to understand how it happens that we raise the question of the truth of religion; it is quite another thing to determine how that question is to be answered. Once it is raised, however, either we must find some way of answering it or find some way in which we can live with the question without destroying the basis of our life.

When we look at the question directly it seems quite evident that a religion cannot examine its own truth. If it tries to do this in its own terms, as a part of the expression of the attitudes and practices of which it is composed, it would of course beg the question. It would be trying to answer a question in terms of what has itself been brought into question.

This is the reason religious dispute is so seldom convincing. To be convinced by an argument, in so far as the conviction is to be a logical one, we must accept the argument's premises. If the argument is about the truth of

2 *The Dilemma of Religious Knowledge,* by Charles A. Bennett (New Haven: Yale University Press, 1930), p. 120.

a religion then the premises themselves are in question. To argue from these premises in favor of them can convince only those who are unaware of what is happening. When we concern ourselves with the doctrines of a religion, and deal with them from the standpoint of that religion itself, then those doctrines are simply accepted. A religion proclaims what it takes to be true, and the hearer accepts or rejects. He is convinced or he is not convinced. To try to justify or establish the truth of what a religion proclaims it is necessary to go beyond what it contains within itself.

Can Theology Establish the Truth of Religion?

One of the facts of life today is that few except theologians take theology seriously. It is not true, at least to the same extent, that only scientists take science seriously or that only artists take art seriously or that only philosophers take philosophy seriously. Even philosophy and science, areas of thought we should expect to find somewhat interested in its truth or falsity, pay little attention to theology. They do not listen to theology; at most they notice only that she has spoken and reply to her only to silence her.

Some explanation of the present-day indifference to theology may be found in the tendency for modern interests to separate themselves from each other, and in the relation of this tendency to certain distinctive features of theology itself. A theology is in one respect a rational system and in another respect it is not; its internal structure of ideas is a rational structure but its foundation is faith. It is composed of a set of doctrines concerning God, man, the world, history, and destiny. These doctrines may be organized in a thoroughly logical order. So far as this is the case a theology is a rational system. But the more complete is its logical order the more evident is the dependence of the whole system upon its basic premises. This is true of any logical system, but it is of special importance in the case of theology because theology admittedly obtains its premises from faith. So although theology is a rational system in its inner structure it is a system which rests on faith, and it neither questions nor inquires into the truth of its premises.

As was pointed out before, with his tendency to divide up life into separate compartments the modern man is unlikely to have any single set of basic principles. Jumping from one set to another as he moves from one activity to another, he feels no need to reconcile his various policies with each other in terms of something fundamental to them all. Even a system of philosophy may be built out of a cluster of hypotheses and inferences which have sprung from a thinker's preoccupation with some technical problem of quite limited scope. Whole philosophies have come out of attempts to deal with such problems as the nature of perception, the status of colors and sounds in the physical world, or the nature of verification and of symbolic utterance. Sometimes we find the philosophizing so quaintly naive that the resulting philosophy describes the kind of a world in which the process of constructing a world view could not possibly take place. It is not surprising that schizophrenia, the splitting up of a mind, is today one of the commonest and most characteristic mental disorders.

Modern inquiry and thinking is so specialized it has become provincial, not in a geographic sense but with respect to its subject matter. There are advantages in this, as there are advantages in many other kinds of specializations; but the disadvantages are precisely those which interfere with the achievement of a unified and integrated point of view.

Each specialized interest has its own assumptions which it does not examine, and the less contact there is between these different areas the easier it is to forget the fact that assumptions are made. So some of the attitudes typical of thought today contain the bland assumption that no assumptions are being made. This is one important reason why other fields of inquiry pay no attention to theology, for theology is a field which never ignores its assumptions; or, if it does now and then ignore some of its assumptions, it never ignores the fact that it makes assumptions. Its very admission that it rests upon faith makes theology seem out of step with the rest of modern thought, and so it is left out of the picture.

When theology does try to ignore its assumptions it gives up its claim to be true, and some theologians have been willing to pay even this price in order to feel at home in our splintered society. These theologians, as Arnold S. Nash points out, "vainly seek to make theology 'scientific' by cutting it free from metaphysics and history and resting it on religious experience. Theology then becomes thinking about our nice feelings rather than thinking about God and His relation to man and the world." [3] President Nathan M. Pusey, of Harvard University, reminds us of the consequences of the neglect of metaphysics when he says "it has now become frighteningly clear that if you try to ignore metaphysical considerations (I would say considerations of ultimate things) or cover them up in bursts of energy, they will rise up in perverted and distorted forms to mock one's thus too-circumscribed efforts." [4]

It is not reason, however, which opens the door to theology, it is faith; and unless the door is opened we cannot enter the structure. Some have

---

[3] *The University and the Modern World* by Arnold S. Nash (New York: The Macmillan Company, 1944), p. 290.

[4] "A Religion for Now," by Nathan M. Pusey, in *Harper's* for December 1953 (New York: Harper and Brothers), pp. 20-21.

insisted, in opposition to this, that a person might become an expert in theology without accepting the truth of its principal tenets, even as an anthropologist might become an expert on some primitive system of magic without himself believing in the effectiveness of the magic he studies. It is true we may come to know a great deal about a theology without a belief in its truth, but there is serious question whether we could think ourselves into it and grasp the full meaning of its doctrines without actually entering through the door of faith. The chief importance of theology, to a greater extent perhaps than in any other field of inquiry, lies in the truth or falsity of its premises. Its premises are of such a nature that adequate understanding of what they mean may require a belief in their truth, just as adequate understanding of another's expression of love may depend upon belief in the truth of the expression. Tremendous consequences hinge upon the truth or falsity of the premises of theology, consequences which completely overshadow its merely historical or cultural or psychological significance. The issues are the issues of man's destiny.

Thus far we have found that theology is important if true, and we have found some of the reasons why it is ignored by other fields of inquiry. Our question now is whether theology itself is competent to determine its own truth or falsity. It is likely that a theology originates in the attempt to defend a religious doctrine which has been challenged. But its defense is confined to showing that the doctrine is implied by the basic beliefs of the religion concerned. In other words theology originates in connection with challenges and objections which arise from within a religion; it is not concerned with attacks which come from outside the religion, except in so far as it may serve to protect from heresy those who would reject heresy solely because it is heresy.

As a religion comes into closer contact with ideas and influences alien or antagonistic to itself, more and more questions arise concerning its basic doctrines. As an answer to these questions theology finds itself inadequate. This, however, has not always prevented theologians from making the attempt, and in making the attempt they are not always clear as to their own purpose and function. They sometimes attempt to defend their theological premises by an appeal to theology. From such confusion was born the discipline known as "apologetics." The fate which the various systems of apologetics have met is the appropriate consequence of the confusion upon which they rest. Apologetics is an illegitimate discipline; for if it assumes its premises it is special pleading or else a mere restatement of the theology it purports to defend, while if it examines its premises it is philosophy and so can plead no case but that of truth itself. Apologetics can disguise its dilemma only by a sleight of hand substitution of rationalizing for reason.

Theology is important, but its importance is in the service it renders to those who accept the religious position to which it gives logical and systematic expression. It is important to him who professes a faith to know what is and what is not consistent with his profession. A little theology quickly cools the overheated religious imagination.

Theology helps prevent extravagance and inconsistency; and it uncovers the less obvious consequences of religious belief. As soon as a religious idea becomes definite enough to pass for a concept it is subject to examination by theology. Thus reason is brought to bear upon it, and only an enemy of reason would venture to say that the long run results of the work of reason can be anything but good.

When we have gone as far as truth will take us in emphasizing the importance of theology we find still echoing in our minds the statement of its limitations. A theology assumes the truth of its own premises; it obtains them from faith and for it their truth is not in question. When question is raised concerning their truth theology has nothing to say. If it is a mistake for other fields of inquiry to ignore theology, it is every bit as serious an error for theology to ignore other fields. This is what happens when theology attempts to assume a position independent of science and philosophy, and attempts to find within itself the warrant of its own truth. In every attempt it may make to insulate itself from other fields, and protect itself from the implications of their discoveries, theology by its own act accepts the very separation from the rest of life and thought to which the modern temper has condemned it. Theology has life in itself only as it permeates all life.

The Unique Position of Philosophy as a Mode of Inquiry

In one important respect philosophy differs from all other methods of seeking knowledge. This difference does not necessarily denote superiority, except with respect to matters to which it is relevant. Nor is philosophy warranted, because of this difference between it and other modes of inquiry, in making any claim of infallibility. Its unique position does not protect philosophy from error.

The distinguishing character of philosophy, to which it owes its special position, is found in the fact that it accepts no assumptions as inaccessible to examination. In this respect philosophy differs from theology; for, as we have seen, theology does not subject its basic premises to rational examination. A theology is constructed because of a conviction that certain primary religious beliefs are true and because it seems important to discover what these beliefs imply and what is inconsistent with their truth.

The difference we have mentioned not only distinguishes philosophy from theology, it also marks it off clearly from the natural sciences, from history, and from the social studies. No science can use its own methods to examine the soundness of those methods. When a scientist finds it necessary to appraise the methods of his science he must shift his position, at least temporarily, from the field of his science to the fields of logic and epistemology, both of which belong to philosophy. Nor can a science examine the truth of its basic assumptions about the objects of its inquiry. It assumes, for example, that knowledge is possible, that there is a world of objects to be known, that the acquisition of knowledge is of value, and that the world it inquires into is a rational order to which the laws of logic and mathematics apply. Similar assumptions are made by history and the social studies, with additional assumptions which apply more directly to their special fields.

To point this out is not to suggest that these assumptions are false. On the contrary we have exceedingly strong reasons to consider them true. The point rather is simply that these modes of inquiry do make assumptions which they themselves are incapable of examining, and if it becomes necessary to attack or to defend any of these assumptions the methods used cannot be the methods of the field of inquiry in which the assumption is made. To pretend to avoid metaphysical assumptions is only to confess failure to recognize them.

Why, then, is not philosophy in the same predicament? How is it possible to justify the assumptions of philosophy except from a standpoint outside philosophy itself? This may seem, at first thought, to rest philosophy on dogma or on arbitrary assertion. But such is not the case. The special position of philosophy results from the special character of its assumptions. The key to the puzzle is the fact that philosophy itself is synonymous with the assertion that in its final nature all actual and possible existence is intelligible.

To deny that existence is intelligible cuts us off from any knowledge of it. Such a denial is the assertion of philosophical skepticism, the assertion that real existence cannot be known. But how can we make such an assertion, and pretend that it is known to be true? As Professor DeWolf says, "It has often been pointed out by the critics of complete philosophical skepticism that to establish skepticism a man would have to be omniscient. How can a thinker know that nothing can ever be known, unless he knows so much about everything there is as to be sure that all is of such a character as to be unknowable?" [5]

But suppose, it may be proposed, that someone questions the intelligibility of existence. How can philosophy assume that which is brought into ques-

---

[5] *The Religious Revolt against Reason* by L. Harold DeWolf (New York: Harper and Brothers, 1949), p. 145.

tion and at the same time justify what it assumes? The answer is that the question itself assumes the very thing it questions, and the role of philosophy in such a dispute is simply to point out that fact. Try as we may to bring reason into question it is only by the use of reason that we can do so. To one who says he rejects reason philosophy's only reply is that the objection cannot be stated without resting the statement upon the very thing it attempts to reject. The act of stating the rejection of reason is one which requires the validity of reason to give it meaning. With the rejection of reason meaning disappears. Existence makes sense, or else it makes sense to say that existence does not make sense; therefore, in not making sense existence does make sense. The intelligibility of existence is the condition which makes it possible for us to make meaningful statements about it.

This becomes clear as soon as we recognize that any statement which claims truth is a statement which rests its claim on such principles of reason as identity and non-contradiction. Unless we admit that what we talk about is what it is, and is not what it is not, our attempt to talk fails. It fails to mean anything. If, then, I try to say that "the rational is false" either I mean it is true that the rational is false, and it is false that the rational is not false, or else my statement means nothing at all. Whatever else it means it has to mean this; and it has to mean this or it means nothing. But the relations by which this minimum meaning operates are logical and rational relationships. So I rest my claim that my denial of reason is true and meaningful upon a relation of reason. If I am at the same time both denying and asserting the same thing, anyone is entitled to ask which I mean. If I answer that I mean both together even though the two are mutually incompatible, then the only remaining course is to reject the statement as meaningless—or perhaps to call in a psychiatrist. With one who attempts to deny the validity of reason we are in the same position we should be with someone who said, "I am going to tell you something important and true but don't believe anything I say." We cannot refute a theory that does not make sense; we can only expose it. But a theory that does not make sense does us this great service, *it* exposes those who think it may be true.

In order that an assertion shall mean any one thing definitely it has to exclude from itself other meanings. Suppose I should utter the sounds appropriate to, "Bladso gellux infism." When I am asked what this means suppose I reply, "Oh, it means everything; there is nothing at all that it does not mean." It would be shorter, and as revealing, simply to say, "It is meaningless; I am merely making up sound combinations." Every meaningful affirmation is also a negation, and every meaningful negation is also an affirmation. Even my assertion that " 'Bladso gellux infism' means everything" is itself meaningless unless this assertion involves the denial that "Bladso gellux infism" has a restricted meaning which excludes other meanings. If, when I say "grass is green," I do not mean "grass is not that which is not green" then I mean nothing at all. But the relation between the two is a logical relation, apprehended by reason, and the one involves the other by virtue of this relation.

Every inquiry has its own assumptions, assumptions bound up with the distinctive methods. Philosophy differs from other inquiries in the fact that its assumptions are the assumptions of any inquiry whatsoever. You accept them or you do not inquire; you do not even inquire about whether you can inquire. Either you accept these assumptions or you do not speak; you accept them or you do not even think, and that includes thinking about not accepting them.

We have here a fundamental principle of our inquiry, and we shall return to this frequently. It is the principle of intelligibility—that whatever is presupposed by the possibility of knowledge cannot itself be brought into question. The furthest we can go is to question the contention that this or that proposition is presupposed by the possibility of knowledge. In so far as the presuppositions of inquiry itself are the presuppositions of philosophy then it follows that no attempt to discredit philosophy as such can be successful. For the attempt to discredit philosophy *is* philosophy in so far as it claims to be true and rests its case on reason and fact; in so far as it does not claim to be true, or does not rest its case on reason and fact, it is senseless and deserves only to be ignored or to have its senselessness pointed out. As Professor Urban says, "Philosophy not only buries its undertakers; it also, by its own inherent logic or dialectic, refutes and reduces to futility those forms of philosophizing which violate the conditions of philosophical intelligibility as such." [6]

The Aim of a Philosophy of Religion

The aim of philosophy is understanding, the discovery of truth, the satisfaction of reason. In the philosophy of religion this aim is directed toward religion. It may be interpreted in two ways, not in conflict with each other but supplementing each other.

There is first the attempt to understand religion, to discover what it is and to uncover the rational meanings which belong to its ideas. Religious ideas are to some degree conceptual; they have logical significance, and by

[6] *Beyond Realism and Idealism* by Wilbur Marshall Urban (London: George Allen and Unwin, 1949; New York; The Macmillan Company), p. 246. See also pp. 134-135. The same problem is discussed in *The Intelligible World* and in *Language and Reality*, both by the same author.

this we mean that it makes sense to raise the question of whether they are true or false. In this aspect of the philosophy of religion we seek to find the rational truth which is contained in religion. This does not mean that all the truth in religion is contained in the rational content we discover, nor does it mean even that we make our chief contact with religious truth by the use of reason. The philosophy of religion is an effort to discover so far as we can what there is in religion which is accessible to our reason.

There is another aspect of the philosophy of religion not adequately expressed in what has been said so far. All knowledge must, in the end, be of a single piece because truth has unity. So far as our knowledge is incomplete the unity of truth may escape us; but when we do not see the unity of truth it is because our knowledge is incomplete, it is not because of any final disruption of any part of truth from any other part. We are like one who has been a short way through a few of the entrances to an enormously complex building. He may know that all the parts he has seen belong to the same building but he may not have gone far enough to see how they fit together.

So far as religion adds to our rational understanding of anything it contributes something to our grasp of the whole pattern of truth. Religion throws light not only on its own objects but on the whole realm of existence, for the objects of religion are related to other things and these relations make a difference to our understanding of the other things. So far as religion has any truth accessible to human reason the philosophy of religion is an essential part of any comprehensive philosophical view. It may well be that religion provides contacts with reality which thought itself cannot give, which are more intimate and more immediate than reason provides. Although we cannot achieve these contacts in philosophy yet a philosophy of religion may help us understand what they are and help us recognize them for what they are. Whatever direct contact with reality religion may provide a comprehensive philosophy must reckon with it, just as a philosophy must take account of our perceptual and aesthetic experience.

When we say that the aim of a philosophy of religion is to try to reach a rational understanding of the truth which religion contains, we do not mean we are primarily concerned with understanding the origins and varieties of religion, and the phases of its development. Those are matters for historians, anthropologists, and psychologists. The kind of understanding which the philosophy of religion seeks is the discovery of what rational grounds there may be for considering its beliefs to be true or false.

Although philosophy is concerned with the rational aspect of religious ideas and beliefs this does not mean that the rational content which philosophy is able to discover is the only content, or even that it is the most important. Nor are we entitled to assume that the only justification of a religious belief is to show rationally that it is true. There may be other and possibly even superior ways of justifying the claim of religious beliefs to be true. Even this, however, does not put religion out of contact with philosophy. For if there is any other than a rational justification of the truth claim of a religious belief the contention that this kind of justification is itself sound must be subjected to rational examination. Otherwise the claim is sheer assertion.[7]

I may be warranted in believing that my sense perception is a reliable guide in my attempt to discover some of the characteristics of physical objects. It is also quite clear that sense perception is not wholly an act of reason, for it includes sensation as well. Yet my claim that perception provides reliable information is itself subject to rational examination. So even though there may be in religion processes beyond our rational acts and though these may bring us into contact with something real in a way which is not the way of rational thought, yet the claim that these processes are effective needs rational justification.

There are religions and religious sects which attempt to deny all contact between religious faith and reason. Even if they were right they could not consistently give any reasons why they were right. So far as they reject reason they renounce any claim of truth which is entitled to the respect of anyone else. If they should happen to have any truth it is an entirely private truth for which they can make no case.

The Difference Between Philosophy and Religion

Philosophy seeks a rational understanding of things and events, of relationships and patterns, in terms of the most general concepts which pertain to knowledge and being. Lack of philosophy is absence of understanding; to lack philosophy is to be naive and provincially minded, to be gullible with respect to current fads of thought, and to be the victim of random associations of ideas and of suggestions planted by those who wish to control the thought of others. It is a kind of ignorance, but it is a special kind of ignorance. It is not like ignorance of chemistry, for example; for although ignorance of chemistry may be a misfortune and on occasion may even have serious consequences, it is not the kind of ignorance which infects the whole outlook and basic judgments of a mind. "No man can live without any basis of philosophy, however primitive, naive, childish or unconscious," Berdyaev

---

[7] See the discussion of revelation and reason in Chapter XXIV, "The Revelation of God."

tells us. "Every man thinks and speaks, makes use of notions, categories, symbols, myths, and gives vent to appreciations. There is always a childish philosophy at the foundation of a childish faith." [8]

Religion has a certain underlying similarity with philosophy in spite of the very important differences between them. It is similar in the fact that it colors a person's whole outlook. So far as it is genuine it is reflected to some degree in a man's every act and every judgment. It is not one compartment of a self, but rather the design of the whole.

Religion, however, is quite different from philosophy; it is a different kind of activity. There is philosophy of religion but there is no such thing as religious philosophy. Where philosophy's activity is rational inquiry and understanding, religion is an appreciation and appropriation of values by means of contact with the ultimate ground of existence. In philosophy we think about things in terms of concepts; in religion we feel ourselves into a scheme of life and perform the acts which express our devotion to its object. Religion does not explain, or perhaps we should say that its explanations are not conceptual explanations; it does not minister primarily to the needs of reason. Quite the contrary, religion claims to put us in touch with existence in a special way; and in so far as religion's claim is just, philosophy can no more take religion's place than it can take the place of eating and loving.[9]

Even though philosophy cannot take the place of religion it is still not necessary for philosophy to depart in order to permit religion to enter. For the contact with existence which religion provides is one of those matters which philosophy most desires to understand. Where religion is the living out of a value scheme, philosophy is the examination and analysis of it. "In the conflict between religion and philosophy, truth is on the side of religion when philosophy claims to replace it in the sphere of salvation and eternal life; but truth is on the side of philosophy when it claims to attain a higher degree of knowledge than that allowed by the elements of naive knowledge incorporated in religion." [10]

Nothing we have said about the difference between philosophy and religion is intended to deny that understanding, as an activity and as a goal, has its own value. But the value of understanding, the highest of all the intellectual virtues, is not a substitute for religion. The value of religion in its highest forms lies in something which understanding alone does not give, it lies in the special contact with reality which it provides and in the transformation of the self which that contact brings about. It may well be that

---

[8] *Solitude and Society* by Nicolas Berdyaev (London: Geoffrey Bles, 1938), p. 18.

[9] See Chapter VIII, "Religious Truth," and Chapter IX, "The Test of Religious Truth."

[10] Berdyaev, *op. cit.*, p. 20.

we are all the better for understanding this work of religion as adequately as we can, but it is something which does not need to be understood in order that it shall take place. Still, the greater the importance we see in religion the more intensely we desire to understand it as well as to experience it. It is this desire that the philosophy of religion attempts to satisfy.

In philosophy, so far as it is true, we come to know and understand reality, but in religion we make contact with it. If reality is the kind which answers our needs and rewards our search for fulfilment, then it is only in *contact* with it that we can find these supports. "And surely," says Professor Bennett, "the most striking historic function of religion has been to lift men from doubt and perplexity to a region of assurance and serenity. If there is any anchorage for human emotions, any one goal for human ambition, any solid foundation for courage to build on, it is religion that has supplied these things. If anywhere we break through from illusion into reality it is in religion that we do so, and any interpretation of faith which ignores or denies this is frankly preposterous." [11]

[11] Bennett, *op. cit.*, p. 17.

EMIL BRUNNER

EMIL BRUNNER (1889-   ), Swiss Protestant theologian, who with Karl Barth in the nineteen twenties revolted against Protestant liberalism and attempted to restate classic Protestant doctrines in contemporary terms. He has written extensively in the field of Christian theology.

The Meaning of Philosophy of Religion for Protestantism*

Philosophy consists in reflection on the connection between all particular facts, and the means it employs to this end is thought investigating the way in which the facts are intellectually founded. But we shall need first to supply the ground for the inquiry into connection by showing that the latter

* From Emil Brunner, *The Philosophy of Religion*, trans. A. J. D. Farrer and Bertram Lee Woolf, pp. 11-21. Published, 1937, Charles Scribner's Sons. Used by permission of Emil Brunner and James Clarke & Co., Ltd.

has intelligible meaning. Hence we must define the problem of philosophy more closely and say that it inquires how far a mental ground is discoverable for the connection between particular facts. By this means we shall become convinced of the necessity, and therefore of the justification, of the inquiry in itself irrespective of its subject matter. Such an inquiry, again, will include that into the meaning of all science, all civilization and indeed human life in general. But when any school of philosophy surveys the more significant expressions of human life, it will discover among them a form of life which on the one hand is in the closest connection with the set of problems peculiar to philosophy, while on the other it has characteristic differences from every school of philosophy, or is even actually opposed to philosophy. This form of life is religion. The kinship between the two rests on the fact that religion as well as philosophy has in view the whole of existence and life; the opposition between them consists in the fact that religion itself claims to supply an answer to the crucial question about reality. It gives this answer in the shape of revelation, and not as the result of the methodical reflection of the intellect, i.e. of an activity within the bounds of reason. Thus philosophy is brought face to face with a most difficult problem, that of showing the meaning and justification of religion within the mental ground known to philosophy. In this way philosophy of religion arises as a part, and perhaps indeed as the culminating point, of philosophy in general.

Provided, however, that the philosopher is serious in his concern about the truth of religion, he cannot avoid listening in the first place to the affirmations of religion about itself—and this always means the affirmations of some specific form of religion. It might of course be the case that religion will have to reject altogether any such classification under philosophy on the plea that it would involve a misinterpretation of religion. In that case the relation between the two would have to be determined conversely, i.e. by starting from religion. Then religion would not have its basis assigned within the bounds of philosophy, but conversely, viz. philosophy, being a special department of man's activity as a reasonable creature, would take its place within the bounds of revealed truth. If such an assertion is not meant to forego every connection with the mind of science, civilization, and philosophy, we must of course make several requirements: that religion should find in her own presuppositions the grounds for thus inverting the relationship between ground and consequence; that it should also report on its mode of supplying these grounds; and once more, that, on the second presupposition, it should make plain the possibility of science, civilization, and philosophy. That would be the way in which, starting from the side of religion, the discussion would have to be carried on with a philosophy originating in the general cultural consciousness. But such an undertaking could be called philosophy of religion only in a secondary sense, and the name as just defined could merely serve to designate the sphere of the discussion.

The state of the case only becomes really clear when, as is incumbent upon us, we look from the stand-point of general possibilities at the special situation that faces us. There are two reasons why we can speak only in a secondary sense of a Christian, and more particularly of a Protestant, philosophy of religion. First, Christian faith, especially in the particular form given to it in Protestant theology, is a fundamentally different thing from every philosophy. To philosophize is to reflect on the mental grounds, with the assumption that ultimate validity belongs to the complex of grounds and consequences developed by natural reason. Christian faith on the other hand involves recognizing that this complex has been broken into by revelation. It is on this revelation that the affirmations of Christian faith are grounded. Theology, which is Christian faith in scientific form, could only lay claim to a scientific character provided it gave clear and exact expression to the fact that its complex of grounds and consequences differs from that of all other sciences as to the final authority it recognizes; provided further that it developed all affirmations purely out of its own presuppositions and thus founded them on that complex; and provided finally, that on this basis it investigated the relations, whether positive or negative, between revealed faith and rational knowledge. Thus theology is on common ground with philosophy in showing the existence of an intelligible connection embracing all things; but this is not, as it is for philosophy, the logos of the natural reasoning process, but the logos of revelation. Hence Christian theology can never be required to make faith rational by giving it scientific form; on the contrary, it has to keep revelation and religion duly apart by means of clearly defined concepts.

It would be to weaken, or rather to do away with, the opposition were we to equate the relation between reason and revelation with that between rational and irrational. Revelation in the Christian sense stands in the same two-fold relation to the irrational as it does to the rational. The irrational (feeling, intuition, etc.) has not more but, on the contrary, less to do with the paradox of revelation than has the logos of reason. In the modern irrationalist philosophies of religion, the irrational is in every case grafted on a rational system (e.g. in the case of Otto and Scholz on an idealistic, and in that of James, on a naturalistic rationalism).

Neither can there be philosophy of religion in the strict sense of the term in the realm of Christian theology, for the further reason that theology has to do not with religion but with revelation. Whatever else religion may be, it is a mode of human life, whereas revelation is a self-disclosure of God. While the philosopher of religion is concerned with historical phenomena, i.e. with the historical religions and their "nature," the theologian is concerned with the ground of all phenomena.

To the philosopher as to the theologian, religion is not the ultimate fact but something that roots in the ultimate. In the former case it is reason that supplies the ultimate ground, while in the latter it is revelation. The aim of theology is thus something quite different from religion, and at bottom is no more closely related to religion than it is to any other department of human life. This conclusion, moreover, follows directly from the fundamental presupposition of theology: its ground, its content, and its standard alike are found not in any consciousness of man's, but in God's self-disclosure.

Christian faith, to which theology gives the form of scientific conceptions, is the knowledge and acknowledgment of God's self-revelation in Jesus Christ. He, the incarnate logos, is the ground, content, and standard of all the affirmations of faith. That is where faith differs from every religion as well as from every philosophy. By Christian faith is meant, not some universal truth, nor yet some universal religious experience, but a definite fact which as such is opposed to every universal, be it religion or philosophy. Not that it denies the existence of a certain universal knowledge of God, religious as well as philosophical: rather it presupposes this. But it does deny that the personal and living God can be generally known from possibilities that lie either in the world or in man's spirit as such. It contends that the living and personal God can be known only by a personal meeting, through His personal word, through that special event to which the Bible, and the Bible alone, bears witness, and the content of which is Jesus Christ. Hence this definite fact is not to be understood merely as an illustration, or an embodiment, or even a symbol; where such language is used concerning this matter it is not Christian faith with which we have to do. On the contrary, the definite fact of revelation takes the place of what is universal, of truth in general, or of the final criterion of valid assertions; the incarnate logos here occupies the position otherwise held by the logos of reason, the essential idea of truth. This is the case because the personal God, who is the ground of all truth, cannot be known as personal by means of idea, but only by personal, concrete revelation; only when He no longer hides Himself, but issues forth and discloses Himself as the ground of all being, all values, and all thought.

This particular fact, this miracle of divine revelation, which by its very particularity is a stumbling block to thinking in universals, is the presupposition of Christian theology. Christian faith consists precisely in taking this peculiar view of ultimate truth. It would cease to be faith, it would indeed give the lie to its own affirmation, if it wanted to ground the truth of this affirmation on a universal truth. Either revelation supplies its own grounds or else it is not revelation. The only man who can look for some other foundation beside the *Deus dixit* is the man who withholds belief from the *Deus dixit* and wants secretly to replace revelation by symbol. Hence theology cannot substantiate its scientific character by such a change in the class of ground and consequent as falsifies faith, but on the contrary, only by giving a logically exact expression to this special, non-universal quality in all its uniqueness. But this means that theology is not a free science void of presuppositions, but one that is closely tied. It is tied to the definite fact of the revelation of God in Jesus Christ. How tied it is appears most clearly in the fact that theology is only possible within the borders of the Christian community or church, and has its definite content and its definite standard in the Bible. Only by perceiving in Scripture the utterance of God does a man become a believer; and only as such, i.e. as a member of the community of believers, is the thinker in a position to think theologically. Theology is in place only in the church, just as in the same way its ground and content are to be found only in the Scriptural revelation.

This again is the starting point for a Protestant philosophy of religion, using this term now in the modified or secondary sense. Such a philosophy must come from theology and, further back still, from faith. It is not the case that it leads towards faith. It is a part of Christian theology as such, i.e. that part in which it carries on the discussion with the common consciousness of truth, i.e. with philosophy; it is that chapter of Christian theology whose business is to start from definitely Christian presuppositions, and give a well-founded description of the relations between revelation and rational knowledge on the one hand, and between revelation and religion on the other. Hence it is not a universal science, of which Christian theology would form a subdivision as being the doctrine of a particular religion. This erroneous view was largely followed in the nineteenth century. The very nature of revealed faith involves reversing the classification of universal and special in this case, because here a particular, viz. revelation, is regarded as ranking above every universal.

Despite the fact then that for us philosophy of religion can be only a branch of theology in general, we have good reason for separating it as a special science from theology; the reason lies in the need of the times, which demands very special attention to this problem; and the need of the times always has determined and always should determine the perspective of theology. Unlike the rest of theology, philosophy of religion is concerned with the formal and general problems of Christian faith, i.e. specifically with the complex of grounds and consequences set forth in the affirmations of faith as distinct from all other affirmations, in other words, with the problem of revelation. Nowhere, however, is it less possible than here to keep form and content apart: what is to be the Christian conception of revelation can only be made clear in connection with the content of that revelation. But it is at least possible to distinguish between form and content. On this distinction will depend the possibility of discussing the problems of philosophy of religion apart from those of theology proper. Such separation involves the further condition that, to a greater extent than in theology as such, philosophy of religion must have its being in the realm of abstract concepts, despite the fact that the conceptions have here just the same wholly concrete and personal basis as they have in the simplest confession of faith ever made by an unlettered man. At bottom, the philosopher of religion knows no more than any plain Christian: he merely knows it in the more exact form of abstract conceptions and in connection with the rational knowledge of his age. The reverse side of this advantage is that the abstract nature of his knowledge imperils the personal character of his faith—which ought to penetrate the said knowledge—even more than does the abstract nature of theology in general.

There is no fundamental difference between a theological and a nontheological expression of Christian faith. All utterance about God, no matter how much of personal earnestness it may have, has always the abstractness of theology. Even the parables of Jesus are theology. And conversely, the very earnestness of a personal, vital faith may lead it in certain circumstances, e.g. in its discussion and contention with the thought of one's age, to avail itself of the most abstract forms conceivable. Yet the primary interest of Christianity is not systematic knowledge, but the relation of a personal faith to revelation. Hence of course faith is constantly directed towards overcoming abstract concepts as completely as possible; and therefore the philosophy of religion must be judged as lying at best on the edge of Christian doctrine and never at its centre.

Revelation meets and fits human consciousness. It is not a matter of indifference that this consciousness should be defined as human, although on the other hand it is not essential to know in what more specific way it is so defined. Faith is indeed bound up with humanity but not with any particular grade of humanity. Of course it presupposes man as man, but not a particular type of humanity, nor yet any particular feature in man. It takes man in his totality, not in some special locus that can be fixed by psychology. The locus in which revelation and the spirit of man meet each other cannot be assigned positively but only negatively: it consists in receptivity. If in place of this we would rather put a particular form of consciousness, we might say that it is "inquiry" when this has assumed the form of a vital need. But although this is a presupposition for faith, it does not designate a particular psychological quality, but, on the contrary, what is universally human. In fact, we can indicate the locus yet more definitely without thereby abandoning what is universally human: the negative point of contact is a consciousness of vital need which is at the same time a consciousness of guilt. Therefore we might fittingly express our meaning as follows: any account of the faith evoked by revelation should be preceded by another account giving the results of man's investigation of universal mental characteristics, which investigation would lead up to the afore-mentioned point of contact. Lack of space obliges us to omit such an account. Ultimately, however, this makes no difference because in every case faith appropriate to revelation must be understood entirely by itself and not by means of any common consciousness of man's. Faith appropriate to revelation can be understood only by revelation, just in the same way as any rational thought can only be understood by its ground in reason, or a sensation of light only by the light-stimulus. Therefore it is necessary to start from revelation as known to faith; in doing so we have only to bear in mind that revelation is always the answer to a question on man's part. But whether man's question, and indeed humanity itself, have their ground in revelation, and only in it can attain their proper meaning; and therefore whether man's question has not its *prius* in God's address to him—these are matters that can be discussed only in connection with the knowledge appropriate to revelation. At all events faith is certain that revelation alone enables us rightly to apprehend that need, that vital incapacity, which is the presupposition of faith; and that thereby revelation itself begets its own presupposition in the crucial sense.

KARL JASPERS (1883-   ) after a medical
education became a psychologist and then
a professor of philosophy at the University
of Heidelberg in Germany. As an existentialist he is concerned with man's immediate existence—especially the experiences of failure,
guilt and death—rather than with the construction of a philosophical system.

Philosophy and Religion*

Throughout the millennia philosophy and religion have stood in alliance
with, or in hostility to one another.

They go hand in hand, originally in the myths and cosmologies, later in
theology,—for philosophy has appeared in the cloak of theology, just as at
other times it has worn the dress of poetry and, most frequently, of science.

But, then, as the two separate, religion becomes for philosophy the great
mystery that it cannot understand. The cult, the claim to revelation, the
claim to power of a community founded on religion, of its organization and
politics, and the interpretation that religion confers upon itself, become
objects of philosophical inquiry.

In this attitude of inquiry lies the germ of the struggle. For philosophy,
the struggle can only take the form of a striving for truth by exclusively
intellectual means.

Neither religion nor philosophy is a clearly defined entity; we cannot take
them as fixed points from which to start on our comparative investigation.
They are both involved in historical transformation, but both conceive of
themselves at all times as vehicles of eternal truth, whose historical garb at
once conceals and transmits the truth. I cannot speak of the one eternal religious truth. Philosophical truth is the *philosophia perennis* to which no one
can lay claim, but with which everyone engaged in philosophical thought is
concerned, and which is present wherever there are true philosophers.

There is no standpoint outside the opposition of philosophy and religion.
Each one of us stands at one of the poles and speaks of some crucial aspect
of the other, without personal experience. Consequently you can expect me

* From Karl Jaspers, *The Perennial Scope of Philosophy*, trans. Ralph Manheim, pp.
75-84, 105-107, 109-112. Copyright, 1949, by Philosophical Library. Used by permission
of Karl Jaspers.

too to be blind in certain points and to misunderstand. I hesitate and yet I must speak. To speak of religion, without being personally involved in it, is questionable, but it is indispensable as a means of expressing one's own clear deficiency, as a means of seeking after the truth, and also of testing religious faith by the questions that thus arise. Religion is no enemy of philosophy, but something that essentially concerns it and troubles it.

But today we are in a situation that I shall illustrate by a personal reference. Because religion is of such prime importance, awareness of my deficiency made me eager to hear what was being said in religious circles. It is among the sorrows of my life spent in the search for truth, that discussion with theologians always dries up at crucial points; they fall silent, state an incomprehensible proposition, speak of something else, make some categoric statement, engage in amiable talk, without really taking cognizance of what one has said—and in the last analysis they are not really interested. For on the one hand they are certain of their truth, terrifyingly certain; and on the other hand they do not regard it as worth while to bother about people like us, who strike them as merely stubborn. And communication requires listening and real answers, forbids silence or the evasion of questions; it demands above all that all statements of faith (which are after all made in human language and directed toward objects, and which constitute an attempt to get one's bearings in the world) should continue to be questioned and tested, not only outwardly, but inwardly as well. No one who is in definitive possession of the truth, can speak properly with someone else,—he breaks off authentic communication in favor of the belief he holds.

I can touch on this great problem only from certain angles and only inadequately, I am concerned in this discussion with throwing light on the original philosophical faith.

Religion, contrasted with philosophy, reveals the following characteristics:

Religion has its cult, is bound up with a peculiar community of men, arising from the cult, and it is inseparable from the myth. Religion always embodies man's practical relation to the transcendent, in the shape of something holy in the world, as delimited from the profane or unholy. Where this is no longer present, or is rejected, the peculiar character of religion has vanished. Almost the whole of mankind, as far as historical memory extends, has lived religiously, and this is an indication that can scarcely be ignored, of the truth and central importance of religion.

Philosophy proper, on the other hand, knows no cult, no community led by a priesthood, no existent invested with a sacred character and set apart from other existents in the world. What religion localizes in a specific place, can for philosophy be present everywhere and always. Philosophy is a product of the individual's freedom, not of socially determined conditions, and it does not carry the sanction of a collectivity. Philosophy has no rites, no roots in a primitive mythology. Men take it from a free tradition and transform it as they make it their own. Although pertaining to man as man, it remains the concern of individuals.

Religion is intent upon embodying its truth in tangible symbols, philosophy pursues only effective subjective certainty.—To religion the God of the philosophers seems threadbare, pale, empty; it disparagingly calls the philosophical state of mind "deism"; to philosophy the tangible symbols of religion seem like deceptive veils and misleading simplifications.—Religion denounces the God of philosophy as a mere abstraction, philosophy distrusts the religious images of God as seductive idols, magnificent as they may be.

Yet, though the manifestations of philosophy and religion seem to clash, there is a contact, and even a convergence in their contents, as may be illustrated by the ideas of God, prayer, revelation.

The Idea of God.   In the West, the idea of the one God arose in Greek philosophy and in the Old Testament. In both cases, a stupendous work of abstraction was effected, but in entirely different ways.

In Greek philosophy monotheism arose as an idea, it was postulated from ethical considerations, it imposed itself on the mind in an atmosphere of philosophic serenity. It did not set its imprint upon masses of men, but upon individuals. Its results were individuals of a high human type and a free philosophy. It was not an effective civilizing agent.

In the Old Testament, on the other hand, monotheism grew up in the passion of battle for the pure, the true, the one God. The abstraction was not accomplished by logic but by a reaction against the images and embodiments of the deity, which veil God more than they reveal him, and a revolt against the seductions of the cult, against Dionysian rites, and against belief in the efficacy of sacrifice. This cult of the one, living God was won in battle against the Baals, against immanent religion with its shallow optimism, its festivals and orgies, its self-complacency and moral indifference.

This true God suffers no image and likeness, sets no store by cult and sacrifice, by temple and rites and laws, but only by righteous actions and love of our fellowmen (Micah, Isaiah, Jeremiah).—The monotheistic abstraction, like nihilism, negates all worldly existence, but actually springs from the spiritual fullness of a mind to which the supra-mundane creator-God with his ethical laws has revealed himself.—This abstraction is not based upon the development of an idea, but upon the word of God, upon God himself, who was experienced in the word which the prophet imparted as the word of God. The force of God's reality refracted in such a prophetic mind, and not the power of an idea, brought forth this monotheism. Hence the miraculous part of it is that in thought content the monotheism of the Greeks and of the Old Testament should coincide, though they differ radically as to the mode of God's presence. The difference is that between philosophy and religion. Consequently it is also the difference between divinity and God,—between transcendence as an intellectual idea, and the living God; the One of philosophy is not the One of the Bible.

But if philosophical clarity prevails, the question arises whether the incomparable faith of the prophets, that moves us so deeply even today, was possible only because they were still intellectually naive, still unaffected by philosophical thought, and accordingly failed to notice that the "word," spoken immediately by God, still embodied a remnant of sensible reality— of the image and likeness which they combated.

Greek and Old Testament monotheism have together dominated the Western idea of God. They interpreted each other. That was possible because the faith of the prophets effected an abstraction that is analogous to philosophical abstraction. The prophetic faith is more powerful than the philosophical idea, because it arises from the direct experience of God. But in intellectual clarity it is inferior to philosophy; hence it was lost in subsequent religious development, even in the Bible.

Prayer. The cult is the act of the community, prayer is an act of the individual in his solitude. The cult exists everywhere, while prayer is discernible here and there in history; in the Bible it becomes distinct only with Jeremiah. The liturgy, in which the cult is embodied, contains a number of texts that are called prayers, because they serve to invoke, praise, and supplicate the godhead. But their salient feature is that they originated in the remotest past, that although they once grew and changed over a period of generations, they have since then retained rigid, immutable forms and are experienced as something permanent. Parts of them have long since become incomprehensible, they either play the role of a mystery or have been endowed with a new, transformed meaning. In contradistinction to this, prayer is individual, existentially present. As a subordinate element of the cult, it is performed by the individual in a fixed form, and then he remains entirely within the sphere of religion. But when it is really personal and primal, prayer stands at the frontier of philosophy, and it becomes philosophy in the moment when it is divested of any pragmatic relation to the godhead or desire to influence the godhead for practical ends. It marks a break with the concreteness of a personal relation to a personal God, which is one of the sources of religion, and a movement toward abstract philosophical contemplation; at first it expresses only devotion and gratitude to God, but later it becomes progressively internalized and man finds in it a firm ground on which to stand. The aim of this contemplation is no longer to achieve practical mundane results, but inward transfiguration. Where such speculative spiritualization developed into genuine contemplation, it was like one continuous prayer. While this contemplation was a part of the whole that is embodied in religion, today it has become separate from religious activity and possible by itself.

Revelation. Religions are based on revelation; this is clearly and consciously the case with the Indian and Biblical religions. Revelation is the immediate utterance of God, localized in time and valid for all men, through word, commandments, action, event. God issues his commandments, he institutes the congregation, founds the cult. Thus the cult of the Christians is founded as an act of God, who instituted the Lord's Supper. Since the content of a religion derives originally from revelation, this content is not valid in itself, but only within a community—the people, the congregation, the church—which is its actual authority and guaranty.

With reference to the efforts to arrive at a philosophical concept of God, these efforts in which each step seems to cancel out the preceding,—we often hear it said that any attempt to arrive at God by thought is vain, and that man knows God and can know God only through revelation. God gave the law, God sent the prophets, He himself descended in the form of his servant, to redeem us on the Cross.

But revelation that is communicated as such, must have a mundane form. Once it is stated, it deteriorates into finiteness, and even into trivial rationality. In speech, its meaning is perverted. The word of man is not the word of God. That part of revelation that concerns man as man, becomes a content of philosophy and as such is valid without revelation. Have we to do with an attenuation of religion, a loss of its substance?—then we call the process secularization. Or have we to do with a purification, a deepening, a distillation or even realization of its primal essence? Both processes would seem to exist. The danger of an emptying by rationalization is coupled with the possibility that man may realize an authentic truth. . . .

3. *Clarification and enhancement of the eternal truth.* By our experience of the tensions, the dialectic and the contradictions striving toward a decision, we can positively apprehend what words can express only abstractly—the truth that we outlined in formulating the basic characteristics of Biblical religion. Let us restate the elements of this truth, which constitutes philosophical faith. They are:

the idea of the one God;

the realization of the absolute nature of the decision between good and evil in finite man;

love as the fundamental actualization of the eternal in man;

the act—both inward and external—as the test of man;

types of moral world order which are always historically absolute, although none of their manifestations is absolute or exclusive;

the incompleteness of the created world, the fact that it does not stand by itself, the inapplicability of all types of order to borderline cases, the experience of the extreme;

the idea that the ultimate and only refuge is with God.

How pale does all we have said seem beside the religious reality. As soon as we set out to discuss the question, we enter upon the plane of philosophical faith. We are thus led automatically to interpret renewal of religious faith as a return to the primal source, as a renewal of the philosophical faith that is implicit in the religious, as a transformation of religion into philosophy (or philosophical religion). But this, though perhaps it will be the road of a minority, will certainly not be that of mankind.

The philosopher cannot possibly tell the theologians and the churches what to do. The philosopher can only hope to help create the preliminary requirements. He would like to help prepare the ground and to help produce awareness of the intellectual situation necessary for the growth of what he himself cannot create.

What more and more people have been saying for half a century continues to be quickly forgotten, though nearly everyone has been saying it: a new era is arising, in which man, down to the very last individual, is subject to a process of transformation more radical than ever before in history. But since the transformation in our objective living conditions goes so deep, the transformation in our forms of religious belief must go correspondingly deeper in order to mould the new, to fructify and spiritualize it. A change is to be expected in what we have called the matter, the dress, the manifestation, the language of faith, a change as far-reaching as all the other changes that have taken place in our era—or else the eternal truth of Biblical religion will recede beyond the horizon of man; he will no longer experience this truth, and it is impossible to say what might take its place. Hence it is in order, that we do everything in our power to restore the eternal truth; we must plumb its very depths and, unconcerned over what is transient and historical, utter this truth in a new language. . . .

Philosophy, whether it affirms or combats religion, withdraws from religion in fact, and yet is constantly concerned with it.

(a) Philosophy takes up the cause of Biblical religion: Western philosophy cannot hide from itself the fact that none of its great philosophers up to and including Nietzsche approached philosophical thought without a thorough knowledge of the Bible. This is no accident. We repeat:

First: Philosophy cannot give man the same thing as religion. Hence it at least leaves the field open for religion. It does not force itself on mankind as the whole and exclusive truth for all men.

Second: Philosophy can scarcely hold its position in the world if the human collectivity does not live in the people through religious faith. Philosophical communication in thought has no compelling force, but only clarifies for the individual man, what arises from within himself. Philosophy would be dispersed among fewer and fewer individuals and finally disappear, if the human collectivity did not live by what becomes clear in philosophical faith. Philosophy cannot realize the sociologically effective transmission of the contents indispensable to man, which occurs solely through religious tradition assimilated from early childhood, thus becoming the vehicle also of philosophy.

Third: The contents of the Bible can be replaced for us by no other book.

(b) Philosophy goes beyond Biblical religion: The development of communications, which has brought all the things ever produced on earth into contact with one another, and which has created a need for ever closer understanding among men, has in addition to the Bible revealed to us two other great religious areas: India with the Upanishads and Buddhism, China with Confucius and Laotse. The soul of the thoughtful man cannot remain closed to the depth of the truth emanating from these sources. The soul strives to extend its horizons without end.

Here an error is likely to crop up. The Enlightenment sought to find the true religion by assembling the best from all religions. The result however was not the authentic truth, purified of historical accident, but a collection of abstractions watered down by rationalism. The source of this universal faith was in fact only a critical, measuring intelligence. The profound meaning, the poignancy was lost. Trivial generalizations remained.

Since all faith is historical, its truth does not lie in a sum of articles of faith, but in a primal source that is historically manifested in various forms. True, the many religions lead to the one truth, but this truth cannot be attained at one stroke, but only along the roads that were really traveled, roads which cannot be traveled all at once and in the same way.

Hence no rational critique can apprehend this truth. On the contrary, man must, in the context of his own destiny, let the truth be revealed to him as it is uttered through tradition, i.e. he must make it his own. In sounding the depths of the past, one can accomplish this only by being given to oneself through inner action.

With regard to religion, philosophy will in practice approve the following propositions: In order to participate in Biblical religion, one must grow up in the tradition of a definite denomination. Every denomination is good to the extent that the people living in it take possession of the Biblical religion as a whole in spite of the special and finite historical degenerations of the particular historical form. Loyalty and historical consciousness bind me to the denomination in which I awakened. A change of religion is difficult without a breach in the soul. But though in every denominational form of Biblical religion the fixation of faith is determined by the specific time in which it occurs, in individual believers the presence of the full Biblical religion is possible and real. The community of the pious cuts across all denominational lines. And the endless struggles, schisms, and condemnations that have occurred in this field can, in Melanchthon's words, be designated as *rabies theologorum*.

WILLIAM
TEMPLE

WILLIAM TEMPLE (1881-1944), the Archbishop of Canterbury, was the best known Anglican theologian of the first half of the twentieth century. He was also a prominent leader in the ecumenical movement in the Christian Churches and was keenly interested in the application of Christian doctrine to contemporary problems.

The Tension Between Philosophy and Religion*

The main type of that tension, then, which we have now to consider, is not caused by particular doctrines either of Religion or of Philosophy, but consists in a sharp difference in mental habit and outlook with reference to the same objects of attention. This may be briefly expressed by saying that *the primary assurances of Religion are the ultimate questions of Philosophy*. Religion finds its fullest expression in absolute surrender to the Object of its worship. But the very existence of that Object is a main theme of philosophical disputation. It is not possible to surrender one's self to what is felt to be an unverified hypothesis; it is not possible to discuss impartially the existence of a Being to whom one is utterly self-surrendered. How then can a religious person be a true philosopher? Or how can a philosopher who has

* From William Temple, *Nature, Man and God*, pp. 34-39, 44-45, 51-56. Copyright, 1934, Macmillan & Co., Ltd. Reprinted by permission of Mrs. Temple, St. Martin's Press, Inc., and Macmillan & Co., Ltd.

not yet solved the problems of existence permit himself the exercise of religion? And if he do not permit himself this exercise, how can he know Religion from within in such a fashion as to qualify himself to pronounce upon its validity and to place it rightly within, or exclude it justly from, his ultimate construction?

That these are grave questions no one who has seriously attempted to combine the two activities is likely to deny. Yet the difficulties are not insuperable in principle, and it seems to be the special duty of some persons at least to engage in the hazardous enterprise of overcoming them.

The divergence of view is specially evident in relation to three central convictions of Religion in its higher forms. These are perhaps different expressions of one truth, but as expressions of it they differ, and it is well to state them separately:

First is the conviction that Spirit is a true source of initiation of processes —a real ἀρχή, a *vera causa*;

Second is the conviction that all existence finds its source (ἀρχή, *vera causa*) in a Supreme Reality of which the nature is Spirit;

Third is the conviction that between that Spirit and ourselves there can be, and to some extent already is, true fellowship, at least such as is involved in our conscious dependence on that Spirit.

The first of these convictions is, as stated, little more than the denial of materialism; but this denial carries positive implications of momentous import. The true nature of spiritual freedom must occupy our attention later; but some aspects of it concern us now. If it were true that by inspection of the Nebula, from which our solar system formed itself, an intelligence of sufficient scope could have predicted all the acts of moral choice that would ever be made by human beings living on this planet, then the whole aspiration and endeavour of Religion would be dismissible as part of the phantasmagoria of a consciousness which emerged only to take note of, never to direct, the process in which it was a transient and ineffectual episode.

Now the sense of the inherent determinism of the physical system, including our bodily organisms, is so strong that some great religions have to a certain extent made terms with it. The Hindu doctrine of Maya is such a compromise. It expresses despair of the spiritual domination of matter; but in order to safeguard both the reality and the supremacy of spirit, it dismisses the material as illusory; the great aim of life which it proposes, is to be delivered from the Wheel of Change (the figure of materialistic Determinism) so that the spiritual reality may exist in its own freedom. This attempt altogether to exclude matter from reality issues in a curiously uncontrolled empire of matter, so that Hinduism, which finds expression in some of the loftiest spiritual philosophy of the world, also makes room for obscenity in connexion with worship itself. You cannot regulate what you do not recognise. If matter is so unreal that spirit, which is real, has neither need for it nor control of it, then in its own sphere it will make havoc. The way to be spiritually effective is not to ignore matter but to use it.

Yet to deny the reality of matter in order to assert that of spirit is less disastrous to Religion than to let the spiritual be swallowed up in the material, as the West is always liable to do. The assertion of the reality and independence of Spirit in the Universe and in Man is a primary necessity for Religion. In the case of Man we may, for the moment, put this at the very lowest and be content to say that the causal process, as it affects human conduct, passes through consciousness and is modified by this passage. If preferred, the same thought may be expressed by saying that, attention having been attracted to the causal process, volition intervenes as an additional determinant of the result. The main point is that consciousness does affect the result, but this does not make the process leading to it other than causal, so that human beings act differently because they are conscious and self-conscious from the way in which they (or rather their bodies) would act if they had no consciousness and self-consciousness.

But while this alone is enough to break the chain of sheer materialistic Determinism, much more is required for the assertion that the Ultimate Ground of the Universe and all things in it is spiritual. This is a claim, not only for the independence of Spirit, but for the universal supremacy of Spirit. It is the claim that Spirit is not only *a* source of initiation, one ἀρχή among others, but is the only ultimate source of the whole World-process. All the more developed religions, which do not deny the reality of matter, have advanced this claim. It is the doctrine of Creation. It is not of direct importance to Religion to assert a date for the act of Creation, or even to assert that it is an act having any date at all; it may be a never-beginning and never-ending activity. But it is of vital importance to Religion to assert that the existence of the world is due to the Will of God. This is the essential notion of Creation, and Religion dare not let it go, unless it is prepared to deny the real existence of the material world. For the only remaining alternative is the acceptance of limitation in the conception of the Supreme Spirit, not only in the sense of an actual finitude which none the less includes or controls all existence, but in the sense of leaving some part of existence outside its control. Such a dualism would be repudiated by Philosophy, which cannot rest in a multiplicity or duality of ultimate principles; and it is entirely fatal to Religion, because to a limited authority only a limited allegiance is due, and absoluteness of allegiance is the very life-breath of Religion.[1]

But this claim to absolute allegiance is one which Philosophy must investigate. Enquiry must be made into its precise meaning, and then into the relation of the claim so interpreted to the facts of common experience. If, for example, it is meant that all things exist only in dependence upon the Will of a Spiritual Being who is good and wise in the ordinary sense of those words, then there is a great deal of experience which cannot be treated as unreal and yet is very hard to appreciate as illustrating the goodness and wisdom of its Author. This is, of course, the familiar problem of Evil, which becomes acute in exact correspondence with the moral sensitiveness of the mind reflecting on it. A mind of low moral sensitiveness may be little troubled by this problem, for it will have a less exalted conception of the divine goodness, and will also be less afflicted by the evil elements in experience. As sensitiveness to moral issues develops, bewilderment before the problem of Evil deepens. It has found no more passionate expression than that given to it in many of the Hebrew Psalms.

That fact alone is sufficient evidence that this problem is not the creation of an alien criticism, but arises out of the heart of religious faith itself. Yet it is inevitable that when rationalising criticism sets to work, it should intensify the perplexity of religious people by seeming to exploit it in a hostile manner. For the aim of the religious person is to stabilise and deepen his faith; the aim of the philosopher is to understand, to "follow the argument wherever it leads," and to regard nothing as assured which is not supported by sufficient evidence. Between these two there is manifest tension; but no one is so intimately aware of that tension as a person who tries wholeheartedly to play both rôles at once.

.   .   .   .

This reflection leads to a new consideration. The difference between Religion and scientific Philosophy [2] in relation to the Object of attention is not only one of temper but also one of method. The latter results from the former. In temper the attitude of Religion is that of assurance; the attitude of Philosophy is that of enquiry. It is hard enough to combine these, and

---

[1] Of course this does not mean that no one may properly be called religious who has not in practice attained to this absoluteness of allegiance; but it is essential to Religion in all its higher phases that the worshipper should regard his Deity as entitled to such allegiance and himself as under obligation to render it.

[2] By the phrase "scientific Philosophy" I mean any philosophy which takes its start from the departmental sciences, ranging from Physics to Epistemology or Ethics, as distinct from a philosophy which takes its start from the deliverances of religious experience as formulated by Theology. Wherever I speak of "Philosophy" without any epithet it is to be understood as "scientific Philosophy" in this sense. Of course Theological Philosophy is no less scientific than this in its own procedure.

probably it can only be done by deliberate alternation. But to combine the resultant methods is harder still. Religion, of which the essence is assurance of fellowship with, or at least of dependence on, the Supreme Spirit, and therefore also of the existence of that Supreme Spirit, necessarily makes its start from that point, and, so far as it enters on the field of Philosophy, seeks to offer explanations of the facts of experience by reference to the character of the Supreme Spirit. This is Theological Philosophy, and I had better here confess my belief that it is in the end the only Philosophy which has any hope of being altogether satisfactory. But it is also most hazardous, and is certain to lead the mind that follows it into all manner of fantasies unless it is constantly checked by a purely critical Philosophy which makes its approach from the other end. In the Middle Ages the course was clear for Theological Philosophy, and the wonder is that it avoided the fantastic as much as it did; yet that element is present in it in sufficient quantity to show the danger.

Theology, which is the science of Religion, starts from the Supreme Spirit and explains the world by reference to Him. Philosophy starts from the detailed experience of men, and seeks to build up its understanding of that experience by reference to that experience alone. Its inevitable and wholesome kinship to Science inclines it to account for everything by the "lowest" category that will in fact account for it; Theology begins with the "highest" category of all and fits in the "lower" categories in the most orderly hierarchy that it can devise in subordination to that "highest" principle. And this difference is inevitable, though it has been exaggerated by the dominant tendencies of European thought from the time of Descartes onwards. With that exaggeration, its causes, and the way to correct it, we shall be concerned in later lectures. Our present concern is with the difference itself, which would still exist if there were no exaggeration at all. The source of the method of Theological Philosophy in the nature of Religion itself has already been made clear. But the method of critical Philosophy is equally inevitable.

.   .   .   .

The inevitability of tension between Religion and Science or the Philosophy which is in line with the scientific impulse is now clear. The method of Natural Theology no doubt requires ideally that the validity of Religion itself should be established before we consider, even cursorily, how this tension may be relieved. For if one of the two parties to it has no real right to exist, the tension is only to be properly relieved by the abolition of that party. Yet for purposes of exposition it is convenient to deal with this whole question of tension together, and the principles to be observed with a view to reconciliation are easily stated, though their detailed application is difficult enough.

First, then, the adherents of Religion must be ready to distinguish between the elements or expression of their faith which are of real spiritual importance, and those which have come to have sentimental value through association with the former. They will not be agreed among themselves about this distinction with regard to any point which is newly called in question. Some will be specially eager to say the point does not matter, so as to avoid the spiritual loss always involved in the tension between Religion and Science; these will be called Latitudinarians or Modernists, according to the fashion of the day; they will usually have intellectual clarity but little spiritual *élan*. Others will hold on till the last possible minute to every questioned phrase, lest what is lost be not only of sentimental but also of spiritual value. These will be called Traditionalists or Obscurantists; they will often have great spiritual force, and often, too, great learning, but as a rule, little intellectual enterprise. Between these two there will be others representing every possible gradation. But all may be loyal to the principle just stated, and may fulfil various necessary parts in winning for it a justly discriminating application. What must be excluded, and is very hard to exclude, is the element of purely personal sentiment. To cling to some belief, when it appears to have no inherent spiritual value and to be discredited by scientific advance, on the ground that it is bound up with what has spiritual value by ties of mere association, is a form of self-assertion which must be condemned by Science and Religion alike. But the nature of spiritual value is such that it is very hard to distinguish between it and personal attachment so that great sympathy is due to those who are perplexed by the need of making such a distinction at all.

The requirements to be made of scientific enquirers are different, though these too are largely various forms of the demand to avoid all self-assertion. Two are perhaps the most important. First it is to be remembered that Science, in following its method of using the "lowest" category applicable, is not entitled to deny the applicability of "higher" categories but is only seeing how far it can go without them. Even if it can cover all the facts and hold them together by means of "lower," as for instance mechanical, categories, it does not necessarily follow that the "higher" categories, such as purpose, have no rightful application at all. Indeed, while an actual machine is an entity of which the unifying principle is mechanical, the natural inference from its existence is that a living intelligence designed and constructed it.[3] And if that is true of a steam-engine, it is hard to see why it should not

---

[3] *I.e.* "living" when it so designed and constructed. All arguments of this type are open to Hume's devastating suggestions in the *Dialogue* of which the following may be quoted: "This world, for aught (any man) knows, is very faulty and imperfect compared to a superior standard; and was only the first rude essay of some infant deity, who afterwards abandoned it, ashamed of his lame performance."

be true of the stellar system or of the cosmos generally. It would be hard to refute the argument which urges that the more perfect the universe is in itself as mechanism, the more forcibly does it suggest an intelligent Creator as its cause. But this carries us past the main point, which is that the positive work of Science, in giving an account of observable facts by its own method, never justifies Science in proceeding to negative inferences concerning other methods of interpretation, provided that these in their turn do not exclude the method of Science.

Secondly, it is to be remembered that there are spheres in which the most characteristic methods of Science are inapplicable. This is true in varying degrees of Ethics and of Art. Our appreciation of Right and Good is independent of argument and experiment. These may certainly affect our estimate of various actions or relationships; we may be persuaded that an action or a social order which we had thought good was in truth bad. But this never touches the ultimate objects of moral judgement. If a man tells me that he finds indulgence in cruelty one of the best things in life, I may try to make him contradict himself, as Socrates did with Callicles in a similar connexion,[4] and so show that he did not really mean what he was saying; or I may try to have him shut up in a prison or an asylum; but I cannot directly attack his proposition by argument. "Our sense of value, and in the end for every man his own sense of value, is ultimate and final." [5]

The realm of Art offers an illustration as clear as that of Ethics. In these days when our minds are chiefly influenced by scientific activity people are often inclined to say that they cannot believe where they have no proof; or at least they demand a balance of probability calculated by formulable laws of evidence. Yet they will without hesitation affirm and even passionately insist on (say) the superiority of Schubert to Mendelssohn, though it would puzzle them to prove it or show it to be manifestly probable.

But it is in personal relationships that the inadequacy of Science is most manifest. We should not recommend a pair of lovers to test the advisability of marriage by making each a psychological analysis of the other. We even use the word "understand" with a different sense in relation to other persons from that which it bears in relation to impersonal objects. To "understand" a person is to have that insight into his character and motives which is another aspect of what is also called sympathy. A wise scientist does not follow only scientific methods, as these are commonly understood, in choosing his wife or expressing his affection for his children.

The heart of Religion is not an opinion about God, such as Philosophy might reach as the conclusion of its argument; it is a personal relationship

4 Plato, Gorgias, 494-495.
5 F. H. Bradley, Essays on Truth and Reality, p. 132.

with God. Its closest analogy is not found in our study of astronomy or any other science, but in our relation to a person whom we trust and love. If Science is not the best of aids in helping the child to determine his relation to his father, no more is it—still less is it—the best of aids in determining the relation of a man to his God.

We have seen that tension between Philosophy and Religion is inevitable; and as both are here assumed to have a rightful place in life, this tension must even be regarded as good. We have seen ways in which it may be alleviated, through the recollection by the adherents of each, what is the real nature and concern of that activity to which they are committed. We may reasonably hope to find here the grounds for an ultimate reconciliation in principle; but that can only be when each is perfect in its own kind. Till then the tension will remain, to the special bewilderment of those who are conscious of an obligation to be loyal to both at once. Yet these may hope that through their travail the progress towards ultimate reconciliation is being made.

Prof. A. Wolf ends his admirable chapter on "Recent and Contemporary Philosophy" in *An Outline of Modern Knowledge* with a warning against the dangers involved in "the unusually friendly relationship which is loudly proclaimed to exist now between science and the Churches"; and he adds this paragraph:

"Contemporary philosophy likewise seems to stand in need of an analogous warning. Considering the fact that so many philosophers were formerly students of theology, the relations between philosophy and theology are naturally expected to be friendly. Among British philosophers, indeed, the number of defenders of the faith seems to be abnormally large. It may be that academic conditions, and institutions like the Gifford Trust, either encourage this tendency or give undue prominence to those who follow it. But philosophy will be in a healthier condition when it has entirely ceased to be a handmaid to theology, and pursues its cosmic problems as independently as possible of vested interests." [6]

Prof. Wolf is more concerned with the welfare of Philosophy; I am, no doubt, more concerned with the welfare of Religion. Consequently my phraseology would differ from his. Yet I agree with him in substance. There not only is, but there ought to be, a tension between Philosophy and Religion. That tension is only relaxed when one of the two assimilates itself excessively to the other. The present atmosphere of friendliness may blunt the edge of philosophic criticism because there is an unwillingness to wound the feelings of religious people; it may also lead Religion to tone down its note of Authority because it does not wish to antagonise its philosophic

[6] *Op. cit.*, p. 592.

friends. But the tension is not to be regretted; it is right in principle and stimulating in effect. And it can be delivered from the danger of doing harm if both parties respect the principle of Justice—τὸ τὰ αὑτοῦ πράττειν. But let no one suppose that this principle is as easy to practice as it is to enunciate.

PAUL
TILLICH

PAUL TILLICH (1886-   ), a German-American philosophical theologian, is now on the faculty of Harvard University. His system reflects a wide-ranging interest in the fields of classical Greek thought, German philosophy, art, history, psychoanalysis and existentialism. *Systematic Theology* is his major work.

Theology and Philosophy: A Question*

Theology claims that it constitutes a special realm of knowledge, that it deals with a special object and employs a special method. This claim places the theologian under the obligation of giving an account of the way in which he relates theology to other forms of knowledge. He must answer two questions: What is the relationship of theology to the special sciences *(Wissenschaften)* and what is its relationship to philosophy? The first question has been answered implicitly by the preceding statement of the formal criteria of theology. If nothing is an object of theology which does not concern us ultimately, theology is unconcerned about scientific procedures and results and vice versa. Theology has no right and no obligation to prejudice a physical or historical, sociological or psychological, inquiry. And no result of such an inquiry can be directly productive or disastrous for theology. The point of contact between scientific research and theology lies in the philosophical element of both, the sciences and theology. Therefore, the question of the relation of theology to the special sciences merges into the question of the relation between theology and philosophy.

The difficulty of this question lies partly in the fact that there is no generally accepted definition of philosophy. Every philosophy proposes a defini-

* Reprinted from *Systematic Theology*, Vol. I, pp. 18-28, by Paul Tillich by permission of The University of Chicago Press. Copyright, 1951, by The University of Chicago Press.

tion which agrees with the interest, purpose, and method of the philosopher. Under these circumstances the theologian can only suggest a definition of philosophy which is broad enough to cover most of the important philosophies which have appeared in what usually is called the history of philosophy. The suggestion made here is to call philosophy *that cognitive approach to reality in which reality as such is the object*. Reality as such, or reality as a whole, is not the whole of reality; it is the structure which makes reality a whole and therefore a potential object of knowledge. Inquiring into the nature of reality as such means inquiring into those structures, categories, and concepts which are presupposed in the cognitive encounter with every realm of reality. From this point of view philosophy is by definition critical. It separates the multifarious materials of experience from those structures which make experience possible. There is no difference in this respect between constructive idealism and empirical realism. The question regarding the character of the general structures that make experience possible is always the same. It is *the* philosophical question.

The critical definition of philosophy is more modest than those philosophical enterprises which try to present a complete system of reality, including the results of all the special sciences as well as the general structures of prescientific experience. Such an attempt can be made from "above" or from "below." Hegel worked from "above" when he filled the categorical forms, developed in his *Logic*, with the available material of the scientific knowledge of his time and adjusted the material to the categories. Wundt worked from "below" when he abstracted general and metaphysical principles from the available scientific material of his time, with the help of which the entire sum of empirical knowledge could be organized. Aristotle worked from both "above" and "below" when he carried through metaphysical and scientific studies in interdependence. This also was the ideal of Leibniz when he sketched a universal calculus capable of subjecting all of reality to mathematical analysis and synthesis. But in all these cases the limits of the human mind, the finitude which prevents it from grasping the whole, became visible. No sooner was the system finished than scientific research trespassed its boundaries and disrupted it in all directions. Only the general principles were left, always discussed, questioned, changed, but never destroyed, shining through the centuries, reinterpreted by every generation, inexhaustible, never antiquated or obsolete. These principles are the material of philosophy.

This understanding of philosophy is, on the other hand, less modest than the attempt to reduce philosophy to epistemology and ethics, which was the goal of the Neo-Kantian and related schools in the nineteenth century, and less modest also than the attempt to reduce it to logical calculus, which has been the goal of logical positivism and related schools in the twentieth century. Both attempts to avoid the ontological question have been unsuccessful. The later adherents of the Neo-Kantian philosophy recognised that every epistemology contains an implicit ontology. It cannot be otherwise. Since knowing is an act which participates in being or, more precisely, in an "ontic relation," every analysis of the act of knowing must refer to an interpretation of being (cf. Nicolai Hartmann). At the same time the problem of values pointed toward an ontological foundation of the validity of value-judgments. If values have no *fundamentum in re* (cf. Plato's identification of the good with the essential structures, the ideas of being), they float in the air of a transcendent validity, or else they are subjected to pragmatic tests which are arbitrary and accidental unless they introduce an ontology of essences surreptitiously. It is not necessary to discuss the pragmatic-naturalistic line of philosophical thought, for, in spite of the anti-metaphysical statements of some of its adherents, it has expressed itself in definite ontological terms such as life, growth, process, experience, being (understood in an all-embracing sense), etc. But it is necessary to compare the ontological definition of philosophy, suggested above, with the radical attempts to reduce philosophy to scientific logic. The question is whether the elimination of almost all traditional philosophical problems by logical positivism is a successful escape from ontology. One's first reaction is the feeling that such an attitude pays too high a price, namely, the price of making philosophy irrelevant. But, beyond this impression, the following argument can be put forward. If the restriction of philosophy to the logic of the sciences is a matter of taste, it need not be taken seriously. If it is based on an analysis of the limits of human knowledge, it is based, like every epistemology, on ontological assumptions. There is always at least one problem about which logical positivism, like all semantic philosophies, must make a decision. What is the relation of signs, symbols, or logical operations to reality? Every answer to this question says something about the structure of being. It is ontological. And a philosophy which is so radically critical of all other philosophies should be sufficiently self-critical to see and to reveal its own ontological assumptions.

Philosophy asks the question of reality as a whole; it asks the question of the structure of being. And it answers in terms of categories, structural laws, and universal concepts. It must answer in ontological terms. Ontology is not a speculative-fantastic attempt to establish a world behind the world; it is an analysis of those structures of being which we encounter in every meeting with reality. This was also the original meaning of metaphysics; but the preposition *meta* now has the irremediable connotation of pointing to a duplication of this world by a transcendent realm of beings. Therefore, it is perhaps less misleading to speak of ontology instead of metaphysics.

Philosophy necessarily asks the question of reality as a whole, the question of the structure of being. Theology necessarily asks the same question, for that which concerns us ultimately must belong to reality as a whole; it must belong to being. Otherwise we could not encounter it, and it could not concern us. Of course, it cannot be one being among others; then it would not concern us infinitely. It must be the ground of our being, that which determines our being or not-being, the ultimate and unconditional power of being. But the power of being, its infinite ground or "being-itself," expresses itself in and through the structure of being. Therefore, we can encounter it, be grasped by it, know it, and act toward it. Theology, when dealing with our ultimate concern, presupposes in every sentence the structure of being, its categories, laws, and concepts. Theology, therefore, cannot escape the question of being any more easily than can philosophy. The attempt of biblicism to avoid nonbiblical, ontological terms is doomed to failure as surely as are the corresponding philosophical attempts. The Bible itself always uses the categories and concepts which describe the structure of experience. On every page of every religious or theological text these concepts appear: time, space, cause, thing, subject, nature, movement, freedom, necessity, life, value, knowledge, experience, being and not-being. Biblicism may try to preserve their popular meaning, but then it ceases to be theology. It must neglect the fact that a philosophical understanding of these categories has influenced ordinary language for many centuries. It is surprising how casually theological biblicists use a term like "history" when speaking of Christianity as a historical religion or of God as the "Lord of history." They forget that the meaning they connect with the word "history" has been formed by thousands of years of historiography and philosophy of history. They forget that historical being is one kind of being in addition to others and that, in order to distinguish it from the word "nature," for instance, a general vision of the structure of being is presupposed. They forget that the problem of history is tied up with the problems of time, freedom, accident, purpose, etc., and that each of these concepts has had a development similar to the concept of history. The theologian must take seriously the meaning of the terms he uses. They must be known to him in the whole depth and breadth of their meaning. Therefore, the systematic theologian must be a philosopher in critical understanding even if not in creative power.

The structure of being and the categories and concepts describing this structure are an implicit or explicit concern of every philosopher and of every theologian. Neither of them can avoid the ontological question. Attempts from both sides to avoid it have proved abortive. If this is the situation, the question becomes the more urgent: What is the relation between the ontological question asked by the philosopher and the ontological question asked by the theologian?

Theology and Philosophy: An Answer

Philosophy and theology ask the question of being. But they ask it from different perspectives. Philosophy deals with the structure of being in itself; theology deals with the meaning of being for us. From this difference convergent and divergent trends emerge in the relation of theology and philosophy.

The first point of divergence is a difference in the cognitive attitude of the philosopher and the theologian. Although driven by the philosophical *erōs*, the philosopher tries to maintain a detached objectivity toward being and its structures. He tries to exclude the personal, social, and historical conditions which might distort an objective vision of reality. His passion is the passion for a truth which is open to general approach, subject to general criticism, changeable in accordance with every new insight, open and communicable. In all these respects he feels no different from the scientist, historian, psychologist, etc. He collaborates with them. The material for his critical analysis is largely supplied by empirical research. Just as all sciences have their origin in philosophy, so they contribute in turn to philosophy by giving to the philosopher new and exactly defined material far beyond anything he could get from a pre-scientific approach to reality. Of course, the philosopher, as a philosopher, neither criticises nor augments the knowledge provided by the sciences. This knowledge forms the basis of his description of the categories, structural laws, and concepts which constitute the structure of being. In this respect the philosopher is as dependent on the scientist as he is dependent on his own pre-scientific observation of reality—often more dependent. This relation to the sciences (in the broad sense of *Wissenschaften*) strengthens the detached, objective attitude of the philosopher. Even in the intuitive-synthetic side of his procedure he tries to exclude influences which are not purely determined by his object.

The theologian, quite differently, is not detached from his object but is involved in it. He looks at his object (which transcends the character of being an object) with passion, fear, and love. This is not the *erōs* of the philosopher or his passion for objective truth; it is the love which accepts saving, and therefore personal, truth. The basic attitude of the theologian is commitment to the content he expounds. Detachment would be a denial of the very nature of this content. The attitude of the theologian is "existential." He is involved—with the whole of his existence, with his finitude and his anxiety, with his self-contradictions and his despair, with the healing forces in him and in his social situation. Every theological statement derives its seriousness from these elements of existence. The theologian, in short, is determined by his faith. Every theology presupposes that the theologian is in the theological circle. This contradicts the open, infinite, and changeable character of philosophical truth. It also differs from the way in which the philosopher is dependent on scientific research. The theologian has no direct relation to the scientist (including the historian, sociologist, psychologist). He deals with him only in so far as philosophical implications are at stake. If he abandons the existential attitude, as some of the "empirical" theologians have done, he is driven to statements the reality of which will not be acknowledged by anybody who does not share the existential presuppositions of the assumedly empirical theologian. Theology is necessarily existential, and no theology can escape the theological circle.

The second point of divergence between the theologian and the philosopher is the difference in their sources. The philosopher looks at the whole of reality to discover within it the structure of reality as a whole. He tries to penetrate into structures of being by means of the power of his cognitive function and its structures. He assumes—and science continuously confirms this assumption—that there is an identity, or at least an analogy, between objective and subjective reason, between the *logos* of reality as a whole and the *logos* working in him. Therefore, this *logos is* common; every reasonable being participates in it, uses it in asking questions and criticising the answers received. There is no particular place to discover the structure of being; there is no particular place to stand to discover the categories of experience. The place to look is all places; the place to stand is no place at all; it is pure reason.

The theologian, on the other hand, must look where that which concerns him ultimately is manifest, and he must stand where its manifestation reaches and grasps him. The source of his knowledge is not the universal *logos* but the Logos "who became flesh," that is, the *logos* manifesting itself in a particular historical event. And the medium through which he receives the manifestation of the *logos* is not common rationality but the church, its traditions, and its present reality. He speaks in the church about the foundation of the church. And he speaks because he is grasped by the power of this foundation and by the community built upon it. The concrete *logos* which he sees is received through believing commitment and not, like the universal *logos* at which the philosopher looks, through rational detachment.

The third point of divergence between philosophy and theology is the difference in their content. Even when they speak about the same object they speak about something different. The philosopher deals with the categories of being in relation to the material which is structured by them. He deals with causality as it appears in physics or psychology; he analyses bio-olgical or historical time; he discusses astronomical as well as microcosmic space. He describes the epistemological subject and the relation of person and community. He presents the characteristics of life and spirit in their dependence on, and independence of, each other. He defines nature and history in their mutual limits and tries to penetrate into ontology and logic of being and nonbeing. Innumerable other examples could be given. They all reflect the cosmological structure of the philosophical assertions. The theologian, on the other hand, relates the same categories and concepts to the quest for a "new being." His assertions have a soteriological character. He discusses causality in relation to a *prima causa*, the ground of the whole series of causes and effects; he deals with time in relation to eternity, with space in relation to man's existential homelessness. He speaks of the self-estrangement of the subject, about the spiritual center of personal life, and about community as a possible embodiment of the "New Being." He relates the structures of life to the creative ground of life and the structures of spirit to the divine Spirit. He speaks of the participation of nature in the "history of salvation," about the victory of being over nonbeing. Here also the examples could be increased indefinitely; they show the sharp divergence of theology from philosophy with respect to their content.

The divergence between philosophy and theology is counterbalanced by an equally obvious convergence. From both sides converging trends are at work. The philosopher, like the theologian, "exists," and he cannot jump over the concreteness of his existence and his implicit theology. He is conditioned by his psychological, sociological, and historical situation. And, like every human being, he exists in the power of an ultimate concern, whether or not he is fully conscious of it, whether or not he admits it to himself and to others. There is no reason why even the most scientific philosopher should not admit it, for without an ultimate concern his philosophy would be lacking in passion, seriousness and creativity. Wherever we look in the history of philosophy, we find ideas and systems which claim to be ultimately relevant for human existence. Occasionally the philosophy of religion openly expresses the ultimate concern behind a system. More often it is the character of the ontological principles, or a special section of a system, such as epistemology, philosophy of nature, politics and ethics, philosophy of history, etc., which is most revealing for the discovery of the ultimate concern and the hidden theology within it. Every creative philosopher is a hidden theologian (sometimes even a declared theologian). He is a theologian in the degree to which his existential situation and his ultimate concern shape his philosophical vision. He is a theologian in the degree to which his intuition of the universal *logos* of the structure of reality as a whole is formed by a particular *logos* which appears to him on his particular place and reveals to him the meaning of the whole. And he is a theologian in the degree to which the particular *logos* is a matter of active commitment within a special community. There is hardly a historically significant philosopher who does not show these marks of a theologian. But the philosopher does not intend to be a theologian. He wants to serve the universal *logos*. He tries to turn away from his existential situation, including his ultimate concern, toward a place above all particular places, toward pure reality. The conflict between the intention of becoming universal and the destiny of remaining particular characterizes every philosophical existence. It is its burden and its greatness.

The theologian carries an analogous burden. Instead of turning away from his existential situation, including his ultimate concern, he turns toward it. He turns toward it, not in order to make a confession of it, but in order to make clear the universal validity, the *logos* structure, of what concerns him ultimately. And he can do this only in an attitude of detachment from his existential situation and in obedience to the universal *logos*. This obliges him to be critical of every special expression of his ultimate concern. He cannot affirm any tradition and any authority except through a "No" and a "Yes." And it is always possible that he may not be able to go all of the way from the "No" to the "Yes." He cannot join the chorus of those who live in unbroken assertions. He must take the risk of being driven beyond the boundary line of the theological circle. Therefore, the pious and powerful in the church are suspicious of him, although they live in dependence upon the work of the former theologians who were in the same situation. Theology, since it serves not only the concrete but also the universal *logos*, can become a stumbling block for the church and a demonic temptation for the theologian. The detachment required in honest theological work can destroy the necessary involvement of faith. This tension is the burden and the greatness of every theological work.

The duality of divergence and convergence in the relation between theology and philosophy leads to the double question: Is there a necessary conflict between the two and is there a possible synthesis between them? Both questions must be answered negatively. Neither is a conflict between theology and philosophy necessary, nor is a synthesis between them possible.

A conflict presupposes a common basis on which to fight. But there is no common basis between theology and philosophy. If the theologian and the philosopher fight, they do so either on a philosophical or on a theological basis. The philosophical basis is the ontological analysis of the structure of being. If the theologian needs this analysis, either he must take it from a philosopher or he must himself become a philosopher. Usually he does both.

If he enters the philosophical arena, conflicts as well as alliances with other philosophers are unavoidable. But all this happens on the philosophical level. The theologian has no right whatsoever to argue for a philosophical opinion in the name of his ultimate concern or on the basis of the theological circle. He is obliged to argue for a philosophical decision in the name of the universal *logos* and from the place which is no place: pure reason. It is a disgrace for the theologian and intolerable for the philosopher if in a philosophical discussion the theologian suddenly claims an authority other than pure reason. Conflicts on the philosophical level are conflicts between two philosophers, one of whom happens to be a theologian, but they are not conflicts between theology and philosophy.

Often, however, the conflict is fought on the theological level. The hidden theologian in the philosopher fights with the professed theologian. This situation is more frequent than most philosophers realise. Since they have developed their concepts with the honest intention of obeying the universal *logos*, they are reluctant to recognize the existentially conditioned elements in their systems. They feel that such elements, while they give colour and direction to their creative work, diminish its truth value. In such a situation the theologian must break the resistance of the philosopher against a theological analysis of his ideas. He can do this by pointing to the history of philosophy, which discloses that in every significant philosopher existential passion (ultimate concern) and rational power (obedience to the universal *logos*) are united and that the truth value of a philosophy is dependent on the amalgamation of these two elements in every concept. The insight into this situation is, at the same time, an insight into the fact that two philosophers, one of whom happens to be a theologian, can fight with each other, and that two theologians, one of whom happens to be a philosopher, can fight with each other; but there is no possible conflict between theology and philosophy because there is no common basis for such a conflict. The philosopher may or may not convince the philosopher-theologian. And the theologian may or may not convert the theologian-philosopher. In no case does the theologian as such stand against the philosopher as such and vice versa.

Thus there is no conflict between theology and philosophy, and there is no synthesis either—for exactly the same reason which ensures that there will be no conflict. A common basis is lacking. The idea of a synthesis between theology and philosophy has led to the dream of a "Christian philosophy." The term is ambiguous. It can mean a philosophy whose existential basis is historical Christianity. In this sense all modern philosophy is Christian, even if it is humanistic, atheistic, and intentionally anti-Christian. No philosopher living within Western Christian culture can deny his dependence on it, as no Greek philosopher could have hidden his dependence on an Apollonian-Dionysian culture, even if he was a radical critic of the gods of Homer. The modern vision of reality and its philosophical analysis is different from that of pre-Christian times, whether one is or is not existentially determined by the God of Mount Zion and the Christ of Mount Golgotha. Reality is encountered differently; experience has other dimensions and directions than in the cultural climate of Greece. No one is able to jump out of this "magic" circle. Nietzsche, who tried to do so, announced the coming of the Anti-Christ. But the Anti-Christ is dependent on the Christ against whom he arises. The early Greeks, for whose Culture Nietzsche was longing, did not have to fight the Christ; indeed, they unconsciously prepared for his coming by elaborating the questions to which he gave the answer and the categories in which the answer could be expressed. Modern philosophy is not pagan. Atheism and anti-Christianity are not pagan. They are anti-Christian in Christian terms. The scars of the Christian tradition cannot be erased; they are a *character indelebilis*. Even the paganism of Nazism was not really a relapse to paganism (just as bestiality is not a relapse to the beast).

But the term "Christian philosophy" is often meant in a different sense. It is used to denote a philosophy which does not look at the universal *logos* but at the assumed or actual demands of a Christian theology. This can be done in two ways: either the church authorities or its theological interpreters nominate one of the past philosophers to be their "philosophical saint" or they demand that contemporary philosophers should develop a philosophy under special conditions and with a special aim. In both cases the philosophical *erōs* is killed. If Thomas Aquinas is officially named *the* philosopher of the Roman Catholic church, he has ceased to be for Catholic philosophers a genuine partner in the philosophical dialogue which goes on through the centuries. And if present-day Protestant philosophers are asked to accept the idea of personality as their highest ontological principle because it is the principle most congenial to the spirit of the Reformation, the work of these philosophers is mutilated. There is nothing in heaven and earth, or beyond them, to which the philosopher must subject himself except the universal *logos* of being as it gives itself to him in experience. Therefore, the idea of a "Christian philosophy" in the narrower sense of a philosophy which is intentionally Christian must be rejected. The fact that every modern philosophy has grown on Christian soil and shows traces of the Christian culture in which it lives has nothing to do with the self-contradicting ideal of a "Christian philosophy."

Christianity does not need a "Christian philosophy" in the narrower sense of the word. The Christian claim that the *logos* who has become concrete in Jesus as the Christ is at the same time the universal *logos* includes the claim that wherever the *logos* is at work it agrees with the Christian message. No philosophy which is obedient to the universal *logos* can contradict the concrete *logos*, the Logos "who became flesh."

SUGGESTED ADDITIONAL READINGS

The Relation of Philosophy of Religion to Theology

Berdyaev, Nicolai A. *Truth and Revelation.* Trans., R. M. French. London: Geoffrey Bles, 1953. An important existentialist compares the meaning of truth as it is used in philosophy with its meaning in the context of religious faith.

Calvin, John. *Institutes of the Christian Religion,* 2 volumes. Trans., John Allen. Philadelphia: Presbyterian Board of Christian Education, n.d. See especially the first seven books of volume I. A classic statement of the truth which theology affirms and its relation to philosophy as seen by a founder of the Reformed tradition in Protestantism.

Collins, James. *God in Modern Philosophy.* Chicago: Henry Regnery Company, 1959. A balanced and careful exposition of the work of many important modern philosophers.

Frank, Erich. *Philosophical Understanding and Religious Truth.* Oxford: Oxford University Press, 1945. A perceptive and sensitive approach to the problem of reconciling philosophy and theology.

Hartshorne, Charles and William L. Reese. *Philosophers Speak of God.* Chicago: University of Chicago Press, 1953. A good source book with critical comment on the work of figures important in the history of philosophy, some of whom are not represented in our selections.

Kaufman, Gordon. "Philosophy of Religion and Christian Theology," *The Journal of Religion* (October, 1957), XXXVII, pp. 233-242. A contemporary American theologian gives expression to one of the widely-held views of the relation between philosophy and theology and indicates possible future relationships between the two disciplines.

Niebuhr, H. Richard. *The Meaning of Revelation.* New York: The Macmillan Company, (Macmillan Paperback series.) A book useful for understanding the foundations of an influential Protestant attitude toward revelation and reason. See especially chapter 1.

Randall, John H., Jr. *The Role of Knowledge in Western Religion.* Boston: Starr King Press, 1958. A brief historical sketch of the chief solutions proposed by Western philosophers and theologians for defining the relation of knowledge to faith.

Tillich, Paul. "Two Types of Philosophy of Religion," *Theology of Culture.* Edited by Robert C. Kimball. New York: Oxford University Press, 1959. An incisive analysis of Augustinian and Thomistic types of philosophy of religion.

Zuurdeeg, Willem F. *An Analytical Philosophy of Religion.* New York: Abindgon Press, 1958. See especially pp. 139f. An independent analytical statement of the relation of philosophy to theology by a contemporary philosopher of religion.

III. *Introduction*

THE PROBLEM OF THE
EXISTENCE OF GOD

Arguments for the existence of God have been undertaken for diverse reasons. Some have undertaken them believing that such arguments will remove unnecessary obstacles to belief, and that in the process of constructing a careful argument they may somehow be opened to the possibility of discovering a God whom they can worship. Others rely on arguments for the existence of God to provide the foundation upon which belief in God must be based. Rather than simply opening up the possibility, arguments prove God's existence and thereby make belief in God mandatory, insofar as the person engaged in the argument is willing to be "rational."

Still others argue that probably few people, if any, initially become theists because of an argument for the existence of God. They contend that the procedure in life is usually quite the reverse—a person believes that there is a God and then looks for arguments to justify his belief. Arguments, in this case, answer one's desire to have rational clarification of what he already takes to be of ultimate significance. Evidently there is a certain ambiguity in this point of view, for one believes and yet desires support for his belief. Consequently, this argument demands unusually careful examination.

For whatever reason a person approaches the question of the existence of God, it is a significant question. The importance of the problem can be no better illustrated than by pointing to the number of philosophers and theologians who have undertaken to struggle with it. Selections included in this section of readings not only indicate the vigor with which this task has been attacked and the great variety of ways devised to answer the question of the existence of God either positively or negatively, but they also provide statements of some major positive positions and of important critiques of these arguments.

The ontological argument, as developed by St. Anselm, provides our beginning point. This argument predicates the necessity of God's existence upon the fact that man is able to conceive of "a being than which nothing greater can be conceived," and that such a perfect being must necessarily exist, or else a still greater, i.e. one who does exist, could be conceived. This argument is not necessarily the oldest nor the most important, but it does represent a position which grows out of the Platonic philosophical tradition and which is reflected in the thought of men ranging from Augustine of the fourth and fifth centuries to modern philosophers such as Hegel. With the selection from Anselm we have included a dialogue which he carried on with an opponent, Gaunilon. In addition, there is included an argument against this proof by Immanuel Kant, the significant eighteenth century German philosopher. While Kant's criticism was not accepted by Hegel, it has been considered crucial by many subsequent philosophers and theologians.

In Thomas Aquinas we have the classical statement of the cosmological arguments for the existence of God. This type of argument begins with the assumption that the existence of things in the ordinary realm of experience calls for an explanation. Is there anything which exists "necessarily," i.e. in and of itself, and which can provide the principle by which all other existence can be explained? The cosmological argument answers this question in the affirmative and attempts to prove the existence of the first cause of all consequent existence. Aquinas holds the belief that these arguments are decisive in providing the foundation for theism. Aquinas' faith in reason and his belief that these arguments can be persuasive for any man willing to approach the matter with an open mind underlies a position which is derived from Aristotle and which is of continuing importance, especially in the Roman Catholic tradition. In contrast to this position, David Hume voices his questions, which remain among the most difficult for a traditional Christian to answer, and Immanuel Kant, in the second selection from his works reprinted in this section, presents his reasons for doubting the legitimacy of the cosmological method of argumentation.

In the selection from Maimonides we have a statement by a medieval Jewish philosopher who argues that no positive statements or predications about God are possible. He says that man is only able to indicate by negations the nature of ultimate reality or God. We can, according to Maimonides, affirm that God exists, but we cannot apply in a positive way any attributes to Him. Nonetheless, for Maimonides, even negations do provide significant knowledge, for they help to delimit the meaning of God and his nature.

W. R. Sorley presents an argument for God proceeding from his belief in the existence of moral values; these he considers to be ultimately a structure of a Supreme Mind. A selection from William Temple's book, *Nature*,

Man and God, argues that the existence of mind, that is, of man as a rational creature, in nature points to another proof of the existence of God. Charles Sanders Peirce presents an argument beginning with the experience of man in his instinctual awareness of the reality of God in the psychophysical universe.

The last and most contemporary statement comes from J. J. C. Smart who represents, from philosophy, the British linguistic analysts. By studying the forms and meaning of the language employed in classical arguments for the existence of God, Professor Smart evaluates their validity. His statement helps to point up the central issues in the arguments and to assess their relative merit.

ST. ANSELM

SAINT ANSELM (1033-1109) was Archbishop of Canterbury and the foremost theologian of the eleventh century. His formulation of the ontological argument has become classic. For a time he served as Abbot of the Monastery at Bec, in Normandy, which was in his day the greatest center of learning in Europe.

The Ontological Argument*

. . . I began to ask myself whether there might be found a single argument which would require no other for its proof than itself alone; and alone would suffice to demonstrate that God truly exists, and that there is a supreme good requiring nothing else, which all other things require for their existence and well-being; and whatever we believe regarding the divine Being.

Although I often and earnestly directed my thought to this end, and at some times that which I sought seemed to be just within my reach, while again it wholly evaded my mental vision, at last in despair I was about to cease, as if from the search for a thing which could not be found. But when I wished to exclude this thought altogether, lest, by busying my mind to no purpose, it should keep me from other thoughts, in which I might be successful; then more and more, though I was unwilling and shunned it, it began to force itself upon me, with a kind of importunity. So, one day, when I was exceedingly wearied with resisting its importunity, in the very conflict of my thoughts, the proof of which I had despaired offered itself, so that I eagerly embraced the thoughts which I was strenuously repelling.

. . . I do not endeavor, O Lord, to penetrate thy sublimity, for in no wise do I compare my understanding with that; but I long to understand in some degree thy truth, which my heart believes and loves. For I do not seek to understand that I may believe, but I believe in order to understand. For this also I believe,—that unless I believed, I should not understand.

Chapter II.

And so, Lord, do thou, who dost give understanding to faith, give me, so far as thou knowest it to be profitable, to understand that thou art as we

* From St. Anselm, *Proslogium*, trans. Sidney Norton Deane, pp. 1-2, 6-9, 149-151, 158-159. Copyright, 1903, Open Court Publishing Company. Reprinted with permission of The Open Court Publishing Company.

162

believe; and that thou art that which we believe. And, indeed, we believe that thou art a being than which nothing greater can be conceived. Or is there no such nature, since the fool hath said in his heart, there is no God? (Psalms xiv. 1) But, at any rate, this very fool, when he hears of this being of which I speak—a being than which nothing greater can be conceived— understands what he hears, and what he understands is in his understanding; although he does not understand it to exist.

For, it is one thing for an object to be in the understanding, and another to understand that the object exists. When a painter first conceives of what he will afterwards perform, he has it in his understanding, but he does not yet understand it to be, because he has not yet performed it. But after he has made the painting, he both has it in his understanding, and he understands that it exists, because he has made it.

Hence, even the fool is convinced that something exists in the understanding, at least, than which nothing greater can be conceived. For, when he hears of this, he understands it. And whatever is understood, exists in the understanding. And assuredly that, than which nothing greater can be conceived, cannot exist in the understanding alone. For, suppose it exists in the understanding alone: then it can be conceived to exist in reality; which is greater.

Therefore, if that, than which nothing greater can be conceived, exists in the understanding alone, the very being, than which nothing greater can be conceived, is one, than which a greater can be conceived. But obviously this is impossible. Hence, there is no doubt that there exists a being, than which nothing greater can be conceived, and it exists both in the understanding and in reality.

Chapter III.

And it assuredly exists so truly, that it cannot be conceived not to exist. For, it is possible to conceive of a being which cannot be conceived not to exist, and this is greater than one which can be conceived not to exist. Hence, if that, than which nothing greater can be conceived, can be conceived not to exist, it is not that, than which nothing greater can be conceived. But this is an irreconcilable contradiction. There is, then, so truly a being than which nothing greater can be conceived to exist, that it cannot even be conceived not to exist; and this being thou art, O Lord, our God.

So truly, therefore, dost thou exist, O Lord, my God, that thou canst not be conceived not to exist; and rightly. For, if a mind could conceive of a being better than thee, the creature would rise above the Creator; and this is most absurd. And, indeed, whatever else there is, except thee alone, can be conceived not to exist. To thee alone, therefore, it belongs to exist more truly than all other beings, and hence in a higher degree than all others. For, whatever else exists does not exist so truly, and hence in a less degree it belongs to it to exist. Why, then, has the fool said in his heart, there is no God, . . . , since it is so evident, to a rational mind, that thou dost exist in the highest degree of all? Why, except that he is dull and a fool?

.   .   .   .

In Behalf of the Fool
An Answer to the Argument of Anselm in the Proslogium
by Gaunilon, a Monk of Marmoutier

5. . . . if it should be said that a being which cannot be even conceived in terms of any fact, is in the understanding, I do not deny that this being is, accordingly, in my understanding. But since through this fact it can in no wise attain to real existence also, I do not yet concede to it that existence at all, until some certain proof of it shall be given.

For he who says that this being exists, because otherwise the being which is greater than all will not be greater than all, does not attend strictly enough to what he is saying. For I do not yet say, no, I even deny or doubt that this being is greater than any real object. Nor do I concede to it any other existence than this (if it should be called existence) which it has when the mind, according to a word merely heard, tries to form the image of an object absolutely unknown to it.

How, then, is the veritable existence of that being proved to me from the assumption, by hypothesis, that it is greater than all other beings? For I should still deny this, or doubt your demonstration of it, to this extent, that I should not admit that this being is in my understanding and concept even in the way in which many objects whose real existence is uncertain and doubtful, are in my understanding and concept. For it should be proved first that this being itself really exists somewhere; and then, from the fact that it is greater than all, we shall not hesitate to infer that it also subsists in itself.

6. For example: it is said that somewhere in the ocean is an island, which, because of the difficulty, or rather the impossibility, of discovering what does not exist, is called the lost island. And they say that this island has an inestimable wealth of all manner of riches and delicacies in greater abundance than is told of the Islands of the Blest; and that having no owner or inhabitant, it is more excellent than all other countries, which are inhabited by mankind, in the abundance with which it is stored.

Now if someone should tell me that there is such an island, I should easily understand his words, in which there is no difficulty. But suppose that he went on to say, as if by a logical inference: "You can no longer doubt that this island which is more excellent than all lands exists somewhere, since you have no doubt that it is in your understanding. And since it is more excellent not to be in the understanding alone, but to exist both in the understanding and in reality, for this reason it must exist. For if it does not exist, any land which really exists will be more excellent than it; and so the island already understood by you to be more excellent will not be more excellent."

If a man should try to prove to me by such reasoning that this island truly exists, and that its existence should no longer be doubted, either I should believe that he was jesting, or I know not which I ought to regard as the greater fool: myself, supposing that I should allow this proof; or him, if he should suppose that he had established with any certainty the existence of this island. For he ought to show first that the hypothetical excellence of this island exists as a real and indubitable fact, and in no wise as any unreal object, or one whose existence is uncertain, in my understanding.

Anselm's Apologetic
In Reply to Gaunilon's Answer in Behalf of the Fool

Chapter III.

But, you say, it is as if one should suppose an island in the ocean, which surpasses all lands in its fertility, and which, because of the difficulty, or rather the impossibility, of discovering what does not exist, is called a lost island; and should say that there can be no doubt that this island truly exists in reality, for this reason, that one who hears it described easily understands what he hears.

Now I promise confidently that if any man shall devise anything existing either in reality or in concept alone (except that than which a greater cannot be conceived) to which he can adapt the sequence of my reasoning, I will discover that thing, and will give him his lost island, not to be lost again.

But it now appears that this being than which a greater is inconceivable cannot be conceived not to be, because it exists on so assured a ground of truth; for otherwise it would not exist at all.

Hence, if any one says that he conceives this being not to exist, I say that at the time when he conceives of this either he conceives of a being than which a greater is inconceivable, or he does not conceive at all. If he does not conceive, he does not conceive of the non-existence of that of which he does not conceive. But if he does conceive, he certainly conceives of a being which cannot be even conceived not to exist. For if it could be conceived not to exist, it could be conceived to have a beginning and an end. But this is impossible.

He, then, who conceives of this being conceives of a being which cannot be even conceived not to exist; but he who conceives of this being does not conceive that it does not exist; else he conceives what is inconceivable. The non-existence, then, of that than which a greater cannot be conceived is inconceivable.

IMMANUEL
KANT

IMMANUEL KANT (1726-1806) was professor at Koenigsberg, Germany, and one of the great philosophers. His writings stimulated much subsequent discussion of theory of knowledge, metaphysics, ethics and religion. The most significant among his many works are *The Critique of Pure Reason* and *The Critique of Practical Reason.*

Sec. IV. - of the Impossibility of an Ontological Proof of the Existence of God*

It is evident from what has been said, that the conception of an absolutely necessary being is a mere idea, the objective reality of which is far from being established by the mere fact that it is a need of reason. On the contrary, this idea serves merely to indicate a certain unattainable perfection, and rather limits the operations than, by the presentation of new objects, extends the sphere of the understanding. But a strange anomaly meets us at the very threshold; for the inference from a given existence in general to an absolutely necessary existence, seems to be correct and unavoidable, while the conditions of the *understanding* refuse to aid us in forming any conception of such a being.

Philosophers have always talked of an *absolutely necessary* being, and

* From Immanuel Kant, *Critique of Pure Reason*, trans. J. M. D. Meiklejohn, pp. 331-337. Published, 1943, Willey Book Company. In the public domain. [Footnote omitted, Eds.]

have nevertheless declined to take the trouble of conceiving, whether—and how—a being of this nature is even cogitable, not to mention that its existence is actually demonstrable. A verbal definition of the conception is certainly easy enough; it is something, the non-existence of which is impossible. But does this definition throw any light upon the conditions which render it impossible to cogitate the non-existence of a thing—conditions which we wish to ascertain, that we may discover whether we think anything in the conception of such a being or not? For the mere fact that I throw away, by means of the word *Unconditioned*, all the conditions which the understanding habitually requires in order to regard anything as necessary, is very far from making clear whether by means of the conception of the unconditionally necessary I think of something, or really of nothing at all.

Nay, more, this chance-conception, now become so current, many have endeavored to explain by examples, which seemed to render any inquiries regarding its intelligibility quite needless. Every geometrical proposition—a triangle has three angles—it was said, is absolutely necessary; and thus people talked of an object which lay out of the sphere of our understanding as if it were perfectly plain what the conception of such a being meant.

All the examples adduced have been drawn, without exception, from *judgments,* and not from *things.* But the unconditioned necessity of a judgment does not form the absolute necessity of a thing. On the contrary, the absolute necessity of a judgment is only a conditioned necessity of a thing, or of the predicate in a judgment. The proposition above-mentioned, does not enounce that three angles necessarily exist, but, upon condition that a triangle exists, three angles must necessarily exist—in it. And thus this logical necessity has been the source of the greatest delusions. Having formed an *a priori* conception of a thing, the content of which was made to embrace existence, we believed ourselves safe in concluding that, because existence belongs necessarily to the object of the conception, (that is, under the condition of my positing this thing as given), the existence of the thing is also posited necessarily, and that it is therefore absolutely necessary—merely because its existence has been cogitated in the conception.

If, in an identical judgment, I annihilate the predicate in thought, and retain the subject, a contradiction is the result; and hence I say, the former belongs necessarily to the latter. But if I suppress both subject and predicate in thought, no contradiction arises; for there is *nothing* at all, and therefore no means of forming a contradiction. To suppose the existence of a triangle and not that of its three angles, is self-contradictory; but to suppose the non-existence of both triangle and angles is perfectly admissible. And so is it with the conception of an absolutely necessary being. Annihilate its existence in thought, and you annihilate the thing itself with all its predicates;

how then can there be any room for contradiction? Externally, there is nothing to give rise to a contradiction, for a thing cannot be necessary externally; nor internally, for, by the annihilation or suppression of the thing itself, its internal properties are also annihilated. God is omnipotent—that is a necessary judgment. His omnipotence cannot be denied, if the existence of a Deity is posited—the existence, that is, of an infinite being, the two conceptions being identical. But when you say, God *does not exist*, neither omnipotence nor any other predicate is affirmed; they must all disappear with the subject, and in this judgment there cannot exist the least self-contradiction.

You have thus seen, that when the predicate of a judgment is annihilated in thought along with the subject, no internal contradiction can arise, be the predicate what it may. There is no possibility of evading the conclusion—you find yourselves compelled to declare: There are certain subjects which cannot be annihilated in thought. But this is nothing more than saying: There exist subjects which are absolutely necessary—the very hypothesis which you are called upon to establish. For I find myself unable to form the slightest conception of a thing which, when annihilated in thought with all its predicates, leaves behind a contradiction; and contradiction is the only criterion of impossibility, in the sphere of pure *a priori* conceptions.

Against these general considerations, the justice of which no one can dispute, one argument is adduced, which is regarded as furnishing a satisfactory demonstration from the fact. It is affirmed, that there is one and only one conception, in which the non-being or annihilation of the object is self-contradictory, and this is the conception of an *ens realissimum*. It possesses, you say, all reality, and you feel yourselves justified in admitting the possibility of such a being. (This I am willing to grant for the present, although the existence of a conception which is not self-contradictory, is far from being sufficient to prove the possibility of an object.) Now the notion of all reality embraces in it that of existence; the notion of existence lies, therefore, in the conception of this possible thing. If this thing is annihilated in thought, the internal possibility of the thing is also annihilated, which is self-contradictory.

I answer: It is absurd to introduce—under whatever term disguised—into the conception of a thing, which is to be cogitated solely in reference to its possibility, the conception of its existence. If this is admitted, you will have apparently gained the day, but in reality have enounced nothing but a mere tautology. I ask, is the proposition, *this or that thing* (which I am admitting to be possible) *exists*, an analytical or a synthetical proposition? If the former, there is no addition made to the subject of your thought by the affirmation of its existence; but then the conception in your minds is identical with the thing itself, or you have supposed the existence of a thing to be possible, and then inferred its existence from its internal possibility—which is but a miserable tautology. The word *reality* in the conception of the thing, and the word *existence* in the conception of the predicate, will not help you out of the difficulty. For, supposing you were to term all positing of a thing, reality, you have thereby posited the thing with all its predicates in the conception of the subject and assumed its actual existence, and this you merely repeat in the predicate. But if you confess, as every reasonable person must, that every existential proposition is synthetical, how can it be maintained that the predicate of existence cannot be denied without contradiction—a property which is the characteristic of analytical propositions, alone?

I should have a reasonable hope of putting an end forever to this sophistical mode of argumentation, by a strict definition of the conception of existence, did not my own experience teach me that the illusion arising from our confounding a logical with a real predicate (a predicate which aids in the determination of a thing) resists almost all the endeavors of explanation and illustration. A *logical predicate* may be what you please, even the subject may be predicated of itself; for logic pays no regard to the content of a judgment. But the determination of a conception is a predicate, which adds to and enlarges the conception. It must not, therefore, be contained in the conception.

Being is evidently not a real predicate, that is, a conception of something which is added to the conception of some other thing. It is merely the positing of a thing, or of certain determinations in it. Logically, it is merely the copula of a judgment. The proposition, *God is omnipotent*, contains two conceptions, which have a certain object or content; the word *is*, is no additional predicate—it merely indicates the relation of the predicate to the subject. Now, if I take the subject (God) with all its predicates (omnipotence being one), and say, *God is*, or, *There is a God*, I add no new predicate to the conception of God, I merely posit or affirm the existence of the subject with all its predicates—I posit the *object* in relation to my *conception*. The content of both is the same; and there is no addition made to the conception, which expresses merely the possibility of the object, by my cogitating the object—in the expression, it *is*—as absolutely given or existing. Thus the real contains no more than the possible. A hundred real dollars contain no more than a hundred possible dollars. For, as the latter indicate the conception, and the former the object, on the supposition that the content of the former was greater than that of the latter, my conception would not be an expression of the whole object, and would consequently be an inadequate conception of it. But in reckoning my wealth there may be said to be more in a hundred real dollars, than in a hundred possible dollars—that is, in the mere conception of them. For the real object—the dollars—

is not analytically contained in my conception, but forms a synthetical addition to my conception (which is merely a determination of my mental state), although this objective reality—this existence—apart from my conception, does not in the least degree increase the aforesaid hundred dollars.

By whatever and by whatever number of predicates—even to the complete determination of it—I may cogitate a thing I do not in the least augment the object of my conception by the addition of the statement, this thing exists. Otherwise, not exactly the same, but something more than what was cogitated in my conception, would exist, and I could not affirm that the exact object of my conception had real existence. If I cogitate a thing as containing all modes of reality except one, the mode of reality which is absent is not added to the conception of the thing by the affirmation that the thing exists; on the contrary, the thing exists—if it exist at all—with the same defect as that cogitated in its conception; otherwise not that which was cogitated, but something different, exists. Now, if I cogitate a being as the highest reality, without defect or imperfection, the question still remains—whether this being exists or not? For although no element is wanting in the possible real content of my conception, there is a defect in its relation to my mental state, that is, I am ignorant whether the cognition of the object indicated by the conception is possible *a posteriori*. And here the cause of the present difficulty becomes apparent. If the question regarded an object of sense merely, it would be impossible for me to confound the conception with the existence of a thing. For the conception merely enables me to cogitate an object as according with the general conditions of experience; while the existence of the object permits me to cogitate it as contained in the sphere of actual experience. At the same time, this connection with the world of experience does not in the least augment the conception, although a possible perception has been added to the experience of the mind. But if we cogitate existence by the pure category alone, it is not to be wondered at, that we should find ourselves unable to present any criterion sufficient to distinguish it from mere possibility.

Whatever be the content of our conception of an object, it is necessary to go beyond it, if we wish to predicate existence of the object. In the case of sensuous objects, this is attained by their connection according to empirical laws with some one of my perceptions; but there is no means of cognizing the existence of objects of pure thought, because it must be cognized completely *a priori*. But all our knowledge of existence (be it immediately by perception, or by inferences connecting some object with a perception) belongs entirely to the sphere of experience—which is in perfect unity with itself—and although an existence out of this sphere cannot be absolutely declared to be impossible, it is a hypothesis the truth of which we have no means of ascertaining.

The notion of a supreme being is in many respects a highly useful idea; but for the very reason that it is an idea, it is incapable of enlarging our cognition with regard to the existence of things. It is not even sufficient to instruct us as to the possibility of a being which we do not know to exist. The analytical criterion of possibility, which consists in the absence of contradiction in propositions, cannot be denied it. But the connection of real properties in a thing is a synthesis of the possibility of which an *a priori* judgment cannot be formed, because these realities are not presented to us specifically; and even if this were to happen, a judgment would still be impossible, because the criterion of the possibility of synthetical cognitions must be sought for in the world of experience, to which the object of an idea cannot belong. And thus the celebrated Leibnitz has utterly failed in his attempt to establish on *a priori* grounds the possibility of this sublime ideal being.

The celebrated ontological or Cartesian argument for the existence of a Supreme Being is therefore insufficient; and we may as well hope to increase our stock of knowledge by the aid of mere ideas, as the merchant to augment his wealth by the addition of noughts to his cash-account.

ST. THOMAS
AQUINAS

THOMAS AQUINAS (c. 1226-1274), Dominican Friar and the greatest of the medieval philosophers, produced a synthesis of Christian faith and Aristotle's metaphysics which has become the official theology of the Roman Catholic Church. His chief works are *Summa Theologica and Summa Contra Gentiles.*

Summa Theologica*

Because the chief aim of sacred doctrine is to teach the knowledge of God, not only as He is in Himself, but also as He is the beginning of things and their last end, and especially of rational creatures, as is clear from what

* From Thomas Aquinas, *Summa Theologica*, Vol. I, pp. 19-27, 1920, Burns, Oates & Washbourne, Ltd. Reprinted with permission of Burns & Oates, Ltd. and Benziger Brothers, Inc.

has been already said, therefore, in our endeavour to expound this science, we shall treat: (1) Of God: (2) Of the rational creature's advance towards God: (3) Of Christ, Who as man, is our way to God.

In treating of God there will be a threefold division:—

For we shall consider (1) whatever concerns the Divine Essence. (2) Whatever concerns the distinctions of Persons. (3) Whatever concerns the procession of creatures from Him.

Concerning the Divine Essence, we must consider:—

(1) Whether God exists? (2) The manner of His existence, or, rather, what is *not* the manner of His existence. (3) Whatever concerns His operations—namely, His knowledge, will, power.

Concerning the first, there are three points of inquiry:—

(1) Whether the proposition "God exists" is self-evident? (2) Whether it is demonstrable? (3) Whether God exists?

First Article
Whether the Existence of God Is Self-Evident?

We proceed thus to the First Article:—

Objection 1. It seems that the existence of God is self-evident. Now those things are said to be self-evident to us the knowledge of which is naturally implanted in us, as we can see in regard to first principles. But as Damascene says (*De Fid. Orth.* i, I, 3), *the knowledge of God is naturally implanted in all.* Therefore the existence of God is self-evident.

Obj. 2. Further, those things are said to be self-evident which are known as soon as the terms are known, which the Philosopher (I *Poster.* iii) says is true of the first principles of demonstration. Thus, when the nature of a whole and of a part is known, it is at once recognized that every whole is greater than its part. But as soon as the signification of the word "God" is understood, it is at once seen that God exists. For by this word is signified that thing than which nothing greater can be conceived. But that which exists actually and mentally is greater than that which exists only mentally. Therefore, since as soon as the word "God" is understood it exists mentally, it also follows that it exists actually. Therefore the proposition "God exists" is self-evident.

Obj. 3. Further, the existence of truth is self-evident. For whoever denies the existence of truth grants that truth does not exist: and, if truth does not exist, then the proposition "Truth does not exist" is true: and if there is anything true, there must be truth. But God is truth itself: *I am the way, the truth, and the life* (John xiv.6). Therefore "God exists" is self-evident.

On the contrary, No one can mentally admit the opposite of what is self-evident; as the Philosopher (*Metaph.* iv., lect. vi.) states concerning the first principles of demonstration. But the opposite of the proposition "God is" can be mentally admitted: *The fool said in his heart, There is no God.* (Ps.lii.I). Therefore, that God exists is not self-evident.

I answer that, A thing can be self-evident in either of two ways; on the one hand, self-evident in itself, though not to us; on the other, self-evident in itself, and to us. A proposition is self-evident because the predicate is included in the essence of the subject, as "Man is an animal," for animal is contained in the essence of man. If, therefore the essence of the predicate and subject be known to all, the proposition will be self-evident to all; as is clear with regard to the first principles of demonstration, the terms of which are common things that no one is ignorant of, such as being and non-being, whole and part, and suchlike. If, however, there are some to whom the essence of the predicate and subject is unknown, the proposition will be self-evident in itself, but not to those who do not know the meaning of the predicate and subject of the proposition. Therefore, it happens, as Boethius says (*Hebdom., the title of which is: "Whether all that is, is good"*), "that there are some mental concepts self-evident only to the learned, as that incorporeal substances are not in space." Therefore I say that this proposition, "God exists," of itself is self-evident, for the predicate is the same as the subject; because God is His own existence as will be here-after shown (Q.III., A.4). Now because we do not know the essence of God, the proposition is not self-evident to us; but needs to be demonstrated by things that are more known to us, though less known in their nature—namely, by effects.

Reply Obj. 1. To know that God exists in a general and confused way is implanted in us by nature, inasmuch as God is man's beatitude. For man naturally desires happiness, and what is naturally desired by man must be naturally known to him. This, however, is not to know absolutely that God exists; just as to know that someone is approaching is not the same as to know that Peter is approaching, even though it is Peter who is approaching; for many there are who imagine that man's perfect good which is happiness, consists in riches, and others in pleasures, and others in something else.

Reply Obj. 2. Perhaps not everyone who hears this word "God" under-stands it to signify something than which nothing greater can be thought, seeing that some have believed God to be a body. Yet, granted that everyone understands that by this word "God" is signified something than which nothing greater can be thought, nevertheless, it does not therefore follow that he understands that what the word signifies exists actually, but only that it exists mentally. Nor can it be argued that it actually exists, unless it be admitted that there actually exists something than which nothing greater can be thought; and this precisely is not admitted by those who hold that God does not exist.

Reply Obj. 3. The existence of truth in general is self-evident, but the existence of a Primal Truth is not self-evident to us.

Second Article
Whether It Can be Demonstrated That God Exists?

We proceed thus to the Second Article:—

Objection 1. It seems that the existence of God cannot be demonstrated. For it is an article of faith that God exists. But what is of faith cannot be demonstrated, because a demonstration produces scientific knowledge; whereas faith is of the unseen (Heb. xi.I). Therefore it cannot be demonstrated that God exists.

Obj. 2. Further, the essence is the middle term of demonstration. But we cannot know in what God's essence consists, but solely in what it does not consist; as Damascene says (*De Fid. Orth.* i.4). Therefore we cannot demonstrate that God exists.

Obj. 3. Further, if the existence of God were demonstrated, this could only be from His effects. But His effects are not proportionate to Him, since He is infinite and His effects are finite; and between the finite and infinite there is no proportion. Therefore, since a cause cannot be demonstrated by an effect not proportionate to it, it seems that the existence of God cannot be demonstrated.

On the contrary, The Apostle says: *The invisible things of Him are clearly seen, being understood by the things that are made* (Rom. 1. 20). But this would not be unless the existence of God could be demonstrated through the things that are made; for the first thing we must know of anything is, whether it exists.

I answer that, Demonstration can be made in two ways: One is through the cause, and is called *a priori*, and this is to argue from what is prior absolutely. The other is through the effect, and is called a demonstration *a posteriori*; this is to argue from what is prior relatively only to us. When an effect is better known to us than its cause, from the effect we proceed to the knowledge of the cause. And from every effect the existence of its proper cause can be demonstrated, so long as its effects are better known to us; because since every effect depends upon its cause, if the effect exists, the cause must pre-exist. Hence the existence of God, in so far as it is not self-evident to us, can be demonstrated from those of His effects which are known to us.

Reply Obj. 1. The existence of God and other like truths about God, which can be known by natural reason, are not articles of faith, but are preambles to the articles; for faith presupposes natural knowledge, even as grace presupposes nature, and perfection supposes something that can be perfected. Nevertheless, there is nothing to prevent a man, who cannot grasp a proof, accepting, as a matter of faith, something which in itself is capable of being scientifically known and demonstrated.

Reply Obj. 2. When the existence of a cause is demonstrated from an effect, this effect takes the place of the definition of the cause in proof of the cause's existence. This is especially the case in regard to God, because, in order to prove the existence of anything, it is necessary to accept as a middle term the meaning of the word, and not its essence, for the question of its essence follows on the question of its existence. Now the names given to God are derived from His effects; consequently, in demonstrating the existence of God from His effects, we may take for the middle term the meaning of the word "God."

Reply Obj. 3. From effects not proportionate to the cause no perfect knowledge of that cause can be obtained. Yet from every effect the existence of the cause can be clearly demonstrated, and so we can demonstrate the existence of God from His effects; though from them we cannot perfectly know God as He is in His essence.

Third Article
Whether God Exists?

We proceed thus to the Third Article:—

Objection 1. It seems that God does not exist; because if one of two contraries be infinite, the other would be altogether destroyed. But the word "God" means that He is infinite goodness. If, therefore, God existed, there would be no evil discoverable; but there is evil in the world. Therefore God does not exist.

Obj. 2. Further, it is superfluous to suppose that what can be accounted for by a few principles has been produced by many. But it seems that everything we see in the world can be accounted for by other principles, supposing God did not exist. For all natural things can be reduced to one principle, which is nature; and all voluntary things can be reduced to one principle, which is human reason, or will. Therefore there is no need to suppose God's existence.

On the contrary, It is said in the person of God: *I am Who am* (Exod. iii. 14).

I answer that, The existence of God can be proved in five ways.

The first and more manifest way is the argument from motion. It is certain, and evident to our senses, that in the world some things are in motion. Now whatever is in motion is put in motion by another, for nothing can be in motion except it is in potentiality to that towards which it is in motion; whereas a thing moves inasmuch as it is in act. For motion is nothing else than the reduction of something from potentiality to actuality. But nothing can be reduced from potentiality to actuality, except by something in the state of actuality. Thus that which is actually hot, as fire, makes wood, which is potentially hot, to be actually hot, and thereby moves and changes it. Now it is not possible that the same thing should be at once in actuality and potentiality in the same respect, but only in different respects. For what is actually hot cannot simultaneously be potentially hot; but it is simultaneously potentially cold. It is therefore impossible that in the same respect and in the same way a thing should be both mover and moved, *i.e.,* that it should move itself. Therefore, whatever is in motion must be put in motion by another. If that by which it is put in motion be itself put in motion, then this also must needs be put in motion by another, and that by another again. But this cannot go on to infinity, because then there would be no first mover, and, consequently, no other mover; seeing that subsequent movers move only inasmuch as they are put in motion by the first mover; as the staff moves only because it is put in motion by the hand. Therefore it is necessary to arrive at a first mover, put in motion by no other; and this everyone understands to be God.

The second way is from the nature of the efficient cause. In the world of sense we find there is an order of efficient causes. There is no case known (neither is it, indeed, possible) in which a thing is found to be the efficient cause of itself; for so it would be prior to itself, which is impossible. Now in efficient causes it is not possible to go on to infinity, because in all efficient causes following in order, the first is the cause of the intermediate cause, and the intermediate is the cause of the ultimate cause, whether the intermediate cause be several, or one only. Now to take away the cause is to take away the effect. Therefore, if there be no first cause among efficient causes, there will be no ultimate, nor any intermediate cause. But if in efficient causes it is possible to go on to infinity, there will be no first efficient cause, neither will there be an ultimate effect, nor any intermediate efficient causes; all of which is plainly false. Therefore it is necessary to admit a first efficient cause, to which everyone gives the name of God.

The third way is taken from possibility and necessity, and runs thus. We find in nature things that are possible to be and not to be, since they are found to be generated, and to be corrupted, and consequently, they are possible to be and not to be. But it is impossible for these always to exist, for that which is possible not to be at some time is not. Therefore, if everything is possible not to be, then at one time there could have been nothing in existence. Now if this were true, even now there would be nothing in existence, because that which does not exist only begins to exist by something already existing. Therefore, if at one time nothing was in existence, it would have been impossible for anything to have begun to exist; and thus even now nothing would be in existence—which is absurd. Therefore, not all beings are merely possible, but there must exist something the existence of which is necessary. But every necessary thing either has its necessity caused by another, or not. Now it is impossible to go on to infinity in necessary things which have their necessity caused by another, as has been already proved in regard to efficient causes. Therefore we cannot but postulate the existence of some being having of itself its own necessity, and not receiving it from another, but rather causing in others their necessity. This all men speak of as God.

The fourth way is taken from the gradation to be found in things. Among beings there are some more and some less good, true, noble, and the like. But "more" and "less" are predicated of different things, according as they resemble in their different ways something which is the maximum, as a thing is said to be hotter according as it more nearly resembles that which is hottest; so that there is something which is truest, something best, something noblest, and, consequently, something which is uttermost being; for those things that are greatest in truth are greatest in being, as it is written in *Metaph.* ii. Now the maximum in any genus is the cause of all in that genus; as fire, which is the maximum of heat, is the cause of all hot things. Therefore there must also be something which is to all beings the cause of their being, goodness, and every other perfection; and this we call God.

The fifth way is taken from the governance of the world. We see that things which lack intelligence, such as natural bodies, act for an end, and this is evident from their acting always, or nearly always, in the same way, so as to obtain the best result. Hence it is plain that not fortuitously, but designedly, do they achieve their end. Now whatever lacks intelligence cannot move towards an end, unless it be directed by some being endowed with knowledge and intelligence; as the arrow is shot to its mark by the archer. Therefore some intelligent being exists by whom all natural things are directed to their end; and this being we call God.

Reply Obj. 1. As Augustine says (*Enchir.* xi.): *Since God is the highest good, He would not allow any evil to exist in His works, unless His omni-*

potence and goodness were such as to bring good even out of evil. This is part of the infinite goodness of God, that He should allow evil to exist, and out of it produce good.

Reply Obj. 2. Since nature works for a determinate end under the direction of a higher agent, whatever is done by nature must needs be traced back to God, as to its first cause. So also whatever is done voluntarily must also be traced back to some higher cause other than human reason or will, since these can change and fail; for all things that are changeable and capable of defect must be traced back to an immovable and self-necessary first principle, as was shown in the body of the *Article.*

DAVID
HUME

DAVID HUME (1711-1776), Scottish empiricist, is one of the most important modern philosophers. His writings stimulated the thought of Immanuel Kant and have continued to influence philosophic study. His writings have been especially important as a background to present-day scientific empiricism.

Dialogues Concerning Natural Religion*

I must own, Cleanthes, said Demea, that nothing can more surprise me, than the light, in which you have, all along, put this argument. By the whole tenor of your discourse, one would imagine that you were maintaining the Being of a God, against the cavils of Atheists and Infidels; and were necessitated to become a champion for that fundamental principle of all religion. But this, I hope, is not by any means a question among us. No man, no man, at least, of common sense, I am persuaded, ever entertained a serious doubt with regard to a truth, so certain and self-evident. The question is not concerning the Being, but the Nature of God. This, I affirm, from the infirmities of human understanding, to be altogether incomprehensible and unknown to us. The essence of that supreme mind, his attributes, the manner of his existence, the very nature of his duration; these

* From David Hume, *Dialogues Concerning Natural Religion,* pp. 437-451, in *The Philosophical Works of Hume,* Vol. II, 1826, Adam Black, William Tait and Charles Tait. In the public domain.

and every particular, which regards so divine a Being, are mysterious to men. Finite, weak, and blind creatures, we ought to humble ourselves in his august presence, and, conscious of our frailties, adore in silence his infinite perfections, which eye hath not seen, ear hath not heard, neither hath it entered into the heart of man to conceive [them]. They are covered in a deep cloud from human curiosity: It is profaneness to attempt penetrating through these sacred obscurities: And, next to the impiety of denying his existence, is the temerity of prying into his nature and essence, decrees and attributes.

But lest you should think, that my *piety* has here got the better of my *philosophy*, I shall support my opinion, if it needs any support, by a very great authority. I might cite all the divines almost, from the foundation of Christianity, who have ever treated of this or any other theological subject: But I shall confine myself, at present, to one equally celebrated for piety and philosophy. It is Father Malebranche, who, I remember, thus expresses himself.[1] "One ought not so much," says he, "to call God a spirit, in order to express positively what he is, as in order to signify that he is not matter. He is a Being infinitely perfect: Of this we cannot doubt. But in the same manner as we ought not to imagine, even supposing him corporeal, that he is clothed with a human body, as the Anthropomorphites asserted, under colour that that figure was the most perfect of any; so, neither ought we to imagine, that the Spirit of God has human ideas, or bears *any* resemblance to our spirit; under colour that we know nothing more perfect than a human mind. We ought rather to believe, that as he comprehends the perfections of matter without being material . . . he comprehends also the perfections of created spirits, without being spirit, in the manner we conceive spirit: That his true name is, *He that is*; or, in other words, Being without restriction, All Being, the Being infinite and universal."

After so great an authority, Demea, replied Philo, as that which you have produced, and a thousand more, which you might produce, it would appear ridiculous in me to add my sentiment, or express my approbation of your doctrine. But surely, where reasonable men treat these subjects, the question can never be concerning the *Being*, but only the *Nature* of the Deity. The former truth, as you well observe, is unquestionable and self-evident. Nothing exists without a cause; and the original cause of this universe (whatever it be) we call God; and piously ascribe to him every species of perfection. Whoever scruples this fundamental truth, deserves every punishment, which can be inflicted among philosophers, to wit, the greatest ridicule, contempt and disapprobation. But as all perfection is entirely relative, we ought never to imagine, that we comprehend the attributes of this divine Being, or to sup-

[1] Recherche de la Verité, liv. 3, chap. 9.

pose, that his perfections have any analogy or likeness to the perfections of a human creature. Wisdom, Thought, Design, Knowledge; these we justly ascribe to him; because these words are honourable among men, and we have no other language or other conceptions by which we can express our adoration of him. But let us beware, lest we think, that our ideas any wise correspond to his perfections, or that his attributes have any resemblance to these qualities among men. He is infinitely superior to our limited view and comprehension; and is more the object of worship in the temple, than of disputation in the schools.

In reality, Cleanthes, continued he, there is no need of having recourse to that affected scepticism, so displeasing to you, in order to come at this determination. Our ideas reach no farther than our experience: We have no experience of divine attributes and operations: I need not conclude my syllogism: You can draw the inference yourself. And it is a pleasure to me (and I hope to you too) that just reasoning and sound piety here concur in the same conclusion, and both of them establish the adorably mysterious and incomprehensible nature of the Supreme Being.

Not to lose any time in circumlocutions, said Cleanthes, addressing himself to Demea, much less in replying to the pious declamations of Philo; I shall briefly explain how I conceive this matter. Look round the world: contemplate the whole and every part of it: You will find it to be nothing but one great machine, subdivided into an infinite number of lesser machines, which again admit of subdivisions, to a degree beyond what human senses and faculties can trace and explain. All these various machines, and even their most minute parts, are adjusted to each other with an accuracy, which ravishes into admiration all men who have ever contemplated them. The curious adapting of means to ends, throughout all nature, resembles exactly, though it much exceeds, the productions of human contrivances; of human design, thought, wisdom, and intelligence. Since therefore the effects resemble each other, we are led to infer, by all the rules of analogy, that the causes also resemble; and that the Author of Nature is somewhat similar to the mind of man; though possessed of much larger faculties, proportioned to the grandeur of the work, which he has executed. By this argument *a posteriori*, and by this argument alone, do we prove at once the existence of a Deity, and his similarity to human mind and intelligence.

I shall be so free, Cleanthes, said Demea, as to tell you, that from the beginning, I could not approve of your conclusion concerning the similarity of the Deity to men; still less can I approve of the mediums, by which you endeavour to establish it. What! No demonstration of the Being of God! No abstract arguments! No proofs *a priori*! Are these, which have hitherto been so much insisted on by philosophers, all fallacy, all sophism? Can we reach no further in this subject than experience and probability? I will not say, that this is betraying the cause of a Deity: But surely, by this affected candour, you give advantage to Atheists, which they never could obtain, by the mere dint of argument and reasoning.

What I chiefly scruple in this subject, said Philo, is not so much, that all religious arguments are by Cleanthes reduced to experience, as that they appear not to be even the most certain and irrefragable of that inferior kind. That a stone will fall, that fire will burn, that the earth has solidity, we have observed a thousand and a thousand times; and when any new instance of this nature is presented, we draw without hesitation the accustomed inference. The exact similarity of the cases gives us a perfect assurance of a similar event; and a stronger evidence is never desired nor sought after. But wherever you depart, in the least, from the similarity of the cases, you diminish proportionately the evidence; and may at last bring it to a very weak *analogy*, which is confessedly liable to error and uncertainty. After having experienced the circulation of the blood in human creatures, we make no doubt that it takes place in Titius and Maevius: But from its circulation in frogs and fishes, it is only a presumption, though a strong one, from analogy, that it takes place in men and other animals. The analogical reasoning is much weaker, when we infer the circulation of the sap in vegetables from our experience, that the blood circulates in animals; and those, who hastily followed that inperfect analogy, are found, by more accurate experiments, to have been mistaken.

If we see a house, Cleanthes, we conclude, with the greatest certainty, that it had an architect or builder; because this is precisely that species of effect, which we have experienced to proceed from that species of cause. But surely you will not affirm, that the universe bears such a resemblance to a house, that we can with the same certainty infer a similar cause, or that the analogy is here entire and perfect. The dissimilitude is so striking, that the utmost you can here pretend to is a guess, a conjecture, a presumption concerning a similar cause; and how that pretension will be received in the world, I leave you to consider.

It would surely be very ill received, replied Cleanthes; and I should be deservedly blamed and detested, did I allow, that the proofs of a Deity amounted to no more than a guess or conjecture. But is the whole adjustment of means to ends in a house and in the universe so slight a resemblance? The economy of final causes? The order, proportion, and arrangement of every part? Steps of a stair are plainly contrived, that human legs may use them in mounting; and this inference is certain and infallible. Human legs are also contrived for walking and mounting; and this inference, I allow, is not altogether so certain, because of the dissimilarity which you remark; but does it, therefore, deserve the name only of presumption or conjecture?

Good God! cried Demea, interrupting him, where are we? Zealous defenders of religion allow, that the proofs of a Deity fall short of perfect evidence! And you, Philo, on whose assistance I depended, in proving the adorable mysteriousness of the Divine Nature, do you assent to all these extravagant opinions of Cleanthes? For what other name can I give them? Or why spare my censure, when such principles are advanced, supported by such an authority, before so young a man as Pamphilus?

You seem not to apprehend, replied Philo, that I argue with Cleanthes in his own way; and by showing him the dangerous consequences of his tenets, hope at last to reduce him to our opinion. But what sticks most with you, I observe, is the representation which Cleanthes has made of the argument *a posteriori*; and finding, that that argument is likely to escape your hold and vanish into air, you think it so disguised, that you can scarcely believe it to be set in its true light. Now, however much I may dissent, in other respects, from the dangerous principles of Cleanthes, I must allow, that he has fairly represented that argument; and I shall endeavour so to state the matter to you, that you will entertain no further scruples with regard to it.

Were a man to abstract from every thing which he knows or has seen, he would be altogether incapable, merely from his own ideas, to determine what kind of scene the universe must be, or to give the preference to one state or situation of things above another. For as nothing which he clearly conceives, could be esteemed impossible or implying a contradiction; every chimera of his fancy would be upon an equal footing; nor could he assign any just reason why he adheres to one idea or system, and rejects the others, which are equally possible.

Again; after he opens his eyes, and contemplates the world as it really is, it would be impossible for him, at first to assign the cause of any one event, much less, of the whole of things or of the universe. He might set his fancy a rambling; and she might bring him in an infinite variety of reports and representations. These would all be possible; but being all equally possible, he would never of himself give a satisfactory account for his preferring one of them to the rest. Experience alone can point out to him the true cause of every phenomenon.

Now, according to this method of reasoning, Demea, it follows (and is, indeed, tacitly allowed by Cleanthes himself) that order, arrangement, or the adjustment of final causes is not, of itself, any proof of design; but only so far as it has been experienced to proceed from that principle. For aught we can know *a priori*, matter may contain the source or spring of order originally within itself, as well as mind does; and there is no more difficulty in conceiving, that the several elements, from an internal unknown cause, may fall into the most exquisite arrangement, than to conceive that their ideas, in the great, universal mind, from a like internal, unknown cause, fall into that arrangement. The equal possibility of both these suppositions is allowed. But by experience we find (according to Cleanthes), that there is a difference between them. Throw several pieces of steel together, without shape or form; they will never arrange themselves so as to compose a watch: Stone, and mortar, and wood, without an architect, never erect a house. But the ideas in a human mind, we see, by an unknown, inexplicable economy, arrange themselves so as to form the plan of a watch or house. Experience, therefore, proves, that there is an original principle of order in mind, not in matter. From similar effects we infer similar causes. The adjustment of means to ends is alike in the universe, as in a machine of human contrivance. The causes, therefore, must be resembling.

I was from the beginning scandalised, I must own, with this resemblance, which is asserted, between the Deity and human creatures; and must conceive it to imply such a degradation of the Supreme Being as no sound Theist could endure. With your assistance, therefore, Demea, I shall endeavour to defend what you justly called the adorable mysteriousness of the Divine Nature, and shall refute this reasoning of Cleanthes, provided he allows that I have made a fair representation of it.

When Cleanthes had assented, Philo, after a short pause, proceeded in the following manner.

That all inferences, Cleanthes, concerning fact, are founded on experience, and that all experimental reasonings are founded on the supposition, that similar causes prove similar effects, and similar effects similar causes; I shall not at present much dispute with you. But observe, I entreat you, with what extreme caution all just reasoners proceed in the transferring of experiments to similar cases. Unless the cases be exactly similar, they repose no perfect confidence in applying their past observation to any particular phenomenon. Every alteration of circumstances occasions a doubt concerning the event; and it requires new experiments to prove certainly, that the new circumstances are of no moment or importance. A change in bulk, situation, arrangement, age, disposition of the air, or surrounding bodies; any of these particulars may be attended with the most unexpected consequences: And unless the objects be quite familiar to us, it is the highest temerity to expect with assurance, after any of these changes, an event similar to that which before fell under our observation. The slow and deliberate steps of philosophers, here, if any where, are distinguished from the precipitate march of the vulgar, who, hurried on by the smallest similitude, are incapable of all discernment or consideration.

But can you think, Cleanthes, that your usual phlegm and philosophy have been preserved in so wide a step as you have taken, when you compared to the universe, houses, ships, furniture, machines and from their similarity in some circumstances inferred a similarity in their causes? Thought, design, intelligence, such as we discover in men and other animals, is no more than one of the springs and principles of the universe, as well as heat or cold, attraction or repulsion, and a hundred others, which fall under daily observation. It is an active cause, by which some particular parts of nature, we find, produce alterations on other parts. But can a conclusion, with any propriety, be transferred from parts to the whole? Does not the great disproportion bar all comparison and inference? From observing the growth of a hair, can we learn any thing concerning the generation of a man? Would the manner of a leaf's blowing, even though perfectly known, afford us any instruction concerning the vegetation of a tree?

But allowing that we were to take the *operations* of one part of nature upon another, for the foundation of our judgment concerning the *origin* of the whole, (which never can be admitted), yet why select so minute, so weak, so bounded a principle as the reason and design of animals is found to be upon this planet? What peculiar privilege has this little agitation of the brain which we call *thought,* that we must thus make it the model of the whole universe? Our partiality in our own favour does indeed present it on all occasions; but sound philosophy ought carefully to guard against so natural an illusion.

So far from admitting, continued Philo, that the operations of a part can afford us any just conclusion concerning the origin of the whole, I will not allow any one part to form a rule for another part, if the latter be very remote from the former. Is there any reasonable ground to conclude, that the inhabitants of other planets possess thought, intelligence, reason, or any thing similar to these faculties in men? When nature has so extremely diversified her manner of operation in this small globe; can we imagine, that she incessantly copies herself throughout so immense a universe? And if thought, as we may well suppose, be confined merely to this narrow corner, and has even there so limited a sphere of action, with what propriety can we assign it for the original cause of all things? The narrow views of a peasant, who makes his domestic economy the rule for the government of kingdoms, is in comparison a pardonable sophism.

But were we ever so much assured, that a thought and reason, resembling the human, were to be found throughout the whole universe, and were its activity elsewhere vastly greater and more commanding than it appears in

this globe; yet I cannot see, why the operations of a world, constituted, arranged, adjusted, can with any propriety be extended to a world, which is
in its embryo-state, and is advancing towards that constitution and arrangement. By observation, we know somewhat of the economy, action, and nourishment of a finished animal; but we must transfer with great caution that
observation to the growth of a foetus in the womb, and still more, to the
formation of an animalcule in the loins of its male parent. Nature, we find,
even from our limited experience, possesses an infinite number of springs
and principles, which incessantly discover themselves on every change of
her position and situation. And what new and unknown principles would
actuate her in so new and unknown a situation as that of the formation of
a universe, we cannot, without the utmost temerity, pretend to determine.

A very small part of this great system, during a very short time, is very
imperfectly discovered to us: and do we thence pronounce decisively concerning the origin of the whole?

Admirable conclusion! Stone, wood, brick, iron, brass, have not, at this
time, in this minute globe of earth, an order or arrangement without human
art and contrivance: therefore the universe could not originally attain its
order and arrangement, without something similar to human art. But is a
part of nature a rule for another part very wide of the former? Is it a rule
for the whole? Is a very small part a rule for the universe? Is nature in one
situation, a certain rule for nature in another situation, vastly different from
the former?

And can you blame me, Cleanthes, if I here imitate the prudent reserve
of Simonides, who, according to the noted story, being asked by Hiero,
What God was? desired a day to think of it, and then two days more; and
after that manner continually prolonged the term, without ever bringing
in his definition or description? Could you even blame me, if I had answered
at first *that I did not know*, and was sensible that this subject lay vastly
beyond the reach of my faculties? You might cry out sceptic and rallier as
much as you pleased: but having found, in so many other subjects much
more familiar, the imperfections and even contradictions of human reason,
I never should expect any success from its feeble conjectures in a subject
so sublime, and so remote from the sphere of our observation. When two
species of objects have always been observed to be conjoined together, I
can *infer, by* custom, the existence of one wherever I *see* the existence of
the other: and this I call an argument from experience. But how this argument can have place, where the objects, as in the present case, are single,
individual, without parallel, or specific resemblance, may be difficult to
explain. And will any man tell me with a serious countenance, that an
orderly universe must arise from some thought and art, like the human;

because we have experience of it? To ascertain this reasoning, it were requisite, that we had experience of the origin of worlds; and it is not sufficient, surely, that we have seen ships and cities arise from human art and contrivance.

Philo was proceeding in this vehement manner, somewhat between jest and earnest, as it appeared to me; when he observed some signs of impatience in Cleanthes, and then immediately stopped short. What I had to suggest, said Cleanthes, is only that you would not abuse terms, or make use of popular expressions to subvert philosophical reasonings. You know, that the vulgar often distinguish reason from experience, even where the question relates only to matter of fact and existence; though it is found, where that *reason* is properly analysed, that it is nothing but a species of experience. To prove by experience the origin of the universe from mind, is not more contrary to common speech, than to prove the motion of the earth from the same principle. And a caviller might raise all the same objections to the Copernican system, which you have urged against my reasonings. Have you other earths, might he say, which you have seen to move? Have. . . .

Yes! cried Philo, interrupting him, we have other earths. Is not the moon another earth, which we see to turn round its centre? Is not Venus another earth, where we observe the same phenomenon? Are not the revolutions of the sun also a confirmation, from analogy, of the same theory? All the planets, are they not earths, which revolve about the sun? Are not the satellites moons, which move round Jupiter and Saturn, and along with these primary planets, round the sun? These analogies and resemblances, with others, which I have not mentioned, are the sole proofs of the Copernican system; and to you it belongs to consider, whether you have any analogies of the same kind to support your theory.

In reality, Cleanthes, continued he, the modern system of astronomy is now so much received by all inquirers, and has become so essential a part even of our earliest education, that we are not commonly very scrupulous in examining the reasons upon which it is founded. It is now become a matter of mere curiosity to study the first writers on that subject, who had the full force of prejudice to encounter, and were obliged to turn their arguments on every side in order to render them popular and convincing. But if we peruse Galilaeo's famous Dialogues concerning the system of the world, we shall find, that that great genius, one of the sublimest that ever existed, first bent all his endeavours to prove, that there was no foundation for the distinction commonly made between elementary and celestial substances. The schools, proceeding from the illusions of sense, had carried this distinction very far; and had established the latter substances to be ingenerable, incorruptible, unalterable, impassible; and had assigned all the opposite qualities to the former. But Galilaeo, beginning with the moon, proved its similarity in every particular to the earth; its convex figure, its natural darkness when not illuminated, its density, its distinction into solid and liquid, the variations of its phases, the mutual illuminations of the earth and moon, their mutual eclipses, the inequalities of the lunar surface, etc. After many instances of this kind, with regard to all the planets, men plainly saw, that these bodies became proper objects of experience; and that the similarity of their nature enabled us to extend the same arguments and phenomena from one to the other.

In this cautious proceeding of the astronomers, you may read your own condemnation, Cleanthes; or rather may see, that the subject in which you are engaged exceeds all human reason and inquiry. Can you pretend to show any such similarity between the fabric of a house, and the generation of a universe? Have you ever seen nature in any such situation as resembles the first arrangement of the elements? Have worlds ever been formed under your eye; and have you had leisure to observe the whole progress of the phenomenon, from the first appearance of order to its final consummation? If you have, then cite your experience, and deliver your theory.

IMMANUEL KANT

IMMANUEL KANT (1726-1806) was professor at Koenigsberg, Germany, and one of the great philosophers. His writings stimulated much subsequent discussion of theory of knowledge, metaphysics, ethics and religion. The most significant among his many works are *The Critique of Pure Reason* and *The Critique of Practical Reason*.

Sec. V.—Of the Impossibility of a Cosmological Proof of the Existence of God*

The *cosmological proof*, which we are about to examine, retains the connection between absolute necessity, and the highest reality; but, instead of

* From Immanuel Kant, *Critique of Pure Reason*, trans. J. M. D. Meiklejohn, pp. 338-347. Published, 1943, Willey Book Company. In the public domain. [Footnote omitted, Eds.]

reasoning from this highest reality to a necessary existence, like the preceding argument, it concludes from the given unconditioned necessity of some being its unlimited reality. The track it pursues, whether rational or sophistical, is at least natural, and not only goes far to persuade the common understanding, but shows itself deserving of respect from the speculative intellect; while it contains, at the same time, the outlines of all the arguments employed in natural theology—arguments which always have been, and still will be, in use and authority. These, however adorned, and hid under whatever embellishments of rhetoric and sentiment, are at bottom identical with the arguments we are at present to discuss. This proof, termed by Leibnitz the *argumentum a contingentia mundi*, I shall now lay before the reader, and subject to a strict examination.

It is framed in the following manner:—If something exists, an absolutely necessary being must likewise exist. Now I, at least, exist. Consequently, there exists an absolutely necessary being. The minor contains an experience, the major reasons from a general experience to the existence of a necessary being. Thus this argument really begins at experience, and is not completely *a priori*, or ontological. The object of all possible experience being the world, it is called the *cosmological* proof. It contains no reference to any peculiar property of sensuous objects, by which this world of sense might be distinguished from other possible worlds; and in this respect it differs from the physico-theological proof, which is based upon the consideration of the peculiar constitution of our sensuous world.

The proof proceeds thus:—A necessary being can be determined only in one way, that is, it can be determined by only one of all possible opposed predicates; consequently, it must be *completely* determined in and by its conception. But there is only a single conception of a thing possible, which completely determines the thing *a priori*: that is, the conception of the *ens realissimum*. It follows that the conception of the *ens realissimum* is the only conception, by and in which we can cogitate a necessary being. Consequently, a supreme being necessarily exists.

In this cosmological argument are assembled so many sophistical propositions, that speculative reason seems to have exerted in it all her dialectical skill to produce a transcendental illusion of the most extreme character. We shall postpone an investigation of this argument for the present, and confine ourselves to exposing the stratagem by which it imposes upon us an old argument in a new dress, and appeals to the agreement of two witnesses, the one with the credentials of pure reason, and the other with those of empiricism; while, in fact, it is only the former who has changed his dress and voice, for the purpose of passing himself off for an additional witness. That it may possess a secure foundation, it bases its conclusions upon experience, and thus appears to be completely distinct from the ontological argument, which places its confidence entirely in pure *a priori* conceptions. But this experience merely aids reason in making one step—to the existence of a necessary being. What the properties of this being are, cannot be learned from experience; and therefore reason abandons it altogether, and pursues its inquiries in the sphere of pure conceptions, for the purpose of discovering what the properties of an absolutely necessary being ought to be, that is, what among all possible things contain the conditions *(requisita)* of absolute necessity. Reason believes that it has discovered these requisites in the conception of an *ens realissimum*—and in it alone, and hence concludes: the *ens realissimum* is an absolutely necessary being. But it is evident that reason has here presupposed that the conception of an *ens realissimum* is perfectly adequate to the conception of a being of absolute necessity, that is, that we may infer the existence of the latter from that of the former—a proposition, which formed the basis of the ontological argument, and which is now employed in the support of the cosmological argument, contrary to the wish and professions of its inventors. For the existence of an absolutely necessary being is given in conceptions alone. But if I say—the conception of the *ens realissimum* is a conception of this kind, and in fact the only conception which is adequate to our idea of a necessary being, I am obliged to admit, that the latter may be inferred from the former. Thus it is properly the ontological argument which figures in the cosmological, and constitutes the whole strength of the latter; while the spurious basis of experience has been of no further use than to conduct us to the conception of absolute necessity, being utterly insufficient to demonstrate the presence of this attribute in any determinate existence or thing. For when we propose to ourselves an aim of this character, we must abandon the sphere of experience, and rise to that of pure conceptions, which we examine with the purpose of discovering whether any one contains the conditions of the possibility of an absolutely necessary being. But if the possibility of such a being is thus demonstrated, its existence is also proved; for we may then assert that, of all possible beings there is one which possesses the attribute of necessity—in other words, this being possesses an absolutely necessary existence. . . .

The following fallacies, for example, are discoverable in this mode of proof: 1. The transcendental principle, Everything that is contingent must have a cause—a principle without significance, except in the sensuous world. For the purely intellectual conception of the contingent cannot produce any synthetical proposition, like that of causality, which is itself without significance or distinguishing characteristic except in the phenomenal world. But in the present case it is employed to help us beyond the limits of its sphere. 2. From the impossibility of an infinite ascending series of causes in the world of sense a first cause is inferred;—a conclusion which the principles of the employment of reason do not justify even in the sphere of experience, and still less when an attempt is made to pass the limits of this sphere. 3. Reason allows itself to be satisfied upon insufficient grounds, with regard to the completion of this series. It removes all conditions (without which, however, no conception of Necessity can take place); and, as after this it is beyond our power to form any other conception, it accepts this as a completion of the conception it wishes to form of the series. 4. The logical possibility of a conception of the total of reality (the criterion of this possibility being the absence of contradiction) is confounded with the transcendental, which requires a principle of the practicability of such a synthesis—a principle which again refers us to the world of experience. And so on.

The aim of the cosmological argument is to avoid the necessity of proving the existence of a necessary being *a priori* from mere conceptions—a proof which must be ontological, and of which we feel ourselves quite incapable. With this purpose, we reason from an actual existence—an experience in general, to an absolutely necessary condition of that existence. It is in this case unnecessary to demonstrate its possibility. For after having proved that it exists, the question regarding its possibility is superfluous. Now, when we wish to define more strictly the nature of this necessary being, we do not look out for some being the conception of which would enable us to comprehend the necessity of its being—for if we could do this, an empirical presupposition would be unnecessary; no, we try to discover merely the negative condition *(conditio sine qua non)*, without which a being would not be absolutely necessary. Now this would be perfectly admissible in every sort of reasoning, from a consequence to its principle; but in the present case it unfortunately happens that the condition of absolute necessity can be discovered in but a single being, the conception of which must consequently contain all that is requisite for demonstrating the presence of absolute necessity, and thus entitle me to infer this absolute necessity *a priori*. That is, it must be possible to reason conversely, and say—the thing, to which the conception of the highest reality belongs, is absolutely necessary. But if I cannot reason thus—and I cannot, unless I believe in the sufficiency of the ontological argument—I find insurmountable obstacles in my new path, and am really no further than the point from which I set out. The conception of a Supreme Being satisfies all questions *a priori* regarding the internal determinations of a thing, and is for this reason an ideal without equal or parallel, the general conception of it indicating it has at the same time an *ens individuum* among all possible things. But the conception does not satisfy the question regarding its existence—which was the purpose of all our inquiries; and although the existence of a necessary being were admitted, we should find it impossible to answer the question—What of all things in the world must be regarded as such?

It is certainly allowable to *admit* the existence of an all-sufficient being—a cause of all possible effects, for the purpose of enabling reason to introduce unity into its mode and grounds of explanation with regard to phenomena. But to assert that such a being *necessarily exists*, is no longer the modest enunciation of an admissible hypothesis, but the boldest declaration of an apodictic certainty; for the cognition of that which is absolutely necessary, must itself possess that character.

The aim of the transcendental ideal formed by the mind is, either to discover a conception which shall harmonize with the idea of absolute necessity, or a conception which shall contain that idea. If the one is possible, so is the other; for reason recognizes that alone as absolutely necessary, which is necessary from its conception. But both attempts are equally beyond our power—we find it impossible to *satisfy* the understanding upon this point, and as impossible to induce it to remain at rest in relation to this incapacity.

Unconditioned necessity, which, as the ultimate support and stay of all existing things, is an indispensable requirement of the mind, is an abyss on the verge of which human reason trembles in dismay. Even the idea of eternity, terrible and sublime as it is, as depicted by Haller, does not produce upon the mental vision such a feeling of awe and terror; for, although it *measures* the duration of things, it does not *support* them. We cannot bear, nor can we rid ourselves of the thought, that a being, which we regard as the greatest of all possible existences should *say to himself*: I am from eternity to eternity; beside me there is nothing except that which exists by my will; *but whence then am I?* Here all sinks away from under us; and the greatest, as the smallest, perfection, hovers without stay or footing in presence of the speculative reason, which finds it as easy to part with the one as with the other.

Many physical powers, which evidence their existence by their effects, are perfectly inscrutable in their nature; they elude all our powers of observation. The transcendental object which forms the basis of phenomena, and, in connection with it, the reason why our sensibility possesses this rather than that particular kind of conditions, are and must ever remain hidden from our mental vision; the fact is there, the reason of the fact we cannot see. But an ideal of pure reason cannot be termed mysterious or *inscrutable*, because the only credential of its reality is the need of it felt by reason, for the purpose of giving completeness to the world of synthetical unity. An ideal is not even given as a cogitable *object*, and therefore cannot be inscrutable; on the contrary, it must, as a mere idea, be based on the constitution of reason itself, and on this account must be capable of explanation and solution. For the very essence of reason consists in its ability to give an account of all our conceptions, opinions, and assertions—upon objective, or, when they happen to be illusory and fallacious, upon subjective grounds.

Detection and Explanation of the Dialectical Illusion in All Transcendental Arguments for the Existence of a Necessary Being

Both of the above arguments are transcendental; in other words, they do not proceed from empirical principles. For, although the cosmological argument professed to lay a basis of experience for its edifice of reasoning, it did not ground its procedure upon the peculiar constitution of experience, but upon pure principles of reason—in relation to an existence given by empirical consciousness; utterly abandoning its guidance, however, for the purpose of supporting its assertions entirely upon pure conceptions. Now what is the cause, in these transcendental arguments, of the dialectical, but natural, illusion, which connects the conceptions of necessity and supreme reality, and hypostatizes that which cannot be anything but an idea? What is the cause of this unavoidable step on the part of reason, of admitting that some-one among all existing things must be necessary, while it falls back from the assertion of the existence of such a being as from an abyss? And how does reason proceed to explain this anomaly to itself, and from the wavering condition of a timid and reluctant approbation—always again withdrawn, arrive at a calm and settled insight into its cause?

It is something very remarkable that, on the supposition that something exists, I cannot avoid the inference, that something exists necessarily. Upon this perfectly natural—but not on that account reliable—inference does the cosmological argument rest. But, let me form any conception whatever of a thing, I find that I cannot cogitate the existence of the thing as absolutely necessary, and that nothing prevents me—be the thing or being what it may—from cogitating its non-existence. I may thus be obliged to admit that all existing things have a necessary basis, while I cannot cogitate any single or individual thing as necessary. In other words, I can never *complete* the regress through the conditions of existence, without admitting the existence of a necessary being; but, on the other hand, I cannot make a *commencement* from this beginning.

It follows from this, that you must accept the absolutely necessary as *out of* and beyond the world, inasmuch as it is useful only as a principle of the highest possible unity in experience, and you cannot discover any such necessary existence in the *world*, the second rule requiring you to regard all empirical causes of unity as themselves deduced.

These remarks will have made it evident to the reader that the ideal of the Supreme Being, far from being an enouncement of the existence of a being in itself necessary, is nothing more than a *regulative principle* of reason, requiring us to regard all connection existing between phenomena as if it has its origin from an all-sufficient necessary cause, and basing upon this the rule of a systematic and necessary unity in the explanation of phenomena. We cannot, at the same time, avoid regarding, by a transcendental *subreptio*, this formal principle as constitutive, and hypostatizing this unity. Precisely similar is the case with our notion of space. Space is the primal condition of all forms, which are properly just so many different limitations of it; and thus, although it is merely a principle of sensibility, we cannot help regarding it as an absolutely necessary and self-subsistent thing—as an object given *a priori* in itself. In the same way, it is quite natural that, as the systematic unity of nature cannot be established as a principle for the empirical employment of reason, unless it is based upon the idea of an *ens realissimum*, as the supreme cause, we should regard this idea as a real object, and this object, in its character of supreme condition, as absolutely necessary, and that in this way a *regulative* should be transformed into a *constitutive* principle. This interchange becomes evident when I regard this supreme being, which, relatively to the world, was absolutely (unconditionally) necessary, as a thing *per se*. In this case, I find it impossible to represent this necessity in or by any conception, and it exists merely in my own mind, as the formal condition of thought, but not as a material and hypostatic condition of existence.

MAIMONIDES

MOSES MAIMONIDES (1135-1204), Medieval
Jewish physician and philosopher, influenced
both Muslim and Christian philosophers and
theologians. In his book, *The Guide of the
Perplexed*, he attempted to combine Biblical
and Aristotelian thought.

The Essence of God and His Attributes Are Identical*

On attributes; remarks more recondite than the preceding. It is known that existence is an accident appertaining to all things, and therefore an element superadded to their essence. This must evidently be the case as regards everything the existence of which is due to some cause; its existence is an element superadded to its essence. But as regards a being whose existence is not due to any cause—God alone is that being, for His existence, as we have said, is absolute—existence and essence are perfectly identical; He is not a substance to which existence is joined as an accident, as an additional element. His existence is always absolute, and has never been a new element or an accident in Him. Consequently God exists without possessing the attribute of existence. Similarly He lives, without possessing the attribute of life; knows, without possessing the attribute of knowledge; is omnipotent without possessing the attribute of omnipotence; is wise, without possessing the attribute of wisdom; all this reduces itself to one and the same entity; there is no plurality in Him, as will be shown. It is further necessary to consider that unity and plurality are accidents supervening to an object according as it consists of many elements or of one. This is fully explained in the book called Metaphysics. In the same way as number is not the substance of the things numbered, so is unity not the substance of the thing which has the attribute of unity, for unity and plurality are accidents belonging to the category of discrete quantity, and supervening to such objects as are capable of receiving them.

To that being, however, which has truly simple, absolute existence, and in which composition is inconceivable, the accident of unity is as inadmissible as the accident of plurality; that is to say, God's unity is not an element superadded, but He is One without possessing the attribute of unity. The investigation of this subject, which is almost too subtle for our understand-

---

* From Moses Maimonides, *The Guide of the Perplexed*, trans. M. Friedländer, Part I, chapters 57-59, pp. 207-220. Published, 1928, George Routledge & Sons, Ltd. In the public domain. [Footnotes omitted, Eds.]

ing, must not be based on current expressions employed in describing it, for these are the great source of error. It would be extremely difficult for us to find, in any language whatsoever, words adequate to this subject, and we can only employ inadequate language. In our endeavour to show that God does not include a plurality, we can only say "He is one," although "one" and "many" are both terms which serve to distinguish quantity. We therefore make the subject clearer, and show to the understanding the way of truth by saying He is one but does not possess the attribute of unity.

The same is the case when we say God is the First . . . , to express that He has not been created; the term . . . , "First," is decidedly inaccurate, for it can in its true sense only be applied to a being that is subject to the relation of time; the latter, however, is an accident to motion which again is connected with a body. Besides the attribute . . . ("first" or "eternal") is a relative term, being in regard to time the same as the terms "long" and "short" are in regard to a line. Both expressions, "created" and "eternal" (or "first"), are equally inadmissible in reference to any being to which the attribute of time is not applicable, just as we do not say "crooked" or "straight" in reference to taste, "salted" or "insipid" in reference to the voice. These subjects are not unknown to those who have accustomed themselves to seek a true understanding of the things, and to establish their properties in accordance with the abstract notions which the mind has formed of them, and who are not misled by the inaccuracy of the words employed. All attributes, such as "the First," "the Last," occurring in the Scriptures in reference to God, are as metaphorical as the expressions "ear" and "eye." They simply signify that God is not subject to any change or innovation whatever; they do not imply that God can be described by time, or that there is any comparison between Him and any other being as regards time, and that He is called on that account "the first" and "the last." In short, all similar expressions are borrowed from the language commonly used among the people. In the same way we use "One" . . . , in reference to God, to express that there is nothing similar to Him, but we do not mean to say that an attribute of unity is added to His essence.

Chapter LVIII

The True Attributes of God Have a Negative Sense

This chapter is even more recondite than the preceding. Know that the negative attributes of God are the true attributes: they do not include any incorrect notions or any deficiency whatever in reference to God, while positive attributes imply polytheism, and are inadequate, as we have already shown. It is now necessary to explain how negative expressions can in a certain sense be employed as attributes, and how they are distinguished from positive attributes. Then I shall show that we cannot describe the Creator by any means except by negative attributes. An attribute does not exclusively belong to the one object to which it is related; while qualifying one thing, it can also be employed to qualify other things, and is in that case not peculiar to that one thing. E.g., if you see an object from a distance, and on enquiring what it is, are told that it is a living being, you have certainly learnt an attribute of the object seen, and although that attribute does not exclusively belong to the object perceived, it expresses that the object is not a plant or a mineral. Again, if a man is in a certain house, and you know that something is in the house, but not exactly what, you ask what is in that house, and are told, not a plant nor a mineral. You have thereby obtained some special knowledge of the thing; you have learnt that it is a living being, although you do not yet know what kind of living being it is. The negative attributes have this in common with the positive, that they necessarily circumscribe the object to some extent, although such circumscription consists only in the exclusion of what otherwise would not be excluded. In the following point, however, the negative attributes are distinguished from the positive. The positive attributes, although not peculiar to one thing, describe a portion of what we desire to know, either some part of its essence or some of its accidents; the negative attributes, on the other hand, do not, as regards the essence of the thing which we desire to know, in any way tell us what it is, except it be indirectly, as has been shown in the instance given by us.

After this introduction, I would observe that,—as has already been shown —God's existence is absolute, that it includes no composition, as will be proved, and that we comprehend only the fact that He exists, not His essence. Consequently it is a false assumption to hold that He has any positive attribute; for He does not possess existence in addition to His essence; it therefore cannot be said that the one may be described as an attribute [of the other]; much less has He [in addition to His existence] a compound essence, consisting of two constituent elements to which the attribute could refer; still less has He accidents, which could be described by an attribute. Hence it is clear that He has no positive attribute whatever. The negative attributes, however, are those which are necessary to direct the mind to the truths which we must believe concerning God; for, on the one hand, they do not imply any plurality, and, on the other, they convey to man the highest possible knowledge of God; e.g., it has been established by proof that some being must exist besides those things which can be perceived by the senses, or apprehended by the mind; when we say of this being, that it exists, we mean that its non-existence is impossible. We then perceive that such a being is not, for instance, like the four elements, which are inanimate, and we therefore say it is living, expressing thereby that it is not dead. We call such a being incorporeal, because we notice that it is unlike the heavens, which are living, but material. Seeing that it is also different from the intellect, which, though incorporeal and living, owes its existence to some cause, we say it is the first . . . , expressing thereby that its existence is not due to any cause. We further notice, that the existence, that is, the essence, of this being is not limited to its own existence, many existences emanate from it, and its influence is not like that of the fire in producing heat, or that of the sun in sending forth light, but consists in constantly giving them stability and order by well-established rule, as we shall show: we say, on that account, it has power, wisdom, and will, i.e., it is not feeble or ignorant, or hasty, and does not abandon its creatures; when we say that it is not feeble, we mean that its existence is capable of produc-ing the existence of many other things; by saying it is not ignorant, we mean "it perceives" or "it lives,"—for everything that perceives is alive—by saying "it is not hasty, and does not abandon its creatures," we mean that all these creatures preserve a certain order and arrangement; they are not left to themselves; or produced aimlessly, but whatever condition they re-ceive from that being is given them with design and intention. We thus learn that there is no other being like unto God, and we say that He is One, i.e., there are not more Gods than one.

It has thus been shown that every attribute predicated of God either de-notes the quality of an action, or—when the attribute is intended to convey some idea of the Divine Being itself, and not of His actions—the negation of the opposite. Even these negative attributes must not be formed and applied to God, except in the way in which, as you know, sometimes an attribute is negatived in reference to a thing, although that attribute can naturally never be applied to it in the same sense, as, e.g., we say, "This wall does not see." Those who read the present work, are aware that, not-withstanding all the efforts of the mind, we can obtain no knowledge of the essence of the heavens—a revolving substance which has been measured by us in spans and cubits, and examined even as regards the proportions of the several spheres to each other and respecting most of their motions—although we know that they must consist of matter and form; but the matter not being the same as sublunary matter, we can only describe the heavens in terms expressing negative properties, but not in terms denoting positive qualities. Thus we say that the heavens are not light, not heavy, not passive and therefore not subject to impressions, and that they do not possess the sensations of taste or smell; or we use similar negative attributes. All this we do, because we do not know their substance. What, then, can be the result of our efforts, when we try to obtain a knowledge of a Being that is free from substance, that is most simple, whose existence is absolute, and not due to any cause, to whose perfect essence nothing can be superadded, and whose perfection consists, as we have shown, in the absence of all defects. All we understand is the fact that He exists, that He is a Being to whom none of all His creatures is similar, who has nothing in common with them, who does not include plurality, who is never too feeble to produce other beings, and whose relation to the universe is that of a steersman to a boat; and even this is not a real relation, a real simile, but serves only to convey to us the idea that God rules the universe; that is, that He gives it duration, and preserves its necessary arrangement. This subject will be treated more fully. Praised be He! In the contemplation of His essence, our comprehension and knowledge prove insufficient; in the examination of His works, how they necessarily result from His will, our knowledge proves to be ignorance, and in the endeavour to extol Him in words, all our efforts in speech are mere weakness and failure!

W. R. SORLEY

WILLIAM SORLEY (1855-1935) was Knight-bridge Professor of Moral Philosophy at Cambridge University from 1900-1933. He sought to ground theism on Moral values. The book from which the selection printed here is taken is his best known work.

The Moral Argument*

The result so far is that the events of the world as a causal system are not inconsistent with the view that this same world is a moral order, that its purpose is a moral purpose. The empirical discrepancies between the two orders, and the obstacles which the world puts in the way of morality, are capable of explanation when we allow that ideals of goodness have not only to be discovered by finite minds, but that for their realisation they need to be freely accepted by individual wills and gradually organized in individual characters. If this principle still leaves many particular difficulties unre-

* From W. R. Sorley, Moral Values and the Idea of God, 3rd edition, pp. 346-352. Copyright, 1919, by Cambridge University Press. Used by permission of Kenneth W. Sorley and Mrs. Geoffrey Bicker-Steth.

solved, it may at least be claimed that it provides the general plan of an explanation of the relation of moral value to experience, and that a larger knowledge of the issues of life than is open to us might be expected to show that the particular difficulties also are not incapable of solution.

This means that it is possible to regard God as the author and ruler of the world, as it appears in space and time, and at the same time to hold that the moral values of which we are conscious and the moral ideal which we come to apprehend with increasing clearness express his nature. But the question remains, Are we to regard morality—its values, laws, and ideal— as belonging to a Supreme Mind, that is, to God? It is as an answer to this question that the specific Moral Argument enters. And here I cannot do better than give the argument in the words of Dr. Rashdall:

"An absolute Moral Law or moral ideal cannot exist *in* material things. And it does not exist in the mind of this or that individual. Only if we believe in the existence of a Mind for which the true moral ideal is already in some sense real, a Mind which is the source of whatever is true in our own moral judgments, can we rationally think of the moral ideal as no less real than the world itself. Only so can we believe in an absolute standard of right and wrong, which is as independent of this or that man's actual ideas and actual desires as the facts of material nature. The belief in God, though not (like the belief in a real and active self) a postulate of there being any such thing as Morality at all, is the logical presupposition of an 'objective' or absolute Morality. A moral ideal can exist nowhere and nohow but in a mind; an absolute moral ideal can exist only in a Mind from which all Reality is derived.[1] Our moral ideal can only claim objective validity in so far as it can rationally be regarded as the revelation of a moral ideal eternally existing in the mind of God." [2]

The argument as thus put may be looked upon as a special and striking extension of the cosmological argument. In its first and most elementary form the cosmological argument seeks a cause for the bare existence of the world and man; to account for them there must be something able to bring them into being: God is the First Cause. Then the order of nature impresses us by its regularity, and we come by degrees to understand the principles of its working and the laws under which the material whole maintains its equilibrium and the ordered procession of its changes: these laws and this order call for explanation, and we conceive God as the Great Lawgiver. But beyond this material world, we understand relations and principles of a still more general kind; and the intellect of man recognizes abstract truths so evident that, once understood, they cannot be questioned, while inferences

[1] "Or at least a mind by which all Reality is controlled."—Dr. Rashdall's footnote.
[2] H. Rashdall, *The Theory of Good and Evil* (1907) Vol. II, p. 212.

are drawn from these which only the more expert minds can appreciate and yet which they recognize as eternally valid. To what order do these belong and what was their home when man as yet was unconscious of them? Surely if their validity is eternal they must have had existence somewhere, and we can only suppose them to have existed in the one eternal mind: God is therefore the God of Truth. Further, persons are conscious of values and of an ideal of goodness, which they recognize as having undoubted authority for the direction of their activity; the validity of these values or laws and of this ideal, however, does not depend upon their recognition: it is objective and eternal; and how could this eternal validity stand alone, not embodied in matter and neither seen nor realised by finite minds, unless there were an eternal mind whose thought and will were therein expressed? God must therefore exist and his nature be goodness.

The argument in this its latest phase has a new feature which distinguishes it from the preceding phases. The laws or relations of interacting phenomena which we discover in nature are already embodied in the processes of nature. It may be argued that they have their reality therein: that in cognising them we are simply cognising an aspect of the actual world in space and time, and consequently that, if the mere existence of things does not require God to account for it (on the ground urged by Hume that the world, being a singular event, justifies no inference as to its cause), then, equally, we are not justified in seeking a cause for those laws or relations which are, after all, but one aspect of the existing world. It may be urged that the same holds of mathematical relations: that they are merely an abstract of the actual order, when considered solely in its formal aspect. It is more difficult to treat the still more general logical relations in the same fashion; but they too receive verification in reality and in our thought so far as it does not end in confusion. But it is different with ethical values. Their validity could not be verified in external phenomena; they cannot be established by observation of the course of nature. They hold good for persons only: and their peculiarity consists in the fact that their validity is not in any way dependent upon their being manifested in the character or conduct of persons, or even on their being recognised in the thoughts of persons. We acknowledge the good and its objective claim upon us even when we are conscious that our will has not yielded to the claim; and we admit that its validity existed before we recognised it.

This leading characteristic makes the theistic argument founded upon moral values or the moral law both stronger in one respect and weaker in another respect than the corresponding argument from natural law and intelligible relations. It is weaker because it is easier to deny the premiss from which it starts—that is, the objective validity of moral law—than it is to deny the objective validity of natural or mathematical or logical relations. But I am here assuming the objective validity of morality as already established by our previous enquiries; and it is unnecessary to go back upon the question. And, granted this premiss, the argument adds an important point. Other relations and laws (it may be said, and the statement is true of laws of nature at any rate) are embodied in actually existing objects. But the same cannot be said of the moral law or moral idea. We acknowledge that there are objective values, although men may not recognise them, that the moral law is not abrogated by being ignored, and that our consciousness is striving towards the apprehension of an ideal which no finite mind has clearly grasped, but which is none the less valid although it is not realised and is not even apprehended by us in its truth and fullness. Where then is this ideal? It cannot be valid at one time and not at another. It must be eternal as well as objective. As Dr. Rashdall urges, it is not in material things, and it is not in the mind of this or that individual; but "it can exist nowhere and nohow but in a mind"; it requires therefore the mind of God.

Against this argument, however, it may be contended that it disregards the distinction between validity and existence. Why is it assumed that the moral ideal must exist somehow and somewhere? Validity, it may be said, is a unique concept, as unique as existence, and different from it. And this is true. At the same time it is also true that the validity of the moral ideal, like all validity, is a validity for existents. Without this reference to existence there seems no meaning in asserting validity. At any rate it is clear that it is for existents—namely, for the realm of persons—that the moral idea is valid. It is also true that the perfect moral ideal does not exist in the volitional, or even in the intellectual, consciousness of these persons: they have not achieved agreement with it in their lives, and even their understanding of it is incomplete. Seeing then that it is not manifested by finite existents, how are we to conceive its validity? Other truths are displayed in the order of the existing world; but it is not so with moral values. And yet the system of moral values has been acknowledged to be an aspect of the real universe to which existing things belong. How are we to conceive its relation to them? A particular instance of goodness can exist only in the character of an individual person or group of persons; an idea of goodness such as we have is found only in minds such as ours. But the ideal of goodness does not exist in finite minds or in their material environment. What then is its status in the system of reality?

The question is answered if we regard the moral order as the order of a Supreme Mind and the ideal of goodness as belonging to this Mind. The

difficulty for this view is to show that the Mind which is the home of goodness may also be regarded as the ground of the existing world. That reality
as a whole, both in its actual events and in its moral order, can be consistently regarded as the expression of a Supreme Mind is the result of the
present argument.

WILLIAM
TEMPLE

WILLIAM TEMPLE (1881-1944), the Archbishop of Canterbury, was the best known
Anglican theologian of the first half of the
twentieth century. He was also a prominent
leader in the ecumenical movement in the
Christian Churches and was keenly interested
in the application of Christian doctrine to
contemporary social problems.

The Proof from the Existence of Mind*

We have directed our attention to the Process which constitutes the world
of Nature. We have seen that, in the course of that Process, Mind appears—
first in rudimentary form, later in fuller development. In this fuller development we see Mind, though occurring within the Process and conditioned by
it, yet capable in steadily increasing measure of selecting the direction of its
own attention, and thereby determining the action which it initiates, even in
the physical sphere. We cannot avoid asking for some explanation of this
Process itself; and when we do so, three points immediately challenge our
attention.

(1) If it is indeed true, as we have found compelling reason to believe,
that Mind thus initiates activity—which includes physical movements—in
the physical sphere, then the physical universe is not a closed system governed only by its own laws. If the tides of the sea retard the rotation of the
earth, then so does every motion on the earth's surface that is caused by the
minds of men, whether that of their own bodies or that of other bodies set
in motion by these. The amount of difference that pygmies like us can make
to astronomical movement is, no doubt, so small as to be negligible by
astronomical science. But the principle stands. The dogma of the closed sys-

* From William Temple, *Nature, Man and God*, pp. 255-257. Copyright, 1934, Macmillan & Co., Ltd. Reprinted with permission of Mrs. Temple, St. Martin's Press, Inc.,
and Macmillan & Co., Ltd. [Footnotes omitted, Eds.]

tem of the physical world must be abandoned if the freedom of Mind is admitted.

(2) Any account of the Process as a whole—of Nature as known to us—must account also for the occurrence of Mind as an element within it. Its explanatory principle must contain the ground of freedom as against naturalistic determinism. It must be of such a character that the occurrence of free minds within the Process is recognisably congruous with that character.

(3) The ground of the universe, by reference to which the universe is explicable or intelligible, must be such that it requires no further explanation of itself. But all ways of accounting for facts or occurrences in terms of physical laws call for further explanation—and that in two ways: they explain what is by reference to what was; but this in turn calls for explanation by reference to what was before that; and the physical law itself is not self-explanatory. Why is it so, and not otherwise?

Now Mind, determined by Good as apprehended, is such a principle of explanation as is required. When Aristotle in Book Lambda of the *Metaphysics* desiderated a first principle of motion, an initiation of Process, he found it in the analogy of an object of desire. The First Mover . . . sets other things in motion, as an object of desire does; without motion on its own part, it sets in motion the bodies of those who desire it. Perhaps Aristotle had in his mind no thought beyond the observation that objects of desire do thus initiate motion while unmoved themselves, so that the notion of an unmoved mover is nothing wholly extravagant. But in fact he indicated a possible explanation of the world-process. When Mind, determined by Good as apprehended, initiates activity, no further explanation is needed. The enquiring mind, confronted with an example of what it perfectly understands as the essential characteristic of its own being, is completely satisfied. Whenever the subject of enquiry is traced to the action of intelligently purposive mind, the enquiry is closed; Mind has recognised itself and is satisfied.

To adopt the hypothesis that the process of nature in all its ranges is to be accounted for by the intelligent purpose of Mind is Theism. This hypothesis, and this alone of any ever suggested, accounts for all the three considerations that were said to arise on a review of the Process as a whole. If the Process is grounded in Mind it is in no way surprising that minds should appear as episodes in the Process, and there is no reason to suppose that the physical universe is a closed system.

CHARLES SANDERS PEIRCE

CHARLES SANDERS PEIRCE (1839-1914), American philosopher, provided a foundation for pragmatism and influenced the development of symbolic logic. He was a major figure in building an indigenous American philosophic tradition.

*Knowledge of God**

492. [We] can know nothing except what we *directly* experience. So all that we can anyway know relates to experience. All the creations of our mind are but patchworks from experience. So that all our ideas are but ideas of real or transposed experiences. A word can mean nothing except the idea it calls up. So that we cannot even *talk* about anything but a knowable object. The unknowable about which Hamilton and the agnostics talk can be nothing but an Unknowable Knowable. The absolutely unknowable is a non-existent existence. The Unknowable is a nominalistic heresy. The nominalists in giving their adherence to that doctrine which is really held by all philosophers of all stripes, namely, that experience is all we know, understand experience in their nominalistic sense as the mere first impressions of sense. These "first impressions of sense" are hypothetical creations of nominalistic metaphysics: I for one deny their existence. But anyway even if they exist, it is not in them that experience consists. By experience must be understood the entire mental product. Some psychologists whom I hold in respect will stop me here to say that, while they admit that experience is more than mere sensation, they cannot extend it to the whole mental product, since that would include hallucinations, delusions, superstitious imaginations and fallacies of all kinds; and that they would limit experience to sense-perceptions. But I reply that my statement is the logical one. Hallucinations, delusions, superstitious imaginations, and fallacies of all kinds are experiences, but experiences misunderstood; while to say that all our knowledge relates merely to sense perception is to say that we can know nothing—not even mistakenly —about higher matters, as honor, aspirations, and love.

493. Where would such an idea, say as that of God, come from, if not

* From Charles Sanders Peirce, *Collected Papers of Charles Sanders Peirce*, ed. Charles Hartshorne and Paul Weiss, Vol. VI, paragraphs 492-503, pp. 338-347. Copyright 1934, 1935, by the President and Fellows of Harvard College. Used by permission of The Belknap Press of Harvard University Press. [Footnotes omitted, Eds.]

from direct experience? Would you make it a result of some kind of reasoning, good or bad? Why, reasoning can supply the mind with nothing in the world except an estimate of the value of a statistical ratio, that is, how often certain kinds of things are found in certain combinations in the ordinary course of experience. And scepticism, in the sense of doubt of the validity of elementary ideas—which is really a proposal to turn an idea out of court and permit no inquiry into its applicability—is doubly condemned by the fundamental principle of scientific method—condemned first as obstructing inquiry, and condemned second because it is treating some other than a statistical ratio as a thing to be argued about. No: as to God, open your eyes—and your heart, which is also a perceptive organ—and you see him. But you may ask, Don't you admit there are any delusions? Yes: I may think a thing is black, and on close examination it may turn out to be bottle-green. But I cannot think a thing is black if there is no such thing to be seen as black. Neither can I think that a certain action is self-sacrificing, if no such thing as self-sacrifice exists, although it may be very rare. It is the nominalists, and the nominalists alone, who indulge in such scepticism, which the scientific method utterly condemns.

The Reality of God

494. The questions can be answered without very long explanations. "Do you believe in the existence of a Supreme Being?" Hume, in his *Dialogues Concerning Natural Religion*, justly points out that the phrase "Supreme Being" is not an equivalent of "God," since it neither implies infinity nor any of the other attributes of God, excepting only Being and Supremacy. This is important; and another distinction between the two designations is still more so. Namely, "God" is a vernacular word and, like all such words, but more than almost any, is *vague*. No words are so well understood as vernacular words, in one way; yet they are invariably vague; and of many of them it is true that, let the logician do his best to substitute precise equivalents in their places, still the vernacular words alone, for all their vagueness, answer the principal purposes. This is emphatically the case with the very vague word "God," which is not made less vague by saying that it imports "infinity," etc., since those attributes are at least as vague. I shall, therefore, if you please, substitute "God," for "Supreme Being" in the question.

495. I will also take the liberty of substituting "reality" for "existence." This is perhaps overscrupulosity; but I myself always use *exist* in its strict philosophical sense of "react with the other like things in the environment."

Of course, in that sense, it would be fetichism to say that God "exists." The word "reality," on the contrary, is used in ordinary parlance in its correct philosophical sense. It is curious that its legal meaning, in which we speak of "real estate," is the earliest, occurring early in the twelfth century. Albertus Magnus, who, as a high ecclesiastic, must have had to do with such matters, imported it into philosophy. But it did not become at all common until Duns Scotus, in the latter part of the thirteenth century began to use it freely. I define the *real* as that which holds its characters on such a tenure that it makes not the slightest difference what any man or men may have *thought* them to be, or ever will have *thought* them to be, here using thought to include, imagining, opining, and willing (as long as forcible *means* are not used); but the real thing's characters will remain absolutely untouched.

496. Of any kind of figment, this is not true. So, then, the question being whether I believe in the reality of God, I answer, Yes. I further opine that pretty nearly everybody more or less believes this, including many of the scientific men of my generation who are accustomed to think the belief is entirely unfounded. The reason they fall into this extraordinary error about their own belief is that they precide (or render precise) the conception, and, in doing so, inevitably change it; and such precise conception is easily shown not to be warranted, even if it cannot be quite refuted. Every concept that is vague is liable to be self-contradictory in those respects in which it is vague. No concept, not even those of mathematics, is absolutely precise; and some of the most important for everyday use are extremely vague. Nevertheless, our instinctive beliefs involving such concepts are far more trustworthy than the best established results of science, if these be precisely understood. For instance, we all think that there is an element of order in the universe. Could any laboratory experiments render that proposition more certain than instinct or common sense leaves it? It is ridiculous to broach such a question. But when anybody undertakes to say *precisely* what that order consists in, he will quickly find he outruns all logical warrant. Men who are given to defining too much inevitably run themselves into confusion in dealing with the vague concepts of common sense.

497. They generally make the matter worse by erroneous, not to say absurd, notions of the function of reasoning. Every race of animals is provided with instincts well adapted to its needs, and especially to strengthening the stock. It is wonderful how unerring these instincts are. Man is no exception in this respect; but man is so continually getting himself into novel situations that he needs, and is supplied with, a subsidiary faculty of *reasoning* for bringing instinct to bear upon situations to which it does not directly apply. This faculty is a very imperfect one in respect to fallibility; but then it is only needed to bridge short gaps. Every step has to be reviewed and criticized;

and indeed this is so essential that it is best to call an uncriticized step of inference by another name. If one does not at all know how one's belief comes about, it cannot be called even by the name of inference. If, with St. Augustine, we draw the inference "I think; therefore, I am," but, when asked how we justify this inference, can only say that we are *compelled to think* that, since we think, we are, this uncriticized inference ought not to be called reasoning, which at the very least conceives its inference to be one of a general class of possible inferences on the same model, and all equally valid. But one must go back and criticize the premisses and the *principles* that guide the drawing of the conclusions. If it could be made out that all the ultimate (or first) premisses were percepts; and that all the ultimate logical principles were as clear as the principle of contradiction, then one might say that one's conclusion was *perfectly* rational. Strictly speaking, it would not be quite so, because it is quite possible for perception itself to deceive us, and it is much more possible for us to be mistaken about the indubitableness of logical principles. But as a matter of fact, as far as logicians have hitherto been able to push their analyses, we have *in no single case*, concerning a matter of *fact*, as distinguished from a matter of mathematical conditional possibility, been able to reach this point. We are in every case either forced by the inexorable critic, sooner or later, to declare, "such and such a proposition or mode of inference I *cannot doubt*; it seems perfectly clear that it is so, but I can't say *why*," or else the critic himself tires before the criticism has been pushed to its very end.

498. If you absolutely cannot doubt a proposition—cannot bring yourself, upon deliberation, to entertain the least suspicion of the truth of it, it is plain that there is no room to desire anything more. Many and many a philosopher seems to think that taking a piece of paper and writing down "I doubt that" is doubting it, or that it is a thing he can do in a minute as soon as he decides what he wants to doubt. Descartes convinced himself that the safest way was to "begin" by doubting everything, and accordingly he tells us he straightway did so, except only his *je pense*, which he borrowed from St. Augustine. Well I guess not; for genuine doubt does not talk of *beginning* with doubting. The pragmatist knows that doubt is an art which has to be acquired with difficulty; and his genuine doubts will go much further than those of any Cartesian. What he does not doubt, about ordinary matters of everybody's life, he is apt to find that no well matured man doubts. They are part of our instincts. Insincts are now known not to be nearly so unchangeable as used to be supposed; and the present "mutation"— theory, which I have *always* insisted must be the way in which species have arisen, is, I am confident, the first beginning of the correct theory, and shows that it is no disproof of the instinctive character of a belief that it relates to

concepts which the primitive man cannot be supposed to have had. Now, this is no confirmation of what one does not doubt. For what one does not doubt cannot be rendered more satisfactory than it already is. Yet while I may entertain, as far as I can search in my mind, no perceptible doubt whatever of any one of a hundred propositions, I may suspect that, among so many, some one that is not true may have slipped in; and, if so, the marvellous inerrancy of instinct may perhaps add a little to my *general* confidence in the whole lot. However, I am far from insisting upon the point. I think the consideration is better adapted to helping us to detect the counterfeit paper doubts, of which so many are in circulation.

499. All the instinctive beliefs, I notice, are vague. The moment they are precided, the pragmatist will begin to doubt them.

500. The fourth part of the first book of Hume's *Treatise of Human Nature* affords a strong argument for the correctness of my view that reason is a mere succedaneum to be used where instinct is wanting, by exhibiting the intensely ridiculous way in which a man winds himself up in silly paper doubts if he undertakes to throw common sense, i.e. instinct, overboard and be perfectly rational. Bradley's *Appearance and Reality* is another example of the same thing, although Bradley is at the opposite pole from Hume in what he *does* admit. But Bradley is in no way as good a case as Hume. Hume endeavours to modify his conclusion by not stating it in the extreme length to which it ought to carry him. But a careful reader will see that if he proves anything at all by all his reasoning, it is that reasoning, as such, is *ipso facto* and essentially illogical, "illegitimate," and unreasonable. And the reason it is so is that either it is bad reasoning, or rests on doubtful premises, or else that those premises have not been thoroughly criticized. Of course not. The moment you come to a proposition which is perfectly satisfactory, so that you can entertain not the smallest suspicion of it, this fact debars you from making any genuine criticism of it. So that what Hume's argument would lead him to is that reasoning is "illegitimate" because its premises are perfectly satisfactory. He candidly confesses that they are satisfactory to himself. But he seems to be dissatisfied with himself for being satisfied. It is easy to see, however, that he pats himself on the back, and is very well satisfied with himself for being so dissatisfied with being satisfied. Bradley's position is equally ridiculous. Another circumstance which goes toward confirming my view that instinct is the great internal source of all wisdom and of all knowledge is that all the "triumphs of science," of which that poor old nineteenth century used to be so vain, have been confined to two directions. They either consist in physical—that is, ultimately, dynamical—explanations of phenomena, or else in explaining things on the basis of our common sense knowledge of human nature. Now dynamics is nothing but an elaboration of

common sense; its experiments are mere imaginary experiments. So it all comes down to common sense in these two branches, of which the one is founded on those instincts about physical forces that are required for the feeding impulsion and the other upon those instincts about our fellows that are required for the satisfaction of the reproductive impulse. Thus, then all science is nothing but an outgrowth from these two instincts.

You will see that all I have been saying is not preparatory to any argument for the reality of God. It is intended as an apology for resting the belief upon instinct as the very bedrock on which reasoning must be built.

501. I have often occasion to walk at night, for about a mile, over an entirely untravelled road, much of it between open fields without a house in sight. The circumstances are not favorable to severe study, but are so to calm meditation. If the sky is clear, I look at the stars in the silence, thinking how each successive increase in the aperture of a telescope makes many more of them visible than all that had been visible before. The fact that the heavens do not show a sheet of light proves that there are vastly more dark bodies, say planets, than there are suns. They must be inhabited, and most likely millions of them with beings much more intelligent than we are. For on the whole, the solar system seems one of the simplest; and presumably under more complicated phenomena greater intellectual power will be developed. What must be the social phenomena of such a world! How extraordinary are the minds even of the lower animals. We cannot appreciate our own powers any more than a writer can appreciate his own style, or a thinker the peculiar quality of his own thought. I don't mean that a Dante did not know that he expressed himself with fewer words than other men do, but he could not admire himself as we admire him; nor can we wonder at human intelligence as we do at that of wasps. Let a man drink in such thoughts as come to him in contemplating the physico-psychical universe without any special purpose of his own; especially the universe of mind which coincides with the universe of matter. The idea of there being a God over it all of course will be often suggested; and the more he considers it, the more he will be enwrapt with Love of this idea. He will ask himself whether or not there really is a God. If he allows instinct to speak, and searches his own heart, he will at length find that he cannot help believing it. I cannot tell how every man will think. I know the majority of men, especially educated men, are so full of pedantries—especially the male sex—that they cannot think straight about these things. But I can tell how a man must think if he is a pragmatist. Now the shower of communications that I have been getting during the last two months causes me to share the expectation that I find so many good judges are entertaining, that pragmatism is going to be the dominant philosophical opinion of the twentieth century. . . .

502. If a pragmaticist is asked what he means by the word "God," he can only say that just as long acquaintance with a man of great character may deeply influence one's whole manner of conduct, so that a glance at his portrait may make a difference, just as almost living with Dr. Johnson enabled poor Boswell to write an immortal book and a really sublime book, just as long study of the works of Aristotle may make him an acquaintance, so if contemplation and study of the physico-psychical universe can imbue a man with principles of conduct analogous to the influence of a great man's works or conversation, then that analogue of a mind—for it is impossible to say that *any* human attribute is *literally* applicable—is what he means by "God." Of course, various great theologians explain that one cannot attribute *reason* to God, nor perception (which always involves an element of surprise and of learning what one did not know), and, in short, that his "mind" is necessarily so unlike ours, that some—though wrongly—high in the church say that it is only negatively, as being entirely different from everything else, that we can attach any meaning to the Name. This is not so; because the discoveries of science, their enabling us to *predict* what will be the course of nature, is proof conclusive that, though we cannot think any thought of God's, we can catch a fragment of His Thought, as it were.

503. Now such being the pragmaticist's answer to the question what he means by the word "God," the question whether there really *is* such a being is the question whether all physical science is merely the figment—the arbitrary figment—of the students of nature, and further whether the *one* lesson the Gautama Boodha, Confucius, Socrates, and all who from any point of view have had their ways of conduct determined by meditation upon the physico-psychical universe, be only their arbitrary notion or be the Truth behind the appearances which the frivolous man does not think of; and whether the superhuman courage which such contemplation has conferred upon priests who go to pass their lives with lepers and refuse all offers of rescue is mere silly fanaticism, the passion of a baby, or whether it is strength derived from the power of the truth. Now the only guide to the answer to this question lies in the power of the passion of love which more or less overmasters every agnostic scientist and everybody who seriously and deeply considers the universe. But whatever there may be of *argument* in all this is as nothing, the merest nothing, in comparison to its force as an appeal to one's own instinct, which is to argument what substance is to shadow, what bed-rock is to the built foundations of a cathedral.

J. J. C. SMART

J. J. C. SMART (1920-   ), professor of
philosophy in the University of Adelaide,
Australia, is interested in the philosophy of
science and the philosophy of religion. He
has contributed a number of articles to important professional journals.

*The Existence of God**

This lecture is not to discuss whether God exists. It is to discuss reasons
which philosophers have given for saying that God exists. That is, to discuss
certain arguments.

First of all it may be as well to say what we may hope to get out of this.
Of course, if we found that any of the traditional arguments for the existence of God were sound, we should get out of our one hour this Sunday
afternoon something of inestimable value, such as one never got out of any
hour's work in our lives before. For we should have got out of one hour's
work the answer to that question about which, above all, we want to know
the answer. (This is assuming for the moment that the question "Does God
exist?" is a proper question. The fact that a question is all right as far as
the rules of ordinary grammar are concerned does not ensure that it has a
sense. For example, "Does virtue run faster than length?" is certainly all
right as far as ordinary grammar is concerned, but it is obviously not a
meaningful question. Again, "How fast does time flow?" is all right as far
as ordinary grammar is concerned, but it has no clear meaning. Now some
philosophers would ask whether the question "Does God exist?" is a proper
question. The greatest danger to theism at the present moment does not
come from people who deny the validity of the arguments for the existence
of God, for many Christian theologians do not believe that the existence
of God can be proved, and certainly nowhere in the Old or New Testaments
do we find any evidence of people's religion having a metaphysical basis.
The main danger to theism today comes from people who want to say that
"God exists" and "God does not exist" are equally absurd. The concept of
God, they would say, is a nonsensical one. . . .)

However, let us assume for the moment that the question "Does God

* From J. J. C. Smart, *New Essays in Philosophical Theology,* ed. by Antony Flew
and Alasdair MacIntyre, pp. 28-29, 31-36, 37-38, 41-45. Copyright 1955 by Student Christian Movement Press, Ltd. Used by permission of Student Christian Movement Press, Ltd.
and J. J. C. Smart.

exist?" is a proper question. We now ask: Can a study of the traditional proofs of the existence of God enable us to give an affirmative answer to this question? I contend that it can not. I shall point out what seems to me to be fallacies in the main traditional arguments for the existence of God. Does proving that the arguments are invalid prove that God does not exist? Not at all. For to say that an argument is invalid is by no means the same thing as to say that its conclusion is false. Still, if we do find that the arguments we consider are all fallacious, what do we *gain* out of our investigation? Well, one thing we gain is a juster (if more austere) view of what philosophical argument can do for us. But, more important, we get a deeper insight into the logical nature of certain concepts, in particular, of course, the concepts of deity and existence. Furthermore we shall get some hints as to whether philosophy can be of any service to theologians, and if it can be of service, some hints as to how it can be of service. I think that it can be, but I must warn you that many, indeed perhaps the majority, of philosophers today would not entirely agree with me here. . . .

One very noteworthy feature which must strike anyone who first looks at the usual arguments for the existence of God is the extreme brevity of these arguments. They range from a few lines to a few pages. St. Thomas Aquinas presents five arguments in three pages! Would it not be rather extraordinary if such a great conclusion should be got so easily? . . . It is my belief that in the case of any metaphysical argument it will be found that if the premises are uncontroversial the argument is unfortunately not valid, and that if the argument is valid the premises will unfortunately be just as doubtful as the conclusion they are meant to support.

With these warnings in mind let us proceed to the discussion of the three most famous arguments for the existence of God. These are:

(1) The Ontological Argument
(2) The Cosmological Argument
(3) The Teleological Argument

The first argument—the ontological argument—really has no premises at all. It tries to show that there would be a contradiction in denying that God exists. It was first formulated by St. Anselm and was later used by Descartes. It is not a convincing argument to modern ears, and St. Thomas Aquinas gave essentially the right reasons for rejecting it. However, it is important to discuss it, as an understanding of what is wrong with it is necessary for evaluating the second argument, that is, the cosmological argument. This argument does have a premiss, but not at all a controversial one. It is that something exists. We should all, I think, agree to that. The teleological argument is less austere in manner than the other two. It tries to argue to the existence of God not purely *a priori* and not from the mere fact of *something* existing, but from the actual features we observe in nature, namely those which seem to be evidence of design or purpose.

We shall discuss these three arguments in order. I do not say that they are the only arguments which have been propounded for the existence of God, but they are, I think, the most important ones. For example, of St. Thomas Aquinas' celebrated "Five Ways" the first three are variants of the cosmological argument, and the fifth is a form of the teleological argument.

The Ontological Argument. This as I remarked, contains no factual premiss. It is a *reductio-ad-absurdum* of the supposition that God does not exist. Now *reductio-ad-absurdum* proofs are to be suspected whenever there is doubt as to whether the statement to be proved is *significant*. For example, it is quite easy, as anyone who is familiar with the so-called Logical Paradoxes will know, to produce a not *obviously* nonsensical statement, such that both it *and* its denial imply a contradiction. So unless we are sure of the significance of a statement we cannot regard a *reductio-ad-absurdum* of its contradictory as proving its truth. This point of view is well known to those versed in the philosophy of mathematics; there is a well-known school of mathematicians, led by Brouwer, who refuse to employ *reductio-ad-absurdum* proofs. However, I shall not press this criticism of the Ontological Argument, for this criticism is somewhat abstruse (though it has been fore-shadowed by Catholic philosophers, who object to the ontological argument by saying that it does not first show that the concept of an infinitely perfect being is a *possible* one). We are at present assuming that "Does God exist?" is a proper question, and if it is a proper question there is no objection so far to answering it by means of a *reductio-ad-absurdum* proof. We shall content ourselves with the more usual criticisms of the ontological argument.

The ontological argument was made famous by Descartes. It is to be found at the beginning of his Fifth Meditation. As I remarked earlier it was originally put forward by Anselm, though I am sorry to say that to read Descartes you would never suspect that fact! Descartes points out that in mathematics we can deduce various things purely *a priori*, "as for example," he says, "when I imagine a triangle, although there is not and perhaps never was in any place . . . one such figure, it remains true nevertheless that this figure possesses a certain determinate nature, form, or essence, which is . . . not framed by me, nor in any degree dependent on my thought; as appears from the circumstance, that diverse properties of the triangle may be demonstrated, for example that its three angles are equal to two right, that its greatest side is subtended by its greatest angle, and the like." Descartes now goes on to suggest that just as having the sum of its angles equal to two right angles is involved in the idea of a triangle, so *existence* is involved in the very idea of an infinitely perfect being, and that it would therefore be as much of a contradiction to assert that an infinitely perfect being does not exist as it is to assert that the three angles of a triangle do not add up to two right angles or that two of its sides are not together greater than the third side. We may then, says Descartes, assert that an infinitely perfect being *necessarily* exists, just as we may say that two sides of a triangle are together *necessarily* greater than the third side.

This argument is highly fallacious. To say that a so-and-so exists is not in the least like saying that a so-and-so has such-and-such a property. It is not to amplify a concept but to say that a concept applies to something, and whether or not a concept applies to something can not be seen from an examination of the concept itself. Existence is not a property. "Growling" is a property of tigers, and to say that "tame tigers growl" is to say something about tame tigers, but to say "tame tigers exist" is not to say something about tame tigers but to say that there are tame tigers. Prof. G. E. Moore once brought out the difference between existence and a property such as that of being tame, or being a tiger, or being a growler, by reminding us that though the sentence "some tame tigers do not *growl*" makes perfect sense, the sentence "some tame tigers do not *exist*" has no clear meaning. The fundamental mistake in the ontological argument, then, is that it treats "exists" in "an infinitely perfect being exists" as if it ascribed a property existence to an infinitely perfect being, just as "is loving" in "an infinitely perfect being is loving" ascribes a property, or as "growl" in "tame tigers growl" ascribes a property: the verb "to exist" in "an infinitely perfect being exists" does not ascribe a property to something already conceived of as existing, but says that the concept of an infinitely perfect being applies to something. The verb "to exist" here takes us right out of the purely conceptual world. This being so, there can never be any *logical contradiction* in denying that God exists. It is worth mentioning that we are less likely to make the sort of mistake that the ontological argument makes if we use the expression "there is a so-and-so" instead of the more misleading form of words "a so-and-so exists."

I should like to mention another interesting, though less crucial, objection to Descartes' argument. He talks as though you can deduce further properties of, say, a triangle, by considering its definition. It is worth pointing out that from the definition of a triangle as a figure bounded by three straight lines you can only deduce trivialities, such as that it is bounded by more than one straight line, for example. It is not at all a contradiction to say that the two sides of a triangle are together not greater than the third side, or that its angles do not add up to two right angles. To get a contradiction you have to bring in the specific axioms of Euclidean geometry. (Remember school

THE PROBLEM OF THE EXISTENCE OF GOD

geometry, how you used to prove that the angles of a triangle add up to two right angles. Through the vertex C of the triangle ABC you drew a line parallel to BA, and so you assumed the axiom of parallels for a start.) Definitions, by themselves, are not deductively potent. Descartes, though a very great mathematician himself, was profoundly mistaken as to the nature of mathematics. However, we can interpret him as saying that from the definition of a triangle, *together with the axioms of Euclidean geometry*, you can deduce various things, such as that the angles of a triangle add up to two right angles. But this just shows how pure mathematics is a sort of game with symbols; you start with a set of axioms, and operate on them in accordance with certain rules of inference. All the mathematician requires is that the axiom set should be *consistent*. Whether or not it has application to reality lies outside pure mathematics. Geometry is no fit model for a proof of real existence.

We now turn to the *Cosmological Argument*. This argument does at least seem more promising than the ontological argument. It does start with a factual premiss, namely that something exists. The premiss that something exists is indeed a very abstract one, but nevertheless it *is* factual, it does give us a foothold in the real world of things, it does go beyond the consideration of mere concepts. The argument has been put forward in various forms, but for present purposes it may be put as follows:

Everything in the world around us is *contingent*. That is, with regard to any particular thing, it is quite conceivable that it might not have existed. For example, if you were asked why you existed, you could say that it was because of your parents, and if asked why they existed you could go still further back, but however far you go back you have not, so it is argued, made the fact of your existence really intelligible. For however far back you go in such a series you only get back to something which itself might not have existed. For a really satisfying explanation of why anything contingent (such as you or me or this table) exists you must eventually begin with something which is not itself contingent, that is, with something of which we cannot say that it might not have existed, that is we must begin with a necessary being. So the first part of the argument boils down to this. *If anything exists an absolutely necessary being must exist. Something exists. Therefore an absolutely necessary being must exist.* . . . the cosmological argument is radically unsound. The trouble comes much earlier than where Kant locates it. The trouble comes in the *first* stage of the argument. For the first stage of the argument purports to argue to the existence of a necessary being. And by "a necessary being" the cosmological argument means "a *logically* necessary being," i.e., "a being whose non-existence is inconceivable in the sort of way that a triangle's having four sides is inconceivable." The trouble is, however, that the concept of a logically necessary being is a self-contradictory concept, like the concept of a round square. For in the first place "necessary" is a predicate of *propositions*, not of things. That is, we can contrast *necessary* propositions such as "3 + 2 = 5," "a thing cannot be red and green all over," "either it is raining or it is not raining," with *contingent* propositions, such as "Mr. Menzies is Prime Minister of Australia," "the earth is slightly flattened at the poles," and "sugar is soluble in water." The propositions in the first class are guaranteed solely by the rules for the use of the symbols they contain. In the case of the propositions of the second class a genuine possibility of agreeing or not agreeing with reality is left open; whether they are true or false depends not on the conventions of our language but on reality. (Compare the contrast between "the equator is 90 degrees from the pole," which tells us nothing about geography but only about our map-making conventions, and "Adelaide is 55 degrees from the pole," which does tell us a geographical fact.) So no informative proposition can be logically necessary. Now since "necessary" is a word which applies primarily to propositions, we shall have to interpret "God is a necessary being" as "The proposition 'God exists' is logically necessary." But this *is* the principle of the ontological argument, and there is no way of getting round it this time in the way that we got out of Kant's criticism. No existential proposition can be logically necessary, for we saw that the truth of a logically necessary proposition depends only on our symbolism, or to put the same thing in another way, on the relationship of concepts. We saw, however, in discussing the ontological argument, that an existential proposition does not say that one concept is involved in another, but that a concept applies to something. An existential proposition must be very different from any logically necessary one, such as a mathematical one, for example, for the conventions of our symbolism clearly leave it open for us either to affirm or deny an existential proposition; it is not our symbolism but reality which decides whether or not we must affirm or deny it.

The demand that the existence of God should be *logically* necessary is thus a self-contradictory one. When we see this and go back to look at the first stage of the cosmological argument it no longer seems compelling, indeed it now seems to contain an absurdity. If we cast our minds back, we recall that the argument was as follows: that if we explain why something exists and is what it is, we must explain it by reference to something else, and we must explain that thing's being what it is by reference to yet another thing, and so on, back and back. It is then suggested that unless we can go back to a logically necessary first cause we shall remain intellectually unsatisfied. We should otherwise only get back to something which might have been otherwise, and with reference to which the same questions can again be asked. This is the argument, but we now see that in asking for a logically necessary first cause we are doing something worse than asking for the moon. It is only *physically* impossible for us to get the moon; if I were a few million times bigger I could reach out for it and give it to you. That is, I know what it would be *like* to give you the moon, though I cannot in *fact* do it. A logically necessary first cause, however, is not impossible in the way that giving you the moon is impossible; no, it is *logically* impossible. "Logically necessary being" is a self-contradictory expression like "round square." It is not any good saying that we would only be intellectually satisfied with a logically necessary cause, that nothing else would do. We can easily have an absurd wish. We should all like to be able to eat our cake and have it, but that does not alter the fact that our wish is an absurd and self-contradictory one. We reject the cosmological argument, then, because it rests on a thorough absurdity. . . .

The cosmological argument, we saw, failed because it made use of the absurd conception of a *logically* necessary being. We now pass to the third argument which I propose to consider. This is the *Teleological Argument*. It is also called "the Argument from Design." It would be better called the argument *to* design, as Kemp Smith does call it, for clearly that the universe has been designed by a great architect is to assume a great part of the conclusion to be proved. Or we could call it "the argument from apparent design." The argument is very fully discussed in Hume's *Dialogues concerning Natural Religion*, to which I should like to draw your attention. In these dialogues the argument is presented as follows: "Look round the world: Contemplate the whole and every part of it: You will find it to be nothing but one great machine, subdivided into an infinite number of lesser machines. . . . The curious adapting of means to ends, throughout all nature, resembles exactly, though it much exceeds, the productions of human contrivance. . . . Since therefore the effects resemble each other, we are led to infer, by all the rules of analogy, that the causes also resemble; and that the Author of nature is somewhat similar to the mind of man; though possessed of much larger faculties, proportioned to the grandeur of the work which he has executed."

This argument may at once be criticized in two ways: (1) We may question whether the analogy between the universe and artificial things like houses, ships, furniture, and machines (which admittedly are designed) is very close. Now in any ordinary sense of language, it is true to say that plants and animals have *not* been designed. If we press the analogy of the universe to a plant, instead of to a machine, we get to a very different conclusion. And why should the one analogy be regarded as any better or worse than the other? (2) Even if the analogy were close, it would only go to suggest that the universe was designed by a *very great* (not infinite) architect, and note, an *architect*, not a *creator*. For if we take the analogy seriously we must notice that we do not create the materials from which we make houses, machines and so on, but only *arrange* the materials.

This, in bare outline, is the general objection to the argument from design, and will apply to any form of it. In the form in which the argument was put forward by such theologians as Paley, the argument is, of course, still more open to objection. For Paley laid special stress on such things as the eye of an animal, which he thought must have been contrived by a wise Creator for the special benefit of the animal. It seemed to him inconceivable how otherwise such a complex organ, so well suited to the needs of the animal, should have arisen. Or listen to Henry More: "For why have we three joints in our legs and arms, as also in our fingers, but that it was much better than having two or four? And why are our fore-teeth sharp like chisels to cut, but our inward teeth broad to grind, [instead of] the fore-teeth broad and the other sharp? But we might have made a hard shift to have lived through in that worser condition. Again, why are the teeth so luckily placed, or rather, why are there not teeth in other bones as well as in the jaw-bones? For they might have been as capable as these. But the reason is, nothing is done foolishly or in vain; that is, there is a divine Providence that orders all things." This type of argument has lost its persuasiveness, for the theory of Evolution explains why our teeth are so luckily placed in our jaw-bones, why we have the most convenient number of joints in our fingers, and so on. Species which did not possess advantageous features would not survive in competition with those which did.

The sort of argument Paley and Henry More used is thus quite unconvincing. Let us return to the broader conception, that of the universe as a whole, which seems to show the mark of a benevolent and intelligent Designer. Bacon expressed this belief forcibly: "I had rather beleave all the Fables in the Legend and the Talmud and the Alcoran than that this Universal Frame is without a Minde." So, in some moods, does the universe strike us. But sometimes, when we are in other moods, we see it very differently. To quote Hume's dialogues again: "Look around this Universe. What an immense profusion of beings, animated and organized, sensible and active! You admire this prodigious variety and fecundity. But inspect a little more narrowly these living existences, the only beings worth regarding. How hostile and destructible to each other! How insufficient all of them for their own happiness! . . . the whole presents nothing but the idea of a blind Nature, impregnated by a great vivifying principle, and pouring forth from her lap, without discernment or parental care, her maimed and abortive children!" There is indeed a great deal of suffering, some part of which is no doubt attributable to the moral choices of men, and to save us from which would conflict with what many people would regard as the greater good of moral freedom, but there is still an immense residue of apparently needless suffering, that is, needless in the sense that it could be prevented by an omnipotent being. The difficulty is that of reconciling the presence of evil and suffering with the assertion that God is both omnipotent and benevolent. If we *already* believe in an omnipotent and benevolent God, then some attempt may be made to solve the problem of evil by arguing that the values in the world form a sort of organic unity, and that making any *part* of the world better would perhaps nevertheless reduce the value of the whole. Paradoxical though this thesis may appear at first sight, it is perhaps not theoretically absurd. If, however, evil presents a *difficulty* to the believing mind, it presents an *insuperable* difficulty to one who wishes to argue rationally from the world as we find it to the existence of an omnipotent and benevolent God. As Hume puts it: "Is the world considered in general, and as it appears to us in this life, different from what a man . . . would *beforehand* expect from a very powerful, wise and benevolent Deity? It must be a strange prejudice to assert the contrary. And from thence I conclude, that, however consistent the world may be, allowing certain suppositions and conjectures, with the idea of such a Deity, it can never afford us an inference concerning his existence."

The teleological argument is thus extremely shaky, and in any case, even if it were sound, it would only go to prove the existence of a very great architect, not of an omnipotent and benevolent Creator.

Nevertheless, the argument has a fascination for us that reason can not easily dispel. Hume, in his twelfth dialogue, and after pulling the argument from design to pieces in the previous eleven dialogues, nevertheless speaks as follows: "A purpose, an intention, a design strikes everywhere the most careless, the most stupid thinker; and no man can be so hardened in absurd systems as at all times to reject it . . . all the sciences almost lead us insensibly to acknowledge a first Author." Similarly Kant, before going on to exhibit the fallaciousness of the argument, nevertheless says of it: "This proof always deserves to be mentioned with respect. It is the oldest, the clearest and the most accordant with the common reason of mankind. It enlivens the study of nature, just as it itself derives its existence and gains ever new vigour from that source. It suggests ends and purposes, where our observation would not have detected them by itself, and extends our knowledge of nature by means of the guiding-concept of a special unity, the principle of which is outside nature. This knowledge . . . so strengthens the belief in a supreme Author of nature that the belief acquires the force of an irresistible conviction." It is somewhat of a paradox that an invalid argument should command so much respect even from those who have demonstrated its invalidity. The solution of the paradox is perhaps somewhat as follows:

The argument from design is no good as an argument. But in those who have the seeds of a genuinely religious attitude already within them the facts to which the argument from design draws attention, facts showing the grandeur and majesty of the universe, facts that are evident to anyone who looks upwards on a starry night, and which are enormously multiplied for us by the advance of theoretical science, these facts have a powerful effect. But they only have this effect on the already religious mind, on the mind which has the capability of feeling the religious type of awe. That is, the argument from design is in reality no argument, or if it is regarded as an argument it is feeble, but it is a potent instrument in heightening religious emotions. . . .

SUGGESTED ADDITIONAL READINGS

The Problem of the Existence of God

Aristotle. *Metaphysics.* See especially sections 1071b-1075a. Upon this work the Aristotelian-Thomistic tradition is built. The book is reading of first importance for students of the philosophy of religion.

Bertocci, Peter A. *Introduction to the Philosophy of Religion.* Prentice-Hall, 1951. See especially chapters XI-XVIII which are a discussion of arguments for the existence of God and a restatement of the teleological argument by an American proponent of personal idealism.

Descartes, René. *Meditations.* Trans., Laurence J. Lafleur. New York: Liberal Arts Press, 1951. (This is a paperback edition). This work provides an incisive discussion of traditional arguments for the existence of God.

Gilson, Etienne. *God and Philosophy.* London: Oxford University Press, 1941. (Also published in paperback by Yale University Press). A Roman Catholic evaluation of the relationship between religion and philosophy, written by an outstanding present-day scholar.

Hartshorne, Charles and William L. Reese. *Philosophers Speak of God.* Chicago: University of Chicago Press, 1953. A comprehensive collection of source materials from Eastern and Western philosophers with brief critical comments.

Malcolm, Norman. "Anselm's Ontological Arguments," *Philosophical Review* (January, 1960), LXIX, pp. 41-62. An excellent contemporary investigation of the intention and validity of Anselm's argument and the arguments of its major critics. See also other articles on Anselm's arguments in the October 1960 and January 1961 issues of the same journal.

Newman, John Henry. *A Grammar of Assent.* New York: Longmans Green, and Company, 1909. (Also published in paperback by Doubleday, Image series). See especially chapter 5. A well-known statement of an argument for the existence of God based on the reality of conscience.

Pascal, Blaise. *Pensées.* Trans., W. F. Trotter. London: J. M. Dent and Sons, Ltd., 1932. (Also published in paperback by E. P. Dutton, Everyman series.) This writing constitutes an argument for the existence of God which is an anticipation of the existentialist approach. See the famous "wager" argument, number 233.

Plato. *The Laws.* Book X. A classic defense of the existence of gods based on Plato's principle of the priority of the spiritual to the material, or the priority of the soul to the body.

Taylor, A. E. *Does God Exist?* New York: The Macmillan Company, 1947. A closely reasoned statement of the moral argument for God's existence.

IV. Introduction

HOW IS GOD KNOWN?

Some Contemporary Answers

In contrast to traditional concern with attempts to prove the existence of God, recent and contemporary theological and philosophical thought has moved in new directions. There are still some, especially among Roman Catholic thinkers, who take the proofs of the existence of God to be of first importance, but, on the whole, current scholarly interest is quite differently oriented.

Arguments for the existence of God were seriously challenged, from the side of philosophy, by the development of logical positivism, which relegated all such questions about ultimate being and meaning to the limbo of "meaningless statements." From this point of view all religious assertions are suspect, for logical positivists maintain that statements such as "God exists" are neither axiomatic nor capable of verification by sense-data. From the camp of the existentialist revolt there has also arisen opposition to the traditional arguments. Existentialist philosophers assert that the basing of religion on the arguments for God's existence leaves out the most important fact of all, namely, that religious truths have no meaning unless they are appropriated by a commitment, resolution or decision of the whole person. Argument for the existence of God is a rational process which may satisfy the mind, but which cannot in itself satisfy the basic demands of one's total experience. Thus, the existentialists have contended that some new way of affirming the reality of God needs to be found.

In theology also there have been new movements which react against the older assumptions about the need for arguments for the existence of God. These can be seen as roughly paralleling the philosophical reactions. On the one hand, there is the reaction of those like Karl Barth who insist on the primacy of God's revelation to man. According to him, God is not found by man, not even by the rigorous exercise of man's reason. Man is found by

God, and man's acknowledgment of God's self-revealing is based upon the fact that this revelation validates itself and not because it is supported by external criteria. On the other hand, there are theologians who follow the lead of the existentialist philosophers. Indeed, the key figure in modern existential philosophy, Sören Kierkegaard, was a theologian. Kierkegaard developed his philosophy because of his awareness of the need for a new understanding of the God-man relationship.

In the selections of this section are writings by some of the thinkers who espouse these different approaches. Jacques Maritain is a contemporary Thomistic philosopher who has carried on the Roman Catholic tradition of establishing God's existence by rational proofs. He has restated the five traditional arguments of Thomas and has, in the selection reprinted here, attempted to formulate again the "eternal approach of man's reason to God." Representing a strong contrast to Maritain are two Protestant theologians, Emil Brunner and Karl Barth. Both Barth and Brunner deny that philosophy, or "natural theology," provides an avenue to the true knowledge of God as he is revealed in Jesus Christ. Further, philosophy cannot provide even a valid beginning point for the understanding of this revelation.

In the selections from A. J. Ayer and E. L. Mascall we have elements of a discussion between a logical positivist and an Anglican theologian on the possibility of religious knowledge. Ayer's statement is one of the clearest and most important attempts to deny the meaningfulness of theological discourse. Mascall attempts to argue against Ayer's assumptions and thereby to establish once again the meaningfulness and validity of theological statement.

The chapter from John Hick's book, *Faith and Knowledge*, asks a crucial question about the nature of religious faith. This selection deals with the problem of cognition in the religious man's awareness of God and the way this is related to his other cognitions. It also illustrates the way in which a linguistic analyst approaches the problem of validating religious faith. An existentialist orientation is presented by the writing of Martin Buber. Buber, in this statement from his influential book, *I and Thou*, emphasizes the importance of man's personal involvement in all encounters with reality. According to Buber, truth of genuinely personal significance is to be found only as man allows reality to "stand over against him," not as subject to his control, but able to speak freely of itself to him. The object of knowledge, which is really a subject, a "Thou" with intrinsic value, can only be known, at the most profound levels, by such a confrontation. And this is pre-eminently true of the ultimate subject, which is God.

Paul Tillich, a German-American philosophical theologian, builds upon the insights of the existentialists' analysis of human existence. In the selection which is included from Tillich's writings we have an attempt to understand the search of man for meaning and purpose in his existence. The questions man asks about himself and his existence, Tillich argues, lead him to ask questions about God, and the meaning, if any, that God has for his life. Tillich believes that answers are provided in God's self-revelation and he tries to indicate what these are.

JACQUES MARITAIN

JACQUES MARITAIN (1882-   ) is a French
Roman Catholic philosopher and an outstanding spokesman for contemporary Thomistic thought. The range of his interests, as
reflected in his writings, is also reminiscent
of the breadth of Thomas. In the United
States he has taught at Chicago, Columbia,
Yale and Princeton Universities.

A New Approach to God*

If civilization is to survive, if the emergent civilization is to achieve the
fulfillment of its potentialities, the coming age must be an age of spiritual as
well as social integration.

Today the human mind is torn and divided between positivism and
irrationalism. The endeavors of pragmatism succeeded in making important
discoveries concerning a number of basic attitudes in thought and morality,
and in what might be called the sociology of knowledge. As a universal system of knowledge and life, as a philosophy, however, pragmatism has been a
failure.

What is essentially needed is a renewal of metaphysics. The conceptions
of modern science—the unification of matter and energy, physical indeter-
minism, the notion of space-time, the new reality recognized both as to
quality and duration—are invaluable means of deciphering material phenomena. A cosmos of electrons and stars in which the stars are the heavenly
laboratories of elements, subjected everywhere to genesis and transmutation,
a universe which is finite but whose limits cannot be attained because of
the curvation of space, and which dynamically evolves in a definite direction,
namely, toward the highest forms of individuation and concentration and
toward a simultaneous degradation of the quality of its total energy—all this
is external description and scientific imagery rather than ontological insight.
Such knowledge can never directly serve the purpose of any philosophical or
metaphysical extrapolations. Yet all this constitutes at the same time a basic
representation of the world incomparably more favorable to the edification
of a philosophy of nature and more open to the deepening labor of meta-

* From Jacques Maritain, "A New Approach to God," *Our Emergent Civilization*, pp.
280-285. Ed. Ruth Nanda Anshen. Copyright, 1947, by Harper & Brothers. Used by
permission of Harper & Brothers.

physical reason than the old Newtonian physics. The opportunity is now given for that reconciliation between science and wisdom for which the human mind thirsts. What the emergent civilization is anticipating, nay, presenting to the world as a tangible possibility and necessity, is a rediscovery of Being, and by the same token a rediscovery of Love.

This means axiomatically a rediscovery of God. The *existential* philosophies which are today in fashion are but a sign of a certain deep want, an inability to find again the sense of Being. This want is now unfulfilled, for these philosophies are still enslaved by irrationalism and seek for the revelation of existence, for ontological ecstasy, in the breaking of reason, in the experience of Despair and Nothingness, of Anguish or Absurdity. True existentialism is the work of reason. The act, by virtue of which I exist and things exist, transcends concepts and ideas; it is a mystery for the intellect. But the intellect lives on this mystery. In its most natural activity it is as ordinary, daily and vulgar as eating or drinking. The act of existing is indeed the very object of every achieved act of the intellect, that is, of judgment. It is perceived by that intellectual intuition, immersed in sense experience, which is the common treasure (all the more precious since it is natural and imbues the depths of our thought) of all our assertions, of all this mysterious activity by means of which we declare either *ita est* or *fiat!* in the face of the world or at the moment of making a decision. Now, when the intellect passes the threshold of philosophy, it does so by becoming aware of this intellectual intuition, freeing its genuine power, and making it the peculiar weapon of a knowledge whose subject matter is Being itself. I do not here refer to Platonic essences. I refer to the act of existing, in so far as it establishes and centers the intelligible structure of reality, as it expands into activity in every being; and as, at its supreme plenitude, it activates and attracts to itself the entire dynamism of nature. At their ontological peak, in the transcendence of the Pure Act and the Absolute, Being, Reason and God are one and the same reality. In the created realm Reason confronts Being and labors to conquer it, both to transfer Being into its own immaterial life and immateriality to be or become Being. In perceiving Being Reason knows God, in an enigmatic but inescapable manner.

But my thesis does not deal only with philosophers and philosophy, but with the mental behavior of the common man. Werner Sombart used to say that the "bourgeois," the man of the "capitalistic" era, was *neither "onto-logical" nor "erotic,"* had lost the sense of Being and the sense of Love. Torture and death have made us aware of the meaning of ontology. Hate has awakened an awareness of the meaning of eros. Let us emerge from sleep, cease to live in the dream or magic of images and formulas, well-systematized words, practical symbols and world-festering kabbala! Once a man is awakened to the reality of existence and the true life of Reason, to the intelligible value of Being, once he has really perceived this tremendous fact, sometimes exhilarating, sometimes disgusting and maddening in the knowledge that I *exist*, he is henceforth taken hold of by the intuition of Being and the implications it involves.

Precisely speaking, this prime intuition is both the intuition of *my* existence and of the existence of things; but first and foremost of the existence of things. When it takes place, I suddenly realize that a given entity, man, mountain or tree, exists and exercises that sovereign activity *to be* in its own way, totally self-assertive and totally implacable, completely independent from me. And at the same time I realize that I also exist but as thrown back into my loneliness and frailty by such affirmation of existence in which I have positively no part, to which I am exactly as naught. So the prime intuition of Being is the intuition of the solidity and inexorability of existence; and, secondly, of the death and nothingness to which *my* existence is liable. And thirdly, in the same flash of intuition, which is but my becoming aware of the intelligible value of Being, I realize that the solid and inexorable existence perceived in anything whatsoever implies—I don't know in what way, perhaps in things themselves, perhaps separately from them—some absolute, irrefragable existence, completely free from nothingness and death. These three intellective leaps—to actual existence as asserting itself independently from me; from this sheer objective existence to my own threatened existence; and from my existence spoiled with nothingness to absolute existence—are achieved within that same and unique intuition which philosophers would explain as the intuitive perception of the essentially analogical content of the first concept, the concept of Being.

Then a quick, spontaneous reasoning, as natural as this intuition (and, as a matter of fact, more or less involved in it) immediately springs forth, as the necessary fruit of such primordial apperception and as enforced by and under its light. I see that my Being, first, is liable to death; and, second, that it depends on the totality of nature, on the universal whole whose part I am; and that Being-with-nothingness, as my own being is, implies, in order to be, Being-without-nothingness. It implies that absolute existence which I confusedly perceived as involved in my primordial intuition of existence. The universal whole, whose part I am, is Being-with-nothingness, from the very fact that I am part of it; so that finally, since the universal whole does not exist by itself, there is another, separate, whole, another Being, transcendent and self-sufficient and unknown in itself and activating all beings, which is Being-without-nothingness, that is, Being by itself.

Thus the inner dynamism of the intuition of existence, or of the intelligible value of Being, causes me to see that absolute existence or Being-without-nothingness transcends the totality of nature, and compels me to face the existence of God.

This is not a new approach to God. It is the eternal approach of man's reason to God. What is new is the manner in which the modern mind has become aware of the simplicity and liberating power, the natural and somehow intuitive characteristics of this eternal approach. The science of the ancients was steeped in philosophy. Their scientific imagery was a pseudo-ontological imagery. Consequently there was a kind of continuum between their knowledge of the physical world and their knowledge of God. The latter appeared as the summit of the former, a summit which was to be climbed through the manifold paths of the causal connections at play in the sublunar world and the celestial spheres. The sense of Being that ruled their universal thought was for them a too usual atmosphere to be felt as a surprising gift. At the same time the natural intuition of existence was so strong in them that their proofs of God could take the form of the most conceptualized and rationalized scientific demonstrations, and be offered as an unrolling of logical necessities, without losing the inner energy of that intuition. Such logical machinery was quickened instinctively by the basic intuition of Being.

We are in a quite different position now. In order to solve the enigma of physical reality and to conquer the world of phenomena, our science has become a kind of Maya—a maya which succeeds and makes us masters of nature. But the sense of Being is absent from it. Thus when we happen to experience the impact of Being upon the mind it appears to us as a kind of intellectual revelation, and we realize clearly both its liberating and its awakening power and the fact that it involves a knowledge which is separated from that sphere of knowledge peculiar to our science. At the same time we realize that the knowledge of God, before being developed into logical and perfectly conceptualized demonstrations, is first and foremost a natural fruit of the intuition of existence, and forces itself upon our mind in the imperative virtue of this intuition.

In other words, we have become aware of the fact that human reason's approach to God, in its primordial vitality, is neither a mere intuition, which would be suprahuman, nor is it that artlike philosophical reasoning by which it is expressed in its achieved form, each step of which is pregnant with involved issues and problems. Human reason's approach to God in its primordial vitality is a *natural* reasoning, that is, intuitive-like or irresistibly vitalized by and maintained within the intellectual flash of the intuition of existence. Then the intuition of existence, grasping in some existing reality Being-with-nothingness, makes the mind grasp by the same stroke the necessity of Being-without-nothingness. And nowhere is there any problem involved, because the illumining power of this intuition takes hold of the mind and obliges it to see. Thus it naturally proceeds, in a primary intuitive flash, from imperative certainty to imperative certainty. I believe that from Descartes to Kierkegaard, the effort of modern thought—to the extent that it has not completely repudiated metaphysics, and if it is cleansed of the irrationalism which has gradually corrupted it—tends to such an awareness of the specific *naturality* of man's knowledge of God, definitely deeper than any logical process scientifically developed. It tends to the awareness of man's knowledge of God, and of the primordial and simple intuitivity in which it originates. Availing itself of any true progress achieved by the critique of knowledge, and realizing its own existential requirements, philosophy must enforce this new awareness and make clear in this way the manner in which the eternal approach of man, of the common man, to God proceeds.

On the other hand, becoming aware of the subconscious life of the spirit, and considering not only our theoretical but also our practical approach to God, philosophy must lay stress on the following fact. When a man experiences, in a primary act of freedom, the impact of the moral good, and is thus awakened to moral life, and directs his life toward the good for the sake of the good, then he directs his life, even without knowing it, toward the absolute Good, and in this way knows God vitally, by virtue of the inner dynamism of his choice of the good, even if he does not know God in any conscious fashion and by means of any conceptual knowledge. Thus Conscience, with its practical intuition of the moral good, and with a practical and preconscious knowledge of the supreme existing Good, has its own approach to God, just as Reason has its own approach with its speculative intuition of existence and with the theoretical and conscious knowledge of the supreme existing Being.

EMIL
BRUNNER

EMIL BRUNNER (1889-   ), Swiss Protestant
theologian, who with Karl Barth in the
nineteen twenties revolted against Protestant
liberalism and attempted to restate classic
Protestant doctrines in contemporary terms.
He has written extensively in the field of
Christian theology.

The "Natural" Knowledge of God: The Problem of the "Theologia Naturalis"*

In recent times, and rightly, the question whether—from the standpoint of the Christian Faith—God can be known outside the historical revelation, is to be answered in the affirmative, or in the negative, is now regarded as a fundamental problem, and like few other problems of this kind, has led to varied and passionate controversies. The very fact of the passionate feeling which has been aroused (a display of emotion which in itself may be deplored) and with which this conflict has been waged, shows that we are here dealing with a decisive question of the first importance. But here, too, the passionate concern for clarity of thought has not always been an advantage; it has indeed led to misunderstandings and misinterpretations which create grave hindrances to the clarification of the problem. Since I myself, by the use of a misleading idea, am bound to admit that I have caused some of the chief misunderstanding, I feel obliged to make yet another attempt to clear up the difficulty.

(i) First of all, we must make a clear distinction between two questions which, unfortunately, are continually being confused with one another: the question of the revelation in Creation, and the question of man's natural knowledge of God. While one side was mainly anxious to deny the validity of a "theologia naturalis," the other side was chiefly concerned to affirm the reality of the revelation in Creation. Now some theologians believed (mistakenly) that their denial of a "theologia naturalis" obliged them also to deny the reality of the revelation in Creation; this was due to their mistaken idea that the acknowledgment of a revelation in Creation must necessarily

---

* From *The Christian Doctrine of God* (pp. 132-136) by Emil Brunner, Tr. by Olive Wyon. Copyright, 1950, by W. L. Jenkins, The Westminster Press. Used by permission of Westminster Press and Lutterworth Press.

lead to the recognition of a *"theologia naturalis."* I myself, however, helped to foster this mistaken equation of the revelation in Creation with Natural Theology (which I contested from the very outset), to this extent, that in the first edition of *Natur und Gnade* I described the Christian doctrine of the revelation in Creation by the misleading expression of a "Christian *theologia naturalis."* On the other side, however, it is evident that the correction of this unfortunate phrase, to which I drew special attention in the second edition of this brochure, has not been noticed.

The affirmation of a revelation in Creation has, in itself, nothing whatever to do with a belief in Natural Theology. A theology which intends to remain true to the Biblical witness to revelation should never have denied the reality of revelation in Creation. All efforts to contest the Biblical evidence for such a revelation must lead to an arbitrary exegesis, and to forced interpretations of the text of the Bible. But even apart from explicit Biblical evidence, the Christian Idea of the Creator should itself force us to admit the reality of a revelation in Creation; for what sort of Creator would not imprint the mark of His Spirit upon His Creation?

(ii) The question whether the "natural man," that is, the man who has not yet been affected by the historical revelation, is in a position to perceive this divine revelation in Creation as such, in accordance with its nature and its meaning, is a quite different question. This question, therefore, has not been answered when we have answered the former question in the affirmative, because between the revelation in Creation and the natural man there stands the fact of Sin.

If it is a mistake, and from the standpoint of the Bible and theology an impossibility, to contest the reality of the revelation in Creation, it is no less mistaken to deny the negative significance of sin for the perception of the truth of the revelation in Creation. Sin not only perverts the will, it also "obscures" the power of perceiving truth where the knowledge of God is concerned. So where a man supports the view of the reality of a *"theologia naturalis"* in the sense of correct, valid knowledge, he is actually denying the reality of sin, or at least its effect in the sphere of man's knowledge of God. Thus, on the one hand, the reality of the revelation in Creation is to be admitted, but, on the other hand, the possibility of a correct and valid natural knowledge of God is to be contested.

(iii) Now, however, the problem is complicated by the fact that when we have said that we must question the possibility of a valid knowledge of God (to the natural man), we have not said all there is to say. There is, it is true, no valid "natural theology," but there is a Natural Theology which, in fact, exists. The place to discuss this, however, is not in connection with the doctrine of God, for here it has no theological validity, but in connexion with the doctrine of Man; for "natural theology" is an anthropological fact, which no one can deny. Human beings, even those who know nothing of the historical revelation, are such that they cannot help forming an idea of God and making pictures of God in their minds. The history of the religions of mankind provides incontrovertible evidence of this fact. The formation of theological ideas is an empirical fact of the reality of sinful humanity. This fact cannot be denied; all that we can contest is how it should be interpreted. From the standpoint of the Christian Faith, on the basis of the Biblical testimony, how are we to interpret this fact?

(iv) The chief passage in the Bible which deals with this question— Romans 1: 19ff.—gives the interpretation which alone can stand the test of theological examination. The fact that sinful human beings cannot help having thoughts about God is due to the revelation in Creation. The other fact, that human beings are not able rightly to understand the nature and meaning of this revelation in Creation is due to the fact that their vision has been distorted by sin.

"Sin obscures men's vision to such an extent that in the place of 'God' they 'know' or imagine 'gods' . . . so that God's revelation in Creation is turned into lying pictures of idols" (*Natur und Gnade*, First ed., p. 14). In this sentence I tried to say three things: (a) that the revelation in Creation is a reality; (b) that Natural Theology, as a legitimate possibility, does not exist; (c) that the fact of Natural Theology as an empirical fact, as something which belongs to the nature of the natural man, is understood in its ambiguity. But the doctrine of the Apostle, in spite of its brevity, takes us a step further.

(v) The Apostle cannot be interested in the theoretical question: how are we to explain the *"theologia naturalis"* of the pagan sinful man or woman; but the question which interests him is this: How should we address the man to whom the message of Jesus Christ is to be proclaimed? This question he answers thus: Sinful man is responsible for his sin, because in the revelation in Creation the possibility is given him of knowing God. He is responsible for his idolatry: he is ἀναπολόγητος, "without excuse." Thus, according to the Biblical teaching, the doctrine of general revelation becomes actual in anthropology. Human responsibility is based upon the general revelation.

The quality that makes man "human" is derived from the revelation in Creation, from the relation which God established at the very outset between man and the Creator. Responsible existence—that is, the existence of man in contrast to that of every other creature, is his existence as *person*. Even sinful man does not cease to be a responsible person; this responsible personal existence, which is grounded in the Creation, cannot be lost.

It is very cheering to note that Karl Barth, in his exposition of the narrative of the Creation in Genesis 1:26ff. has come to the same conclusion. The fact that man has been created in the Image of God (taught in this passage) means responsible existence, the "Thou"-relation with the Creator, which is the basis of the "Thou"-relation with one's fellow man; and *this* fact: namely, that we have been created in the Image of God, cannot be lost (*Kirchl. Dogm.*, III, I, p. 224).

The Fall does not mean that man ceases to be responsible, but that he ceases to understand his responsibility aright, and to live according to his responsibility. Sin, far from eliminating responsibility, and thus *this* vestige of the *Imago Dei*, is, on the contrary, a witness to God-willed responsibility, just as the sinful illusion of idolatry is a witness to the God-given revelation in Creation. The idolatrous images of man—whether they be the massive structures of wood or brass, or the idolatrous abstractions of speculative theology—accuse man, because to him has been given another possibility of the knowledge of God. It is sin which makes idols out of the revelation in Creation.

(vi) This Biblical view of the natural man, and of his *theologia naturalis*, can, and must, be examined in the light of historic facts. What is the result of this examination?

The history of religions shows that mankind cannot help producing religious ideas, and carrying on religious activities. It also shows the confusion caused by sin. The multiplicity of religious ideas of God, and of the "gods," is so vast, and so contradictory, that it is impossible to gather it all up in one positive conception, as the result of research; to reach such a result by a process of elimination is not the task of religion itself but of philosophy. Whither it leads will be shown directly.

Within this welter of religious conceptions of God it is impossible to discover one common denominator. The "higher religions" are contrasted with the primitive religions, and the contradictions are too great to be overcome. There is no common element which could do justice at the same time to the polytheistic personalism of the one, and the monistic impersonalism of the other. (Cf. my *Religionsphilosophie protestantischer Theologie*, pp. 51ff. and *Offenbarung und Vernunft*, pp. 215ff.)

(vii) From the beginning of Greek philosophy men have continually tried to reach a clear and certain knowledge of God, not along the path of religion, but by the way of philosophy, by the speculative thought, and thus to overcome the irrationalism of the purely religious formation of ideas. These philosophical doctrines of God now confront one another in irreconcilable opposition. Above all, none of them can possibly be combined with the Christian Idea of God. The relation of the "God" of Plato or of Aristotle with the God of the Biblical revelation is that of the Either-Or. The same may be said of every other idea of God which has been attained purely by philosophical speculation. The reason for this will be given in the next chapter: the God of thought *must* differ from the God of revelation. The God who is "conceived" by thought is not the one who discloses Himself; from this point of view He is an intellectual idol. (Cf. *Offenbarung und Vernuft*, pp. 43ff. and Chapters 20-23.)

KARL
BARTH

KARL BARTH (1886-   ), Swiss Protestant theologian and prolific writer, was the chief figure in the revolt of the nineteen twenties against Protestant liberalism. Barth's *Church Dogmatics* is a major contribution to twentieth century theology.

The Christian Understanding of Revelation*

What is this revelation, what is the subject of the revelation of which we have been speaking? What is the frame of mind which is open to receive what we call revelation? What is the theory of cognition for which revelation in the Christian sense is a valid object of knowledge?

And on the other hand: is there a conception of the world, a basic view of existence which can include what we have called God? If the general conception of the world and the general pattern of human thought are the criteria, can such a thing as revelation exist in the Christian sense at all? Does this God exist, of whom we have spoken as the subject of this revelation? What are we in fact talking about? Are we possibly talking nonsense, talking about a non-ens? There are theories of knowledge which can account for what we have called the self-revelation of that which exists, and there are ontologies which can embrace the gods corresponding to these revelations. But as far as one can see there is no theory of knowledge and no pattern of thought which can embrace revelation in the Christian sense of the term. We can work through the whole history of philosophy from Thales to Martin Heidegger, and we shall be forced to the same conclusion. There is no room for revelation in the Christian sense in any human inquiry or any human faculty of reason. And the same applies to what we have called God in the

* From Karl Barth, *Against the Stream*, ed. Ronald Gregor Smith, pp. 210-216. Copyright, 1954, by Student Christian Movement Press. Used by permission of the publisher.

Christian sense. There may be conceptions of the world which provide for gods, but the God of Christianity cannot appear in any imaginable human conception of the world. Try to map out a conception of the world in which God, as understood in Christian thought, would have room!—And so we must say that if a purely human conception of the world is the measure of all things, then neither revelation nor God in the Christian sense exist at all. We would in fact have been speaking about "nothing" when we were speaking about revelation and God.

We have not, however, been speaking about "nothing," but about a reality, something incomparably more real than anything that can be called real in the sphere of human thought and knowledge. When the Christian language speaks of revelation and God it means a reality which is very insignificant-looking and outwardly most unpromising; it speaks quite simply of a single concrete fact in the midst of the numberless host of facts and the vast stream of historical events; it speaks of a single human person living in the age of the Roman Empire: it speaks of Jesus Christ. When the Christian language speaks of God it does so not on the basis of some speculation or other, but looking at this fact, this story, this person. It cannot place this fact in relationship to any system of principles and ideas which would illuminate its importance and significance; it cannot explain and establish it from any other source; it makes no presuppositions when it points to this event. Its sole concern is with the event itself; all it can do is to refer to the existence, or rather, more precisely, the presence of this fact and the reception of the news of its presence as recorded in a tiny sheaf of news about the existence of this Person.

With its eyes concentrated on this news, Christianity speaks of revelation and of God as the subject of this revelation. Looking at this fact, it speaks with absolute assurance. Here—but only here—it sees revelation (in the sense of the criteria we have stated) and it sees God (again, in the sense of the criteria we have stated). Revelation in the Christian sense takes place and God in the Christian sense is, in accordance with the news of Jesus Christ, His words and deeds, His death and resurrection. That is what we now have to expound and, once again, we propose, for the sake of clarity, to make ten points. Each point will be based on a certain item of the good news of the gospel.

1. "And the times of this ignorance God winked at; but now commandeth all men everywhere to repent. Because he hath appointed a day, in the which he will judge the world in righteousness by that man whom he hath ordained" (Acts 17: 30ff.).

This is the news: Because judgment is pronounced on all men in the one man, and their being and non-being decided, revelation in the Christian sense takes place, and not as an approximate but an original and final revelation. And He who makes the decision in the Person of this one man is God.

2. "If any man sin, we have an advocate with the Father, Jesus Christ the righteous. And he is the propitiation for our sins; and not for ours only, but also for the sins of the whole world" (I John 2: 1ff.).

Since, in accordance with this news, man in this one Jesus Christ, in this offering of Jesus Christ as a propitiation for our sins, is accepted by God, revelation takes place, and not for the imperilling but for the salvation of man. It is God who does this.

3. "I am the light of the world." "The light shineth in darkness; and the darkness comprehended it not" (John 8: 12 and 1: 5).

Since, in accordance with this news, Jesus Christ came into the darkness as the light of the world, since, therefore, Jesus Christ is and remains absolutely new for man, revelation takes place in the Christian sense, and not as a relative but as an absolute revelation. And it is God who shines in Jesus Christ.

4. "For all have sinned, and come short of the glory of God; being justified freely by his grace through the redemption that is in Christ Jesus" (Rom. 3: 23f.).

Since, in accordance with this news, the event that is called redemption takes place in Jesus Christ, in this one person, the event that cannot proceed from any man and which no man can bring about, but which has been brought about by this One revelation in the Christian sense takes place. Without all, but for all! And therefore not as a special, but as a general revelation which concerns all and is meant for all. And it is God whose honour is so high and whose grace reaches so deep.

5. "No man hath seen God at any time; the only begotten Son, which is in the bosom of the Father, he hath declared him" (John 1: 18).

Inasmuch as what is hidden from all men is revealed in this One, the one exclusive revelation takes place. And it is God that makes Himself known in the One.

6. "Ye have not chosen me, but I have chosen you and ordained you that ye should go and bring forth fruit" (John 15: 16).

Inasmuch as this happens, inasmuch as this One chooses others and calls them to Himself, revelation in the Christian sense takes place; revelation that man cannot bring about by himself but which he receives as a gift. And it is God that has this freedom of choice in relation to man and exercises it in the One.

7. "I am the vine, ye are the branches: he that abideth in me, and I in him, the same bringeth forth much fruit; for without me ye can do nothing" (John 15: 5).

Inasmuch as this One, Jesus Christ, has and exercises such sovereignty over His own, revelation takes place, revelation that cannot be capitalised, but is and remains free. And the origin and the essense of this sovereignty is God. 8. "Jesus Christ the same yesterday and today and for ever" (Heb. 13: 8).

Revelation as an event that has happened, is happening and will happen in the future, which fulfills time in all its three constituents, is not approximate, but complete and final. And the Lord of this time is the eternal God. 9. "For we are his workmanship, created in Christ Jesus unto good works, which God hath ordained that we should walk in them" (Eph. 2: 10).

Inasmuch as this necessity of a definite change comes into force in this One Jesus Christ, revelation takes place: practical, not speculative revelation. And it is God who thus disposes the way of man.

10. "In the beginning was the Word and the Word was with God and the Word was God. The same was in the beginning with God. All things were made by him, and without him was not anything made that was made" (John 1: 1f.).

Inasmuch as this creative Word, which is superior to all being, is spoken and heard in Him, revelation takes place: transcendent, not immanent revelation. Revelation from the origin of all being. And it is God who speaks this Word.

The concept of revelation and the concept of God in the Christian sense coincide, therefore, in the contemplation of Jesus Christ, in which they are both related to reality. And in contemplation of Him it is decided that God is and what God is; that God is a person and not a neutral thing. And that revelation is His acting and speaking and not a blind occurrence or an unarticulated sound.

5

When it refers to God's revelation as the Word of God, Christianity means Jesus Christ. What is a word? A word obviously differs from a mere sound in that it is formed with the definite intention of calling on others to make a common cause. When I utter the simple word: "Look!" I call on others to look at something I think I have seen myself. Or if I say: "Listen!", I call them to listen to something I think I have heard myself. The primary intention of words is quite simply to be heard by others. Words cannot compel, they can only make an appeal. But every word has in view, in some sense or other, the obedient response of other persons. When I utter words I want to induce others to listen and conform to my wishes. In this sense too revelation is a word: God wants our interest, He wants us to listen, He wants to call us to decision, He wants us to obey His Word.

When we speak about the Word, and particularly this Word of God, a certain uneasiness is liable to come over us. Is what we are discussing really no more than a word? Are words not "sound and smoke clouding the glow of heaven?" "In the beginning was the Word? I cannot possibly esteem the Word so highly; I must translate it differently: in the beginning was the Deed," as Goethe says. What have we to say to that? Simply that the argument overlooks the fact that the "glow of heaven" and the "Deed" without words are phenomena which may be most impressive, but in relation to which it is possible for man to remain free and aloof and which are in any case something essentially different from what we have discerned as revelation in the Christian sense. Secondly, in contrast to all mere words and all empty words, revelation in the Christian sense is both Word and Deed at one and the same time. It is not merely the "glow of heaven" but a consuming fire and a blinding light. According to Heb. 1: 3 the Word of revelation is "his enabling word on whom all creation depends for its support" (cf. John 1: 3). Jesus Christ is the Word. Inasmuch as what happens in Him, happened and happens and will happen, the word of revelation is spoken. The whole criticism of the concept "the word" is superfluous as far as this Word is concerned. And thus we might take leave of Dr. Faust by suggesting he might have done better not to have tried to translate the Word differently! Incidentally, it is significant that immediately after the translation the Devil appears!

Revelation in the Christian sense is the Word of God, the Word spoken in divine Majesty. He to whom man belongs, to whom man cannot refuse to listen without calling himself into question, who calls man to decision, summons us to make common cause with Him. Neutrality towards the Word of God is impossible; we cannot say Yes and No at the same time. Obedience to the Word of God is not merely one of several possibilities. We do not confront this Word like Hercules at the crossroads. This is a case where there is only one possibility, the possibility of obedience. Man's genuine freedom does not consist in an ability to evade this Word. If he does not submit to it he chooses the impossible possibility, he chooses *nihil*.

Because revelation in the Christian sense is the Word of God, it is impossible to adopt the attitude of a mere onlooker towards it. The revelation of God can only be searched, understood and judged in the act of obedience, of listening, which leads to decision—or it will not be searched, understood and judged at all. We cannot think and talk *about* the revelation of God; we can only reflect on what the Word itself says to us. We can only speak out of the revelation itself; otherwise we shall be thinking and talking about something else.

Since revelation in the Christian sense is the Word of God, we cannot bring it forward as if it were an object outside ourselves. I cannot demonstrate the revelation of God to you in the way that my colleague in the Chemistry Department demonstrates his objects. Because it is the Word of God, the revelation of God cannot be recommended and defended; it has no advocates and no propagandists. And, finally, one cannot profess one's belief in it by protesting and asserting that it exists. Revelation can only be believed in by becoming worthy of belief. Revelation can only be attested as any other unknown fact is attested by someone who happens to know it. Revelation can only be presupposed in our thinking and our speaking, and in our Christian theology and preaching too, in the way that certain axioms or objective facts are presupposed in every branch of knowledge, when the belief and the testimony and the presupposition are only forms of that one possible decision, the decision of obedience. *Omnis recta cognitio ab obedientia nascitur*, Calvin says. Thus it is with revelation because it is the Word of God.

A. J. AYER

A. J. AYER (1910-   ), Wykeham Professor of Logic at Oxford University, has been the leading exponent of logical positivism in Great Britain. He is best known for his book, *Language, Truth and Logic*, which was first published in 1936.

Is Religious Knowledge Possible?*

This mention of God brings us to the question of the possibility of religious knowledge. We shall see that this possibility has already been ruled out by our treatment of metaphysics. But, as this is a point of considerable interest, we may be permitted to discuss it at some length.

It is now generally admitted, at any rate by philosophers, that the existence of a being having the attributes which define the god of any non-animistic religion cannot be demonstratively proved. To see that this is so, we have only to ask ourselves what are the premises from which the existence of such a god could be deduced. If the conclusion that a god exists is to be demonstratively certain, then these premises must be certain; for, as the conclusion of a deductive argument is already contained in the premises, any uncer-

* From A. J. Ayer, *Language, Truth and Logic*, Second Edition, pp. 114-120. Copyright, 1946, Victor Gollancz. Reprinted by permission of A. J. Ayer and of Dover Publications, Inc., N. Y. 14, N. Y.

tainty there may be about the truth of the premises is necessarily shared by it. But we know that no empirical proposition can ever be anything more than probable. It is only *a priori* propositions that are logically certain. But we cannot deduce the existence of a god from an *a priori* proposition. For we know that the reason why *a priori* propositions are certain is that they are tautologies. And from a set of tautologies nothing but a further tautology can be validly deduced. It follows that there is no possibility of demonstrating the existence of a god.

What is not so generally recognized is that there can be no way of proving that the existence of a god, such as the God of Christianity, is even probable. Yet this also is easily shown. For if the existence of such a god were probable, then the proposition that he existed would be an empirical hypothesis. And in that case it would be possible to deduce from it, and other empirical hypotheses, certain experiential propositions which were not deducible from those other hypotheses alone. But in fact this is not possible. It is sometimes claimed, indeed, that the existence of a certain sort of regularity in nature constitutes sufficient evidence for the existence of a god. But if the sentence "God exists" entails no more than that certain types of phenomena occur in certain sequences, then to assert the existence of a god will be simply equivalent to asserting that there is the requisite regularity in nature; and no religious man would admit that this was all he intended to assert in asserting the existence of a god. He would say that in talking about God, he was talking about a transcendent being who might be known through certain empirical manifestations, but certainly could not be defined in terms of those manifestations. But in that case the term "god" is a metaphysical term. And if "god" is a metaphysical term, then it cannot be even probable that a god exists. For to say that "God exists" is to make a metaphysical utterance which cannot be either true or false. And by the same criterion, no sentence which purports to describe the nature of a transcendent god can possess any literal significance.

It is important not to confuse this view of religious assertions with the view that is adopted by atheists, or agnostics.[1] For it is characteristic of an agnostic to hold that the existence of a god is a possibility in which there is no good reason either to believe or disbelieve; and it is characteristic of an atheist to hold that it is at least probable that no god exists. And our view that all utterances about the nature of God are nonsensical, so far from being identical with, or even lending any support to, either of these familiar contentions, is actually incompatible with them. For if the assertion that there is a god is nonsensical, then the atheist's assertion that there is no god is

[1] This point was suggested to me by Professor H. H. Price.

equally nonsensical, since it is only a significant proposition that can be significantly contradicted. As for the agnostic, although he refrains from saying either that there is or that there is not a god, he does not deny that the question whether a transcendent god exists is a genuine question. He does not deny that the two sentences "There is a transcendent god" and "There is no transcendent god" express propositions one of which is actually true and the other false. All he says is that we have no means of telling which of them is true, and therefore ought not to commit ourselves to either. But we have seen that the sentences in question do not express propositions at all. And this means that agnosticism also is ruled out.

Thus we offer the theist the same comfort as we gave to the moralist. His assertions cannot possibly be valid, but they cannot be invalid either. As he says nothing at all about the world, he cannot justly be accused of saying anything false, or anything for which he has insufficient grounds. It is only when the theist claims that in asserting the existence of a transcendent god he is expressing a genuine proposition that we are entitled to disagree with him.

It is to be remarked that in cases where deities are identified with natural objects, assertions concerning them may be allowed to be significant. If, for example, a man tells me that the occurrence of thunder is alone both necessary and sufficient to establish the truth of the proposition that Jehovah is angry, I may conclude that, in his usage of the words, the sentence "Jehovah is angry" is equivalent to "It is thundering." But in sophisticated religions, though they may be to some extent based on men's awe of natural process which they cannot sufficiently understand, the "person" who is supposed to control the empirical world is not himself located in it; he is held to be superior to the empirical world, and so outside it; and he is endowed with super-empirical attributes. But the notion of a person whose essential attributes are non-empirical is not an intelligible notion at all. We may have a word which is used as if it named this "person," but, unless the sentences in which it occurs express propositions which are empirically verifiable, it cannot be said to symbolize anything. And this is the case with regard to the word "god," in the usage in which it is intended to refer to a transcendent object. The mere existence of the noun is enough to foster the illusion that there is a real, or at any rate a possible entity corresponding to it. It is only when we enquire what God's attributes are that we discover that "God," in this usage, is not a genuine name.

It is common to find belief in a transcendent god conjoined with belief in an after-life. But, in the form which it usually takes, the content of this belief is not a genuine hypothesis. To say that men do not ever die, or that the state of death is merely a state of prolonged insensibility, is indeed to express a significant proposition, though all the available evidence goes to show that it is false. But to say that there is something imperceptible inside a man, which is his soul or his real self, and that it goes on living after he is dead, is to make a metaphysical assertion which has no more factual content than the assertion that there is a transcendent god.

It is worth mentioning that, according to the account which we have given of religious assertions, there is no logical ground for antagonism between religion and natural science. As far as the question of truth or falsehood is concerned, there is no opposition between the natural scientist and the theist who believes in a transcendent god. For since the religious utterances of the theist are not genuine propositions at all, they cannot stand in any logical relation to the propositions of science. Such antagonism as there is between religion and science appears to consist in the fact that science takes away one of the motives which make men religious. For it is acknowledged that one of the ultimate sources of religious feeling lies in the inability of men to determine their own destiny; and science tends to destroy the feeling of awe with which men regard an alien world, by making them believe that they can understand and anticipate the course of natural phenomena, and even to some extent control it. The fact that it has recently become fashionable for physicists themselves to be sympathetic towards religion is a point in favour of this hypothesis. For this sympathy towards religion marks the physicists' own lack of confidence in the validity of their hypotheses, which is a reaction on their part from the anti-religious dogmatism of nineteenth-century scientists, and a natural outcome of the crisis through which physics has just passed.

It is not within the scope of this enquiry to enter more deeply into the causes of religious feeling, or to discuss the probability of the continuance of religious belief. We are concerned only to answer those questions which arise out of our discussion of the possibility of religious knowledge. The point which we wish to establish is that there cannot be any transcendent truths of religion. For the sentences which the theist uses to express such "truths" are not literally significant.

An interesting feature of this conclusion is that it accords with what many theists are accustomed to say themselves. For we are often told that the nature of God is a mystery which transcends the human understanding. But to say that something transcends the human understanding is to say that it is unintelligible. And what is unintelligible cannot significantly be described. Again, we are told that God is not an object of reason but an object of faith. This may be nothing more than an admission that the existence of God must be taken on trust, since it cannot be proved. But it may also be an assertion that God is the object of a purely mystical intuition, and cannot therefore be defined in terms which are intelligible to the reason. And I think there are many theists who would assert this. But if one allows that it is impossible to define God in intelligible terms, then one is allowing that it is impossible for a sentence both to be significant and to be about God. If a mystic admits that the object of his vision is something which cannot be described, then he must also admit that he is bound to talk nonsense when he describes it.

For his part, the mystic may protest that his intuition does reveal truths to him, even though he cannot explain to others what these truths are; and that we who do not possess this faculty of intuition can have no ground for denying that it is a cognitive faculty. For we can hardly maintain *a priori* that there are no ways of discovering true propositions except those which we ourselves employ. The answer is that we set no limit to the number of ways in which one may come to formulate a true proposition. We do not in any way deny that a synthetic truth may be discovered by purely intuitive methods as well as by the rational method of induction. But we do say that every synthetic proposition, however it may have been arrived at, must be subject to the test of actual experience. We do not deny *a priori* that the mystic is able to discover truths by his own special methods. We wait to hear what are the propositions which embody his discoveries, in order to see whether they are verified or confuted by our empirical observations. But the mystic, so far from producing propositions which are empirically verified, is unable to produce any intelligible propositions at all. And therefore we say that his intuition has not revealed to him any facts. It is no use his saying that he has apprehended facts but is unable to express them. For we know that if he really had acquired any information, he would be able to express it. He would be able to indicate in some way or other how the genuineness of his discovery might be empirically determined. The fact that he cannot reveal what he "knows," or even himself devise an empirical test to validate his "knowledge," shows that his state of mystical intuition is not a genuinely cognitive state. So that in describing his vision the mystic does not give us any information about the external world; he merely gives us indirect information about the condition of his own mind.

These considerations dispose of the argument from religious experience, which many philosophers still regard as a valid argument in favour of the existence of a god. They say that it is logically possible for men to be immediately acquainted with God, as they are immediately acquainted with a sense-content, and that there is no reason why one should be prepared to believe a man when he says that he is seeing a yellow patch, and refuse to believe him when he says that he is seeing God. The answer to this is that if the man who asserts that he is seeing God is merely asserting that he is experiencing a peculiar kind of sense-content, then we do not for a moment deny that his assertion may be true. But, ordinarily, the man who says that he is seeing God is saying not merely that he is experiencing a religious emotion, but also that there exists a transcendent being who is the object of this emotion; just as the man who says that he sees a yellow patch is ordinarily saying not merely that his visual sense-field contains a yellow sense-content, but also that there exists a yellow object to which the sense-content belongs. And it is not irrational to be prepared to believe a man when he asserts the existence of a yellow object, and to refuse to believe him when he asserts the existence of a transcendent god. For whereas the sentence "There exists here a yellow-coloured material thing" expresses a genuine synthetic proposition which could be empirically verified, the sentence "There exists a transcendent god" has, as we have seen, no literal significance.

We conclude, therefore, that the argument from religious experience is altogether fallacious. The fact that people have religious experiences is interesting from the psychological point of view, but it does not in any way imply that there is such a thing as religious knowledge, any more than our having moral experiences implies that there is such a thing as moral knowledge. The theist, like the moralist, may believe that his experiences are cognitive experiences, but, unless he can formulate his "knowledge" in propositions that are empirically verifiable, we may be sure that he is deceiving himself. It follows that those philosophers who fill their books with assertions that that they intuitively "know" this or that moral or religious "truth" are merely providing material for the psycho-analyst. For no act of intuition can be said to reveal a truth about any matter of fact unless it issues in verifiable propositions. And all such propositions are to be incorporated in the system of empirical propositions which constitutes science.

E. L. MASCALL

E. L. MASCALL (1905-   ), Anglican theologian, has published extensively and contributed to a revival of interest in the Thomistic tradition in theology. His books, *He Who
Is*, *Words and Images* and *Existence and
Analogy*, are significant contributions to philosophy of religion.

Is Theological Discourse Possible?*

I. Theology and Verification

There is nothing new in the discovery that a peculiar problem is raised by
the fact that human beings from time to time make utterances which pur-
port to be statements about God, that is to say, which claim to speak about
the ineffable and to describe the indescribable. There is a whole branch of
traditional Christian theology—the doctrine of analogy—whose main concern
is with this problem. There is, however, something new about the way in
which the matter has been raised in recent years; and it is a way which, if it
is valid, is highly destructive not only of Christian theism as it has usually
been understood but of any religion which involves belief in a transcendent
deity. Little excuse should therefore be needed for devoting some space to its
discussion.

Some preliminary remarks may help to clarify the issue. In the first place,
it should be observed that, although the problem of theological discourse
and the problem of theological knowledge are not identical, they are very
closely connected and it is practically impossible to discuss either of them
without also discussing the other. Talking about God and knowing God are
not necessarily identical or even co-extensive; there may be such a thing as
wordless knowledge. Nevertheless we cannot talk about even wordless knowledge without using words to discuss it; and our discussion of it is likely to
be very unprofitable if at the same time we make no attempt to discuss its
object. I shall try not to confuse the two activities, but it will be quite impossible to separate them.

Again, we must recognise that it is impossible to separate the question
whether God can be talked about from the question of the kind of things

* From E. L. Mascall, *Words and Images*, pp. 1-14. Copyright, 1957, The Ronald
Press Company. Used by permission of The Ronald Press Company, New York, and
Longmans Green & Co., Ltd., London, 1957. [Footnotes omitted, Eds.]

that people say when they talk about him. The word "God" must have some content if our statements about God are to be intelligible at all; and if we say what the content is we are inevitably saying things about him. We shall thus be discussing in this book not one question but a number of closely related ones; and we may note that some of the confusion in which the subject has been involved has been due to a failure to distinguish between them.

I shall begin by examining the position that was put forward by Mr. (now Professor) A. J. Ayer in 1936 in his famous little book *Language, Truth and Logic*, in spite of the fact that nobody, perhaps not even Professor Ayer himself, appears to hold exactly that position today. This seems to me to be worth while for two reasons. In the first place, there are a good many people alive whose philosophical studies ended about that date, and, since Professor Ayer's book was given something of the character of a manifesto, as the statement of a philosophy which was to end philosophising, there may still be point in making a brief reference to it, in spite of the large number of criticisms, of various degrees of penetration, which have appeared since it was published. In the second place, most of what has been written on the question in recent years has derived, either directly or indirectly, from Professor Ayer's thesis, even if only by way of reaction against it; and it is in practice almost impossible to take any other starting point for our discussion. It ought in fairness to be recognised that, ten years after its first publication, Professor Ayer added to his book a new Introduction which contained certain modifications of his original position; but how firmly entrenched that position was is shown by how few and insignificant those modifications were.

The basis of Ayer's system was the famous "verification principle," in formulating which Ayer claimed to be simply expressing in the most clear-cut way the fundamentally empirical character of the tradition in British philosophy which derives from the great eighteenth-century Scottish philosopher David Hume. The principle had indeed been already stated in the most extreme form by philosophers of the Viennese School, in particular by M. Schlick, for whom the sole criterion of the meaningfulness of a statement was the possibility of verifying it by sense-experience. This is what Ayer called "verifiability in the strong sense": "A proposition is said to be verifiable, in the strong sense of the term, if, and only if, its truth could be conclusively established in experience." For Ayer, however, verifiability in the strict sense seemed to be far too drastic a criterion of meaningfulness; for it would dismiss as meaningless many statements which he was convinced were undoubtedly meaningful. It would rule out general statements, such

as "Arsenic is poisonous," which could not be conclusively verified so long
as any fragment of arsenic remained unconsumed, statements about inaccessible events and objects, such as "There are mountains on the other side
of the moon," whose unverifiability might be overcome by a sufficient development of the science of astronautics, and also statements about the past,
such as "Napoleon was defeated at Waterloo," which could be conclusively
verified only by the impossible method of going back in time to the year
1815 and observing what happened. Ayer therefore adopted a mitigated or
"weak" verification principle, according to which a statement is meaningful
if it is possible for experience to render it *probable*; "the question that must
be asked about any putative statement of fact is not, Would any observations make its truth or falsehood logically certain? but simply, Would any
observations be relevant to the determination of its truth or falsehood? And
it is only if a negative answer is given to this second question that we conclude that the statement under consideration is nonsensical." Some minor
modifications were made in Ayer's second edition, but they do not affect
our present considerations.

For Ayer, then (and here I mean the Ayer of the two editions of *Language,
Truth and Logic*), a statement which purports to be a statement of fact
is genuine and meaningful if, and only if, some possible empirical observations can be specified which would be relevant to the determination of its
truth or falsehood. He does, indeed, recognise that there is another kind
of meaningful statement, but these are not statements of fact; they are
simply tautologies, like the statement "Either all the ants that there are
are carnivorous or there is at least one ant that is not," and they provide
no information about any matter of fact whatever.

Having laid down his verification principle, Ayer then proceeds by the
use of it to dismiss as meaningless and nonsensical all ethical, metaphysical
and theological statements. Ethical statements emerge from the trial with
a reprieve, but only with the loss of their status as statements; they survive
as expressions and stimulants of feeling, or as exhortations to action. Metaphysical and theological statements, on the other hand, receive the shortest
of shrift; for they claim to make factual assertions about entities which are
not objects of sense-experience, and this is the unforgivable sin. "We are
often told," writes Ayer, "that the nature of God is a mystery which
transcends the human understanding. But to say that something transcends
the human understanding is to say that it is unintelligible. And what is
unintelligible cannot significantly be described." (I will only comment in
passing on the ambiguity in the use of the word "transcends" in the first
two sentences of this quotation.) Nor will Ayer have any truck with mystical
experience as anything more than a psychological phenomenon. "The mystic,

so far from producing propositions which are empirically verified, is unable to produce any intelligible propositions at all. . . . It is no use his saying that he has apprehended facts but is unable to express them. For we know that if he really had acquired any information, he would be able to express it." ("Do we?" we might interpose.) And again:

If the man who asserts that he is seeing God is merely asserting that he is experiencing a peculiar kind of sense-content, then we do not for a moment deny that his assertion may be true. But, ordinarily, the man who says that he is seeing God is saying not merely that he is experiencing a religious emotion, but also that there exists a transcendent being who is the object of this emotion; just as the man who says that he sees a yellow patch is ordinarily saying not merely that his visual sense-field contains a yellow sense-content, but also that there exists a yellow object to which the sense-content belongs. And it is not irrational to be prepared to believe a man when he asserts the existence of a yellow object, and to refuse to believe him when he asserts the existence of a transcendent God. For whereas the sentence 'There exists here a yellow-coloured material thing' expresses a genuine synthetic proposition which could be empirically verified, the sentence 'There exists a transcendent god' has, as we have seen, no literal significance.

We are not concerned at the moment with Ayer's theory of ethical statements; we are, however, concerned with his theory of theological statements, and also with his theory of metaphysical statements in so far as theological statements are themselves metaphysical. And there are, I think, at least four important comments to be made on his use of the verification principle.

First, there is something very suspicious about the fact that the verification principle had to be mitigated. In its original "strong" form it had all the downright simplicity that a fundamental philosophical principle might be expected to have. But, writes Ayer, "it seems to me that if we adopt conclusive verifiability as our criterion of significance, as some positivists have proposed, our argument will prove too much." "Too much for what?" we might inquire, with a notion that the answer is "Too much for Ayer." It would be a manly, robust and, as Ayer himself says, a heroic course to apply the principle ruthlessly regardless of the casualties that might result. But this would demolish many types of statement whose meaningfulness Ayer wishes to preserve, such as the statements already quoted about arsenic and the mountains on the far side of the moon and Napoleon. Why should they not be in fact demolished? Is it because Ayer has some independent criterion of significance and is trimming the verification principle to conform to it? It looks as if this is the case. But if so, why should we not trim the principle a little more in order to let in ethical, metaphysical or even (sit venia verbis) theological statements? Who is to decide where the line is to be drawn?

Secondly, what sort of statement is the verification principle itself? Ayer undoubtedly thinks it is meaningful, but it does not obviously belong to either of the two types of meaningful statement which he recognises. If he had taken the heroic course of nailing his colours to the mast of the "strong" form of the principle, some sort of case might have been made for the point of view that the principle was a tautology, that "meaningful" and "empirically verifiable" were simply synonyms or at least that "empirically verifiable" was part of the content of "meaningful." Even so, I think, the assertion would have been questionable, for we have, I would maintain, only to think of the phrases "empirically verifiable" and "meaningful" to see that they do not *mean* the same thing. Some philosophers might have held that, in spite of this difference of meaning, "Meaningful entails empirically verifiable" was a synthetic *a priori* truth, but this way is not open to Ayer, who denies that there are such things as synthetic *a priori* truths. Is the principle, then, an empirical generalisation? That is to say, has Ayer examined a large variety of statements for meaningfulness and concluded that all those that were meaningful conformed to the principle and that all those that were meaningless did not conform to it? I have suggested that this is almost what he seems to claim to have done, in the somewhat arbitrary way in which he has mitigated the verification principle. However, in the Introduction to his second edition he denies this explicitly, when he writes as follows: "While I wish the principle of verification itself to be regarded, not as an empirical hypothesis, but as a definition, it is not supposed to be entirely arbitrary." What, in this sentence, is the force of the statement "it is not supposed to be entirely arbitrary" it is indeed difficult to see; but its introduction seems to manifest a reprehensible desire to run with the hare and hunt with the hounds. For the assertion that the principle is a definition makes it impossible to question its truth, while the assertion that it is not entirely arbitrary suggests that some ground for its assertion is to be found in experience. This dual character is, however, just what Ayer elsewhere alleges that no statement can have, and one of his chief grievances against metaphysical and theological statements is that they—or some of them—claim to have it. This assertion that the verification principle is a definition will, however, bring us to our third comment.

For, if Ayer simply defines "meaningful" as equivalent to "verifiable in the weak sense or else tautological," no harm is done to either metaphysical or theological statements by saying that, in *this* sense, they are meaningless or nonsensical. What would be harmful would be a demonstration that they were meaningless in the common or garden sense of "unintelligible," and this is in fact nowhere proved. If the verification principle is simply a definition, it can assert nothing, for the function of definitions is not to make assertions but to register our linguistic conventions; if, on the other hand, it is a statement of fact, then it is a synthetic proposition, and, in virtue of the very assertion which it makes, itself needs empirical verification. Ayer seems in fact to have fallen into the snare in which the empiricists customarily claim to find the metaphysicians, that of packing into their principles the conclusions which they want to get out of them, as a conjuror inserts the rabbit into the hat before he comes on to the stage. This is the method of which Lord Russell has remarked that it has many advantages, but that they are the advantages which theft has over honest toil. But in fact, in his second edition Ayer makes a number of admissions which are extremely damaging to his former thesis. Thus he admits that there may be definitions of "meaning" according to which statements which are neither tautological nor empirically verifiable may be meaningful and that there is some proper use of the word "understanding" according to which such statements may be capable of being understood. He adds that this will not be the sense in which scientific hypothesis or common sense statements are understood, but I do not imagine that anyone ever thought that it was. He tells us that he would still defend the use of the criterion of verifiability as a methodological principle, but this remark as it stands is nothing more than an interesting statement of his own preferences and habits. His final admission is that for the effective elimination of metaphysics the criterion needs to be supported by detailed analyses of particular metaphysical arguments, and this is very remarkable. For it reduces the verification principle to the level of a generalisation from experience, namely the experience of examining a number of metaphysical arguments, and as long as any metaphysical arguments remain unexamined (which will presumably be always the case, as their number is potentially infinite) there is always the possibility that one of them will turn out to be valid and at the same time to violate the verification principle. If one compares the bold assertions in Ayer's first edition with the somewhat tentative and hedging remarks in the relevant passages of the second, one is tempted to feel that one is witnessing a very skilful rearguard action, in which Ayer rapidly oscillates between a number of positions, treating the verification principle at one moment as a definition, at another as a truth of logic and at another as an empirically verified generalisation. To be convicted of this procedure would leave some philosophical systems unabashed, but for Ayer's it is fatal. For the absolute distinction between truths of logic and statements of empirical fact is its basic doctrine, and it is precisely for their violation of this doctrine that it condemns its competitors. Nothing could therefore be more damaging to it than the discovery that it has itself fallen into the commission, in however small a degree, of this unforgivable sin.

My fourth criticism of Ayer is that, having made the apparently innocent and plausible assertion that all meaningful assertions must have some reference to experience, he then goes on to limit the meaning of experience in the narrowest and most arbitrary way to the experience of the bodily senses. Once again, we want to know what is the logical status of this assumption. If it is alleged to be a tautology, it seems pretty clear that this allegation is false, for there is nothing logically impossible in an experience which is not an experience of sense impressions upon the physical organs of the body. If, on the other hand, it is alleged to be an empirical generalisation, there is a good deal of experience, namely mystical experience in the broadest sense, which *prima facie* contradicts it and which certainly ought not to be dismissed without detailed examination. But in Ayer's book such an examination is nowhere made. The remarks which he does pass upon mystical experience are, however, highly revealing.

We do not deny *a priori* [he writes] that the mystic is able to discover truths by his own special methods. We wait to hear what are the propositions which embody his discoveries, in order to see whether they are verified or confuted by our empirical observations. But the mystic, so far from producing propositions which are empirically verified, is unable to produce any intelligible propositions at all. And therefore we say that his intuition has not revealed to him any facts. It is no use his saying that he has apprehended facts but is unable to express them. For we know that if he really had acquired any information, he would be able to express it . . . So that in describing his vision the mystic does not give us any information about the external world; he merely gives us indirect information about the condition of his own mind.

Everything here turns upon the way in which the word "empirical" has been smuggled into the second sentence of this passage. We may grant that if the mystic's language bore no relation whatever to the experience of any of his hearers or readers it could convey nothing to them. But this is not the case. The mystics do in fact use a great deal of language derived from sensory experience, the language of sight and touch and taste, while they emphasize that these words are not to be taken in their ordinary crude applications. They also at times appeal to non-sensory experiences which they assume that some at least of their hearers will have had and will be able to identify as of essentially the same type as their own. This use of language is undoubtedly odd, and it will certainly be misinterpreted by anyone who supposes that the only intelligible use of language derived from sense experience is its use in the registration of the occurrence of sense-phenomena. When Ayer waits for the mystic to enunciate propositions which are verified or confuted by empirical observation, he will certainly be disappointed. The mystic does not produce, at least as a general rule, propositions which are empirically verified, and, if he does, these will not be theological propositions. But to say that he does not produce any intelligible theological propositions at all is to make a dogma into a wall which hides the most obvious facts. Anyone who takes the trouble to study diligently the writings of the mystics can verify this for himself. Mystical theology, like other pursuits (physical science for example), has its own way of talking, which can be misleading or even flatly unintelligible to the complete outsider. The way in which its language is related to the reality with which it is concerned is as indirect and raises at least as many problems as the language which physical science uses to deal with the reality with which *it is* concerned. And, unlike the subject-matter of physics, the subject-matter of mystical theology is supremely mysterious and needs (so its practitioners tell us) for its understanding not merely training in a technique but purity of heart and religious devotion. It is furthermore alleged that, in the present life, very few persons are privileged to apprehend this reality with full immediacy and intensity. All this is true, yet the fact remains that the language of mystical experience, like, on a lower level, the language of dogmatic theology, can in fact be understood by those who are prepared to learn to do this. That finite minds can apprehend a transcendent and infinite reality and that human language can communicate information about it is no doubt very surprising, but it happens to be true; and to rule the language either of dogmatic or of mystical theology out of court, on the grounds that it fails to conform to an externally imposed prejudice as to what types of statement ought to be intelligible, is simply to exclude from consideration great tracts of reality and to confine oneself within a constricted and impoverished world. In Berkeley's phrase, it is to cast dust in one's eyes and then complain that one cannot see. I shall discuss this matter in more detail later on. At the moment I merely wish to make it plain that I am far from asserting that all our knowledge of God, or even the greater part of it, is derived from mystical experience in the strict sense, that is to say from a direct experimental awareness of God in which the senses play no part. But I do want to point out that Ayer's denial of the possibility of such awareness rests upon a sheer ambiguity in the use of the word "empirical," which is used first in an extremely general sense in order to make the verification principle plausible and then in an extremely specialised sense in order to rule out all experience except that of sense-phenomena.

It is, I would maintain, clear to anyone who approaches the matter with an open mind, that the fundamental criterion of meaningfulness is not sense-verifiability but intelligibility, that is to say that in order to know whether a statement has meaning you should see whether it is possible to understand it. This statement is of course a tautology, and therein lies its strength. For meaningfulness is a primary notion, which cannot be described in terms of anything else. As Mr. J. O. Wisdom has said, "with statements that can be understood independently of verification, to say that the verification provides the meaning is to confuse the meaning of a statement with the evidence for its truth." I am far from denying that the verification principle has a very considerable use, if a limited one, as a methodological principle. If you are uncertain whether a statement is significant or not it may be very useful to inquire what you would do in order to test its truth or falsehood. And this may involve subjecting it to the criterion of sense-verifiability. But the validity of this process depends upon its being the kind of statement to which the process is appropriate, and this can only be determined by examining it to see what kind of statement it is. I think that in fact a good many of the statements made by idealist philosophers are indefinite and confused, that they frequently fall into ambiguity and sometimes simply make mistakes in their arguments; they are not the only philosophers to go astray in these ways. But one of the difficulties in getting to grips with Ayer's strictures upon theology arises from the fact that he seems to have read very little theology, and to have a totally inadequate notion of the way that theologians think and the things that they say. This is a provocative statement, but I hope to provide justification for it in the course of this book.

JOHN HICK

JOHN HICK (1922-   ), English analytical philosopher and Presbyterian clergyman, has taught at Cornell and is now Stuart Professor of Christian Philosophy at Princeton Theological Seminary. His book, *Faith and Knowledge*, is his major publication.

The Nature of Faith*

We come now to our main problem. What manner of cognition is the religious man's awareness of God, and how is it related to his other cognitions?

We have already taken stock in a general way of our situation as cognizing beings. We become conscious of the existence of other objects in the uni-

* From John Hick, *Faith and Knowledge*, pp. 109-133. © 1957 by Cornell University, Cornell University Press. Reprinted by permission of The Cornell University Press.

verse, whether things or persons, either by experiencing them for ourselves or by inferring their existence from evidences within our experience. We have also noted that the awareness of God reported by the ordinary religious believer is of the former kind. He professes, not to have inferred that there is a God, but that God as a living being has entered into his own experience. He claims to enjoy something which he describes as an experience of God.

The ordinary believer does not, however, report an awareness of God as existing in isolation from all other objects of experience. His consciousness of the divine does not involve a cessation of his consciousness of a material and social environment. It is not a vision of God in solitary glory, filling the believer's entire mind and blotting out his normal field of perception. Whether such phrases correctly describe the mystic's goal, the ultimate Beatific Vision which figures in Christian doctrine, is a question for a later chapter.[1] But at any rate the ordinary person's religious awareness here on earth is not of that kind. He claims instead an apprehension of God meeting him in and through his material and social environments. He finds that in his dealings with the world of men and things he is somehow having to do with God, and God with him. The moments of ordinary life possess, or may possess, for him in varying degrees a religious significance. As has been well said, religious experience is "the whole experience of religious persons." [2] The believer meets God not only in moments of worship, but also when through the urgings of conscience he feels the pressure of the divine demand upon his life; when through the gracious actions of his friends he apprehends the divine grace; when through the marvels and beauties of nature he traces the hand of the Creator; and he has increasing knowledge of the divine purpose as he responds to its behests in his own life. In short, it is not apart from the course of mundane life, but in it and through it, that the ordinary religious believer claims to experience, however imperfectly and fragmentarily, the divine presence and activity.

This at any rate, among the variety of claims to religious awareness which have been and might be made, is the claim whose epistemological credentials we are to examine. Can God be known through his dealings with us in the world which he has made? The question concerns human experience, and the possibility of an awareness of the divine being mediated through awareness of the world, the supernatural through the natural.

In answer to this query I shall try to show in the present chapter that "mediated" knowledge, such as is postulated by this religious claim, is already a common and accepted feature of our cognitive experience. To this end we must study a basic characteristic of human experience, which I shall

---

[1] See ch. 7.
[2] William Temple, *Nature, Man and God* (London, 1934), p. 334.

call "significance," together with the correlative mental activity by which it is apprehended, which I shall call "interpretation." We shall find that interpretation takes place in relation to each of the three main types of existence, or orders of significance, recognized by human thought—the natural, the human, and the divine; and that in order to relate ourselves appropriately to each, a primary and unevidenceable act of interpretation is required which, when directed toward God, has traditionally been termed "faith." Thus I shall try to show that while the object of religious knowledge is unique, its basic epistemological pattern is that of all our knowing.

This is not to say that the logic of theistic belief has no peculiarities. It does indeed display certain unique features; and these (I shall try to show) are such as follow from the unique nature of its object, and are precisely the peculiarities which we should expect if that object is real. In the present chapter, then, we shall take note of the common epistemological pattern in which religious knowledge partakes, and in the following chapter we shall examine some special peculiarities of religious knowing.

"Significance" seems to be the least misleading word available to name the fundamental characteristic of experience which I wish to discuss. Other possible terms are "form" and "meaning." But "form," as the word is used in the traditional matter-form distinction, would require careful editing and commentary to purge it of unwanted Aristotelian associations. "Meaning," on the other hand, has been so overworked and misused in the past, not only by plain men and poets, but also by theologians and philosophers,[3] as to be almost useless today, except in its restricted technical use as referring to the equivalence of symbols. We may perhaps hope that after a period of exile the wider concept of "meaning" will be readmitted into the philosophical comity of notions. Indeed Professor Brand Blanshard has already braved the post-Ogden and Richards ban by using the phrase "perceptual meaning."[4] I propose here, however, to use the less prejudged term "significance."

By significance I mean that fundamental and all-pervasive characteristic of our conscious experience which de facto constitutes it for us the experience of a "world" and not of a mere empty void or churning chaos. We find ourselves in a relatively stable and ordered environment in which we have come to feel, so to say, "at home." The world has become intelligible to us, in the sense that it is a familiar place in which we have learned to act and react in appropriate ways. Our experience is not just an unpredictable kaleidoscope of which we are bewildered spectators, but reveals to us a familiar, settled cosmos in which we live and act, a world in which we can adopt purposes and adapt means to ends. It is in virtue of this homely, familiar, intelligible

---

[3] Cf. Ogden and Richards, The Meaning of Meaning (7th ed.; London, 1945), ch. 8.
[4] The Nature of Thought (London, 1939), I, chs. 4-6.

character of experience—its possession of significance—that we are able to inhabit and cope with our environment.

If this use of "significance" be allowed it will, I think, readily be granted that our consciousness is essentially consciousness of significance. Mind could neither emerge nor persist in an environment which was totally nonsignificant to it. For this reason it is not possible to define "significance" ostensively by pointing to contrasting examples of significant and nonsignificant experience. In its most general form at least, we must accept the Kantian thesis that we can be aware only of that which enters into a certain framework of basic relations which is correlated with the structure of our own consciousness. These basic relations represent the minimal conditions of significance for the human mind. The totally nonsignificant is thus debarred from entering into our experience. A completely undifferentiated field, or a sheer "buzzing, booming confusion," would be incapable of sustaining consciousness. For our consciousness is (to repeat) essentially consciousness of significance. Except perhaps in very early infancy or in states of radical breakdown, the human mind is always aware of its environment as having this quality of fundamental familiarity or intelligibility. Significance, then, is simply the most general characteristic of our experience.

Significance, so defined, has an essential reference to action. Consciousness of a particular kind of environmental significance involves a judgment, implicit or explicit, as to the appropriateness of a particular kind, or range of kinds, of action in relation to that environment. The distinction between types of significance is a distinction between the reactions, occurrent and dispositional, which they render appropriate. For the human psychophysical organism has evolved under the pressure of a continual struggle to survive, and our system of significance-attributions has as a result an essentially pragmatic orientation. Our outlook is instinctively empirical and practical. Physiologically we are so constituted as to be sensitive only to a minute selection of the vast quantity and complexity of the events taking place around us—that precise selection which is practically relevant to us. Our ears, for example, are attuned to a fragment only of the full range of sound waves, and our eyes to but a fraction of the multitudinous variations of light. Our sense organs automatically select from nature those aspects in relation to which we must act. We apprehend the world only at the macroscopic level at which we have practical dealings with it. As Professor Kemp Smith has said, "The function of sense-perception, as of instinct, is not knowledge but power, not insight but adaptation." [5] For an animal to apprehend more of its environment than is practically relevant to it would prove

---

[5] *Prolegomena to an Idealist Theory of Knowledge*, (London, 1924), pp. 32-33.

a fatal complication; it would be bemused and bewildered, and unable to react selectively to the stimuli indicating danger, food, and so on. And it is equally true at the human level that the significance of a given object or situation for a given individual consists in the practical *difference* which the existence of that object makes to that individual. It is indeed one of the marks of our status as dependent beings that we live by continual adaptation to our environment; and from this follows the essentially practical bearing of that which constitutes significance for us.

Although the locus of significance is primarily our environment as a whole, we can in thought divide this into smaller units of significance. We may accordingly draw a provisional distinction between two species of significance, object-significance and situational significance, and note the characteristics of significance first in terms of the former.

Every general name, such as "hat," "book," "fire," "house," names a type of object-significance. For these are isolable aspects of our experience which (in suitable contexts) render appropriate distinctive patterns of behavior. The word "hat," for example, does not name a rigidly delimited class of objects but a particular *use* to which things can be put, namely, as a covering for the head. Objects are specially manufactured for this use; but if necessary many other items can be made to fulfill the function of hat. This particular way of treating things, as headgear, is the behavioral correlate of the type of object-significance which we call "being a hat." Indeed the boundaries of each distinguishable class of objects are defined by the two *foci* of (1) physical structure and (2) function in relation to human interests. Our names are always in part names for functions or uses or kinds of significance as apprehended from the standpoint of the agent.

Significance, then, is a relational concept. A universe devoid of consciousness would be neither significant nor nonsignificant. An object or a sense-field is significant *for* or *to* a mind. We are only concerned here with significance for the human mind, but it is well to remember that the lower animals also are aware of their environment as being significant, this awareness being expressed not in words or concepts but in actions and readinesses for action.

There is, I hope, no suggestion of anything occult about this fundamental feature of our experience which I am calling "significance." The difficulty in discussing it is not novelty but, on the contrary, overfamiliarity. It is so completely obvious that we can easily overlook its importance, or even its existence. There is also the related difficulty that we do not apprehend significance as such, but only each distinguishable aspect of our experience as having its own particular type of significance. For significance is a genus which exists only in its species. Just as we perceive the various colors, but never color in general, so we perceive this and that kind of significance, but never significance *simpliciter*.

After this preliminary characterization of the nature of significance, we may take note of the mental activity of interpretation which is its subjective correlate. The word "interpretation" suggests the possibility of differing judgments; we tend to call a conclusion an interpretation when we recognize that there may be other and variant accounts of the same subject matter. It is precisely because of this suggestion of ambiguity in the given, and of alternative modes of construing data, that "interpretation" is a suitable correlate term for "significance."

Two uses of "interpretation" are to be distinguished. In one of its senses, an interpretation is a (true or false) *explanation*, answering the question, Why? We speak, for example, of a metaphysician's interpretation of the universe. In its other sense, an interpretation is a (correct or incorrect) *recognition*,[6] or attribution of significance, answering the question, What? ("What is that, a dog or a fox?") These two meanings are closely connected. For all explanation operates ultimately in terms of recognition. We explain a puzzling phenomenon by disclosing its context, revealing it as part of a wider whole which does not, for us, stand in need of explanation. We render the unfamiliar intellectually acceptable by relating it to the already recognizable, indicating a connection or continuity between the old and the new. But in the unique case of the universe as a whole the distinction between explanation and recognition fails to arise. For the universe has no wider context in terms of which it might be explained; an explanation of it can therefore only consist in a perception of its significance. In this case, therefore, interpretation is both recognition and explanation. Hence the theistic recognition, or significance-attribution, is also a metaphysical explanation or theory. However, although the explanatory and recognition aspects of theistic faith are inseparable, they may usefully be distinguished for purposes of exposition. In the present chapter we shall be examining interpretation, including the religious interpretation, as a recognition, or perception of significance; and in the following chapter, as an explanation.

An act of recognition, or of significance-attribution, is a complex occurrence dealing with two different types of ambiguity in the given. There are, on the one hand, interpretations which are mutually exclusive (e.g., "That is a fox" and "That is a dog," referring to the same object), and on the other hand interpretations which are mutually compatible (e.g., "That

---

[6] This is a slightly off-dictionary sense of "recognition," equating it, not with the identification of the appearances of an object at different times as appearances of the same object, but with the apprehension of what has been discussed above as the "significance" of objects.

is an animal" and "That is a dog"; or "He died by asphyxiation" and "He was murdered"). Of two logically alternative interpretations only one (at most) can be the correct interpretation. But two compatible interpretations may both be correct. We shall be concerned henceforth with this latter kind of difference, in which several levels or layers or orders of significance are found in the same field of data.

The following are some simple examples of different levels or orders of object-significance.

(a) I see a rectangular red object on the floor in the corner. So far I have interpreted it as a "thing" (or "substance"), as something occupying space and time. On looking more closely, however, I see that it is a red-covered book. I have now made a new interpretation which includes my previous one, but goes beyond it.

(b) There is a piece of paper covered with writing. An illiterate savage can perhaps interpret it as something made by man. A literate person, who does not know the particular language in which it is written, can interpret it as being a document. But someone who understands the language can find in it the expression of specific thoughts. Each is answering the question, "What is it?" correctly, but answering it at different levels. And each more adequate attribution of significance presupposes the less adequate ones.

This relationship between types of significance, one type being superimposed upon and interpenetrating another, is a pattern which we shall find again in larger and more important spheres.

We have already noted that significance is essentially related to action. The significance of an object to an individual consists in the practical difference which that object makes to him, the ways in which it affects either his immediate reactions or his more long-term plans and policies. There is also a reciprocal influence of action upon our interpretations. For it is only when we have begun to act upon our interpretations, and have thereby verified that our environment is capable of being successfully inhibited in terms of them, that they become fully "real" modes of experience. Interpretations which take the dispositional form of readinesses for action, instead of immediate overt activity, borrow this feeling of "reality" from cognate interpretations which are being or have already been confirmed in action. (For example, when I see an apple on the sideboard, but do not immediately eat it, I nevertheless perceive it as entirely "real" because I have in the past verified similar interpretations of similar apple-like appearances.) It is by acting upon our interpretations that we build up an apprehension of the world around us; and in this process interpretations, once confirmed, suggest and support further interpretations. The necessity of acting-in-terms-of to "clinch" or confirm an interpretation has its importance, as we shall note later, in relation to the specifically religious recognition which we call theistic faith.

We have been speaking so far only of object-significance. But, as already indicated, object-significance as contrasted with situational significance is an expository fiction. An object absolutely per se and devoid of context would have no significance for us. It can be intelligible only as part of our familiar world. What significance would remain, for example, to a book without the physical circumstance of sight, the conventions of language and writing, the acquired art of reading, and even the literature of which the book is a part and the civilization within which it occurs? An object owes its significance as much to its context as to itself; it is what it is largely because of its place in a wider scheme of things. We are indeed hardly ever conscious of anything in complete isolation. Our normal consciousness is of groups of objects standing in recognizable patterns of relations to one another. And it is the resulting situation taken as a whole that carries significance for us, rendering some ranges of action and reaction appropriate and others inappropriate. We live and plan and act all the time in terms of the situational significance of our environment; although of course our interest may focus at any given moment upon a particular component object within the current situation.

We do not, it is true, as plain men generally think of the familiar situations which constitute our experience from moment to moment as having "significance" and of our actions as being guided thereby. But in the fundamental sense in which we are using the term, our ordinary consciousness of the world is undoubtedly a continuous consciousness of significance. It is normally consciousness of a routine or humdrum significance which is so familiar that we take it entirely for granted. The significance for me, for example, of my situation at the present moment is such that I go on quietly working; this is the response rendered appropriate by my interpretation of my contemporary experience. No fresh response is required, for my routine reactions are already adjusted to the prevailing context of significance. But this significance is none the less real for being undramatic.

The component elements of situational significance are not only physical objects—tables, mountains, stars, houses, hats, and so on—but also such nonmaterial entities as sounds and lights and odors and, no less important, such psychological events and circumstances as other peoples' thoughts, emotions, and attitudes. Thus the kinds of situational significance in terms of which we act and react are enormously complex. Indeed the philosopher who would trace the morphology of situational significance must be a dramatist and poet as well as analyst. Attempts at significance-mapping have been undertaken by some of the existentialist writers: what they refer to as the "existential" character of experience is the fact that we are ourselves by definition *within* any relational system which constitutes a situation for us. However, these writers have usually been concerned to bring out the more strained and hectic aspects of human experience, presenting it often as a vivid night-mare of metaphysical anxieties and perils. They are undoubtedly painting from real life, particularly in this frightened age, but I venture to think that they are depicting it in a partial and one-sided manner.

A "situation" may be defined, then, as a state of affairs which, when selected for attention by an act of interpretation, carries its own distinctive practical significance for us. We may be involved in many different situations at the same time and may move by swift or slow transitions of interpretation from one to another. There may thus occur an indefinitely complex inter-penetration of situations. For example I am, let us say, sitting in a room playing a game of chess with a friend. The game, isolated by the brackets of imagination, is a situation in itself in which I have a part to play as one of the two competing intelligences presiding over the chess board. Here is an artificial situation with its conventional boundaries, structure, and rules of procedure. But from time to time my attention moves from the board to the friend with whom I am playing, and I exchange some conversation with him. Now I am living in another situation which contains the game of chess as a sub-situation. Then suddenly a fire breaks out in the building, and the attention of both of us shifts at once to our wider physical situation; and so on. There are the wider and wider spatial situations of the block, the city, the state, continent, globe, Milky Way, and finally, as the massive permanent background situation inclusive of all else, the physical universe. And there are also the widening circles of family, class, nation, civilization, and all the other groupings within the inclusive group of the human species as a whole. The complex web of interplays within and between these two expanding series gives rise to the infinite variety of situations of which our human life is composed.

Finally, enfolding and interpenetrating this interlocking mass of finite situations there is also, according to the insistent witness of theistic religion, the all-encompassing situation of being in the presence of God and within the sphere of an on-going divine purpose. Our main concern, after these pro-longed but unavoidable preliminaries, is to be with this alleged ultimate and inclusive significance and its relation to the more limited and temporary significances through which it is mediated.

Our inventory, then, shows three main orders of situational significance, corresponding to the threefold division of the universe, long entertained by human thought, into nature, man, and God. The significance for us of the physical world, nature, is that of an objective environment whose character and "laws" we must learn, and toward which we have continually to relate ourselves aright if we are to survive. The significance for us of the human world, man, is that of a realm of relationships in which we are responsible agents, subject to moral obligation. This world of moral significance is, so to speak, superimposed upon the natural world, so that relating ourselves to the moral world is not distinct from the business of relating ourselves to the natural world but is rather a particular manner of so doing. And likewise the more ultimately fateful and momentous matter of relating ourselves to the divine, to God, is not distinct from the task of directing ourselves within the natural and ethical spheres; on the contrary, it entails (without being reducible to) a way of so directing ourselves.

In the case of each of these three realms, the natural, the human, and the divine, a basic act of interpretation is required which discloses to us the existence of the sphere in question, thus providing the ground for our multifarious detailed interpretations within that sphere.

Consider first the level of natural significance. This is the significance which our environment has for us as animal organisms seeking pleasure and survival and shunning pain and death. In building houses, cooking food, avoiding dangerous precipices, whirlpools, and volcanoes, and generally conducting ourselves prudently in relation to the material world, we are all the time taking account of what I am calling (for want of a better name) the *natural* significance of our environment.

We have already noted some instances of natural significance when discussing the recognition of objects and situations. It is a familiar philosophical tenet, and one which may perhaps today be taken as granted, that all conscious experience of the physical world contains an element of interpretation. There are combined in each moment of experience a presented field of data and an interpretive activity of the subject. The perceiving mind is thus always in some degree a selecting, relating and synthesizing agent, and experiencing our environment involves a continuous activity of interpretation. "Interpretation" here is of course an unconscious and habitual process, the process by which a sense-field is perceived, for example, as a three-dimensional room, or a particular configuration of colored patches within that field as a book lying upon a table. Interpretation in this sense is generally recognized as a factor in the genesis of sense perception. We have now to note, however, the further and more basic act of interpretation which reveals to us the very existence of a material world, a world which we explore and inhabit as our given environment. In attending to this primary interpretative act we are noting the judgment which carries us beyond the solipsist predicament into an objective world of enduring, causally interacting objects, which we share with other people. Given the initial rejection of solipsism (or rather given the interpretative bias of human nature, which has prevented all but the most enthusiastic of philosophers from falling into solipsism) we can, I think, find corroborations of an analogical kind to support our belief in the unobserved continuance of physical objects and the reality of other minds. But the all-important first step, or assumption, is unevidenced and unevidenceable—except for permissive evidence, in that one's phenomenal experience is "there" to be interpreted either solipsistically or otherwise. But there is no event within our phenomenal experience the occurrence or nonoccurrence of which is relevant to the truth or falsity of the solipsist hypothesis. That hypothesis represents one possible interpretation of our experience as a whole, and the contrary belief in a plurality of minds existing in a common world represents an alternative and rival interpretation.

It may perhaps be objected that it does not make any practical difference whether solipsism be true or not, and that these are not therefore two *different* interpretations of our experience. For if our experience, phenomenally considered, would be identical on either hypothesis, then the alternative (it will be said) is a purely verbal one; the choice is merely a choice of synonyms. I do not think, however, that this is the case. Phenomenally, there is no difference between a dream in which we know that we are dreaming and one in which we do not. But, nevertheless, there is a total difference between the two experiences—total not in the sense that every, or indeed any, isolable aspects of them differ, but in the sense that the two experiences taken as wholes are of different kinds. We are aware of precisely the same course of events, but in the one case this occurs within mental brackets, labeled as a dream, while in the other case we are ourselves immersed within the events and live through them as participants. The phenomena are apprehended in the one case as dream constituents and in the other case as "real." And the difference caused by a genuine assent to solipsism would be akin to the sudden realization during an absorbing dream that it *is* only a dream. If the solipsist interpretation were to be seriously adopted and wholeheartedly believed, experience would take on an unreal character in contrast with one's former nonsolipsist mode of experience. Our personal relationships in particular, our loves and friendships, our hates and enmities, rivalries and cooperations, would have to be treated not as transsubjective meetings with other personalities, but as dialogues and dramas with oneself. There would be only one person in existence, and other "people," instead of being apprehended as independent centers of intelligence and purpose, would be but human-like appearances. They could not be the objects of affection or enmity, nor could their actions be subjected to moral judgment in our normal nonsolipsist sense. In short, although it must be very difficult, if not impossible, for the sanely functioning mind seriously to assent to solipsism and to apperceive in terms of it, yet this does represent at least a logically possible interpretation of experience, and constitutes a *different* interpretation from our ordinary belief in an independently existing world of things and persons. It follows that our normal mode of experience is itself properly described as an interpretation, an interpretation which we are unable to justify by argument but which we have nevertheless no inclination or reason to doubt. Indeed as Hume noted, nature has not left this to our choice, "and has doubtless esteem'd it an affair of too great importance to be trusted to our uncertain reasonings and speculations. We may well ask, What causes induce us to believe in the existence of body [i.e., matter]? but 'tis vain to ask, Whether there be body or not? That is a point, which we must take for granted in all our reasonings." [7]

But the ordering of our lives in relation to an objective material environment thus revealed to us by a basic act of interpretation is not the most distinctively human level of experience. It is characteristic of mankind to live not only in terms of the natural significance of his world but also in the dimension of personality and responsibility. And so we find that presupposing consciousness of the physical world, and supervening upon it, is the kind of situational significance which we call "being responsible" or "being under obligation." The sense of moral obligation, or of "oughtness," is the basic datum of ethics. It is manifested whenever someone, in circumstances requiring practical decision, feels "obligated" to act, or to refrain from acting, in some particular way. When this occurs, the natural significance of his environment is interpenetrated by another, ethical significance. A traveler on an unfrequented road, for example, comes upon a stranger who has met with an accident and who is lying injured and in need of help. At the level of natural significance this is just an empirical state of affairs, a particular configuration of stone and earth and flesh. But an act or reflex of interpretation at the moral level reveals to the traveler a situation in which he is under obligation to render aid. He feels a categorical imperative laid upon him, demanding that he help the injured man. The situation takes on for him a peremptory ethical significance, and he finds himself in a situation of inescapable personal responsibility.

As has often been remarked, it is characteristic of situations exhibiting moral significance that they involve, directly or indirectly, more than one person. The other or others may stand either in an immediate personal relationship to the moral agent or, as in large-scale social issues, in a more remote causal relationship. (The sphere of politics has been defined as that of the *im*personal relationships between persons.) Ethical significance, as the distinctive significance of situations in which persons are components, in-

[7] *Treatise*, bk. I, pt. IV, sec. 2 (Selby-Bigge's ed., pp. 187-188).

cludes both of these realms. To feel moral obligation is to perceive (or misperceive) the practical significance for oneself of a situation in which one stands in a responsible relationship to another person or to other people. That the perception of significance in personal situations sets up (in Kant's terms) a categorical imperative, while natural situations give rise only to hypothetical imperatives, conditional upon our own desires, is a defining characteristic of the personal world.

Clearly, moral significance presupposes natural significance. For in order that we may be conscious of moral obligations, and exercise moral intelligence, we must first be aware of a stable environment in which actions have foreseeable results, and in which we can learn the likely consequences of our deeds. It is thus a precondition of ethical situations that there should be a stable medium, the world, with its own causal laws, in which people meet and in terms of which they act. Indeed the two spheres of significance, the moral and the physical, entirely interpenetrate. For all occasions of obligation have reference, either immediately or ultimately, to overt action. Relating oneself to the ethical sphere is thus a particular manner of relating oneself to the natural sphere: ethical significance is mediated to us in and through the natural world.

As in the case of natural situational significance, we can enter the sphere of ethical significance only by our own act of interpretation. But at this level the interpretation is a more truly voluntary one. That is to say, it is not forced upon us from outside, but depends upon an inner capacity and tendency to interpret in this way, a tendency which we are free to oppose and even to overrule. If a man chooses to be a moral solipsist, or absolute egoist, recognizing no responsibility toward other people, no one can prove to him that he has any such responsibilities. The man who, when confronted with some standard situation having ethical significance, such as a bully wantonly injuring a child, fails to see it as morally significant, could only be classified as suffering from a defect of his nature analogous to physical blindness. He can of course be compelled by threats of punishment to conform to a stated code of behavior; but he cannot be compelled to feel moral obligation. He must see and accept for himself his own situation as a responsible being and its obverse of ethical accountability.

Has this epistemological paradigm—of one order of significance superimposed upon and mediated through another—any further application? The contention of this essay is that it has. As ethical significance interpenetrates natural significance, so religious significance interpenetrates both ethical and natural. The divine is the highest and ultimate order of significance, mediating neither of the others and yet being mediated through both of them.

But what do we mean by religious significance? What is it that, for the

ethical monotheist, possesses this significance, and in what does the significance consist?

The primary locus of religious significance is the believer's experience as
a whole. The basic act of interpretation which reveals to him the religious
significance of life is a uniquely "total interpretation," whose logic will be
studied in the next chapter. But we must at this point indicate what is
intended by the phrase, "total interpretation," and offer some preliminary
characterization of its specifically theistic form.

Consider the following imagined situation. I enter a room in a strange
building and find that a militant secret society appears to be meeting there.
Most of the members are armed, and as they take me for a fellow member
I judge it expedient to acquiesce in the role. Subtle and bloodthirsty plans
are discussed for a violent overthrow of the constitution. The whole situation
is alarming in the extreme. Then I suddenly notice behind me a gallery in
which there are batteries of arc lights and silently whirring cameras, and I
realize that I have walked by accident onto the set of a film. This realization
consists in a change of interpretation of my immediate environment. Until
now I had automatically interpreted it as being "real life," as a dangerous
situation demanding considerable circumspection on my part. Now I interpret it as having practical significance of a quite different kind. But there
is no corresponding change in the observable course of events. The meeting
of the "secret society" proceeds as before, although now I believe the state
of affairs to be quite other than I had previously supposed it to be. The same
phenomena are interpreted as constituting an entirely different practical
situation. And yet not quite the same phenomena, for I have noticed important new items, namely, the cameras and arc lights. But let us now in
imagination expand the room into the world, and indeed expand it to include
the entire physical universe. This is the strange room into which we walk at
birth. There is no space left for a photographers' gallery, no direction in
which we can turn in search of new clues which might reveal the significance
of our situation. Our interpretation must be a *total* interpretation, in which
we assert that the world as a whole (as experienced by ourselves) is of this
or that kind, that is to say, affects our plans and our policies in such and
such ways.

The monotheist's faith-apprehension of God as the unseen Person dealing
with him in and through his experience of the world is from the point of
view of epistemology an interpretation of this kind, an interpretation of the
world as a whole as mediating a divine presence and purpose. He sees in his
situation as a human being a significance to which the appropriate response
is a religious trust and obedience. His interpretative leap carries him into
a world which exists through the will of a holy, righteous, and loving Being

who is the creator and sustainer of all that is. Behind the world—to use an almost inevitable spatial metaphor—there is apprehended to be an omnipotent, personal Will whose purpose toward mankind guarantees men's highest good and blessedness. The believer finds that he is at all times in the presence of this holy Will. Again and again he realizes, either at the time or in retrospect, that in his dealings with the circumstances of his own life he is also having to do with a transcendent Creator who is the determiner of his destiny and the source of all good.

Thus the primary religious perception, or basic act of religious interpretation, is not to be described as either a reasoned conclusion or an unreasoned hunch that there is a God. It is, putatively, an apprehension of the divine presence within the believer's human experience. It is not an inference to a general truth, but a "divine-human encounter," a mediated meeting with the living God.

As ethical significance presupposes natural, so religious significance presupposes both ethical and natural. Entering into conscious relation with God consists in large part in adopting a particular style and manner of acting towards our natural and social environments. For God summons men to serve him *in* the world, and in terms of the life of the world. Religion is not only a way of cognizing but also, and no less vitally, a way of living. To see the world as being ruled by a divine love which sets infinite value upon each individual and includes all men in its scope, and yet to live as though the world were a realm of chance in which each must fight for his own interests against the rest, argues a very dim and wavering vision of God's rule. So far as that vision is clear it issues naturally in a trust in the divine purpose and obedience to the divine will. We shall be able to say more about this practical and dispositional response, in which the apprehension of the religious significance of life so largely consists, when we come in Chapter 9 to examine a particular form of theistic faith. At present we are concerned only with the general nature of the awareness of God.

Rudolf Otto has a somewhat obscure doctrine of the schematization of the Holy in terms of ethics.[8] Without being committed to Otto's use of the Kantian notion, or to his general philosophy of religion, we have been led to a parallel conception of the religious significance of life as schematized in, mediated through, or expressed in terms of, its natural and moral significance. As John Oman says of the Hebrew prophets,

What determines their faith is not a theory of the Supernatural, but an attitude towards the Natural, as a sphere in which a victory of deeper meaning than the visible and of more abiding purpose than the fleeting can be won. . . .

[8] *The Idea of the Holy*, trans. by J. W. Harvey (London, 1923), ch. 7.

The revelation of the Supernatural was by reconciliation to the Natural: and this was made possible by realising in the Natural the meaning and purpose of the Supernatural.[9]

In one respect this theistic interpretation is more akin to the natural than to the ethical interpretation. For while only *some* situations have moral significance, *all* situations have for embodied beings a continuous natural significance. In like manner the sphere of the basic religious interpretation is not merely this or that isolable situation, but the uniquely total situation constituted by our experience as a whole and in all its aspects, up to the present moment.

But on the other hand the theistic interpretation is more akin to the ethical than to the natural significance-attribution in that it is clearly focused in some situations and imperceptible in others. Not all the moments of life mediate equally the presence of God to the ordinary believer. He is not continuously conscious of God's presence (although possibly the saint is), but conscious rather of the divine Will as a reality in the background of his life, a reality which may at any time emerge to confront him in absolute and inescapable demand. We have already observed how one situation may interpenetrate another, and how some sudden pressure or intrusion can cause a shift of interpretation and attention so that the mind moves from one interlocking context to another. Often a more important kind of significance will summon us from a relatively trivial kind. A woman may be playing a game of bridge when she hears her child crying in pain in another room; and at once her consciousness moves from the artificial world of the game to the real world in which she is the mother of the child. Or an officer in the army reserve may be living heedless of the international situation until sudden mobilization recalls him to his military responsibility. The interrupting call of duty may summon us from trivial or relatively unimportant occupations to take part in momentous events. Greater and more ultimate purposes may without warning supervene upon lesser ones and direct our lives into a new channel. But the final significance, which takes precedence over all others as supremely important and overriding, is (according to theism) that of our situation as being in the presence of God. At any time a man may be confronted by some momentous decision, some far-reaching moral choice either of means or of ends, in which his responsibility as a servant of God intrudes upon and conflicts with the requirements of his earthly "station and its duties," so that the latter pales into unimportance and he acts in relation to a more ultimate environment whose significance magisterially overrules his customary way of life. When the call of God is clearly heard

[9] *The Natural and the Supernatural* (Cambridge, 1931), p. 448.

other calls become inaudible, and the prophet or saint, martyr or missionary, the man of conscience or of illumined mind may ignore all considerations of worldly prudence in responding to a claim with which nothing else whatever may be put in the balance.

To recapitulate and conclude this stage of the discussion, the epistemological point which I have sought to make is this. There is in cognition of every kind an unresolved mystery. The knower-known relationship is in the last analysis *sui generis*: the mystery of cognition persists at the end of every inquiry—though its persistence does not prevent us from cognizing. We cannot explain, for example, how we are conscious of sensory phenomena as constituting an objective physical environment; we just find ourselves interpreting the data of our experience in this way. We are aware that we live in a real world, though we cannot prove by any logical formula that it *is* a real world. Likewise we cannot explain how we know ourselves to be responsible beings subject to moral obligations; we just find ourselves interpreting our social experience in this way. We find ourselves inhabiting an ethically significant universe, though we cannot prove that it *is* ethically significant by any process of logic. In each case we discover and live in terms of a particular aspect of our environment through an appropriate act of interpretation; and having come to live in terms of it we neither require nor can conceive any further validation of its reality. The same is true of the apprehension of God. The theistic believer cannot explain *how* he knows the divine presence to be mediated through his human experience. He just finds himself interpreting his experience in this way. He lives in the presence of God, though he is unable to prove by any dialectical process that God exists.

To say this is not of course to demonstrate that God *does* exist. The outcome of the discussion thus far is rather to bring out the similarity of epistemological structure and status between men's basic convictions in relation to the world, moral responsibility, and divine existence. If our line of thought in Chapter I has been sound, these three parallel convictions all qualify, as instances of rational certainty, for the title of knowledge. The aim of the present chapter has thus been to show how, if there be a God, he is known to mankind, and how such knowledge is related to other kinds of human knowing. I hope that at least the outline of a possible answer to these questions has now been offered. . . .

MARTIN
BUBER

MARTIN BUBER (1878-   ), Austrian-Jewish existentialist theologian, has made contributions in the fields of sociology, Old Testament studies and Judaic studies as well as in theology. He is now professor of Social Philosophy at Hebrew University in Jerusalem.

I and Thou*

Men have addressed their eternal *Thou* with many names. In singing of Him who was thus named they always had the *Thou* in mind: the first myths were hymns of praise. Then the names took refuge in the language of *It*; men were more and more strongly moved to think of and to address their eternal *Thou* as an *It*. But all God's names are hallowed, for in them He is not merely spoken about, but also spoken to.

Many men wish to reject the word God as a legitimate usage, because it is so misused. It is indeed the most heavily laden of all the words used by men. For that very reason it is the most imperishable and most indispensable. What does all mistaken talk about God's being and works (though there has been, and can be, no other talk about these) matter in comparison with the one truth that all men who have addressed God had God Himself in mind? For he who speaks the word God and really has *Thou* in mind (whatever the illusion by which he is held), addresses the true *Thou* of his life, which cannot be limited by another *Thou*, and to which he stands in a relation that gathers up and includes all others.

But when he, too, who abhors the name, and believes himself to be godless, gives his whole being to addressing the *Thou* of his life, as a *Thou* that cannot be limited by another, he addresses God.

. . . .

Every real relation with a being or life in the world is exclusive. Its *Thou* is freed, steps forth, is single, and confronts you. It fills the heavens. This does not mean that nothing else exists; but all else lives in *its* light. As long as the presence of the relation continues, this its cosmic range is inviolable. But as soon as a *Thou* becomes *It*, the cosmic range of the relation appears

---

* From Martin Buber, *I and Thou*, trans. Ronald Gregor Smith, pp. 75-76, 78-83, 95-96, 99-101, 109-116. Published, 1937, T. & T. Clark. Reprinted with permission of T. & T. Clark and Charles Scribner's Sons.

as an offence to the world, its exclusiveness as an exclusion of the universe.

In the relation with God unconditional exclusiveness and unconditional inclusiveness are one. He who enters on the absolute relation is concerned with nothing isolated any more, neither things nor beings, neither earth nor heaven; but everything is gathered up in the relation. For to step into pure relation is not to disregard everything but to see everything in the *Thou*, not to renounce the world but to establish it on its true basis. To look away from the world, or to stare at it, does not help a man to reach God; but he who sees the world in Him stands in His presence. "Here world, there God" is the language of *It*; "God in the world" is another language of *It*; but to eliminate or leave behind nothing at all, to include the whole world in the *Thou*, to give the world its due and its truth, to include nothing beside God but everything in Him—this is full and complete relation.

Men do not find God if they stay in the world. They do not find Him if they leave the world. He who goes out with his whole being to meet his *Thou* and carries to it all being that is in the world, finds Him who cannot be sought.

Of course God is the "wholly Other"; but He is also the wholly Same, the wholly Present. Of course He is the *Mysterium Tremendum* that appears and overthrows; but He is also the mystery of the self-evident, nearer to me than my *I*.

If you explore the life of things and of conditioned being you come to the unfathomable, if you deny the life of things and of conditioned being you stand before nothingness, if you hallow this life you meet the living God.

Man's sense of *Thou*, which experiences in the relations with every particular *Thou* the disappointment of the change to *It*; strives out but not away from them all to its eternal *Thou*; but not as something is sought: actually there is no such thing as seeking God, for there is nothing in which He could not be found. How foolish and hopeless would be the man who turned aside from the course of his life in order to seek God; even though he won all the wisdom of solitude and all the power of concentrated being he would miss God. Rather is it as when a man goes his way and simply wishes that it might be the way: in the strength of his wish his striving is expressed. Every relational event is a stage that affords him a glimpse into the consummating event. So in each event he does not partake, but also (for he is waiting) does partake, of the one event. Waiting, not seeking, he goes his way; hence he is composed before all things, and makes contact with them which helps them. But when he has *found*, his heart is not turned from them, though everything now meets him in the one event. He blesses every cell that sheltered him, and every cell into which he will yet turn. For this finding is not the end, but only the eternal middle, of the way.

It is a finding without seeking, a discovering of the primal, of origin. His sense of *Thou*, which cannot be satiated till he finds the endless *Thou*, had the *Thou* present to it from the beginning; the presence had only to become wholly real to him in the reality of the hallowed life of the world.

God cannot be inferred in anything—in nature, say, as its author, or in history as its master, or in the subject as the self that is thought in it. Something else is not "given" and God then elicited from it; but God is the Being that is directly, most nearly, and lastingly, over against us, that may properly only be addressed, not expressed.

Men wish to regard a feeling (called feeling of dependence, and recently, more precisely, creaturely feeling) as the real element in the relation with God. In proportion as the isolation and definition of this element is accurate, its unbalanced emphasis only makes the character of complete relation the more misunderstood.

What has already been said of love is even more unshakably valid here. Feelings are a mere accompaniment to the metaphysical and metapsychical fact of the relation, which is fulfilled not in the soul but between *I* and *Thou*. A feeling may be considered ever so essential, it remains nevertheless subject to the dynamic of the soul, where one feeling is outstripped, outdone, and abolished by another. In distinction from relation a feeling has its place in a scale. But above all, every feeling has its place within a polar tension, obtaining its colour and significance not from itself alone, but also from the opposite pole: every feeling is conditioned by its opposite. Thus the absolute relation (which gathers up into reality all those that are relative, and is no more a part, as these are, but is the whole that completes and unifies them all), in being reduced to the status of an isolated and limited feeling, is made into a relative psychological matter.

If the soul is the starting-point of our consideration, complete relation can be understand only in a bipolar way, only as the *coincidentia oppositorum*, as the coincidence of oppositions of feeling. Of course, the one pole—suppressed by the person's basic religious attitude—often disappears from the reflective consciousness, and can only be recalled in the purest and most ingenuous consideration of the depths of the being.

Yes; in pure relation you have felt yourself to be simply dependent, as you are able to feel in no other relation—and simply free, too, as in no other time or place: you have felt yourself to be both creaturely and creative. You had the one feeling then no longer limited by the other, but you had both of them limitlessly and together.

You know always in your heart that you need God more than everything; but do you not know too that God needs you—in the fulness of His eternity needs you? How would man be, how would you be, if God did not need him, did not need you? You need God, in order to be—and God needs you, for the very meaning of your life. In instruction and in poems men are at pains to say more, and they say too much—what turgid and presumptuous talk that is about the "God who becomes"; but we know unshakably in our hearts that there is a becoming of the God that is. The world is not divine sport, it is divine destiny. There is divine meaning in the life of the world, of man, of human persons, of you and of me.

Creation happens to us, burns itself into us, recasts us in burning—we tremble and are faint, we submit. We take part in creation, meet the Creator, reach out to Him, helpers and companions.

Two great servants pace through the ages, prayer and sacrifice. The man who prays pours himself out in unrestrained dependence, and knows that he has—in an incomprehensible way—an effect upon God, even though he obtains nothing from God; for when he no longer desires anything for himself he sees the flame of his effect burning at its highest.—And the man who makes sacrifice? I cannot despise him, this upright servant of former times, who believed that God yearned for the scent of his burnt-offering. In a foolish but powerful way he knew that we can and ought to give to God. This is known by him, too, who offers up his little will to God and meets Him in the grand will. "Thy will be done," he says, and says no more; but truth adds for him "through me whom Thou needest."

What distinguishes sacrifice and prayer from all magic?—Magic desires to obtain its effects without entering into relation, and practises its tricks in the void. But sacrifice and prayer are set "before the Face", in the consummation of the holy primary word that means mutual action: they speak the *Thou*, and then they hear.

To wish to understand pure relation as dependence is to wish to empty one of the bearers of the relation, and hence the relation itself, of reality.

.   .   .   .

Man's religious situation, his *being there* in the Presence, is characterized by its essential and indissoluble antinomy. The nature of its being determines that this antinomy is indissoluble. He who accepts the thesis and rejects the antithesis does injury to the significance of the situation. He who tries to think out a synthesis destroys the significance of the situation. He who strives to make the antinomy into a relative matter abolishes the significance of the situation. He who wishes to carry through the conflict of the antinomy other than with his life transgresses the significance of the situation. The significance of the situation is that it is lived, and nothing but lived, continually, ever anew, without foresight, without forethought, without prescription, in the totality of its antinomy.

Comparison of the religious with the philosophical antinomy will make this clear. Kant may make the philosophical conflict between necessity and freedom into a relative matter by assigning the former to the world of appearances and the latter to the world of being, so that in their two settings they are no longer really opposed, but rather reconciled—just as the worlds for which they are valid are reconciled. But if I consider necessity and freedom not in worlds of thought but in the reality of my standing before God, if I know that "I am given over for disposal" and know at the same time that "It depends on myself," then I cannot try to escape the paradox that has to be lived by assigning the irreconciliable propositions to two separate realms of validity; nor can I be helped to an ideal reconciliation by any theological device: but I am compelled to take both to myself, to be lived together, and in being lived they are one.

. . . .

Every real relation in the world is exclusive, the Other breaks in on it and avenges its exclusion. Only in the relation with God are unconditioned exclusiveness and unconditioned inclusiveness one and the same, in which the whole universe is implied.

Every real relation in the world rests on individuation, this is its joy— for only in this way is mutual knowledge of different beings won—and its limitation—for in this way perfect knowledge and being known are foregone. But in the perfect relation my *Thou* comprehends but is not my Self, my limited knowledge opens out into a state in which I am boundlessly known.

Every real relation in the world is consummated in the interchange of actual and potential being; every isolated *Thou* is bound to enter the chrysalis state of the *It* in order to take wings anew. But in pure relation potential being is simply actual being as it draws breath, and in it the *Thou* remains present. By its nature the eternal *Thou* is eternally *Thou*; only our nature compels us to draw it into the world and the talk of *It*.

The world of *It* is set in the context of space and time.

The world of *Thou* is not set in the context of either of these.

Its context is in the Centre, where the extended lines of relations meet— in the eternal *Thou*.

In the great privilege of pure relation the privileges of the world of *It* are abolished. By virtue of this privilege there exists the unbroken world of *Thou*: the isolated moments of relations are bound up in a life of world solidarity. By virtue of this privilege formative power belongs to the world of *Thou*: spirit can penetrate and transform the world of *It*. By virtue of this privilege we are not given up to alienation from the world and the loss of reality by the *I*—to domination by the ghostly. Reversal is the recognition of the Centre and the act of turning again to it. In this act of the being the buried relational power of man rises again, the wave that carries all the spheres of relation swells in living streams to give new life to our world

Perhaps not to our world alone. For this double movement, of estrangement from the primal Source, in virtue of which the universe is sustained in the process of becoming, and of turning towards the primal Source, in virtue of which the universe is released in being, may be perceived as the metacosmical primal form that dwells in the world as a whole in its relation to that which is not the world—form whose twofold nature is represented among men by the twofold nature of their attitudes, their primary words, and their aspects of the world. Both parts of this movement develop fraught with destiny, in time, and are compassed by grace in the timeless creation that is, incomprehensibly, at once emancipation and preservation, release and binding. Our knowledge of twofold nature is silent before the paradox of the primal mystery.

.   .   .   .

What is the eternal, primal phenomenon, present here and now, of that which we term revelation? It is the phenomenon that a man does not pass, from the moment of the supreme meeting, the same being as he entered into it. The moment of meeting is not an "experience" that stirs in the receptive soul and grows to perfect blessedness; rather, in that moment something happens to the man. At times it is like a light breath, at times like a wrestling-bout, but always—it *happens*. The man who emerges from the act of pure relation that so involves his being has now in his being something more that has grown in him, of which he did not know before and whose origin he is not rightly able to indicate. However the source of this new thing is classified in scientific orientation of the world, with its authorised efforts to establish an unbroken causality, we, whose concern is real consideration of the real, cannot have our purpose served with subconsciousness or any other apparatus of the soul. The reality is that we receive what we did not hitherto have, and receive it in such a way that we know it has been given to us. In the language of the Bible, "Those who wait upon the Lord shall renew their strength." In the language of Nietzsche, who in his account remains loyal to reality, "We take and do not ask who it is there that gives."

Man receives, and he receives not a specific "content" but a Presence, a Presence as power. This Presence and this power include three things, undivided, yet in such a way that we may consider them separately. First, there is the whole fulness of real mutual action, of the being raised and bound up in relation: the man can give no account at all of how the binding in relation is brought about, nor does it in any way lighten his life—it makes life heavier, but heavy with meaning. Secondly, there is the inexpressible confirmation of meaning. Meaning is assured. Nothing can any longer be meaningless. The question about the meaning of life is no longer there. But were it there, it would not have to be answered. You do not know how to exhibit and define the meaning of life, you have no formula or picture for it, and yet it has more certitude for you than the perceptions of your senses. What does the revealed and concealed meaning purpose with us, desire from us? It does not wish to be explained (nor are we able to do that) but only to be done by us. Thirdly, this meaning is not that of "another life," but that of this life of ours, not one of a world "yonder" but that of this world of ours, and it desires its confirmation in this life and in relation with this world. This meaning can be received, but not experienced; it cannot be experienced but it can be done, and this is its purpose with us. The assurance I have of it does not wish to be sealed within me, but it wishes to be born by me into the world. But just as the meaning itself does not permit itself to be transmitted and made into knowledge generally current and admissible, so confirmation of it cannot be transmitted as a valid Ought; it is not prescribed, it is not specified on any tablet, to be raised above all men's heads. The meaning that has been received can be proved true by each man only in the singleness of his being and the singleness of his life. As no prescription can lead us to the meeting, so none leads from it. As only acceptance of the Presence is necessary for the approach to the meeting, so in a new sense is it so when we emerge from it. As we reach the meeting with the simple *Thou* on our lips, so with the *Thou* on our lips we leave it and return to the world.

That before which, in which, out of which, and into which we live, even the mystery, has remained what it was. It has become present to us and in its presentness has proclaimed itself to us as salvation; we have "known" it, but we acquire no knowledge from it which might lessen or moderate its mysteriousness. We have come near to God, but not nearer to unveiling being or solving its riddle. We have felt release, but not discovered a "solution." We cannot approach others with what we have received, and say "You must know this, you must do this." We can only go, and confirm its truth. And this, too, is no "ought," but we can, we *must*.

This is the eternal revelation that is present here and now. I know of no revelation and believe in none whose primal phenomenon is not precisely this. I do not believe in a self-naming of God, a self-definition of God before men. The Word of revelation is *I am that I am*. That which reveals is that which reveals. That which is *is*, and nothing more. The eternal source of strength streams, the eternal contact persists, the eternal voice sounds forth, and nothing more.

The eternal *Thou* can by its nature not become *It*; for by its nature it cannot be established in measure and bounds, not even in the measure of the immeasurable, or the bounds of boundless being; for by its nature it cannot be understood as a sum of qualities, not even as an infinite sum of qualities raised to a transcendental level; for it can be found neither in nor out of the world; for it cannot be experienced, or thought; for we miss Him, Him who is, if we say "I believe that He is"—"He" is also a metaphor, but "Thou" is not.

And yet in accordance with our nature we are continually making the eternal *Thou* into *It*, into some thing—making God into a thing. Not indeed out of arbitrary self-will; God's history as a thing, the passage of God as Thing through religion and through the products on its brink, through its bright ways and its gloom, its enhancement and its destruction of life, the passage away from the living God and back again to Him, the changes from the present to establishment of form, of objects, and of ideas, dissolution and renewal—all are one way, are *the* way.

What is the origin of the expressed knowledge and ordered action of the religions? How do the Presence and the power of the revelation (for all religions necessarily appeal to some kind of revelation, whether through the medium of the spoken word, or of nature, or of the soul: there are only religions of revelation)—how do the Presence and the power received by men in revelation change into a "content"?

The explanation has two layers. We understand the outer psychical layer when we consider man in himself, separated from history, and the inner factual layer, the primal phenomenon of religion, when we replace him in history. The two layers belong together.

Man desires to possess God; he desires a continuity in space and time of possession of God. He is not content with the inexpressible confirmation of meaning, but wants to see this confirmation stretched out as something that can be continually taken up and handled, a continuum unbroken in space and time that insures his life at every point and every moment. Man's thirst for continuity is unsatisfied by the life-rhythm of pure relation, the interchange of actual being and of a potential being in which only our power to enter into relation, and hence the presentness (but not the primal Presence) decreases. He longs for extension in time, for duration. Thus God becomes an object of faith. At first faith, set in time, completes the acts of relation; but gradually it replaces them. Resting in belief in an *It* takes the place of the continually renewed movement of the being towards concentration and going out to the relation. The "Nevertheless I believe" of the fighter who knows remoteness from as well as nearness to God is more and more completely transformed into the certainty of him who enjoys profits, that nothing can happen to him, since he believes that there is One who will not let anything happen to him.

Further, man's thirst for continuity is unsatisfied by the life-structure of pure relation, the "solitude" of the *I* before the *Thou*, the law that man, though binding up the world in relation in the meeting, can nevertheless only as a person approach and meet God. He longs for extension in space, for the representation in which the community of the faithful is united with its God. Thus God becomes the object of a cult. The cult, too, completes at first the acts of relation, in adjusting in a spatial context of great formative power the living prayer, the immediate saying of the *Thou*, and in linking it with the life of the senses. It, too, gradually replaces the acts of relation, when the personal prayer is no longer supported, but displaced, by the communal prayer, and when the act of the being, since it admits no rule, is replaced by ordered devotional exercises.

Actually, however, pure relation can only be raised to constancy in space and time by being embodied in the whole stuff of life. It cannot be preserved, but only proved true, only done, only done up into life. Man can do justice to the relation with God in which he has come to share only if he realises God anew in the world according to his strength and to the measure of each day. In this lies the only authentic assurance of continuity. The authentic assurance of duration consists in the fact that pure relation can be fulfilled in the growth and rise of beings into *Thou*, that the holy primary word makes itself heard in them all. Thus the time of human life is shaped into a fulness of reality, and even though human life neither can nor ought to overcome the relation of *It*, it is so penetrated with relation that relation wins in it a shining streaming constancy: the moments of supreme meeting are then not flashes in darkness but like the rising moon in a clear starlit night. Thus, too, the authentic assurance of constancy in space consists in the fact that men's relations with their true *Thou*, the radial lines that proceed from all the points of the *I* to the Centre, form a circle. It is not the periphery, the community, that comes first, but the radii, the common quality of relation with the Centre. This alone guarantees the authentic existence of the community.

Only when these two arise—the binding up of time in a relational life of salvation and the binding up of space in the community that is made one by its Centre—and only so long as they exist, does there arise and exist, round about the invisible altar, a human cosmos with bounds and form, grasped with the spirit out of the universal stuff of the aeon, a world that is house and home, a dwelling for man in the universe.

Meeting with God does not come to man in order that he may concern himself with God, but in order that he may confirm that there is meaning in the world. All revelation is summons and sending. But again and again man brings about, instead of realisation, a reflexion to Him who reveals:

he wishes to concern himself with God instead of with the world. Only, in such a reflexion, he is no longer confronted by a *Thou*, he can do nothing but establish an It-God in the realm of things, believe that he knows of God as of an *It*, and so speak about Him. Just as the "self"-seeking man, instead of directly living something or other, a perception or an affection, reflects about his perceptive or reflective *I*, and thereby misses the truth of the event, so the man who seeks God (though for the rest he gets on very well with the self-seeker in the one soul), instead of allowing the gift to work itself out, reflects about the Giver—and misses both.

God remains present to you when you have been sent forth; he who goes on a mission has always God before him: the truer the fulfilment the stronger and more constant His nearness. To be sure, he cannot directly concern himself with God, but he can converse with Him. Reflexion, on the other hand, makes God into an object. Its apparent turning towards the primal source belongs in truth to the universal movement away from it; just as the apparent turning away of the man who is fulfilling his mission belongs in truth to the universal movement towards the primal source.

PAUL
TILLICH

PAUL TILLICH (1886-   ), German-American philosophical theologian, is now on the faculty of Harvard University. His system reflects a wide-ranging interest in the fields of classical Greek thought, German philosophy, art, history, psychoanalysis and existentialism. *Systematic Theology* is his major work.

Courage and Transcendence*

Courage is the self-affirmation of being in spite of the fact of nonbeing. It is the act of the individual self in taking the anxiety of nonbeing upon itself by affirming itself either as part of an embracing whole or in its individual selfhood. Courage always includes a risk, it is always threatened by nonbeing, whether the risk of losing oneself and becoming a thing within the whole of things or of losing one's world in an empty self-relatedness.

* From Paul Tillich, *The Courage to Be*, pp. 155-156, 167-190. Copyright, 1952, Yale University Press. Used by permission of Yale University Press.

Courage needs the power of being, a power transcending the nonbeing which is experienced in the anxiety of fate and death, which is present in the anxiety of emptiness and meaninglessness, which is effective in the anxiety of guilt and condemnation. The courage which takes this threefold anxiety into itself must be rooted in a power of being that is greater than the power of oneself and the power of one's world. Neither self-affirmation as a part nor self-affirmation as oneself is beyond the manifold threat of nonbeing. Those who are mentioned as representatives of these forms of courage try to transcend themselves and the world in which they participate in order to find the power of being-itself and a courage to be which is beyond the threat of nonbeing. There are no exceptions to this rule; and this means that every courage to be has an open or hidden religious root. For religion is the state of being grasped by the power of being-itself. In some cases the religious root is carefully covered, in others it is passionately denied; in some it is deeply hidden and in others superficially. But it is never completely absent. For everything that is participates in being-itself, and everybody has some awareness of this participation, especially in the moments in which he experiences the threat of nonbeing. This leads us to a final consideration, the double question: How is the courage to be rooted in being-itself, and how must we understand being-itself in the light of the courage to be? The first question deals with the ground of being as source of the courage to be, the second with courage to be as key to the ground of being.

.   .   .   .

Fate and the Courage To Accept Acceptance

As the symbolic figures of death and the devil show, the anxiety of this period [the Reformation—Eds.] was not restricted to the anxiety of guilt. It was also an anxiety of death and fate. The astrological ideas of the later ancient world had been revived by the Renaissance and had influenced even those humanists who joined the Reformation. We have already referred to the Neo-Stoic courage, expressed in some Renaissance pictures, where man directs the vessel of his life although it is driven by the winds of fate. Luther faced the anxiety of fate on another level. He experienced the connection between the anxiety of guilt and the anxiety of fate. It is the uneasy conscience which produces innumerable irrational fears in daily life. The rustling of a dry leaf horrifies him who is plagued by guilt. Therefore conquest of the anxiety of guilt is also conquest of the anxiety of fate. The courage of confidence takes the anxiety of fate as well as the anxiety of guilt into itself.

It says "in spite of" to both of them. This is the genuine meaning of the doctrine of providence. Providence is not a theory about some activities of God; it is the religious symbol of the courage of confidence with respect to fate and death. For the courage of confidence says "in spite of" even to death.

Like Paul, Luther was well aware of the connection of the anxiety of guilt with the anxiety of death. In Stoicism and Neo-Stoicism the essential self is not threatened by death, because it belongs to being-itself and transcends nonbeing. Socrates, who in the power of his essential self conquered the anxiety of death, has become the symbol for the courage to take death upon oneself. This is the true meaning of Plato's so-called doctrine of immortality of the soul. In discussing this doctrine we should neglect the arguments for immortality, even those in Plato's *Phaedon*, and concentrate on the image of the dying Socrates. All the arguments, skeptically treated by Plato himself, are attempts to interpret the courage of Socrates, the courage to take one's death into one's self-affirmation. Socrates is certain that the self which the executioners will destroy is not the self which affirms itself in his courage to be. He does not say much about the relation of the two selves, and he could not because they are not numerically two, but one in two aspects. But he makes it clear that the courage to die is the test of the courage to be. A self-affirmation which omits taking the affirmation of one's death into itself tries to escape the test of courage, the facing of nonbeing in the most radical way.

The popular belief in immortality which in the Western world has largely replaced the Christian symbol of resurrection is a mixture of courage and escape. It tries to maintain one's self-affirmation even in the face of one's having to die. But it does this by continuing one's finitude, that is one's having to die, infinitely, so that the actual death never will occur. This, however, is an illusion and, logically speaking, a contradiction in terms. It makes endless what, by definition, must come to an end. The "immortality of the soul" is a poor symbol for the courage to be in the face of one's having to die.

The courage of Socrates (in Plato's picture) was based not on a doctrine of the immortality of the soul but on the affirmation of himself in his essential, indestructible being. He knows that he belongs to two orders of reality and that the one order is transtemporal. It was the courage of Socrates which more than any philosophical reflection revealed to the ancient world that everyone belongs to two orders.

But there was one presupposition in the Socratic (Stoic and Neo-Stoic) courage to take death upon oneself, namely the ability of every individual to participate in both orders, the temporal and the eternal. This presupposition is not accepted by Christianity. According to Christianity we are estranged from our essential being. We are not free to realize our essential being, we are bound to contradict it. Therefore death can be accepted only through a state of confidence in which death has ceased to be the "wages of sin." This, however, is the state of being accepted in spite of being unacceptable. Here is the point in which the ancient world was transformed by Christianity and in which Luther's courage to face death was rooted. It is the being accepted into communion with God that underlies this courage, not a questionable theory of immortality. The encounter with God in Luther is not merely the basis for the courage to take upon oneself sin and condemnation, it is also the basis for taking upon oneself fate and death. For encountering God means encountering transcendent security and transcendent eternity. He who participates in God participates in eternity. But in order to participate in him you must be accepted by him and you must have accepted his acceptance of you.

Luther had experiences which he describes as attacks of utter despair (Anfechtung), as the frightful threat of a complete meaninglessness. He felt these moments as satanic attacks in which everything was menaced: his Christian faith, the confidence in his work, the Reformation, the forgiveness of sins. Everything broke down in the extreme moments of this despair, nothing was left of the courage to be. Luther in these moments, and in the descriptions he gives of them, anticipated the descriptions of them by modern Existentialism. But for him this was not the last word. The last word was the first commandment, the statement that God is God. It reminded him of the unconditional element in human experience of which one can be aware even in the abyss of meaninglessness. And this awareness saved him.

It should not be forgotten that the great adversary of Luther, Thomas Münzer, the Anabaptist and religious socialist, describes similar experiences. He speaks of the ultimate situation in which everything finite reveals its finitude, in which the finite has come to its end, in which anxiety grips the heart and all previous meanings fall apart, and in which just for this reason the Divine Spirit can make itself felt and can turn the whole situation into a courage to be whose expression is revolutionary action. While Luther represents ecclesiastical Protestantism, Münzer represents evangelical radicalism. Both men have shaped history, and actually Münzer's views had even more influence in America than Luther's. Both men experienced the anxiety of meaninglessness and described it in terms which had been created by Christian mystics. But in doing so they transcended the courage of confidence which is based on a personal encounter with God. They had to receive elements from the courage to be which is based on mystical union. This leads to a last question: whether the two types of the courage to accept

acceptance can be united in view of the all-pervasive presence of the anxiety
of doubt and meaninglessness in our own period.

Absolute Faith and the Courage To Be

We have avoided the concept of faith in our description of the courage
to be which is based on mystical union with the ground of being as well
as in our description of the courage to be which is based on the personal
encounter with God. This is partly because the concept of faith has lost its
genuine meaning and has received the connotation of "belief in something
unbelievable." But this is not the only reason for the use of terms other
than faith. The decisive reason is that I do not think either mystical union
or personal encounter fulfills the idea of faith. Certainly there is faith in
the elevation of the soul above the finite to the infinite, leading to its union
with the ground of being. But more than this is included in the concept
of faith. And there is faith in the personal encounter with the personal God.
But more than this is included in the concept of faith. Faith is the state of
being grasped by the power of being-itself. The courage to be is an expression
of faith and what "faith" means must be understood through the courage
to be. We have defined courage as the self-affirmation of being in spite of
nonbeing. The power of this self-affirmation is the power of being which is
effective in every act of courage. Faith is the experience of this power.

But it is an experience which has a paradoxical character, the character
of accepting acceptance. Being-itself transcends every finite being infinitely;
God in the divine-human encounter transcends man unconditionally. Faith
bridges this infinite gap by accepting the fact that in spite of it the power
of being is present, that he who is separated is accepted. Faith accepts "in
spite of;" and out of the "in spite of" of faith the "in spite of" of courage is
born. Faith is not a theoretical affirmation of something uncertain, it is the
existential acceptance of something transcending ordinary experience. Faith
is not an opinion but a state. It is the state of being grasped by the power
of being which transcends everything that is and in which everything that
is participates. He who is grasped by this power is able to affirm himself
because he knows that he is affirmed by the power of being-itself. In this
point mystical experience and personal encounter are identical. In both of
them faith is the basis of the courage to be.

This is decisive for a period in which, as in our own, the anxiety of doubt
and meaninglessness is dominant. Certainly the anxiety of fate and death
is not lacking in our time. The anxiety of fate has increased with the degree
to which the schizophrenic split of our world has removed the last remnants
of former security. And the anxiety of guilt and condemnation is not lacking

either. It is surprising how much anxiety of guilt comes to the surface in psychoanalysis and personal counseling. The centuries of puritan and bourgeois repression of vital strivings have produced almost as many guilt feelings as the preaching of hell and purgatory in the Middle Ages.

But in spite of these restricting considerations one must say that the anxiety which determines our period is the anxiety of doubt and meaning-lessness. One is afraid of having lost or of having to lose the meaning of one's existence. The expression of this situation is the Existentialism of today.

Which courage is able to take nonbeing into itself in the form of doubt and meaninglessness? This is the most important and most disturbing ques-tion in the quest for the courage to be. For the anxiety of meaninglessness undermines what is still unshaken in the anxiety of fate and death and of guilt and condemnation. In the anxiety of guilt and condemnation doubt has not yet undermined the certainty of an ultimate responsibility. We are threatened but we are not destroyed. If, however, doubt and meaninglessness prevail one experiences an abyss in which the meaning of life and the truth of ultimate responsibility disappear. Both the Stoic who conquers the anxiety of fate with the Socratic courage of wisdom and the Christian who conquers the anxiety of guilt with the Protestant courage of accepting forgiveness are in a different situation. Even in the despair of having to die and the despair of self-condemnation meaning is affirmed and certitude preserved. But in the despair of doubt and meaninglessness both are swallowed by nonbeing.

The question then is this: Is there a courage which can conquer the anxiety of meaninglessness and doubt? Or in other words, can the faith which accepts acceptance resist the power of nonbeing in its most radical form? Can faith resist meaninglessness? Is there a kind of faith which can exist together with doubt and meaninglessness? These questions lead to the last aspect of the problem discussed in these lectures and the one most relevant to our time: How is the courage to be possible if all the ways to create it are barred by the experience of their ultimate insufficiency? If life is as meaningless as death, if guilt is as questionable as perfection, if being is no more meaningful than nonbeing, on what can one base the courage to be?

There is an inclination in some Existentialists to answer these questions by a leap from doubt to dogmatic certitude, from meaninglessness to a set of symbols in which the meaning of a special ecclesiastical or political group is embodied. This leap can be interpreted in different ways. It may be the expression of a desire for safety; it may be as arbitrary as, according to Existentialist principles, every decision is; it may be the feeling that the Christian message is the answer to the questions raised by an analysis of human existence; it may be a genuine conversion, independent of the theoretical situation. In any case it is not a solution of the problem of radical doubt. It gives the courage to be to those who are converted but it does not answer the question as to how such a courage is possible in itself. The answer must accept, as its precondition, the state of meaninglessness. It is not an answer if it demands the removal of this state; for that is just what cannot be done. He who is in the grip of doubt and meaninglessness cannot liberate himself from this grip; but he asks for an answer which is valid within and not outside the situation of his despair. He asks for the ultimate foundation of what we have called the "courage of despair." There is only one possible answer, if one does not try to escape the question: namely that the acceptance of despair is in itself faith and on the boundary line of the courage to be. In this situation the meaning of life is reduced to despair about the meaning of life. But as long as this despair is an act of life it is positive in its negativity. Cynically speaking, one could say that it is true to life to be cynical about it. Religiously speaking, one would say that one accepts oneself as accepted in spite of one's despair about the meaning of this acceptance. The paradox of every radical negativity, as long as it is an active negativity, is that it must affirm itself in order to be able to negate itself. No actual negation can be without an implicit affirmation. The hidden pleasure produced by despair witnesses to the paradoxical character of self-negation. The negative lives from the positive it negates.

The faith which makes the courage of despair possible is the acceptance of the power of being, even in the grip of nonbeing. Even in the despair about meaning being affirms itself through us. The act of accepting meaninglessness is in itself a meaningful act. It is an act of faith. We have seen that he who has the courage to affirm his being in spite of fate and guilt has not removed them. He remains threatened and hit by them. But he accepts his acceptance by the power of being-itself in which he participates and which gives him the courage to take the anxieties of fate and guilt upon himself. The same is true of doubt and meaninglessness. The faith which creates the courage to take them into itself has no special content. It is simply faith, undirected, absolute. It is undefinable, since everything defined is dissolved by doubt and meaninglessness. Nevertheless, even absolute faith is not an eruption of subjective emotions or a mood without objective foundation.

An analysis of the nature of absolute faith reveals the following elements in it. The first is the experience of the power of being which is present even in face of the most radical manifestation of nonbeing. If one says that in this experience vitality resists despair one must add that vitality in man is proportional to intentionality. The vitality that can stand the abyss of meaninglessness is aware of a hidden meaning within the destruction of meaning. The second element in absolute faith is the dependence of the experience of nonbeing on the experience of being and the dependence of the experience of meaninglessness on the experience of meaning. Even in the state of despair one has enough being to make despair possible. There is a third element in absolute faith, the acceptance of being accepted. Of course, in the state of despair there is nobody and nothing that accepts. But there is the power of acceptance itself which is experienced. Meaninglessness, as long as it is experienced, includes an experience of the "power of acceptance." To accept this power of acceptance consciously is the religious answer of absolute faith, of a faith which has been deprived by doubt of any concrete content, which nevertheless is faith and the source of the most paradoxical manifestation of the courage to be.

This faith transcends both the mystical experience and the divine-human encounter. The mystical experience seems to be nearer to absolute faith but it is not. Absolute faith includes an element of skepticism which one cannot find in the mystical experience. Certainly mysticism also transcends all specific contents, but not because it doubts them or has found them meaningless; rather it deems them to be preliminary. Mysticism uses the specific contents as grades, stepping on them after having used them. The experience of meaninglessness, however, denies them (and everything that goes with them) without having used them. The experience of meaninglessness is more radical than mysticism. Therefore it transcends the mystical experience.

Absolute faith also transcends the divine-human encounter. In this encounter the subject-object scheme is valid: a definite subject (man) meets a definite object (God). One can reverse this statement and say that a definite subject (God) meets a definite object (man). But in both cases the attack of doubt undercuts the subject-object structure. The theologians who speak so strongly and with such self-certainty about the divine-human encounter should be aware of a situation in which this encounter is prevented by radical doubt and nothing is left but absolute faith. The acceptance of such a situation as religiously valid has, however, the consequence that the concrete contents of ordinary faith must be subjected to criticism and transformation. The courage to be in its radical form is a key to an idea of God which transcends both mysticism and the person-to-person encounter.

The Courage To Be As the Key To Being-Itself

Nonbeing Opening Up Being

The courage to be in all its forms has, by itself, revelatory character. It shows the nature of being, it shows that the self-affirmation of being is an affirmation that overcomes negation. In a metaphorical statement (and every assertion about being-itself is either metaphorical or symbolic) one could say that being includes nonbeing but nonbeing does not prevail against it. "Including" is a spatial metaphor which indicates that being embraces itself and that which is opposed to it, nonbeing. Nonbeing belongs to being, it cannot be separated from it. We could not even think "being" without a double negation: being must be thought as the negation of the negation of being. This is why we describe being best by the metaphor "power of being." Power is the possibility a being has to actualize itself against the resistance of other beings. If we speak of the power of being-itself we indicate that being affirms itself against nonbeing. In our discussion of courage and life we have mentioned the dynamic understanding of reality by the philosophers of life. Such an understanding is possible only if one accepts the view that nonbeing belongs to being, that being could not be the ground of life without nonbeing. The self-affirmation of being without nonbeing would not even be self-affirmation but an immovable self-identity. Nothing would be manifest, nothing expressed, nothing revealed. But nonbeing drives being out of its seclusion, it forces it to affirm itself dynamically. Philosophy has dealt with the dynamic self-affirmation of being-itself wherever it spoke dialectically, notably in Neoplatonism, Hegel, and the philosophers of life and process. Theology has done the same whenever it took the idea of the living God seriously, most obviously in the trinitarian symbolization of the inner life of God. Spinoza, in spite of his static definition of substances (which is his name for the ultimate power of being), unites philosophical and mystical tendencies when he speaks of the love and knowledge with which God loves and knows himself through the love and knowledge of finite beings. Nonbeing, (that in God which makes his self-affirmation dynamic) opens up the divine self-seclusion and reveals him as power and love. Nonbeing makes God a living God. Without the No he has to overcome in himself and in his creature, the divine Yes to himself would be lifeless. There would be no revelation of the ground of being, there would be no life.

But where there is nonbeing there is finitude and anxiety. If we say that nonbeing belongs to being-itself, we say that finitude and anxiety belong to being-itself. Wherever philosophers or theologians have spoken of the divine blessedness they have implicitly (and sometimes explicitly) spoken of the anxiety of finitude which is eternally taken into the blessedness of the divine infinity. The infinite embraces itself and the finite, the Yes includes itself and the No which it takes into itself, blessedness comprises itself and the anxiety of which it is the conquest. All this is implied if one says that being includes nonbeing and that through nonbeing it reveals itself. It is a highly symbolic language which must be used at this point. But its symbolic character does not diminish its truth; on the contrary, it is a condition of its truth. To speak unsymbolically about being-itself is untrue.

The divine self-affirmation is the power that makes the self-affirmation of the finite being, the courage to be, possible. Only because being-itself has the character of self-affirmation in spite of nonbeing is courage possible. Courage participates in the self-affirmation of being-itself, it participates in the power of being which prevails against nonbeing. He who receives this power in an act of mystical or personal or absolute faith is aware of the source of his courage to be.

Man is not necessarily aware of this source. In situations of cynicism and indifference he is not aware of it. But it works in him as long as he maintains the courage to take his anxiety upon himself. In the act of the courage to be the power of being is effective in us, whether we recognize it or not. Every act of courage is a manifestation of the ground of being, however questionable the content of the act may be. The content may hide or distort true being, the courage in it reveals true being. Not arguments but the courage to be reveals the true nature of being-itself. By affirming our being we participate in the self-affirmation of being-itself. There are no valid arguments for the "existence" of God, but there are acts of courage in which we affirm the power of being, whether we know it or not. If we know it, we accept acceptance consciously. If we do not know it, we nevertheless accept it and participate in it. And in our acceptance of that which we do not know the power of being is manifest to us. Courage has revealing power, the courage to be is the key to being-itself.

Theism Transcended

The courage to take meaninglessness into itself presupposes a relation to the ground of being which we have called "absolute faith." It is without a *special* content, yet it is not without content. The content of absolute faith is the "God above God." Absolute faith and its consequence, the courage that takes the radical doubt, the doubt about God, into itself, transcends the theistic idea of God.

Theism can mean the unspecified affirmation of God. Theism in this sense does not say what it means if it uses the name of God. Because of the traditional and psychological connotations of the word God such an empty theism can produce a reverent mood if it speaks of God. Politicians, dictators, and other people who wish to use rhetoric to make an impression on their audience like to use the word God in this sense. It produces the feeling in their listeners that the speaker is serious and morally trustworthy. This is especially successful if they can brand their foes as atheistic. On a higher level people without a definite religious commitment like to call themselves theistic, not for special purposes but because they cannot stand a world without God, whatever this God may be. They need some of the connotations of the word God and they are afraid of what they call atheism. On the highest level of this kind of theism the name of God is used as a poetic or practical symbol, expressing a profound emotional state or the highest ethical idea. It is a theism which stands on the boundary line between the second type of theism and what we call "theism transcended." But it is still too indefinite to cross this boundary line. The atheistic negation of this whole type of theism is as vague as the theism itself. It may produce an irreverent mood and angry reaction of those who take their theistic affirmation seriously. It may even be felt as justified against the rhetorical-political abuse of the name God, but it is ultimately as irrelevant as the theism which it negates. It cannot reach the state of despair any more than the theism against which it fights can reach the state of faith.

Theism can have another meaning, quite contrary to the first one: it can be the name of what we have called the divine-human encounter. In this case it points to those elements in the Jewish-Christian tradition which emphasize the person-to-person relationship with God. Theism in this sense emphasizes the personalistic passages in the Bible and the Protestant creeds, the personalistic image of God, the word as the tool of creation and revelation, the ethical and social character of the kingdom of God, the personal nature of human faith and divine forgiveness, the historical vision of the universe, the idea of a divine purpose, the infinite distance between creator and creature, the absolute separation between God and the world, the conflict between holy God and sinful man, the person-to-person character of prayer and practical devotion. Theism in this sense is the nonmystical side of biblical religion and historical Christianity. Atheism from the point of view of this theism is the human attempt to escape the divine-human encounter. It is an existential—not a theoretical—problem.

Theism has a third meaning, a strictly theological one. Theological theism is, like every theology, dependent on the religious substance which it conceptualizes. It is dependent on theism in the first sense insofar as it tries to prove the necessity of affirming God in some way; it usually develops the so-called arguments for the "existence" of God. But it is more dependent on theism in the second sense insofar as it tries to establish a doctrine of God which transforms the person-to-person encounter with God into a doctrine about two persons who may or may not meet but who have a reality independent of each other.

Now theism in the first sense must be transcended because it is irrelevant, and theism in the second sense must be transcended because it is one-sided. But theism in the third sense must be transcended because it is wrong. It is bad theology. This can be shown by a more penetrating analysis. The God of theological theism is a being beside others and as such a part of the whole of reality. He certainly is considered its most important part, but as a part and therefore as subjected to the structure of the whole. He is supposed to be beyond the ontological elements and categories which constitute reality. But every statement subjects him to them. He is seen as a self which has a world, as an ego which is related to a thou, as a cause which is separated from its effect, as having a definite space and an endless time. He is a being, not being-itself. As such he is bound to the subject-object structure of reality, he is an object for us as subjects. At the same time we are objects for him as a subject. And this is decisive for the necessity of transcending theological theism. For God as a subject makes me into an object which is nothing more than an object. He deprives me of my subjectivity because he is all-powerful and all-knowing. I revolt and try to make *him* into an object, but the revolt fails and becomes desperate. God appears as the invincible tyrant, the being in contrast with whom all other beings are without freedom and subjectivity. He is equated with the recent tyrants who with the help of terror try to transform everything into a mere object, a thing among things, a cog in the machine they control. He becomes the model of everything against which Existentialism revolted. This is the God Nietzsche said had to be killed because nobody can tolerate being made into a mere object of absolute knowledge and absolute control. This is the deepest root of atheism. It is an atheism which is justified as the reaction against theological theism and its disturbing implications. It is also the deepest root of the Existentialist despair and the widespread anxiety of meaninglessness in our period.

Theism in all its forms is transcended in the experience we have called absolute faith. It is the accepting of the acceptances without somebody or something that accepts. It is the power of being-itself that accepts and gives the courage to be. This is the highest point to which our analysis has brought us. It cannot be described in the way the God of all forms of theism can be described. It cannot be described in mystical terms either. It transcends both mysticism and personal encounter, as it transcends both the courage to be as a part and the courage to be as oneself.

The God Above God and the Courage To Be

The ultimate source of the courage to be is the "God above God"; this is the result of our demand to transcend theism. Only if the God of theism is transcended can the anxiety of doubt and meaninglessness be taken into the courage to be. The God above God is the object of all mystical longing, but mysticism also must be transcended in order to reach him. Mysticism does not take seriously the concrete and the doubt concerning the concrete. It plunges directly into the ground of being and meaning, and leaves the concrete, the world of finite values and meanings, behind. Therefore it does not solve the problem of meaninglessness. In terms of the present religious situation this means that Eastern mysticism is not the solution of the problems of Western Existentialism, although many people attempt this solution. The God above the God of theism is not the devaluation of the meanings which doubt has thrown into the abyss of meaninglessness; he is their potential restitution. Nevertheless absolute faith agrees with the faith implied in mysticism in that both transcend the theistic objectivation of a God who is a being. For mysticism such a God is not more real than any finite being, for the courage to be such a God has disappeared in the abyss of meaninglessness with every other value and meaning.

The God above the God of theism is present, although hidden in every divine-human encounter. Biblical religion as well as Protestant theology are aware of the paradoxical character of this encounter. They are aware that if God encounters man God is neither object nor subject and is therefore above the scheme into which theism has forced him. They are aware that personalism with respect to God is balanced by a transpersonal presence of the divine. They are aware that forgiveness can be accepted only if the power of acceptance is effective in man—biblically speaking, if the power of grace is effective in man. They are aware of the paradoxical character of every prayer, of speaking to somebody to whom you cannot speak because he is not "somebody," of asking somebody of whom you cannot ask anything because he gives or gives not before you ask, of saying "thou" to somebody who is nearer to the I than the I is to itself. Each of these paradoxes drives the religious consciousness toward a God above the God of theism.

The courage to be which is rooted in the experience of the God above the God of theism unites and transcends the courage to be as a part and the courage to be as oneself. It avoids both the loss of oneself by participation and the loss of one's world by individualization. The acceptance of the God above the God of theism makes us a part of that which is not also a part but is the ground of the whole. Therefore our self is not lost in a larger whole, which submerges it in the life of a limited group. If the self participates in the power of being-itself it receives itself back. For the power of being acts through the power of the individual selves. It does not swallow them as every limited whole, every collectivism, and every conformism does.

This is why the Church, which stands for the power of being-itself or for the God who transcends the God of the religions, claims to be the mediator of the courage to be. A church which is based on the authority of the God of theism cannot make such a claim. It inescapably develops into a collectivist or semicollectivist system itself.

But a church which raises itself in its message and its devotion to the God above the God of theism without sacrificing its concrete symbols can mediate a courage which takes doubt and meaninglessness into itself. It is the Church under the Cross which alone can do this, the Church which preaches the Crucified who cried to God who remained his God after the God of confidence had left him in the darkness of doubt and meaningless-ness. To be as a part in such a church is to receive a courage to be in which one cannot lose one's self and in which one receives one's world.

Absolute faith, or the state of being grasped by the God beyond God, is not a state which appears beside other states of the mind. It never is something separated and definite, an event which could be isolated and described. It is always a movement in, with, and under other states of the mind. It is the situation on the boundary of man's possibilities. It *is* this boundary. Therefore it is both the courage of despair and the courage in and above every courage. It is not a place where one can live, it is without the safety of words and concepts, it is without a name, a church, a cult, a theology. But it is moving in the depth of all of them. It is the power of being, in which they participate and of which they are fragmentary expressions.

One can become aware of it in the anxiety of fate and death when the traditional symbols, which enable men to stand the vicissitudes of fate and the horror of death have lost their power. When "providence" has become a superstition and "immortality" something imaginary that which once was the power in these symbols can still be present and create the courage to be in spite of the experience of a chaotic world and a finite existence. The Stoic courage returns as the absolute faith which says Yes to being without seeing anything concrete which could conquer the nonbeing in fate and death.

And one can become aware of the God above the God of theism in the anxiety of guilt and condemnation when the traditional symbols that enable men to withstand the anxiety of guilt and condemnation have lost their power. When "divine judgment" is interpreted as a psychological complex and forgiveness as a remnant of the "father-image," what once was the power in those symbols can still be present and create the courage to be in spite of the experience of an infinite gap between what we are and what we ought to be. The Lutheran courage returns but not supported by the faith in a judging and forgiving God. It returns in terms of the absolute faith which says Yes although there is no special power that conquers guilt. The courage to take the anxiety of meaninglessness upon oneself is the boundary line up to which the courage to be can go. Beyond it is mere non-being. Within it all forms of courage are re-established in the power of the God above the God of theism. *The courage to be is rooted in the God who appears when God has disappeared in the anxiety of doubt.*

SUGGESTED ADDITIONAL READINGS

How Is God Known?

Some Contemporary Answers

Baillie, John, *Our Knowledge of God*. New York: Charles Scribner's Sons, 1939. See especially chapters 18 and 19. A contemporary Scottish theologian whose work represents a continuation and modification of the liberal tradition in Christian theology.

D'Arcy, Martin C. *The Nature of Belief*. London: Sheed and Ward, 1937. See especially pp. 297f. Explanation by a Roman Catholic theologian of the nature of knowledge of God.

Heschel, Abraham J. *God In Search of Man, A Philosophy of Judaism*. Philadelphia: The Jewish Publication Society of America, 1956. (Also published in paperback by Meridian Books.) An outstanding Jewish theologian defines basic elements in a Jewish understanding of God.

Inge, W. R. *Christian Mysticism*. New York: Charles Scribner's Sons, 1899. A careful and sympathetic scholar provides a clear, balanced account of the meaning and significance of mysticism.

James, William. "The Will to Believe," *Essays on Faith and Morals*. New York: Longmans, Green & Company, 1943. Famous pragmatic argument for the meaningfulness of belief in God's existence.

Jones, Rufus. *Pathways To The Reality of God*. New York: The Macmillan Company, 1931. A twentieth century American philosopher and Quaker mystic explains in contemporary terms what mystics conceive to be the means to knowledge of God.

Kaplan, Mordecai M. *The Meaning of God In Modern Jewish Religion*. New York: Jewish Reconstructionist Foundation, Inc., 1947. A Jewish naturalistic approach that argues that God is to be understood as life's creative force.

Kroner, Richard. *How Do We Know God?* New York: Harper & Brothers, 1943. A German-American philosophical theologian argues that faith is basically a response of man's will and mind to God.

Marcel, Gabriel. *The Philosophy of Existence*. Trans., Manya Harari. London: Harvill Press, 1948. French Roman Catholic existentialist philosopher expresses his conception of how God may be known.

Revelation. Edited by John Baillie and Hugh Martin. London: Faber & Faber, Ltd., 1937. A collection of essays on revelation by prominent representatives from several branches of the Christian tradition, Eastern Orthodox, Roman Catholic and Protestant.

Whitehead, Alfred North. *Process and Reality*. New York: The Macmillan Company, 1929. (Also published in paperback by Harper & Brothers, Torchbook, The Academy Library).

——— *Science and the Modern World*. New York: The Macmillan Company, 1925. (Also published in paperback by The New American Library of World Literature, Mentor Series.) See especially chapter X. These works by a distinguished contemporary philosopher include statements on the necessity of God in the order of the universe.

V. Introduction

RELIGIOUS LANGUAGE

One of the most important new areas of concern in philosophy of religion is that of the analysis of religious language. This concern stems from the wider philosophic study of the use and meaning of all language. Turning from the idea that the objective of philosophy is to create a unified system or world-view, many philosophers in recent times have undertaken the quite different effort of analyzing the usages of language. Development of this area has come swiftly in recent decades.

On the Continent this movement found its main impetus among a group of philosophers centered in Vienna. Taking their lead from the new directions in logic indicated by the work of Bertrand Russell and Alfred North Whitehead and from the writings of Ludwig Wittgenstein, these men, often called "logical positivists," undertook the work of making explicit both the realm and task of logic and the realm of empirical verification. Under the leadership of such men as Moritz Schlick and Rudolf Carnap (who later came to America), along with A. J. Ayer in England, this school accepted as a central concern the creation of a simplified and precise linguistic system.

In England philosophers who had been influenced by F. H. Bradley (a figure transitional between idealism and linguistic analysis), G. E. Moore, and more lately by Wittgenstein, who came to live in England, became interested in language as it is ordinarily used in any given field, and undertook the work of analyzing the ways in which language is employed in its various modes. These philosophers raised the question of what people mean by what they say, whether the person be speaking of science, art, morals, religion, or whatever. Their interest was not in creating an ideal or logically exact language, as was that of the Continental logical positivists, but rather in making an analysis of the usages of language in its "natural" modes.

Other philosophers were also at work. Among the most influential was Ernst Cassirer, who developed his philosophy in Germany and then in America. The major contribution of Cassirer to this effort has been his analysis of the place of myth in human thought and expression. His writings have made an impression on the work of many subsequent philosophers, especially in the United States. One of the best known of his followers is Suzanne Langer, whose book, *Philosophy In A New Key*, is a basic introduction to the role of symbol-making in human thought.

Concern for the meaning of specifically religious language and symbols was awakened by other influences. Religious thinkers became seriously concerned with the question: Does the biblical message, wrapped as it is in prescientific myth and symbol, have any relevance to the modern, scientific man? Rudolf Bultmann and Reinhold Niebuhr stand out as theologians who have endeavored to examine the use of myth in the Bible and who have investigated the validity and discussed the relevance of religious language. One of the most pressing questions is whether there is an essential truth to be found in the biblical message, and if so, what is it, and how can it be extracted? The primary approach followed has been to study the use and meaning of the forms of expression found in the Bible.

In philosophy of religion at the present time work is being done in a number of areas involving examination of religious language. Some thinkers are reinvestigating the Medieval scholastic discussion of the analogical relation of human language to the reality of God, while others are concentrating on the nature and form of biblical language. One of the growing movements of the time is found among those who follow the English linguistic analysts in their attempt to understand the unique character of religious language. Language in every distinct area has its own peculiar usages, and the realm of religion is no exception. The analysis of religious language ranges beyond theological statements, although these are also included, for it is concerned to understand the nature and function of religious language as it is found in worship and symbolization, as well as in formal statement.

Selections reprinted after this introduction present illustrations of the work being done in these areas. Robert Calhoun's essay is an exceptionally clear statement of the role of language in religion. In the concluding section of his article, that which deals with three problems of language in religion, Professor Calhoun sketches a setting for the work which is reported in the other articles.

In the essay of Rudolf Bultmann we have a major figure in the contemporary discussion of biblical language making a case for fresh interpretation of the essential meaning of the New Testament message, separated from its husks of mythology. Bultmann also gives some indication of how he thinks this work should be done. Ronald Hepburn evaluates Bultmann's use of the word "myth" from the perspective of linguistic analysis and finds fault with the definition proposed by Bultmann.

John Wilson introduces us more directly to the general intention of linguistic analysis in philosophy. His article can well serve as a clear statement
of some of the possible ways to delineate the forms of religious statements
and to assess their validity. Both John Wisdom and R. B. Braithwaite demonstrate at a more advanced level the same interest. Wisdom's article is of historical importance as one of the early, influential essays in the area. In it,
Wisdom discusses the question "Is belief in gods reasonable?" He makes
suggestions both for understanding the question and for assessing its validity.
The Braithwaite selection provides us with an empiricist orientation and a
new attempt to evaluate the relation between religious and moral statements.
Braithwaite is most provocative in his discussion of religious "stories."

Paul Tillich is a contemporary Protestant thinker who undertakes to
clarify the intention and meaning of symbols in religion. His essay attempts
to show that symbols taken from the world of ordinary sensory experience
can be the means by which man's ultimate religious concern finds expression.
E. L. Mascall provides a contemporary discussion of the meaning of analogy
in religious language. The discussion of analogy has been an important interest throughout the history of Christian thought. It continues to retain
its importance in the Thomistic tradition, and, to a lesser extent, in other
philosophical traditions.

ROBERT L. CALHOUN

ROBERT L. CALHOUN (1896-   ) is Professor of Historical Theology at Yale Divinity School. His interests range from Greek philosophy to contemporary theological problems. He has written in the field of Christian ethics as well as in the history of Christian thought.

The Place of Language in Religion*

Religion is not primarily talk, nor symbolic behavior of any kind. It is not primarily ceremony, nor preaching and listening, not even reflective meditation, though all these have their due places in it. First of all, religion is response, deeper and more inclusive than speech or thought, to revelation— to the impact of reality apprehended as divine. In the broadest sense of the term, such reality is numinous, "a mystery full of terror and fascination." In simpler religious communities, the mystery may be found in natural objects, animals, persons, in particular places, times, or events, even in man-made implements hallowed by antiquity and tradition or by dramatic association with a crisis in human living. The gods of unsophisticated peoples are indefinite in number and often transitory in divine status. But in more discriminating religion, the divine is identified sooner or later with the ultimate in man's universe. Mystery and numinous quality are not left behind, but they are apprehended now as characters not of serpents or stars or sorcerers, but of the abiding ground of all particular existence and worth—God beyond all finite things and events, apprehended as overwhelmingly great and good. Our central concern here is with religion of this latter sort.

The primary response of one who finds himself at grips with what he takes to be ultimate reality is an all-inclusive response like the turning of a plant toward the light. It involves thought, feeling, and action, and the still deeper impulses—below the threshold of conscious experience—from which decision and action arise. Religion involves the whole self, in a commitment at once inescapable and spontaneously affirmative, like the commitment of a free mind to evident truth or of a perceptive heart to a beloved person, community, or cause. Such commitment is not calculating, arbitrary, or avoidable, given the situation that evokes it. But neither is it coerced, involuntary,

* From Robert L. Calhoun, "The Language of Religion," *The Unity of Knowledge*, ed. Lewis Leary, Doubleday & Co., Inc., pp. 252-262. Copyright, 1955, by Columbia University. Used by permission of Columbia University.

or enslaving. It is the affirmation of one who can do no other, yet who in such affirmation is enhanced and emancipated. Such response to the presence of God is worship that continually seeks expression in devoted work. Both are integral and inseparable components in primary religion.

This primary response finds characteristic if not inevitable elaboration in the life of religious communities whose members have been drawn into such commitment and seek then to reaffirm, to interpret, and to communicate their experience. First in this social or corporate elaboration of religion is the development of cultus or liturgy, a system of ceremonial acts in which renewal of worship is sought or sensibly embodied. Here sacraments are central—enacted means of communication between worshipers and God, and among members of the community both past and present. In a broad sense the whole liturgy is sacramental: a blending of speech and action, light and shadow, color, tone, rhythm, fragrance into a complex act *(leitourgia)* of affirmation and reception of meaning, in the presence of reality beyond the fabric of symbols. Secondly, there is a more or less elaborate system of verbalization—evangelism in the usual restricted sense of spoken and written conveyance of "the gospel" of God's living presence and acts: proclamation, reflective interpretation, and systematic teaching. In the terminology of the early Christian Church, these interrelated phases of evangelism were called *kērygma* (preaching, testimony, announcement as by a herald), spontaneous, declaratory, and particularized rather than general, critical, or systematic; *theologia* (more reflective, critical, reasoned discourse about God and man), seeking to classify, order, interpret, and defend the substance of the *kērygma* as coherent and relevant doctrine (*doctrina, dogma*) suitable, as the name suggests, for systematic study and teaching; and *catechēsis* (instruction) in which both the gist of the first-hand, eyewitness proclamation (*kērygma*) and some part of the growing system of interpretation (*theologia, doctrina*) are carefully expounded for learners. This is the area with which the major part of this paper is chiefly concerned. Thirdly, there is in every religious community more or less elaborate maintenance of organization and discipline: allocation of office, function, and authority; moral rules or norms embodied in individual and corporate living. Finally, there is active concern for the welfare of neighbors within and outside the organized community, normally expressed in practical service (*diakonia*), the everyday acts of devoted living.

If something like this account be accepted, the place of language in religion is most obvious in the first two of these elaborated phases: liturgy and evangelism. Man's primary response in worship to the impact of God's presence is concrete and immediate rather than reflective and articulate, *erleben* rather than *erkennen*. This is not to say it is irrational, nor that symbolism and language have no place in it. If neither of these statements were true, it is hard to see how theology could get a foothold as an integral component in religious life at all. If the primary response of man to God were as simply immediate and ineffable as toothache or salt taste, theology would be as external to the experience as the effort to verbalize a sensation is to the simple intuition itself. But since the religious response involves the whole person, it has an internal structure that lends itself to reflection and symbolic communication as a simple sensation does not. At the same time, like a concrete experience of love or loyalty, a concrete moment of worship is not *eo ipso* reflective, critical, even articulate. These are characteristics rather of the elaborated moments of religion, in which the implicit meanings of the primary moment are spelled out in growing detail—but never completely.

This situation is sometimes obscured by ambiguous use of the term revelation. This term refers properly to the primary moment of religion, in which God is said to reveal or disclose his presence to the worshiper and thereby to evoke the primary religious response. Sometimes this revelation is understood as consisting of propositions given as guaranteed truth. In that event, verbalization would of course be conspicuous from the very start. "The word of the Lord" to Amos or Isaiah would consist of information, instructions, and commands in verbal form. But in common with a substantial body of interpreters, this paper takes revelation to consist not in dictated propositions but in arresting events—impacts, confrontations—whose meaning is partly verbalized in further reflection.

The modes and functions of language in religion can now be examined a bit more directly, though very briefly. It seems convenient to look first at liturgy and especially at sacrament as a very inclusive and characteristic form of the language of religion, whose nature, presuppositions, and intent can help to illuminate the more precisely verbal and conceptual language of theology. It goes without saying that the latter is needed likewise for illumination of the former. The two are not separable without serious damage to both.

An essential presupposition of all genuine liturgy, as distinct from the "vain repetitions" of rote memory and habit, is the real communion or participation (*koinōnia*) of men with one another and with reality beyond themselves; and the possibility of heightening, clarifying, renewing, and extending this communion both for present worshipers and for other men. Liturgy is a complex of symbolic acts intended to express the communion that is already real, and by communication to help extend and to enhance it. *Koinōnia* is neither identity nor uniformity. It is a mutual involvement of beings that are radically other, yet profoundly interrelated. Thus, each man is radically other than his neighbor, incapable of occupying his neighbor's perspective instead of his own. Yet each is so bound up with his neighbors that without them he could not be himself, and he is able to recognize this bond. Thus also man is radically other than God, the ultimate ground of his existence, the perfect truth and right by which he is judged. Yet in moments of arresting confrontation he is able to recognize and acknowledge his dependence on the radically Other, and to find himself in his wrongness not only condemned but forgiven and accepted, reconciled, reaffirmed. This paradoxical conquest of alienation, this profound communion in radical otherness—of man from man, and of man from God—is what liturgy seeks to affirm, to mediate, and to articulate in symbolic action.

The symbols, as already noted, are of many sorts. But to fulfill their function they must be sacramental. That is to say, among other things, they must be not mere external pointers but concrete media embodying or exemplifying the communion they seek to convey. They must be like friendly handclasps or like gifts offered and received, not like calling cards or polite salutations. They must be saturated in memory, individual and corporate, so that they can call up in vivid presence the long past and enable those who share in them to share in the life of a community enduring through time. They must be rooted in the hungers and hopes of our common humanity, speaking in their many-dimensional gestures not a local dialect only but a universal language. At the same time, like any concrete living tongue as against an artificially abstracted Esperanto, they are sure to manifest the peculiarities of particular traditions and to be susceptible of incalculably various understanding. Their virtue as sacramental symbols would not be enhanced if they could be reduced to simple freedom from ambiguity. To convey a living sense of participation in the whole fabric of human life and in a specific community diversified in time and space and modes of existence, they must point in many directions at once, like a musical theme amid variations, and be themselves actual segments or foci of the communal experience they signify. Finally, they must point beyond human life to reality that transcends it yet effectively enters into it: the producing and sustaining source of our life, the goal and norm by which we are judged, the transforming influence—the divine grace—by which we are corrected, renewed, and led into unforeseen dimensions of shared living.

Sacraments are signs and symbols, and in that sense components in the language of religion. A sacrament is at once an affirmation and a reminder of the reality from which the affirmation has its meaning. *Sacramentum* is the soldier's oath of loyalty, and the legionary standard—marked SPQR—by which he swears. It is "the outward, visible sign of an inward, spiritual grace," a "means (*medium*) of grace," a "symbol and occasion of the working of the Holy Spirit." As such it is also to be called *mysterion*, as in the Greek Church, at once sign and vehicle of the presence of God. Whether

God's grace is mediated exclusively, or at least in exceptional and indispensable ways by particular liturgical acts, such as ceremonial washing or common meal, or whether such acts are peculiarly effective reminders of the working of grace through all sorts of channels—the spoken word in prayer and in preaching, the everyday acts of faithful service—is a question long and widely debated among religious people. It need not detain us here, but it may serve to direct our thought from liturgy as enacted language to the more specifically verbal expressions of theology and doctrine.

Here again we meet, from the early generations in Christian history, the term *symbolon,* as a name for a concise theological formula: a *credo* or formula for confession of faith in token of commitment and of membership in a committed community. The confessional formulae called symbols or creeds speedily found place in the liturgy—first for each new convert in the ceremony of baptism by which he was inducted into the Church, and thereafter as an integral part of each regular service of worship. This is a simple instance of the way in which cultus has been affected by reflective thought, by theology. The meaning of the whole liturgy is thus reoriented and further defined by the systematic effort toward verbalization. On the other hand, theological effort has proceeded in its own terms, mostly nonliturgical. Creeds and confessions have multiplied and expanded into sizable theological treatises approved by the community, related to its liturgy, but not included in it. Yet the initial intent of the whole dogmatic enterprise is clearly preserved in the use of the name symbolics for the study of all these creeds and confessions. They too, like liturgical acts of worship, intend to signify and in some sense to serve as media for the presence of God. The words they employ and the ordering of the words are never the carefully sterilized terms and propositions of algebra, of theoretical physics, or of clinical medicine. Their function as affirmations of active commitment requires a vocabulary and a syntax that have something of the urgency, ambivalence, and particularity of momentous action. They are not simple, exact results of exact reasoning—though much arduous, closely reasoned effort to attain exactitude enters into their formation. Rather they are what Plato called "articles of faith," hammered out in the midst of hard thinking yet grounded at bottom not in reasoning as such, but in rational conviction of the sort exemplified by Socrates, and serving as touchstones for genuine reasoning about God.

Such reasoning is theology, always inseparable from and pervaded by faith, never able to dispense with language in which a subjective or confessional moment is essential. At the same time, the task of theology is very largely an objective task as well. This means not merely that it is communicative as well as expressive, semantic and not simply emotive. Liturgy also, as we have urged, is communicative. Beyond that, theology is analytic, critical, interpretative, argumentative, and systematic. It seeks far more extensively than liturgy to distinguish and point out explicitly the factors involved in the primary confrontation of God and man—in revelation and religious response. It seeks to clarify and test by the familiar tests of internal coherence and empirical relevance the affirmations of religious conviction, recognizing that no more than those of love or intense loyalty, or of artistic or musical discernment can such affirmations be translated into alien terms or subordinated to alien requirements. It seeks to illuminate from various angles their characteristic structure and implications, their interconnections with other modes of human experience, and their actual sources and modifications in the course of history. It seeks, finally, to exhibit them as at once an ordered whole of which every component involves every other, and an effort to speak of mystery that is never reducible to the dimensions of any human experience or discourse.

In theology, therefore, both language and methods are employed that find place also in many sciences, in history, in philosophy, in the study of poetry and other literature, and especially in everyday personal relations. Excepting a comparatively few technical terms, indeed, there is no vocabulary peculiar to theology. What is peculiar is the perspective in which familiar words are used. That perspective, as already affirmed more than once, is determined by the impact of divine revelation and the distinctive response of faith. From this situation arise the most difficult problems for theological discourse, and the most characteristic efforts to solve them without dissolving them away.

Three Problems for Language in Religion

The root of these difficulties is familiar. The ordinary use of language is to direct attention to some objectively perceptible component of the speaker's world—an "it" to which one can point by a verbal gesture. Whether it is a sensible object (chair, planet, galaxy) or an intelligible object (Euclidean line, equality, sovereignty), words can be found or made that can indicate it with fair precision. The words are not *like* it, but in the context of human observation and converse, they come to have a conventionally accepted congruence with it. And this can come about the more easily because the words are at least of the same experiential order as the objects to which they point: the words also are objects, and as such can serve most readily as labels or finger posts for other objects. The attention of an observer ordinarily moves with least difficulty from one objective "it" to another.

When we seek to call attention to a subject, an "I," the task is notoriously much harder. David Hume even declared it impossible to point out a subject *qua* subject at all. Immanuel Kant agreed with him, but went on to explore in the immense, painstaking argument of the first two *Critiques* both reasons and methods for dealing concretely, actively, and significantly with subjects, even though they cannot be observed and described as if they were objects. Here also verbal signs provide a usable medium, since each of us is himself a subject, comes to know himself as such in active, responsible relations with others, and so can recognize and acknowledge others in the common matrix of social, historical existence.

But God is neither an observable "It" nor a finite "I." At least this is the conviction to which reflective religion sooner or later has come, in all the great traditions known to me. And only for such religion does the special problem of language arise. For such religion, God is not merely numinous but radically transcendent—incommensurable with finite things and persons, as Creator with creatures, Perfect with imperfect, Infinite with finite, and so on. Moreover, if it be true, as many religious thinkers have held, that God is the ground of rational order, the presupposition of all discourse, then trying to talk or to think articulately *about* him is a little like trying to see oneself as observing subject, the presupposed ground of all one's seeing. This last difficulty might perhaps be outflanked, in Kant's way or some other; indeed, to be able to see and state the problem seems to imply that in some sense one is already beyond it—if only the right forms of speech could be found to express what the situation implies.

But all our language is relative to the objective phenomena we observe and to the finite existence we share. More than that, all of it is culturally conditioned, like our own minds, so that any words we can use have special reference not even to the whole of human experience or of finite existence, but only to some part of it. How can such constricted language be used in valid reference to God?

One familiar answer is often associated with mysticism: recourse to some *via negativa* or *via remotionis*. Since God is incommensurable with the finite things from which our languages derive and to which they properly refer, the only true assertions about God are negative assertions, denying of him all predicates drawn from our experience of things in time and space, or of persons in human history. But such negation has at least one tremendous affirmation as its base: that God is transcendent, incommensurable with all that is finite. Hence, unless one is to keep wholly silent, avoiding even negative assertions, it seems necessary to probe further after some ground for affirmation. Three such efforts to undergird affirmations about God may be noticed briefly here: the ways of mythology, of analogy, and of paradox.

The earliest, simplest, most concrete form of religious discourse was myth.

Indeed, one major theory holds that language itself arises in the matrix of mythical experience, and achieves independent status and conceptual form only after a long maturing within the context of myth. In the mythical perspective, "all things are full of gods," in Thales' well-known words. Earth and heaven interpenetrate freely, because the gods are beings in space and time, gifted with powers beyond those of men, appearing and disappearing at will, but very far from radically transcendent. This is the stage of mythical experience and discourse that Paul Tillich calls "unbroken myth." It is precritical and untroubled by misgivings about the direct applicability of mythical picture-language to divine beings, who are man's near neighbors and kinsmen in a finite world.

But with progress in critical thought concerning gods and men, this early confidence is shattered. Whenever the many gods are subordinated to one god, and the one at length absorbs or displaces the rest, the crucial step is not far off. That step is taken when the one god is declared to be the Ultimate, radically other than man, uncontainable in space and to me, incommensurable with any finite existence. Then the question is posed sharply whether mythical experience and discourse concerning God must not be abandoned. Tillich says no. Any discourse concerning God is inevitably mythical, in the sense that predicates derived from experiences with finite beings in space and time are affirmed of God, in the context of such apprehension of a numinous transcendent as Otto has described and we have noticed above. But myth as now used, says Tillich, is "broken myth," no longer naively assumed to be an actual description of divine reality but recognized as usable *faute de mieux* to signalize the presence of a transcendent other that cannot be described at all. To substitute nonmythical language (that is, a carefully desiccated technical vocabulary of some sort) would serve no good purpose. No technical vocabulary is more adequate for symbolizing the Ultimate Being, and it would have for religious discourse the great disadvantage of failing to convey effectively even the human side of the religious situation: man's awe in the presence of God.

A second way of trying to cope with the problem is the familiar scholastic theory of analogy. From one point of view, this may be taken as an effort to find a theoretic basis for such discourse as "broken myth" provides. The term *analogia*, in the sense of proportion, was not unfamiliar in Greek mathematics, and Plato used it in that sense. Aristotle extended its range into the vocabulary of logic and the theory of knowledge, as a *via media* between univocal predication that applies a term to more than one subject, with essentially identical meaning, and equivocal predication that applies a term to more than one subject, with essentially different meanings. Analogical predication applies a term to more than one subject, with meanings that are not essentially identical but that bear a certain proportion to one another, and signalize a corresponding proportionality between the subjects themselves.

When this conception was first applied to the problem of religious discourse I do not know. The second-century Platonist (?) and hostile critic of Christianity named Celsus, whom we know only through Origen's polemic against him, included "the method of analogy" among philosophic methods suited for discourse about God. Origen himself follows suit, subordinating analogy along with all other philosophic methods to revelation and the "rule of faith." Augustine gives the method and its underlying principle a central place in his work *On the Trinity*, arguing that since man is created *ad imaginem* dei, it is not improper to seek in the personal existence of man analogies that may help to illustrate, not to prove, the Church's doctrine of the true Being of God. Substantially this same line is developed in the two *Summae* of Thomas Aquinas. He too sets out from the relation between Creator and creature, being careful to warn against saying, "God is like man"—as if man were the standard—whereas the truth is that man is in some sense like God. God is the Origin, man the derivative being. The Being of God—self-existent, perfect—is not the being of man—dependent, imperfect. Yet between them is such *analogia entis* that some predicates, such as rational, just, and merciful, can be affirmed *analogice* of man and of God.

To most Roman Catholic thought today, this doctrine seems valid and essential. But there are competent theologians who reject it, because it narrows too much the gulf between Creator and creatures. Some of them, like Karl Barth, are quite willing to talk of analogy in a different context, provided not by creation as such but by incarnation, and apprehended not by natural reason but by faith—an *analogia fidei* instead of an *analogia entis*. On this view, the self-disclosure of God in Jesus Christ as God-man, the Word of God incarnate, is the indispensable break-through from God's side that makes theological discourse possible. Analogies now can be found between various aspects of life in the Church and the life of the incarnate Word, though not directly between creatures as such and their Creator. One may question whether this account as it stands is self-complete. Its stress on the need for divine initiative in revelation to make theological discourse feasible may be welcomed. But such revelation is not provided *in vacuo*. It is provided in and through created being. That is what incarnation means, in one essential perspective. And whether the existing relation between created being and Creator be called *analogia entis* or not, it seems a requisite component in the situation in which *analogia fidei* can be realized.

There is a third way in which this problem has been dealt with: the way of paradoxical or dialectical affirmation. These terms are among the hall-marks of Sören Kierkegaard's thought, with leaders in the Protestant Refor-mation and Kant preceding him, and the dialectical theology of our day, often strongly tinged with such theistic existentialism as that of Buber, following and transforming some of his suggestions. Although most dialec-tical theologians, like Martin Luther and John Calvin, are wary of mysticism, their treatment of this problem of theological affirmation has strong bonds, both negative and positive, to the great mystics' thought on the same problem. The rejection of mysticism centers mainly on denial of any basic identification of man and God, and insistence on the primacy of faith—personal commitment in response to revelation—rather than immediate intuition. But there is also clear reaffirmation of a characteristic doctrine of the mystics: that any attempt to speak of the inexpressible Fullness of God must take the form of joint affirmation and denial, the sort of dialectical affirmation which, unlike Hegel's, can never pass smoothly to a synthesis in which antitheses are wholly combined. The Being of God is and remains Mystery.

Our affirmations then must have the paradoxical character of state-ments in which contraries are declared to be inseparable and equally neces-sary. This is not contradiction. A self-contradictory term or proposition tries verbally to combine strictly incompatible elements each of which is intel-ligible in isolation from the other. Square circles and uncreated creatures are of that sort. But finding life by losing it, mercy that judges more search-ingly than condemnation, God everywhere present and nowhere included, at once immanent and radically transcendent—these are terms whose com-ponents cannot have in isolation the meanings they have when combined. The incarnate Word, the God-man is the supreme instance, for Kierkegaard, "The Paradox" that enables corrupted man as no teacher can do—not even Socrates, the very model of genuine teachers—to apprehend truth and reality that is radically *other* than he, of a different order of magnitude, incommensurable with his weakness and distortion of mind. The light he requires is not in him, and no Socrates can bring it into view. The light must be *given* to him, and that means he must be transformed. When the light comes, he still cannot talk simply of what he sees. He must speak in paradoxes, for the truth is not simple, objective, formulable, and never his to possess.

Implicit in all three of these proffered answers, and explicit in most of their variant forms, is the presupposition of divine self-disclosure and human faith. Faith as total personal response is much more than cognitive belief, and differently related to reasoning, knowledge, and speech. It is not a substitute for any of these, nor a first or a final leap beginning or completing a process of thought. If one may venture a concluding paradox, it is the personal context, climate, active disposition in which thought and discourse of God must go on, subject at every step to their testing yet never subordinate to them and never exhausted in what they may find to say.

RUDOLF
BULTMANN

RUDOLF BULTMANN (1884-   ), Professor of New Testament at Marburg University, 1921-1951, has undertaken the study of the Christian scripture from an existentialist orientation. Existentialist philosophy, he believes, helps to open the true meaning of the biblical message.

New Testament and Mythology*

The Task of Demythologizing the New Testament Proclamation

A. The Problem

1. The Mythical View of the World and the Mythical Event of Redemption.

The cosmology of the New Testament is essentially mythical in character. The world is viewed as a three-storied structure, with the earth in the centre, the heaven above, and the underworld beneath. Heaven is the abode of God and of celestial beings—the angels. The underworld is hell, the place of torment. Even the earth is more than the scene of natural, everyday events, of the trivial round and common task. It is the scene of the supernatural activity of God and his angels on the one hand, and of Satan and his daemons on the other. These supernatural forces intervene in the course of nature and in all that men think and will and do. Miracles are by no means rare. Man is not in control of his own life. Evil spirits may take possession of him. Satan may inspire him with evil thoughts. Alternatively, God may inspire his thought and guide his purposes. He may

* From Rudolf Bultmann, *Kerygma and Myth*, ed. Hans W. Bartsch, trans. Reginald H. Fuller, pp. 1-16. Published, 1954, Society for the Publication of Christian Knowledge. Used by permission of the publisher. [Footnotes omitted, Eds.]

grant him heavenly visions. He may allow him to hear his word of succour or demand. He may give him the supernatural power of his Spirit. History does not follow a smooth unbroken course; it is set in motion and controlled by these supernatural powers. This aeon is held in bondage by Satan, sin, and death (for "powers" is precisely what they are), and hastens towards its end. That end will come very soon, and will take the form of a cosmic catastrophe. It will be inaugurated by the "woes" of the last time. Then the Judge will come from heaven, the dead will rise, the last judgment will take place, and men will enter into eternal salvation or damnation.

This then is the mythical view of the world which the New Testament presupposes when it presents the event of redemption which is the subject of its preaching. It proclaims in the language of mythology that the last time has now come. "In the fulness of time" God sent forth his Son, a pre-existent divine Being, who appears on earth as a man. He dies the death of a sinner on the cross and makes atonement for the sins of men. His resurrection marks the beginning of the cosmic catastrophe. Death, the consequence of Adam's sin, is abolished, and the daemonic forces are deprived of their power. The risen Christ is exalted to the right hand of God in heaven and made "Lord" and "King." He will come again on the clouds of heaven to complete the work of redemption, and the resurrection and judgement of men will follow. Sin, suffering and death will then be finally abolished. All this is to happen very soon; indeed, St. Paul thinks that he himself will live to see it.

All who belong to Christ's Church and are joined to the Lord by Baptism and the Eucharist are certain of resurrection to salvation, unless they forfeit it by unworthy behaviour. Christian believers already enjoy the first instalment of salvation, for the Spirit is at work within them, bearing witness to their adoption as sons of God, and guaranteeing their final resurrection.

2. The Mythological View of the World Obsolete.

All this is the language of mythology, and the origin of the various themes can be easily traced in the contemporary mythology of Jewish Apocalyptic and in the redemption myths of Gnosticism. To this extent *the kerygma is incredible to modern man, for he is convinced that the mythical view of the world is obsolete.* We are therefore bound to ask whether, when we preach the Gospel to-day, we expect our converts to accept not only the Gospel message, but also the mythical view of the world in which it is set. If not, does the New Testament embody a truth which is quite independent of its mythical setting? If it does, theology must undertake the task of stripping the Kerygma from its mythical framework, of "demythologizing" it.

Can Christian preaching expect modern man *to accept the mythical view of the world as true?* To do so would be both senseless and impossible. It would be senseless, because there is nothing specifically Christian in the mythical view of the world as such. It is simply the cosmology of a pre-scientific age. Again, it would be impossible, because no man can adopt a view of the world by his own volition—it is already determined for him by his place in history. Of course such a view is not absolutely unalterable, and the individual may even contribute to its change. But he can do so only when he is faced by a new set of facts so compelling as to make his previous view of the world untenable. He has then no alternative but to modify his view of the world or produce a new one. The discoveries of Copernicus and the atomic theory are instances of this, and so was romanticism, with its discovery that the human subject is richer and more complex than enlightenment or realism had allowed, and nationalism, with its new realization of the importance of history and the tradition of peoples.

It may equally well happen that truths which a shallow enlightenment had failed to perceive are later rediscovered in ancient myths. Theologians are perfectly justified in asking whether this is not exactly what has happened with the New Testament. At the same time it is impossible to revive an obsolete view of the world by a mere fiat, and certainly not a mythical view. For all our thinking to-day is shaped for good or ill by modern science. A blind acceptance of the New Testament mythology would be irrational, and to press for its acceptance as an article of faith would be to reduce Christian faith to the level of a human achievement. Wilhelm Herrmann pointed this out many years ago, and one would have thought that his demonstration was conclusive. It would involve a sacrifice of the intellect which could have only one result—a curious form of schizophrenia and insincerity. It would mean accepting a view of the world in our faith and religion which we should deny in our everyday life. Modern thought as we have inherited it provides us with *a motive for criticizing the New Testament view of the world.*

Man's knowledge and mastery of the world have advanced to such an extent through science and technology that it is no longer possible for anyone seriously to hold the New Testament view of the world—in fact, there is hardly anyone who does. What meaning, for instance, can we attach to such phrases in the creed as "descended into hell" or "ascended into heaven?" We no longer believe in the three-storied universe which the creeds take for granted. The only honest way of reciting the creeds is to strip the mythological framework from the truth they enshrine—that is, assuming that they contain any truth at all, which is just the question that theology has to ask. No one who is old enough to think for himself supposes that God lives in a local heaven. There is no longer any heaven in the traditional sense of the word. The same applies to hell in the sense of a mythical underworld beneath our feet. And if this is so, we can no longer accept the story of Christ's descent into hell or his Ascension into heaven as literally true. We can no longer look for the return of the Son of Man on the clouds of heaven or hope that the faithful will meet him in the air (I Thess. 4.15ff.).

Now that the forces and the laws of nature have been discovered, we can no longer believe *in spirits, whether good or evil.* We know that the stars are physical bodies whose motions are controlled by the laws of the universe, and not daemonic beings which enslave mankind to their service. Any influence they may have over human life must be explicable in terms of the ordinary laws of nature; it cannot in any way be attributed to their malevolence. Sickness and the cure of disease are likewise attributable to natural causation; they are not the result of daemonic activity or of evil spells. *The miracles of the New Testament* have ceased to be miraculous, and to defend their historicity by recourse to nervous disorders or hypnotic effects only serves to underline the fact. And if we are still left with certain physiological and psychological phenomena which we can only assign to mysterious and enigmatic causes, we are still assigning them to causes, and thus far are trying to make them scientifically intelligible. Even occultism pretends to be a science.

It is impossible to use electric light and the wireless and to avail ourselves of modern medical and surgical discoveries, and at the same time to believe in the New Testament world of daemons and spirits. We may think we can manage it in our own lives, but to expect others to do so is to make the Christian faith unintelligible and unacceptable to the modern world.

The mythical eschatology is untenable for the simple reason that the parousia of Christ never took place as the New Testament expected. History did not come to an end, and, as every schoolboy knows, it will continue to run its course. Even if we believe that the world as we know it will come to an end in time, we expect the end to take the form of a natural catastrophe, not of a mythical event such as the New Testament expects. And if we explain the parousia in terms of modern scientific theory, we are applying criticism to the New Testament, albeit unconsciously.

But natural science is not the only challenge which the mythology of the New Testament has to face. There is the still more serious challenge presented by *modern man's understanding of himself.*

Modern man is confronted by a curious dilemma. He may regard himself as pure nature, or as pure spirit. In the latter case he distinguishes the essential part of his being from nature. In either case, however, *man is essentially a unity.* He bears the sole responsibility for his own feeling, thinking, and willing. He is not, as the New Testament regards him, the victim of a strange dichotomy which exposes him to the interference of powers outside himself. If his exterior behaviour and his interior condition are in perfect harmony, it is something he has achieved himself, and if other people think their interior unity is torn asunder by daemonic or divine interference, he calls it schizophrenia.

Although biology and psychology recognize that man is a highly dependent being, that does not mean that he has been handed over to powers outside of and distinct from himself. This dependence is inseparable from human nature, and he needs only to understand it in order to recover his self-mastery and organize his life on a rational basis. If he regards himself as spirit, he knows that he is permanently conditioned by the physical, bodily part of his being, but he distinguishes his true self from it, and knows that he is independent and responsible for his mastery over nature.

In either case he finds *what the New Testament has to say about the "Spirit"* (πνεῦμα) and the sacraments utterly strange and incomprehensible. Biological man cannot see how a supernatural entity like the πνεῦμα can penetrate within the close texture of his natural powers and set to work within him. Nor can the idealist understand how a πνεῦμα working like a natural power can touch him and influence his mind and spirit. Conscious as he is of his own moral responsibility, he cannot conceive how baptism in water can convey a mysterious something which is henceforth the agent of all his decisions and actions. He cannot see how physical food can convey spiritual strength, and how the unworthy receiving of the Eucharist can result in physical sickness and death (I Cor. 11.30). The only possible explanation is that it is due to suggestion. He cannot understand how anyone can be baptized for the dead (I Cor. 15.29).

We need not examine in detail the various forms of modern *Weltanschauung*, whether idealist or naturalist. For the only criticism of the New Testament which is theologically relevant is that which arises *necessarily* out of the situation of modern man. The biological *Weltanschauung* does not, for instance, arise necessarily out of the contemporary situation. We are still free to adopt it or not as we choose. The only relevant question for the theologian is the basic assumption on which the adoption of a biological as of every other *Weltanschauung* rests, and that assumption is the view of the world which has been moulded by modern science and the modern conception of human nature as a self-subsistent unity immune from the interference of supernatural powers.

Again, the biblical doctrine that *death is the punishment of sin* is equally abhorrent to naturalism and idealism, since they both regard death as a simple and necessary process of nature. To the naturalist death is no problem at all, and to the idealist it is a problem for that very reason, for so far from arising out of man's essential spiritual being it actually destroys it. The idealist is faced with a paradox. On the one hand is a spiritual being, and therefore essentially different from plants and animals, and on the other hand he is the prisoner of nature, whose birth, life, and death are just the same as those of the animals. Death may present him with a problem, but he cannot see how it can be a punishment for sin. Human beings are subject to death even before they have committed any sin. And to attribute human mortality to the fall of Adam is sheer nonsense, for guilt implies personal responsibility, and the idea of original sin as an inherited infection is sub-ethical, irrational, and absurd.

The same objections apply to *the doctrine of the atonement*. How can the guilt of one man be expiated by the death of another who is sinless— if indeed one may speak of a sinless man at all? What primitive notions of guilt and righteousness does this imply? And what primitive idea of God? The rationale of sacrifice in general may of course throw some light on the theory of the atonement, but even so, what a primitive mythology it is, that a divine Being should become incarnate, and atone for the sins of men through his own blood! Or again, one might adopt an analogy from the law courts, and explain the death of Christ as a transaction between God and man through which God's claims on man were satisfied. But that would make sin a juridicial matter; it would be no more than an external trans- gression of a commandment, and it would make nonsense of all our ethical standards. Moreover, if the Christ who died such a death was the pre-existent Son of God, what could death mean for him? Obviously very little, if he knew that he would rise again in three days!

The *resurrection of Jesus* is just as difficult, if it means an event whereby a supernatural power is released which can henceforth be appropriated through the sacraments. To the biologist such language is meaningless, for he does not regard death as a problem at all. The idealist would not object to the idea of a life immune from death, but he could not believe that such a life is made available by the resuscitation of a corpse. If that is the way God makes life available for man, his action is inextricably involved in a nature miracle. Such a notion he finds intolerable, for he can see God at work only in the life of the spirit (which is for him the only real life) and in the transformation of his personality. But, quite apart from the in- credibility of such a miracle, he cannot see how an event like this could be the act of God, or how it could affect his own life.

Gnostic influence suggests that this Christ, who died and rose again, was not a mere human being but a God-man. His death and resurrection were not isolated facts which concerned him alone, but a cosmic event in which we are all involved. It is only with effort that modern man can think himself back into such an intellectual atmosphere, and even then he could never accept it himself, because it regards man's essential being as nature and redemption as a process of nature. And as for the pre-existence of Christ, with its corollary of man's translation into a celestial realm of light, and the clothing of the human personality in heavenly robes and a spiritual body—all this is not only irrational but utterly meaningless. Why should salvation take this particular form? Why should this be the fulfilment of human life and the realization of man's true being?

B. The Task before Us

1. Not Selection or Subtraction.

Does this drastic criticism of the New Testament mythology mean the complete elimination of the kerygma?

Whatever else may be true, we cannot save the kerygma by selecting some of its features and subtracting others, and thus reduce the amount of mythology in it. For instance, it is impossible to dismiss St Paul's teaching about the unworthy reception of Holy Communion or about baptism for the dead, and yet cling to the belief that physical eating and drinking can have a spiritual effect. If we accept one idea, we must accept everything which the New Testament has to say about Baptism and Holy Communion, and it is just this one idea which we cannot accept.

It may of course be argued that some features of the New Testament mythology are given greater prominence than others: not all of them appear with the same regularity in the various books. There is for example only one occurrence of the legends of the Virgin birth and the Ascension; St Paul and St John appear to be totally unaware of them. But, even if we take them to be later accretions, it does not affect the mythical character of the event of redemption as a whole. And if we once start subtracting from the kerygma, where are we to draw the line? The mythical view of the world must be accepted or rejected in its entirety.

At this point absolute clarity and ruthless honesty are essential both for the academic theologian and for the parish priest. It is a duty they owe to themselves, to the Church they serve, and to those whom they seek to win for the Church. They must make it quite clear what their hearers are expected to accept and what they are not. At all costs the preacher must not leave his people in the dark about what he secretly eliminates, nor must he be in the dark about it himself. In Karl Barth's book *The Resurrection of the Dead* the cosmic eschatology in the sense of "chronologically final history" is eliminated in favour of what he intends to be a nonmythical "ultimate history". He is able to delude himself into thinking that this is exegesis of St. Paul and of the New Testament generally only because he gets rid of everything mythological in I Corinthians by subjecting it to an interpretation which does violence to its meaning. But that is an impossible procedure.

If the truth of the New Testament proclamation is to be preserved, the only way is to demythologize it. But our motive in so doing must not be to make the New Testament relevant to the modern world at all costs. The question is simply whether the New Testament message consists exclusively of mythology, or whether it actually demands the elimination of myth if it is to be understood as it is meant to be. This question is forced upon us from two sides. First there is the nature of myth in general, and then there is the New Testament itself.

2. The Nature of Myth.

The real purpose of myth is not to present an objective picture of the world as it is, but to express man's understanding of himself in the world in which he lives. Myth should be interpreted not cosmologically, but anthropologically, or better still, existentially. Myth speaks of the power or the powers which man supposes he experiences as the ground and limit of his world and of his own activity and suffering. He describes these powers in terms derived from the visible world, with its tangible objects and forces, and from human life, with its feelings, motives, and potentialities. He may, for instance, explain the origin of the world by speaking of a world egg or a world tree. Similarly he may account for the present state and order of the world by speaking of a primeval war between the gods. He speaks of the other world in terms of this world, and of the gods in terms derived from human life.

Myth is an expression of man's conviction that the origin and purpose of the world in which he lives are to be sought not within it but beyond it—that is, beyond the realm of known and tangible reality—and that this realm is perpetually dominated and menaced by those mysterious powers which are its source and limit. Myth is also an expression of man's awareness that he is not lord of his own being. It expresses his sense of dependence not only within the visible world, but more especially on those forces which hold sway beyond the confines of the known. Finally, myth expresses man's belief that in this state of dependence he can be delivered from the forces within the visible world.

Thus myth contains elements which demand its own criticism—namely, its imagery with its apparent claim to objective validity. The real purpose of myth is to speak of a transcendent power which controls the world and man, but that purpose is impeded and obscured by the terms in which it is expressed.

Hence the importance of the New Testament mythology lies not in its imagery but in the understanding of existence which it enshrines. The real question is whether this understanding of existence is true. Faith claims that it is, and faith ought not to be tied down to the imagery of New Testament mythology.

3. *The New Testament Itself.*

The New Testament itself invites this kind of criticism. Not only are there rough edges in its mythology, but some of its features are actually contradictory. For example, the death of Christ is sometimes a sacrifice and sometimes a cosmic event. Sometimes his person is interpreted as the Messiah and sometimes as the Second Adam. The kenosis of the pre-existent Son (Phil. 2.6ff.) is incompatible with the miracle narratives as proofs of his messianic claims. The Virgin birth is inconsistent with the assertion of his pre-existence. The doctrine of the Creation is incompatible with the conception of the "rulers of this world" (I Cor. 2.6ff.), the "god of this world" (2 Cor. 4.4) and the "elements of this world" στοιχεῖα τοῦ κόσμου, (Gal. 4. 3). It is impossible to square the belief that the law was given by God with the theory that it comes from the angels (Gal. 3. 19f.).

But the principal demand for the criticism of mythology comes from a curious contradiction which runs right through the New Testament. Sometimes we are told that human life is determined by cosmic forces, at others we are challenged to a decision. Side by side with the Pauline indicative stands the Pauline imperative. In short, man is sometimes regarded as a cosmic being, sometimes as an independent "I" for whom decision is a matter of life or death. Incidentally, this explains why so many sayings in the New Testament speak directly to modern man's condition while others remain enigmatic and obscure. Finally, attempts at demythologization are sometimes made even within the New Testament itself. But more will be said on this point later.

4. *Previous Attempts at Demythologizing.*

How then is the mythology of the New Testament to be reinterpreted? This is not the first time that theologians have approached this task. Indeed, all we have said so far might have been said in much the same way thirty or forty years ago, and it is a sign of the bankruptcy of contemporary theology that it has been necessary to go all over the same ground again. The reason for this is not far to seek. The liberal theologians of the last century were working on the wrong lines. They threw away not only the mythology but also the kerygma itself. Were they right? Is that the treatment the New Testament itself required? That is the question we must face to-day. The last twenty years have witnessed a movement away from criticism and a return to a naive acceptance of the kerygma. The danger both for the theological scholarship and for the Church is that this uncritical resuscitation of the New Testament mythology may make this Gospel message unintelligible to the modern world. We cannot dismiss the critical labours of earlier generations without further ado. We must take them up and put them to constructive use. Failure to do so will mean that the old battles between orthodoxy and liberalism will have to be fought out all over again, that is assuming that there will be any Church or any theologians to fight them at all! Perhaps we may put it schematically like this: whereas the older liberals used criticism to *eliminate* the mythology of the New Testament, our task to-day is to use criticism to *interpret* it. Of course it may still be necessary to eliminate mythology here and there. But the criterion adopted must be taken not from modern thought, but from the understanding of human existence which the New Testament itself enshrines.

To begin with, let us review some of these earlier attempts at demythologizing. We need only mention briefly the allegorical interpretation of the New Testament which has dogged the Church throughout its history. This method spiritualizes the mythical events so that they become symbols of processes going on in the soul. This is certainly the most comfortable way of avoiding the critical question. The literal meaning is allowed to stand and is dispensed with only for the individual believer, who can escape into the realm of the soul.

It was characteristic of the older liberal theologians that they regarded mythology as relative and temporary. Hence they thought they could safely eliminate it altogether, and retain only the broad, basic principles of religion and ethics. They distinguished between what they took to be the essence of religion and the temporary garb which it assumed. Listen to what Harnack has to say about the essence of Jesus' preaching of the Kingdom of God and its coming: "The kingdom has a triple meaning. Firstly, it is something supernatural, a gift from above, not a product of ordinary life. Secondly, it is a purely religious blessing, the inner link with the living God; thirdly, it is the most important experience that a man can have, that on which everything else depends; it permeates and dominates his whole existence, because sin is forgiven and misery banished." Note how completely the mythology is eliminated: "The kingdom of God comes by coming to the individual, by entering into his *soul* and laying hold of it."

It will be noticed how Harnack reduces the kerygma to a few basic principles of religion and ethics. Unfortunately this means that *the kerygma has ceased to be kerygma:* it is no longer the proclamation of the decisive act of God in Christ. For the liberals the great truths of religion and ethics are timeless and eternal, though it is only within human history that they are realized, and only in concrete historical processes that they are given clear expression. But the apprehension and acceptance of these principles does not depend on the knowledge and acceptance of the age in which they first took shape, or of the historical persons who first discovered them. We are all capable of verifying them in our own experience at whatever period we happen to live. History may be of academic interest, but never of paramount importance for religion.

But the New Testament speaks of an *event* through which God has wrought man's redemption. For it, Jesus is not primarily the teacher, who certainly had extremely important things to say and will always be honoured for saying them, but whose person in the last analysis is immaterial for those who have assimilated his teaching. On the contrary, his person is just what the New Testament proclaims as the decisive event of redemption. It speaks of this person in mythological terms, but does this mean that we can reject the kerygma altogether on the ground that it is nothing more than mythology? That is the question.

Next came the History of Religions school. Its representatives were the first to discover the extent to which the New Testament is permeated by mythology. The importance of the New Testament, they saw, lay not in its teaching about religion and ethics but in its actual religion and piety; in comparison with that all the dogma it contains, and therefore all the mythological imagery with its apparent objectivity, was of secondary importance or completely negligible. The essence of the New Testament lay in the religious life it portrayed; its high-watermark was the experience of mystical union with Christ, in whom God took symbolic form.

These critics grasped one important truth. Christian faith is not the same as religious idealism; the Christian life does not consist in developing the individual personality, in the improvement of society, or in making the world a better place. The Christian life means a turning away from the world, a detachment from it. But the critics of the History of Religions school failed to see that in the New Testament this detachment is essentially eschatological and not mystical. Religion for them was an expression of the human yearning to rise above the world and transcend it: it was the discovery of a supramundane sphere where the soul could detach itself from all earthly care and find its rest. Hence the supreme manifestation of religion was to be found not in personal ethics or in social idealism but in the cultus regarded as an end in itself. This was just the kind of rel/gous life portrayed in the New Testament, not only as a model and pattern, but as a challenge and inspiration. The New Testament was thus the abiding source of power which enabled man to realize the true life of religion, and Christ was the eternal symbol for the cultus of the Christian Church. It will be noticed how the Church is here defined exclusively as a worshipping community, and this represents a great advance on the older liberalism. This school rediscovered the Church as a *religious* institution. For the idealist there was really no place for the Church at all. But did they succeed in recovering the meaning of the Ecclesia in the full, New Testament sense of the word? For in the New Testament the Ecclesia is invariably a phenomenon of salvation history and eschatology.

Moreover, if the History of Religions school is right, the kerygma has once more ceased to be kerygma. Like the liberals, they are silent about a decisive act of God in Christ proclaimed as the event of redemption. So we are still left with the question whether this event and the person of Jesus, both of which are described in the New Testament in mythological terms, are nothing more than mythology. Can the kerygma be interpreted apart from mythology? Can we recover the truth of the kerygma for men who do not think in mythological terms without forfeiting its character as kerygma?

5. An Existentialist Interpretation the Only Solution.

The theological work which such an interpretation involves can be sketched only in the broadest outline and with only a few examples. We must avoid the impression that this is a light and easy task, as if all we have to do is to discover the right formula and finish the job on the spot. It is much more formidable than that. It cannot be done single-handed. It will tax the time and strength of a whole theological generation.

The mythology of the New Testament is in essence that of Jewish apocalyptic and the Gnostic redemption myths. A common feature of them both is their basic dualism, according to which the present world and its human inhabitants are under the control of daemonic, satanic powers, and stand in need of redemption. Man cannot achieve this redemption by his own efforts; it must come as a gift through a divine intervention. Both types of mythology speak of such an intervention: Jewish apocalyptic of an imminent world crisis in which this present aeon will be brought to an end and the new aeon ushered in by the coming of the Messiah, and Gnosticism of a Son of God sent down from the realm of light, entering into this world in the guise of a man, and by his fate and teaching delivering the elect and opening up the way for their return to their heavenly home.

The meaning of these two types of mythology lies once more not in their imagery within its apparent objectivity but in the understanding of human existence which both are trying to express. In other words, they need to be interpreted existentially. A good example of such treatment is to be found in Hans Jonas's book on Gnosticism.

Our task is to produce an existentialist interpretation of the dualistic mythology of the New Testament along similar lines. When, for instance, we read of daemonic powers ruling the world and holding mankind in bondage, does the understanding of human existence which underlies such language offer a solution to the riddle of human life which will be acceptable even to the nonmythological mind of to-day? Of course we must not take this to imply that the New Testament presents us with an anthropology like that which modern science can give us. It cannot be proved by logic or demonstrated by an appeal to factual evidence. Scientific anthropologies always take for granted a definite understanding of existence, which is invariably the consequence of a deliberate decision of the scientist, whether he makes it consciously or not. And that is why we have to discover whether the New Testament offers man an understanding of himself which will challenge him to a genuine existential decision.

RONALD W. HEPBURN

RONALD HEPBURN (1927-   ), British analytical philosopher, formerly at Aberdeen, is
now head of the department of philosophy
at Nottingham University. His major interest
is in philosophy of religion. His book, *Christianity and Paradox*, is a contribution to this
field.

Demythologizing and the Problem of Validity*

It might seem as if the title I have chosen were either bombastic and
empty, or claimed nothing less than the entire field of myth and the Bible
as its theme. For does not every theologian aim at producing *valid* theology
and is not "the problem of validity" only another name for the theologian's
problems as a whole? Yet it is all too easy in theology to muffle this question
of validity, for all its importance, to veil and camouflage inadvertently the
logical nature of what is being undertaken. Nothing is harder than to write
so transparently that the reader is kept aware of exactly what claims are
essential to the validity of the doctrine or theory concerned, and what are
subsidiary, carefully distinguishing the logical from the psychological, the
historical from the metaphysical—at every stage. This is far more than a
peripheral matter of expositional technique: for to allow the logical structure
of a theology to shine through its presentation is not only to prepare the way
for assessing its validity; it is to have commenced assessment already. In this
field clarification and verification constantly merge into one another. To see
clearly what a theology demands is to begin seeing how plausible or im-
plausible are those demands.

This is, of course, true not only of theology. If a piece of empirical science
is dressed up to look like *a priori* mathematics, we shall be tempted to use
quite inappropriate methods for testing its truth or falsity—looking for internal consistency in the use of symbols instead of conformity with a range
of phenomena in the outside world. A mistaken account of ethics (say a
crude subjectivism) can suggest irrelevant tests for moral rightness and wrongness (such as the occurrence of certain kinds of sentiments). But however

* From Ronald W. Hepburn, *New Essays In Philosophical Theology*, ed. Antony Flew
and Alasdair MacIntyre, pp. 227-242. Published, 1955, by Student Christian Movement
Press. Used by permission of Student Christian Movement Press and The Macmillan
Company. [Footnotes omitted, Eds.]

319

widely spread this danger, the theologian is exposed to it in a unique way. Notoriously, his utterances about God put constant severe strain upon the vocabulary with which he is compelled to work: the lines of communication between the senses which he gives his words and ordinary use are ever on the point of being ruptured—a truth which he may learn from Kant as well as from Wittgenstein. It is, therefore, of paramount importance that he should show as far as he can what functions his language is performing—when literal, when symbolical, when descriptive, when evaluative.

In what follows, I want to ask how far the contributors to the recent debate on demythologizing have been alert to this problem of meaning and validity. How far, in particular, does Bultmann's *New Testament and Mythology* reveal an awareness of them? If my conclusions are unsympathetic, this must not be taken as evidence of a sceptical indifference to the subject itself. The relations between historical fact, mythological statement and existential concern are inescapably fundamental to the New Testament study of our day. It is rather my sense of their ultimacy which prompts this criticism of the procedures employed by one major protagonist in the debate.

The pith of my criticism is simply this: that Bultmann's methods and terminology tend to insulate his claims against the possibility of verification or falsification (using these words in their widest sense); that this happens not in conjunction with a reasoned assertion that theological disagreements are by nature unsettleable, but *by default* through ambiguities and confusions in crucial terms, which effectively prevent the question of validity being raised as it ought to be raised and even deny the language whereby this could be done.

My remarks may be grouped under five headings.

1. The Definition of Myth

Any instability in the concept of myth itself would be found to imperil the discussion at point after point. Yet Bultmann neither offers a satisfactory definition, nor abides by the definition he does offer. "Mythology," he writes (p. 10) "is the use of imagery to express the other worldly in terms of this world and the divine in terms of human life, the other side in terms of this side." By his own test this definition itself is partly couched in mythological language, which is cause enough for bewilderment. And it is sufficiently wide in its scope to include all pictorial, analogical and symbolical speech whatever. Now in another place Bultmann concedes that *all* utterance about God is analogical, and therefore (if the first definition is to stand) irreducibly mythological. Bultmann cannot mean this. For if it were true, it would make demythologizing a logically impossible task; and the contrast he constantly wishes to make between "mere mythology" and authentic existentialist interpretation would be robbed of its basis. Perplexity does not end here: in a discussion on the expression "act of god" (p. 196f.) Bultmann decides against calling this "mythological language," on the ground that "mythological thought regards the divine activity . . . as an interference with the course of nature," and "acts of God," to Bultmann, are not of this sort. Therefore to speak of such acts is not to speak mythologically, but *analogically*. This conclusion, however, violates his original definition of myth in two ways at once:

(1) Bultmann is saying: "the expression 'act of God' is not mythological language, but analogical," whereas on his definition this antithesis could not be made, since "myth" is there plainly the "genus" word, with "analogy," "pictorial image," etc., as species.

(2) The mythological has been redefined as that which depicts God as "interfering in the course of nature"; while the first definition concerned itself only with myth as a form of language and said nothing at all about the *content* of any particular myths.

The contrast mentioned a moment ago between "just mythology" and "existentialist interpretation" (p. 110) reminds us that Bultmann frequently uses "myth" and its cognates as pejoratives. For example: Bultmann may well be right when he claims that the New Testament myths are *in origin* Jewish and Gnostic. But he goes on to say that they are also Jewish and Gnostic "in essence"—a very different claim (pp. 3, 15). "Identical in essence with X," implies "containing no more than X," "of the same value as X." Part of Bultmann's failure to justify his transition from "in origin" to "in essence" may be due to just this pejorative innuendo carried by "myth" which militates against the scrutiny and evaluation of each individual myth (and modification of myth) on its own merits.

Here, then, in the definition of "myth," is one point at which greater logical rigour is urgently required, if the discussion is to be set on a secure foundation.

2. The Flight from the Evidential

Bultmann's reluctance to face problems of validity manifests itself in a recurrent pattern of argumentation which could be schematized in roughly the following way.

(a) A fact or argument appears, which *prima facie* is hostile to the validity of the Christian position;

(b) Bultmann turns aside from its negative evidential implication; and
(c) transforms the hostile fact in such a way as to make it yield positive
support for a modified and freshly secured theological view.

The suspicion grows, as one reads, that no evidence at all would be admitted as finally detrimental to Bultmann's position. If he actually believes
this (and it is not an *absurd* belief to hold), it ought to be clearly exhibited
as the crucial tenet it undoubtedly would be, and argued for as such.

Two simple examples may bring out this pattern of thought.

(1) On page 11 of *Kerygma and Myth* Bultmann describes how antinomies are generated by conflicting imagery in the New Testament. "The
virgin birth is inconsistent with the assertion of [Christ's] pre-existence,"
so is the creation doctrine with talk about the "rulers of this world," and the
law as God-given with the statement that it came from the angels. To Bultmann all this implies, "Rise, therefore, *above* the mythological."

(2) Christ failed to return in the way the disciples had at first expected.
We ought, says Bultmann, to profit from their mistake; recognizing that the
Last Things are mythological conceptions, not historical.

In both cases a difficulty is metamorphosed into a theologically acceptable "truth." But in each case too Bultmann has side-stepped an equally
important sceptical option—without giving adequate reasons for so doing.
In the first case we might say: "Conflicting views? then so much the worse
for the reliability of the documents!"; and in the second case: "Jesus did
not come, because the disciples were simply and tragically wrong about him."
Plausibility can be given to evasive moves like these in individual instances,
but only so long as the by-passed sceptical options are never gathered together and faced *cumulatively* as a challenge, more or less formidable, to
the Christian position.

One may go further: the whole category of the evidential is repeatedly
pushed aside by Bultmann as of no importance, or, worse, as a snare. He
speaks scornfully of the "provable": "It is precisely its immunity from
proof which secures the Christian proclamation against the charge of being
mythological" (p. 44). The language of myth is concrete and pictorial, concerned with stones rolling away and men rising into the sky, suggesting in
many cases events that might be captured by the camera. Not so the truths
of non-mythological Christian belief: for to Bultmann the removal of Christianity from the realm of myth up-grades it in value. So much so, that the
reader is prepared to accept, if he is off-guard, that to remove it from the
realm of the "provable" must also be an act of up-grading, to be welcomed
like a release from a long-standing bondage. But in this way Bultmann has

again omitted to argue for a vital proposition, namely that absence of evidence does not disqualify a religion from being acceptable by reasonable men, or that "unprovable" here is not equivalent to "baseless" or "unfounded," as it undeniably is in many contexts.

In speaking of faith Bultmann makes this turn of thought particularly plain: "It is impossible to prove that faith is related to its object . . . it is just here that its strength lies" (p. 201). Once more the absence of evidence is taken as a commendation. For if the relation of faith to God *were* provable, then, says Bultmann, God would be reduced to the status of one item among others in the furniture of the universe: and only "in that realm (are we) justified in demanding proof". Unfortunately this latter sentence begs the question. It assumes that we know already—have had convincingly shown to us—that there are in fact two "realms"—a belief which should surely appear as part of the end-product, not as the initial presupposition of a reasoned theology. Again, a sceptical option demands attention but does not receive it; that is, "If God's being cannot be established, there *may* be no God."

The furthest Bultmann goes in this extraordinary and fascinating flight from the evidential is to transform the failure to obtain proof into an aggressive refusal to accept any *possible* proof. Thus he rejects I Cor. 15.3-8 as evidence for the resurrection, not explicitly on critical grounds, but in his own words—"that line of argument is fatal *because* it tries to adduce a proof for the *Kerygma*" (p. 112; my italics).

This trend of thought, yoked with his critical standpoint, leads Bultmann to speak evasively and ambiguously of the Biblical narratives. As Schleiermacher could say of the ascension only that "something happened," so Bultmann says of the resurrection with similar cloudiness, "I have no intention whatever of denying the uniqueness of the first Easter Day" (p. 111), selecting a vocabulary which permits the retention of a reverent attitude but leaves altogether unclear the nature of the event towards which the attitude is adopted, and therefore leaves equally unclear what procedure could show whether the attitude was an *appropriate* one or not.

An avowed historical agnosticism about the events of Jesus' life would be quite unexceptionable. What one finds in Bultmann, however, is something more positive and dogmatic. At many crucial points he casts about in his mind for an interpretation of an event which he thinks adequate to the existential seriousness of Christianity and proceeds to *read back* his interpretation into the original documents however these may resist the treatment, and however many critical questions may be begged. It is one thing to say, "I have no idea what happened at the ascension, but it provides an excellent symbol for Christ's oneness with the Father": quite another thing to say, "The ascension did not happen—*could* not have happened: it is an excellent symbol, etc., etc." To speak of the "unique and final revelation of God in history" may be misleading as Bultmann claims, in its tendency to lead to thinking of that revelation as a *revelatum*, an event which happened once in the remote past, to which we have access only by historical documents; in Bultmann's words, "something which took place in the past and is now an object of detached observation" (p. 111). But anxiety on this score has gone too far when it results in a fight against history itself; and it cannot be invoked as justification for abandoning the evidential as such.

It is hardly an exaggeration to say that Bultmann would feel an *embarrassment* at the very possibility that certain events might after all have taken place just as the documents narrate them. Doubtless a Christian ought not to see a miracle as a divine conjuring trick, but should interpret the miraculous in personal and moral categories. But that does not give Bultmann warrant to say, "the God of revelation is the God of judgment and forgiveness, *not* the Cause of abnormal phenomena" (p. 121; my italics). It may also be true that in the believer's passage from death into life "outwardly everything remains as before, but inwardly his relation to the world has been radically changed" (p. 20), but Bultmann is over-eager to make this inner invisible event the paradigm not only of conversion but of the New Testament message in its entirety, for the most momentous divine activity still leaves "undisturbed" the "closed weft of history" (p. 197). Can he also consistently say, "It is indeed part of the *skandalon* that . . . our salvation is One who is involved in all the relativity of history" (p. 111)? For he is as anxious to *escape* the level of the verifiable as the logical positivists were to remain within it, in making verifiability the touchstone of meaningfulness. Both are guilty through excess of zeal: the positivists in their belief that any simple verification procedure could prove adequate to every possible experience, Bultmann in refusing to make plain what states of affairs would be incompatible with Christian belief, or just how different the world would have to be before belief would have to be declared senseless.

The historian's task would be impossible, were he forbidden to fill out imaginatively the reconstruction of events to which his sources bear witness. Yet at what point legitimate interpretation fades into fanciful and irresponsible refashioning of the past is often a hard question. We have no guarantee that any ingenious device we may introduce into a production of Shakespeare was actually present in the poet's mind when he wrote his play; how much more uncertain is the assurance of Bultmann that the demythologized, existentialist account of the New Testament proclamation does not in fact distort that proclamation, for all its philosophical attractiveness.

3. Fact and Language

A theology which aims at being logically transparent must carefully distinguish issues of fact from matters of linguistic convenience. Now, the very word "demythologize" strongly suggests a venture in translation, the substitution of more literal language for pictorial and symbolic language. Yet this is thoroughly deceptive. If the ascension, say, is amenable to demythologizing, that is to say something not only about the language in which the "event" is described, but to decide also about the actual status of the event itself, to deny that Jesus did in fact rise into the air. And no linguistic investigation could lead by itself to such conclusions. Put it differently: to qualify for mythhood a statement must be (on Bultmann's definition) actually about "the other world" or "the other side." The process of demythologizing must accordingly consist of at least two phases, of which the first is the recognition that the scriptural account concerned is mythological in nature; while the second phase re-interprets its substance nonmythologically. But the question whether any particular narration *is* mythical cannot be settled by Bultmann or anyone else while acting in the capacity of *translator*. An event such as a piece of prophetic symbolism may be historical (Jesus did enter Jerusalem in triumph, did curse the fig tree) and at the same time be mythological in Bultmann's sense. Or the alleged event may not have happened and the narrative still retain mythological value. What one must insist is that whether or not the imagery, etc., of the narrative yields itself to translation into existentialist terms, this does nothing to tell us which of those possibilities is more likely to be true. Yet Bultmann repeatedly suggests that "X is described in mythological terms" implies "X cannot have happened as narrated," and does not make it plain that the latter judgment required a quite distinct investigation.

Two brief examples of this may be hazarded. First, the expression "the cross" is indispensable in devotional language; but the very reasons which make it valuable there make it a dangerous and slippery term in a theology like Bultmann's—namely its conflation of two distinguishable conceptions, the actual crucifixion of Jesus at Calvary and the "meaning" that event can have for the Christian. This span of meaning permits a theologian to keep his reader in a state of sustained uncertainty about exactly what historical claim, if any, he is making when he speaks of the "cross."

Second, "Take . . . the case of a child being sacrificed in order to ensure the success of an enterprise or to avert misfortune. Such a practice implies a 'crude mythological conception of God' " (p. 108). Here the rejection of a primitive view of sacrifice (as in the stories of Iphigenia and Jeptha's daughter) appears to be part and parcel with Bultmann's general impatience with the mythological: its repudiation is represented as involved in the passage from myth to non-myth. But is this not misleading in the extreme? What is "crude" about the sacrifice theory is not its mythological nature, but its *moral* inadequacy. Abandoning it is not a piece of linguistic spring-cleaning but a value-judgment, logically quite different.

There may be at least a hint of this fact-language conflation on page 7 of *Kerygma and Myth* where Bultmann says: "The only criticism of the New Testament which is theologically relevant is that which arises *necessarily* out of the situation of modern man" (Bultmann's italics). One such "necessity" is disbelief in the miraculous as interference in the order of nature. Now, as Austin Farrer remarks in the same volume, some modern men do not find such a belief impossible. But Bultmann whisks his reader past the possible objection, aided by this word "necessarily" which is always ready to take on the logician's sense of "analytically, logically necessary," therefore not falsifiable by any matter of fact. Again the controversial is made to seem less controversial, and objections on the score of validity are glided over by the hint that the truth of the statement is guaranteed by linguistic convention, that its denial involves contradiction.

4. Myth and Oblique Language

The project of demythologizing raises in an acute form the general problem of the religious use of language, the logical nature of statements about God. We may start with Bultmann's crucial statement, ". . . there are certain concepts which are fundamentally mythological, and with which we shall never be able to dispense—e.g. the idea of transcendence. In such cases, however, the original mythological meaning has been lost, and they have become mere metaphors or ciphers" (pp. 102f.). "*Mere* metaphors," note; the phrase suggests that these concepts are "as near literal as makes no difference." But in fact it makes a great deal of difference. The gulf between literal (or direct) and oblique language cannot be bridged so lightheartedly. For if propositions about God are irreducibly oblique—that is, symbolical, analogical and so on, then to demythologize is not to remove all obliqueness, but only obliqueness of certain sorts: on the other hand, if it is possible to speak literally of God, then demythologizing is quite a different activity, not one of translation out of one code into another, but rather of *decoding* altogether. The question which should be of greatest concern to the theologian is not whether this or that myth may be re-expressed in language less flagrantly pictorial, more abstract in appearance, but whether or not the circle of myth, metaphor and symbol is a closed one: and if closed then in what way propositions about God manage to *refer*. Bultmann's first definition of "myth" gave the word a sense sufficiently extended to include every kind of oblique language; yet in practice he gives very little scrutiny indeed to this general issue, and even (as we have noticed) contrasts the mythological with the analogical—a procedure for which his definition gives no warrant. That is to say: the nature of demythologizing as an enterprise must remain logically obscured so long as we leave unsettled the question "Is any direct talk of God possible, or can one talk only obliquely of him?" How inattention to this question can enfeeble the debate can be brought out as follows.

Bultmann's critics have often pointed out that his existentialist terminology is no less mythological than the New Testament ideas from which he wishes to deliver us. Bultmann is prepared to admit this: even "transcendence" is a mythological concept, but one (he is assured) in which myth is merely vestigial, neutralized, reduced to the harmless status of "mere metaphor or cipher." But the more searching objection can still be made that this *appearance* of directness and abstract sterility can be (logically) a menace. If the demythologized talk of God is still oblique, then it should display its obliqueness overtly, for to carry it surreptitiously may be rather like treating measles by hiding the rash with face-powder. For all we know, the suppressed picture, the latent myth, may still be doing the work in the expression concerned; and the "cashing" of it may be impossible without once more reverting to the concealed, but active, myth.

The importance of this may be made plainer by referring to a perceptive article by Ian Crombie, where he considers the challenge to religious belief presented recently by certain linguistic philosophers. In particular, it had been argued that a proposition like "God loves me" appears at first sight to be rich in meaning but is in fact qualified out of existence as soon as we attempt to describe in detail what precisely it claims. Although there are certain sorts of behaviour which give good grounds for denying that one human being loves another, the Christian is expected to go on saying "God loves me" even when his child is born blind and he himself succumbs to an incurable disease. Even the proposition "God exists" is eroded away to emptiness by successive qualifications: "he exists—*but* is invisible, inaudible, intangible, not *in* the world nor a name for the world as a whole. . . ." Now, in his article, Crombie granted that any attempt to speak literally, directly of God was indeed bound to fail. Nevertheless, we can still speak of him—in "parable" (using the word in an extended sense). We say "God loves us"; what this is like as an experience in God's own being we have not the least idea (nor, without taking in the hereafter, can we exhaustively verify or falsify it): for to predicate "loving" or "acting" or "suffering" of One who infinite and unconditioned is at once to snap the links with every intelligible use of these words. But if we think of "God loves us" as a parable, an oblique utterance, the word "loves" is being used not in a stretched sense but with its everyday familiar meaning. Without knowing what it is like for God to love, we do know now what thoughts of God and what sorts of behaviour are appropriate and what not. We accept one parable about God, rather than another, on the authority, primarily, of Jesus Christ. The parabolic is only one of the two "parents" of religious belief: the other is what might be called "undifferentiated theism," and springs from a sense of the contingency (or beauty, etc.) of the world, giving a "direction" in which the revealed parable can be referred.

Professor Tillich, in a conversation, once pointed out to me how closely this analysis followed the pattern of his own treatment of the same problem, however different his starting-point. Tillich maintains that all propositions about God are symbolic, except one: for without one direct proposition the oblique language, despite its internal coherence, would have no anchor in reality; the flotilla of symbols would be adrift, unpiloted. To Tillich this one direct proposition is "God is Being-itself," and its resemblance to Crombie's "undifferentiated theism" is obvious enough.

Neither Crombie nor Tillich was engaged on a project of demythologizing. None the less, my point is that demythologizing is only an artificially broken off segment of the problem with which they *were* grappling, and that both of them permit the logical structure of their enterprises to shine through with a clarity impossible to the close disciple of Bultmann. Thus Crombie's presentation, if acceptable, makes it at once plain what sort of procedure is relevant to establishing its truth: each "parent" of belief requires a separate justification. With the theistic, for instance, we must ask how far it is exposed to the general difficulties of the classical arguments of natural theology despite its prelinguistic character: with the parabolic we must investigate the grounds on which we accept Jesus' authority in uttering the parable.

5. The Existentialist Interpretation

So far I have been trying to lay bare some of the pitfalls which beset Bultmann's enterprise, ways in which the problem of validity tends to be side-stepped in demythologizing and the logic of religious statements obscured rather than clarified. Something must be said in conclusion (however briefly), about the other half of the total programme—the revision of the Kerygma in existentialist terms. Do existentialist modes of thought, as Bultmann adopts them, help or hinder the fashioning of a theology whose logical structure reveals itself through its presentation and terminology?

In the first place, there is an undeniable advance from a sentimentalist analysis of belief (as in Schleiermacher) to an existentialist analysis. The advance is comparable to that recent progress from the positivist's dichotomy between "descriptive and emotive" language to the recognition of the variety of actual linguistic functions as seen in the writing of philosophers like Wisdom and Austin. Existentialism provides the theologian (the poet and novelist too) with a rich vocabulary in which to express important elements of the human situation—decision, commitment, dereliction, anguish and many more. Indeed, its theological adaptability is not matter for surprise, since the roots of existentialism go back as far as Pascal and Augustine.

But the adoption of a twentieth-century existentialist terminology is not without its dangers. Certain of these were admirably discussed in Christopher Evans' broadcast review of *Kerygma and Myth*. It is as a tentative supplement to what he said there that I hazard these three additional criticisms.

The first is the most formidable, but space will permit only its bare statement. Overwhelmingly concerned with the phenomenology of faith and the life of faith, existentialist thought is in continual peril of failing to emerge from the subjectivist circle at all. A subjectivist account can provide an informative description of what it is like to think and act *as if* there were a God, of the "inward" metamorphosis which accompanies belief. But it is unable to go further (and it is only here that the question of validity becomes relevant) unable to say whether the belief is justified or unjustified, whether or not there exists a Being before whom the believer has taken up the attitude of faith.

A second danger arises from the almost unlimited hospitality which existentialist thought gives to the paradoxical. Even granting that there are situations in which one is forced to say, "This is a paradox—an enigma, a mystery," there are others in which the proper response is, "This is paradoxical, contradictory and nonsensical." The more cautious a theologian is of paradox, the less he revels in it for its own dramatic sake—the less likely he will be to revere the nonsensical and the invalid when he ought to be dismissing them. His ideal language is one which (by its reluctance to resort to paradox in all but unavoidable contexts) reduces the risk of such confusions as far as possible. Again, it is not an insensitivity to the value of metaphor and analogy in exposition that prompts the suspicion that existentialist language is frequently over-tolerant also of those. In sentences like "we possess the present through encounter" (p. 116, *K.a.M.*) the adoption of the language of drama in the field of general philosophy has begotten a metaphorical mode of speech in which cogent argumentation or criticism is desperately hard. Distortion is inevitable when all relations come to be conceived on the model of interpersonal encounter.

Finally, an existentialist dramatic vocabulary tends on occasion illicitly to prescribe to the theologian what questions he should or should not pursue, where his inquiry should start and (worse still) where it should end. Bultmann writes: "It is not for us to question [the] credentials" of the "word of preaching," "It is we who are questioned" (p. 41). Perhaps: but this alluring language of drama cannot justify the theologian's evasion of that abiding and ultimate question—"*on what grounds* ought I to assume an attitude of obedience before the New Testament and not before, say, the Koran?" On another page we read: "I think I may take for granted that the right question to frame with regard to the Bible—at any rate within the Church—is the question of human existence" (pp. 191f., *ibid.*), as if by the weightiness of existential utterance itself one could smother the thousand and one *other* questions—of historicity, integrity of text, interpretation—which likewise clamour for their answer, and concern Churchmen as much as unbelievers. Here existentialism has become Bultmann's master, not his servant. So long as it provides the means of expressing what without its terms would be inexpressible, theologians can do nothing but respect it: but it is time to protest when it proceeds arbitrarily to impose limits upon critical examination, whether of doctrine or document.

The quest for a language that is adequate to describe our experience in all its multifariousness is the common task of philosophers and theologians. They must resist equally the artificial truncation of language on dogmatic positivist lines and any language ("inflationary" language, Isaiah Berlin would call it) which is given to the multiplication of metaphysical or theological entities beyond necessity, and from crying mystery where there is not always mystery but sometimes only muddle. In each case a defective linguistic instrument is an obstacle not only to clarity in exposition but also to the attainment of validity.

JOHN
WILSON

JOHN WILSON (1928-   ), teacher in England, has attempted to interpret the importance of linguistic analysis for philosophy of religion. He has written two books which serve as introductions to analytical philosophy, *Language and Christian Belief* and *Language and the Pursuit of Truth.*

*Verification and Religious Language**

Let us begin by taking a superficial glance at the language of religion. In religious works of literature, creeds, ritual, and so on we come across different types of sentences which have (or appear to have) different uses. On this superficial level, we can list these without difficulty:

1. Sentences expressing commands, injunctions, exhortations, wishes, etc., such as "Thou shalt love the Lord thy God," "Let us love one another," and so on.

2. Sentences expressing moral views, such as "Brethren, these things ought not so to be," "It is not good for man to be alone," etc.

3. Sentences expressing factual truths, often historical, such as "Christ was born in Bethlehem," "Mary was a virgin," etc.

4. Sentences giving information about the meanings of words, expressing analytic truths. A statement like "A sacrament is an outward and visible sign of an inward and spiritual grace" is analytic, and should be taken as informing the hearer about the meaning of "sacrament."

5. Sentences which appear to be informative, but informative about the supernatural or metaphysical rather than the natural or physical world. For instance, "God exists," "Christ is the Son of God," and so on.

So far the philosopher has not yet got to work. But when he does, it is likely that he will be tempted to make two changes in our scheme above. The first does not concern us here: it involves merging what I have called "moral views" with "commands, injunctions, etc.," at least to some extent. The second is to attempt to distribute sentences in (5), metaphysical sentences, among the other classes, in such a way that the possibility of supernaturally informative sentences is excluded. He could say, for instance, that

* From John Wilson, *Language and Christian Belief*, pp. 1-15. Copyright, 1958, St. Martin's Press. Used by permission of Macmillan & Co., Ltd. and St. Martin's Press, Inc.

some of these sentences are really analytic, and others really commands: this is one of the commonest ways in which this particular move is made.

Let us look, for example, at one of the ablest attempts to make this kind of move which have recently appeared. It has been made by Professor Braithwaite. He regards religious belief as primarily the intention or resolution to adopt a certain way of life, this intention being supported by what he calls "stories": that is, what appear to be empirical statements of fact, statements about the world, which are however not verifiable in the way that ordinary empirical statements are verifiable. (Presumably the only sense in which they could be said to be verifiable at all is the sense in which we say that a statement in a story or work of fiction is verifiable, i.e. within the context of the work as a whole.) These statements are believed because the religious believer finds them psychologically helpful, inasmuch as they bolster up his intention to adopt the way of life which he has chosen. But they are not central to religious belief; and we should verify whether a man is to be regarded as adhering to or following a certain religion, not by seeing how many "stories" or how much of any "story" he accepts as true, but by seeing how far he genuinely tries to carry out his intention to adopt a religious way of life. This intention, according to Braithwaite, has a great deal in common with what is expressed in ethical statements. Religion, in fact, is an ethical outlook bolstered up with "stories."

I have chosen to mention this particular attempt to deal with religious statements because it is typical as well as skilful. Its typicality consists in trying to show that metaphysical statements, statements about the supernatural are other than they appear: in particular, that they cannot be regarded as genuinely informative. This in itself is not a misconceived attempt: plenty of statements are not what they appear. But it is necessary to be very careful in assigning statements to classes in this way; and I do not think that writers of this kind have always kept a firm grasp of certain necessary points in connection with the use of language.

The most important of these is the point that it is primarily people who mean, and not statements. Language does not exist in the abstract, but is used by people with certain intentions, who desire to communicate. The appropriate question, therefore, is really not "What does such-and-such a statement mean?" but "What does so-and-so mean by this statement?" The same point applies to verification: we should ask not "How is this statement verified?" but "How do people who make this statement verify it?" This point may seem trivial. But to appreciate it entails appreciating that we may get different answers to our questions. It is easy to assume that statements have single meanings and single methods of verification; and though this may be generally true of other informative statements, it may not be true of metaphysical statements. Indeed, the answers which are given to a question about the meaning of a religious belief show a remarkable variety of opinion, even amongst those who share a common religion.

It would be erroneous to suppose, therefore, that because there is no standard meaning or verification for religious statements they are meaningless and unverifiable. Nearly all philosophers today admit that they are meaningful; indeed, it was never possible to hold that they were meaningless without adopting a monopolistic and unfairly restricted sense of "meaning." But it is an equal mistake to suppose that because all religious believers are not agreed upon what is to count as evidence for the truth of their statements, therefore nothing counts or could ever count. It may not be at all clear how these statements are to be verified or falsified, but this does not entail that they are not verifiable or falsifiable in principle. Neither does it entail that they are not informative.

In other words, the religious believer may meet the cross-questioning of the philosopher with a straight *nolle prosequi*. He may say simply, "This statement is intended by me as informative." The philosopher cannot sensibly reply, "No, it's not." He may point to a lack of agreed meaning and verification, show that most if not all other informative statements have agreed meaning and verification, and so on, but he cannot deny the speaker's intention: and he cannot show that the intention cannot in principle be fulfilled. For it may be possible to provide meaning and verification for the statement, or to agree on them. What the philosopher can try to do, however, is to show that whatever the intentions of the speaker, the statement is not actually informative. He will try to do this by showing that being informative, in the case of all statements, depends on the existence of agreed verification.

The religious believer is here faced with two alternatives. He can either say that his statements are not, after all, informative, thereby evading the attack altogether: or say that established meaning and verification is not in fact necessary for informative statements, thereby standing up to it. This is the crux of the matter, the rock which all metaphysics and religious belief must either escape or be wrecked on. And it seems to me tragic that religious believers do not realise that neither of the two alternatives I have mentioned are at all satisfactory.

First, the attempt to evade the attack. The attempt must fail, because it is these allegedly informative assertions which give to any religion its importance and distinctive character. Statements which lay down language-rules ("A sacrament is an outward and visible sign of an inward and spiritual grace"), historical statements ("The man Jesus Christ was crucified in Palestine during the reign of Tiberius"), exhortations ("Brethren, let us love one another"), and moral injunctions ("Judge not"), all have obvious uses; but they would, none of them, have any peculiarly religious interest unless backed by a number of assertions about the supernatural. Thus, we are only interested in defining "sacrament" clearly because it is held that the Son of God instituted certain sacraments: historical statements about Jesus concern us only because we believe certain metaphysical statements about Him: and exhortations and injunctions have religious force only because they derive from supernatural fact—hence we see arguments like: "Let us love one another, for love is of God." Most Christians, except under philosophical cross-examination, would surely regard the "good news" of the Gospel as factually informative. To say "There is a God" is to state a fact: God is real in the same *sense*, though not in the same way, as physical objects are real: [1] and the information which religious beliefs contain is not only supposed to be genuine, but of the utmost importance in the conduct of our lives.

The second alternative, that of claiming that statements can be informative without being verifiable in the sense required by philosophers, is more difficult to prove unsatisfactory. To begin with, many believers would hold that there was evidence for their beliefs. For some Christians, for instance, the supposed majesty and order of the natural universe is a proof of God's existence: to others, the life and personality of Christ is verification for His divinity: and so on. They might also admit that certain things counted against their beliefs: that the existence of pain and evil, for instance, counted against their belief in a loving and omnipotent God. Why is it, then, that philosophers still wish to insist that religious statements may not be verifiable? What precisely is this test of verification which they claim that all informative statements must pass?

The philosopher's point may be better made (as one or two philosophers have themselves suggested) in terms of falsification rather than verification; and the principle may be stated thus: "If a statement is not decisively falsifiable, in principle as well as in practice, then the statement is not informative." Of course this statement is itself somewhat vague: we may wonder what the phrase "in principle" means, for instance. But the reasons for making it are tolerably clear. If you are trying to tell somebody that something is the case, this logically excludes certain other things being the case. For example, suppose I say, "There is a tiger in the room." Asked what evidence there was for this statement, or how it could be verified, I should mention pieces of evidence like there being a growling noise, a large striped

----

[1] This point is of central importance to my thesis: I have tried to expand and elucidate it on pp. 13-14.

animal with teeth and four legs, and so on. To say "there is a tiger" entails there being a large striped animal, etc., because they are part of the meaning of the statement. The statement is vacuous without them. "There is a tiger" is only informative if there is actually a large striped animal. Consequently, it must be decisively falsifiable: falsifiable, that is, if the pieces of evidence could not be found. Of course, the absence of only some of the evidence would not falsify it decisively: the growl might be absent, for instance, and there might still be a tiger. But there comes a time when the absence of evidence is overwhelming. An animal with three legs and no growl might still be a tiger; but an animal with no legs at all and a trunk could not be.

Moreover, statements are informative to the same degree as they are falsifiable or vulnerable. For the more precise information they give, the easier it is to upset them. "There is something in the room" is very uninformative and not very vulnerable: "there is an animal in the room" slightly more informative, but *ipso facto* more vulnerable: because more criteria have to be satisfied for "animal" than for "something"—the statement has to pass more verification-tests. "There is a six-foot tiger exactly in the middle of the room, possessing only four teeth and pointing its tail consistently at an angle of seventy-eight degrees" is very precise, and very vulnerable. To put this more generally, any informative statement specifies that a part of reality is such-and-such; and the more precise the specification—the more the specification specifies, so to speak—then the more things there might be wrong with it.

If, then, a statement's truth is consistent with any evidence that might be forthcoming, it cannot be at all informative. Making a statement of this kind would be like saying: "There is a tiger in the room, and nothing could count as evidence which decisively falsifies this truth." Of course if there actually is a tiger, then the statement cannot actually be decisively falsified: for it is true. But it is still decisively falsifiable as a statement: for there is no logical compulsion about its being true. To say "nothing could count as evidence against the existence of God" might mean "since God exists, there can be no decisive evidence against it": but it might also mean that the statement "God exists" is logically exempt from decisive evidence against it. And if this is true, then it cannot be informative. For saying "God exists" is a particular instance of saying "Such-and-such is the case"; and it is always logically possible that such-and-such is not the case. Whether it is or not precisely constitutes the test which any informative statement must pass.

Since therefore neither of these two alternatives is satisfactory, religious believers have to face up to the problem of providing their religious statements with established meaning and verification. In view of the points mentioned, they should be anxious rather than unwilling to make it clear what would decisively falsify the statements, since their informativeness corresponds to their falsifiability. Just how this process of giving verification to religious statements is to be gone through, I shall endeavour to explain in the next essay. So far as we are here concerned, the point I wish to establish is that our fifth class of statements—those apparently informative about the super-natural world—must be claimed as genuinely informative, with all that this implies. If they are to be merged with any other class, it must be with the third: those expressing factual truths, or what are generally known as empirical statements.

Providing statements with verification, however, is not an arbitrary process; and there is one further point which must be allowed to the philosopher. Informative statements inform us about something in our experience, and must therefore be verifiable ultimately by our experience. I do not mean, of course, that they are about something which we are actually touching, seeing, feeling, etc., or which we have touched, seen, felt, etc. "There is a tiger in the room" is informative even though we may never have seen a tiger. But they must be about something of which we could in principle have experience: for if they were not, they would not inform us about anything at all which had any connection with our lives and interests. To say "There is a tiger in the room" would be senseless, and certainly not informative, if I added "but nobody could ever have any experience of such a thing." The whole interest of making such a statement is that, if we enter the room, we can expect to experience certain things—growls, stripes, being eaten, and so on. Statements which are of public interest and are informative, like this one, are based on the experiences of some people, and on the possibility that other people may also have similar experiences. This is the purpose of informative communication.

Past writers have attempted to discover many loopholes which might enable them to avoid this point also; and it is impossible to demonstrate that all of them are culs-de-sac. A typical loophole is to say that God "transcends" human experience, and that therefore we cannot expect to verify statements about God by human experience; though of course the first of these two statements need not be understood in such a way that the second follows from it. But the same dilemma presents itself. Either "God" stands for something at least partly within our experience, so that statements with the word "God" in them are to that extent experimentally verifiable: or else "God" does not stand for something within our actual or potential experience, in which case (to put it bluntly) statements about God can have no possible interest for us, and may well be meaningless. Of course this dilemma could be put more forcibly. We could say that if a descriptive word is supposed to refer to something which could not be experienced, then it seems doubtful whether it describes anything at all: since to be a thing involves the capability of being experienced, and can only be known through experience.

Nor need the Christian attempt to take evasive action over the issue of verification in any other way. Philosophers have been concerned to clarify the logical characteristics of informative assertions by various observations. They have said that they must be meaningful and verifiable: that we must know what would count as evidence for or against them: that their verification must ultimately be conducted by somebody's experience: that unless these conditions were satisfied they could not qualify for truth or falsehood, and so on. All this can be accepted; and there seems little use in trying to break out of the circle of these observations at any point, e.g. by saying that Christian assertions are "true" in the sense of "illuminating," or can be "verified" "by the Christian way of life itself." For though the points being made here may be valid and important, they are insufficient; because Christian assertions are also supposed, by Christians themselves, to be true and verifiable in the (possibly more usual) sense in which philosophers have used these words.

This attempt to put religious assertions in the same logical boat, as it were, with straightforward empirical statements looks naïve and old-fashioned, because it suggests a naïve and old-fashioned view of religious language. We are accustomed to regard religious language as inadequate for its purposes; in particular, it is said to be "metaphor" or "analogy." When challenged at every point, the metaphor becomes "eroded" or "evaporates," until nothing may be left. Hence the Christian and the philosopher seem both driven to the view that the metaphorical assertions cannot be informative, and must be in a different logical category from empirical statements, with a different sort of meaning and verification, if indeed they have any verification at all. But this is deceptive; because a metaphor may assert something quite as precise and informative as any other assertion. A word used metaphorically or analogically may lose something of its straightforward meaning; but it may gain some other significance. For example, "sugar is sweet" may be a straightforward empirical assertion, and "Mary is sweet" a metaphor; but it would be wrong to suppose that what we are saying about Mary is less definite or meaningful than what we are saying about sugar. The word "sweet" simply means different things, and has a different method of verification, in either case. This might well be true of religious assertions. They are expressed in language borrowed from non-religious contexts, just as "Mary is sweet" uses a word borrowed from taste-experience; but this language may well have a new and precise significance, though of course the fact that the same word is used suggests that there are points of contact between the two uses—points which might help to make the new use more comprehensible to someone who did not understand the metaphorical meaning.

One essential task which religious believers have to perform, therefore, is to give the individual words in religious language a clear and unambiguous descriptive meaning where such meaning is required. This applies both to what we might call technical religious words—words like "God," "soul," "grace," and so on—and also to words used metaphorically—"love," "father," "kingdom," etc. Hitherto many believers have clung desperately to these words, but have been more able to say what they do not mean than what they do. Yet if religious language is ever to be genuinely and importantly informative, it is important that the criteria for the use of these words should be clear. If this task is not achieved, we shall be reduced to saying, as the Vedantist says when asked to describe his deity, "Not this, not this."

To many people this might seem to imply that God is an object, much like a table or an elephant, Who can be immediately and wholly comprehended by experience: the only slight difference being that a different kind of experience is required. Yet this is plainly absurd; and a God of this kind is not the sort of God in which anybody believes. But we must be careful to understand the point. I have said earlier in this chapter that God is real in the same sense, though not in the same way, that physical objects are real. He must be real in the same sense: for the word "real" has, in fact, only one sense—either something is real and exists, or it is unreal and does not exist. "Real" and "exists" are definitely not ambiguous words. But He is not (putting it roughly) real in the same *way*, because He is not the same sort of thing as a table or an elephant: indeed, we might say that He is not a *thing* at all, and certainly that He is not an object. Briefly, then, my contention is that if God is real and exists, the unambiguous logic and language of statements about existence, and the verification needed for these statements, must apply to God as much as to anything else, for these are part and parcel of what we mean by words like "exist" and "real;" but this is not to deny that much of His nature may be mysterious and uncomprehended by men. In much the same way, we might hold that love, or Martians, or the fourth dimension exist and are real: we might be able to give these words and phrases clear and unambiguous descriptive meanings and verification-methods: but they might still be very different from other things, highly mysterious, and largely uncomprehended.

Instead of the Vedantist's "Not this, not this", Christians must be able to say, "At least this, and at least this." They must be able to assert definitely about God, whilst admitting that there is far more to be known about Him than we can perhaps ever hope to know. Moreover, as we come to learn more about God, there is nothing in logic to prevent our expanding the meaning of the word "God". In just such a way the word "desire" has, since Freudian psychology, become expanded to include the concept of unconscious desires. In the light of new experience, words change their meaning in order to incorporate and communicate the experience. A due observance of logic, therefore, does nothing to remove the mystery of God on which Christians rightly insist; but it does serve the useful purpose of reminding us that if we are to talk meaningfully about God at any particular time, we must know what the word "God" is agreed to mean at that time, and that we can ultimately know this only by reference to experience.

Another and equally important task for believers is to adopt a firm and unambiguous classification of the statements and sentences in their religion. Much that is spoken and written about religion is vitiated by the absence of such a classification; and it is particularly difficult for non-believers to achieve a firm grasp of the logical structure of religious doctrine. It is annoying, for instance, to argue at length about whether the soul is immortal, only to find after a time that the word "soul" is being used to mean "the immortal part of man". This of course makes the statement "The soul is immortal" analytic or tautologous, and therefore not empirically informative. In trying to assess the truth of a complex metaphysical system, such as the doctrines of the Roman church, it is essential to be clear about which statements are supposed to be informative and verifiable, and which are supposed to follow by deductive arguments from other statements. For example, if we were intended to accept a number of statements on the authority of Christ, the Bible, the Church or some other source, we should be particularly interested in verifying the statements which were relevant to showing that source to be reliable, and not waste time in examining the statements deduced from its reliability.

This task of establishing meaning and verification, and classifying statements in religious belief according to their logic, has hardly been started. Hitherto Christian apologists have been chiefly interested in trying to collect and assess evidence for their beliefs, not realising the importance of the (logically prior) question of what is to count as evidence. Until this question is settled, it is unlikely that many people will be convinced by this collected "evidence": for it may not be evidence to them at all. One cannot tell whether something is evidence for a statement or not unless one first knows what sort of statement it is supposed to be, and what sorts of things count as evidence for it. And it is this lack of clarity, if I may be permitted to conclude with a sociological sidelight, which has engendered a situation in which many intelligent people are now neither convinced of, nor hostile to, Christian belief, but merely uninterested in it.

JOHN WISDOM (1904-   ), professor of philosophy at Cambridge University, has written on an unusually large number of topics.
He has been a leading figure among British
analytical philosophers. His book, *Philosophy
and Psycho-Analysis*, is a major contribution
in their field of study.

"Gods"*

1. The existence of God is not an experimental issue in the way it was.
An atheist or agnostic might say to a theist "You still think there are spirits
in the trees, nymphs in the streams, a God of the world." He might say this
because he noticed the theist in time of drought pray for rain and make
a sacrifice and in the morning look for rain. But disagreement about whether
there are gods is now less of this experimental or betting sort than it used
to be. This is due in part, if not wholly, to our better knowledge of why
things happen as they do.

It is true that even in these days it is seldom that one who believes in
God has no hopes or fears which an atheist has not. Few believers now
expect prayer to still the waves, but some think it makes a difference to
people and not merely in ways the atheist would admit. Of course with people, as opposed to waves and machines, one never knows what they won't do
next, so that expecting prayer to make a difference to them is not so definite
a thing as believing in its mechanical efficacy. Still, just as primitive people
pray in a business-like way for rain so some people still pray for others with a
real feeling of doing something to help. However, in spite of this persistence
of an experimental element in some theistic belief, it remains true that
Elijah's method on Mount Carmel of settling the matter of what god or gods
exist would be far less appropriate to-day than it was then.

**2. Belief in gods is not merely a matter of expectation of a world to
come.** Someone may say "The fact that a theist no more than an atheist
expects prayer to bring down fire from heaven or cure the sick does not
mean that there is no difference between them as to the facts, it does not
mean that the theist has no expectations different from the atheist's. For

* From John Wisdom, *Philosophy and Psycho-Analysis*, pp. 149-159. Published, 1953,
by Basil Blackwell. Used by permission of the publishers.

very often those who believe in God believe in another world and believe that God is there and that we shall go to that world when we die."

This is true, but I do not want to consider here expectations as to what one will see and feel after death nor what sort of reasons these logically unique expectations could have. So I want to consider those theists who do not believe in a future life, or rather, I want to consider the differences between atheists and theists in so far as these differences are not a matter of belief in a future life.

3. What are these differences? And is it that theists are superstitious or that atheists are blind?   A child may wish to sit a while with his father and he may, when he has done what his father dislikes, fear punishment and feel distress at causing vexation, and while his father is alive he may feel sure of help when danger threatens and feel that there is sympathy for him when disaster has come. When his father is dead he will no longer expect punishment or help. Maybe for a moment an old fear will come or a cry for help escape him, but he will at once remember that this is no good now. He may feel that his father is no more until perhaps someone says to him that his father is still alive though he lives now in another world and one so far away that there is no hope of seeing him or hearing his voice again. The child may be told that nevertheless his father can see him and hear all he says. When he has been told this the child will still fear no punishment nor expect any sign of his father, but now, even more than he did when his father was alive, he will feel that his father sees him all the time and will dread distressing him and when he has done something wrong he will feel separated from his father until he has felt sorry for what he has done. Maybe when he himself comes to die he will be like a man who expects to find a friend in the strange country where he is going, but even when this is so, it is by no means all of what makes the difference between a child who believes that his father lives still in another world and one who does not.

Likewise one who believes in God may face death differently from one who does not, but there is another difference between them besides this. This other difference may still be described as belief in another world, only this belief is not a matter of expecting one thing rather than another here or hereafter, it is not a matter of a world to come but of a world that now is, though beyond our senses.

We are at once reminded of those other unseen worlds which some philosophers "believe in" and others "deny", while non-philosophers unconsciously "accept" them by using them as models with which to "get the hang of" the patterns in the flux of experience. We recall the timeless entities whose changeless connections we seek to represent in symbols, and the values which stand firm [1] amidst our flickering satisfaction and remorse, and the physical things which, though not beyond the corruption of moth and rust, are yet more permanent than the shadows they throw upon the screen before our minds. We recall, too, our talk of souls and of what lies in their depths and is manifested to us partially and intermittently in our own feelings and the behaviour of others. The hypothesis of mind, of other human minds and of animal minds, is reasonable because it explains for each of us why certain things behave so cunningly all by themselves unlike even the most ingenious machines. Is the hypothesis of minds in flowers and trees reasonable for like reasons? Is the hypothesis of a world mind reasonable for like reasons—someone who adjusts the blossom to the bees, someone whose presence may at times be felt—in a garden in high summer, in the hills when clouds are gathering, but not, perhaps, in a cholera epidemic?

4. The question "Is belief in gods reasonable?" has more than one source. It is clear now that in order to grasp fully the logic of belief in divine minds we need to examine the logic of belief in animal and human minds. But we cannot do that here and so for the purposes of this discussion about divine minds let us acknowledge the reasonableness of our belief in human minds without troubling ourselves about its logic. The question of the reasonableness of belief in divine minds then becomes a matter of whether there are facts in nature which support claims about divine minds in the way facts in nature support our claims about human minds.

In this way we resolve the force behind the problem of the existence of gods into two components, one metaphysical and the same which prompts the question "Is there *ever any* behaviour which gives reason to believe in *any* sort of mind?" and one which finds expression in "Are there other mind-patterns in nature beside the human and animal patterns which we can easily detect, and are these other mind-patterns super-human?"

Such over-determination of a question syndrome is common. Thus, the puzzling questions "Do dogs think?", "Do animals feel?" are partly metaphysical puzzles and partly scientific questions. They are not purely metaphysical; for the reports of scientists about the poor performances of cats in cages and old ladies' stories about the remarkable performances of their pets are not irrelevant. But nor are these questions purely scientific; for the stories never settle them and therefore they have other sources. One other source is the metaphysical source we have already noticed, namely, the difficulty about getting behind an animal's behaviour to its mind, whether it is a non-human animal or a human one.

[1] In another world, Dr. Joad says in the *New Statesman* recently.

But there's a third component in the force behind these questions, these disputes have a third source, and it is one which is important in the dispute which finds expression in the words "I believe in God", "I do not". This source comes out well if we consider the question "Do flowers feel?" Like the questions about dogs and animals this question about flowers comes partly from the difficulty we sometimes feel over inference from *any* behaviour to thought or feeling and partly from ignorance as to what behaviour is to be found. But these questions, as opposed to a like question about human beings, come also from hesitation as to whether the behaviour in question is *enough* mind-like, that is, is it enough similar to or superior to human behaviour to be called "mind-proving"? Likewise, even when we are satisfied that human behaviour shows mind and even when we have learned whatever mind-suggesting things there are in nature which are not explained by human and animal minds, we may still ask "But are these things sufficiently striking to be called a mind-pattern? Can we fairly call them manifestations of a divine being?"

"The question," someone may say, "has then become merely a matter of the application of a name. And 'What's in a name?' "

5. But the line between a question of fact and a question of decision as to the application of a name is not so simple as this way of putting things suggests. The question "What's in a name?" is engaging because we are inclined to answer both "Nothing" and "Very much". And this "Very much" has more than one source. We might have tried to comfort Heloise by saying "It isn't that Abelard no longer loves you, for this man isn't Abelard"; we might have said to poor Mr. Tebrick in Mr. Garnet's *Lady into Fox* "But this is no longer Silvia." But if Mr. Tebrick replied "Ah, but it is!" this might come not at all from observing facts about the fox which we have not observed, but from noticing facts about the fox which we had missed, although we had in a sense observed all that Mr. Tebrick had observed. It is possible to have before one's eyes all the items of a pattern and still to miss the pattern. Consider the following conversation:

"And I think Kay and I are pretty happy. We've always been happy."
Bill lifted up his glass and put it down without drinking.
"Would you mind saying that again," he asked.
"I don't see what's so queer about it. Taken all in all, Kay and I have really been happy."
"All right," Bill said gently, "Just tell me how you and Kay have been happy."
Bill had a way of being amused by things which I could not understand.
"It's a little hard to explain," I said. "It's like taking a lot of numbers that don't look alike and that don't mean anything until you add them all together."
I stopped, because I hadn't meant to talk to him about Kay and me.

PHILOSOPHY OF RELIGION

"Go ahead," Bill said. "What about the numbers." And he began to smile.

"I don't know why you think it's so funny," I said. "All the things that two people do together, two people like Kay and me, add up to something. There are the kids and the house and the dog and all the people we have known and all the times we've been out to dinner. Of course, Kay and I do quarrel sometimes but when you add it all together, all of it isn't as bad as the parts of it seem. I mean, maybe that's all there is to anybody's life."

Bill poured himself another drink. He seemed about to say something and checked himself. He kept looking at me.[2]

Or again, suppose two people are speaking of two characters in a story which both have read [3] or of two friends which both have known, and one says "Really she hated him," and the other says "She didn't, she loved him." Then the first may have noticed what the other has not although he knows no incident in the lives of the people they are talking about which the other doesn't know too, and the second speaker may say "She didn't, she loved him" because he hasn't noticed what the first noticed, although he can remember every incident the first can remember. But then again he may say "She didn't, she loved him" not because he hasn't noticed the patterns in time which the first has noticed but because though he has noticed them he doesn't feel he still needs to emphasize them with "Really she hated him." The line between using a name because of how we feel and because of what we have noticed isn't sharp. "A difference as to the facts," "a discovery," "a relevation," these phrases cover many things. Discoveries have been made not only by Christopher Columbus and Pasteur, but also by Tolstoy and Dostoievsky and Freud. Things are revealed to us not only by the scientists with the microscopes, but also by the poets, the prophets, and the painters. What is so isn't merely a matter of "the facts." For sometimes when there is agreement as to the facts there is still argument as to whether defendant did or did not "exercise reasonable care," was or was not "negligent."

And though we shall need to emphasize how much "There is a God" evinces an attitude to the familiar [4] we shall find in the end that it also evinces some recognition of patterns in time easily missed and that, therefore, difference as to there being any gods is in part a difference as to what is so and therefore as to the facts, though not in the simple ways which first occurred to us.

6. Let us now approach these same points by a different road.

6.1. How it is that an explanatory hypothesis, such as the existence of

[2] *H. M. Pulham, Esq.*, p. 320, by John P. Marquand.

[3] E.g. Havelock Ellis's autobiography.

[4] "Persuasive Definitions," *Mind*, July, 1938, by Charles Leslie Stevenson, should be read here. It is very good. [Also in his *Ethics and Language*, Yale, 1945.—Editors.]

God, may start by being experimental and gradually become something quite different can be seen from the following story:

Two people return to their long neglected garden and find among the weeds a few of the old plants surprisingly vigorous. One says to the other "It must be that a gardener has been coming and doing something about these plants." Upon inquiry they find that no neighbour has ever seen anyone at work in their garden. The first man says to the other "He must have worked while people slept". The other says "No, someone would have heard him and besides, anybody who cared about the plants would have kept down these weeds." The first man says "Look at the way these are arranged. There is purpose and a feeling for beauty here. I believe that someone comes, someone invisible to mortal eyes. I believe that the more carefully we look the more we shall find confirmation of this." They examine the garden ever so carefully and sometimes they come on new things suggesting that a gardener comes and sometimes they come on new things suggesting the contrary and even that a malicious person has been at work. Besides examining the garden carefully they also study what happens to gardens left without attention. Each learns all the other learns about this and about the garden. Consequently, when after all this, one says, "I still believe a gardener comes" while the other says "I don't" their different words now reflect no difference as to what they have found in the garden, no difference as to what they would find in the garden if they looked further and no difference about how fast untended gardens fall into disorder. At this stage, in this context, the gardener hypothesis has ceased to be experimental, the difference between one who accepts and one who rejects it is now not a matter of the one expecting something the other does not expect. What is the difference between them? The one says "A gardener comes unseen and unheard. He is manifested only in his works with which we are all familiar", the other says "There is no gardener" and with this difference in what they say about the gardener goes a difference in how they feel towards the garden, in spite of the fact that neither expects anything of it which the other does not expect.[5]

But is this the whole difference between them—that the one calls the garden by one name and feels one way towards it, while the other calls it by another name and feels in another way towards it? And if this is what the difference has become then is it any longer appropriate to ask "Which is right?" or "Which is reasonable?"

And yet surely such questions *are* appropriate when one person says to

[5] [For an extended discussion of the implications of this story see "The *University* Discussion" in *New Essays In Philosophical Theology*, eds. Antony Flew and Alaisdair MacIntyre (New York: The Macmillan Company, 1955), pp. 96f., Eds.]

another "You still think the world's a garden and not a wilderness, and that
the gardener has not forsaken it" or "You still think there are nymphs of
the streams, a presence in the hills, a spirit of the world." Perhaps when
a man sings "God's in His heaven" we need not take this as more than
an expression of how he feels. But when Bishop Gore or Dr. Joad write
about belief in God and young men read them in order to settle their religious doubts the impression is not simply that of persons choosing exclama-
tions with which to face nature and the "changes and chances of this mortal
life". The disputants speak as if they are concerned with a matter of scientific fact, or of trans-sensual, trans-scientific and metaphysical fact, but
still of fact and still a matter about which reasons for and against may be
offered, although no scientific reasons in the sense of field surveys for fossils
or experiments on delinquents are to the point.

6.2. *Now can an interjection have a logic?* Can the manifestation of an
attitude in the utterance of a word, in the application of a name, have a
logic? When all the facts are known how can there still be a question of
fact? How can there still be a question? Surely as Hume says ". . . after
every circumstance, every relation is known, the understanding has no further
room to operate"? [6]

6.3. When the madness of these questions leaves us for a moment *we can
all easily recollect disputes which though they cannot be settled by experiment are yet disputes in which one party may be right and the other wrong
and in which both parties may offer reasons and the one better reasons than
the other. This may happen in pure and applied mathematics and logic.*
Two accountants or two engineers provided with the same data may reach
different results and this difference is resolved not by collecting further
data but by going over the calculations again. Such differences indeed share
with differences as to what will win a race, the honour of being among the
most "settlable" disputes in the language.

6.4. *But it won't do to describe the theistic issue as one settlable by such
calculation,* or as one about what can be deduced in this *vertical* fashion
from the facts we know. No doubt dispute about God has sometimes, perhaps especially in mediaeval times, been carried on in this fashion. But
nowadays it is not and we must look for some other analogy, some other
case in which a dispute is settled but not by experiment.

6.5. *In courts of law* it sometimes happens that opposing counsel are
agreed as to the facts and are not trying to settle a question of further
fact, are not trying to settle whether the man who admittedly had quarrelled

---

[6] Hume, *An Enquiry concerning the Principles of Morals.* Appendix I.

with the deceased did or did not murder him, but are concerned with whether Mr. A who admittedly handed his long-trusted clerk signed blank cheques did or did not exercise reasonable care, whether a ledger is or is not a document,[7] whether a certain body was or was not a public authority.

In such cases we notice that the process of argument is not a *chain* of demonstrative reasoning. It is a presenting and representing of those features of the case which *severally co-operate* in favour of the conclusion, in favour of saying what the reasoner wishes said, in favour of calling the situation by the name by which he wishes to call it. The reasons are like the legs of a chair, not the links of a chain. Consequently although the discussion is *a priori* and the steps are not a matter of experience, the procedure resembles scientific argument in that the reasoning is not *vertically* extensive but *horizontally* extensive—it is a matter of the cumulative effect of several independent premises, not of the repeated transformation of one or two. And because the premises are severally inconclusive the process of deciding the issue becomes a matter of weighing the cumulative effect of one group of severally inconclusive items against the cumulative effect of another group of severally inconclusive items, and thus lends itself to description in terms of conflicting "probabilities". This encourages the feeling that the issue is one of fact— that it is a matter of guessing from the premises at a further fact, at what is to come. But this is a muddle. *The dispute does not cease to be* a priori *because it is a matter of the cumulative effect of severally inconclusive premises.* The logic of the dispute is not that of a chain of deductive reasoning as in a mathematic calculation. But nor is it a matter of collecting from several inconclusive items of information an expectation as to something further, as when a doctor from a patient's symptoms guesses at what is wrong, or a detective from many clues guesses the criminal. It has its own sort of logic and its own sort of end—the solution of the question at issue is a decision, a ruling by the judge. But it is not an arbitrary decision though the rational connections are neither quite like those in vertical deductions nor like those in inductions in which from many signs we guess at what is to come; and though the decision manifests itself in the application of a name it is no more merely the application of a name than is the pinning on of a medal merely the pinning on of a bit of metal. Whether a lion with stripes is a tiger or a lion is, if you like, merely a matter of the application of a name.

[7] *The Times*, March 2nd, 1945. Also in *The Times* of June 13th, 1945, contrast the case of Hannah V. Peel with that of the cruiser cut in two by a liner. In the latter case there is not agreement as to the facts. See also the excellent articles by Dr. Glanville L. Williams in the *Law Quarterly Review*, "Language and the Law," January, and April 1945, and "The Doctrine of Repugnancy," October, 1943, January, 1944, and April, 1944. The author, having set out how arbitrary are many legal decisions, needs now to set out how far from arbitrary they are—if his readers are ready for the next phase in the dialectic process.

Whether Mr. So-and-So of whose conduct we have so complete a record
did or did not exercise reasonable care is not merely a matter of the application of a name or, if we choose to say it is, then we must remember that
with this name a game is lost and won and a game with very heavy stakes.
With the judges' choice of a name for the facts goes an attitude, and the
declaration, the ruling, is an exclamation evincing that attitude. But *it is an
exclamation which not only has a purpose but also has a logic*, a logic
surprisingly like that of "futile", "deplorable", "graceful", "grand", "divine".

6.6. *Suppose two people are looking at a picture or natural scene.* One
says "Excellent" or "Beautiful" or "Divine"; the other says "I don't see it".
He means he doesn't see the beauty. And this reminds us of how we felt
the theist accuse the atheist of blindness and the atheist accuse the theist
of seeing what isn't there. And yet surely each sees what the other sees. It
isn't that one can see part of the picture which the other can't see. So
the difference is in a sense not one as to the facts. And so it cannot be
removed by the one disputant discovering to the other what so far he hasn't
seen. It isn't that the one sees the picture in a different light and so, as
we might say, sees a different picture. Consequently the difference between
them cannot be resolved by putting the picture in a different light. And
yet surely this is just what can be done in such a case—not by moving
the picture but by talk perhaps. To settle a dispute as to whether a piece
of music is good or better than another we listen again, with a picture we
look again. Someone perhaps points to emphasize certain features and we
see it in a different light. Shall we call this "field work" and "the last of
observation" or shall we call it "reviewing the premises" and "the beginning
of deduction (horizontal)"?

If in spite of all this we choose to say that a difference as to whether
a thing is beautiful is not a factual difference we must be careful to remember that there is a procedure for settling these differences and that this
consists not only in reasoning and redescription as in the legal case, but
also in a more literal resetting-before with re-looking or re-listening.

6.7. *And if we say as we did at the beginning that when a difference
as to the existence of a God is not one as to future happenings then it is
not experimental and therefore not as to the facts, we must not forthwith
assume that there is no right and wrong about it,* no rationality of irrationality, no appropriateness or inappropriateness, no procedure which tends to
settle it, *nor even that this procedure is in no sense a discovery of new facts.*
After all even in science this is not so. Our two gardeners even when they
had reached the stage when neither expected any experimental result which
the other did not, might yet have continued the dispute, each presenting
and representing the features of the garden favouring his hypothesis, that is,

fitting his model for describing the accepted fact; each emphasizing the pattern he wishes to emphasize. True, in science, there is seldom or never a pure instance of this sort of dispute, for nearly always with difference of hypothesis goes some difference of expectation as to the facts. But scientists argue about rival hypotheses with a vigour which is not exactly proportioned to difference in expectations of experimental results.

The difference as to whether a God exists involves our feelings more than most scientific disputes and in this respect is more like a difference as to whether there is beauty in a thing.

R. B. BRAITHWAITE

R. B. BRAITHWAITE (1900-   ), Knight-bridge Professor of Moral Philosophy at Cambridge, is mainly interested in philosophy of science, but he is also concerned with interpreting religious belief in such a way as to make it empirically tenable.

An Empiricist's View of the Nature of Religious Belief *

The meaning of any statement, then, will be taken as being given by the way it is used. The kernel for an empiricist of the problem of the nature of religious belief is to explain, in empirical terms, how a religious statement is used by a man who asserts it in order to express his religious conviction.

Since I shall argue that the primary element in this use is that the religious assertion is used as a moral assertion, I must first consider how moral assertions are used. According to the view developed by various moral philosophers since the impossibility of regarding moral statement as verifiable propositions was recognized, a moral assertion is used to express an *attitude* of the man making the assertion. It is not used to assert the proposition that he has the attitude—a verifiable psychological proposition; it is used to show forth or evince his attitude. The attitude is concerned with the action which he asserts to be right or to be his duty, or the state of affairs which he asserts

* From R. B. Braithwaite, *An Empiricist's View of the Nature of Religious Belief*, pp. 11-26. Published, 1955, by Cambridge University Press. Used by permission of Cambridge University Press.

to be good; it is a highly complex state, and contains elements to which various degrees of importance have been attached by moral philosophers who have tried to work out an "ethics without propositions." One element in the attitude is a feeling of approval towards the action; this element was taken as the fundamental one in the first attempts, and views of ethics without propositions are frequently lumped together as "emotive" theories of ethics. But discussion of the subject during the last twenty years has made it clear, I think, that no emotion or feeling of approval is fundamental to the use of moral assertions; it may be the case that the moral asserter has some specific feeling directed on to the course of action said to be right, but this is not the most important element in his "pro-attitude" towards the course of action: what is primary is his intention to perform the action when the occasion for it arises.

The form of ethics without propositions which I shall adopt is therefore a conative rather than an emotive theory: it makes the primary use of a moral assertion that of expressing the intention of the asserter to act in a particular sort of way specified in the assertion. A utilitarian, for example, in asserting that he ought to act so as to maximize happiness, is thereby declaring his intention to act, to the best of his ability, in accordance with the policy of utilitarianism: he is not asserting any proposition, or necessarily evincing any feeling of approval; he is subscribing to a policy of action. There will doubtless be empirical propositions which he may give as reasons for his adherence to the policy (e.g. that happiness is what all, or what most people, desire), and his having the intention will include his understanding what is meant by pursuing the policy, another empirically verifiable proposition. But there will be no specifically moral proposition which he will be asserting when he declares his intention to pursue the policy. This account is fully in accord with the spirit of empiricism, for whether or not a man has the intention of pursuing a particular behaviour policy can be empirically tested, both by observing what he does and by hearing what he replies when he is questioned about his intentions.

Not all expressions of intentions will be moral assertions: for the notion of morality to be applicable it is necessary either that the policy of action intended by the asserter should be a general policy (e.g. the policy of utilitarianism) or that it should be subsumable under a general policy which the asserter intends to follow and which he would give as the reason for his more specific intention. There are difficulties and vaguenesses in the notion of a general policy of action, but these need not concern us here. All that we require is that, when a man asserts that he ought to do so-and-so, he is using the assertion to declare that he resolves, to the best of his ability, to do so-and-so. And he will not necessarily be insincere in his assertion if he suspects, at the time of making it, that he will not have the strength of character to carry out his resolution.

The advantage this account of moral assertions has over all others, emotive non-propositional ones as well as cognitive propositional ones, is that it alone enables a satisfactory answer to be given to the question: What is the reason for my doing what I think I ought to do? The answer it gives is that, since my thinking that I ought to do the action is my intention to do it if possible, the reason why I do the action is simply that I intend to do it, if possible. On every other ethical view there will be a mysterious gap to be filled somehow between the moral judgment and the intention to act in accordance with it: there is no such gap if the primary use of a moral assertion is to declare such an intention.

Let us now consider what light this way of regarding moral assertions throws upon assertions of religious conviction. The idealist philosopher McTaggart described religion as "an emotion resting on a conviction of a harmony between ourselves and the universe at large," [1] and many educated people at the present time would agree with him. If religion is essentially concerned with emotion, it is natural to explain the use of religious assertions on the lines of the original emotive theory of ethics and to regard them as primarily evincing religious feeling or emotions. The assertion, for example, that God is our Heavenly Father will be taken to express the asserter's feeling secure in the same way as he would feel secure in his father's presence. But explanations of religion in terms of feeling, and of religious assertions as expressions of such feelings, are usually propounded by people who stand outside any religious system; they rarely satisfy those who speak from inside. Few religious men would be prepared to admit that their religion was a matter merely of feeling: feelings—of joy, of consolation, of being at one with the universe—may enter into their religion, but to evince such feelings is certainly not the primary use of their religious assertions.

This objection, however, does not seem to me to apply to treating religious assertions in the conative way in which recent moral philosophers have treated moral statements—as being primarily declarations of adherence to a policy of action, declarations of commitment to a way of life. That the way of life led by the believer is highly relevant to the sincerity of his religious conviction has been insisted upon by all the moral religions, above all, perhaps, by Christianity. "By their fruits ye shall know them." The view which I put forward for your consideration is that the intention of a Christian to follow a Christian way of life is not only the criterion for the sincerity of his belief in the assertions of Christianity; it is the criterion for the meaning-

---

[1] J. M. E. McTaggart, *Some Dogmas of Religion* (1906), p. 3.

fulness of his assertions. Just as the meaning of a moral assertion is given by its use in expressing the asserter's intention to act, so far as in him lies, in accordance with the moral principle involved, so the meaning of a religious assertion is given by its use in expressing the asserter's intention to follow a specified policy of behaviour. To say that it is belief in the dogmas of religion which is the cause of the believer's intending to behave as he does is to put the cart before the horse: it is the intention to behave which constitutes what is known as religious conviction.

But this assimilation of religious to moral assertions lays itself open to an immediate objection. When a moral assertion is taken as declaring the intention of following a policy, the form of the assertion itself makes it clear what the policy is with which the assertion is concerned. For a man to assert that a certain policy ought to be pursued, which on this view is for him to declare his intention of pursuing the policy, presupposes his understanding what it would be like for him to pursue the policy in question. I cannot resolve not to tell a lie without knowing what a lie is. But if a religious assertion is the declaration of an intention to carry out a certain policy, what policy does it specify? The religious statement itself will not explicitly refer to a policy, as does a moral statement; how then can the asserter of the statement know what is the policy concerned, and how can he intend to carry out a policy if he does not know what the policy is? I cannot intend to do something I know not what.

The reply to this criticism is that, if a religious assertion is regarded as representative of a large number of assertions of the same religious system, the body of assertions of which the particular one is a representative specimen is taken by the asserter as implicitly specifying a particular way of life. It is no more necessary for an empiricist philosopher to explain the use of a religious statement taken in isolation from other religious statements than it is for him to give a meaning to a scientific hypothesis in isolation from other scientific hypotheses. We understand scientific hypotheses, and the terms that occur in them, by virtue of the relation of the whole system of hypotheses to empirically observable facts; and it is the whole system of hypotheses, not one hypothesis in isolation, that is tested for its true-value against experience. So there are good precedents, in the empiricist way of thinking, for considering a system of religious assertions as a whole, and for examining the way in which the whole system is used.

If we do this the fact that a system of religious assertions has a moral function can hardly be denied. For to deny it would require any passage from the assertion of a religious system to a policy of action to be mediated by a moral assertion. I cannot pass from asserting a fact, of whatever sort, to intending to perform an action, without having the hypothetical intention to intend to do the action if I assert the fact. This holds however widely fact is understood—whether as an empirical fact or as a non-empirical fact about goodness or reality. Just as the intention-to-act view of moral assertions is the only view that requires no reason for my doing what I assert to be my duty, so the similar view of religious assertions is the only one which connects them to ways of life without requiring an additional premiss. Unless a Christian's assertion that God is love (*agape*)—which I take to epitomize the assertions of the Christian religion—be taken to declare his intention to follow an agapeistic way of life, he could be asked what is the connexion between the assertion and the intention, between Christian belief and Christian practice. And this question can always be asked if religious assertions are separated from conduct. Unless religious principles are moral principles, it makes no sense to speak of putting them into practice.

The way to find out what are the intentions embodied in a set of religious assertions, and hence what is the meaning of the assertions, is by discovering what principles of conduct the asserter takes the assertions to involve. These may be ascertained both by asking him questions and by seeing how he behaves, each test being supplemental to the other. If what is wanted is not the meaning of the religious assertions made by a particular man but what the set of assertions would mean were they to be made by anyone of the same religion (which I will call their *typical* meaning), all that can be done is to specify the form of behaviour which is in accordance with what one takes to be the fundamental moral principles of the religion in question. Since different people will take different views as to what these fundamental moral principles are, the typical meaning of religious assertions will be different for different people. I myself take the typical meaning of the body of Christian assertions as being given by their proclaiming intentions to follow an agapeistic way of life, and for a description of this way of life—a description in general and metaphorical terms, but an empirical description nevertheless—I should quote most of the Thirteenth Chapter of I Corinthians. Others may think that the Christian way of life should be described somewhat differently, and will therefore take the typical meaning of the assertions of Christianity to correspond to their different view of its fundamental moral teaching.

My contention then is that the primary use of religious assertions is to announce allegiance to a set of moral principles: without such allegiance there is no "true religion." This is borne out by all the accounts of what happens when an unbeliever becomes converted to a religion. The conversion is not only a change in the propositions believed—indeed there may be no specifically intellectual change at all; it is a change in the state of will. An excellent instance is C. S. Lewis's recently published account of his conversion from an idealist metaphysic—"a religion [as he says] that cost nothing"—to a theism where he faced (and he quotes George MacDonald's phrase) "something to be neither more nor less nor other than *done*." There was no intellectual change, for (as he says) "there had long been an ethic (theoretically) attached to my Idealism": it was the recognition that he had to do something about it, that "an attempt at complete virtue must be made." [2] His conversion was a re-orientation of the will.

In assimilating religious assertions to moral assertions I do not wish to deny that there are any important differences. One is the fact already noticed that usually the behaviour policy intended is not specified by one religious assertion in isolation. Another difference is that the fundamental moral teaching of the religion is frequently given, not in abstract terms, but by means of concrete examples—of how to behave, for instance, if one meets a man set upon by thieves on the road to Jericho. A resolution to behave like the good Samaritan does not, in itself, specify the behaviour to be resolved upon in quite different circumstances. However, absence of explicitly recognized general principles does not prevent a man from acting in accordance with such principles; it only makes it more difficult for a questioner to discover upon what principles he is acting. And the difficulty is not only one way round. If moral principles are stated in the most general form, as most moral philosophers have wished to state them, they tend to become so far removed from particular courses of conduct that it is difficult, if not impossible, to give them any precise content. It may be hard to find out what exactly is involved in the imitation of Christ; but it is not very easy to discover what exactly is meant by the pursuit of Aristotle's *eudaemonia* or of Mill's *happiness*. The tests for what it is to live agapeistically are as empirical as are those for living in quest of happiness; but in each case the tests can best be expounded in terms of examples of particular situations.

A more important difference between religious and purely moral principles is that, in the higher religions at least, the conduct preached by the religion concerns not only external but also internal behaviour. The conversion involved in accepting a religion is a conversion, not only of the will, but of the heart. Christianity requires not only that you should behave towards your neighbour as if you loved him as yourself: it requires that you should love him as yourself. And though I have no doubt that the Christian concept of *agape* refers partly to external behaviour—the agapeistic behaviour for which there are external criteria—yet being filled with *agape* includes more than behaving agapeistically externally: it also includes an agapeistic frame of mind. I have said that I cannot regard the expression of a feeling of any

[2] C. S. Lewis, *Surprised by Joy* (1955), pp. 198, 212-13.

sort as the primary element in religious assertion; but this does not imply that intention to feel in a certain way is not a primary element, nor that it cannot be used to discriminate religious declarations of policy from declarations which are merely moral. Those who say that Confucianism is a code of morals and not, properly speaking, a religion are, I think, making this discrimination.

The resolution proclaimed by a religious assertion may then be taken as referring to inner life as well as to outward conduct. And the superiority of religious conviction over the mere adoption of a moral code in securing conformity to the code arises from a religious conviction changing what the religious man wants. It may be hard enough to love your enemy, but once you have succeeded in doing so it is easy to behave lovingly towards him. But if you continue to hate him, it requires a heroic perseverance continually to behave as if you loved him. Resolutions to feel, even if they are only partly fulfilled, are powerful reinforcements of resolutions to act.

But though these qualifications may be adequate for distinguishing religious assertions from purely moral ones, they are not sufficient to discriminate between assertions belonging to one religious system and those belonging to another system in the case in which the behaviour policies, both of inner life and of outward conduct, inculcated by the two systems are identical. For instance, I have said that I take the fundamental moral teaching of Christianity to be the preaching of an agapeistic way of life. But a Jew or a Buddhist may, with considerable plausibility, maintain that the fundamental moral teaching of his religion is to recommend exactly the same way of life. How then can religious assertions be distinguished into those which are Christian, those which are Jewish, those which are Buddhist, by the policies of life which they respectively recommend if, on examination, these policies turn out to be the same?

Many Christians will, no doubt, behave in a specifically Christian manner in that they will follow ritual practices which are Christian and neither Jewish nor Buddhist. But though following certain practices may well be the proper test for membership of a particular religious society, a church, not even the most ecclesiastically-minded Christian will regard participation in a ritual as the fundamental characteristic of a Christian way of life. There must be some more important difference between an agapeistically policied Christian and an agapeistically policied Jew than that the former attends a church and the latter a synagogue.

The really important difference, I think, is to be found in the fact that the intentions to pursue the behaviour policies, which may be the same for different religions, are associated with thinking of different *stories* (or sets of stories). By a story I shall here mean a proposition or set of propositions which are straight-forwardly empirical propositions capable of empirical test and which are thought of by the religious man in connexion with his resolution to follow the way of life advocated by his religion. On the assumption that the ways of life advocated by Christianity and by Buddhism are essentially the same, it will be the fact that the intention to follow this way of life is associated in the mind of a Christian with thinking of one set of stories (the Christian stories) while it is associated in the mind of a Buddhist with thinking of another set of stories (the Buddhist stories) which enables a Christian assertion to be distinguished from a Buddhist one.

A religious assertion will, therefore, have a propositional element which is lacking in a purely moral assertion, in that it will refer to a story as well as to an intention. The reference to the story is not an assertion of the story taken as a matter of empirical fact: it is a telling of the story, or an alluding to the story, in the way in which one can tell, or allude to, the story of a novel with which one is acquainted. To assert the whole set of assertions of the Christian religion is both to tell the Christian doctrinal story and to confess allegiance to the Christian way of life.

The story, I have said, is a set of empirical propositions, and the language expressing the story is given a meaning by the standard method of understanding how the story-statements can be verified. The empirical story-statements will vary from Christian to Christian; the doctrines of Christianity are capable of different empirical interpretations, and Christians will differ in the interpretations they put upon the doctrines. But the interpretations will all be in terms of empirical propositions. Take, for example, the doctrine of Justification by means of the Atonement. Matthew Arnold imagined it in terms of

> . . . a sort of infinitely magnified and improved Lord Shaftesbury, with a race of vile offenders to deal with, whom his natural goodness would incline him to let off, only his sense of justice will not allow it; then a younger Lord Shaftesbury, on the scale of his father and very dear to him, who might live in grandeur and splendour if he liked, but who prefers to leave his home, to go and live among the race of offenders, and to be put to an ignominious death, on condition that his merits shall be counted against their demerits, and that his father's goodness shall be restrained no longer from taking effect, but any offender shall be admitted to the benefit of it on simply pleading the satisfaction made by the son; —and then, finally, a third Lord Shaftesbury, still on the same high scale, who keeps very much in the background, and works in a very occult manner, but very efficaciously nevertheless, and who is busy in applying everywhere the benefits of the son's satisfaction and the father's goodness.[3]

Arnold's "parable of the three Lord Shaftesburys" got him into a lot of trouble: he was "indignantly censured" (as he says) for wounding "the

[3] Matthew Arnold, *Literature and Dogma* (1873), pp. 306-7.

feelings of the religious community by turning into ridicule an august doctrine, the object of their solemn faith." [4] But there is no other account of the Anselmian doctrine of the Atonement that I have read which puts it in so morally favourable a light. Be that as it may, the only way in which the doctrine can be understood verificationally is in terms of human beings—mythological beings, it may be, who never existed, but who nevertheless would have been empirically observable had they existed.

For it is not necessary, on my view, for the asserter of a religious assertion to believe in the truth of the story involved in the assertions: what is necessary is that the story should be entertained in thought, i.e. that the statement of the story should be understood as having a meaning. I have secured this by requiring that the story should consist of empirical propositions. Educated Christians of the present day who attach importance to the doctrine of the Atonement certainly do not believe an empirically testable story in Matthew Arnold's or any other form. But it is the fact that entertainment in thought of this and other Christian stories forms the context in which Christian resolutions are made which serves to distinguish Christian assertions from those made by adherents of another religion, or of no religion.

[4] Matthew Arnold, *God and the Bible* (1875), pp. 18-19.

PAUL TILLICH

PAUL TILLICH (1886-   ), a German-American philosophical theologian, is now on the faculty of Harvard University. His system reflects a wide-ranging interest in the fields of classical Greek thought, German philosophy, art, history, psychoanalysis and existentialism. *Systematic Theology* is his major work.

Symbols of Faith*

1. The Meaning of Symbol

Man's ultimate concern must be expressed symbolically, because symbolic language alone is able to express the ultimate. This statement demands explanation in several respects. In spite of the manifold research about the meaning and function of symbols which is going on in contemporary philosophy, every writer who uses the term "symbol" must explain his understanding of it.

Symbols have one characteristic in common with signs; they point beyond themselves to something else. The red sign at the street corner points to the order to stop the movement of cars at certain intervals. A red light and the stopping of cars have essentially no relation to each other, but conventionally they are united as long as the convention lasts. The same is true of letters and numbers and partly even words. They point beyond themselves to sounds and meanings. They are given this special function by convention within a nation or by international conventions, as the mathematical signs. Sometimes such signs are called symbols; but this is unfortunate because it makes the distinction between signs and symbols more difficult. Decisive is the fact that signs do not participate in the reality of that to which they point, while symbols do. Therefore, signs can be replaced for reasons of expediency or convention, while symbols cannot.

This leads to the second characteristic of the symbol: It participates in that to which it points: the flag participates in the power and dignity of the nation for which it stands. Therefore, it cannot be replaced except after an historic catastrophe that changes the reality of the nation which it symbolizes. An attack on the flag is felt as an attack on the majesty of the group in which it is acknowledged. Such an attack is considered blasphemy.

The third characteristic of a symbol is that it opens up levels of reality which otherwise are closed for us. All arts create symbols for a level of reality which cannot be reached in any other way. A picture and a poem reveal elements of reality which cannot be approached scientifically. In the creative work of art we encounter reality in a dimension which is closed for us without such works. The symbol's fourth characteristic not only opens up dimensions and elements of reality which otherwise would remain unapproachable but also unlocks dimensions and elements of our soul which correspond to the dimensions and elements of reality. A great play gives us not only a new vision of the human scene, but it opens up hidden depths of our own being. Thus we are able to receive what the play reveals to us in reality. There are within us dimensions of which we cannot become aware except through symbols, as melodies and rhythms in music.

Symbols cannot be produced intentionally—this is the fifth characteristic. They grow out of the individual or collective unconscious and cannot function without being accepted by the unconscious dimension of our being. Symbols which have an especially social function, as political and religious symbols, are created or at least accepted by the collective unconscious of the group in which they appear.

The sixth and last characteristic of the symbol is a consequence of the fact that symbols cannot be invented. Like living beings, they grow and they die. They grow when the situation is ripe for them, and they die when the situation changes. The symbol of the "king" grew in a special period of history, and it died in most parts of the world in our period. Symbols do not grow because people are longing for them, and they do not die because of scientific or practical criticism. They die because they can no longer produce response in the group where they originally found expression.

These are the main characteristics of every symbol. Genuine symbols are created in several spheres of man's cultural creativity. We have mentioned already the political and the artistic realm. We could add history and, above all, religion, whose symbols will be our particular concern.

2. Religious Symbols

We have discussed the meaning of symbols generally because, as we said, man's ultimate concern must be expressed symbolically! One may ask: Why can it not be expressed directly and properly? If money, success or the nation is someone's ultimate concern, can this not be said in a direct way without symbolic language? Is it not only in those cases in which the content of the ultimate concern is called "God" that we are in the realm of symbols? The answer is that everything which is a matter of unconditional concern is made into a god. If the nation is someone's ultimate concern, the name of the nation becomes a sacred name and the nation receives divine qualities which far surpass the reality of the being and functioning of the nation. The nation then stands for and symbolizes the true ultimate, but in an idolatrous way. Success as ultimate concern is not the natural desire of actualizing potentialities, but is readiness to sacrifice all other values of life for the sake of a position of power and social predominance. The anxiety about not being a success is an idolatrous form of the anxiety about divine condemnation. Success is grace; lack of success, ultimate judgment. In this way concepts designating ordinary realities become idolatrous symbols of ultimate concern.

The reason for this transformation of concepts into symbols is the character of ultimacy and the nature of faith. That which is the true ultimate transcends the realm of finite reality infinitely. Therefore, no finite reality can express it directly and properly. Religiously speaking, God transcends his own name. This is why the use of his name easily becomes an abuse or a blasphemy. Whatever we say about that which concerns us ultimately, whether or not we call it God, has a symbolic meaning. It points beyond itself while participating in that to which it points. In no other way can faith express itself adequately. The language of faith is the language of symbols. If faith were what we have shown that it is not, such an assertion could not be made. But faith, understood as the state of being ultimately concerned, has no language other than symbols. When saying this I always expect the question: Only a symbol? He who asks this question shows that he has not understood the difference between signs and symbols nor the power of symbolic language, which surpasses in quality and strength the power of any nonsymbolic language. One should never say "only a symbol," but one should say "not less than a symbol." With this in mind we can now describe the different kinds of symbols of faith.

The fundamental symbol of our ultimate concern is God. It is always present in any act of faith, even if the act of faith includes the denial of God. Where there is ultimate concern, God can be denied only in the name of God. One God can deny the other one. Ultimate concern cannot deny its own character as ultimate. Therefore, it affirms what is meant by the word "God." Atheism, consequently, can only mean the attempt to remove any ultimate concern—to remain unconcerned about the meaning of one's existence. Indifference toward the ultimate question is the only imaginable form of atheism. Whether it is possible is a problem which must remain unsolved at this point. In any case, he who denies God as a matter of ultimate concern affirms God, because he affirms ultimacy in his concern. God is the fundamental symbol for what concerns us ultimately. Again it would be completely wrong to ask: So God is nothing but a symbol? Because the next question has to be: A symbol for what? And then the answer would be: For God! God is symbol for God. This means that in the notion of God we must distinguish two elements: the element of ultimacy, which is a matter of immediate experience and not symbolic in itself, and the element of concreteness, which is taken from our ordinary experience and symbolically applied to God. The man whose ultimate concern is a sacred tree has both the ultimacy of concern and the concreteness of the tree which symbolizes his relation to the ultimate. The man who adores Apollo is ultimately concerned, but not in an abstract way. His ultimate concern is symbolized in the divine figure of Apollo. The man who glorifies Jahweh, the God of the Old Testament, has both an ultimate concern and a concrete image of what concerns him ultimately. This is the meaning of the seemingly cryptic statement that God is the symbol of God. In this qualified sense God is the fundamental and universal content of faith.

It is obvious that such an understanding of the meaning of God makes the discussions about the existence or non-existence of God meaningless. It is meaningless to question the ultimacy of an ultimate concern. This element in the idea of God is in itself certain. The symbolic expression of this element varies endlessly through the whole history of mankind. Here again it would be meaningless to ask whether one or another of the figures in which an ultimate concern is symbolized does "exist." If "existence" refers to something which can be found within the whole of reality, no divine being exists. The question is not this, but: which of the innumerable symbols of faith is most adequate to the meaning of faith? In other words, which symbol of ultimacy expresses the ultimate without idolatrous elements? This is the problem, and not the so-called "existence of God"—which is in itself an impossible combination of words. God as the ultimate in man's ultimate concern is more certain than any other certainty, even that of oneself. God as symbolized in a divine figure is a matter of daring faith, of courage and risk.

God is the basic symbol of faith, but not the only one. All the qualities we attribute to him, power, love, justice, are taken from finite experiences and applied symbolically to that which is beyond finitude and infinity. If faith calls God "almighty," it uses the human experience of power in order to symbolize the content of its infinite concern, but it does not describe a highest being who can do as he pleases. So it is with all the other qualities and with all the actions, past, present and future, which men attribute to God. They are symbols taken from our daily experience, and not information about what God did once upon a time or will do sometime in the future. Faith is not the belief in such stories, but it is the acceptance of symbols that express our ultimate concern in terms of divine actions.

Another group of symbols of faith are manifestations of the divine in things and events, in persons and communities, in words and documents. This whole realm of sacred objects is a treasure of symbols. Holy things are not holy in themselves, but they point beyond themselves to the source of all holiness, that which is of ultimate concern.

3. Symbols and Myths

The symbols of faith do not appear in isolation. They are united in "stories of the gods," which is the meaning of the Greek word "mythos"— myth. The gods are individualized figures, analogous to human personalities, sexually differentiated, descending from each other, related to each other in love and struggle, producing world and man, acting in time and space. They participate in human greatness and misery, in creative and destructive works. They give to man cultural and religious traditions, and defend these sacred rites. They help and threaten the human race, especially some families, tribes or nations. They appear in epiphanies and incarnations, establish sacred places, rites and persons, and thus create a cult. But they themselves are under the command and threat of a fate which is beyond everything that is. This is mythology as developed most impressively in ancient Greece. But many of these characteristics can be found in every mythology. Usually the mythological gods are not equals. There is a hierarchy, at the top of which is a ruling god, as in Greece; or a trinity of them, as in India; or a duality of them, as in Persia. There are savior-gods who mediate between the highest gods and man, sometimes sharing the suffering and death of man in spite of their essential immortality. This is the world of the myth, great and strange, always changing but fundamentally the same: man's ultimate concern symbolized in divine figures and actions. Myths are symbols of faith combined in stories about divine-human encounters.

Myths are always present in every act of faith, because the language of faith is the symbol. They are also attacked, criticized, and transcended in each of the great religions of mankind. The reason for this criticism is the very nature of the myth. It uses material from our ordinary experience. It puts the stories of the gods into the framework of time and space although it belongs to the nature of the ultimate to be beyond time and space. Above all, it divides the divine into several figures, removing ultimacy from each of them without removing their claim to ultimacy. This inescapably leads to conflicts of ultimate claims, able to destroy life, society, and consciousness.

The criticism of the myth first rejects the division of the divine and goes beyond it to one God, although in different ways according to the different types of religion. Even one God is an object of mythological language, and if spoken about is drawn into the framework of time and space. Even he loses his ultimacy if made to be the content of concrete concern. Consequently, the criticism of the myth does not end with the rejection of the polytheistic mythology.

Monotheism also falls under the criticism of the myth. It needs, as one says today, "demythologization." This word has been used in connection with the elaboration of the mythical elements in stories and symbols of the Bible, both of the Old and the New Testaments—stories like those of the Paradise, of the fall of Adam, of the great Flood, of the Exodus from Egypt, of the virgin birth of the Messiah, of many of his miracles, of his resurrection and ascension, of his expected return as the judge of the universe. In short, all the stories in which divine-human interactions are told are considered as mythological in character, and objects of demythologization. What does this negative and artificial term mean? It must be accepted and supported if it points to the necessity of recognizing a symbol as a symbol and a myth as a myth. It must be attacked and rejected if it means the removal of symbols and myths together. Such an attempt is the third step in the criticism of the myth. It is an attempt which never can be successful, because symbol and myth are forms of the human consciousness which are always present. One can replace one myth by another, but one cannot remove the myth from man's spiritual life. For the myth is the combination of symbols of our ultimate concern.

A myth which is understood as a myth, but not removed or replaced, can be called a "broken myth." Christianity denies by its very nature any unbroken myth, because its presupposition is the first commandment: the affirmation of the ultimate as ultimate and the rejection of any kind of idolatry. All mythological elements in the Bible, and doctrine and liturgy should be recognized as mythological, but they should be maintained in their symbolic form and not be replaced by scientific substitutes. For there is no substitute for the use of symbols and myths: they are the language of faith.

The radical criticism of the myth is due to the fact that the primitive mythological consciousness resists the attempt to interpret the myth of myth. It is afraid of every act of demythologization. It believes that the broken myth is deprived of its truth and of its convincing power. Those who live in an unbroken mythological world feel safe and certain. They resist, often fanatically, any attempt to introduce an element of uncertainty by "breaking the myth," namely, by making conscious its symbolic character. Such resistance is supported by authoritarian systems, religious or political, in order to give security to the people under their control and unchallenged power to those who exercise the control. The resistance against demythologization expresses itself in "literalism." The symbols and myths are understood in their immediate meaning. The material, taken from nature and history, is used in its proper sense. The character of the symbol to point beyond itself to something else is disregarded. Creation is taken as a magic act which happened once upon a time. The fall of Adam is localized on a special geographical point and attributed to a human individual. The virgin birth of the Messiah is understood in biological terms, resurrection and ascension as physical events, the second coming of Christ as a telluric, or cosmic, catastrophe. The presupposition of such literalism is that God is a being, acting in time and space, dwelling in a special place, affecting the course of events and being affected by them like any other being in the universe. Literalism deprives God of his ultimacy and, religiously speaking, of his majesty. It draws him down to the level of that which is not ultimate, the finite and conditional. In the last analysis it is not rational criticism of the myth which is decisive but the inner religious criticism. Faith, if it takes its symbols literally, becomes idolatrous! It calls something ultimate which is less than ultimate. Faith, conscious of the symbolic character of its symbols, gives God the honor which is due him.

One should distinguish two stages of literalism, the natural and the reactive. The natural stage of literalism is that in which the mythical and the literal are indistinguishable. The primitive period of individuals and groups consists in the inability to separate the creations of symbolic imagination from the facts which can be verified through observation and experiment. This stage has a full right of its own and should not be disturbed, either in individuals or in groups, up to the moment when man's questioning mind breaks the natural acceptance of the mythological visions as literal. If, however, this moment has come, two ways are possible. The one is to replace the unbroken by the broken myth. It is the objectively demanded way, although it is impossible for many people who prefer the repression of their questions to the uncertainty which appears with the breaking of the myth. They are forced into the second stage of literalism, the conscious one, which is aware of the questions but represses them, half consciously, half unconsciously. The tool of repression is usually an acknowledged authority with sacred qualities like the Church or the Bible, to which one owes unconditional surrender. This stage is still justifiable, if the questioning power is very weak and can easily be answered. It is unjustifiable if a mature mind is broken in its personal center by political or psychological methods, split in his unity, and hurt in his integrity. The enemy of a critical theology is not natural literalism but conscious literalism with repression of and aggression toward autonomous thought.

Symbols of faith cannot be replaced by other symbols, such as artistic ones, and they cannot be removed by scientific criticism. They have a genuine standing in the human mind, just as science and art have. Their symbolic character is their truth and their power. Nothing less than symbols and myths can express our ultimate concern.

One more question arises, namely, whether myths are able to express every kind of ultimate concern. For example, Christian theologians argue that the word "myth" should be reserved for natural myths in which repetitive natural processes, such as the seasons, are understood in their ultimate meaning. They believe that if the world is seen as a historical process with beginning, end and center, as in Christianity and Judaism, the term "myth" should not be used. This would radically reduce the realm in which the term would be applicable. Myth could not be understood as the language of our ultimate concern, but only as a discarded idiom of this language. Yet history proves that there are not only natural myths but also historical myths. If the earth is seen as the battleground of two divine powers, as in ancient Persia, this is an historical myth. If the God of creation selects and guides a nation through history toward an end which transcends all history, this is an historical myth. If the Christ—a transcendent, divine being—appears in the fullness of time, lives, dies and is resurrected, this is an historical myth. Christianity is superior to those religions which are bound to a natural myth. But Christianity speaks the mythological language like every other religion. It is a broken myth, but it is a myth: otherwise Christianity would not be an expression of ultimate concern.

E. L. MASCALL

E. L. MASCALL (1905-   ), Anglican theologian, has published extensively and contributed to a revival of interest in the Thomistic tradition in theology. His books, *He Who
Is*, *Words and Images* and *Existence and
Analogy*, are significant contributions to philosophy of religion.

The Doctrine of Analogy*

One preliminary remark may be made before the discussion is opened, namely that the function of the doctrine of analogy is not to make it possible for us to talk about God in the future but to explain how it is that we have been able to talk about him all along. In spite of all that has been said by positivists, logical and other, we do in fact find ourselves talking about God, and talking about him in a way that is significant. It is, I would maintain, transparently clear to anyone whose judgment is not shackled by a predetermined dogma that, if two men respectively affirm and deny that God exists, they are in fact disagreeing about the nature of reality, and not merely expressing different emotional or aesthetic attitudes. There is, un-fortunately, a recurrent tendency among philosophers, in analysing the mental activities of human beings in general, to assume that until their analysis and criticism have been satisfactorily completed, nobody has the right to make any affirmations at all; so deeply has Cartesianism entered into our heritage. The consequence is that the plain man laughs at the philosophers and goes on his own way without them. Against this tendency we are, as I see it, bound to assert that the task of any philosophical critique is to account for, to render precise and, if necessary, to correct the body of doctrine that the human mind has acquired by the natural exercise of its own powers, but not, except in a purely relative and *ex post facto* way, to

* From E. L. Mascall, *Existence and Analogy*, pp. 94-115. Published 1949, by Long-mans, Green & Co., Ltd. Used by permission of the publishers. [Footnotes omitted, Eds.]

provide a justification for the activity of thought itself. To forget this is to doom oneself to a kind of intellectual suicide. For the critical philosopher is himself the heir of his past; before he was a philosopher at all he was a man, and before he was a man he was a child. To enter a second time into the womb and to be born again equipped with a fully developed critique of knowledge is a sheer impossibility. The fact is that, however fallible it may be, the human mind does acquire knowledge by the exercise of the powers which it possesses, and a sane philosophy will recognize this fact. To return, then, to the subject of our present discussion, the doctrine of analogy is not concerned to discover whether discourse about God is antecedently possible, or to endow it with a possibility that was originally absent, but to account for the fact that discourse about God has, as matter of experience, been taking place in spite of various considerations that might seem at first sight to rule its possibility out of court.

I would further add that the question of analogy does not arise at all in the mere proof of the existence of God; it arises only when, having satisfied ourselves that the existence of finite being declares its dependence upon self-existent being, we then apprehend that no predicate can be attributed to finite and to self-existent being univocally. Penido's remarks seem to me to be of the first importance here. "Formally," he writes, "the problem of analogy is a problem of nature, not of existence. We can arrive at the existence of God without *explicit* recourse to analogy, while it is impossible to think about the divine nature without conceiving it as equivocal, univocal or analogous to our own." And again: "It is quite true that the proofs of God are analogical *realities*, otherwise they would prove nothing. But they do not fall under the jurisdiction of the *method* of analogy, as theology employs it. Let us distinguish carefully—without separating them and still more without opposing them—the problem of analogical knowledge and the metaphysical problem of analogy. The former belongs in full right to the treatise on God, while it is only after the treatise on creation that we can approach the latter in its fullness. . . . Does this mean that analogy in no way depends on the *quinque viae?* By no means. Analogy begins at the precise point where the rational demonstration ends." We had no need of any doctrine of analogy in the last chapter, in arguing from the existence of finite beings to the existence of God. When, however, the argument was complete, we saw that the God whose existence we were now asserting was a being of so radically different an order from everything else in our experience that it became a real question whether the word "God" in that context meant anything at all. There can be little satisfaction in demonstrating the existence of a being whom the very demonstration shows to be altogether inapprehensible. God would seem to have slipped from between our hands at the very moment when we had at last laid hold on him. It is at this point that the doctrine of analogy becomes altogether necessary, and it is for this reason that its full investigation only began among Christian philosophers who gave primacy of place to the existential approach to God.

The doctrine, as we find it in the Thomist tradition, appears in at least three distinct departments of philosophy, namely the metaphysical or onto-logical, the epistemological or psychological, and the logical or linguistic. This is only what we might expect in a fundamentally realist philosophy, which holds that words are not merely noises and that thought is not merely about ideas, but that speech with its words and thought with its ideas are ultimately about things. It is well to make this point clear at the start or we shall find ourselves puzzled to know what precisely is the question with which analogy is concerned. Is it "How can we talk about God?" or "How can we think about God?" or "How are things related to God?" In fact it is about all three, and we need not be worried by the way in which it slips from one to the other, so long as our attitude is confidently realist. I shall, however, take the first question as my starting-point and consider the prob-lem of analogical predication.

Is it possible, we therefore ask, for statements expressed in human lan-guage to mean anything when made about God—that is to say, are theolog-ical statements meaningful or meaningless? (The relevance of this discussion to the questions raised by the logical positivists will be immediately clear to those who have any acquaintance with their works.) Starting from a famous distinction made by Aristotle, we remark that, even within the realm of discourse about finite beings, one and the same word, when ap-plied to two things, sometimes bears the same sense in both applications and sometimes different ones. In the former case it is used *univocally* (συνωνύμως), as when Carlo and Fido are both called dogs. Even if Carlo is a great Dane and Fido a Pomeranian, we mean the same thing about each of them when we call them both *dogs*; the characteristics in each that distinguish Carlo as a Dane from Fido as a Pomeranian, while they cannot be found in their totality except in dogs, are additional to caninity as such. But sometimes we use words purely equivocally (ὁμωνύμως), as when we apply the word "mug" both to a drinking utensil and to the victim of a fraud. (The neglect of this distinction can lead to unfortunate consequences, as the choirboys found who were starting a cricket team, when they asked the vicar for one of the bats which the verger had led them to believe were in the belfry.) But in addition to these two uses, it is alleged, a word is sometimes applied to two objects in senses that are neither wholly different nor yet wholly the same, as when we say that Mr. Jones and Skegness [1] are

---

[1] A seaside health resort. Eds.

both healthy, the former because he *enjoys*, and the latter because it *induces*, health; in this case we are said to use the term "healthy" *analogically* (ἀνάλογως).

At first sight the introduction of this mode of predication might seem to be unnecessary and trivial, and certainly Aristotle did not accord to it anything like as much attention as the scholastics do. We might be tempted to suppose that analogy is only a dignified kind of univocity, and that it is quite sufficient to say that the healthiness of Mr. Jones and the healthiness of Skegness are merely two ways of being healthy, just as the Danishness of Carlo and the Pomeranianity of Fido are merely two ways of being canine. Or, alternatively, we might go to the other extreme and say that analogy is only equivocity in sheep's clothing, that to enjoy health and to induce health are two altogether different activities and that only for the sake of economy in words can there be any justification for using the same term "healthy" *tout court* to denote them both. Furthermore, it might be asked, even if we admit this *tertium quid* of analogy, can we ever be quite sure when it applies? When we say that Mr. Jones is alive and that an oyster is alive, is the difference between the life of Mr. Jones and the life of the oyster something additional to a quality, namely life, which is found univocally in both, as the Danishness of Carlo and the Pomeranianity of Fido are additional to their common caninity? Or, on the other hand, is the life which is attributed to Mr. Jones and to the oyster, as the scholastics would say, an analogical perfection, contracted to each subject not by external *differentiae* but by different internal modes of participation? Can one possibly settle this kind of question? Can we even give the distinction any real meaning?

Now, so long as we are merely considering qualities and properties of finite beings, the introduction of analogical discourse, in addition to univocal and equivocal, might well appear to be an unnecessary and artificial complication. There are, however, two instances in which it—or something like it—seems to be unavoidable, namely when we are discussing transcendentals and when we are discussing God. And it is worth noting that, in Christian thought, it is precisely the necessity of talking about God that has given rise to the great development which the doctrine of analogy has undergone. Let us consider these instances in order.

The transcendentals, in scholastic thought, are those six primary notions— *ens, res, unum, aliquid, verum* and *bonum*—which, because of their very universality, refuse to fall in any of the Aristotelian categories, but cut across them all. The last five ultimately reduce to the first, so it will be sufficient to consider that. What, then, is meant by the analogy of being? Why is it denied that being is univocal? Simply because there is nothing outside being by which it could be differentiated. When we say that Carlo and Fido are both dogs, the word "dog" means precisely the same when applied to each of them; the differences that distinguish them as dogs are, as we have seen, extrinsic to caninity as such. But when we say that Carlo and Fido are both *beings*, the differences that distinguish them as beings cannot be extrinsic to being as such, for being, in its altogether universal reference, must embrace everything, including differences; if differences were not instances of being, they would be non-existent, and then no two things could be distinct from each other. So the scholastics tell us, being is not a genus, since there is nothing outside it which could act as a differentia to it, to subdivide it into species; nevertheless everything is an instance of being, and being is differentiated by its own inherent analogical variety. To be is to be in a certain way, and the way is the very heart of the being. So the whole order of things, of *entia*, from the triune Deity down to the speck of dust and the electron, consists of nothing more and nothing less than analogical instances of being: self-existent being and dependent being, actual being and possible being, substantial being and accidental being, real being and notional being, not in any pantheistic or monistic sense, as if being were some kind of cosmic material, a metaphysical modelling-clay appearing now in this shape and now in that, but in the far more profound sense that every being must *be*, and must be in some determinate way, and—the theist will add—in the sense that the way in which it has being depends in the last resort upon its relation to the self-existent Being which is the prime analogate of all.

Now what is true about beings as such in their relation to one another must be true *a fortiori* about finite beings in their relation to the God who is self-existent Being. If being is not a genus, then the supreme Being transcends all genera, and the principle of analogy, which we have seen applies even between creatures when they are considered as they participate in the transcendentals, will apply with even greater force when creatures are brought into comparison with the altogether transcendent God and when God is spoken about in words whose meaning is derived from their application to finite things. Here, if anywhere, the distinction between the *perfectio significata* and the *modus significandi* will hold; here, if anywhere, will the classical definition of analogy apply, namely that it is the application of a concept to different beings in ways that are simply diverse from each other and are only the same in a certain respect, *simpliciter diversa et eadem secundum quid*. It is noticeable that St. Thomas does not deny that analogues are equivocal but only that they are purely so.

Let us now proceed to consider in more detail this classical doctrine of analogy. The precise classification of the various types of analogy that can be distinguished is to this day a matter of considerable controversy; the method that I shall adopt will, however, bring out the salient points.

II.

In the first place, we may distinguish between analogy *duorum ad tertium* and analogy *unius ad alterum*; this is the fundamental distinction made by St. Thomas in both the *Summa Theologica* and the *Summa contra Gentiles*. Analogy *duorum ad tertium* is the analogy that holds between two beings in consequence of the relation that each of them bears to a third (the analogy considered is, it must be noticed, between the *two*; the *tertium* only comes in as something in the background to which they are both related). For example, if the adjective "healthy" is applied both to Skegness and to the complexion of Mr. Jones who lives there, this double attribution of the adjective can only be seen to be legitimate if it is grasped that in its strict and primary application the adjective applies neither to Skegness nor to the complexion but to Mr. Jones. It is he who is (in the scholastic sense) *formally* healthy and is the *prime analogate*. His complexion is healthy only in the sense that it is a *sign* of health in him, Skegness is healthy only in the sense that it *induces* health in him (or in others like him); we cannot rationally justify the attribution of the same predicate "healthy" to things as diverse as a complexion and a seaside town except by referring them both to human beings to whom the predicate formally and properly belongs.

This type of analogy can, however, have little or no application to the case where we are attributing the same predicate to God and to a creature, for there is no being antecedent to God to whom the predicate can apply more formally and properly than it applies to him. We therefore pass to the other type of analogy, analogy *unius ad alterum*, which is founded not upon diverse relations which each of the analogates bears to a third, but upon a relation which one of them bears to the other. And this type of analogy itself subdivides into two.

The former of these sub-types is that which is known as analogy of *attribution* or of *proportion*, analogy *unius ad alterum* in the strict sense. In this case the predicate belongs formally and properly to one of the analogates (which is thus not merely *an* analogate but is the *prime* analogate), and only relatively and derivatively to the other. Thus it is by an analogy of attribution or proportion that Mr. Jones and his complexion are both described as healthy; health is found formally and properly in Mr. Jones, and his complexion is described as healthy only because it bears a certain relation to his health, namely the relation of being a sign of it. In its theological application, where the analogates concerned are God and a creature, the relation upon which the analogy is based will be that of creative causality; creatures are related to God as his effects, by all those modes of participation by the creature in the perfection of its creator which are indicated, for example, by the Thomist Five Ways. Thus when we say that God and Mr. Jones are both good or that they are both beings, remembering that the content which the word "good" or "being" has for us is derived from our experience of the goodness and the being of creatures, we are, so far as analogy of attribution is concerned, saying no more than that God has goodness or being in whatever way is necessary if he is to be able to produce goodness and being in his creatures. This would not seem necessarily to indicate anything more than the perfections which are found formally in various finite modes in creatures exist *virtually* in God, that is to say, that he is able to produce them in the creatures; it does not seem to necessitate that God possesses them formally himself (In the case of Mr. Jones, of course, his complexion did indicate his formal possession of health, but there is, literally, all the difference in the world between the relation between two analogates in the finite realm and that between God and a creature.) Analogy of attribution certainly does not exclude the formal possession of the perfections by God, but it does not itself ascribe it to him. The mode in which the perfection which exists in the secondary analogate also exists in the prime analogate will depend on the relation between them; and if this relation is merely that the latter analogate is the *cause* of the former, the possession by the latter of a perfection that exists formally in the former will not, so far as the present mode of analogy is concerned, be necessarily anything more than a virtual one. Creatures are good (formally but finitely), God is the cause of them and of all that they have, therefore the word "good" applied to God need not mean any more than that he is able to produce goodness. It is at this point that the second sub-type of analogy comes to the rescue.

This is analogy of proportionality, also called analogy *plurium ad plura*. In it there is a direct relation of the mode in which a perfection is participated to the being by which it is participated, independently of any relation to a prime analogate. (There may be a prime analogate, and indeed some would maintain that there must be, but it does not come in at this stage.) A spurious, though sometimes useful, form of this type of analogy is *metaphor*, in which there is not a formal participation of the same characteristic in the different analogates but only a similarity of effects. Thus, to take a classic example, the lion is called the king of the beasts because he bears to savage animals a relation similar to that which a king bears to his subjects, but no one would assert that kingship is to be found formally in the lion. Again, God is described as being angry, because his relation to the punishments which he imposes is similar to that which an angry man has to the injuries which he inflicts, but no one (at least, no scholastic philosopher) would say that anger was to be found formally in God. In the strict sense, an analogy of proportionality implies that the analogue under discussion is found formally in each of the analogates but in a mode that is determined by the nature of the analogate itself. Thus, assuming that life is an analogous and not a univocal concept, it is asserted that cabbages, elephants, men and God each possess life formally (that is each of them is, quite literally and un-metaphorically, *alive*), but that the cabbage possesses life in the mode proper to a cabbage, the elephant in that proper to an elephant, the man in that proper to a man, and finally God in that supreme, and by us unimaginable, mode proper to self-existent Being itself. This is commonly expressed in the following quasi-mathematical form, from which, in fact, the name "analogy of proportionality" is derived.

$$\frac{\text{life of cabbage}}{\text{essence of cabbage}} = \frac{\text{life of elephant}}{\text{essence of elephant}}$$
$$= \frac{\text{life of man}}{\text{essence of man}} = \frac{\text{life of God}}{\text{essence of God}}$$

We must, however, beware of interpreting the equal sign too literally. For the point is not that the life of the cabbage is determined by the essence of the cabbage in the *same* way as that in which the life of the man is determined by the essence of the man, but that the way in which cabbage essence determines cabbage life is proper to cabbagehood, while the way in which the human essence determines human life is proper to manhood. But at this point various objections rapidly spring to the mind.

In the first place, it may be asked, has not the remark just made landed us in an infinite regress? We began by denying the univocity of the identity,

$$\text{life of cabbage} = \text{life of man,}$$

and substituted for it the proportionality:

$$\frac{\text{life of cabbage}}{\text{essence of cabbage}} = \frac{\text{life of man}}{\text{essence of man}}$$

But we now have denied that the equal sign in this latter equation really signifies equality and have substituted for it a proposition which, in quasi-mathematical form, can be written as follows:

$$\frac{\text{way in which life of cabbage is determined by essence of cabbage}}{\text{essence of cabbage}}$$
$$= \frac{\text{way in which life of man is determined by essence of man}}{\text{essence of man}}$$

And again we shall have to remember that the equal sign means not identity but similarity, and shall now have to write:

$$\frac{\text{way in which way-in-which-life-of-cabbage-is-determined-by-essence-of-cabbage is determined by essence of cabbage}}{\text{essence of cabbage}}$$

$$= \frac{\text{way in which way-in-which-life-of-man-is-determined-by-essence-of-man is determined by essence of man}}{\text{essence of man}}$$

and so *ad infinitum*.

To put this more briefly, if we write L for "life of" and E for "essence of," c for "cabbage" and m for "man," and use A/B to signify "determination of A by B," we began by denying Lc = Lm, and put in its place

$$Lc/Ec \;=\; Lm/Em;$$

then we said that what we really meant was

$$(Lc/Ec)/Ec \;=\; (Lm/Em)/Em;$$

then we found that for this we should have to substitute

$$[(Lc/Ec)/Ec]/Ec \;=\; [(Lm/Em)/Em]/Em.$$

The next stage will be

$$\{[(Lc/Ec)/Ec]/Ec\}/Ec \;=\; \{[(Lm/Em)/Em]/Em\}/Em,$$

and so we shall go on for ever, at each successive stage denying progressively more complicated relationships between cabbages and men, and never managing to assert a relationship which we shall not immediately have to deny. And at the end of it we shall have nothing but a series of negations:

$$Lc \neq Lm,$$
$$Lc/Ec \neq Lm/Em,$$
$$(Lc/Ec)/Ec \neq (Lm/Em)/Em,$$
$$[(Lc/Ec)/Ec]/Ec \neq [(Lm/Em)/Em]/Em, \qquad \text{etc.}$$

Our proportionality has completely collapsed, and all we are left with is the fact that cabbages have nothing in common with men except the fact that, for no valid reason, men have described them both as being alive. In fact, the introduction of analogy as a *via media* between univocity and equivocity has turned out to be nothing more than an imposing piece of mystification. This is the first objection of which we must take account; it is obviously a serious one. It strikes, not in particular at the analogical application of terms to God, but to analogical predication as such. I shall not attempt a full reply until I have stated another objection which is concerned with the specifically theological case, but I shall offer a few observations in passing.

First, then, we may remark that the objection, while on the surface plausible, has something of the appearance of a conjuring trick. It brings to mind two somewhat similar feats of philosophical legerdemain. The first is Lewis Carroll's *What the Tortoise said to Achilles*. In this problem, which its originator did not perhaps intend to be taken as seriously as it really demands, Achilles maintained that, if two premisses A and B logically implied a conclusion Z, then anybody who saw this and also accepted A and B as true would have to accept Z as true also. The tortoise objected that this would only be the case if he accepted a further proposition C, namely that if A and B are true then Z must be true. Achilles was thus forced to modify his original assertion, so that it now took the form "Anyone who accepts A, B and C as true must accept Z as true also." But again the tortoise objected that this involved the acceptance of another proposition D, which was that, if A and B and C are all true, Z must be true as well. And so on for ever! This corresponds, of course, to the well-known fact that the principle of inference is incapable of formal symbolic statement within the logical calculus to which it applies. A logical system cannot, as it were, operate under its own steam, without help from outside; we shall derive from this fact a pointer towards the solution of our present problem. The other puzzle to which I wish to refer is one which its originator took much more seriously: I mean Mr. F. H. Bradley's famous argument that relations are illusions. It is, he urged, of the essence of a relation to unite terms, but how is each term united to the relation? It can only be by another relation, but if so, what unites the term to this? To make the first relation intelligible we have to presuppose an infinite sequence of relations antecedent to it, and none of these is yet intelligible. Hence, Mr. Bradley concluded, relations are mere illusion. Lord Russell has caustically remarked that if Bradley's argument were valid it would prove that chains are impossible—and yet they exist. Dr. C. D. Broad has dealt with Bradley's problem in some detail. He takes as an instance of it the fact that A is father of B. "Here," he writes, "we have a perfectly intelligible statement, involving the non-formal relation of *fatherhood*. At the next stage we get the fact that A is referent to *fatherhood*, and the fact that B is relatum to *fatherhood*. The 'relations' introduced at this stage are purely formal. At the next stage we get the fact that A is referent to *referent to*, that *fatherhood* is relatum to *referent to*, that *fatherhood* is referent to *referent to*, and that B is relatum to *referent to*. Thus no new 'relations' are introduced at this or any subsequent stage. The fact that at every stage after the first the relating relations are purely formal and are merely repeated shows that we are now embarked on the self-evidently impossible task of explaining, by means of particular relational judgments, that general relational form which is presupposed by all relational judgments whatever." We might, in fact, say that, while it is of the essence of relations to unite terms, they are not themselves terms in this context (though, of course, in another context they may become terms, as when we pick out two relations, or a relation and a term, and ask what is the relation between them). Similarly, in the case of analogy of proper proportionality, we might reply to our objector that we are simply concerned with the fact that essences determine their qualities, and that the truth of this is not in the least affected by the fact that they can only do this if they also determine the way in which they determine their qualities, and the way in which they determine the way in which they determine their qualities, and so on to the crack of doom. *Ce n'est que le premier pas qui coûte.*

Such a reply would, I think, go a very long way, though I am doubtful whether it is altogether sufficient. For the fact remains that we have denied that our equal signs really stand for equality and we have not indicated anything definite that they do stand for. Can we in some way re-establish this bond that we have broken? Clearly we cannot by analogy of proportionality, but I shall suggest that we can by analogy of attribution, and that the two types of analogy, while either in separation is insufficient, can in combination do what is required. But this is an anticipation. I will pass on now to consider the second objection, which is specially concerned with analogical discourse about God.

III.

Let us therefore see what happens when we attribute life both to a creature and to God; any other perfection which can be formally predicated of God would, of course, do as well. Analogy of proportionality asserts:

$$\frac{\text{life of man}}{\text{essence of man}} = \frac{\text{life of God}}{\text{essence of God}}$$

Now, the objector urges, even if the first objection has been successfully overcome, so that we have no longer to bother about the fact that the equal sign does not indicate an exact identity of relationship, our formula will not in fact tell us in what sense life is to be predicated of God. For the essence of God is as little known to us as is his life; indeed his life is, formally considered, identical with it. Our equation has therefore two unknowns and cannot be solved. Nor can we get out of our difficulty by comparing essence with existence and saying that the essence of a being will correspond to, and be determined by, the act in virtue of which it exists:

$$\frac{\text{essence of man}}{\text{existential act of man}} = \frac{\text{essence of God}}{\text{existential act of God}}$$

Once again, both the terms on the right-hand side are unknown. Sheer agnosticism seems to be the outcome. What reply can we make?

Some scholastic philosophers, of whom Garrigou-Lagrange is one, claim to answer this objection, while remaining in the realm of analogy of proportionality, by denying that there are two unknown terms on the right-hand side. This last-mentioned writer, for example, taking the analogy

$$\frac{\text{creature}}{\text{its being}} = \frac{\text{first cause}}{\text{its being}}$$

asserts that only the fourth term is in fact unknown. "We have," he says, "(1) *the very confused concept of being in general*, which a child possesses from the moment of its first intellectual knowledge, (2) *the concept of finite being*, of which we know positively the finite mode and which is nothing else than the essence of the things that we see, stones, plants, animals, etc., (3) *the concept of analogous being*, imperfectly abstracted from the finite mode . . . ; it is a precision of the first very confused concept possessed by the child, and the metaphysician acquires it by recognizing that the formal notion of being does not in itself include the finite mode which accompanies it in the creature, (4) *the concept of the divine being*, the cause of created beings. These latter," he continues, "not having in their essence the reason of their existence, require a cause which exists of itself. In the concept of the divine being, the divine mode is expressed only in a negative and relative way, e.g. as non-finite or as supreme being. What is positive in this analogical knowledge of God is what God has that is proportionally common to him and the creature." Again, he writes, "*being* designates *that which* has relation to existence; this relation is implied in the very nature of that which exists and it is essentially varied according as it is necessary or contingent. The created essence in its inmost entity is altogether relative to its contingent existence, which it can lose; the uncreated essence is conceived only relatively to that necessary existence with which it is identified. . . . Analogous perfections are thus not pure relations. They are perfections which imply in the creature a composition of two correlative elements, potentiality and act, but which in God are pure act. Our intelligence conceives that they are realized more fully according as they are purified of all potentiality; in God they exist therefore in the pure state.

We thus see that there are not two unknowns in the proportionalities set up by theology."

For this distinguished French Dominican, therefore, the third term in the formula is given us as that in which essence and existence are identical, and this gives us a limited and analogical, but nevertheless genuine, knowledge of the fourth term, while remaining within the realm of analogy of proportionality. We can transfer the notion of any perfection from a finite being to God, remembering that the difference of mode is that which corresponds to the difference between a being whose essence involves merely a possibility of existence and one whose essence involves existence of necessity. Of course, we do not know positively what the mode of the perfection in God is; to demand that would be to demand a quidditative knowledge of the divine essence and to abolish analogy altogether in favor of univocity. We are given all that we have a right to ask for; the comparison of the finite and the infinite modes of perfection is based on a comparison of the relations to existence which are proper to finite essence and to the divine essence respectively.

Now all this seems very satisfactory so far as it goes, but does it go far enough? Is it sufficient simply to base the comparison of the finite and infinite modes of a perfection upon a comparison of the finite and infinite modes of the essence-existence relation, without bringing in an explicit reference to the concrete relation which the creature has to God? There are indeed traces in Garrigou-Lagrange's own discussion of an awareness of the need of this further step; the very form in which he writes the formula last quoted suggests this. For he does not describe the finite being as a being in whom essence does not necessarily involve existence, but as a "creature"; and he does not describe God as a being whose essence necessarily involves existence, but as the "first cause." "In these equations," he writes, "two created terms are known directly, one uncreated term is known indirectly *by way of causality* and we infer the fourth term which is known indirectly in a *positive* manner as regards what is analogically common with creatures and in a *negative* and relative manner as regards its proper divine mode." And the first cause and the creature are directly related by the relation of creation, which thus, as it were, cuts horizontally across the analogy of proportionality with an analogy of attribution. The equal sign does not, as we have seen earlier, express a mathematical identity, but, on the other hand, the two sides of the formula are not left in complete separation. They are bound together by an analogy of attribution *unius ad alterum*, of the creature to God in the case which we have just been considering. In the cases considered earlier, where the two sides of the formula both refer to finite beings, the linking analogy is an analogy *duorum ad tertium*, which holds in view the fact that each of the analogates is in an analogy of attribution *unius ad alterum*, of itself to God. The figure below, Fig. 4, may help to make this plain.

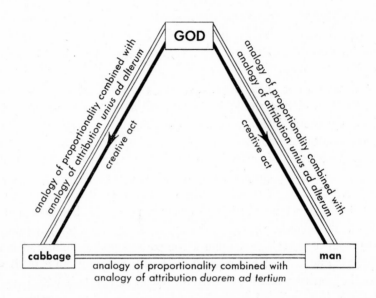

analogy of proportionality combined with
analogy of attribution *duorem ad tertium*

The conclusion would thus seem to be that, in order to make the doctrine of analogy really satisfactory, we must see the analogical relation between God and the world as combining in a tightly interlocked union both analogy of attribution and analogy of proportionality. Without analogy of proportionality it is very doubtful whether the attributes which we predicate of God can be ascribed to him in more than a merely virtual sense; without analogy of attribution it hardly seems possible to avoid agnosticism. Which of the two forms of analogy is prior to the other has been, and still is, a hotly debated question among scholastic philosophers. Sylvester of Ferrara, in his great commentary on the *Summa contra Gentiles*, asserted the primacy of attribution and alleged that in this he was expressing the true thought of St. Thomas, but the "prince of commentators" Cajetan, in his luminous little treatise *De Nominum Analogia*, asserted that only proportionality was analogy in the true and strict sense and the majority of Thomists have followed him, down to Garrigou-Lagrange, Penido, and Maritain at the present day, though Descoqs is a notable exception.

SUGGESTED ADDITIONAL READINGS

Religious Language

Aquinas, St. Thomas. "The Names of God," *Summa Theologica*. Book I, Question 12, Articles 1-12. One of the fountainheads of discussion of the nature of the analogical knowledge of God.

Cajetan (Tommaso de Vio). *The Analogy of Names*. Trans., Edward A. Bushinski and Henry J. Koren. Pittsburg: Duquesne University Press, 1953. Cajetan sets forth here an influential examination of analogy in religious language.

Cassirer, Ernst. *Language and Myth. Trans.*, Suzanne K. Langer. New York: Harper and Brothers, 1946. (Also published in paperback by Dover Publications, Inc.) An investigation of the mythical element in human thinking by a man who helped make this an important area of study in modern philosophy.

Cusa, Nicholaus. *Of Learned Ignorance*. Trans., Germain Heron. London: Routledge & Paul, 1954. See especially chapters 24-26. A medieval philosopher discourses on the impossibility of a positive knowledge of the attributes of God.

Faith and Logic. Edited by Basil Mitchell. Boston: Beacon Press, 1957. A collection of essays by British philosophers and theologians that analyze religious concepts.

Farrer, Austin M. *The Glass of Vision*. London: Dacre Press, 1948. A provocative discussion of symbols as the media of religious knowledge.

Kerygma and Myth. Edited by Hans W. Bartsch. Trans., Reginald Fuller. London: Society for the Publication of Christian Knowledge, 1954. A collection of essays which assess the possibility and legitimacy of removing the mythological concepts from the New Testament in an effort to interpret its message.

Langer, Suzanne K. *Philosophy In A New Key*. Cambridge, Mass.: Harvard University Press, 1942. (Also published in paperback by The New American Library of World Literature, Mentor Series). A good interpretation of the role of myth in knowledge.

Niebuhr, Reinhold. "The Truth In Myths," *The Nature of Religious Experience*. Edited by J. S. Bixler. New York: Harper & Brothers, 1937. pp. 117-135. A leading American theologian's argument that meaning can be found in religious myth.

Newman, John Henry. A *Grammar of Assent*. New York: Longmans, Green & Company, 1909. (Also published in paperback by Doubleday, Image series.) An early and often referred to discussion of the meaning of religious language and an assessment of its validity.

Stace, W. T. *Time and Eternity*. Princeton, New Jersey: Princeton University Press, 1952. (Also published in paperback by Princeton University Press.) Professor Stace's work asserts the impossibility of predicating positive attributes to God.

VI. *Introduction*

THE PROBLEM OF EVIL

Consideration of the problem of evil is as old as man's thinking about the meaning of his existence. The reality of moral and physical evil has always interposed itself upon man's attempt to understand the present significance and the ultimate reason for his own existence. Epidemics, floods, and earthquakes on the natural plane, the bloody struggle for life among animals, and the personal disorder, inhumanity and seeming meaninglessness in human existence are brute facts which force themselves upon us.

Some explanation of evil, however difficult to achieve, seems imperative if one is to be able to find meaning in existence. Such meaning has been found by some men in the courageous endurance of bludgeoning by meaningless forces; others have found it in attempts to turn evil into some ultimate good. However the problem is met, the fact of evil does force men back to the questions of the source and purpose, if there is a purpose, of evil.

In no area has the question of the nature of the universe and the problem of evil come to sharper focus than in religion. In order to reconcile the existence of evil with a belief in God the problem is devastatingly simple: either God is responsible for evil or He is in some way limited. If God cannot prevent the appearance and progress of evils in the world, it would seem that He is not all-powerful. The result in this case would be to affirm an ultimate dualism between God and demonic forces. If God can, but will not, prevent them, it would appear that He is not all-good. This conclusion would cut the main nerve of most religious faith (though some religions have worshipped evil gods). A second group of theists refuse to accept this either/or and have affirmed God's goodness, even though it meant the acceptance of a finite or limited God. Others who represent a third position feel forced to give up the belief in a God entirely if He cannot be considered both all-good and all-powerful.

A fourth group seeking to explain the presence of evil in the world have attempted to avoid the positing of an antithesis between goodness and omnipotence by arguing that God alone is ultimate and that, in the final analysis, evil has no reality. They claim that what is called evil is either an absence of being or an illusion. A fifth group maintain that evil is indeed one of the real facts of life, but, in the total scope of things, it is instrumental in the gaining of some ultimate good. Such a belief affirms the idea that God can use even the negativity of evil in the achievement of His benevolent purpose in creating the world. Still others, who represent a sixth group, view evil not as an instrument, but as an impediment to God's purpose. In this case God will not use evil, He will fight against it and defeat it. Here evil has no constructive end; it must be directly confronted and destroyed.

A seventh alternative is represented by thinkers for whom the metaphysical problem of evil is artificial. For instance, humanists sometimes prefer to stress a practical, instrumental approach to specific evils, confident that the careful and persistent application of scientific technology to specific problems will in piecemeal fashion gradually eliminate evil.

These are not all of the alternative ways in which men have dealt with the fact of evil, but they indicate some of the major approaches by which the problem has been met. In the selections which follow are writings of important thinkers who have spoken to this problem and who have attempted to achieve some solution.

Our selection from the works of Augustine is representative of the position which denies that evil has any ultimate status in being, while recognizing its limiting and perverse influence in man's present experience. Augustine calls evil the "privation" or absence of being. This evil he roots in an evil will which he calls "Pride." Spinoza recognizes the reality of evil as an obstruction to the self-fulfillment of human life, but, at the same time, maintains that the distinction between good and evil as such does not exist in the infinite intellect of God who fulfills Himself. Leibnitz justifies the existence of evil by saying that this is the best world that could have been created and that even evil can become an instrument to the perfection of the whole creation.

In Josiah Royce we have an absolute idealistic position. Royce finds evil a necessity for the completion of God's life, for only by struggle with evil in the temporal world can God in His eternity be triumphantly perfect. William Temple approaches the problem of evil from the standpoint of a concern with human sin. While he does not see evil as limited to sin, nor to be accounted for solely in terms of sin, he does see sin as the most immediate, and experientially the most devastating, form of evil.

Radoslav Tsanoff approaches the question with the frank recognition that this is a world of good and evil. Neither fact can be expunged from the context in which life is lived. The problem he deals with is the possibility of correlating these two realities. Having recognized that evil exists, man is able to fight against it and wrest some value and goodness out of life. John Stuart Mill also acknowledges the reality of evil. Indeed, the fact of evil looms so starkly before him that the only explanation he believes natural religion is able to give is one which recognizes the limited power of God. Such a limitation implies that a struggle against an awesome foe must be waged if good is to be won.

F. R. Tennant addresses the problem of physical evil. He examines many of the traditional arguments and then attempts to make his own case. This he does by discussing the relation between nature's harmony and evil's disruptive negations. Nicolai Berdyaev takes us to a different approach. For him the problem of evil comes to clearest focus in the problem of death and the only meaningful answer to evil, for him, is to be found in "rebirth" through conversion to Christian faith.

SAINT AUGUSTINE

SAINT AUGUSTINE (345-430) was Bishop of Hippo in North Africa and probably the most important theologian in the first millennium of the Christian era. In his work he attempted to combine Platonic thought with Christian theology. *The Confessions* and *The City of God* are among the best known of his works.

The City of God*

13. That in Adam's Sin An Evil Will Preceded the Evil Act

Our first parents fell into open disobedience because already they were secretly corrupted; for the evil act had never been done had not an evil will preceded it. And what is the origin of our evil will but pride? For "pride is the beginning of sin." And what is pride but the craving for undue exaltation? And this is undue exaltation, when the soul abandons Him to whom it ought to cleave as its end, and becomes a kind of end to itself. This happens when it becomes its own satisfaction. And it does so when it falls away from that unchangeable good which ought to satisfy it more than itself. This falling away is spontaneous; for if the will had remained steadfast in the love of that higher and changeless good by which it was illumined to intelligence and kindled into love, it would not have turned away to find satisfaction in itself, and so become frigid and benighted; the woman would not have believed the serpent spoke the truth, nor would the man have preferred the request of his wife to the command of God, nor have supposed that it was a venial transgression to cleave to the partner of his life even in a partnership of sin. The wicked deed, then—that is to say, the transgression of eating the forbidden fruit—was committed by persons who were already wicked. That "evil fruit" could be brought forth only by "a corrupt tree." But that the tree was evil was not the result of nature; for certainly it could become so only by the vice of the will, and vice is contrary to nature. Now, nature could not have been depraved by vice had it not been made out of nothing. Consequently, that it is a nature, this is because it is made by God; but that it falls away from Him, this is because it is made out of nothing. But man did not so fall away as to become absolutely nothing;

* From St. Augustine, *The City of God*, trans. Marcus Dods, Book XIV, 13, 14, pp. 460-462. Copyright, 1950, by Randon House, Inc. In the public domain. [Footnotes omitted, Eds.]

but being turned towards himself, his being became more contracted than it was when he clave to Him who supremely is. Accordingly, to exist in himself, that is, to be his own satisfaction after abandoning God, is not quite to become a nonentity, but to approximate to that. And therefore the holy Scriptures designate the proud by another name, "self-pleasers." For it is good to have the heart lifted up, yet not to one's self, for this is proud, but to the Lord, for this is obedient, and can be the act only of the humble. There is, therefore, something in humility which, strangely enough, exalts the heart, and something in pride which debases it. This seems, indeed, to be contradictory, that loftiness should debase and lowliness exalt. But pious humility enables us to submit to what is above us; and nothing is more exalted above us than God; and therefore humility, by making us subject to God, exalts us. But pride, being a defect of nature, by the very act of refusing subjection and revolting from Him who is supreme, falls to a low condition; and then comes to pass what is written: "Thou castedst them down when they lifted up themselves." For he does not say, "when they had been lifted up," as if first they were exalted, and then afterwards cast down; but "when they lifted up themselves" even then they were cast down—that is to say, the very lifting up was already a fall. And therefore it is that humility is specially recommended to the city of God as it sojourns in this world, and is specially exhibited in the city of God, and in the person of Christ its King; while the contrary vice of pride, according to the testimony of the sacred writings, specially rules his adversary the devil. And certainly this is the great difference which distinguishes the two cities of which we speak, the one being the society of the godly men, the other of the ungodly, each associated with the angels that adhere to their party, and the one guided and fashioned by love of self, the other by love of God.

The devil, then, would not have ensnared man in the open and manifest sin of doing what God had forbidden, had man not already begun to live for himself. It was this that made him listen with pleasure to the words, "Ye shall be as gods," which they would much more readily have accomplished by obediently adhering to their supreme and true end than by proudly living to themselves. For created gods are gods not by virtue of what is in themselves, but by a participation of the true God. By craving to be more, man becomes less; and by aspiring to be self-sufficing, he fell away from Him who truly suffices him. Accordingly, this wicked desire which prompts man to please himself as if he were himself light, and which thus turns him away from that light by which, had he followed it, he would himself have become light—this wicked desire, I say, already secretly existed in him, and the open sin was but its consequence. For that is true which is written, "Pride goeth before destruction, and before honour is humility;"

that is to say, secret ruin precedes open ruin, while the former is not counted ruin. For who counts exaltation ruin, though no sooner is the Highest forsaken than a fall is begun? But who does not recognise it as ruin, when there occurs an evident and indubitable transgression of the commandment? And consequently, God's prohibition had reference to such an act as, when committed, could not be defended on any pretence of doing what was righteous. And I make bold to say that it is useful for the proud to fall into an open and indisputable transgression, and so displease themselves, as already, by pleasing themselves, they had fallen. For Peter was in a healthier condition when he wept and was dissatisfied with himself, than when he boldly presumed and satisfied himself. And this is averred by the sacred Psalmist when he says, "Fill their faces with shame, that they may seek Thy name, O Lord;" that is that they who have pleased themselves in seeking their own glory may be pleased and satisfied with Thee in seeking Thy glory.

14. Of the Pride in the Sin, Which Was Worse Than the Sin Itself

But it is a worse and more damnable pride which casts about for the shelter of an excuse even in manifest sins, as these our first parents did, of whom the woman said, "The serpent beguiled me, and I did eat;" and the man said, "The woman whom Thou gavest to be with me, she gave me of the tree, and I did eat." Here there is no word of begging pardon, no word of entreaty for healing. For though they do not, like Cain, deny that they have perpetrated the deed, yet their pride seeks to refer its wickedness to another—the woman's pride to the serpent, the man's to the woman. But where there is a plain transgression of a divine commandment, this is rather to accuse than to excuse oneself. For the fact that the woman sinned on the serpent's persuasion, and the man at the woman's offer, did not make the transgression less, as if there were any one whom we ought rather to believe or yield to than God.

BENEDICT
SPINOZA

BENEDICT SPINOZA (1632-1677), seventeenth
century rationalistic philosopher, produced
one of the most thoroughgoing monistic systems in western thought. He was traditionally
of the Jewish faith but was excommunicated
because of his unorthodox views.

*The Ethics**

Appendix.—In the foregoing I have explained the nature and properties
of God. I have shown that he necessarily exists, that he is one: that he is,
and acts solely by the necessity of his own nature; that he is the free cause of
all things, and how he is so; that all things are in God, and so depend on
him, that without him they could neither exist nor be conceived; lastly, that
all things are predetermined by God, not through his free will or absolute fiat,
but from the very nature of God or infinite power. I have further, where occasion offered, taken care to remove the prejudices, which might impede the
comprehension of my demonstrations. Yet there still remain misconceptions
not a few, which might and may prove very grave hindrances to the understanding of the concatenation of things, as I have explained it above. I have
therefore thought it worth while to bring these misconceptions before the bar
of reason.

All such opinions spring from the notion commonly entertained, that all
things in nature act as men themselves act, namely, with an end in view. It
is accepted as certain, that God himself directs all things to a definite goal
(for it is said that God made all things for man, and man that he might
worship him). I will, therefore, consider this opinion, asking first, why it
obtains general credence, and why all men are naturally so prone to adopt it?
secondly, I will point out its falsity; and, lastly, I will show how it has given
rise to prejudices about good and bad, right and wrong, praise and blame,
order and confusion, beauty and ugliness, and the like. However, this is not
the place to deduce these misconceptions from the nature of the human
mind: it will be sufficient here, if I assume as a starting point, what ought
to be universally admitted, namely, that all men are born ignorant of the
causes of things, that all have the desire to seek for what is useful to them,

* From Benedict Spinoza, *The Chief Works of Benedict De Spinoza*, trans. R. H. M.
Elwes, pp. 74-81. Published, 1889, by George Bell & Sons. In the public domain.

and that they are conscious of such desire. Herefrom it follows, first, that men think themselves free in asmuch as they are conscious of their volitions and desires, and never even dream, in their ignorance, of the causes which have disposed them so to wish and desire. Secondly, that men do all things for an end, namely, for that which is useful to them, and which they seek. Thus it comes to pass that they only look for a knowledge of the final causes of events, and when these are learned, they are content, as having no cause for further doubt. If they cannot learn such causes from external sources, they are compelled to turn to considering themselves, and reflecting what end would have induced them personally to bring about the given event, and thus they necessarily judge other natures by their own. Further, as they find in themselves and outside themselves many means which assist them not a little in their search for what is useful, for instance, eyes for seeing, teeth for chewing, herbs and animals for yielding food, the sun for giving light, the sea for breeding fish, &c., they come to look on the whole of nature as a means for obtaining such conveniences. Now as they are aware, that they found these conveniences and did not make them, they think they have cause for believing, that some other being has made them for their use. As they look upon things as means, they cannot believe them to be self-created; but, judging from the means which they are accustomed to prepare for themselves, they are bound to believe in some ruler or rulers of the universe endowed with human freedom, who have arranged and adapted everything for human use. They are bound to estimate the nature of such rulers (having no information on the subject) in accordance with their own nature, and therefore they assert that the gods ordained everything for the use of man, in order to bind man to themselves and obtain from him the highest honour. Hence also it follows, that everyone thought out for himself, according to his abilities, a different way of worshipping God, so that God might love him more than his fellows, and direct the whole course of nature for the satisfaction of his blind cupidity and insatiable avarice. Thus the prejudice developed into superstition, and took deep root in the human mind; and for this reason everyone strove most zealously to understand and explain the final causes of things; but in their endeavour to show that nature does nothing in vain, i.e., nothing which is useless to man, they only seem to have demonstrated that nature, the gods, and men are all mad together. Consider, I pray you, the result: among the many helps of nature they were bound to find some hindrances, such as storms, earthquakes, diseases, &c.: so they declared that such things happen, because the gods are angry at some wrong done them by men, or at some fault committed in their worship. Experience day by day protested and showed by infinite examples, that good and evil fortunes fall to the lot of pious and impious alike; still they would not abandon their inveterate prejudice, for it was more easy for them to class such contradictions among other unknown things of whose use they were ignorant, and thus to retain their actual and innate condition of ignorance, than to destroy the whole fabric of their reasoning and start afresh. They therefore laid down as an axiom, that God's judgments far transcend human understanding. Such a doctrine might well have sufficed to conceal the truth from the human race for all eternity, if mathematics had not furnished another standard of verity in considering solely the essence and properties of figures without regard to their final causes. There are other reasons (which I need not mention here) besides mathematics, which might have caused men's minds to be directed to these general prejudices, and have led them to the knowledge of the truth.

I have now sufficiently explained my first point. There is no need to show at length, that nature has no particular goal in view, and that final causes are mere human figments. This, I think, is already evident enough, both from the causes and the foundations on which I have shown such prejudice to be based, and also from Prop. xvi., and the Corollary of Prop. xxxii., and, in fact, all those propositions in which I have shown, that everything in nature proceeds from a sort of necessity, and with the utmost perfection. However, I will add a few remarks, in order to overthrow this doctrine of a final cause utterly. That which is really a cause it considers as an effect, and *vice versâ*: it makes that which is by nature first to be last, and that which is highest and most perfect to be most imperfect. Passing over the questions of cause and priority as self-evident, it is plain from Props. xxi., xxii., xxiii. that that effect is most perfect which is produced immediately by God; the effect which requires for its production several intermediate causes is, in that respect, more imperfect. But if those things which were made immediately by God were made to enable him to attain his end, then the things which come after, for the sake of which the first were made, are necessarily the most excellent of all.

Further, this doctrine does away with the perfection of God: for, if God acts for an object, he necessarily desires something which he lacks. Certainly, theologians and metaphysicians draw a distinction between the object of want and the object of assimilation; still they confess that God made all things for the sake of himself, not for the sake of creation. They are unable to point to anything prior to creation, except God himself, as an object for which God should act, and are therefore driven to admit (as they clearly must), that God lacked those things for whose attainment he created means, and further that he desired them.

We must not omit to notice that the followers of this doctrine, anxious to display their talent in assigning final causes, have imported a new method of argument in proof of their theory—namely, a reduction, not to the impossible, but to ignorance; thus showing that they have no other method of exhibiting their doctrine. For example, if a stone falls from a roof on to someone's head, and kills him, they will demonstrate by their new method, that the stone fell in order to kill the man; for, if it had not by God's will fallen with that object, how could so many circumstances (and there are often many concurrent circumstances) have all happened together by chance? Perhaps you will answer that the event is due to the facts that the wind was blowing, and the man was walking that way. "But why," they will insist, "was the wind blowing, and why was the man at that very time walking that way?" If you again answer, that the wind had then sprung up because the sea had begun to be agitated the day before, the weather being previously calm, and that the man had been invited by a friend, they will again insist: "But why was the sea agitated, and why was the man invited at that time?" So they will pursue their questions from cause to cause, till at last you take refuge in the will of God—in other words, the sanctuary of ignorance. So, again, when they survey the frame of the human body, they are amazed; and being ignorant of the causes of so great a work of art, conclude that it has been fashioned, not mechanically, but by divine and supernatural skill, and has been so put together that one part shall not hurt another.

Hence anyone who seeks for the true causes of miracles, and strives to understand natural phenomena as an intelligent being, and not to gaze at them like a fool, is set down and denounced as an impious heretic by those, whom the masses adore as the interpreters of nature and the gods. Such persons know that, with the removal of ignorance, the wonder which forms their only available means for proving and preserving their authority would vanish also. But I now quit this subject, and pass on to my third point.

After men persuaded themselves, that everything which is created is created for their sake, they were bound to consider as the chief quality in everything that which is most useful to themselves, and to account those things the best of all which have the most beneficial effect on mankind. Further, they were bound to form abstract notions for the explanation of the nature of things, such as *goodness, badness, order, confusion, warmth, cold, beauty, deformity,* and so on; and from the belief that they are free agents arose the further notions *praise* and *blame, sin* and *merit.*

I will speak of these latter hereafter, when I treat of human nature; the former I will briefly explain here.

Everything which conduces to health and the worship of God they have called *good,* everything which hinders these objects they have styled *bad;* and inasmuch as those who do not understand the nature of things do not verify phenomena in any way, but merely imagine them after a fashion, and mistake their imagination for understanding, such persons firmly believe that there is an *order* in things, being really ignorant both of things and their own nature. When phenomena are of such a kind, that the impression they make on our senses requires little effort of imagination, and can consequently be easily remembered, we say that they are *well-ordered*; if the contrary, that they are *ill-ordered* or *confused*. Further, as things which are easily imagined are more pleasing to us, men prefer order to confusion—as though there were any order in nature, except in relation to our imagination—and say that God has created all things in order; thus, without knowing it, attributing imagination to God, unless, indeed, they would have it that God foresaw human imagination, and arranged everything, so that it should be most easily imagined. If this be their theory, they would not, perhaps, be daunted by the fact that we find an infinite number of phenomena, far surpassing our imagination, and very many others which confound its weakness. But enough has been said on this subject. The other abstract notions are nothing but modes of imagining, in which the imagination is differently affected, though they are considered by the ignorant as the chief attributes of things, inasmuch as they believe that everything was created for the sake of themselves; and, according as they are affected by it, style it good or bad, healthy or rotten and corrupt. For instance, if the motion which objects we see communicate to our nerves be conducive to health, the objects causing it are styled *beautiful*; if a contrary motion be excited, they are styled *ugly*.

Things which are perceived through our sense of smell are styled fragrant or fetid; if through our taste, sweet or bitter, full-flavoured or insipid; if through our touch, hard or soft, rough or smooth, &c.

Whatsoever affects our ears is said to give rise to noise, sound, or harmony. In this last case, there are men lunatic enough to believe, that even God himself takes pleasure in harmony; and philosophers are not lacking who have persuaded themselves, that the motion of the heavenly bodies gives rise to harmony—all of which instances sufficiently show that everyone judges of things according to the state of his brain, or rather mistakes for things the forms of his imagination. We need no longer wonder that there have arisen all the controversies we have witnessed, and finally scepticism: for, although human bodies in many respects agree, yet in very many others they differ; so that what seems good to one seems bad to another; what seems well ordered to one seems confused to another; what is pleasing to one displeases another, and so on. I need not further enumerate, because this is not the place to treat the subject at length, and also because the fact is sufficiently well known. It is commonly said: "So many men, so many minds; everyone is wise in his own way; brains differ as completely as palates." All of which proverbs show, that men judge of things according to their mental disposition, and rather imagine than understand: for, if they understood phenomena, they would, as mathematics attest, be convinced, if not attracted, by what I have urged.

We have now perceived, that all the explanations commonly given of nature are mere modes of imagining, and do not indicate the true nature of anything, but only the constitution of the imagination; and, although they have names, as though they were entities, existing externally to the imagination, I call them entities imaginary rather than real; and, therefore, all arguments against us drawn from such abstractions are easily rebutted.

Many argue in this way. If all things follow from a necessity of the absolutely perfect nature of God, why are there so many imperfections in nature? such, for instance, as things corrupt to the point of putridity, loathsome deformity, confusion, evil, sin, &c. But these reasoners are, as I have said, easily confuted, for the perfection of things is to be reckoned only from their own nature and power; things are not more or less perfect, according as they delight or offend human senses, or according as they are serviceable or repugnant to mankind. To those who ask why God did not so create all men, that they should be governed only by reason, I give no answer but this: because matter was not lacking to him for the creation of every degree of perfection from highest to lowest; or, more strictly, because the laws of his nature are so vast, as to suffice for the production of everything conceivable by an infinite intelligence, as I have shown in Prop. xvi.

Such are the misconceptions I have undertaken to note; if there are any more of the same sort, everyone may easily dissipate them for himself with the aid of a little reflection.

G. W. LEIBNITZ

GOTTFRIED W. LEIBNITZ (1646-1716), mathematician, versatile man of affairs and rationalistic philosopher, made important contributions to the development of calculus and
logic and was known for his philosophical
system of spiritualistic pluralism. *Monodology*
is his most important work.

The Theodicy*

Abridgment of the Argument Reduced to Syllogistic Form

Some intelligent persons have desired that this supplement should be made
[to the Theodicy], and I have the more readily yielded to their wishes as
in this way I have an opportunity to again remove certain difficulties and to
make some observations which were not sufficiently emphasized in the work
itself.

I. *Objection.* Whoever does not choose the best is lacking in power, or
in knowledge, or in goodness.

God did not choose the best in creating this world.

Therefore God has been lacking in power, or in knowledge, or in goodness.

Answer. I deny the minor, that is, the second premise of this syllogism:
and our opponent proves it by this

Prosyllogism. Whoever makes things in which there is evil, which could
have been made without any evil, or the making of which could have been
omitted, does not choose the best.

God has made a world in which there is evil; a world, I say, which could
have been made without any evil, or the making of which could have been
omitted altogether.

Therefore God has not chosen the best.

Answer. I grant the minor of this prosyllogism; for it must be confessed
that there is evil in the world which God has made, and that it was possible
to make a world without evil, or even not to create a world at all, for its
creation depended on the free will of God; but I deny the major, that is,
the first of the two premises of the prosyllogism, and I might content myself
with simply demanding its proof; but in order to make the matter clearer,

* From Gottfried W. Leibnitz, *The Philosophical Works of Leibnitz,* trans. George
M. Duncan, pp. 194-197, 202-204. Published, 1890, by Tuttle, Morehouse & Taylor. In
the public domain.

I have wished to justify this denial by showing that the best plan is not always that which seeks to avoid evil, since it may happen that *the evil be accompanied by a greater good*. For example, a general of the army will prefer a great victory with a slight wound to a condition without wound and without victory. We have proved this more fully in the large work by making it clear, by instances taken from mathematics and elsewhere, that an imperfection in the part may be required for a greater perfection in the whole. In this I have followed the opinion of St. Augustine, who has said a hundred times, that God permitted evil in order to bring about good, that is, a greater good; and that of Thomas Aquinas (in libr. II. sent. dist. 32, qu. I, art. 1), that the permitting of evil tends to the good of the universe. I have shown that the ancients called Adam's fall *felix culpa,* a happy sin, because it had been retrieved with immense advantage by the incarnation of the Son of God, who has given to the universe something nobler than anything that ever would have been among creatures except for this. And in order to a clear understanding, I have added, following many good authors, that it was in accordance with order and the general good that God gave to certain creatures the opportunity of exercising their liberty, even when he foresaw that they would turn to evil, but which he could so well rectify; because it was not right that, in order to hinder sin, God should always act in an extraordinary manner.

To overthrow this objection, therefore, it is sufficient to show that a world with evil might be better than a world without evil; but I have gone even farther in the work, and have even proved that this universe must be in reality better than every other possible universe.

II. *Objection.* If there is more evil than good in intelligent creatures, then there is more evil than good in the whole work of God.

Now, there is more evil than good in intelligent creatures.

Therefore there is more evil than good in the whole work of God.

Answer. I deny the major and the minor of this conditional syllogism. As to the major, I do not admit it at all, because this pretended deduction from a part to the whole, from intelligent creatures to all creatures, supposes tacitly and without proof that creatures destitute of reason cannot enter into comparison nor into account with those which possess it. But why may it not be that the surplus of good in the non-intelligent creatures which fill the world, compensates for, and even incomparably surpasses, the surplus of evil in the rational creatures? It is true that the value of the latter is greater; but, in compensation, the other are beyond comparison the more numerous, and it may be that the proportion of number and of quantity surpasses that of value and of quality.

As to the minor, that is no more to be admitted; that is, it is not at all to be admitted that there is more evil than good in the intelligent creatures. There is no need even of granting that there is more evil than good in the human race, because it is possible, and in fact very probable, that the glory and the perfection of the blessed are incomparably greater than the misery and the imperfection of the damned, and that here the excellence of the total good in the smaller number exceeds the total evil in the greater number. The blessed approach the Divinity, by means of the Divine Mediator, as near as may suit these creatures, and make such progress in good as is impossible for the damned to make in evil, approach as nearly as they may to the nature of demons. God is infinite, and the devil is limited; good may and does advance *ad infinitum*, while evil has its bounds. It is therefore possible, and is credible, that in the comparison of the blessed and the damned, the contrary of that which I have said might happen in the comparison of intelligent and non-intelligent creatures, takes place; namely, it is possible that in the comparison of the happy and the unhappy, the proportion of degree exceeds that of number, and that in the comparison of intelligent and non-intelligent creatures, the proportion of number is greater than that of value. I have the right to suppose that a thing is possible so long as its impossibility is not proved; and indeed that which I have here advanced is more than a supposition.

But in the second place, if I should admit that there is more evil than good in the human race, I have still good grounds for not admitting that there is more evil than good in all intelligent creatures. For there is an inconceivable number of genii, and perhaps of other rational creatures. And an opponent could not prove that in all the City of God, composed as well of genii as of rational animals without number and of an infinity of kinds, evil exceeds good. And although in order to answer an objection, there is no need of proving that a thing is, when its mere possibility suffices; yet, in this work, I have not omitted to show that it is a consequence of the supreme perfection of the Sovereign of the universe, that the kingdom of God be the most perfect of all possible states or governments, and that consequently the little evil there is, is required for the consummation of the immense good which is there found.

. . . .

VIII. *Objection.* He who cannot fail to choose the best, is not free.
God cannot fail to choose the best.
Hence, God is not free.

Answer. I deny the major of this argument; it is rather true liberty and the most perfect, to be able to use one's free will for the best, and to always exercise this power without ever being turned from it either by external force or by internal passions, the first of which causes slavery of the body, the second, slavery of the soul. There is nothing less servile than to be always led toward the good, and always by one's own inclination, without any constraint and without any displeasure. And to object therefore that God had need of external things, is only a sophism. He created them freely; but having proposed to himself an end, which is to exercise his goodness, wisdom determined him to choose those means best fitted to attain this end. To call this a *need* is to take that term in an unusual sense which frees it from all imperfection, just as when we speak of the wrath of God.

Seneca has somewhere said that God commanded but once but that he obeys always, because he obeys the laws which he willed to prescribe to himself; *semel jussit semper paret.* But he had better have said that God always commands and that he is always obeyed; for in willing, he always follows the inclination of his own nature, and all other things always follow his will. And as this will is always the same, it cannot be said that he obeys only that will which he formerly had. Nevertheless, although his will is always infallible and always tends toward the best, the evil, or the lesser good, which he rejects, does not cease to be possible in itself; otherwise the necessity of the good would be geometrical (so to speak), or metaphysical and altogether absolute; the contingency of things would be destroyed, and there would be no choice. But this sort of necessity, which does not destroy the possibility of the contrary, has this name only by analogy; it becomes effective, not by the pure essence of things, but by that which is outside of them, above them,—namely, by the will of God. This necessity is called moral, because, to the sage, *necessity* and *what ought to be* are equivalent things; and when it always has its effect, as it really has in the perfect sage, that is, in God, it may be said that it is a happy necessity. The nearer creatures approach to it, the nearer they approach to perfect happiness. Also this kind of necessity is not that which we try to avoid and which destroys morality, rewards and praise. For that which it brings, does not happen whatever we may do or will, but because we will it well. And a will to which it is natural to choose well, merits praise so much the more; also it carries its reward with it, which is sovereign happiness. And as this constitution of the divine nature gives entire satisfaction to him who possesses it, it is also the best and the most desirable for the creatures who are all dependent on God. If the will of God did not have for a rule the principle of the best, it would either tend toward evil, which would be the worst; or it would be in some way indifferent to good and to evil, and would be guided by chance: but a will which would allow itself always to act by chance, would not be worth more for the government of the universe than the fortuitous concourse of atoms, without there being any divinity therein. And even if God should abandon himself to chance only in some cases and in a certain way (as he would do, if he did not always work towards the best and if he were capable of preferring a lesser good to a greater, that is, an evil to a good, since that which prevents a greater good is an evil), he would be imperfect, as well as the object of his choice; he would not merit entire confidence; he would act without reason in such a case, and the government of the universe would be like certain games, equally divided between reason and chance. All this proves that this objection which is made against the choice of the best, perverts the notions of the free and of the necessary, and represents to us even the best as evil; to do which is either malicious or ridiculous.

JOSIAH ROYCE

JOSIAH ROYCE (1855-1916), professor of philosophy at Harvard College, was the best known American advocate of absolute idealism. He developed and defended his philosophy against the views of his colleague, William James.

The Problem of Job*

There remains a fourth doctrine as to our problem. This doctrine is in essence the thesis of philosophical idealism, a thesis which I myself feel bound to maintain, and, so far as space here permits, to explain. The theoretical basis of this view, the philosophical reasons for the notion of the divine nature which it implies, I cannot here explain. That is another argument. But I desire to indicate how the view in question deals with Job's problem.

This view first frankly admits that Job's problem is, upon Job's presuppositions, simply and absolutely insoluble. Grant Job's own presupposition that God is a being other than this world, that he is its external creator and ruler, and then all solutions fail. God is then either cruel or helpless, as regards all real finite ill of the sort that Job endures. Job, moreover, is right in demanding a reasonable answer to his question. The only possible answer is, however, one that undertakes to develop what I hold to be the

* From Josiah Royce, *Studies In Good and Evil*, pp. 13-28. Copyright, 1898, by D. Appleton & Company. In the public domain.

immortal soul of the doctrine of the divine atonement. The answer to Job is: God is not in ultimate essence another being than yourself. He is the Absolute Being. You truly are one with God, part of his life. He is the very soul of your soul. And so, here is the first truth: When you suffer, *your sufferings are God's sufferings*, not his external work, not his external penalty, not the fruit of his neglect, but identically his own personal woe. In you God himself suffers, precisely as you do, and has all your concern in overcoming this grief.

The true question then is: Why does God thus suffer? The sole possible, necessary, and sufficient answer is, Because without suffering, without ill, without woe, evil, tragedy, God's life could not be perfected. This grief is not a physical means to an external end. It is a logically necessary and eternal constituent of the divine life. It is logically necessary that the Captain of your salvation should be perfect through suffering. No outer nature compels him. He chooses this because he chooses his own perfect selfhood. He is perfect. His world is the best possible world. Yet all its finite regions know not only of joy but of defeat and sorrow, for thus alone, in the completeness of his eternity, can God in his wholeness be triumphantly perfect.

This, I say, is my thesis. In the absolute oneness of God with the sufferer, in the concept of the suffering and therefore triumphant God, lies the logical solution of the problem of evil. The doctrine of philosophical idealism is, as regards its purely theoretical aspects, a fairly familiar metaphysical theory at the present time. One may, then, presuppose here as known the fact that, for reasons which I have not now to expound, the idealist maintains that there is in the universe but one perfectly real being, namely, the Absolute, that the Absolute is self-conscious, and that his world is essentially in its wholeness the fulfillment *in actu* of an all-perfect ideal. We ourselves exist as fragments of the absolute life, or better, as partial functions in the unity of the absolute and conscious process of the world. On the other hand, our existence and our individuality are not illusory, but are what they are in an organic unity with the whole life of the Absolute Being. This doctrine once presupposed, our present task is to inquire what case idealism can make for the thesis just indicated as its answer to Job's problem.

In endeavoring to grapple with the theoretical problem of the place of evil in a world that, on the whole, is to be conceived, not only as good, but as perfect, there is happily one essentially decisive consideration concerning good and evil which falls directly within the scope of our own human experience, and which concerns matters at once familiar and momentous as well as too much neglected in philosophy. When we use such words as good, evil, perfect, we easily deceive ourselves by the merely abstract meanings which we associate with each of the terms taken apart from the other. We forget the experiences from which the words have been abstracted. To these experiences we must return whenever we want really to comprehend the words. If we take the mere words, in their abstraction, it is easy to say, for instance, that if life has any evil in it at all, it must needs not be so perfect as life would be were there no evil in it whatever. Just so, speaking abstractly, it is easy to say that, in estimating life, one has to set the good over against the evil, and to compare their respective sums. It is easy to declare that, since we hate evil, wherever and just so far as we recognize it, our sole human interest in the world must be furthered by the removal of evil from the world. And thus viewing the case, one readily comes to say that if God views as not only good but perfect a world in which we find so much evil, the divine point of view must be very foreign to ours, so that Job's rebellious pessimism seems well in order, and Prometheus appears to defy the world-ruler in a genuinely humane spirit. Shocked, however, by the apparent impiety of this result, some teachers, considering divine matters, still misled by the same one-sided use of words, have opposed one falsely abstract view by another, and have strangely asserted that the solution must be in proclaiming that since God's world, the real world, in order to be perfect, must be without evil, what we men call evil must be a mere illusion—a mirage of the human point of view— a dark vision which God, who sees all truth, sees not at all. To God, so this view asserts, the eternal world in its wholeness is not only perfect, but has merely the perfection of an utterly transparent crystal, unstained by any color of ill. Only mortal error imagines that there is any evil. There is no evil but only good in the real world, and that is why God finds the world perfect, whatever mortals dream.

Now neither of these abstract views is my view. I consider them both the result of a thoughtless trust in abstract words. I regard evil as a distinctly real fact, a fact just as real as the most helpless and hopeless sufferer finds it to be when he is in pain. Furthermore, I hold that God's point of view is not foreign to ours. I hold that God willingly, freely, and consciously suffers in us when we suffer, and that our grief is his. And despite all this I maintain that the world from God's point of view fulfills the divine ideal and is perfect. And I hold that when we abandon the one-sided abstract ideas which the words good, evil, and perfect suggest, and when we go back to the concrete experiences upon which these very words are founded, we can see, even within the limits of our own experience, facts which make these very paradoxes perfectly intelligible, and even commonplace.

As for that essentially pernicious view, nowadays somewhat current amongst a certain class of gentle but inconsequent people—the view that all evil is *merely* an illusion and that there is no such thing in God's world—

I can say of it only in passing that it is often advanced as an idealistic view, but that, in my opinion, it is false idealism. Good idealism it is to regard all finite experience as an appearance, a hint, often a very poor hint, of deeper truth. Good idealism it is to admit that man can err about truth that lies beyond his finite range of experience. And very good idealism it is to assert that all truth, and so all finite experience, exists in and for the mind of God, and nowhere outside of or apart from God. But it is not good idealism to assert that any facts which fall within the range of finite experience are, even while they are experienced, mere illusions. God's truth is inclusive, not exclusive. What you experience God experiences. The difference lies only in this, that God sees in unity what you see in fragments. For the rest, if one said, "The source and seat of evil is only the error of mortal mind," one would but have changed the name of one's problem. If the evil were but the error, the error would still be the evil, and altering the name would not have diminished the horror of the evil of this finite world.

V.

But I hasten from the false idealism to the true; from the abstractions to the enlightening insights of our life. As a fact, idealism does not say: The finite world is, as such, a mere illusion. A sound idealism says, whatever we experience is a fragment, and as far as it goes, a genuine fragment of the truth of the divine mind. With this principle before us, let us consider directly our own experiences of good and of evil, to see whether they are as abstractly opposed to each other as the mere words often suggest. We must begin with the elementary and even trivial facts. We shall soon come to something deeper.

By good, as we mortals experience it, we mean something that, when it comes or is expected, we actively welcome, try to attain or keep, and regard with content. By evil in general, as it is in our experience, we mean whatever we find in any sense repugnant and intolerable. I use the words repugnant and intolerable because I wish to indicate that words for evil frequently, like the words for good, directly refer to our actions as such. Commonly and rightly, when we speak of evil, we make reference to acts of resistance, of struggle, of shrinking, of flight, of removal of ourselves from a source of mischief—acts which not only follow upon the experience of evil, but which serve to define in a useful fashion what we mean by evil. The opposing acts of pursuit and of welcome define what we mean by good. By the evil which we experience we mean precisely whatever we regard as something to be gotten rid of, shrunken from, put out of sight, of hearing, or of memory, eschewed, expelled, assailed, or otherwise directly or indirectly resisted. By good we mean whatever we regard as something to be welcomed, pursued, won, grasped, held, persisted in, preserved. And we show all this in our acts in presence of any grade of good or evil, sensuous, aesthetic, ideal, moral. To shun, to flee, to resist, to destroy, these are our primary attitudes towards ill; the opposing acts are our primary attitudes towards the good; and whether you regard us as animals or as moralists, whether it is a sweet taste, a poem, a virtue, or God that we look to as good, and whether it is a burn or a temptation, an outward physical foe, or a stealthy, inward, ideal enemy, that we regard as evil. In all our organs of voluntary movement, in all our deeds, in a turn of the eye, in a sigh, a groan, in a hostile gesture, in an act of silent contempt, we can show in endlessly varied ways the same general attitude of repugnance.

But man is a very complex creature. He has many organs. He performs many acts at once, and he experiences his performance of these acts in one highly complex life of consciousness. As the next feature of his life we all observe that he can at the same time shun one object and grasp at another. In this way he can have at once present to him a consciousness of good and a consciousness of ill. But so far in our account these sorts of experience appear merely as facts side by side. Man loves, and he *also* hates, loves this, and hates that, assumes an attitude of repugnance towards one object, while he welcomes another. So far the usual theory follows man's life, and calls it an experience of good and ill as mingled but exclusively and abstractly opposed facts. For such a view the final question as to the worth of a man's life is merely the question whether there are more intense acts of satisfaction and of welcome than of repugnance and disdain in his conscious life.

But this is by no means an adequate notion of the complexity of man's life, even as an animal. If every conscious act of hindrance, of thwarting, of repugnance, means just in so far an awareness of some evil, it is noteworthy that men can have and can show just such tendencies, not only towards external experiences, but towards their own acts. That is, men can be seen trying to thwart and to hinder even their own acts themselves, at the very moment when they note the occurrence of these acts. One can consciously have an impulse to do something, and at that very moment a conscious disposition to hinder or to thwart as an evil that very impulse. If, on the other hand, every conscious act of attainment, of pursuit, of reinforcement, involves the awareness of some good, it is equally obvious that one can show by one's acts a disposition to reinforce or to emphasize or to increase, not only the externally present gifts of fortune, but also one's own deeds, in so far as one observes them. And in our complex lives it is common enough to find ourselves actually trying to reinforce and to insist upon a situation which involves for us, even at the moment of its occurrence, a great deal of repugnance. In such cases we often act as if we felt the very thwarting of our own primary impulses to be so much of a conscious good that we persist in pursuing and reinforcing the very situation in which this thwarting and hindering of our own impulses is sure to arise.

In brief, as phenomena of this kind show, man is a being who can to a very great extent find a sort of secondary satisfaction in the very act of thwarting his own desires, and thus of assuring for the time his own dissatisfactions. On the other hand, man can to an indefinite degree find himself dissatisfied with his satisfactions and disposed to thwart, not merely his external enemies, but his own inmost impulses themselves. But I now affirm that in all such cases you cannot simply say that man is preferring the less of two evils, or the greater of two goods, as if the good and the evil stood merely side by side in his experience. On the contrary, in such cases, man is not merely setting his acts or his estimates of good and evil side by side and taking the sum of each; but he is making his own relatively primary acts, impulses, desires, the objects of all sorts of secondary impulses, desires, and reflective observations. His whole inner state is one of tension; and he is either making a secondary experience of evil out of his estimate of a primary experience of good, as is the case when he at once finds himself disposed to pursue a given good and to thwart this pursuit as being an evil pursuit; or else he is making a secondary experience of good out of his primary experience of evil, as when he is primarily dissatisfied with his situation, but yet secondarily regards this very dissatisfaction as itself a desirable state. In this way man comes not only to love some things and also to hate other things, he comes to love his own hates and to hate his own loves in an endlessly complex hierarchy of superposed interests in his own interests.

Now it is easy to say that such states of inner tension, where our conscious lives are full of a warfare of the self with itself, are contradictory or absurd states. But it is easy to say this only when you dwell on the words and fail to observe the facts of experience. As a fact, not only our lowest but our highest states of activity are the ones which are fullest of this crossing, conflict, and complex interrelation of loves and hates, of attractions and repugnances. As a merely physiological fact, we begin no muscular act without at the same time initiating acts which involve the innervation of opposing sets of muscles, and these opposing sets of muscles hinder each other's freedom. Every sort of control of movement means the conflicting play of opposed muscular impulses. We do nothing simple, and we will no complex act without willing what involves a certain measure of opposition between the impulses or partial acts which go to make up the whole act.

If one passes from single acts to long series of acts, one finds only the more obviously this interweaving of repugnance and of acceptance, of pursuit and of flight, upon which every complex type of conduct depends.

One could easily at this point spend time by dwelling upon numerous and relatively trivial instances of this interweaving of conflicting motives as it appears in all our life. I prefer to pass such instances over with a mere mention. There is, for instance, the whole marvelous consciousness of play, in its benign and in its evil forms. In any game that fascinates, one loves victory and shuns defeat, and yet as a loyal supporter of the game scorns anything that makes victory certain in advance; thus as a lover of fair play preferring to risk the defeat that he all the while shuns, and partly thwarting the very love of victory that from moment to moment fires his hopes. There are, again, the numerous cases in which we prefer to go to places where we are sure to be in a considerable measure dissatisfied; to engage, for instance, in social functions that absorbingly fascinate us despite or even in view of the very fact that, as long as they continue, they keep us in a state of tension which makes us, amongst other things, long to have the whole occasion over. Taking a wider view, one may observe that the greater part of the freest products of the activity of civilization, in cere- monies, in formalities, in the long social drama of flight, of pursuit, of re- partee, of contest and of courtesy, involve an elaborate and systematic delaying and hindering of elemental human desires, which we continually outwit, postpone and thwart, even while we nourish them. When students of human nature assert that hunger and love rule the social world, they recognize that the elemental in human nature is trained by civilization into the service of the highest demands of the Spirit. But such students have to recognize that the elemental rules the higher world only in so far as the elemental is not only cultivated, but endlessly thwarted, delayed, out- witted, like a constitutional monarch, who is said to be a sovereign, but who, while he rules, must not govern.

But I pass from such instances, which in all their universality are still, I admit, philosophically speaking, trivial, because they depend upon the accidents of human nature. I pass from these instances to point out what must be the law, not only of human nature, but of every broader form of life as well. I maintain that this organization of life by virtue of the tension of manifold impulses and interests is not a mere accident of our imperfect human nature, but must be a type of the organization of every rational life. There are good and bad states of tension, there are conflicts that can only be justified when resolved into some higher form of harmony. But I insist that, in general, the only harmony that can exist in the realm of the spirit is the harmony that we possess when we thwart the present but more elemental impulse for the sake of the higher unity of experience; as when we rejoice in the endurance of the tragedies of life, because they show us the depth of life, or when we know that it is better to have loved and lost than never to have loved at all, or when we possess a virtue in the moment of victory over the tempter. And the reason why this is true lies in the fact that the more one's experience fulfills ideals, the more that experience presents to one, not of ignorance, but of triumphantly wealthy acquaintance with the facts of manifold, varied and tragic life, full of tension and thereby of unity. Now this is an universal and not merely human law. It is not those innocent of evil who are fullest of the life of God, but those who in their own case have experienced the triumph over evil. It is not those naturally ignorant of fear, or those who, like Siegfried, have never shivered, who possess the genuine experience of courage; but the brave are those who have fears, but control their fears. Such know the genuine virtues of the hero. Were it otherwise, only the stupid could be perfect heroes.

To be sure it is quite false to say, as the foolish do, that the object of life is merely that we may "know life" as an irrational chaos of experiences of good and of evil. But knowing the good in life is a matter which concerns the form, rather than the mere content of life. One who knows life wisely knows indeed much of the content of life; but he knows the good of life in so far as, in the unity of his experience, he finds the evil of his experience not abolished, but subordinated, and in so far relatively thwarted by a control which annuls its triumph even while experiencing its existence.

VI.

Generalizing the lesson of experience we may then say: It is logically impossible that a complete knower of truth should fail to know, to experience, to have present to his insight, the fact of actually existing evil. On the other hand, it is equally impossible for one to know a higher good than comes from the subordination of evil to good in a total experience. When one first loving, in an elemental way, whatever you please, himself hinders, delays, thwarts his elemental interest in the interest of some larger whole of experience, he not only knows more fact, but he possesses a higher good than would or could be present to one who was aware neither of the elemental impulse, nor of the thwarting of it in the tension of a richer life. The knowing of the good, in the higher sense, depends upon contemplating the overcoming and subordination of a less significant impulse, which survives even in order that it should be subordinated. Now this law, this form of the knowledge of the good, applies as well to the existence of moral as to that of sensuous ill. If moral evil were simply destroyed and wiped away from the external world, the knowledge of moral goodness would also be destroyed. For the love of moral good is the thwarting of lower loves for the sake of the higher organization. What is needed, then, for the definition of the divine knowledge of a world that in its wholeness is perfect, is not a divine knowledge that shall ignore, wipe out and utterly make naught the existence of any ill, whether physical or moral, but a divine knowledge to which shall be present that love of the world as a whole which is fulfilled in the endurance of physical ill, in the subordination of moral ill, in the thwarting of impulses which survive even when subordinated, in the acceptance of repugnances which are still eternal, in the triumph over an enemy that endures even through its eternal defeat, and in the discovery that the endless tension of the finite world is included in the contemplative consciousness of the repose and harmony of eternity. To view God's nature thus is to view his nature as the whole idealistic theory views him, not as the Infinite One beyond the finite imperfections, but as the being whose unity determines the very constitution, the lack, the tension, and relative disharmony of the finite world.

The existence of evil, then, is not only consistent with the perfection of the universe, but is necessary for the very existence of that perfection. This is what we see when we no longer permit ourselves to be deceived by the abstract meanings of the words good and evil into thinking that these two opponents exist merely as mutually exclusive facts side by side in experience, but when we go back to the facts of life and perceive that all relatively higher good, in the trivial as in the more truly spiritual realm, is known only in so far as, from some higher reflective point of view, we accept as good the thwarting of an existent interest that is even thereby declared to be a relative ill, and love a tension of various impulses which even thereby involves, as the object of our love, the existence of what gives us aversion or grief. Now if the love of God is more inclusive than the love of man, even as the divine world of experience is richer than the human world, we can simply set no human limit to the intensity of conflict, to the tragedies of existence, to the pangs of finitude, to the degree of moral ill, which in the end is included in the life that God not only loves, but finds the fulfillment of the perfect ideal. If peace means satisfaction, acceptance of the whole of an experience as good, and if even we, in our weakness, can frequently find rest in the very presence of conflict and of tension, in the very endurance of ill in a good cause, in the hero's triumph over temptation, or in the mourner's tearless refusal to accept the lower comforts of forgetfulness, or to wish that the lost one's preciousness had been less painfully revealed by death—well, if even we know our little share of this harmony in the midst of the wrecks and disorders of life, what limit shall we set to the divine power to face this world of his own sorrows, and to find peace in the victory over all its ills.

But in this last expression I have pronounced the word that serves to link this theory as to the place of evil in a good world with the practical problem of every sufferer. Job's rebellion came from the thought that God, as a sovereign, is far off, and that, for his pleasure, his creature suffers. Our own theory comes to the mourner with the assurance: "Your suffering, just as it is in you, is God's suffering. No chasm divides you from God. He is not remote from you even in his eternity. He is here. His eternity means merely the completeness of his experience. But that completeness is inclusive. Your sorrow is one of the included facts." I do not say: "God sympathizes with you from without, would spare you if he could, pities you with helpless external pity merely as a father pities his children." I say: "God here sorrows, not *with* but *in* your sorrow. Your grief is identically his grief, and what you know as your loss, God knows as his loss, just in and through the very moment when you grieve."

But hereupon the sufferer perchance responds: "If this is God's loss, could he not have prevented it? To him are present in unity all the worlds; and yet he must lack just this for which I grieve." I respond: "He suffers here that he may triumph. For the triumph of the wise is no easy thing. Their lives are not light, but sorrowful. Yet they rejoice in their sorrow, not, to be sure, because it is mere experience, but because, for them, it becomes part of a strenuous whole of life. They wander and find their home even in wandering. They long, and attain through their very love of longing. Peace they find in triumphant warfare. Contentment they have most of all in endurance. Sovereignty they win in endless service. The eternal world contains Gethsemane."

Yet the mourner may still insist: "If my sorrow is God's, his triumph is not mine. Mine is the woe. His is the peace." But my theory is a philosophy. It proposes to be coherent. I must persist: "It is your fault that you are thus sundered from God's triumph. His experience in its wholeness cannot now be yours, for you just as you—this individual—are now but a fragment, and see his truth as through a glass darkly. But if you see his truth at all, through even the dimmest light of a glimmering reason, remember, that truth is in fact your own truth, your own fulfillment, the whole from which your life cannot be divorced, the reality that you mean even when you most doubt, the desire of your heart even when you are most blind, the perfection that you unconsciously strove for even when you were an infant, the complete Self apart from whom you mean nothing, the very life that gives your life the only value which it can have. In thought, if not in the fulfillment of thought, in aim if not in attainment of aim, in aspiration if not in the presence of the revealed fact, you can view God's triumph and peace as your triumph and peace. Your defeat will be no less real than it is, nor will you falsely call your evil a mere illusion. But you will see not only the grief but the truth, your truth, your rescue, your triumph."

Well, to what ill-fortune does not just such reasoning apply? I insist: our conclusion is essentially universal. It discounts any evil that experience may contain. All the horrors of the natural order, all the concealments of the divine plan by our natural ignorance, find their general relation to the unity of the divine experience indicated in advance by this account of the problem of evil.

"Yes," one may continue, "ill-fortune you have discovered, but how about moral evil? What if the sinner now triumphantly retorts: 'Aha! So my will is God's will. All then is well with me.'" I reply: What I have said disposes of moral ill precisely as definitely as of physical ill. What the evil will is to the good man, whose goodness depends upon its existence, but also upon the thwarting and the condemnation of its aim, just such is the sinner's will to the divine plan. God's will, we say to the sinner, is your will. Yes, but it is your will thwarted, scorned, overcome, defeated. In the eternal world you are seen, possessed, present, but your damnation is also seen including and thwarting you. Your apparent victory in this world stands simply for the vigor of your impulses. God wills you not to triumph. And that is the use of you in the world—the use of evil generally—to be hated but endured, to be triumphed over through the very fact of your presence, to be willed down even in the very life of which you are a part.

But to the serious moral agent we say: What you mean when you say that evil in this temporal world ought not to exist, and ought to be suppressed, is simply what God means by seeing that evil ought to be and is endlessly thwarted, endured, but subordinated. In the natural world you are the minister of God's triumph. Your deed is his. You can never clean the world of evil; but you can subordinate evil. The justification of the presence in the world of the morally evil becomes apparent to us mortals only in so far as this evil is overcome and condemned. It exists only that it may be cast down. Courage, then, for God works in you. In the order of time you embody in outer acts what is for him the truth of his eternity.

WILLIAM
TEMPLE

WILLIAM TEMPLE (1881-1944), the Archbishop of Canterbury, was the best known
Anglican theologian of the first half of the
twentieth century. He was also a prominent
leader in the ecumenical movement in the
Christian Churches and was keenly interested
in the application of Christian doctrine to
contemporary social problems.

Finitude and Evil*

We have two questions to consider, which may or may not turn out to
be identical—the cause of evil, and the justification of its occurrence. First
we must enquire how evil finds a place in the world-process as we have conceived it, and secondly, whether, when its origin is so understood, its occurrence is compatible with the belief that the world is created and ruled by a
God who is both infinite Goodness and infinite Power.

In the first stages of its existence the world exhibits neither life nor consciousness. At a certain point of its development life appears in rudimentary
vegetable form. This life is void of consciousness. But again at a certain point
in its development, life exhibits consciousness. Consciousness supervenes
upon an organic existence which has already established a habitual routine.
That routine includes the process in which one organism becomes food for
another. If there is no consciousness, that cannot be called evil. If the organism that becomes the food of another is conscious, there is perhaps already
evil in that combination of facts. But this seems less than certain; for the
merely conscious organism lives in the present, and an extremely constricted
present, so that consciousness perishes almost if not quite simultaneously
with the occurrence of the event which in combination with continued consciousness would be evil. At this level then there is perhaps a very little evil,
perhaps none at all. But once more at a certain stage in development consciousness becomes self-consciousness. The organism is now not only conscious of its environment as offering occasions for satisfying appetite, or for
flight from danger. It is now conscious also of itself as distinct from its

* From William Temple, *Nature, Man and God*, pp. 359-375. Copyright, 1935, Macmillan & Co., Ltd. Used by permission of Mrs. Temple, St. Martin's Press, Inc., and
Macmillan & Co., Ltd. [Footnotes omitted, Eds.]

environment, and of possible states of itself as distinct from its actual state. It is, in Green's phrase, a self-distinguishing and self-seeking consciousness. Its time-span is increased. The "present" is now for it a longer stretch of clock-time, and it has memory of a past and anticipation of a future. Events now have value for it, and it is become a centre of value-judgements.

As we look back we see that at any stage which we choose to isolate, prior to the human, there was a possible balance or harmony comprising the best possible good at that stage. It was in principle possible that each self-conscious organism should pursue its own interest in such ways that the good of life should on the whole at least outweigh the evil. There seems to be no doubt that life in the jungle is, on balance, good. The larger beasts must kill the smaller to maintain themselves; but though this involves for the smaller beasts moments of terror, it seems clear from the accounts of naturalists that even for them enjoyment of life is the prevailing tone or colour of experience. And though there is already some problem concerning the occurrence of any evil at all, yet at this level there is reason to be satisfied with a balance of good over evil. That is not all that we have to say about it. But it is all that arises at this stage; and at this stage it is enough. For the stage at which evil may be taken up into good and made part of its own excellence is the stage of definite moral values. If life at the animal stage is good on the whole, then as a whole it is good, and no question of its justification arises. If later developments appear to offer a justification of the subordinate element of evil which it contains, that is to be welcomed in the interest of a completely rational interpretation of the world; but even without it we can safely pronounce that the best understanding we can frame of the animal world offers no obstacle to a reasonable Theism.

It is with the advent of man that the problem assumes proportions so overwhelming. Mind, as known in man, early achieves a certain detachment from its basis in the physical organism by its use of "free ideas." But it actually holds these ideas by means of its capacity as imagination. The mind cannot think without either percept or image. The use of the Figure in Geometry is more than a convenience; it is a necessity. But it need not be drawn on paper or on a blackboard. It can be constructed in imagination. The mind is not strictly thinking about the Figure—the triangle ABC, for example; it is thinking about the universal triangle; but it can only do this by means of a particular triangle, taking care to avoid reference to any peculiarity of the particular triangle. Now imagination, just because it exists to offer particular instances of general qualities, offers to desire the stimulus which the appropriate physical objects offer to appetite. Hence comes a great, and in principle unlimited, expansion of the life of desire, which initially functions only as expressive of the vital needs of the organism or as stimulated by ap-

propriate objects in the physical environment. Desire as so expanded may
take the form of aspiration or of lust. No doubt it always takes in fact both
forms at first, and one way of expressing the purpose of educational discipline
is to say that it aims at directing the whole force of desire away from lust
towards aspiration. When this process is corrective rather than preventive it
is commonly called "sublimation."

From these considerations it is clear that so far as Evil is a product of
exaggerated or misdirected desire, the condition of its occurrence is identical
with the condition that makes possible all the higher ranges of human life.
The ancient Hebrews had ample justification for tracing sin to the "Evil
imagination." But to imagination also must be traced the possibility of all
forms of distinctively human excellence. All depends on how it is used. To
take up the thought of our earlier discussion of Freedom, all depends on the
direction of attention; and this is largely within the mind's own control.

But this gives us rather the mechanism of evil as known in men than its
mainspring. If the mind can control the direction of its attention, why does
it so often give it a bad direction? It is easy to answer by attributing this to
perversion or sin in the mind. But that hardly helps us. What is the source
and nature of this perversion of mind? That any man ever chose evil, knowing it to be evil *for him*, is to me quite incredible. He may say, under an
impulse of defiance, "Evil, be thou my good;" but his pursuit of it is then
due to the fact that he has adopted it as his good and not because it is evil.
To desire evil strictly for its own sake is impossible. To hate the human race
so as to desire as good for one's self what is evil for all others, and even because it is evil for all others, is possible; but this evil for others is still desired
as supposedly good for him who desires it.

In other words, a man is governed by what effectively appears good to him,
which we shall henceforth term "the apparent good." And what appears
good depends on the condition of his mind. It is not a reflective judgement
with which we are now concerned. No one, probably, *thinks* cruelty good—
certainly not as a general proposition, and hardly in a particular instance. Yet
men do cruel things; they do them because at the moment those things
appear good through gratification of some lust for self-assertion, or through
their power to allay some panic fear. A man's character determines his apparent good at any moment; his apparent good determines his conduct.

If this process is working out to a bad result it is because the apparent
good is not the real good. Sometimes it is possible to change the apparent
good by setting beside it some presentation of the real good. There are many
who habitually gain control of evil desires by turning their attention to the
Figure of Christ, in contrast with which the object of the evil desire appears
no longer good but abhorrent. Sometimes again it is possible to think out the

full implication of what presents itself as good, and to see that taken in its real completeness it is bad. But as a rule the real good will be impotent against the apparent good unless it can be made equally apparent; and this means that it must be presented to the mind in some form apprehensible by the senses or in imagination. A man may know as a matter of general principle that stealing is not only wrong but bad—bad, that is, for him. But if he sufficiently desires an object that is within his grasp, he may none the less take it unless there is also before him the sorrow of the person robbed, or the penalty which he is likely to bring upon himself. Most of us have been able to master our covetousness of possessions sufficiently to be free from these temptations. The force of temptation is more felt in the region of bodily appetites, or of personal resentments, or of professional or commercial ambition, or of political sentiment. But the principle is the same. There may be a genuine apprehension of the true good in conceptual form; but this will not prevail against the vivid attraction of an apparent good unless it is presented in a form that is as effectively apparent. Imagination is usually the connecting link between thought and volition, and if the apparent good is to be changed otherwise than by conversion of the character, it must chiefly be through the occupation of the imagination with the things—and the relevant things—that are "pure, honourable and of good report."

But we have not yet come to the heart of the problem. Why is there a difference between the apparent and the real good? or, to put the question more usefully, why are we such that what appears to us good is other than the real good? For there is here an unquestionable bias or tendency to evil in human nature. Theologians have called this Original Sin; and if those words mean that every human being has in one respect or another such a bias or tendency to evil, they do not stand for a mysterious doctrine but for an evident and vitally important fact. Our task is to relate that fact to belief in the divine government of the world; but it will assist us if we first enquire further into the ground of the fact in human nature and its place in the world process as our argument has led us to envisage this.

The point which here concerns us is this. Mind arises within the world process as one of its episodes; but it is a peculiar episode in two ways. First, it is peculiar because it is able to take the process in which it occurs within the embrace of its awareness and its comprehension. Viewed from one standpoint, a man is a trifling occurrence—a midget breathing and moving for a brief span in one corner of a universe overwhelmingly vast. Viewed from another standpoint, he is himself the master of that universe, able to comprehend it as it can never comprehend him, and bending the mighty forces of nature to serve his purposes. He tames the force of lightning, turning it on and off with a switch. He regulates the waves of ether, bidding them carry accounts of his very games round the globe. To his lightest whim the august energy of Nature must be subservient. There may be rational minds domiciled in other planets, or in stars and nebulae. On the planet called Earth such minds have appeared, and their achievements make even the suns look small. That is one way in which Mind is peculiar as an episode in the world process.

The other, which more concerns us now, is this. Till Mind appeared as an episode in the world process, all other episodes had value in potentiality only, not in actuality—so far at least as the process itself supplied the condition of its actualisation. In the sight of God, and it may be also of spirits other than those born in the world process, that process and its episodes had value. But with the coming of minds there came also for the first time episodes within the process supplying to other episodes the condition for the actualisation of their value. Here, even more than in the impressive achievements lately enumerated, is the supreme peculiarity and distinction of mind. *The human mind is a focus of appreciation. It has knowledge of good and evil. The winning of that knowledge is called the Fall of Man, because acts, which before he won it were merely instinctive reactions to environment, become through that knowledge sins against the light. Again, because they are done against the light, they are done with a new degree of self-assertion. And, once more, because imagination is so potent to stimulate desire, there is an additional impulse to those acts. Man in so far as he is evil is worse than any animal; and in every man there is the bias or tendency to evil.* We are now in a position to track this to its source.

Mind, as it occurs as an episode in the world-process, takes the form of finite minds. It is indeed confined within extremely narrow limitations. It cannot attain to any grasp of the true proportions and perspective of the world in which it is set. Certain things have a value for it and are its apparent good. There is no inherent and absolute necessity for this to be other than the real good; yet the probability of divergence is so great as to amount to certainty for all practical purposes. The finite, and indeed very narrowly limited, mind appreciates the gigantic fact of good and evil. But its limitations hinder it from apprehending the full significance of these, or the true nature of the various objects which present themselves as apparent goods. *The mind by a necessary tendency of its own nature attaches more importance to values which find their actualisation in itself than to those which find it elsewhere; or to put it crudely, each man cares more about what seems to be good for him than about goods which he does not expect personally to enjoy. Even so far as he knows of these, they take a second place for him; and about many of them he knows nothing. So he becomes not only the subject of his own value judgements, which he can never cease to be,*

*but also the centre and criterion of his own system of values, which he is
quite unfit to be.*

Accordingly, as man rose above sub-human forms of life through the development of mind within his psycho-physical organism as an increasingly
dominant factor, he found himself self-centred. The animal also is self-
centred. But in the animal this is an innocent state, because it is merely a
given fact of nature; the animal self does not compare its actual condition
with a conceived or imagined ideal; it is a consciousness but not a "self-
distinguishing and self-seeking consciousness." Consequently it is self-centred
without being self-assertive. But as soon as consciousness advances to full
self-consciousness, so that the self, disinguishing itself from its environment,
not only chooses what appetites it shall satisfy but even what ends it shall
pursue, self-centredness becomes self-assertion. The good-for-self is alone
effectively apparent good, and good in a fuller sense, though recognised to
be real, is relatively powerless as motive. It is not utterly necessary that this
should be so; and therefore it is not true to say that God made man selfish,
or predestined him to sin. But that it should be so was "too probable not
to happen"; and it is true to say that God so made the world that man was
likely to sin, and the dawn of moral self-consciousness was likely to be more
of a "fall" than an ascent. Human sin was not a necessary episode in the
divine plan; but was always so closely implicated in the divine plan that
it must be held to fall within the divine purpose. To the problem thus presented we must return at a later stage.

The individual members of human society are not mutually exclusive
atoms of consciousness. Each is a partly self-determining, self-integrating
system of experience; but the content of that experience is derived from
environment. The part of that content with which we are now concerned
is derived from social environment. We are, in part, reciprocally determining
beings. We make each other what we are. Therefore the existence of one
self-centred soul would spread an evil infection through all who come within
its range of influence. This happens both positively by suggestion and negatively by repulsion. If A is self-centred, B tends to become so by imitation;
but also B becomes so in self-defence. The instincts of gregariousness and of
fear combine to produce the same result. And this process continues, so
that A and B perpetually develop their own and one another's self-centredness. Actual human society is to a large extent, though never completely,
that network of competing selfishnesses, all kept in check by each one's
selfish fear of the others, which Glaucon describes in Plato's *Republic*
and which Hobbes made the basis of his political philosophy in the
Leviathan.

This may, perhaps, be called an evolutionary account of the origin of moral evil. But it must be sharply distinguished from any theory of moral evil which accounts for it by reference to a survival of animal impulses into the rational stage of development. The centre of trouble is not the turbulent appetites, though they are troublesome enough, and the human faculty for imagination increases their turbulence. But the centre of trouble is the personality as a whole, which is self-centred and can only be wholesome and healthy if it is God-centred. This whole personality in action is the will; and it is the will which is perverted. Our primary need is not to control our passions by our purpose, but to direct our purpose itself to the right end. It is the form taken by our knowledge of good and evil that perverts our nature. We know good and evil, but know them amiss. We take them into our lives, but we mis-take them. The corruption is at the centre of rational and purposive life.

The suggestion which we have repudiated belongs to the phase of "faculty-psychology." This presented the soul as a complex entity in which reason and passion exist side by side. Passion, according to this view, comes from our animal ancestors and is already strongly developed when reason appears; reason at first is feeble, and very slowly develops capacity to control passion; the devices of education aim at keeping passion in check while the development of reason is hastened. At last it may be hoped that reason will take complete control, and then all will be well.

Of course that picture is not wholly false. But it is more false than true, because it misses the most vital point. That point is that reason itself as it exists in us is vitiated. We wrongly estimate the ends of life, and give preference to those which should be subordinate, because they have a stronger appeal to our actual, empirical selves. That is why the very virtues of one generation lead to the miseries of the next; for they are contaminated with the evil principle, and it is truly said that "our righteousnesses are filthy rags." *We totally misconceive alike the philosophic and the practical problem of evil if we picture it as the winning of control over lawless and therefore evil passions by a righteous but insufficiently powerful reason or spirit. It is the spirit which is evil; it is reason which is perverted; it is aspiration itself which is corrupt.*

And yet it cannot be said that the principle of selfhood is evil. To say that would be to accuse the constitution of the universe itself and therefore also God its Creator. Moreover it would be, for us at least, self-contradictory. For we have found that the essential condition of Good is the discovery by mind of itself in its object, which reaches its culmination in the love that binds different souls into the unity of perfect fellowship. If the highest good is found in personal relationships, it must be ludicrous to contend that persons or selves are inherently evil in principle. But the persons or selves which occur in the World Process are finite; they are extremely limited in range of apprehension. Their own well-being is dependent on the principle of the Whole in which they are no more than episodes; but this is not within their apprehension; if they so ordered their scale of values as to conform to it, that would seem to be a lucky accident which had occurred against all the balance of probability. Some of them at least must be expected to order that scale wrongly because of the falsified perspective due to their limited range of apprehension; and that will be enough, as we saw, to infect the race. It is still more likely that all will thus err, and then mutually infect with error one another. Because it was not necessary that we should err, we cannot say that our sin is itself God's act; it is our fault, not His, in the first instance. But that we are finite selves is directly due to God's act, and we cannot doubt that God foresaw the issues of conferring selfhood upon finite beings, so that sin falls within His purpose, and is even part of it, though it can not be said that He directly willed or wills it. What He faced was a probability so great as to be distinguishable only in thought from certainty. "I speak after the manner of men"; of course there is, for God's *eternal* knowledge, no such thing as "probability" but apprehension of all reality in its ordered completeness. Yet that distinction in thought is important. For it means that God did not directly cause any man to sin.

The sin of each man is a new element in the World Process. It is what, being himself, he contributes to it. And its essence is not that he is a self, but that being a self he is self-centred. What matters to him bulks larger in his estimate of value than what matters equally or even more to others. He does not love his neighbour as himself, but allows himself to count for more in the direction of his attention, and therewith his life, than his neighbour does. It is not wicked to be finite; but it is so improbable as to be beyond all reasonable estimate of practical possibility that finite selves, if left to themselves, should not be wicked.

When once the spiritual principle of evil had established itself through the adoption of themselves as centres of their systems of value by all, or by any, selves, its calamitous authority would spread apace. Each would infect, and be infected by, the others. The great system of mutual support in evil would be established, which Dr. Inge describes as "co-operative guilt with limited liability." As was noted above, it spreads itself in two different ways, both by positive suggestion, and by putting on the defensive those who find that their neighbours, being self-centred, will attack them if interest so prompts. The young soul, still plastic and rather timidly making its adventure in the world, sees that others fend for themselves, and resolves to do the like; it also finds that in a world so conducted it is likely to be overwhelmed unless it does the like. However small its own perversion, resulting from its own finitude, may have been, it is firmly rooted in self as its centre by its intercourse with others who were perhaps at the outset in their own outlook and estimate of the goods of life no more perverted than itself. And in each this process is intensified by the activity of imagination, which not only stimulates desire beyond its proper province, so that it becomes lust, but also, being specially responsive to fear, exaggerates the peril proceeding from the rivalries and antagonisms of the competing individuals and groups, poisoning all thought and feeling with rancour and bitterness.

This is the account of that indubitable fact, called by theologians Original Sin, which coheres with our general account of the World Process and of man's place within it. Because mind when it appears in that process is finite, and even narrowly restricted in scope, it attaches undue importance to those goods and evils which it apprehends as affecting itself; its perspectives are falsified; what is near at hand looks larger than it is, and what is far off, smaller than it is. This initial aberration of (probably) every finite mind is magnified by the activity of imagination and by the reciprocity of social influence till the Apostolic catalogue is no exaggerated account of the state of man: "foolish, disobedient, deceived, serving divers lusts and pleasures, living in malice and envy, hateful, hating one another."

It is not suggested that this is a complete account of human nature or of any actual phase of human society. But the evil aspect of human nature and society is all that has been said and more. It is no solution of the difficulty which such a view presents to Theism, to say that there is also much good in human nature. If the world is the creation of Almighty Righteousness, we should expect to find good in abundance; that causes no perplexity; but the occurrence of any, even minute, instance of evil causes great perplexity.

With that perplexity, however, we are not yet in a position to deal. Our present endeavour is to apprehend with substantial accuracy the actual moral situation of mankind. And for this purpose it is necessary to allow its fair place to the good that is in human nature despite its perversions, and (no less important) to those potentialities for good which are bound up with the very source and occasion of evil.

First, then, we notice that the earliest experience of the child is almost always predominantly good. The love for its mother which is part of the child's first conscious apprehension is almost purely good. It is not a perfect good, because it is a love wherein from the outset self-interest plays a part. It is in some respects truly disinterested, but is also in a certain sense self-centred. It is φιλία—the love of friendship, where the well-being of the self is an element in the complex of motives determining the friendly relation, not ἀγάπη—the love of utter self-giving and self-forgetfulness. Therefore it can be stifled and quenched; for if no kindness meets it, its element of self-regard will turn acid within it and corrode it till it vanishes away. Ἀγάπη cannot be so quenched; for as in it the self has been freely given from the outset, the absence of kindness only lets it prove its quality more perfectly. It is necessary to notice this contrast here, not in order to cast a blight upon the loveliness of a child's love, but to remind ourselves both of its possible decay and of the more splendid love which is alone divine and safe from evil infection.

That earliest experience, being good, creates in the soul a tendency which is not easily quite obliterated. And if the home be happy, and early years are spent in a society where love prevails, the good tendency may often be established so firmly that nothing can now prevent its becoming the controlling determinant of character throughout life. Yet the soul will still have its own element of perversion due to self-centredness, and is inevitably hardened in this by the play upon it of the selfishness in the world, from which even its early home is sure not to have been quite exempt. Nor can it be said that every soul trained in a loving home is less selfish than every soul trained under the pressure of grinding selfishness. There are some whose natural responsiveness to the goodness and beauty of the world gives them a centre outside themselves, which is only established the more firmly in resistance to the shocks administered by selfish surroundings.

"Centre" is a spatial, even a geometrical term. Its main suggestion in this context is clear enough, but we must not be misled by its limitations. A circle can only have one centre, but a soul can have two or more. If precision of geometrical metaphor is to be more nearly observed we may then speak of these as foci. Certainly it is the fact that very few, if any, lives are wholly self-centred; that could only happen through great spiritual mutilation, a mutilation which is perhaps impossible. For though our reason, as empirically active, is perverted, yet the essential principle of reason is incorruptible, and those mystics are probably right who hold that in every soul there is a divine spark which never consents to sin. Life cannot be fully integrated about the self as centre; it can only be fully integrated when it becomes God-centred. For God is the real centre of the real world: His purpose is its controlling principle; only in Him therefore can all creatures find a centre which brings them all to harmony with one another and with themselves. But God is immanent in the world, making Himself apprehensible through the Truth, the Beauty, the Goodness which call forth from men the allegiance of discipleship. Consequently there is a constant lure to every soul to find itself at home with Him, and this influence works in the world side by side with that influence of inter-reticulated evil which was earlier described. The soul which all through life is fashioning itself by the exercise of its mental freedom under the pressure of all these forces, good and evil, pursues its difficult and commonly wayward course, with always some element of self-seeking, and almost always some element also of sheer self-giving.

In the process of history the pressure of self-seeking and the impulse of self-giving tend increasingly to converge, making outward conformity to standards of sound morality easier, but also for many souls making progress in inward and spiritual morality more difficult. Selfishness, for its own sake, puts a check upon its expression in acts. If each fights hard for his own hand, no man's hand will retain what it has grasped. Covetousness itself will prompt a prohibition of stealing; for the thief who ignores his neighbour's property rights desires to be protected in his own. As selfishness learns by experience it attains to prudence, and those who zealously follow the best policy will about as often as not be honest. Outward morality is thus encouraged even by the immoral principle itself. Some genuine progress is thus made; but to an almost equal extent conscience is confused and the edge of its witness blunted.

Moral and social progress is, no doubt, mainly due to the activity of positive good influences. But it is of great importance, both practical and theoretical, to notice that lower motives, and even that principle of self-centredness which is the very fount of moral evil, play their part in the empirical development of good. Very often the wisdom of a trainer of character or a reformer of institutions is shown in the extent to which he can secure that the lower motives support the higher in promoting right conduct. Often the elimination of self-centredness is best assisted through the stage of enlisting it in support of what public spirit and even the highest claims of absolute morality require. Few actions are guided by one motive alone, and the vital question in practice is not whether the motive of an action was noble or mean, but whether the just order of priority among motives has been maintained, so that when divergence arises the higher check and control the lower, and the lower do not control or check the higher. The argument, frequent on the lips of a certain kind of moral idealist, that virtuous conduct sustained by fear of the consequences of vice is worthless, only proves that he who uses it is a bungler. Even if nothing sustained the virtuous conduct except fear, it would still be better than vicious conduct, both because it is beneficial instead of harmful to society and because its own excellence at least has the opportunity of making its appeal to the conscience of the person acting, so that imperceptibly another and better foundation for the virtuous conduct may be fashioned. Moreover, impulses which are refused any expression in conduct may atrophy, provided that the energy represented by them is utilised in other ways. It is quite possible for character to improve under the pressure of disciplinary sanctions, and for self-regard to be partly undermined by appeal to self-regarding motives.

Even more evident is the improvement in social relationships which may be assisted by the considerations of an enlightened selfishness. To a quite appreciable extent respect for law rests on the need of every citizen for the law's protection. So through the action of self-regarding motives men may be led to an appreciation of justice. So far as civilisation needs prisons and a police force, the general good is served through appeal to particular interest.

Yet when all this is admitted, it is still true that the self-regarding principle is a precarious support of moral progress, and that a point is reached in connexion with each successive phase of development in individual or society, at which it becomes a barrier to further advance. Where it exists—which is everywhere—the practical statesman and the practical pastor must alike recognise it as a fact and allow for it in the plans which they make to assist social or moral progress; they will try to enlist it as an ally in an advance that is really dictated by higher principles than itself. But man cannot be saved, nor either individual or society attain to perfection, except by the total elimination of self-centredness. Only by truly disinterested love does man enter into completeness of fellowship with God.

RADOSLAV A. TSANOFF

RADOSLAV A. TSANOFF (1887-   ), Emeritus Professor of Philosophy at Rice Institute, has dealt in his philosophical work with the areas of ethics, history of philosophy and philosophy of religion. His study of the problem of evil is probably his most important contribution.

The Nature of Evil*

Our survey of the problem of evil and of the alternative proposed solutions has revealed several sources of confusion. The endeavor to recognize and to clear up these confusions has suggested a better way out. The theory which is now presented in conclusion makes no presumptuous claims to originality or novelty: enough if it preserve the sound elements of other doctrines and avoid their confusion of issues, unwarranted preconceptions, insufficient respect for fact, and undue complacency or depression.

One thing seems clear at the very outset: this is a world of good *and* evil, however we may have to define the two. Wholesale and unqualified condemnation of the world, and likewise suave dismissal of evil as unreal are plainly at variance with the facts of life, are indeed self-refuting views. Value, whatever its more adequate definition, has this essential character of bipolarity: it is positive or negative, in whatever field we may examine it. Truth implies and is meaningless apart from error; virtue is similarly related and opposed to vice, beauty and justice and happiness to their respective opposites. "In the scale of existence," Dean Inge writes, "there are no minus signs. . . . But . . . the moral standard is essentially dualistic, and the dualism cannot be transcended without transcending the standpoint of morality." [1] Using the terms good and evil in the broadest sense to designate value positive and negative, we are bound to say that, if either is admissible, both must be. We have them both on our hands, both actual. Our problem is to understand the relation between them, and the essential character of the world which the perception of their relation serves to reveal. So axiology and cosmology may contribute to each other.

* From Radoslav A. Tsanoff, *The Nature of Evil*, pp. 387-393, 397-401. Copyright, 1931, The Macmillan Company. Used by permission of R. A. Tsanoff. [Footnoes have been renumbered, Eds.]

[1] *The Philosophy of Plotinus*, Vol. I, p. 133.

The attempted reduction of evil to finitude is a virtual rejection of the clear point with which we start, and, as we have seen, leads not to the solution but to the abandonment of the problem of evil. The reduction of good and evil to pleasure and pain ignores the variety and complexity of value, and, instead of simplifying our problem, serves only to confuse it. The reduction of good and evil to self-denial and self-assertion narrows the range of value unduly and even in this narrow range is disclosed as artificial and as dictated by theological and other preconceptions rather than as warranted by experience.

The essential defects of the theories just reviewed are two. First, the outright dismissal of evil or its reduction to finitude involves an evasion of the characteristic problem of value and, in particular, by reducing moral to metaphysical evil, rules out ethics. Second, the proposed equating of good and evil with pleasure and pain, or with self-denial and self-assertion, mistakenly looks for sheep and goats in the world, treating good and evil as distinct things or aspects or qualities, as if we could say of x that it is and remains good and the good, and of y that it is evil and the evil in the world.

The realm of value is too vast and complex to be thus forced in the frame of any such x and y. This undue simplification of the problem of evil, furthermore, overlooks the fact that truth, for instance, has no status in isolation but is always relative to a context, and not only may but characteristically does lose, in another context, its truth character and is disclosed as an error. And likewise with the other values. The value-character of reality, in other words, is not to be sought in individual things or aspects or qualities that stay put, that can be isolated and exhibited for praise or execration. Good and evil, truth and error, beauty and justice and the rest are what they are always in relation, in certain contexts, and in different contexts and relations may and do disclose a metamorphosis: the sheep turn out to be also goats! Yet even if philosophy of value could be formulated with offhand simplicity in terms of pleasure-pain or benevolence-selfishness, the real problem of theodicy would still remain: How are we to estimate a world in which sheep and goats have thus been picked out and opposed to each other?

Value positive or negative is not to be located in certain areas of existence but is a fundamental and ultimate character of all existence. No thing *is* value, but in all things value of some sort may be sought, recognized, enhanced, frustrated. The value-character of reality is a character which is postulated, and in being postulated involves a demand for its realization or a demand for its negation, and in both demands a fundamental recognition of higher and lower and an incipient or determined preference. Valuation is thus bound up with conative experience; it implies a moving world in which interest stimulates will-activity, in which intelligence is not a mere passive recipient of the factual, but an active participant, preferring, demanding, resisting. The true is what we should believe and maintain; the beautiful is what we should enjoy and cherish; the good is what we should pursue, do, love, and uphold; and so with the other values, and in all these cases the chosen value is the preferred claimant setting us in opposition to rival invasions of interest.[2]

The world discloses value only in and to personal experience. Values are personal in reference and connotation. This main principle, which commands weighty support, has found classical expression in Green's formula: Values are always "relative to value for, of, or in a person."[3] Some of the reasons for upholding this view have been stated in the last chapter of my work, *The Problem of Immortality*, and perhaps need not be rehearsed.

This principle of the relation of value and personality, however, is liable to a certain grave misinterpretation. It may be expressed in the doctrine that value is *merely* personal, that nature is indifferent to value, that value of whatever sort is merely read into nature by persons, is as it were a poetic fiction of reality. In support of this opinion is cited the mere factuality of existence as physical science deals with it. But does the physical-scientific view of nature exhaust reality? Is not scientific activity itself, and the possibility of physical *science*, an indication that the range of reality transcends factual-mechanistic categories? What would be the chemical formulae of a true and of an untrue chemical theory? Nature, in the full and only proper sense of the word, is not merely factual and indifferent to value, for nature includes human nature, includes scientific, logical activity and its standards, aesthetic creation and contemplation, moral endeavor and ideals, religious worship. These are all in and of nature, quite as real certainly as atoms, electrons, positive and negative charges. An utterly impersonal universe would not allow of value or valuation, but the universe is not wholly impersonal. That values are essentially bound up with personality is thus nowise a reflection on their reality; indeed, quite the contrary, if we only consider the range of being that is exemplified in personality. Value is personal; its range and roots are the range and roots of personality, and these, after all, reach over all nature. To ignore this last is to ignore the problem "how a universe without mind or value could produce mind and value."[4]

Personal activity may not be as common as mechanical process, but this observation is neither surprising nor relevant to the reflection it is intended

---

[2] Cf. Urban, *Valuation*, pp. 54, 63, and also Professor Urban's articles on Value in the *Journal of Philosophy*, Vols. XIII, XIV; Sorley, *Moral Values and the Idea of God*, pp. 54-131, 134, 498. Cf. also A. P. Brogan, "The Implication of Meliorism concerning the Relation between Value and Existence," in the *Proceedings of the Sixth International Congress of Philosophy*, pp. 308ff.

[3] *Prolegomena to Ethics*, Section 184.

[4] E. S. Brightman, *Religious Values*, p. 135.

to convey. The apex of the pyramid is not any the less apex because it covers less area than the base. Was there a long time during which there was neither man nor man's thinking and valuation in nature? All the more clearly, then, should we recognize that nature among its other capacities had and has the making of human nature in it. The lower we perceive the sub-human range of nature to extend, the clearer evidence should we find, in nature's attainment unto personality, of its essentially dynamic, upward-reaching character. So John Keats wrote words of wisdom which Bernard Bosanquet was to interpret and develop: "The world is the vale of soul-making." [5] But we should also recognize the arduousness of this attainment. We should be on our guard not to oversimplify our cosmology either in the manner of the subjective idealist or in the manner of the materialist.

Personality and valuation serve to exhibit more adequately and as it were in fuller maturity characteristics and capacities which reality manifests less adequately and in germ and bud at lower levels of existence. The clear perception of the values of life evident to critical intelligence may enable us, without any anthropomorphism or mythology, to perceive the promise of them all along the line. So far is nature from being indifferent to worth.

It is the essence and nature of everything, Spinoza told us, to endeavor to persist in its own being. In a world of things and processes different in character, difference and conflict-in-relation are just what we should expect. It is of the essence of fire to set the green wood aflame, and it is of the essence of the moisture and the sap in the wood to delay flaming and to extinguish the fire. It is the nature of the invading horde of germs to take hold, multiply and take possession of the organism, and it is the nature of the organism to resist the infection which threatens its health and life. It is as natural for a dog's ravenous hunger to cause it to snap the bone out of another dog's mouth as it is for our social sense and reason to control appetite. The "flesh" and the "spirit" are both "nature," each in its sphere persisting, each in relation to the other and overarching to dominate the other. Our life, and the world we live in, may be conceived as a vast concourse of activities self-persisting, counteracting, conflicting.

But this cosmic concourse is a scale or hierarchy of activities. Things are not indifferently on a par; the difference among them is gradational. What the specific order of gradation is, in different fields of experience, constitutes the special problem of the philosophy of value in its various branches, logical, aesthetic, ethical. The meaning of the terms "higher" and "lower" is itself ever-expanding: signifying difference in complexity and range of categories, enhanced self-realization and self-judgment. The hierarchy points from mech-

[5] Cf. Bosanquet, *The Value and Destiny of the Individual*, pp. 63ff.

anism to life and consciousness, from unconscious and non-rational to self-conscious and rational activity, from law-conforming process to action on principle and in pursuit of ideal ends.

That there is some sort of hierarchy, however, that there is higher and lower in the world, is not a conclusion of valuation but its prime presupposition. Its very outlook is gradational. The first axiom of the philosophy of value is: there is a hierarchy of being, or there is higher and lower in the world, some things are preferable, better, worthier than others. Grant this way of looking at the world, for unless we do the problems of value not only cannot be solved but cannot even arise: what, from such a point of view, is evil?

In this gradational view of things, evil is literally *degradation*, the surrender of the higher to the lower in the scale of being, the effective down-pulling incursion of the lower against the higher. This definition of evil would apply irrespective of the judgment as to what in any specific case is higher or lower, for such difference of judgment would involve a corresponding difference of judgment as to what in the circumstances is evil, and would reaffirm this fundamental conception of the nature of evil.

The perception of the cosmic process as gradational in character and the personal response to this perception find expression in the various categories of the philosophy of value. Thus the self-maintenance of the higher and its reaching to everer full realization and enhancement is progress, whether cosmic, biologic or human-social. Man's degrading surrender to a lower incursion involves him in varieties of vice. His effective resistance to the baser invasion is virtue. His self-satisfaction at any stage of advancement is complacency and marks stagnation: this we may call the sin against the Holy Ghost. His sense of inability to maintain himself on high ground or to attain ground still higher, if due to the conviction that the universe is callous or hostile to the enhancement of worth, gives rise to a consciousness of frustration, the tragic sense of life. . . .

The view of existence which is here developed recognizes unflinchingly the actuality of evil, but is not on that account plunged in pessimistic despair. It is nowise to be mistaken for the complacent theory of evil as the mere shadow in the picture or the discord swelling the larger harmony. Evil is not "somehow good," any more than sinking is somehow rising. Evil is evil and the opposite of good, contrary in course and direction. But it is a fact that what at a lower level and from a lower point of view passes for good and at that level is good discloses from a higher point of view its insufficiency, and adherence to it at the higher level becomes evil. So again St. Augustine writes: "He who inordinately loves the good which any nature possesses, even though he obtain it, himself becomes evil in the good, and wretched because deprived of a greater good." [6] In that sense, but in that sense only, we could well say that all good is somehow evil. So far at any rate is the view here advocated removed from complacency.

Thus it is the destiny of every good theory to open up vistas of inquiry, realms of evidence, new problems which in the end indicate the short-comings of the theory and cause it to be replaced by one more adequate. It is the destiny of every truth in the end to help prove itself an error and itself again an element in a higher truth. In the entire realm of value every solution is but the better setting of a new problem, every achievement but the clearer recognition of a greater task. Spinoza's principle which we recognized is only one half of the truth; our dynamic universe requires also the other half, which Unamuno has expressed so eloquently in his disturbed and disturbing book, *The Tragic Sense of Life:* "Every created being not only tends to preserve itself in itself, but to perpetuate itself, and, moreover, to invade all other beings, to be others without ceasing to be itself, to extend its limits to the infinite but without breaking them." [7] Not bare identity of structure, nor yet change and bare sequence of discretes, but growth, unfolding and genuine enhancement of perfection, active, arduous, and inexhaustible, characterize the world-process.

The vaster the field of attainment and advance, the greater is the range of possible error and frustration. Indeed the perception of a certain value as in some respects inadequate and unworthy is the first step in the attainment of the higher and worthier value. The criticism and the collapse of the lower truth are the birth-pangs of the new truth; remorse and repentance, the thresholds to saintliness. Life does not lose but gains in tragic hazard as it gains in prospect and in dignity. Not self-sufficiency and bland placidity, but vigilant aspiration marks the heroic soul: its ideals are always in the van and its march to higher values never ceases. Far from content to accept the adulation of those with lower standards, it is ever keenly aware of the vast unattained and, by it judging its own attainment, finds itself ever short of the mark. Didn't James Martineau write somewhere: "The blessings of a satisfied conscience are least experienced where they are most deserved"? So we read of Leonardo da Vinci: "What to others appears perfection is to him teeming with error." [8] So Socrates' high conception of knowledge led him to count himself ignorant. So Jesus: "Why callest thou me good?" [9]

---

[6] *Ibid.*, XII; English translation of Augustine's *Works*, Vol. I, p. 491.

[7] *The Tragic Sense of Life*, p. 208.

[8] Merejkovsky, *The Romance of Leonardo da Vinci*, transl. by Herbert Trench, Vol. I, p. 211. Cf. Carl Hilty, *Happiness*, transl. by F. G. Peabody, 1903, p. 107: "My impression is that there is not one of us who has ever, even for a single day, done his whole duty."

[9] Matthew, xix: 16.

It is of the essence of value, then, that it recognizes no final terminus or conclusion. The target, to borrow a phrase from Professor Boodin,[10] is a moving target. Perfection has its base, of course, but its base is always a springboard. Perfection is perfectibility. All along the line of human endeavor this truth is demonstrated, and on the higher peaks of achievement it stands out most clearly. Theology, to be sure, has demanded a conception of God in terms of absolute perfection, a perfection all past perfect or present absolute, without prospect or problems. But, as we have endeavored to indicate elsewhere,[11] this conception of divine perfection carries over inappropriate mechanistic notions of completeness and plenitude into the realm of value. If we conceive of God as the Apogee of Value, then God's perfection must be dynamic: it is not the alleged terminus of perfectibility, but its cosmic course, its heart and soul. Matthew Arnold wrote of "the enduring power not ourselves which *makes for* righteousness." [12] The core of reality is this eternal perfectibility: the heavens declare it; evolution cosmic, biologic, or human-social discloses it; man's logical, aesthetic, and moral activity reveals its sublime range. Man's idea of God is his gesture towards the dizzy utmost of value, the infinite reach and endless span of it. When our vigor fails and our lot seems hopeless, and the abyss wells up to engulf us and our ideals, when wild Nature seems to mock our helpless dignity, and dull scepticism whispers harsh doubts of the reality of value, and all that is worthy in our world is "scientifically" exhibited as ephemeral and episodic, then the very tragedy which the cosmos thus reënacts in our experience serves to save us from despair: in our own loyal aspiration after values we find our conviction that they are in and of Reality and abiding. And this conviction of the ultimate reality, conservation, enhancement of value is man's faith in God.

In God is no stagnant plenitude but plenitude of ideal activity, no dull placidity but ever-heroic redemption of the world from the hazard of settling back. "My Father worketh hitherto, and I work." [13] Not less than myself but more is God thus resistant to the evil tug of the downpulling and the inert and the complacent. For just this upward-urging, ever more perfectly active character of the cosmos is what we can intelligently mean by God. And the evil tug is not outside of God or alien to the divine nature, but just as in finite beings so in the cosmic system of them, in God, it is the negative moment, the obverse of positive enhancement and ideal activity. For there can be no higher without its corresponding lower.

There is accordingly no coming to terms with evil, not ever. Only he

---

[10] *Cosmic Evolution*, p. 45.
[11] *The Problem of Immortality*, pp. 345ff.
[12] *Literature and Dogma*, Chapter I.
[13] John, v: 17.

straightforwardly "accepts the universe" who accepts it unreservedly as a battleground of achievement, only he who in thus accepting it is clearly aware of evils to be resisted and overcome. It has been said that the way to understand best the articles of the Creed is to keep clearly in mind the heresies which they were meant to combat. So the pursuit of truth is through the clearance of error, and virtue is in resistance to vice, and beauty is won through the refusal of ugliness. But this does not mean that error or vice or ugliness are accepted as any the less evil because they are conditions of good: they *are—to be resisted.* The only view of the world that might justify pessimistic despair would be a view that perceived no evil in it, nothing perverse, nothing lower to surmount or overcome, and therefore nothing higher to challenge our endeavor: no problem, no task, no hazard of defeat or frustration: dull, placid monotony! There is a reported saying of Machiavelli: "The worst misfortune in life is not sickness, nor poverty, nor grief; but tediousness." [14] Pessimistic philosophy, as we have seen, may have the reverse effect of that intended by the pessimist: it may be a goad to the sluggish. Evil and the perception of it are conditions for heroic recognition and pursuit of value, be it truth, beauty, goodness; for "powers subjected to no strain . . . atrophy and eventually disappear." [15] In this sense evil is always only relative to good; but, paradoxically, if we refuse to perceive and resist it as evil, then it becomes evil absolute and utterly damns the very man who makes his peace with it.

This is the outlook for a world that admits of valuation: this contest, contact and conflict, of higher and lower, ever persisting, each achievement opening new prospects, raising new problems, imposing new duties, facing new hazards. There is a grim element in this idea; we can apply to our purpose words which Plato wrote in the *Theaetetus:* "Evils . . . can never pass away; for there must always remain something which is antagonistic to good." [16] But another version of this truth, and one more inspiriting, is Emerson's: "Within every man's thought is a higher thought: within the character he exhibits today, a higher character." [17] Good and evil are not distinct realities and have no status in isolation; they are always relative to each other. Evil is that ever-present side or factor in the actual world, by resistance to which a possible worthier side or nature affirms itself and gains reality through attainment. This contest is at the heart of things; it has neither beginning nor end, and it makes our world significant and stirring. The gradational theory of the nature of evil thus expresses essential characteristics of

[14] Merejkovsky, *The Romance of Leonardo da Vinci*, Book XIII, Chap. x.
[15] E. C. Wilm, *The Problem of Religion*, p. 172; cf. Émile Lasbax, *Le problème du mal*, 1919, p. 372.
[16] *Theaetetus*, 176.
[17] Quoted from McComb, *The Future Life in the Light of Modern Inquiry*, p. 94.

PHILOSOPHY OF RELIGION

our logical, aesthetic, and moral activity, does justice to the complexity and dynamic hierarchy of nature, and points to an idea of perfection which does not nullify the fundamental character of value of which perfection is rightly conceived as the apogee.

JOHN STUART MILL

JOHN STUART MILL (1806-1873), British moral philosopher, economist and logician, was the most important English utilitarian thinker. He strongly defended individual rights and capitalism and made improvements in the statement of the method of induction in logic. He identified himself with liberal political and social movements of his time.

*Attributes**

The question of the existence of a Deity, in its purely scientific aspect, standing as is shown in the First Part, it is next to be considered, given the indications of a Deity, what *sort* of a Deity do they point to? What attributes are we warranted, by the evidence which Nature affords of a creative mind, in assigning to that mind?

It needs no showing that the power if not the intelligence, must be so far superior to that of Man, as to surpass all human estimate. But from this to Omnipotence and Omniscience there is a wide interval. And the distinction is of immense practical importance.

It is not too much to say that every indication of Design in the Kosmos is so much evidence against the Omnipotence of the Designer. For what is meant by Design? Contrivance: the adaptation of means to an end. But the necessity for contrivance—the need of employing means—is a consequence of the limitation of power. Who would have recourse to means if to attain his end his mere word was sufficient? The very idea of means implies that the means have an efficacy which the direct action of the being who employs them has not. Otherwise they are not means, but an incumbrance. A man does not use machinery to move his arms. If he did, it could only be when paralysis had deprived him of the power of moving them by volition. But if the employment of contrivance is in itself a sign of limited power, how

* From John Stuart Mill, *Three Essays on Religion*, pp. 176-195. Published, 1884, Henry Holt & Company. In the public domain.

much more so is the careful and skilful choice of contrivances? Can any wisdom be shown in the selection of means, when the means have no efficacy but what is given them by the will of him who employs them, and when his will could have bestowed the same efficacy on any other means? Wisdom and contrivance are shown in overcoming difficulties, and there is no room for them in a Being for whom no difficulties exist. The evidences, therefore, of Natural Theology distinctly imply that the author of the Kosmos worked under limitations; that he was obliged to adapt himself to conditions independent of his will, and to attain his ends by such arrangements as those conditions admitted of.

And this hypothesis agrees with what we have seen to be the tendency of the evidences in another respect. We found that the appearances in Nature point indeed to an origin of the Kosmos, or order in Nature, and indicate that origin to be Design but do not point to any commencement, still less creation, of the two great elements of the Universe, the passive element and the active element, Matter and Force. There is in Nature no reason whatever to suppose that either Matter or Force, or any of their properties, were made by the Being who was the author of the collocations by which the world is adapted to what we consider as its purposes; or that he has power to alter any of those properties. It is only when we consent to entertain this negative supposition that there arises a need for wisdom and contrivance in the order of the universe. The Deity had on this hypothesis to work out his ends by combining materials of a given nature and properties. Out of these materials he had to construct a world in which his designs should be carried into effect through given properties of Matter and Force, working together and fitting into one another. This did require skill and contrivance, and the means by which it is effected are often such as justly excite our wonder and admiration: but exactly because it requires wisdom, it implies limitation of power, or rather the two phrases express different sides of the same fact.

If it be said, that an Omnipotent Creator, though under no necessity of employing contrivances such as man must use, thought fit to do so in order to leave traces by which man might recognize his creative hand, the answer is that this equally supposes a limit to his omnipotence. For if it was his will that men should know that they themselves and the world are his work, he, being omnipotent, had only to will that they should be aware of it. Ingenious men have sought for reasons why God might choose to leave his existence so far a matter of doubt that men should not be under an absolute necessity of knowing it, as they are of knowing that three and two make five. These imagined reasons are very unfortunate specimens of casuistry; but even did we admit their validity, they are of no avail on the supposition

of omnipotence, since if it did not please God to implant in man a complete
conviction of his existence, nothing hindered him from making the conviction fall short of completeness by any margin he chose to leave. It is
usual to dispose of arguments of this description by the easy answer, that
we do not know what wise reasons the Omniscient may have had for leaving
undone things which he had the power to do. It is not perceived that this
plea itself implies a limit to Omnipotence. When a thing is obviously good
and obviously in accordance with what all the evidences of creation imply
to have been the Creator's design, and we say we do not know what good
reason he may have had for not doing it, we mean that we do not know to
what other, still better object—to what object still more completely in
the line of his purposes, he may have seen fit to postpone it. But the necessity of postponing one thing to another belongs only to limited power.
Omnipotence could have made the object compatible. Omnipotence does
not need to weigh one consideration against another. If the Creator, like
a human ruler, had to adapt himself to a set of conditions which he did not
make, it is as unphilosophical as presumptuous in us to call him to account
for any imperfections in his work; to complain that he left anything in it
contrary to what, if the indications of design prove anything, he must have
intended. He must at least know more than we know, and we cannot judge
what greater good would have had to be sacrificed, or what greater evil
incurred, if he had decided to remove this particular blot. Not so if he be
omnipotent. If he be that, he must himself have willed that the two
desirable objects should be incompatible; he must himself have willed that
the obstacle to his supposed design should be insuperable. It cannot therefore *be* his design. It will not do to say that it was, but that he had other
designs which interfered with it; for no one purpose imposes necessary limitations on another in the case of a Being not restricted by conditions of
possibility.

   Omnipotence, therefore, cannot be predicated of the Creator on grounds
of natural theology. The fundamental principles of natural religion as deduced from the facts of the universe, negative his omnipotence. They do
not, in the same manner, exclude omniscience: if we suppose limitation
of power, there is nothing to contradict the supposition of perfect knowledge and absolute wisdom. But neither is there anything to prove it. The
knowledge of the powers and properties of things necessary for planning
and executing the arrangements of the Kosmos, is no doubt as much in
excess of human knowledge as the power implied in creation is in excess
of human power. And the skill, the subtlety of contrivance, the ingenuity
as it would be called in the case of a human work, is often marvellous. But
nothing obliges us to suppose that either the knowledge or the skill is infinite.

THE PROBLEM OF EVIL

We are not even compelled to suppose that the contrivances were always the best possible. If we venture to judge them as we judge the works of human artificers, we find abundant defects. The human body, for example, is one of the most striking instances of artful and ingenious contrivances which nature offers, but we may well ask whether so complicated a machine could not have been made to last longer, and not to get so easily and frequently out of order. We may ask why the human race should have been so constituted as to grovel in wretchedness and degradation for countless ages before a small portion of it was enabled to lift itself into the very imperfect state of intelligence, goodness and happiness which we enjoy. The divine power may not have been equal to doing more; the obstacles to a better arrangement of things may have been insuperable. But it is also possible that they were not. The skill of the Demiourgos was sufficient to produce what we see; but we cannot tell that this skill reached the extreme limit of perfection compatible with the material it employed and the forces it had to work with. I know not how we can even satisfy ourselves on grounds of natural theology, that the Creator foresees all the future; that he foreknows all the effects that will issue from his own contrivances. There may be great wisdom without the power of foreseeing and calculating everything: and human workmanship teaches us the possibility that the workman's knowledge of the properties of the things he works on may enable him to make arrangements admirably fitted to produce a given result, while he may have very little power of foreseeing the agencies of another kind which may modify or counteract the operation of the machinery he has made. Perhaps a knowledge of the laws of nature on which organic life depends, not much more perfect than the knowledge which man even now possesses of some other natural laws, would enable man, if he had the same power over the materials and the forces concerned which he has over some of those of inanimate nature, to create organized beings not less wonderful nor less adapted to their conditions of existence than those in Nature.

Assuming then that while we confine ourselves to Natural Religion we must rest content with a Creator less than Almighty; the question presents itself, of what nature is the limitation of his power? Does the obstacle at which the power of the Creator stops, which says to it: Thus far shalt thou go and no further, lie in the power of other Intelligent Beings; or in the insufficiency and refractoriness of the materials of the universe; or must we resign ourselves to admitting the hypothesis that the author of the Kosmos, though wise and knowing, was not all-wise and all-knowing, and may not always have done the best that was possible under the conditions of the problem?

The first of these suppositions has until a very recent period been and in many quarters still is, the prevalent theory even of Christianity. Though attributing, and in a certain sense sincerely, omnipotence to the Creator, the received religion represents him as for some inscrutable reason tolerating the perpetual counteraction of his purposes by the will of another Being of opposite character and of great though inferior power, the Devil. The only difference on this matter between popular Christianity and the religion of Ormuzd and Ahriman, is that the former pays its good Creator the bad compliment of having been the maker of the Devil and of being at all times able to crush and annihilate him and his evil deeds and counsels, which nevertheless he does not do. But, as I have already remarked, all forms of polytheism, and this among the rest, are with difficulty reconcileable with an universe governed by general laws. Obedience to law is the note of a settled government, and not of a conflict always going on. When powers are at war with one another for the rule of the world, the boundary between them is not fixed but constantly fluctuating. This may seem to be the case on our planet as between the powers of good and evil when we look only at the results; but when we consider the inner springs, we find that both the good and the evil take place in the common course of nature, by virtue of the same general laws originally impressed—the same machinery turning out now good, now evil things, and oftener still, the two combined. The division of power is only apparently variable, but really so regular that, were we speaking of human potentates, we should declare without hesitation that the share of each must have been fixed by previous consent. Upon that supposition indeed, the result of the combination of antagonist forces might be much the same as on that of a single creator with divided purposes.

But when we come to consider, not what hypothesis may be conceived, and possibly reconciled with known facts, but what supposition is pointed to by the evidences of natural religion; the case is different. The indications of design point strongly in one direction, the preservation of the creatures in whose structure the indications are found. Along with the preserving agencies there are destroying agencies, which we might be tempted to ascribe to the will of a different Creator: but there are rarely appearances of the recondite contrivance of means of destruction, except when the destruction of one creature is the means of preservation to others. Nor can it be supposed that the preserving agencies are wielded by one Being, the destroying agencies by another. The destroying agencies are a necessary part of the preserving agencies: the chemical compositions by which life is carried on could not take place without a parallel series of decompositions. The great agent of decay in both organic and inorganic substances is oxidation, and it is only by oxidation that life is continued for even the length of a minute. The imperfections in the attainment of the purposes which the appearances indicate, have not the air of having been designed. They are like the unintended results of accidents insufficiently guarded against, or of a little excess or deficiency in the quantity of some of the agencies by which the good purpose is carried on, or else they are consequences of the wearing out of a machinery not made to last for ever: they point either to shortcomings in the workmanship as regards its intended purpose, or to external forces not under the control of the workman, but which forces bear no mark of being wielded and aimed by any other and rival intelligence.

We may conclude, then, that there is no ground in Natural Theology for attributing intelligence or personality to the obstacles which partially thwart what seem the purposes of the Creator. The limitation of his power more probably results either from the qualities of the material—the substances and forces of which the universe is composed not admitting of any arrangements by which his purposes could be more completely fulfilled; or else, the purposes might have been more fully attained, but the Creator did not know how to do it; creative skill, wonderful as it is, was not sufficiently perfect to accomplish his purposes more thoroughly.

We now pass to the moral attributes of the Deity, so far as indicated in the Creation; or (stating the problem in the broadest manner) to the question, what indications Nature gives of the purposes of its author. This question bears a very different aspect to us from what it bears to those teachers of Natural Theology who are incumbered with the necessity of admitting the omnipotence of the Creator. We have not to attempt the impossible problem of reconciling infinite benevolence and justice with infinite power in the Creator of such a world as this. The attempt to do so not only involves absolute contradiction in an intellectual point of view but exhibits to excess the revolting spectacle of a jesuitical defence of moral enormities.

On this topic I need not add to the illustrations given of this portion of the subject in my Essay on Nature. At the stage which our argument has reached there is none of this moral perplexity. Grant that creative power was limited by conditions the nature and extent of which are wholly unknown to us, and the goodness and justice of the Creator may be all that the most pious believe; and all in the work that conflicts with those moral attributes may be the fault of the conditions which left to the Creator only a choice of evils.

It is, however, one question whether any given conclusion is consistent with known facts, and another whether there is evidence to prove it: and if we have no means for judging of the design but from the work actually produced, it is a somewhat hazardous speculation to suppose that the work designed was of a different quality from the result realized. Still, though the ground is unsafe we may, with due caution, journey a certain distance on it. Some parts of the order of nature give much more indication of contrivance than others; many, it is not too much to say, give no sign of it at all. The signs of contrivance are most conspicuous in the structure and processes of vegetable and animal life. But for these, it is probable that the appearances in nature would never have seemed to the thinking part of mankind to afford any proofs of a God. But when a God had been inferred from the organization of living beings, other parts of Nature, such as the structure of the solar system, seemed to afford evidences, more or less strong, in confirmation of the belief: granting, then, a design in Nature, we can best hope to be enlightened as to what that design was, by examining it in the parts of Nature in which its traces are the most conspicuous.

To what purpose, then, do the expedients in the construction of animals and vegetables, which excite the admiration of naturalists, appear to tend? There is no blinking the fact that they tend principally to no more exalted object than to make the structure remain in life and in working order for a certain time: the individual for a few years, the species or race for a longer but still a limited period. And the similar though less conspicuous marks of creation which are recognized in inorganic Nature, are generally of the same character. The adaptations, for instance, which appear in the solar system consist in placing it under conditions which enable the mutual action of its parts to maintain instead of destroying its stability, and even that only for a time, vast indeed if measured against our short span of animated existence, but which can be perceived even by us to be limited: for even the feeble means which we possess of exploring the past, are believed by those who have examined the subject by the most recent lights, to yield evidence that the solar system was once a vast sphere of nebula or vapour, and is going through a process which in the course of ages will reduce it to a single and not very large mass of solid matter frozen up with more than arctic cold. If the machinery of the system is adapted to keep itself at work only for a time, still less perfect is the adaptation of it for the abode of living beings since it is only adapted to them during the relatively short portion of its total duration which intervenes between the time when each planet was too hot and the time when it became or will become too cold to admit of life under the only conditions in which we have experience of its possibility. Or we should perhaps reverse the statement, and say that organization and life are only adapted to the conditions of the solar system during a relatively short portion of the system's existence.

The greater part, therefore, of the design of which there is indication in Nature, however wonderful its mechanism, is no evidence of any moral attributes, because the end to which it is directed, and its adaptation to which end is the evidence of its being directed to an end at all, is not a moral end: it is not the good of any sentient creature, it is but the qualified permanence, for a limited period, of the work itself, whether animate or inanimate. The only inference that can be drawn from most of it, respecting the character of the Creator, is that he does not wish his works to perish as soon as created; he wills them to have a certain duration. From this alone nothing can be justly inferred as to the manner in which he is affected towards his animate or rational creatures.

After deduction of the great number of adaptations which have no apparent object but to keep the machine going, there remain a certain number of provisions for giving pleasure to living beings, and a certain number of provisions for giving them pain. There is no positive certainty that the whole of these ought not to take their place among the contrivances for keeping the creature or its species in existence; for both the pleasures and the pains have a conservative tendency; the pleasures being generally so disposed as to attract to the things which maintain individual or collective existence, the pains so as to deter from such as would destroy it.

When all these things are considered it is evident that a vast deduction must be made from the evidences of a Creator before they can be counted as evidences of a benevolent purpose: so vast indeed that some may doubt whether after such a deduction there remains any balance. Yet endeavouring to look at the question without partiality or prejudice and without allowing wishes to have any influence over judgment, it does appear that granting the existence of design, there is a preponderance of evidence that the Creator desired the pleasure of his creatures. This is indicated by the fact that pleasure of one description or another is afforded by almost everything, the mere play of the faculties, physical and mental, being a never-ending source of pleasure, and even painful things giving pleasure by the satisfaction of curiosity and the agreeable sense of acquiring knowledge; and also that pleasure, when experienced, seems to result from the normal working of the machinery, while pain usually arises from some external interference with it, and resembles in each particular case the result of an accident. Even in cases when pain results, like pleasure, from the machinery itself, the appearances do not indicate that contrivance was brought into play purposely to produce pain: what is indicated is rather a clumsiness in the contrivance employed for some other purpose. The author of the machinery is no doubt accountable for having made it susceptible of pain; but this may have been a necessary condition of its susceptibility to pleasure; a supposition which avails nothing on the theory of an Omnipotent Creator but is an extremely probable one in the case of a contriver working under the limitation of inexorable laws and indestructible properties of matter. The suscepti-

bility being conceded as a thing which did enter design, the pain itself
usually seems like a thing undesigned; a casual result of the collision of
the organism with some outward force to which it was not intended to
be exposed, and which, in many cases, provision is even made to hinder it
from being exposed to. There is, therefore, much appearance that pleasure
is agreeable to the Creator, while there is very little if any appearance that
pain is so: and there is a certain amount of justification for inferring, on
grounds of Natural Theology alone, that benevolence is one of the attributes
of the Creator. But to jump from this to the inference that his sole or
chief purposes are those of benevolence, and that the single end and aim
of Creation was the happiness of his creatures, is not only not justified by
any evidence but is a conclusion in opposition to such evidence as we have.
If the motive of the Deity for creating sentient beings was the happiness
of the beings he created, his purpose, in our corner of the universe at least,
must be pronounced, taking past ages and all countries and races into account, to have been thus far an ignominious failure; and if God had no
purpose but our happiness and that of other living creatures it is not credible
that he would have called them into existence with the prospect of being
so completely baffled. If man had not the power by the exercise of his own
energies for the improvement both of himself and of his outward circumstances, to do for himself and other creatures vastly more than God had
in the first instance done, the Being who called him into existence would
deserve something very different from thanks at his hands. Of course it may
be said that this very capacity of improving himself and the world was given
to him by God, and that the change which he will be thereby enabled
ultimately to effect in human existence will be worth purchasing by the
sufferings and wasted lives of entire geological periods. This may be so;
but to suppose that God could not have given him these blessings at a
less frightful cost, is to make a very strange supposition concerning the
Deity. It is to suppose that God could not, in the first instance, create anything better than a Bosjesman or an Andaman islander, or something still
lower; and yet was able to endow the Bosjesman or the Andaman islander
with the power of raising himself into a Newton or a Fénelon. We certainly
do not know the nature of the barriers which limit the divine omnipotence;
but it is a very odd notion of them that they enable the Deity to confer on
an almost bestial creature the power of producing by a succession of efforts
what God himself had no other means of creating.

Such are the indications of Natural Religion in respect to the divine
benevolence. If we look for any other of the moral attributes which a certain class of philosophers are accustomed to distinguish from benevolence,
as for example Justice, we find a total blank. There is no evidence whatever

in Nature for divine justice, whatever standard of justice our ethical opinions may lead us to recognize. There is no shadow of justice in the general arrangements of Nature; and what imperfect realization it obtains in any human society (a most imperfect realization as yet) is the work of man himself, struggling upwards against immense natural difficulties, into civilization, and making to himself a second nature, far better and more unselfish than he was created with. But on this point enough has been said in another Essay, already referred to, on Nature.

These, then, are the net results of Natural Theology on the question of the divine attributes. A Being of great but limited power, how or by what limited we cannot even conjecture; of great, and perhaps unlimited intelligence, but perhaps, also, more narrowly limited than his power: who desires, and pays some regard to, the happiness of his creatures, but who seems to have other motives of action which he cares more for, and who can hardly be supposed to have created the universe for that purpose alone. Such is the Deity whom Natural Religion points to; and any idea of God more captivating than this comes only from human wishes, or from the teaching of either real or imaginary Revelation. . . .

F. R. TENNANT

FREDERICK R. TENNANT (1866-1957) was lecturer in theology and philosophy of religon from 1909-1931 at Cambridge University. His concern for a valid rational theology and a broad empirical approach are reflected in his important work, *Philosophical Theology*.

The Problem of Evil*

The problem of evil has thus far been discussed with almost exclusive reference to evil of the moral kind. And the solution that has been presented consists in shewing the tenability of the belief that in our developing world all things work together, as a whole, for the highest conceivable good. The possibility of moral evil and the actuality of its consequences are inevitable concomitants of the "best possible" evolutionary world. It

* From F. R. Tennant, *Philosophical Theology*, II, 197-205. Published, 1930, Cambridge University Press. Used by permission of Cambridge University Press.

is not maintained that everything is good, or that "whatever is, is right," or that partial evil is not evil because it is a condition of universal good. Nor is it implied that every particular evil is directly essential to the emergence of some particular good, or that it has its necessary place, like a dissonance in music, in the harmony of the world-process. When it is asserted that all things work together for good, by "all things" is not meant each and every single thing, but the sum of things regarded as one whole or complex, the universe as a coherent order.

It is by adhering to this general view that the theist can best face the problem presented by the existence of that form of evil for which human freedom is not necessarily, and generally not at all, responsible: the physical evil, or the pain and suffering occasioned by the course of Nature in sentient beings. Indeed any other position than that which has just been summarised seems obviously inadequate as a basis for the explanation of the forthcomingness of physical ills. In order to reconcile the suffering inflicted by the material world upon mankind and other sentient creatures with the goodness and power of the Creator it is both superfluous and insufficient to seek to shew that in every particular case pain is essential to some special end, or that in each single instance suffering may fulfil some particular providential purpose. To attempt a theodicy on these lines is as hopeless as it would be to-day to develope a teleological argument from particular instances of adaptedness, after the manner of Paley. But, as there is a wider teleology than Paley's so is there a wider theodicy than that which consists in pleading that human and animal pain are sometimes prophylactic—a warning against danger, or that human suffering is sometimes punitive or purgatorial, and thus subservient to benign ends. These assertions are undoubtedly true, and there is no need to belittle their import. But by themselves they will not carry us far towards a theodicy. They but touch the fringe of the problem: or, to change the metaphor, they do not go to the root of the matter. It is useless, again, to minimise the pain of the sentient world, or even to reduce our possibly extravagant and unscientific estimate of its intensity, except for the purpose of arguing that, in spite of pain, animal life is probably happy on the whole: otherwise a single pang of useless or superfluous pain is enough to raise our problem. It involves faulty psychology to assert that pain is the necessary background to pleasure; for a lesser pleasure would seem to yield a sufficient contrast to render the enjoyment of intenser pleasure possible. And if pain be sometimes stimulating, educational, preventive, or remedial, as well as sometimes stunting, crushing, and provocative of moral evil, this fact is only significant for an estimation of the worth-whileness of sentient life. The knife may be necessary to cure the disease, but why the necessity of the disease? The escape from mortal danger

THE PROBLEM OF EVIL 439

may require the painful warning, but why the mortal danger? Or, speaking generally, what are we to make of the remoter evil which renders the nearer evil necessary or salutary? The real problem obviously lies further back than these particular and partial solutions reach. It must be shewn that pain is either a necessary by-product of an order of things requisite for the emergence of the higher goods, or an essential instrument to organic evolution, or both. Short of this, we cannot refute the charge that the world is a clumsy arrangement or an imperfectly adjusted mechanism.

It can be argued, however, that the former of the foregoing alternatives is applicable in the case of human suffering, while the latter of them can be invoked to meet especially the case of animal pain. The suffering of the lower animals is not merely an accidental superfluity emerging out of the evolutionary process, but is essentially instrumental to organic progress. It renders unnecessary a large amount of inheritance of specialised structure and function, and so prevents the suppression of plasticity; and, as the "sensitive edge" turned towards danger, or as prophylactic, it is of value for organic progressiveness. Although evil, it is also good for something. Much of human suffering, and many of the outrages of this present life upon our rational prudences and our most sacred affections, on the other hand, seem to be good for nothing, or to be non-essential for the realisation of goodness. If a man already has it in him to meet pain with fortitude and patience, he is not necessarily one whit the better man after actually enduring excruciating tortures; and if an all-powerful being "appointed" him such tortures, merely in order that his fortitude might pass from potentiality to actuality, such a being would be but a super-brute. However, it can be argued that the forthcomingness of our suffering is inevitably incidental to a moral order in a developing world. It issues ultimately out of what is inappropriately called metaphysical evil, or is a necessary outcome of a determinate cosmos of the particular kind that can sustain rational and moral life. The problem which it raises will therefore be solved if it can be maintained that no suffering such as we experience is superfluous to the cosmos as a coherent system and a moral order, however excessive pain often may be as a means to the accomplishment of specific ends such as are attainable by discipline and chastening.

It cannot be too strongly insisted that a world which is to be a moral order must be a physical order characterised by law or regularity. The routine of Nature may be differently described by the spiritualist, the dualist, etc.; but the diversity of these ultimate explanations of law does not affect the present problem. The theist is only concerned to invoke the fact that law-abidingness, on the scale which science is able to assert its subsistence in Nature as already *naturata*, is an essential condition of the world being a theatre of moral life. Without such regularity in physical phenomena there could be no probability to guide us: no prediction, no prudence, no accumulation of ordered experience, no pursuit of premeditated ends, no formation of habit, no possibility of character or of culture. Our intellectual faculties could not have developed. And, had they been innate, they would have wasted themselves, as Comte observed, in wild extravagances and sunk rapidly into incurable sloth; while our nobler feelings would have been unable to prevent the ascendancy of the lower instincts, and our active powers would have abandoned themselves to purposeless agitation. All this is obvious; but it has often been ignored in discussion of the problem of physical evil. Nevertheless, Nature's regularity is the key to this problem. Once let it be admitted that, in order to be a theatre for moral life, the world must be largely characterised by uniformity or constancy, and most significant consequences will be seen to follow. It becomes idle to complain, as some writers have done, that the orderliness of the world is too dear at the cost of the suffering and hardship which it entails, and might more or less be dispensed with for the benefit of the sentient and rational beings which people the world. As Hume admitted, if the "conducting of the world by general laws" were superseded by particular volitions, no man could employ his reason in the conduct of his life. And without rationality, morality is impossible: so, if the moral status of man be the goal of the evolutionary process, the reign of law is a *sine quâ non*. It is a condition of the forthcomingness of the highest good, in spite of the fact that it is not an unmixed good but a source of suffering. We cannot have the advantages of a determinate order of things without its logically or its causally necessary disadvantages. Nor can we be evaluating subjects without capacity to feel. The disadvantages, viz. particular ills, need not be regarded, however, as directly willed by God as ends in themselves or as particular means, among other equally possible but painless means, to particular ends. To make use of an ancient distinction, we may say that God wills them consequently, not antecedently. That is to say, they are not desired as such, or in themselves, but are only willed because the moral order, which is willed absolutely or antecedently by God, cannot be had without them. Now to will a moral order is to will the best possible world; and it also involves adoption of what we necessarily, if somewhat anthropomorphically, must call a determinate world-plan. Such a determinate method of procedure to realise a definite end in an evolutionary world, however, rules out once and for all any other possible goals and methods. As Dr. Martineau has put it, the cosmical equation being defined, only such results as are compatible with the values of its roots can be worked out, and these must be worked out. All determination is negation. If two consequences follow from a system of propositions, or two physical properties are involved in a configuration of particles, we cannot have the one without the other, though the one may be pleasing or beneficial to man and the other may be painful, or in its immediate effects hurtful. And such a result by no means implies lack of benevolence or of power on the part of the Creator, so long as power does not include inconsistency or indeterminateness. It simply bespeaks the inexorableness of logic, the compatibility of things, and the self-consistency of the Supreme Being. That painful events occur in the causal chain is a fact; but, that there could be a determinate evolutionary world of unalloyed comfort, yet adapted by its law-abidingness to the developement of rationality and morality, is a proposition the burden of proving which must be allotted to the opponent of theism. One can only add that, in so far as experience in this world enables us to judge, such proof seems impossible. To illustrate what is here meant: if water is to have the various properties in virtue of which it plays its beneficial part in the economy of the physical world and the life of mankind, it cannot at the same time lack its obnoxious capacity to drown us. The specific gravity of water is as much a necessary outcome of its ultimate constitution as its freezing-point, or its thirst-quenching and cleansing functions. There cannot be assigned to any substance an arbitrarily selected group of qualities, from which all that ever may prove unfortunate to any sentient organism can be eliminated, especially if one organism's meat is to be another's poison, and yet the world, of which that substance forms a part, be a calculable cosmos. Mere determinateness and fixity of nature involves such and such concatenations of qualities, and rule out others. Thus physical ills follow with the same necessity as physical goods from the determinate "world-plan" which secures that the world be a suitable stage for intelligent and ethical life.

And if this be so, the disadvantages which accrue from the determinateness and regularity of the physical world cannot be regarded either as absolute or as superfluous evils. They are not absolute evils because they are parts of an order which subserves the highest good in providing opportunity for moral developement. And they are not superfluous ills because they are the necessary outcome of that order. They are collateral effects of what, in itself or as a whole, is good because instrumental to the highest good. They are not good, when good is hedonically defined; but they are good for good, when good is otherwise defined, rather than good for nothing.

As in the case of moral evil, so also in the case of physical evil, appeal has sometimes been made from necessary linkages and conditionings to a supposed possibility of their being over-ridden by divine omnipotence. And as it was found absurd to suppose that God could make developing beings at the same time morally free and temptationless, so it involves absurdity to suppose that the world could be a moral order without being a physical cosmos. To save mankind from the painful consequences which flow from a determinate world-order, such as the earthquake and the pestilence, would involve renunciation of a world-order, and therefore of a moral order, and the substitution of a chaos of incalculable miracle. Doubtless some directive agency, or the introduction of new streams of causation into the course of Nature, is conceivable without subversion of such regularity as is requisite for human prudence and without the stultification of our science. But the general suspension of painful events, requisite on the vast scale presupposed in the elimination of physical ills, would abolish order and convert a cosmos into an unintelligible chaos in which anything might succeed upon anything. We should have to "renounce reason" if we would thus be "saved from tears," as Martineau says.

Physical evil, then, must necessarily be. And the goodness of God is vindicated if there be no reason to believe that the world-process involves more misery than Nature's uniformity entails. It is not incumbent on the theist to prove that particular evils are never greater than we judge to be necessary for the production of particular salutary effects: that difficult task confronts only the particular kind of theism which is concerned to dispense with proximate causes and a more or less autonomous world, and regards God as the sole and immediate cause of every natural event, and of every incident in a personal life. According to the theodicy which has here been sketched, it is not necessary to suppose that every specific form of suffering that man undergoes—e.g. the agony of tetanus or of cancer—is antecedently willed by God as a means to some particular end. It can be admitted that excruciating pains are more severe than they need be for evoking virtues such as patience and fortitude, and that to assign them to God's antecedent will would be to attribute devilishness to the Deity. Moreover, the fact that some human beings are born as abortions, as imbecile or insane, seems to be inexplicable on the view that every form of suffering is a particular providence, or an antecedently willed dispensation for educating and spiritually perfecting the person on whom the affliction falls; while to suppose that suffering is inflicted on one person for the spiritual edification of another is again to conceive of God as immoral. But the hardest fact of all for human equanimity, in presence of physical and mental evil, is that the apportionment of suffering among individuals is entirely irreconcilable by us with any divine plan of adjustment of particular afflictions to the particular needs, circumstances, and stages of moral developement, of individual sufferers. Even more distressing to human thought than the goading intensity of some kinds of pain is the seemingly chaotic distribution of human ills. If we could trace the utility of particular sufferings with their varying degrees of endurableness, or discern any adaptation of pain to the person's sensibility, moral state, and need of awakening or chastening, then philosophy might be able to agree with the simple-minded piety which assigns a special purpose to every instance of suffering, and finds therein the visitation or appointment of an all-wise and all-good God. But the wind is not tempered to the shorn lamb; the fieriest trials often overtake those who least need torments to inspire fear, to evoke repentance, or to perfect patience, and also those who, through no fault of their own, lack the mature religious faith and moral experience by which alone they could understand how affliction may be endured for their souls' good. "All things come alike to all: there is one event to the righteous and to the wicked"—to those who may be enabled, and to those who are unable, to profit by severe trial.

Disastrous as these facts are to the extremer forms of the doctrine of divine immanence in Nature, they are compatible with theism such as allows to the created world somewhat of delegated autonomy. According to the wider theodicy which has here been presented, the human afflictions arising from our relations with the physical world are not willed as such by God at all, or for any purpose. They are rather inevitable, if incidental, accompaniments or by-products of the world-order which, as a whole, and by means of its uniformity, is a pre-requisite of the actualisation of the highest good that we can conceive a world as embodying. The world is none the less God's world for its callousness to man; but its autonomy, not the particular incidence of each single ill, is what the religious should attribute to his "appointment."

Further, man himself does not deem his suffering to be an excessive price to pay for the dignity of his ethical status, once he recognises physical evil to be inevitable in a moral world. He is then not compelled to see in his suffering self a mere means either to the perfecting of the race, or to the realisation of a divine purpose, or to the manifestation of the "glory" of God. And this is an important consideration for any theodicy. For man is an end for himself, whatever else he may be. My ills can only be justified to me if the remoter advantage of there being ills at all be mine: not humanity's, or even God's, alone. But in that the remoter advantage is the enjoyment of rational and ethical dignity, the individual man can acquiesce in God's purpose for the world: God's ideal may be his also. It is the assurance that God is fulfilling us individually as well as Himself, and fulfilling us for ourselves as well as for Himself, that makes human life in this bitter-sweet world endurable by the sensitively and delicately minded, the tender-hearted, believer. It is because a being of the earth, yet so God-like as man, could not be moulded into the image of God *save from within himself*, as a person or a free agent, that man can account the payment of the sometimes exorbitant price of the chance of learning love inevitable.

If the doctrine of a future life be a corollary of theism, or an implication of the moral purposiveness and meaning which may reasonably be read into the cosmos, it can be invoked to throw further light on the problem of evil. The balance of felicity and unhappiness in an individual life cannot be struck so long as we confine our thought to experience of the present world alone, if we have reason to believe that the earth is "no goal, but starting-point for man." We may then venture to add to our knowledge the faith that "the sufferings of this present time are not worthy to be compared with the glory that shall be revealed." Pain is indeed none the less pain, nor any kind of evil the less evil, for that it shall be done away, or compensated, or because it is a necessary means or by-product. But its hideousness is somewhat trans-figured if, besides being involved in the "best possible" world, it can be seen to have been "but for a moment" in the time-span of just men made perfect. It is not the reality of evil that is here under consideration, but simply the worth-whileness of this life in which evil has a temporary and necessary place. That should not be estimated by looking only at what may now be seen; but for the idea of compensation hereafter theodicy and theistic religion have no further use. They do not ask us to tolerate the evils of the present world, and to abstain from blaming the Creator for them, because of a compensation stored up for us in another world: they rather insist that in this life, with all its evils, we may already discern the world-purpose of God to be a reign of love.

This life acquires, indeed, a new aspect if death be but translation to an-other mansion in the Father's house, and exchange of one kind of service for another. And it is a question whether theism, in asserting the world-ground to be a Spirit and the Father of spirits, and in ascribing to the world the role of ministering to rational and moral life, can stop short of adding the doctrine of a future life to its fundamental articles of belief, without stulti-fying its previously reached interpretation of the world and man. For it would not be a perfectly reasonable world which produced free beings, with God-ward aspirations and illimitable ideals, only to cut them off in everlasting death, mocking their hopes and frustrating their purposes. Such spirits, even with their moral status, would after all be pawns, not children of God. Certainly a God who can be worshipped by moral beings must be a respecter of the persons whom He has moulded into His own image. Hence theists generally regard the Supreme Being as a God, not of the dead, but of the living.

NICOLAS BERDYAEV

NICOLAS A. BERDYAEV (1874-1948), émigré
Russian philosopher and leading lay-theologian of the Russian Orthodox Church, is
well-known for his eschatological philosophy
of history, existentialist interpretation of
Christian ethics, and penetrating criticisms of
extreme rationalism.

Evil*

Suffering and evil are connected with each other, but they are not identical.
Suffering may not be an evil; it may even be a good. The existence of evil
is the greatest mystery in the life of the world and causes the greatest embarrassment to official theological doctrine and to all monistic philosophy.
A rationalistic solution of the problem of evil is just as beset with difficulty
as a solution of the problem of freedom. It can be asserted and with good
grounds, that evil has no positive existence and that it can only allure by
what it filches from good. But none the less evil not only exists but it
prevails in the world. What may be called non-being may have an existential
significance; nonentity has great existential significance, although it would
be untrue to say that it exists. One of the attempts to solve the problem of
evil, and to reconcile it with the possibility of theodicy, amounts to this, that
evil is present only in the parts, whereas in the whole there is only good.
It was thus that St. Augustine thought, and Leibnitz, and indeed in the
last resort, most forms of theodicy adopt the same position, for they admit
that God uses evil for the purposes of good. But that sort of doctrine is
based upon the denial of the unconditional significance of all personality,
and it is a characteristic rather of ancient moral philosophy than of Christian. It means the prevalence of the aesthetic point of view over the ethical.

It is in fact true that in this empirical world there is no good divine
teleological principle, and indeed there cannot be in a world which is recognized as fallen. It might be said that such exists for separate groups of
phenomena but not for the whole phenomenal world, not as a connecting
link among these phenomena for the sake of Good. The traditional doctrine
of Providence is compelled to deny the evil and injustice of the world and

* From Nicolas Berdyaev, *The Divine and The Human*, trans. R. M. French, pp. 86-97.
Published, 1949, by Geoffrey Bles, Ltd. Used by permission of Geoffrey Bles. [Footnotes
omitted, Eds.]

it finds a way out of the difficulty in the fact that instead of evil it recognizes simply the existence of sin. There is in our world an insurmountable conflict between the individual and the race. The individual life, both human and animal, is fragile and menaced to an extraordinary degree, but at the same time our racial life has an extraordinary productive power, and is always begetting life afresh. The doctrine which sees evil only in the parts and does not see it in the whole, is at the mercy of race and is indifferent to the individual. The genius of race is cunning; it is always prompting unhappy man to accept false justifications, and by means of these it holds him in bondage; and historical and social life is, therefore, based upon an accumulation of such falsehood. A lie may be self-deception, when a man becomes the plaything of the commonplace social forces of life. A lie may also take the form of a defence of life against attacks upon it. The question of truth and falsehood is a fundamental moral question.

Man seeks to find refuge from the tormenting question of evil in the realm of neutrality, and by doing so seeks to conceal his treachery to God. But in the deeper sense there is no neutrality; the neutral is on the surface. It might even be said that the devil is neutral. It is a mistake to suppose that the devil is the polar opposite of God. The pole which is the direct opposite of God is again God, the other face of God; extremes meet. The devil is the prince of this world and he takes cover in neutrality. In religious life in general, and in the Christian life, belief in demons and in the devil has played an enormous role. It has been one of the solutions of the problem of evil. When the devil is regarded as the source of evil, objectivization of the interior drama of the human soul takes place. The devil is an existential reality but is certainly not an objective reality in the world of things like the realities of the natural world. He is a reality of spiritual experience, of the path along which man goes. The idea of the devil has been greatly abused socially. Men and women have been held in fear by it, and the kingdom of the devil has been expanded to enormous dimensions, new areas have been continually added to it. Thus a real spiritual reign of terror has been established. Liberation of the soul from the demons which torment it is possible only in a purified spiritual religion. Demonology and demonolatry have existed only on the path which man follows towards the kingdom of spirit, towards the kingdom of freedom and love, towards the Kingdom of God.

The fight against evil easily acquires an evil character itself; it becomes infected by evil. There is a sinister moral dialectic of Manichaean dualism. Too great foes of evil become evil themselves. This is a paradox of the conflict with evil and with evil men and things. The good become evil for the sake of victory over evil and do not believe in the use of other methods than evil in the conflict against evil. Kindliness invites an attitude of disdain, it appears to be uninteresting and insipid. Malice, on the other hand, imposes itself and appears more interesting and more attractive. Those engaged in the struggle think that malice is more intelligent than kindness. Here the problem lies in the fact that actually it is impossible to give effect to the purposes of good, to good ends; this too easily leads to evil and the employment of evil means. It is necessary to be within the good and to radiate the good. It is only the Gospel which overcomes this rebirth of the conflict with evil in the form of a new evil, and regards the condemnation of sinners as a new sin. One must behave with humanity and kindliness even to the devil. There is a dialectic of one's behaviour to the enemy and to evil. You begin by fighting in the name of good against the enemy, against the evil, but you end by being yourself permeated with evil. The problem of one's attitude to the enemy is the fundamental moral problem of our time. The enemy is ceasing to be regarded as a man, there must be no human attitude towards him. In this respect the greatest apostasy from the truth of the Gospel has taken place. I do not think that there are any hopelessly demoniacal natures, that is to say natures over whom the doom of demoniacal possession hangs, just as I do not think that demoniacal nations have existed. What exists is simply a demoniacal condition of people and nations and, therefore, a final judgment is possible upon nobody.

As there is a dialectic of the attitude to the enemy in virtue of which he who fights an evil enemy in the name of good becomes evil, so also there is a dialectic of humility in virtue of which it is turned into passivity in the face of evil, and into accommodation to evil. In the same way there is a dialectric of punishment for crime which turns the punishment itself into a crime. There is in human beings an irresistible need for a scapegoat, for an enemy who is to blame for all their misfortunes and whom they can and even should hate. It may be the Jews, heretics, masons, Jesuits, Jacobins, Bolshevists, bourgeois, international secret societies, and so forth. Revolution always requires an enemy for its nourishment and if there is no enemy it invents one. The same is true of counter-revolution. When the scapegoat is found man begins to feel better. This is an objectivization of evil, an ejection of it into external reality. The State rightly carries on a fight against crime, and against external expressions of evil which are unduly vigorous, but nevertheless the State itself commits crime and does evil. As "the most cold-blooded of monsters" (the expression is Nietzche's) it commits crime, it creates evil without passion and in the abstract. In upholding law and right the State defends the good but it creates its own particular evil. The evil need to experience the joy of cruelty is objectivized, the collective sense of satisfaction in being the cause of pain, in having the right to punish and to be present at the infliction of punishment.

The relations between good and evil are not simple and there is a complex existential dialectic in them. Good may be reborn as evil and evil may be reborn as good. The very distinction between good and evil has been an unhealthy and morbid division and has borne the impress of having passed through the Fall. There is something servile in the interpretation of sin as crime which infringes the will of God and calls for legal proceedings on the part of God. To overcome this servile conception means movement within, movement in depth. Sin is dividedness, a state of deficiency, incompleteness, dissociation, enslavement, hatred, but it is not disobedience and not formal violation of the will of God. It is impossible and inadmissible to construct an ontology of evil. The idea of an eternal hell is, therefore, absurd and evil. Evil is but a pathway, a testing, a disruption; to fall into sin is above all else a testing of freedom. Man moves towards the light through the darkness. Dostoyevsky revealed this more profoundly than anyone.

Evil is usually explained in terms of freedom. This is the most widespread explanation of evil. But freedom is a mystery which does not lend itself to rationalization. The traditional doctrine of the schools about the freedom of the will is static and reveals very little of the mystery of the rise of evil. It remains incomprehensible how out of the good nature of man and of the devil himself, out of heavenly life in the rays of the light of God, there could arise—thanks to the freedom of the creature (freedom which it understood to be the highest gift of God and a mark of likeness to God)—how there could arise evil and the evil life of man and of the world, evil which is reminiscent of hell. It is necessary to concede the existence of an uncreated freedom which precedes being and is submerged in the irrational sphere, in what Boehme calls the *Ungrund*, though he gave a somewhat different meaning to it. The recognition of such a freedom, preceding being, preceding creation, premundane, sets before man the creative task of continuing the creation of the world, and makes evil itself a path, a grievous experience, but not an ontological principle which passes over into eternity (hell). Freedom must be understood dynamically, as engaged in a dialectic process. There are contradictions in freedom, and varying conditions and laws belong to it. Evil raises the eschatological problem in an acute form and it is removed and overcome only eschatologically.

The fight against evil must be carried on and evil must be finally overcome, and at the same time the experience of evil has been a path which leads not only downwards but upwards also. It is not evil itself which has been an upward path, but the spiritual strength of the resistance aroused by it and the knowledge which was born of it. Evil is meaningless, and at the same time it has the highest meaning. In the same way freedom is the antithesis of necessity and bondage, but it can be reborn as necessity and bondage, it can pass into its opposite. Man must go through the testing of all possibilities, he must pass through the experience of the knowledge of good and evil, and evil itself may become a dialectic moment of good. And evil must be overcome immanently, that is to say, there must take place what Hegel called *Aufhebung*, when the negative is overcome, and all the positive enters into the subsequent stage. Thus even atheism may become a dialectic moment in the knowledge of God. It is the lot of man to pass through atheism, through communism, and many other such things in order that he may move out towards the light by an immanent, enriching, act of overcoming. What is needed is not the destruction of those who are "evil" but their enlightenment. Evil can be vanquished only from within, not by violent prohibition alone, nor can it be destroyed by force. Yet at the same time external limits ought to be set to the manifestations of evil which are destructive of life. Both a spiritual and a social conflict ought to be carried on against evil, and the social conflict cannot avoid having recourse to force in the conditions of this world. But the spiritual conflict, on the other hand, can only be carried on as a process of enlightenment and transfiguration, not by resort to violence.

The experience of evil cannot in itself enrich, if one surrenders to it. It is only that positive radiant spiritual power which is brought out in the overcoming of evil, which is able to enrich. Light presupposes darkness, good presupposes evil, creative development presupposes not only "this" but also "the other." It was Boehme and Hegel who understood this best. Evil has the mastery in this world, but it is not to evil that the last word belongs. Evil can be a dialectic moment in the unfolding development of created things, but only because through it the good which is opposed to it is disclosed. The idea of hell and the torments of hell was an eternalization of evil; it represents a failure of strength in the face of it. Evil presupposes freedom and there is no freedom without the freedom of evil, that is to say there is no freedom in a state of compulsory good. But evil is directed against freedom; it seeks to destroy it and to enthrone slavery. According to Kierkegaard man becomes an ego through sin; only he who goes down into hell knows heaven, and he who is the farther from God may be the nearer to God. In Kierkegaard's view the begetting of children is the primary sin. Baader says that life is born in pain and makes its appearance only after a descent into hell. There is a flash of light on the frontier between the world of darkness and the world of light. At the outset evil behaves towards us as towards a master, later on it treats us as fellow-workers and in the end itself becomes the master. All ideas are dynamic, they presuppose contradiction and a process which arises from contradiction.

Two opposite causes give rise to evil in man. Either a vacuum is formed in the soul and proves attractive to evil, or a passion which has become an *idée fixe*, and crowded out everything else, degenerates into evil. Such passions are, for instance, ambition, avarice, jealousy, hatred. The passion is not yet evil in itself but it easily becomes an evil and leads to the loss of inward freedom. A passion for death is also possible. It is difficult for a man in whom moral and religious consciousness had been already formed to commit the first transgression, but the first offence easily gives rise to the second offence, and the man enters into a magical atmosphere of delinquency. This is admirably depicted by Shakespeare in Macbeth. It is difficult to enter upon the path of terrorism, but afterwards it is difficult to stop and bring it to an end. Evil is above all the loss of integrality; it is a breaking away from the spiritual centre, and the formation of autonomous parts which begin to carry on an independent existence of their own. The good in man, on the other hand, is inner integrality, interior unity, the subordination of the life of the soul and of bodily life to a spiritual principle. Evil belongs to this world and, given an apophatic interpretation of the divine, it cannot be transferred to the life beyond. The idea of hell was not a victory over evil but rather an immortalization of it.

In the face of the tormenting problem of evil, both optimism and pessimism are alike untrue. What is needed is to be more of a pessimist in the recognition of evil in this phenomenal world where the prince of this world reigns, and more of an optimist in the denial of it in the world beyond. The concrete knowledge of life, the vision of all its secrets in detail, is a very bitter knowledge. The coming of a better life is merely symbolized in revolutions, political or religious, the better life itself does not come, the entirely new man does not make his appearance. Always the very basest expressions of human life come to light anew; in oppression and persecution, whether it be religious, national, or political, whether it be the outcome of class feeling or belongs to the realm of ideas. Collective enthusiasm easily ends in the setting up of a Gestapo or a Cheka. The life of man in civilization has an irresistible tendency to disintegration, corruption, to collapse into fatuity. Then appears the desire to save oneself by movement in the opposite direction, to take refuge in nature, in the country, in labour, asceticism, monasticism; but this movement also easily leads to ossification or to dissolution.

It is an astounding thing that when people repent they do not, as a rule, repent for that for which they needed to repent. Torquemada did not repent of his actual sin as an inquisitor, he was convinced that he was serving God. Christian people desire not so much a real change and transformation of their nature as absolution for their sins. Religious ideologies and beliefs become a matter of fresh hatred and hostility. The religion of love and forgiveness enshrines a struggle for power. States and societies are always offensive and aggressive, so that human personality is obliged to be always on the defensive. The love of woman may have a redemptive saving significance (in *The Flying Dutchman*; in the case of Sollweg in *Peer Gynt*; or Jouhandot in *Véronique*). Here the image of the Mother of God is, as it were, always meeting us. But the love of woman can much more often be a cause of ruin. Propitiatory blood sacrifices should have had a redemptive significance, but, as it was, they expressed the cruelty and bloodthirstiness of man. And to this very day bloody human sacrifices are offered for the sake of ideas and beliefs which have all the appearance of nobility. All this bitter knowledge of life is not final knowledge, it is not knowledge of the last things. Behind all the darkness of the world and human life a light is hidden, and there are other moments when this light is so strong that it blinds us. Man ought to look evil straight in the face, to allow himself no illusions about it, but never to be overwhelmed by it. Truth lies beyond optimism and pessimism. The absurdity of the world is not a denial of the existence of meaning. The exposure of lack of meaning presupposes the existence of meaning. The evil of the world presupposes the existence of God, without it, it would be impossible to get to know Him.

Nobility, the quality which I call true aristocracy, requires of a man the recognition of his guilt. In its depths, conscience, which is frequently covered up and suppressed, is always a consciousness of guilt. The necessary thing is to take upon oneself as much guilt as possible and to put as little as possible of it upon other people. The aristocrat is not one who is proudly conscious of himself as first, as a privileged being, and who safeguards his position as such. The aristocrat is the man who is aware of the guilt and sinfulness of this first place, this privileged position of his. The sense that one is being continually affronted is on the other hand, precisely a plebian feeling. But it is all too easy to condemn the *ressentiment* of the oppressed and those whose position in society comes last. Max Scheler has done this, and most unjustly, from the point of view of a Nietzscheanized Christianity. The *ressentiment*, into which envy enters is indisputably not a noble sentiment, but there may be all too good grounds for its existence, and it is not for him who is to blame for the *ressentiment* of the humiliated, to busy himself with accusations of it. None the less the most profound thing is not the consciousness of one's own sinfulness (which may remain in the sphere of psychology and ethics), but the metaphysical consciousness of the position of man in the world; man who has infinite struggling aspirations while placed in the circumstances of a finite and compressed existence. In this lies the fall of man, and in this lies the origin of the formation by unenlightened passions of illusory false worlds.

Man finds difficulty in enduring the fact that he is in this world as a mortal creature and that everything which happens in him and with him is mortal. Hence the problem of evil is above all the problem of death. Victory over evil is victory over death. Evil is death; victory over evil is the resuscitation of life, rebirth to a new life. Murder, hatred, revenge, treachery and perfidy, debauchery, slavery, are death. The victory of God—manhood over the last enemy, death, is victory over evil. It is the victory of love, of freedom and creativeness, over hatred, slavery and inertia, the victory of personality over impersonality. The last enemy, death, has a positive meaning too. The tragic sense of death is connected with an acute sense of personality, of personal destiny. For the life of the race there is nothing tragic in death. The life of the race always renews itself and continues, it finds compensation for itself. Death appals the most developed and individualized organism most of all. With an acute sense of personality is associated an acute sense of evil also. The positive meaning of death lies in the fact that its inevitability for the individual personal existence is evidence of the unattainability of the infinite enterprizes of life, and of the impossibility of realizing fullness of life within the limits of this world and this time.

Death, that final evil, is one of the paths to eternity. Endless life in the conditions of our limited existence would be a nightmare. To pass through death is just as necessary for our personal destiny in eternity, as the end of the world is necessary for the accomplishment of its eternal destiny. The antinomies and problems of human life and of the life of the world are insoluble in this aeon, and, therefore, a transition to another aeon is necessary. For this reason fear of death is not the only possibility; there is also an attraction of death. The thought of death is sometimes a consolation to a man when the contradictions of his life become intolerable, when the evil around him grows too dense. Freud regarded the instinct of death not only as of a higher order than the sexual instinct but as the sole elevated instinct in man. Heidegger is likewise compelled to recognize death as higher than *Dasein*, which is submerged in the humdrum and prosaic, in *das Man*. The last word in his philosophy belongs to death. It is an interesting fact that to the German spirit there is in general something attractive about death, victory and death. Wagner's music was permeated with the sense of victory and death; Nietzsche preached the will to power and an ecstatic joy in life, but in his perpetually tragic feeling about life the most profound and final thing was *Amor fati*. There has been depth in the German spirit but there has been no resuscitating strength.

That resuscitating strength does exist in the Russian spirit, and Fedorov represented the summit of its expression. And it is not a matter of chance that the principal festival of Russian Orthodoxy is the Feast of the Resurrection of Christ. It is thus that Christianity is understood. The source of victory over the evil of life in this world is not in death and it is not in birth, but in resurrection. The experience of the evil of the world destroys, but the creative power of resurrection conquers evil and death. Christian ethics in respect of evil as a whole and of individual evils can but be paradoxical. In Christ the God-Man and in the divine-human process, the transfiguration of the whole cosmos is being made ready. It is impossible to think of evil and of freedom, which is connected with evil, in an ontological and static way. They must be thought of dynamically in the language of spiritually existential experience.

SUGGESTED ADDITIONAL READINGS

The Problem of Evil

The Bible. Job. A dramatic presentation which deals with the problem of evil and the omnipotence of God.

Brightman, Edgar S. *A Philosophy of Religion.* New York: Prentice-Hall, 1940. See especially pp. 248f. An American personal idealistic philosopher feels that evil implies a limited God.

Ferré, Nels F. S. *Evil and The Christian Faith.* New York: Harper & Brothers, 1947. See especially pp. 123-137. A clear explanation of evil and its relation to the Christian faith by a Protestant theologian.

Laird, John. *Mind and Deity.* New York: Philosophical Library, 1941. See especially chapter 6. A Scottish philosopher discusses evil in relation to the providence of God.

Lewis, C. S. *The Problem of Pain.* New York: The Macmillan Company, 1950. Discussion of pain by a well-known apologist for the Christian faith.

Lewis, Edwin. *The Creator and The Adversary.* New York: Abingdon-Cokesbury Press, 1948. A good exposition of the relation of evil to belief in God from the perspective of a Protestant theologian who struggles with the question of a limited God.

Maimonides, Moses. *Guide of the Perplexed.* Trans., M. Friedländer. New York: Hebrew Publishing Co., n.d. (Also published in paperback by Dover Publications, Inc.) See especially Part III. A well-known medieval Jewish philosopher insists that God is not responsible for evil.

Petit, Francois. *The Problem of Evil.* Trans., Christopher Williams. New York: Hawthorn Books, 1959. A recent statement which deals with this problem from a Roman Catholic point of view.

Rashdall, Hastings. *The Theory of Good and Evil,* vol. II. London: Oxford University Press, 1924. British philosopher and theologian committed to personal idealism offers a major study quite inclusive in its coverage.

Weiss, Paul. "Good and Evil." *Review of Metaphysics* (September, 1949), III, 1, no. 9, pp. 81-94. An American philosopher considers evil to be the conflict of opposing goods and evaluates traditional arguments as they may be seen by those accepting this position.

VII. *Introduction*

IMMORTALITY AND ESCHATOLOGY

The possibility of life after death has engaged man's interest from the earliest times. The reality of posthumous existence is usually a fundamental assurance of theistic religions, although in some forms of religion the belief has been absent or inconspicuous. In the western philosophical tradition there has been ambivalence toward this idea: some philosophers have accepted immortality, while others have considered it an unsettled question or have denied its possibility altogether.

Those philosophers and theologians who have defended the belief in immortality have generally based their positions on one of two different foundations. Some have predicated their belief on what they take to be the indestructible nature of the human soul or of human values. Others have based their faith in immortality on a belief that God is able to resurrect man and to give him new life. The former argument derives from a belief in a special quality in man typically asserted by the Greek, and more particularly, the Platonic point of view. Platonists see man as a unique being who has an intrinsic conformity with ultimate reality. This relationship is described in terms of the presence of an indestructible element in man, rational and simple, namely, a soul. This soul substance is in this world enmeshed in a material shell or body. The effort of man's philosophic or religious quest is to "tend the soul" or to understand rationally his relationship to ultimate reality and thereby to escape the corrupting and timebinding imprisonment of the flesh. Death, then, is the release of the soul from the prison of the body.

The argument for the future life in terms of resurrection involves different assumptions. On this view man is understood to be a mortal being, and death is seen as a final end. Only if some new creative act is executed is there hope for man to escape death. God the Creator performs such acts. In His graciousness He has provided for the giving of new life to man, a new life which overcomes the threat of death and annihilation.

In the historical development of western thought these approaches have sometimes been considered antithetical and sometimes complementary. Often in Christian interpretations one can see illustrated the way in which these two approaches have been taken to be complementary. For instance, it is sometimes maintained that man has an immortal soul, but that only by an act of God can the soul enter into the relationship with God which is its ultimate purpose.

These traditional arguments have also been supplemented, and sometimes supplanted, by other approaches. One of these supplementary approaches sets the discussion in terms of a unique quality of life in the present which may also extend into the future. In this view, death and life are not seen primarily as physical events, but in terms of meanings and purposes, or in terms of what is perhaps more generally called life's present significance. It is at this point that one can see the relevance of eschatology to our discussion.

In recent decades, the use of the word "eschatology" and the employment of "eschatological" categories have increased. While there are different nuances of meaning in the word, its basic import can be indicated. The word itself means the study of the last things: such as death, judgment, heaven and hell. In recent times the term has tended to be used by those who believe that the time of the final events, when life's ultimate meaning will be revealed, is at hand. Intimately associated with this position is the question: how does the end come? Does it bring all normal history to a close and usher in a new era? Or does it come within the present time in the form of new meaning and new significance for the current order of things?

In the minds of many contemporary interpreters the terminus and the subsequent new beginning of life come when an individual finds meaning in life. This, then, brings what are considered by some to be qualities inhering only in a future life after death into the realm of man's present existence. The claim of many who would bring the last things into man's present experience, is that man, in escaping meaninglessness, finds *life*; that is, his present mortal existence assumes a new, eternal dimension. This dimension includes the "meaning" that was incorporated in the ideas of death, judgment, heaven and hell. Those of this persuasion emphasize man's finitude, consequent alienation from God, and estrangement from God's purpose. They feel that the world is broken or frustrated, and that it can be fulfilled or completed only by God's action. Such action can take place in man's present experience and provide him with a new dimension of meaning. Most proponents of this view hold that this new level of existence extends beyond the eventual fact of physical death.

But not all thinkers believe it is possible to demonstrate that life can assume such a radically new dimension in the present or that it can reach beyond death. Materialists, rationalists and humanists have often rejected these claims as untenable and unworthy of men who have the courage to face reality.

From these alternative possibilities it becomes apparent that a person's belief about the possibility of life after death is derived from his metaphysical or religious commitments. Thus materialism and behaviorism, which explain human life completely in terms of physical functions, exclude the possibility of immortality, whereas others who accept the eternal reality of values often argue that the ultimate extinction of persons as organized centers of value cannot be admitted. It is, of course, possible to accept the eternality of objective value without drawing the inference of human immortality.

A. E. Taylor, in his selection which follows, examines Christian concepts of immortality and makes interpretative comments on their development in terms of his own ethical interests. Oscar Cullmann in his essay defends the New Testament conception of resurrection and attempts to distinguish it from Greek conceptions of immortality.

The French philosopher, Jacques Maritain, provides a characteristic Thomistic interpretation and defense of the immortality of the soul, while Andrew Seth Pringle-Pattison gives an interesting and provocative interpretation of eternal life as a new dimension in the present. C. D. Broad, an English philosopher, offers in the selection from his work a carefully reasoned analysis of the argument from the continuity of nature as it bears on the possibility of human survival beyond physical death.

F. R. Tennant conveniently classifies the arguments both for and against immortality, with brief comments on their significance. The student who has read the other selections will want to evaluate both Tennant's analysis and his interpretation of the meaning of classical types of argument for immortality. The approach of Ian T. Ramsey to the question of human immortality reflects his concern with empiricism and linguistic analysis. Our final selection is from Nicolas Berdyaev, who, from the perspective of an existentialist orientation, recognizes the threat of death to meaningful living and who proclaims that there is purpose for life despite this threat.

ALFRED E. TAYLOR

A. E. TAYLOR (1869-1954) taught philosophy at Aberdeen and Edinburgh and made contributions in the fields of history of philosophy, ethics and religion. His books, *Faith of A Moralist* and *Plato, The Man and His Work*, are among his best known.

The Christian Hope of Immortality*

Let us begin our examination, then, by setting down briefly some of the leading characteristics that seemed to us to distinguish an "immortality" such as it is reasonable at least to hope for from one which would be a mere arbitrary fancy without any rational justification.

(1) It is the attainment of a completed rational selfhood, or personality, conscious of itself and in harmonious possession both of all its own internal resources and of its "environment." Since it is only in and through intercourse with one another that personality is developed and maintained in us, such a life can only be that of a *society* of persons of one heart and mind from which the veil of mystery now making each of us so much a riddle to the rest, and the self-centred "private interest" which sets barriers to community of will, purpose, and sympathy have been eliminated.

(2) It is a life communicated to those who share in it, in the first instance, from the supreme personality presupposed by the very existence of the world and of ourselves. At that fountain our personality is fed; if we enter into and share the life of one another, in the way proper to moral persons, it is because we are all admitted to be sharers in His life. The "brotherhood of all men," so often dreamed of and longed for, is only possible in so far as all men recognize themselves as "sons of God."

(3) It is no privilege reserved to an *élite* of the richly dowered and gifted, but a heritage open to all mankind, high and low, learned and unlearned, refined or homely, bond or free, in virtue of their common endowment with the capacity for personality.

(4) But, though it is thus, in the end, an inheritance and a gift, it is a gift which has to be appropriated by genuine effort on our own part. We can render ourselves increasingly fit for it by steady and strenuous endeavour,

* From A. E. Taylor, *The Christian Hope of Immortality*, pp. 45-63. Published, 1947, The Macmillan Company. Reprinted by permission of F. E. A. Taylor.

or we can fail more and more to appropriate it by our own carelessness and sloth. Even in what we now see of human life, we are familiar enough with the fact that as a man uses or abuses his opportunities, he tends to grow more and more into true personality or to degenerate from it. It is possible to "save one's soul," but equally possible to lose it; eternal life can be won, but it can also be thrown away. And thus, in the end, we must expect it to be with each of us strictly "according to his works," good or evil, though we must never allow ourselves to forget that it is only the supreme Wisdom which knows the full good and evil of any man's "work" as it truly is; the account is not to be rendered to me, and my judgment of the quality of any man's work, and particularly perhaps of that of my own, must always be uncertain. To judge you or myself with the judgment of God, I should need first to see myself or you with the "all-seeing" eyes of the reader of all hearts, and that vision is not vouchsafed to us in our earthly pilgrimage.

(It should hardly be necessary, though to obviate a certain kind of criticism it may be judicious to say that in speaking of the Christian representation of the life to come, our attention will be confined to the few and reticent statements definitely made in the New Testament. We are not in the least concerned with the sometimes rather grotesque pictorial imagery of certain types of popular hymn or sermon. Such utterances are no part of the authoritative teaching of the Christian Church; their language, as everyone understands, is purely metaphorical, and the metaphors employed, being so largely borrowed from Old Testament poetry, are often not those which would spontaneously commend themselves to a modern European imagination, not to add that many of them have the further glaring fault of improperly transferring to the eternal life of "blessed spirits" in Heaven language used in the Apocalypse expressly of the "new Jerusalem" of an earthly "millennium." The golden streets, gates of pearl and foundations of precious stones, for example, all belong to the seer's imaginative description of the renovated terrestrial city; they have nothing to do with "Heaven" and "eternity.")

If we turn, then, to the four points we have just specified and take them in order, we shall, I believe, find that on each and all of them the teaching of Christianity exhibits a complete agreement with what we have called our natural and reasonable anticipations, but at the same time does more than merely repeat those anticipations; it adds something of its own, strictly in conformity with the "natural light," but yet not discoverable apart from an actual historical disclosure, first through the "prophets," and finally through the teaching, and even more, the life, death, and resurrection of our Lord Jesus Christ. Christianity—that is, if it is what it professes to be—is really a *revelation*, a disclosure of God's purposes for us, made from the side of God

Himself, and, at the same time, the God to whom it bears witness is no other
than the God to whom the careful and unbiased use of our own intelligence
has been directing us. It is certainly a faith, but no less certainly, rightly
apprehended a reasonable faith.

As to the first of our four points, we may note that the one thing definitely
said about the hope held out to the Christian in the New Testament is that
it is a being fully alive and fully conscious of the whole truth about our
Maker, ourselves, and the world. Thus in the fourth Gospel the Evangelist's
leading thought is that the divine Christ who, in the fullness of time has
appeared among men, is Himself an eternal living personality, and has come
into our midst in order to impart such personality to us. He was "in the
beginning with God" and "was God." All creation was made "through Him,"
and, the writer goes on to explain—if we follow what seems the most probable
punctuation—"that which was made was life in Him, and the life was the
light of men." The life, that is, which is eternally inherent in the Christ is
no blind "life force;" it is an intelligent personality, like that we find in a
most imperfect measure in ourselves at our best, and aspire to possess in a
fuller manner. So in the great prayer of Chapter xvii, our Lord describes the
eternal life, which it is His mission to bestow on those who believe, as consisting in knowledge of "the only true God and Jesus Christ whom He has
sent." What this implies is expressed in so many words in the first Epistle
of John, where, amid all the reserve with which the writer confesses that we
know and can know little or nothing, at present, of what eternal life is ("it
doth not yet appear what we shall be"), he also insists that at least we shall
be "like Him," because "we shall see Him as He is." That is, the knowledge
of God as He is will transform us, as we attain to it, into God's likeness,
since our personality inevitably shapes itself on the model of that which
supplies the food of its habitual contemplation and meditation.

St. Paul again strikes the same note both in his reserves and in his cer-
tainties. He, too, will commit himself to no rash theosophic dreams of the
future which lies before him; as he tells his Corinthian converts "what God
had prepared for them that love Him" is something which "has not entered
into man's heart," something transcending all our imaginative speculation;
here on earth the best of us only see the reality dimly, through a mirror, so
to say, and "in a riddle;" it is elsewhere, "yonder" as the Neo-Platonist
philosophers were fond of saying, that it will be for us to see it as it is, and
without the distortions which arise from the interposition of the "mirror,"
to "know even as we are known." Here our most certain knowledge is beset
all around with a penumbra of obscurity and darkness; as the old proverb
says, as soon as we pursue any of our inquiries more than a very little way,
we come upon the inexplicable, *omnia abeunt in mysterium;* "yonder" there

will be no unintelligibilities left, our vision will have the limpid transparency of God's, and our wills will be in perfect harmony with themselves and one another because our vision is clear. We shall be what we are here at best seeking to become, persons in full and conscious possession of our own personality.

The tradition of the great Christian divines has always been true to the lines thus laid down in the New Testament. The Greek Fathers did not shrink from translating the Johannine language about likeness to God as the result of "seeing Him as He is," into the formula that the process of attaining eternal life is one of *theosis (deification)*, becoming ourselves divine, and the formula was retained by the Western Church, though with a preference for replacing the word *deification*, which might be misunderstood as though it were meant to efface the impassable gulf between the Creator and His creatures, by the less dangerous term, *deiformity*. If even that word sounds too presumptuous to certain modern ears we may gloss it by saying that in view of the thorough-going rationalism of medieval Christian thought, to achieve deiformity means neither more nor less than what we have ourselves spoken of as the attainment of an assured and conscious complete personality. When the great men of the Middle Ages spoke of human life as a pilgrimage of the soul to God, they did not mean, as an Indian Yogi might, that the goal of the pilgrim's journey is to lose himself in the impersonal. "The dewdrops slip into the boundless sea" may be a pretty phrase, but to the Christian ear it is charged with deadly heresy; the goal, as Christians have seen it, is not to lose one's personal self, but to find it for the first time and to find it beyond all possibility of loss. Certainly, according to the Gospels, the man who is set on keeping a dwarfish and misgrown self with its trivial lusts and limited and conflicting loves, will in the end lose himself, but he who is ready to set this more than half unreal self on the hazard will end by finding himself "unto life eternal," he will find the personality which God meant to be his, and he is the only man who will do so.

As to our second point, it would be wasting words to take up unnecessary space in dwelling on the fact that eternal life is always represented in the New Testament as a *gift* from God. It is enough for us to remember that St. Paul lays special stress on the contrast between the death which is the *wage* of sin and the eternal life which is not a wage but a free gift of God, and that the same thought reappears in the fourth Gospel when we find Christ saying that He grants it to His disciples to have life in themselves, as the Father has granted it to Him to have life in Himself. It is more to our purpose to note that the gift is not represented in the New Testament as bestowed on men by the fact of their creation. Men are not thought of as already sons of God and heirs of eternal life in virtue of their birth into the world as men; that is a modern "humanitarian" remodelling of the thought; according to the New Testament, men acquire sonship to God and the inheritance of eternal life by being "adopted" into the Christian fellowship; they are adopted, not natural sons of the Father in Heaven. This is why the first step on the way to eternal life can be called by St. Paul being a *"new* creation," and in the fourth Gospel being "born *again*," and why in the Epistle of St. Peter God is said to have "begotton us again unto a lively hope *by the resurrection of Jesus Christ."* Those who are still outside the Christian fellowship are said, on the contrary, to be without hope in the world, and are spoken of not as sons of God, but as "children of wrath." The Christian conception is that eternal life is a gift which Christ is empowered to confer on His followers, and only on them, though sight is never lost of the fact that any man is potentially a son of God, since any man may be re-born into the Christian fellowship.

This is not to say that the New Testament writers teach the doctrine of the "natural mortality of the soul." As their constant references to judgment to come show, they accept as something familiar to themselves and their readers the belief that we all survive what we call the death of the body. It is possible, no doubt, by a suitable exegesis to read into their writings a doctrine of "conditional immortality," if that phrase is taken to mean that the final doom of the man who distinctly rejects Christ and His gift is complete dissolution of personality, but we cannot force on them the thought this dissolution is effected at the death of the present body. That, they assume, we shall all survive. But such mere survival, even if indefinitely prolonged, is not what they mean by "incorruptibility" or eternal life. They keep those names for the new quality of life enjoyed by the man who is "with the Lord" and "sees Him as He is." This is a point which is unfortunately obscured when Christian thinkers set themselves, as they have often done in the past, to try to demonstrate the immortality of the soul by reasoning based simply on a theory of *its* nature, without any reference to God, except perhaps as the Creator of the soul and of everything else. It is therefore, perhaps, from the Christian point of view a gain that arguments of this kind have fallen under suspicion, even excessive suspicion, ever since Kant's vigorous onslaught on them in the *Critique of Pure Reason.* An "immortality" which could be demonstrated without any reference to God would be only an indefinite survival which might conceivably prove to be the fact in a world where there was no God at all; this is not the "better life" that any religiously minded man, least of all a Christian, is particularly interested in.

It should be hardly necessary to remark, again, that there is a complete

absence from the New Testament of any trace of the insidious tendency
to regard God's gift of a full and completed personality as restricted to some
little aristocracy of the intellectually highly endowed. "Heaven," as Christianity conceives it, is not reserved for "superior persons"; it is full of "common people." This is, indeed, a direct consequence of the way in which,
in the New Testament, the "promises" are regularly made not to the isolated
individual, but to the whole society of the "re-born." They are promises to
a "you," not to a "thou." We can, of course, understand how, in the necessary reaction of modern times against the coarsening and hardening of the
original thought of the Gospel into the notion of a "salvation" to be mechanically earned by membership of a particular visible organization, men's
minds should have been driven in the opposite direction, to the point of
regarding "religion" as a purely private affair between the individual soul
and its God. But neither this extreme "protestantism" (which, of course,
was never contemplated by the original Protestants) nor its opposite, an
extreme "institutionalism" has any true warrant in the New Testament.
According to the New Testament, "salvation" certainly depends on a *personal* relation between God and the individual soul; if a man has not in
him "the spirit of Christ," he is none of Christ's, no matter what he may
seem to be from his superficial inclusion in any visible organization. But the
personal relation is not a *private* one. It carries with it, and should normally
show itself by, a relation of the most intimate kind to all the other persons
who together constitute "the body of Christ." Hence the inseparability of
the love of God, which is the first commandment of the New Law from
the love of one's neighbour, which is the second, and the apostle's insistence
that absence of the love of the brethren may be taken as proof of the absence
of love of God. This is, in fact, a consequence of the very nature of personality itself. Personality can only develop in an atmosphere of reciprocal
intimate and loving fellowship between persons; the closer and more intimate
this fellowship, the more real the personality attained by those who share
in it; a narrow and "self-centred" person (even when, as may be often the
case, his isolation is rather his misfortune than his fault) is not fully a
person. St. Paul's way of putting this is to say that in virtue of the fact
that each of us is a "member" of the body of Christ, we are also "members
of one another." Disease or weakness of one limb or organ of a living
body inevitably has its effect on the health and strength of the whole, and
the reason for the closeness of this connection between the different organs
is precisely that all are related as "organs" to the life of the single self,
which *is* not any of the "organs" but finds its expression through them all.

    It is not meant that there is no distinction between the magnitude of
the tasks executed by different organs; the very perfection of organization

demands that there should be distinction and discrimination. But all alike, conspicuous or inconspicuous, primary or secondary, have their own special communication to make to the single life of the whole, and all are alike alive with its life. So in the Christian fellowship, not all who belong to it are apostles, or teachers, or share in the gifts of wisdom and knowledge to the same degree, but all are alike alive with the distinctive Christian life, all have in principle been "re-born into eternity." In the community of the re-born there are no barriers of race, or colour, or class, and the degree to which any man has attained possession of *his* true personality is not to be measured by the place he holds in any scale drawn up with a view to mundane standards. A simple uninstructed man may rank much higher in the scale of genuine personality than a great scholar or man of science; an indigent negro than a "cultivated English gentlemen." Those of us whose work in the world is discharged in one of the so-called "learned professions," perhaps, need particularly to be warned that whenever we yield to the temptation to confuse spiritual worth with intellectual attainments, or delicate taste, or "culture," as the word is commonly understood, we are deserting the Christian standard.

Finally, though the eternal life spoken of in the New Testament is, in its origin, a free gift bestowed by God, it is one which has to be appropriated by the recipient, and the appropriation involves a lifetime of work and care. The gift may always be thrown away by our own wilfulness or carelessness, and none of us is secure against these faults. Hence the need that "he who seems to stand" should take unremitting care "lest he fall." No New Testament writer is more emphatic in his declarations that eternal life is not a "wage" or "salary" for services rendered but a gift than St. Paul, but it is he also who most expressly enjoins his converts to "work out their own salvation" in "fear and trembling," and openly envisages the possibility that, even in himself, negligence might end in "becoming a castaway." The High Calvinists of a bygone age were accustomed to find the warrant for their assertion "once in grace, always in grace" in certain passages of the Epistle to the Romans; yet it is clear that the author of the epistle would never have ventured to say of himself what some of his exponents have said, that he *knew* himself to be now and for ever finally "in grace."

If it is a paradox to say that something which is a free gift of God may also be forfeited unless we strive towards it diligently and unremittingly, it is a paradox which runs through the whole New Testament. No honest exegesis can get rid of the patent fact that, when all is said, the New Testament doctrine of man's destiny is no mere message of comfort for the indolent; there is a side to it which is distinctly disquieting. Eternal life can be won, and won by him who will, but it can also be thrown away, and apparently—though the New Testament, intelligently read, is not very explicit in this—finally thrown away. That any man has actually made such a final "great refusal" is, perhaps, more than the New Testament ever says, but at least, for each of us, there is the possibility of making it. It is emphatically *not* the Christian doctrine that the persistent "waster" has only to pass through the portals of death to find himself in a world which automatically "makes this world right." And this also is as it should be if what is at stake is personality itself. Personality cannot be thrust upon us from without; it has to be asserted by each of us for himself by resolute concentration of thought and will, and if a man "lets himself drift," he rapidly sinks to a more impersonal level. If I choose, I can degrade myself into something like a mere self of momentary impulses and feelings, and we all find that we are too apt to act thus, especially as age steals over us. We have no reason to suppose that it can be otherwise in the hereafter.

If what we have so far said is true, then, we may fairly claim for the Christian hope that, when rightly understood, it is no fantastic dream, pleasing but baseless; in substance it accords with anticipations which are independently inevitable in all of us, just because we are reasonable creatures in a universe where reason is at home. But Christianity also gives a new and determinate character to these anticipations, which would otherwise remain vague and uncertain, and because it does this, we rightly receive it as a "revelation." It is wholly misleading to speak of Christianity, in the fashion of the eighteenth-century latitudinarians, as "the religion of nature republished," with the implication that it contains only what might have been, and presumably was, equally well known to the reflective and devout of all ages, and that the mission of our Lord was no more than to remind the thoughtless of what they had allowed themselves to forget. Christ, according to the New Testament, did not come into the world simply to help men to "brush up" their "natural religion" as middle-aged men may "brush up" the French and Latin they learned in their schooldays. He came primarily not to *teach* us something in the short course of His earthly life, but to *do* something for us which no mere teacher could do; so far as He came to teach, it was to teach us something we did not know before, and without Him could not know at all.

What the New Testament adds to the statement that eternal life is the gift of God is, in the first place, that the gift has been bestowed on us specifically through Christ, and that Christ is no mere envoy through whom a far-away God has conveyed a message to us, but one who is Himself both a man of our own flesh and blood and also divine, "one with the Father." (The New Testament writers do not, of course, use the technical terminology which was subsequently developed for the express purpose of putting an end to discussions about their meaning, but it is recognized to-day by the scholars of all shades of personal opinion that the New Testament everywhere presents Christ as a divine being who may rightly receive the adoration due to God, and whose acts are rightly described as acts of God. It is just the impossibility of reducing the Lord Jesus of "primitive Christianity" to purely human dimensions which leads ingenious but ill-balanced writers in our own times to make attempts, discountenanced by all serious historians, Christian or non-Christian, to get rid altogether of the historical Jesus Christ and to reduce Him to a "myth." Preposterous [1] as the device is, it is prompted by the sound perception that the Christ of our earliest documents is *already* presented as a divine being.)

Now here is, as has been said—for example, by Dr. E. R. Bevan—the characteristically new note of the New Testament as compared with the Old. Ezekiel, in particular, had said long before that God would once more gather together his people, now scattered in bondage, as a shepherd might go out into the wilderness and collect his strayed flock. But to the Jewish reader this had apparently meant only that God would raise up in the future some wonderful human leader who would gather together again the "dispersion" of Israel. It would be, after all, only this wonderful man who could actually go out into the desert to reassemble the "sheep"; God would only be concerned in the business as the far-off being who had sent him on his costly and perilous errand, as a monarch may sit comfortably at home in his palace and send out devoted servants on a distant enterprise; the undertaking would be God's only on the principle that *qui facit per alium facit per se*. The courage and devotion would really be those of the envoy, and, to the strictly logical mind, they would be proof of *his* goodness, but no proof of the goodness of the sovereign to whom they cost nothing. Christianity, on the other hand, declared that it was actual fact that the divine shepherd had Himself come into the wilderness after the strayed sheep and had faced all its hardships and privations in His own person. The historical

---

[1] How preposterous is shown, for example, by the theory of some literary men that the Jesus of the Gospels is identical with the Joshua of the Old Testament. We are thus to assume (1) that Joshua was an old and forgotten Hebrew divinity, and (2) that at the Christian era there was, for some unknown reason, a revival of the cult of this obsolete god. But there is not one scrap of evidence that Joshua was ever regarded by any Israelite as being a deity. His story, as we have it in the Old Testament, is simply that of a successful leader of Hebrew tribes in their first penetration into the country of the Canaanites, and there is no reason to think that anyone had ever supposed him to be anything else. We do not even hear that the Israelites made a colossal statue of him and hammered nails into it for luck. The Germans did this sort of thing for Hindenburg some 20 years ago, but a man who should assert that Hindenburg was a resurrected Wotan would only make himself ridiculous.

events were thus witnesses to the self-forgetting love, not of a great teacher or prophet, but of the very Lord of creation Himself. "So God loved the world" thus came to have a depth of meaning for Christians which it had never had for an Israelite, and the new significance of the thought gave a new meaning to the Christian life as a response to this love; it was possible henceforth for life to be inspired by a supreme, grateful love, not simply to a great human benefactor, but to the Maker of "all things visible and invisible."

The result is a changed attitude to the whole drama of human life and death. Even in a world morally indifferent—as the world depicted in Shakespeare's greatest tragedies sometimes looks to be—to good and bad; even in a world definitely and positively evil, we could still feel love and devotion to a human benefactor who had at least protected us, to the best of his power, against "fortune's spite"; some of us might steel ourselves, when he fell, to fall not utterly unmanned by his side. But in an evil world we should certainly know, and in an indifferent world we should have over-powering reasons for believing that our hero and we were at best falling together in a forlorn hope. The order of things would be against us, and our highest courage would be the courage of despair dying "game to the last." Now despair can for a time nerve to vigorous achievement, but as a permanent attitude it is not invigorating but enervating. At least, it must be so with us, who are not wolves or weasels but men, reasonable animals. If we are once firmly convinced that the order of things is irrevocably against our ideals, we cannot avoid the paralyzing suspicion that these ideals, how-ever much we cherish them, are futile and arbitrary, and we shall come to ask ourselves doubtingly whether they are, after all, worth the blood and tears they cost, whether mankind had not better do without them.

This is why, for my own part, I doubt very much whether a virile human morality can flourish apart from some conviction about the universal world-order which, thought out, proves to imply belief in God and His goodness. One may say, no doubt, that "value" and "existence" have nothing to do with one another, but belong to wholly different worlds of thought; one may say "What we need as inspiration to action is not belief in the *exist-ence* of any thing or any person, but belief in the *worth* of courage and love," and the like. But divorced from belief in the overpowering actuality of the "love whose smile kindles the universe," your declaration "I believe in love" only means "I personally choose to regard love as supremely good"; and if your only reason for your profession is a *Hoc volo, sic jubeo*, why should you not change your choice? *Le peu de chose que sont les hommes!* and if *l'amour* is, to put it brutally, only an episode in the career of these little creatures, *le peu de chose qu'est l'amour*.[2] It is, you will say, what I care most about. But it is not what all men, perhaps not what many men, care most about, and it may be that to-morrow, or next year, I shall have changed my scale of "values"; if these values are no more than creations of my personal will, there is nothing sacred about them, they arise and perish as my fancy flickers, like the "fancy values of commerce." There can, indeed, be no worth except in relation to some will which finds satisfaction in it, but the will to which genuine and abiding worth has this relation cannot be merely your mutable willing or mine; it can only be a "living will that shall endure when all that seems shall suffer shock." To the good man love is sacred and duty is sacred, but neither could be so if they were mere expressions of his own will as this individual man; the good man is not an idolator of himself and his private will. And if I, or all mankind, were to-morrow to turn against the old sanctities and tread love and duty under our feet, they would lose nothing of their sacredness; it would not really be they, but our own wills, which would be profaned.

Now if the central doctrine of the Christian is true, then we have such a certainty as the world cannot otherwise afford that love and duty are indeed sacred. For then it is a fact that the Master of all things has not merely told us to be loving and dutiful and will hold us to account if we fail; He has Himself, in the person of the historical Lord Jesus, entered into the life of humanity, has Himself led the life of selfless love and duty to the bitter end, and triumphed over all the obstacles that beset it; we, who have still the obstacles and hindrances to conflict with, have received from him not merely the inspiration of His teaching and example, but the certainty that the values which are sustained by the eternal "living will" are precisely those which were affirmed in practice by the Lord Jesus and are dearest to our own hearts—love, dutifulness, humility, courage, patience. We know, then, that, however appearances may be against them, these values can "never fail"; they are the foundation-stones on which the frame of things is built. This is why an apostle can speak of the faith of the Christian fellowship as one which conquers the world. It is not merely that, to quote Blake, "a strong persuasion that a thing is so makes it so"; for you cannot make falsehood into truth by the violence of your "persuasion" of the falsehood. The "world-conquering" quality of the Christian faith, if it is not an illusion, depends, first and foremost, on the nature of the person towards whom it is directed. It can conquer the world because, if it is true

---

[2] Rupert Brooke wrote of the First World War as a welcome recall from "all the little emptiness of love." Presumably the kind of "love" he had in his mind was none of the loftiest, but if the noblest love we know is, after all, *only* the "idiosyncrasy" of a particular species of animal, is it not all, in the end, "little" and "empty"?

at all, it is a confidence based on a real disclosure of the character of the unseen source of the world. If the mind of God has been truly disclosed by the life, death, and triumph of Jesus, then it is certain that God's world is not really either indifferent or hostile to our highest human aspirations, and for the true "members of Christ's body" eternal life ceases to be only what Plato had called it, a "great hope," and becomes a fact. It is the confidence in the fact which accounts for the strange "joy" so characteristic of the obscure, toil-worn despised and persecuted first Christians in the midst of a world full of pleasures, refined or sordid, but, as students of the period have so often noted, as deficient in joy as it was avid of pleasure.

These considerations also explain what might otherwise seem a singular fact about the history of Christian theology. When the Church set itself to codify and formulate its convictions it was not content with the emphatic assertion of the divinity of its founder; it insisted no less emphatically on his genuine and complete humanity. If it was declared deadly heresy to pronounce him in any way "inferior to the Father as touching this divinity," it was an equal heresy to abate anything from his humanity. You were not to withhold from him any jot of the worship due to the supreme Creator; equally you were not to exempt him from anything incidental to full human normality—hunger, thirst, weariness, pain, temptation. He was to be thought of neither as a deity of second rank, nor as a "superman." This, more than anything else, was what perplexed and shocked the ordinary outsider. He would not have found it incredible that a god, at any rate a minor god, should show himself in the visible form of a man. But that a god should feel genuine want or pain, should shed tears at the grave of a friend, should be insulted, beaten, crucified, and should feel the pain and shame of such things was a veritable scandal. Yet obviously if the life of Christ is to be evidence that *our* highest human values are also the eternal and absolute values, it is precisely this union in one historical person of Deity and complete humanity which must be maintained. To whittle away either the divinity or the humanity—to be either "Liberal Protestant" or Docetist—is to surrender the very "ground of all our hopes."

OSCAR CULLMANN

OSCAR CULLMANN (1902-) continental
Protestant theologian, has taught at Basel, the
Sorbonne and in America. His major field
of study is the New Testament. Among his
most important works are *Christ and Time*
and *The Christology of the New Testament.*

Immortality of the Soul or Resurrection of the Dead?*

The Wages of Sin: Death

Body and Soul—Flesh and Spirit

Yet the contrast between the Greek idea of the immortality of the soul
and the Christian belief in the resurrection is still deeper. The belief in
the resurrection presupposes the Jewish connexion between death and *sin*.
Death is not something natural, willed by God, as in the thought of the
Greek philosophers; it is rather something unnatural, abnormal, opposed
to God. The Genesis narrative teaches us that it came into the world only
by the sin of man. Death is a curse, and the whole creation has become
involved in the curse. The sin of man has necessitated the whole series of
events which the Bible records and which we call the story of redemption.
Death can be conquered only to the extent that sin is removed. For "death
is the wages of sin." It is not only the Genesis narrative which speaks thus.
Paul says the same thing (Romans 6^{23}), and this is the view of death held
by the whole of primitive Christianity. Just as sin is something opposed to
God, so is its consequence, death. To be sure, God can make use of death
(1 Corinthians 15^{35ff}, John 12^{24}), as He can make use of Satan to man.

Nevertheless, death *as such* is the enemy of God. For God is Life and the
Creator of life. It is not by the will of God that there are withering and
decay, dying and sickness, the by-products of death working in our life. All
these things, according to Christian and Jewish thinking, come from human
sin. Therefore, every healing which Jesus accomplishes is not only a driving
back of death, but also an invasion of the province of sin; and therefore
on every occasion Jesus says: "Your sins are forgiven." Not as though there

* From Oscar Cullmann, *Immortality of the Soul or Resurrection of the Dead?* pp.
28-47. Copyright, 1958, The Epworth Press. Used by permission of The Epworth Press
and the Macmillan Company. [Footnotes omitted, Eds.]

470

were a corresponding sin for every individual sickness; but rather, like the presence of death, the fact that sickness exists at all is a consequence of the sinful condition of the whole of humanity. Every healing is a partial resurrection, a partial victory of life over death. That is the Christian point of view. According to the Greek interpretation, on the contrary, bodily sickness is a corollary of the fact that the body is bad in itself and is ordained to destruction. For the Christian an anticipation of the Resurrection can already become visible, even in the earthly body.

That reminds us that the body is in no sense bad in itself, but is, like the soul, a gift of our Creator. Therefore, according to Paul, we have duties with regard to our body. God is the *Creator* of all things. The Greek doctrine of immortality and the Christian hope in the resurrection differ so radically because Greek thought has such an entirely different interpretation of creation. The Jewish and Christian interpretation of creation excludes the whole Greek dualism of body and soul. For indeed the visible, the corporeal, is just as truly God's creation as the invisible. God is the maker of the body. The body is not the soul's prison, but rather a temple, as Paul says (1 Corinthians 6[19]): the temple of the Holy Spirit! The basic distinction lies here. Body and soul are not opposites. God finds the corporeal "good" after He has created it. The Genesis story makes this emphasis explicit. Conversely, moreover, sin also embraces the whole man, not only the body, but the soul as well; and its consequence, death, extends over all the rest of creation. Death is accordingly something dreadful, because the whole visible creation, including our body, is something wonderful, even if it is corrupted by sin and death. Behind the pessimistic interpretation of death stands the optimistic view of creation. Wherever, as in Platonism, death is thought of in terms of liberation, there the visible world is not recognized directly as God's creation.

Now, it must be granted that in Greek thought there is also a very positive appreciation of the body. But in Plato the good and beautiful in the corporeal are not good and beautiful in virtue of corporeality but rather, so to speak, *in spite of* corporeality: the soul, the eternal and the only substantial reality of being, shines faintly through the material. The corporeal is not the real, the eternal, the divine. It is merely that through which the real appears—and then only in debased form. The corporeal is meant to lead us to contemplate the pure archetype, freed from all corporeality, the invisible Idea.

To be sure, the Jewish and Christian points of view also see something else besides corporeality. For the whole creation is corrupted by sin and death. The creation which we see is not as God willed it, as He created it; nor is the body which we wear. Death rules over all; and it is not necessary for annihilation to accomplish its work of destruction before this fact becomes apparent—it is already obvious in the whole outward form of all things. Everything, even the most beautiful, is marked by death. Thus it might seem as if the distinction between Greek and Christian interpretation is not so great after all. And yet it remains radical. Behind the corporeal appearance Plato senses the incorporeal, transcendent, pure Idea. Behind the corrupted creation, under sentence of death, the Christian sees the future creation brought into being by the resurrection, just as God willed it. The contrast, for the Christian, is not between the body and the soul, not between outward form and Idea, but rather between the creation delivered over to death by sin and new creation; between the corruptible, fleshly body and the incorruptible resurrection body.

This leads us to a further point: the Christian interpretation of man. The anthropology of the New Testament is not Greek, but is connected with Jewish conceptions. For the concepts of body, soul, flesh, and spirit (to name only these), the New Testament does indeed use the same words as the Greek philosopher. But they mean something quite different, and we understand the whole New Testament amiss when we construe these concepts only from the point of view of Greek thought. Many misunderstandings arise thus. . . . There are good monographs on the subject, not to mention the appropriate articles in the *Theologisches Wörterbuch*. A complete study would have to treat separately the anthropologies of the various New Testament authors, since on this point there exist differences which are by no means unimportant. Of necessity I can deal here only with a few cardinal points which concern our problem, and even this must be done somewhat schematically, without taking into account the nuances which would have to be discussed in a proper anthropology. In so doing, we shall naturally have to rely primarily upon Paul, since only in his writings do we find an anthropology which is definable in detail, even though he too fails to use the different ideas with complete consistency.

The New Testament certainly knows the difference between body and soul, or more precisely, between the inner and outer man. This distinction does not, however, imply opposition, as if the one were by nature good, the other by nature bad. Both belong together, both are created by God. The inner man without the outer has no proper, full existence. It requires a body. It can, to be sure, somehow lead a shady existence without the body, like the dead in Sheol according to the Old Testament, but that is not a *genuine life*. The contrast with the Greek soul is clear: it is precisely apart from the body that the Greek soul attains to full development of its life. According to the Christian view, however, it is the inner man's very nature which demands the body.

And what now is the role played by the flesh (σάρξ) and spirit (πνεῦμα)? Here it is especially important not to be misled by the secular use of the Greek words, though it is found in various places even in the New Testament and even within individual writers whose use of terminology is never completely uniform. With these reservations, we may say that according to the use which is characteristic, say, for Pauline theology, flesh and spirit in the New Testament are two *transcendent* powers which can enter into man from without; but *neither is given with human existence as such*. On the whole it is true that the Pauline anthropology, contrary to the Greek, is grounded in *Heilsgeschichte*. "Flesh" is the power of sin or the power of death. It seizes the outer and the inner man *together*. *Spirit* (πνεῦμα) is its great antagonist: the power of creation. It also seizes the outer and inner man *together*. Flesh and spirit are active powers, and as such they work within us. The flesh, the power of death, entered man with the sin of Adam; indeed it entered the whole man, inner and outer; yet in such a way that it is very closely linked with the body. The inner man finds itself less closely connected with the flesh; although through guilt this power of death has more and more taken possession even of the inner man. The spirit, on the other hand, is the great power of life, the element of the resurrection; God's power of creation is given to us through the Holy Spirit. In the Old Testament the Spirit is at work only from time to time in the prophets. In the End-time in which we live—that is, since Christ has broken the power of death in His own death and has arisen—this power of life is at work in all members of the community (Acts 2[16]: "In the last days"). Like the flesh, it too already takes possession of the whole man, inner and outer. But whereas, in this age, the flesh has established itself to a substantial degree in the body, though it does not rule the inner man in the same inescapable way, the quickening power of the Holy Spirit is already taking possession of the inner man so decisively that the inner man is "renewed from day to day," as Paul says (2 Corinthians 4[16]). The whole Johannine Gospel emphasizes the point. We are already in the state of resurrection, that of eternal life—not immortality of soul: the new era is already inaugurated. The body, too, is already in the power of the Holy Spirit.

Wherever the Holy Spirit is at work we have what amounts to a momentary retreat of the power of death, a certain foretaste of the End. This is true even in the body, hence the healings of the sick. But here it is a question only of a retreat, not of a final transformation of the body of death into a resurrection body. Even those whom Jesus raised up in His lifetime will die again, for they did not receive a resurrection body, the transformation of the fleshly body into a spiritual body does not take place until the End. Only then will the Holy Spirit's power of resurrection take such complete possession of the body that it transforms it in the way it is already transforming the inner man. It is important to see how different the New Testament anthropology is from that of the Greeks. Body and soul are both originally good in so far as they are created by God; they are both bad in so far as the deadly power of the flesh has hold of them. Both can and must be set free by the quickening power of the Holy Spirit.

Here, therefore, deliverance consists not in a release of soul from body but in a release of both from flesh. We are not released from the body; rather the body itself is set free. This is made especially clear in the Pauline Epistles, but it is the interpretation of the whole New Testament. In this connexion one does not find the differences which are present among the various books on other points. Even the much-quoted saying of Jesus in Matthew 10²⁸ in no way presupposes the Greek conception. "Fear not them that kill the body, but cannot kill the soul." It might seem to presuppose the view that the soul has no need of the body, but the context of the passage shows that this is not the case. Jesus does not continue: "Be afraid of him who kills the soul"; rather "Fear him who can slay both soul *and* body in Gehenna." That is, fear God who is able to give you over completely to death; to wit, when He does not resurrect you to life. We shall see, it is true, that the soul is the starting-point of the resurrection, since, as we have said, it can already be possessed by the Holy Spirit in a way quite different from the body. The Holy Spirit already lives in our inner man. "By the Holy Spirit who dwells in you (already)," says Paul in Romans 8¹¹, "God will also quicken your mortal bodies." Therefore, those who kill only the body are not to be feared. It can be raised from the dead. Moreover, it must be raised. The soul cannot always remain without a body. And on the other side we hear in Jesus' saying in Matthew 10²⁸ that the soul can be killed. The soul is not immortal. There must be resurrection for both; for since the Fall the whole man is "sown corruptible." For the inner man, thanks to the transformation by the quickening power of the Holy Spirit, the resurrection can take place already in this present life: through the "renewal from day to day." The flesh, however, still maintains its seat in our body. The transformation of the body does not take place until the End, when the whole creation will be made new by the Holy Spirit, when there will be no death and no corruption.

The resurrection of the body, whose substance will no longer be that of the flesh, but that of the Holy Spirit, is only a part of the *whole new creation*. "We wait for a new heaven *and* a new earth," says 2 Peter 3¹³. The Christian hope relates not only to my individual fate, but to the entire creation. Through sin the whole creation has become involved in death. This we hear not only in Genesis, but also in Romans 8¹⁹ᶠᶠ, where Paul writes that the whole creation from now on waits longingly for deliverance. This deliverance will come when the power of the Holy Spirit transforms all matter, when God in a new act of creation will not *destroy* matter, but set it free from the flesh, from corruptibility. Not eternal Ideas, but concrete objects will then rise anew, in the new, incorruptible life-substance of the Holy Spirit; and among these objects belongs our body as well.

Because resurrection of the body is a new act of creation which embraces everything, it is not an event which begins with each individual death, but only at the *End*. It is not a transition from this world to another world, as is the case of the immortal soul freed from the body; rather it is the transition from the present age to the future. It is tied to the whole process of redemption.

Because there is sin there must be a process of redemption enacted in time. Where sin is regarded as the source of death's lordship over God's creation, there this sin and death must be vanquished together, and there the Holy Spirit, the only power able to conquer death, must win all creatures back to life in a continuous process.

Therefore the Christian belief in the resurrection, as distinct from the Greek belief in immortality, is tied to a *divine total process* implying deliverance. Sin and death must be conquered. *We* cannot do this. *Another* has done it for us; and He was able to do it only in that He betook himself to the province of death—that is, He himself died and expiated sin, so that death as the wages of sin is overcome. Christian faith proclaims that Jesus had done this and that He arose *with* body and soul after He was fully and really dead. Here God has consummated the miracle of the new creation expected at the End. Once again He has created life as in the beginning. At this one point, in Jesus Christ, this has already happened! Resurrection, not only in the sense of the Holy Spirit's taking possession of the *inner* man, but also resurrection of the *body*. This is a new creation of matter, an incorruptible matter. Nowhere else in the world is there this new spiritual matter. Nowhere else is there a spiritual body—only here in Christ.

The First-Born From the Dead

Between the Resurrection of Christ and the Destruction of Death

We must take into account what it meant for the Christians when they proclaimed: Christ is risen from the dead! Above all we must bear in mind what death meant for them. We are tempted to associate these powerful affirmations with the Greek thought of the immortality of the soul, and in this way to rob them of their content. Christ is risen: that is, we stand in the new era in which death is conquered, in which corruptibility is no more. For if there is really *one* spiritual body (not an immortal soul, but a spirited body) which has emerged from a fleshly body, then indeed the power of death is broken. Believers, according to the conviction of the first Christians, should no longer die: this was certainly their expectation in the earliest days. It must have been a problem when they discovered that Christians continued to die. But even the fact that men continue to die no longer has the same significance after the Resurrection of Christ. The fact of death is robbed of its former significance. Dying is no longer an expression of the absolute lordship of Death, but only one of Death's last contentions for lordship. Death cannot put an end to the great fact that there is *one* risen Body.

We ought to try simply to understand what the first Christians meant when they spoke of Christ as being the "first-born from the dead." However difficult it may be for us to do so, we must exclude the question whether or not we can accept this belief. We must also at the very start leave on one side the question whether Socrates or the New Testament is right. Otherwise we shall find ourselves continually mixing alien thought-processes with those of the New Testament. We should for once simply listen to what the New Testament says. Christ the first-born from the dead! His body the first Resurrection body, the first Spiritual Body. Where this conviction is present, the whole of life and the whole of thought must be influenced by it. The whole thought of the New Testament remains for us a book sealed with seven seals if we do not read behind every sentence there this other sentence: Death has already been overcome (death, be it noted, not the body); there is already a new creation (a new creation, be it noted, not an immortality which the soul has always possessed) the resurrection age is already inaugurated.

Granted that it is only inaugurated, but still it is decisively inaugurated. *Only* inaugurated: for death is at work, and Christians still die. The disciples experienced this as the first members of the Christian community died. This necessarily presented them with a difficult problem. In 1 Corinthians 11[30] Paul writes that basically death and sickness should no longer occur. We still die, and still there is sickness and sin. But the Holy Spirit is already effective in our world as the power of new creation; He is already at work visibly in the primitive community in the diverse manifestations of the Spirit. In my book *Christ and Time* I have spoken of a tension between present and future, the tension between "already fulfilled" and "not yet consummated." This tension belongs *essentially* to the New Testament and is not introduced as a secondary solution born of embarrassment, as Albert Schweitzer's disciples and Rudolph Bultmann maintain. This tension is already present in and with Jesus. He proclaims the Kingdom of God for the future; but on the other hand, He proclaims that the Kingdom of God has already broken in, since He Himself with the Holy Spirit is indeed repulsing death by healing the sick and raising the dead (Matthew 12²⁸, 11³ᶠᶠ, Luke 10¹⁸) in anticipation of the victory over death which He obtains in His own death. Schweitzer is not right when he sees as the original Christian hope *only* a hope in the future; nor is C. H. Dodd when he speaks *only* of a realized eschatology; still less Bultmann when he resolves the original hope of Jesus and the first Christians into Existentialism. It belongs to the very stuff of the New Testament that it thinks in temporal categories, and this is because the belief that in Christ the resurrection is achieved in the starting-point of all Christian living and thinking. When one starts from this principle, then the chronological tension between "already fulfilled" and "not yet consummated" constitutes the *essence* of the Christian faith. Then the metaphor I use in *Christ and Time* characterizes the whole New Testament situation: the decisive battle has been fought in Christ's death and Resurrection; only V-day is yet to come.

Basically the whole contemporary theological discussion turns upon this question: Is *Easter the* starting-point of the Christian Church, of its existence, life, and thought? If so, we are living in an interim time.

In that case, the faith in resurrection of the New Testament becomes the cardinal point of all Christian belief. Accordingly, the fact that there is a resurrection body—Christ's body—defines the first Christians' whole interpretation of time. If Christ is the "first-born from the dead," then this means that the End-time is already present. But it also means that a temporal interval separates the First-born from all other men who are not yet "born from the dead." This means then that we live in an interim time, between Jesus' Resurrection, which has already taken place, and our own, which will not take place until the End. It also means, moreover, that the quickening Power, the Holy Spirit, is already at work among us. Therefore Paul designates the Holy Spirit by the same term—ἀπαρχή, first-fruits (Romans 8²³)—as he uses for Jesus Himself (1 Corinthians 15²³). There is then already a foretaste of the resurrection. And indeed in a twofold way: our inner man is already being renewed from day to day by the Holy Spirit (2 Corinthians 4¹⁶; Ephesians 3¹⁶); the body also has already been laid hold of by the Spirit, although the flesh still has its citadels within it. Wherever the Holy Spirit appears, the vanquished power of death recoils, even in the body. Hence miracles of healing occur even in our still mortal body. To the despairing cry in Romans 7²⁴, "Who shall deliver me from this body of death?" the whole New Testament answers: The Holy Spirit!

The foretaste of the End, realized through the Holy Spirit, becomes most clearly visible in the early Christian celebration of the breaking of bread. Visible miracles of the Spirit occur there. There the Spirit tries to break through the limits of imperfect human language in the speaking with tongues. And there the community passes over into direct connexion with the Risen One, not only with His soul, but also with His Resurrection Body. Therefore we hear in 1 Corinthians 10[16]: "The bread we break, is it not communion with the body of Christ?" Here in communion with the brethren we come nearest to the Resurrection Body of Christ; and so Paul writes in the following Chapter 11 (a passage which has received far too little consideration): if this Lord's Supper were partaken of by all members of the community in a completely worthy manner, then union with Jesus' Resurrection Body would be so effective in our bodies that even now there would be no more sickness or death (1 Corinthians 11[28-30])—a singularly bold assertion. Therefore the community is described as the body of Christ, because here the spiritual body of Christ is present, because here we come closest to it; here in the common meal the first disciples at Easter saw Jesus' Resurrection Body, His Spiritual Body.

Yet in spite of the fact that the Holy Spirit is already so powerfully at work, men still die; even after Easter and Pentecost men continue to die as before. Our body remains mortal and subject to sickness. Its transformation into the spiritual body does not take place until the whole creation is formed anew by God. Then only, for the first time, there will be nothing but Spirit, nothing but the power of life, for then death will be destroyed with finality. Then there will be a new substance for all things visible. Instead of the fleshly matter there appears the spiritual. That is, *instead of corruptible matter there appears the incorruptible*. The visible and the invisible will be spirit. But let us make no mistake: this is certainly not the Greek sense of bodiless Idea! A new heaven *and* a new earth! That is the Christian hope. And then will our bodies also rise from the dead. Yet not as fleshly bodies, but as spiritual bodies.

The expression which stands in the ancient Greek texts of the Apostles' Creed is quite certainly not biblical: "I believe in the resurrection of the flesh!" Paul could not say that. Flesh and blood cannot inherit the Kingdom. Paul believes in the resurrection of the *body*, not of the *flesh*. The flesh is the power of death, which must be destroyed. This error in the Greek creed made its entrance at a time when the biblical terminology had been misconstrued in the sense of Greek anthropology. Our body, moreover (not merely our soul), will be raised at the End, when the quickening power of the Spirit makes all things new, all things without exception.

An incorruptible body! How are we to conceive this? Or better, how did the first Christians conceive of it? Paul says in Philippians 3[21] that at the End Christ will transform our lowly body into the body of his own glory (δόξα), just as in 2 Corinthians 3[18]; "we are being transformed into his own likeness from glory to glory (ἀπὸ δόξης εἰς δόξαν)." This glory (δόξα) was conceived by the first Christians as a sort of light-substance; but this is only an imperfect comparison. Our language has no word for it. Once again I refer to Grünewald's painting of the Resurrection. He may have come closest to what Paul understood as the spiritual body.

JACQUES MARITAIN

JACQUES MARITAIN (1882-   ) is a French Roman Catholic philosopher, and an outstanding spokesman for contemporary Thomistic thought. The range of his interests, as reflected in his writings, is also reminiscent of the breadth of Thomas. In the United States he has taught at Chicago, Columbia, Yale and Princeton Universities.

III. Personal Immortality*

The Existence of the Soul

It is of this immortality, and of the way in which the Scholastics established its rational certainty, that I should now like to speak.

We must of course realize that we have a soul before we can discuss whether it is immortal. How does St. Thomas Aquinas proceed in this matter?

He observes first that man has an activity, the activity of the intellect, which is in itself immaterial. The activity of the intellect is immaterial because the proportionate or "connatural" object of the human intellect is not, like the object of the senses, a particular and limited category of things, or rather a particular and limited category of the qualitative properties of things. The proportionate or "connatural" object of the intellect is the nature of the sense-perceivable things considered in an all-embracing manner, whatever the sense concerned may be. It is not only—as for sight—color or the colored thing (which absorbs and reflects such or such rays of light) nor—as for hearing—sound or the sound-source; it is the whole universe and

* Reprinted with the permission of Charles Scribner's Sons and Geoffrey Bles, Ltd., from *The Range of Reason* by Jacques Maritain (pp. 54-61), copyright 1952, Jacques Maritain. [Footnotes omitted, Eds.]

texture of sense-perceivable reality which can be known by the intellect, because the intellect does not stop at qualities, but pierces beyond, and proceeds to look at essence (that which a thing *is*). This very fact is a proof of the spirituality, or complete immateriality of our intellect; for every activity in which matter plays an intrinsic part is limited to a given category of material objects, as is the case for the senses, which perceive only those properties which are able to act upon their physical organs.

There is already, in fact, a certain immateriality in sense-knowledge: knowledge, as such, is an immaterial activity, because when I am in the act of knowing, I become, or am, the very thing that I know, a thing other than myself, insofar as it is other than myself. And how can I be, or become, other than myself, if it is not in a supra-subjective or immaterial manner? Sense-knowledge is a very poor kind of knowledge; insofar as it is knowledge, it is immaterial, but it is an immaterial activity intrinsically conditioned by, and dependent upon, the material functioning of the sense-organs. Sense-knowledge is the immaterial achievement, the immaterial actuation and product of a living bodily organ; and its very object is also something half material, half immaterial, I mean a physical quality *intentionally* or immaterially present in the medium by which it acts on the sense-organ (something comparable to the manner in which a painter's idea is immaterially present in his paint-brush).

But with intellectual knowledge we have to do with an activity which is in itself completely immaterial. The human intellect is able to know whatever participates in being and truth; the whole universe can be inscribed in it; this means that, in order to be known, the object known by the intellect has been stripped of any existential condition of materiality. This rose, which I see, has contours; but Being, of which I am thinking, is more spacious than space. The object of the intellect is universal, for instance that universal or de-individualized object which is apprehended in the idea of man, of animal, of atom; the object of the intellect is a universal which remains what it is while being identified with an infinity of individuals. And this is only possible because things, in order to become objects of the mind, have been entirely separated from their material existence. To this it must be added that the operation of our intellect does not stop at the knowledge of the nature of sense-perceivable things; it goes further; it knows by analogy the spiritual natures; it extends to the realm of merely possible things; its field has infinite magnitude.

Thus, the objects known by the human intellect, taken not as things existing in themselves, but precisely as objects determining the intellect and united with it, are purely immaterial.

Furthermore, just as the condition of the *object* is immaterial, so is the condition of the *act* which bears upon it, and is determined or specified by it. The object of the human intellect is, as such, purely immaterial; the act of the human intellect is also purely immaterial.

And, moreover, if the act of the intellectual power is purely immaterial, that *power* itself is also purely immaterial. In man, this thinking animal, the intellect is a purely spiritual power. Doubtless it depends upon the body, upon the conditions of the brain. Its activity can be disturbed or hindered by a physical disorder, by an outburst of anger, by a drink or a narcotic. But this dependence is an *extrinsic* one. It exists because our intelligence cannot act without the joint activity of the memory and the imagination, of the internal senses and external senses, all of which are organic powers residing in some material organ, in some special part of the body. As for the intellect itself, it is not *intrinsically* dependent upon the body since its activity is immaterial; the human intellect does not reside in any special part of the body. It is not contained by the body, but rather contains it. It uses the brain, since the organs of the internal senses are in the brain; yet the brain is not an organ of the intelligence; there is no part of the organism whose act is intellectual operation. The intellect has no organ.

Finally, since intellectual power is spiritual, or purely immaterial in itself, its *first substantial root*, the subsisting principle from which this power proceeds and which acts through its instrumentality, is also spiritual.

So much for the spirituality of the intellect. Now, thought or the operation of the intellect is an act and emanation of man as a unit; and when I think, it is not only my intellect which thinks: it is I, my own self. And my own self is a bodily self; it involves matter; it is not a spiritual or purely immaterial subject. The body is an essential part of man. The intellect is not the whole man.

Therefore the intellect, or rather the substantial root of the intellect, which must be as immaterial as the intellect, is only a part, albeit an essential part, of man's substance.

But man is not an aggregate, a juxtaposition of two substances; man is a natural whole, a single being, a single substance.

Consequently, we must conclude that the essence or substance of man is single, but that this single substance itself is a compound, the components of which are the body and the spiritual intellect: or rather matter, of which the body is made, and the spiritual principle, one of the powers of which is the intellect. Matter—in the Aristotelian sense of prime matter, or of that root potentiality which is the common stuff of all corporeal substance —matter, substantially united with the spiritual principle of the intellect, is ontologically molded, shaped from within and in the innermost depths of being, by this spiritual principle as by a substantial and vital impulse, in order to constitute that body of ours. In this sense, Saint Thomas, after Aristotle, says that the intellect is the form, the substantial form of the human body.

That is the Scholastic notion of the human soul. The human soul, which is the root principle of the intellectual power, is the first principle of life of the human body, and the substantial form, the *entelechy*, of that body. And the human soul is not only a substantial form or entelechy, as are the souls of plants and animals according to the biological philosophy of Aristotle; the human soul is also a spirit, a spiritual substance able to exist apart from matter, since the human soul is the root principle of a spiritual power, the act of which is intrinsically independent of matter. The human soul is both a soul and a spirit, and it is its very substantiality, subsistence and existence, which are communicated to the whole human substance, in order to make human substance be what it is, and to make it subsist and exist. Each element of the human body is human, and exists as such, by virtue of the immaterial existence of the human soul. Our body, our hands, our eyes exist by virtue of the existence of our souls.

The immaterial soul is the first substantial root not only of the intellect, but of all that which, in us, is spiritual activity; and it is also the first substantial root of all our other living activities. It would be inconceivable that a non-spiritual soul, that kind of soul which is not a spirit and cannot exist without informing matter—namely, the souls of plants or animals in Aristotelian biology—should possess a power or faculty *superior* to its own degree in being, that is, immaterial, or act through a supra-material instrumentality independent of any corporeal organ and physical structure. But when it is a question of a spirit which is a soul, or of a *spiritual soul*, as the human soul is, then it is perfectly conceivable that such a soul should have, aside from immaterial or spiritual faculties, other powers and activities which are organic and material, and which, relating to the union between soul and body, pertain to a level of being *inferior* to that of the spirit.

The Spirituality of the Human Soul

Thus, the very way in which the Scholastics arrived at the existence of the human soul also established its spirituality. Just as the intellect is spiritual, that is to say intrinsically independent of matter in its operation and in its nature, so also, and for the same reason, the human soul, the substantial root of the intellect, is spiritual, that is, intrinsically independent of matter in its nature and in its existence; it does not live by the body, the body lives by it. The human soul is a spiritual substance which, by its substantial union with matter, gives existence and countenance to the body.

That is my second point. As we have seen, the Scholastics demonstrated it by a metaphysical analysis of the intellect's operation, carefully distinguished from the operation of the senses. They adduced, of course, much other evidence in support of their demonstration. In their consideration of the intellect, they observed, for instance, that the latter is capable of *perfect reflection*, that is, of coming back entirely upon itself—not in the manner of a sheet of paper, half of which can be folded on the other half, but in a complete manner, so that it can grasp its whole operation and penetrate it by knowledge, and can contain itself and its own principle, the existing self, in its own knowing activity, a perfect reflection or self-containing of which any material agent, extended in space and time, is essentially incapable. Here we are confronted with that phenomenon of self-knowledge, of *prise de conscience* or becoming aware of oneself, which is a privilege of the spirit, as Hegel (after St. Augustine) was to emphasize, and which plays so tremendous a part in the history of humanity and the development of its spiritual energies.

In the same way it is possible to show that the human will, which is rooted in the intellect, and which is able to determine itself, or to master the very motive or judgment which determines it and is made efficacious by the will itself, is spiritual in its operation and nature. Every material agent is subject to the universal determinism. Free will is the privilege, the glorious and weighty privilege, of an agent endowed with immaterial power.

We are responsible for ourselves; we choose for ourselves and decide on our own ends and our own destinies. We are capable of spiritual, suprasensuous love, and desire and joy, which are naturally intermingled with our organic and sensuous emotions, but which are in themselves affections of the spiritual will, and are awakened through the immaterial light of intellectual insight. We delight in beauty, we desire perfection and justice, we love truth, we love God, we love all men—not only the members of our social group, or our family, our class or nation—but all men because they are human beings, and children of God. The saints, those men who are called everywhere spiritual men, experience a contemplation which establishes their souls in a peace superior to and stronger than the whole world, and they go through inner trials, crucifixions and deaths which only a life superior to and stronger than biological existence can suffer and go through —and still remain alive. And we ourselves know that we can deliberate about ourselves, judge our own actions, cling to what is good because it is

good and for no other reason; all of us know more or less obscurely that
we are persons, that we have rights and duties, that we preserve human
dignity within ourselves. Each one of us can, at certain moments in his
existence, descend into the innermost depths of the Ego, to make there
some external pledge or gift of himself, or face some irrefutable judgment
of his conscience; and each one of us, on such occasions, alone with himself, feels that he is a universe unto himself, immersed in, but not dominated by, the great star-studded universe.

Through all these convergent ways, we may realize and experience in a
certain measure, and in a concrete fashion, that living reality of our spiritual
roots, or of what is above time in us, which the philosophical proofs make
intellectually certain, but in the abstract manner of scientific knowledge.

The Immortality of the Human Soul

The third point follows immediately from the second. The immortality
of the human soul is an immediate corollary of its spirituality. A soul which
is spiritual in itself, intrinsically independent of matter in its nature and
existence, cannot cease existing. A spirit—that is, a "form" which needs
nothing other than itself (save the influx of the Prime Cause) to exercise
existence—once existing cannot cease existing. A spiritual soul cannot be
corrupted, since it possesses no matter; it cannot be disintegrated, since it
has no substantial parts; it cannot lose its individual unity, since it is self-
subsisting, nor its internal energy, since it contains within itself all the
sources of its energies. The human soul cannot die. Once it exists, it cannot
disappear; it will necessarily exist forever, endure without end.

Thus, philosophic reason, put to work by a great metaphysician like
Thomas Aquinas, is able to prove the immortality of the human soul in
a demonstrative manner. Of course, this demonstration implies a vast and
articulate network of metaphysical insights, notions and principles (relating
to essence and nature, substance, act and potency, matter and form, operation, etc.) the validity of which is necessarily presupposed. We can appreciate fully the strength of the Scholastic demonstration only if we realize
the significance and full validity of the metaphysical notions involved. If
modern times feel at a loss in the face of metaphysical knowledge, I fancy
that it is not metaphysical knowledge which is to blame, but rather modern
times and the weakening of reason they have experienced.

It is not surprising, on the other hand, that the philosophical demonstration I have just summarized is an abstract and a difficult one. The great and
fundamental truths which are spontaneously grasped by the natural instinct

of the human mind are always the most arduous for philosophic reason to establish. With regard to the immortality of the human soul, philosophic reason must use the very refined and elaborate concept of immateriality, a concept remote from the natural understanding, not only of primitive men, but of everyone who thinks with his imagination rather than with his intellect. Were not certain monks of Asia Minor, in the early Christian centuries, indignant at the idea that God is an Immaterial Being? They did not use the English language, yet they were convinced that to be *immaterial*, or deprived of matter, actually meant to be something immaterial, or nothing at all. They surely believed in the immortality of the soul, but it is doubtful whether they would have understood the strength of the argument we have used.

Primitive men did not philosophize; but, for all that, they had their own way, an instinctive, non-conceptual way, of believing in the soul's immortality. It was a belief rooted in an obscure experience of the self, and in the natural aspirations of the spirit in us to overcome death. We need not embark on an analysis of this natural and instinctive, non-philosophical belief in immortality. I should like merely to quote a passage from a book by the late scientist Pierre Lecomte du Noüy. Speaking of prehistoric man, he said: "Not only did the Neanderthal Man, who lived in Paleolithic times, bury his dead, but sometimes he buried them in a common ground. An example of this is the Grotte des Enfants near Mentone. Because of this respect he had for his dead, we have reached an anatomical knowledge of the Neanderthal Man that is more perfect than that which we have of certain races which have recently become extinct, or which still exist, such as the Tasmanians. This is no longer a question of instinct. We are dealing already with the dawn of human thought, which reveals itself in a kind of revolt against death. And revolt against death implies love for those who have gone as well as the hope that their disappearance is not final. We see these *ideas*, the first perhaps, develop progressively alongside the first artistic feelings. Flat rocks in the shape of dolmens are placed so as to protect the faces and heads of those who are buried. Later, ornaments, weapons, food, and the colors which serve to adorn the body, are placed in the tombs. The idea of finality is unbearable. The dead man will awaken, he will be hungry, he will have to defend himself, he will want to adorn himself."

The same author goes on to observe that because the primordial notions, like those of good and evil, or of immortality, were spontaneously born in the most primitive human beings, those notions would deserve for that very reason to be examined and scrutinized as possessing absolute value.

I think that these views expressed by Lecomte de Noüy are true and thought-provoking. A *priori* it is probable that the great and basic ideas, the prime ideas, which are contained in the myths of primitive man, and are handed down in the common heritage of mankind, are more sound than illusory, and deserve respect more than contempt. At the same time, we are free to prefer a genuine philosophical demonstration.

ANDREW SETH
PRINGLE - PATTISON

ANDREW SETH PRINGLE-PATTISON (1856-1931) was professor of Logic and Metaphysics at Edinburgh and an influential figure in the British revival of Idealism, though he remained a critic of many aspects of Hegelianism. He was particularly interested in the philosophy of religion.

*Eternal Life**

In the theory of Karma, reincarnation is not put forward as the goal of desire. So much at least will be evident from the discussion in the preceding lecture. Christian writers are accustomed to speak of "the hope of immortality," and theologians frequently use the phrase "a blessed immortality;" but, for the millions who really believe in it, reincarnation is not a "hope," it is rather, one might say, a "doom" to which they must submit. It is explicitly part of the wheel of becoming; and the endlessness of the process, instead of being an attraction ("On and always on," as Tennyson says), operates on the imagination like a nightmare. The sustaining hope is that, after the lapse of ages, release from the wheel may be attained, that is to say, the cessation of finite or separate being, either by absorption into Brahma or, as it would seem in Buddhism, by actual extinction. It is obvious, therefore, that if we mean by immortality simply an endless continuance of our individual existence, opinions may differ as to the desirability of such a gift or endowment.

Twenty years ago the American Branch of the Society for Psychical Research issued a *questionnaire* on "Human Sentiment with regard to a Future Life," and the first two questions were:

* From A. Seth Pringle-Pattison, *The Idea of Immortality*, pp. 131-147. Published, 1922, The Clarendon Press. Used by permission of The Clarendon Press. [Footnotes omitted, Eds.]

(1) Would you prefer to live after death or not?

(2) If you would prefer to live after death, do you desire a future life whatever the conditions might be, or, if that is not so, what would have to be its character to make the prospect seem tolerable?

The replies received were not very instructive and perhaps not sufficiently representative, but Plutarch has left us his answers to the precise terms of these two questions, and he professes to speak for the vast majority of mankind. "The hope of eternity and the yearning for life," he writes, "is the oldest, as it is the greatest, of human desires." "I might almost say that all men and women would readily submit themselves to the teeth of Cerberus, and to the punishment of carrying water in a sieve, if only they might remain in existence and escape the doom of annihilation." Milton has put the same sentiment in the mouth of one of the rebel angels contemplating the alternative of annihilation in an access of the divine wrath. But the nearest modern parallel to Plutarch's passage is perhaps to be found in Heine's lines shortly before his death; and the force of the feeling they represent will be best realized if we remember that they were written from the "mattress-grave" in Paris, where he had lingered for so many years:

> O Gott, wie hässlich bitter ist das Sterben!
> O Gott, wie süss und traulich lässt sich's leben
> In diesem traulich süssen Erdennest!

The words recall Claudio's passionate recoil from the thought of impending death in *Measure for Measure:*

> This sensible warm motion to become
> A kneaded clod.

But Claudio's ignoble dread, like Hamlet's hesitation, is due not to the idea of extinction, but to "what we fear of death," "what dreams may come."

> The weariest and most loathèd worldly life
> That age, ache, penury, and imprisonment
> Can lay on nature, is a paradise
> To what we fear of death.

Heine was not troubled by such fears: it was just the blankness of death that wrung the words from him. "How our soul struggles against the thought of the cessation of our personality, of eternal annihilation! The *horror vacui* which we ascribe to nature is really inborn in the human heart!" So he had written some years earlier in the well-known postscript to his *Romanzero.* Yet the attitude which these two writers so vehemently express is certainly

not universal. We have just seen how widely divergent is the voice of
Eastern philosophy and Eastern religion. As it has been neatly put, the width
of the divergence between East and West may be estimated from the fact
that "the destiny which in one hemisphere has been propounded as the final
reward of virtue is regarded in the other as the extreme penalty of obstinate
wickedness." Where the theory of annihilation has found favour in Christian
circles, its acceptance has usually been due to a recoil from the thought of
the eternal duration of future punishment. But the profound weariness and
sense of oppression, which the thought of the endlessness of future existence
is capable of engendering, is not confined to the East. In the West, too, it is
found prompting the hope—

> That even the weariest river
> Winds somewhere safe to sea.

Eternal rest is the deepest longing of many an over-driven body and tortured
soul.

> Sleep after toil, port after stormy seas,
> Ease after war, death after life, does greatly please.

Buddha avowedly links his doctrine to the thought of the suffering or
sorrow which accompanies all finite existence, and Brahmanism emphasizes
the emptiness, the illusory character of the finite. But it is not merely the
pessimism of Eastern thought that underlies its view here. Perhaps we should
not be wrong in saying that the East is naturally more speculative than the
West, and therefore thinks out and realizes more fully the implications of a
metaphysical idea like that of endlessness. The Western temperament, with
its active bias, is content for the most part to take the doctrine of immortality
pragmatically, as equivalent to the belief that death does not end all, without
developing its further consequences. Only, perhaps, in connexion with the
doctrine of eternal punishment has there been any vivid attempt to realize
and to apply these consequences. The unendingness of the penal fire was a
theme on which preachers loved to dilate as embodying a horror greater even
than the cruelty of the tortures depicted.

Questi non hanno speranza di morte is one of Dante's most terrible lines.
Yet it does not require the experience of the damned to produce this sense
of intolerableness. It is sufficient to concentrate our thoughts, or we might
better say our imagination, on mere endlessness or pure succession. A personal immortality, so conceived, instead of being felt as a state of blessedness,
oppresses us like a burden too heavy to be borne. "Is it never to end?"
[I quote one homely utterance.] "The thought appals. I, little I, to live a

million years—and another million—and another! My tiny light to burn for ever." We did not require, in short, to wait for Hegel to tell us that the endless progress in time or in space is the false infinite. The feeling is instinctive. It is the aimlessness of the process which afflicts the mind; for it is a progress which leads nowhere, which has no goal, seeing that, after ages of forward movement, you are precisely as distant from the imagined end as when you started.

But this impression is produced, it will be said, only because we allow ourselves to be gorgonized by the idea of empty time and the endless succession of its moments, apart from the experiences which fill them. As each moment of time, looked at thus abstractly, is exactly like every other, progress inevitably appears as a change which is no change. But if we think of the content of our experiences, it is argued, the afflicting illusion will disappear. In thinking of an immortal life we may, and ought to, think of it, not as the simple continuance of a being in existence at the same level of all his powers and attainments, but as a progress or advance in a real sense, a continuous growth towards the stature of a perfect humanity. The idea of growth, it is urged, liberates us from the oppressiveness of an unchanging identity. With ever new insights opened to us, and ever new conquests achieved, there can be no question of existence palling upon the taste. In the nature of things, the process can have no end; but, absorbed in each stage as it opens before us, we need not be distracted by the empty thought of the series of future stages still to be traversed. The future, in such a case, would not break upon us until it was present. It is clear, I think, that we are here on the road to a more satisfactory theory, but the improvement lies rather in the stress laid on the quality of the experiences than on the idea of growth as such. Kant's argument for the immortality of the soul based on the conception of the moral life as an infinite process of approximation to perfect virtue, might, I suppose, be taken as a typical application, from the ethical side, of the idea of growth. But such a process is still perilously like the *progressus in indefinitum*; it has, indeed, often been attacked on that ground. The infinite distance of the goal—nay, its explicit unreachableness—is the thought which inspires the argument; and hence the spectre of the future is inevitably conjured up with all the tension of the time-process. Unless we can rise to some experience satisfying in itself, we are not likely to reach a tenable theory of immortality. And, if we are to realize such an experience, we must pass beyond morality to religion, in which the life of finite struggle and endeavour is somehow transcended—where we escape, therefore, from the implications of the time-process, of which the moral life, in the strict sense of the word, is the typical expression.

Accordingly we find both theologians and philosophers insisting on the idea of an "eternal life," not as something in the future, a continuance of existence after our earthly life is ended, but as an experience, a state of being, to be enjoyed here and now. So, for example, in Schleiermacher's famous declaration: "The goal and the character of the religious life is not the immortality desired and believed in by many. . . . It is not the immortality that is outside of time, behind it or rather after it, and which still is in time. It is the immortality which we can have now in this temporal life. In the midst of finitude to be one with the Infinite, and in every moment to be eternal, that is the immortality of religion." The idea is very commonly put forward, as it is in this passage of Schleiermacher's, in opposition to banal and selfishly personal conceptions of a future life, which have nothing religious about them; and hence such statements are often interpreted as implying that the enjoyment of the eternal life described is limited to the opportunities afforded by the present life. They are taken as definitely negating the idea of personal immortality in any ordinary sense of the term. This negative attitude is, no doubt, adopted by many: they put forward the possibility of realizing eternal life here and now *in place of* the further life which we ordinarily mean by immortality. Schleiermacher himself, at least during the earlier part of his career, seems to have held such a view. There is recounted in Dr. Martineau's *Study of Religion* the touching story of his ineffectual efforts to console a young widow whose husband, according to Schleiermacher's teaching, had "melted away into the great ALL." But eternity and immortality are by no means necessarily exclusive terms: on the contrary, our experience here and now may carry in it "the power of an endless life," and be in truth the only earnest or guarantee of such a life.

It is a commonplace of philosophical criticism that the term "eternal," when strictly and properly used, does not mean endless continuance *in* time, but a quality of experience which transcends time altogether. Thus in Spinoza, where the contrast is specially emphasized, eternity means rational necessity. We know things "under a certain form of eternity" when we see them not as isolated contingent events, but as necessary parts of a single system, each integral to the whole. It is of the nature of reason (*de natura rationis*) so to regard things, and the perception of this timeless necessity is a very real experience. Mr. Bertrand Russell has told our own generation afresh, in this connexion, that "mathematics, rightly viewed, possesses not only truth but supreme beauty—a beauty cold and austere like that of sculpture . . . yet sublimely pure, and capable of a stern perfection such as only the greatest art can show. The true spirit of delight, the exaltation, the sense of being more than man, which is the touchstone of the highest excellence, is to be found in mathematics as surely as in poetry." For Spinoza the necessity of reason is not divorced, as with Mr. Russell, from actual existence. It is Spinoza's vision of the universe as in all its parts a system of divine necessity which creates in him "the intellectual love of God," that supreme emotion which expels all lower or merely selfish desires, because it is itself joy and peace, the perfect satisfaction of the mind *(vera mentis acquiescentia)*. "All our happiness or unhappiness," he tells us, "depends solely on the quality of the object on which our love is fixed. . . . But love towards an object eternal and infinite feeds the mind with a joy that is pure with no tinge of sadness." Such is the life of "thoughts immortal and divine" of which we found Plato and Aristotle also speaking as opening up to the thinker a present immortality. For Spinoza this "eternal life" is realized in the intellectual vision of truth and harmony; and, as he twice over reminds us in the *Short Treatise*, Truth—the ultimate or all-embracing Truth—is God Himself. This is the "intuition" *(scientia intuitiva)* in which knowledge culminates.

But Art, or, to put it more widely, the perception of Beauty, also yields us experiences under a similar "form of eternity."

> A thing of beauty is a joy for ever:
> Its loveliness increases; it will never
> Pass into nothingness.

Art, it has been said, is the wide world's memory of things. Think only of some of the great stories which have delighted generation after generation, the tale of Troy, the wanderings of Odysseus, the history of Don Quixote. Think of the figures of drama, every turn of whose fate is graven upon our mind and heart, "forms more real than living man," who trod the boards centuries before our coming, and on whom the curtain will rise as many ages after we have gone. Or take the forms bequeathed to us by the sculptor's art, or some melody of immortal loveliness. Perhaps this sense of bodiless immortality is most vividly realized by the ordinary person in the case of a musical work, as the sounds fill the air and the instruments give its harmonies and sequences once more a brief existence for the bodily ear.

In Art, as Schopenhauer loved to insist, the objects we contemplate have the eternity and universality of the Platonic Ideas. They are lifted out of the stream of becoming which constitutes individual existence; and in contemplating them we are emancipated from the tyranny of the Will, that is to say, of selfish desire. In aesthetic perception our knowledge is pure and disinterested; our objectivity is complete. "The subject and the object mutually fill and penetrate each other completely." Science, based on the principle of causality, is constantly investigating the relations of its object to other things, and is involved, thereby, in an endless quest. "Art is everywhere at its goal, for it plucks the object of its contemplation out of the world's course, and has it isolated before it. And this particular thing, which in that stream was a small perishing part, becomes to art the representative of the whole, an equivalent of the endless multitude in space and time. The course of time stops; relations vanish for it; only the essential, the Idea, is its object." Our individuality has fallen from us: "we are only that *one* eye of the world which looks out from all knowing creatures, but only in man can become perfectly free from the service of the will." "Then all at once the peace which we were always seeking, but which fled from us on the former path of the desires, comes to us of its own accord and it is well with us: we keep a Sabbath from the penal slavery of the will; the wheel of Ixion stands still." Many, accordingly, have celebrated Art in this strain, as the only refuge of the spirit from the miseries and weariness of the actual world,

> The weariness, the fever, and the fret,
> Here where men sit and hear each other groan.

To such natures—to Keats, from whom I have quoted, to Goethe and Schiller at certain points in their career—Art thus becomes a religion, or at least is made to do duty for one. Such moments, however, of selfless contemplation and aesthetic enjoyment cannot be more than intermittent, Schopenhauer confesses, and therefore Art cannot achieve that perfect and final deliverance which we seek from the misery of existence. For that we must go, he teaches, to religion, to a religion like Buddhism, which inculcates the resolute extermination of the will to live.

It is in religion, after all, that the term "eternal life" is most familiar to us. It occurs constantly in the New Testament as the designation of a frame of mind or spiritual attitude which is intended to be realized here and now. The meaning of the phrase in early Christian usage can hardly be fully understood, however, without a glance at the Jewish apocalyptic beliefs, so prominent in men's minds at the time, with which it was at first closely associated, but with which it comes to be in a sense contrasted. We have seen in a previous Lecture how slow was the growth of an effective doctrine of a future life among the Hebrews. When it did arise, it was associated with the national hope of a Messianic kingdom. "The day of Jahveh," originally conceived simply as a judgement on the enemies of Israel executed by the national god, and the inauguration of a new period of material prosperity under his protection, had been transformed by the prophets into the idea of a day of judgement upon Israel itself for the nation's sins; and with the rise of a true monotheism (from the seventh century onwards) this judgement was extended to include all the nations of the earth. The result of the prophesied judgement was to be the establishment of the righteous and penitent remnant of Israel under a prince of the house of David, or a dynasty of such warrior kings and righteous rulers. Other nations—the Gentiles—were either to be destroyed, according to the bitter nationalism of some of the prophets, or, according to the larger-hearted, brought into this divinely established kingdom by conversion. The kingdom was to be set up on this present earth and would last for ever, and the righteous dead of Israel were to be raised from Sheol to participate in its blessedness.

This was the first form of the apocalyptic idea, but in course of time—about the close of the second century B.C.—it came to be realized that the earth (whether as we know it or as transformed into "a new heaven and a new earth") was unfit to be the scene of such an eternal kingdom: the Kingdom of God could be realized only in a spiritual world to come. The idea of a Messianic reign of the saints upon earth was not abandoned, but it was conceived as temporary in duration (sometimes as lasting a thousand years), and as a prelude to the final judgement which inaugurates the eternal kingdom of God. The important point, however, remains the same, namely, the sharp distinction drawn between "the present age," in which the powers of wickedness hold sway, and "the coming age," when the divine kingdom will be realized. The appearance of the Messiah, now conceived as a supernatural being—"the Son of man" or "the Son of God"—is the event which is to mark the advent, or at least the near approach, of the new age. Such were the convictions of the religious part of the Jewish nation in the time of Jesus, and this eschatology meets us everywhere in the New Testament. The sense of the imminence of the coming of the Kingdom is universal. "The Kingdom of Heaven is at hand" was the text of John the Baptist's preaching, and the phrase was appropriated and applied by Jesus in his own way. The first idea which the words roused in the minds of his hearers was the thought of this future dispensation, to be ushered in catastrophically by the appearance of the Messiah on the clouds of heaven to judge the world. Jesus himself appears to have shared the general belief that this event would take place within the life-time of those whom he was addressing: "There be some standing here which shall not taste of death, till they see the Son of man coming in his Kingdom." "This generation shall not pass, till all these things be fulfilled." When he sent out the Twelve on their preaching mission, he is represented as saying that, before their return, the expected event would have taken place: "Verily I say unto you, Ye shall not have gone over the cities of Israel, till the Son of man be come." We need not wonder, therefore, if, in spite of the rest of their Master's teaching about the spiritual nature of the Kingdom, the disciples continued to give his sayings about it this future reference, and had to be rebuked for the thoroughly mundane hopes of reward and distinction which they linked with its establishment.

Yet, from the beginning of his teaching, Jesus made the inheritance of this kingdom dependent on purely spiritual conditions. He taught not simply, like John the Baptist or the prophets before him, that the kingdom of heaven was at hand, but that it was already a present fact—"in their midst" or "within them;" and, in so doing, he stepped out of the ranks of the Hebrew prophets and came forward as the bearer of a new message from God to man. And the gospel he proclaimed was not a promise of future reward for certain beliefs about himself, but, as every genuinely religious message must be, a gospel of deliverance, a message of present salvation: "Come unto me, all ye that labour and are heavy laden, and I *will give you rest.* Take my yoke upon you and learn of me; for I am meek and lowly in heart: and *ye shall find rest unto your souls.*" It is an insight which changes the face of the world and "makes all things new." Above all it is an insight into what salvation really means. Not a password enabling a man to escape dire penalties in the future or admitting him to great rewards, but a change of the inner man, the adoption of a new attitude towards life and its happenings. The changed attitude is not to be understood as the condition of salvation, in the sense that salvation is something different from the spiritual state and externally added to it. As St. Paul says, "To be spiritually minded *is* life and peace." This, then, is the salvation of the soul, the only salvation that matters, as the Platonic Socrates had already so impressively insisted: and when Jesus says "A man's *life* consisteth not in the abundance of the things which he possesseth," or "What shall it profit a man if he shall gain the whole world and lose his own *soul?*," the words "life" and "soul" are clearly used in the Platonic sense and not in an eschatological reference. Hence we have the antithesis of "life" and "death," so recurrent in the New Testament, both terms being used to signify a present spiritual state. The message of the Gospel is continually referred to as a message of "life," and the change it effects is described as a passage from "death unto life." The antithesis is equated by St. Paul with his own favourite contrast between the flesh and the spirit. "To be carnally minded is death; but to be spiritually minded is life and peace." "The law of the spirit of life in Christ Jesus hath made me free from the law of sin and death. . . . The body is dead because of sin, but the spirit is life because of righteousness." He also inweaves with his statement that other sense of "death," contained in the most characteristic teaching of Jesus, that "whosoever will save his life shall lose it: and whosoever will lose his life for my sake shall find it." This is, in his own emphatic phrase, the very "word of the cross," life through death. We must die to self —to selfish desires and egoistic cravings—before we can find our true self in that wider life which is at once the love of the brethren and the love of God. In this sense, St. Paul protests, he dies daily: only by dying with Christ, "crucifying the flesh with the passions and the lusts thereof," can we share with him the higher life to which he showed the way. As sharing that life, "walking in Him," "complete in Him," St. Paul describes believers as already "risen with Christ." Thus the death and resurrection of Jesus, which he accepted (we know) as historical facts, and his own resurrection, to which he undoubtedly looked forward as a future event, became for the Apostle, as a religious thinker, a description of the eternal nature of the spiritual life, symbols of an experience daily realized. It is in this sense that Christ is said to have brought *life and immortality* to light through the gospel. "This gift to men" [I purposely quote a strictly orthodox commentator] "is not the inculcation of the truth of an endless existence, nor any dogma of the soul's deathless perpetuity, but the revelation of a higher life."

Life, in the mystical sense indicated, often more specifically "eternal life," is the very burden of the Fourth Gospel and the Johannine Epistles. "I am come," says the Johannine Christ, "that they might have life, and that they might have it more abundantly." "He that eateth my flesh and drinketh my blood hath eternal life." This spiritual sense both of life and of resurrection forms the kernel of the Lazarus story, where it is expressly emphasized against the literalism of Martha. "Martha saith unto him, I know that he shall rise again in the resurrection at the last day. Jesus said unto her, I am the resurrection and the life: he that believeth in me, though he were dead, yet shall he live: and whosoever liveth and believeth in me shall never die." So again: "The hour cometh *and now is*, when the dead shall hear the voice of the Son of God, and they that hear shall live." This is the same spiritual sense of life and resurrection as an accomplished fact that we have in St. Paul. The dead here are the spiritually dead who are to be quickened or made alive. "This is life eternal, that they should know thee, the only true God, and Jesus Christ whom thou hast sent." Similarly in the Epistles: "God hath given to us eternal life, and this life is in his Son. He that hath the Son hath life." "We know that we have passed from death unto life, because we love the brethren. He that loveth not his brother abideth in death." "He that loveth not, knoweth not God; for God is love. . . . If we love one another, God abideth in us, and his love is perfected in us." "This is the true God, and eternal life."

The emphatic present tense throughout these passages is evidence sufficient of the writer's meaning. Eternal life is not a state of existence to follow upon physical death, but an all-satisfying present experience of the love of God in Christ. It is, as the theologians say, "participation in the being of the spiritual Christ." The fruit of such an experience (to quote St. Paul's list) is "love, joy, peace." "My peace I give unto you," says the Johannine Christ. "These things have I spoken unto you, that your joy might be full." "And ye shall know the truth, and the truth shall make you free." This is the eternal life in the midst of time which is claimed by the saints as an immediate experience, one which time can neither increase nor diminish, one to which considerations of time are, in fact, indifferent, because we are at rest in the present.

Needless to say, such experience is not the exclusive property of any single faith. Much controversy has raged, for example, round the meaning of the Buddhist Nirvana. The term is ordinarily translated nothingness or annihilation. At his death, we are told, the perfected saint becomes extinct, like the flame of an expiring fire. That appears to be the natural result of the insight he has gained into the root of all evil and the way of deliverance; and the term is so applied by Buddhists themselves. Yet the Buddha himself, when urged by his disciples, expressly declined to answer yea or nay to the question whether the man who has won deliverance will exist or not after death —on the ground that "this is a matter which does not make for things needful to salvation, nor for that which concerns a holy life." What he had taught, he said, was only the cause of suffering and the path which leads to its cessation. The primary reference of the word is, therefore, not to any future event—to what may happen after death—but to the insight on which that ultimate deliverance may be supposed to follow—to the extinction of all the fires of desire and the perfect peace resulting therefrom. Nirvana, in its original intention, is that immediate emancipation from all the passions and cares of life which renunciation brings with it, a state of mind to be attained here and now, the peace which the world can neither give nor take away, and which is the supreme and only blessedness. "There is no spot, O King, East, South, West, or North, above, below or beyond, where Nirvana is situate, and yet Nirvana is, and he who orders his life aright . . . may realize it, whether he live in Greece, in China, in Alexandria or Kosala." Apart from the fundamental pessimism of Buddhism, the words of Jesus and those of the Buddha often strikingly resemble one another in their recurring emphasis on rest and peace. And the language of Buddhist hymns is not so different from that of Christian devotion. Take, for instance, these short examples rendered by Mrs. Rhys Davids:—

Nirvana have I realized, and gazed
Into the mirror of the Holy Law.
I, even I, am healed of my hurt.
Low is my burden laid, my task is done,
My heart is wholly set at liberty.

.   .   .   .

Nor is there any bliss greater than peace.
These things to know, e'en as they really are,
This is Nirvana, crown of happiness.

Religion is thus, as Hegel has finely said, "the realm where all the riddles of the world are solved, all the contradictions of probing thought are unveiled, and all pangs of feeling cease, the region of eternal truth, of eternal rest. The whole complexity of human relations, activities, enjoyments, everything that man values and esteems, wherein he seeks his happiness, his glory, his pride —all find their final centre in religion, in the thought, the consciousness, the feeling of God. . . . God is known in religion. Religion just means being occupied with this object. In this occupation the spirit casts off all its finitude; in it it finds its satisfaction and perfect freedom. All nations accordingly have looked upon this religious consciousness as their true dignity, as the Sunday of their lives; every care and anxiety, this 'bank and shoal of time' itself, vanishes in this aether, in the immediate feeling of devotion or of hope."

It is, then, on the possibility of such experiences as we have been considering that any valid theory of immortality must be based. Their reality is beyond dispute, whether reached in the apprehension of Truth, through Beauty, or through Goodness. By whatever gate a man may enter, the eternal foundations of the world are there discovered to him, and he knows that in his hold on these realities lies all that is worth striving for, all that is of value in his life. The being of these realities and his own relation to them "stand sure" beyond the risks of time and change, even the change which we call death. He who has tasted eternal life is not wont to be troubled in heart about the question of his personal survival; for such survival would mean nothing to him, if he were separated from the object in which he has found his true life. His immortality lies for him in his union with the eternal object on which his affections are set, and he seeks no other assurance.

C. D. BROAD

C. D. BROAD (1887-   ) was before his re-
tirement Knightbridge Professor of philosophy at Cambridge University. He is well-
known in America and Great Britain for his
careful analytical writings. His main contributions have been in the areas of ethics and
epistemology, as well as in the discussion of
immortality.

The Mind and Its Place in Nature*

Ought we to attach any weight to this primitive belief which nearly every one has in his own survival? The mere fact that it is held without reasons is no conclusive objection to it; for, unless some propositions can be known to be true without reasons, no proposition can be known to be true for reasons. We must, therefore, consider the belief on its merits without prejudice. Now it seems perfectly clear that it is not a self-evident proposition like an axiom, which becomes more certain the more carefully we inspect it. Nor can it be regarded as a postulate; *i.e.*, as a proposition which, though not self-evident and incapable of either proof or disproof by experience, has to be assumed in order to organise experience and to furnish a motive for research. Certain propositions which we use in induction seem to me to be postulates in this sense; the proposition that John Jones will survive the death of his body seems to me to be quite plainly nothing of the kind. In fact I think that the belief represents nothing more profound than an easily explicable limit of our powers of imagination. Naturally all my experience of myself has been of myself as conscious and active. There have indeed been gaps during dreamless sleep or fainting fits, but consciousness has revived and the gaps have been bridged by memory. Again, at every moment I have been obliged for practical purposes to think of myself as going to exist at later moments; it is therefore a breach with the mental habits of a lifetime to envisage a moment after which the series of my conscious states shall have finally ended. This practical difficulty, due to habit, seems the sole and sufficient explanation of our primitive belief in our own indefinite continuance; and it obviously provides no evidence for the truth of that belief.

I think then that we must conclude that a mere contemplation of the world as it appears in ordinary experience furnishes no trace of support for

* From C. D. Broad, *The Mind and Its Place in Nature*, pp. 523-533. Published, 1925, by Kegan Paul, Trench, Trubner & Company, Ltd. Used by permission of Routledge & Kegan Paul, Ltd., and Humanities Press, Inc.

the belief in survival. Ought we to hold that the absence of all evidence *for* constitutes evidence *against?* This is a somewhat delicate question. Sometimes the absence of evidence for a proposition makes strongly against it, and sometimes it does not. If I look carefully round a room and, seeing no one, say: "There is no one in the room," my evidence is purely negative; but it is almost conclusive against the proposition: "There is someone in the room." But the fact that I did not see a tuberculosis bacillus in the room would be quite irrelevant to the question whether there was one there. Finding no evidence for a proposition is evidence against it only if the proposition be such that, if it were true, there ought to be some observable evidence for it.

Now the proposition: "Some men survive the death of their bodies" is not precisely in the position of either of the two quoted above. I know enough about human bodies and about tuberculosis bacilli to be sure that one of the former could hardly be present in a room without my finding it, but that one of the latter could not be seen by the naked eye even if it were present. I know very much less about the conditions under which one human spirit can make its presence known to another; but I do know something about it. I am a human spirit connected with a body, and all other spirits of whose existence I am certain are in the same position. Setting aside the phenomena treated by Psychical Research, I know that one such spirit can make its presence known to another only by moving its own body, thence agitating the air or the ether, and thence affecting another human body. My friend dies; I remain alive and connected with my body. Communication with me, therefore, presumably requires the same complex and roundabout series of material changes as before. Its very complexity and indirectness make it not unlikely that, even if my friend has survived, some necessary link in this mechanism will have broken down. Hence the absence of evidence for his survival cannot be regarded logically as very strong evidence against it.

The present position, therefore, is that at the level of ordinary experience there is not the faintest trace of evidence for survival, though there is a pretty general belief in it. The causes of this belief have been enumerated and seen not to be reasons. But the absence of evidence for the belief cannot be taken as strong evidence against it, in view of what we know about the means by which embodied human spirits have to communicate with each other.

Is there at this level any *positive* evidence *against* survival? I think that there are two sets of facts which impress common-sense and are interpreted in this direction. One is the apparently haphazard way in which men are born and die. Human beings are constantly brought into the world thoughtlessly and by mistake; many children live for a few minutes or hours and then die; many are born idiotic. The general impression produced is that the claim to permanence for creatures whose earthly lives begin and end in these trivial ways is somewhat ridiculous. An unwanted child is produced, let us say, in a drunken orgy; and in six weeks dies of neglect or is killed by its mother. Does it seem likely that a being whose earthly career is started and stopped by such causes is a permanent and indestructible part of the universe, or indeed that it survives the death of its body at all?

The second fact which is felt to bear in the same direction is the continuity between men and animals. The bodies of each begin and cease to be animated by minds through precisely similar physical and physiological causes. No doubt the mind of any living man differs, not merely quantitatively, but also qualitatively from that of any living animal; still the most primitive men can hardly have differed appreciably from the highest animals in their mental endowments. Did *Pithecanthropus erectus* and does every Australian aborigine survive the death of his body? If they do, have not the higher animals almost an equal claim? And, if you grant this for cats and monkeys, will you not be forced in the end to grant it for lice and earwigs? If, on the other hand, you deny that any animal survives, on the ground that their minds are not complex or important enough to be permanent factors in the universe, how can you be sure that any man yet born has possessed a mind complex and important enough for survival? The two facts quoted above do, I am sure, exert a considerable influence against the view that men survive the death of their bodies. I am conscious that they affect me personally more than any others. But the question remains: "Have they any logical right to exert this influence?"

I am inclined to think on reflection that the first argument is wholly fallacious. It really involves the illegitimate introduction of a judgment of value into a question of fact. And the judgment of value is itself a rather superficial one. It is thought that, because the occasioning causes of birth and death are often trivial, therefore what seems to begin with birth and to end with death cannot be important enough to survive. But (*a*) you cannot argue from the triviality of a cause to the impermanence of its effect. (*b*) The cause is trivial only in the irrelevant ethical sense that it does not involve a considered and deliberate choice by a virtuous human being. There is really no logical transition from "This is caused by the careless or criminal action of a human being" to: "This is the kind of thing whose existence is transitory." (*c*) When we say that the cause is trivial we make the common mistake of taking for *the* cause some necessary cause-factor which happens to be specially noticeable or of special practical interest. The complete cause of the birth of a child or the death of a man must be of almost unthinkable complexity, whether the child be begotten or the man be killed carelessly or with deliberate forethought. This is true even if we confine ourselves to the material conditions; and we are not really in a position to say that the *complete* conditions of so singular an event as the manifestation of a new mind through a new body are contained in the material world.

The second argument is of course of a well-known general type. It tries to show by continuity of cases that, if a man asserts one proposition, he ought in consistency not to deny a certain other proposition which he would like to deny. Arguments of this kind can be met in one of two ways. (1) We may point out that an argument from continuity is reversible, and that the direction in which one turns it is arbitrary. We might just as well argue by continuity from the supposed immortality of men to the immortality of earwigs as from the supposed mortality of earwigs to the mortality of men. The actual direction in which the argument is used presupposes that we are *already* pretty certain that earwigs are mortal, and much more doubtful whether men are immortal. This no doubt is true. But it immediately raises the question: "Why are we practically certain that earwigs are mortal?" This question cannot be answered by considerations of continuity, but only by reflecting on the special peculiarities of earwigs. (2) When we raise this question two answers are possible. (*a*) We may find on reflection that we have no good reason for thinking that earwigs are unlikely to be immortal. In that case the argument from continuity to the case of men will prove nothing. Or (*b*) we may find that those characteristics of earwigs which make it very unlikely that they are immortal are obviously not present in men. In that case the argument from continuity will also prove nothing about men. At most it will show that it is difficult for us to say with confidence about certain intermediate forms of living being whether they are likely to be mortal or not. Let us then consider the question why we think it very unlikely that earwigs should be immortal; and let us also consider whether the reasons, whatever they may be, apply to men also.

In the first place it might be said that an earwig's mind has very little value, and therefore it is unworthy to be a permanent factor in the universe. And it might be argued that it is therefore unlikely to survive. But (*a*) this would be an ethical argument of a kind which we have already dismissed. And (*b*), even if it were valid, it is obvious that most human minds are enormously more valuable than the mind of any earwig; so that it would not be inconsistent to think it likely that human minds are immortal and unlikely that the minds of earwigs are so. All that we should be entitled to say is (*a*) that it is not certain even that any human mind is valuable enough to be immortal; and (*b*) that, if it were certain, there would be intermediate cases, *e.g.*, cats, about which the probabilities are about equally balanced.

But the differences between the minds of men and those of the lower animals are never *mere* differences of value. Presumably an earwig's mind has very little unity, complexity, or comprehensiveness. Now it is arguable that such a very simple mind is not very likely to survive bodily death. But (*a*) I do not think that what we know of nature suggests any straight-forward connexion between unity and complexity on the one hand and stability on the other. Both the very simple and the highly comprehensive seem to be fairly stable, though for different reasons. The very simple, like the electron, is stable because of its comparative indifference to changes in external conditions. The highly unified and comprehensive complex, like the solar system, tends to be stable because it contains so much within itself that there is little left over to disturb it. It is therefore quite in accordance with what we know of the order of nature to suppose that the simplicity of the earwig's mind gives it a particularly good chance of survival. (*b*) Suppose, on the other hand, that we do hold that the simplicity of the earwig's mind makes it very unlikely to survive. Then we must admit that the human mind is enormously less simple and more comprehensive and highly unified. Hence it would be perfectly consistent to hold that the human mind is likely to survive because of its unity and comprehensiveness and that the earwig's mind is unlikely to survive because of its simplicity and poverty of content. Thus on neither alternative does the argument from continuity make it unreasonable to hold that the human mind is likely to survive. As before, all that we can legitimately conclude from the argument from continuity is (*a*) that it is uncertain whether any human mind even is complex and comprehensive enough to survive; and (*b*) that, if it were certain, there would be cases of intermediate complexity, *e.g.*, cats, about which the probabilities would be nearly equally balanced.

Again, some people no doubt shrink from admitting the possibility of survival to the lower animals out of horror at the immense number of minds which there would be if none, even of the lowest kind, died with the death of their bodies. This shrinking from mere numerical vastness seems to me to be childish. We have no reason to suppose that the universe is conducted in accordance with the Law of Parsimony; and it may well be that the world exhibits a profusion in the item of minds which would horrify the inhabitants of Aberdeen. Thus I do not think that this consideration makes it specially improbable that earwigs should be immortal.

Lastly, the following argument might be used to suggest that the minds of the lower animals are very unlikely to survive the death of their bodies. The characteristic activities and experiences of animals seem to be specially and exclusively directed to preserving their own lives and those of their offspring. If we judge living things teleologically (and, in practice it is hard to avoid doing this) it does seem that an animal accomplishes "all that is in it" when it succeeds in keeping itself alive long enough to produce young and to start them in the world. It is hard to see what "purpose" would be served by the individual survival of an earwig which dies at a reasonable age after bringing up a family of little earwigs. I do not know what weight to attach to such an argument as this. The principle of judging living beings and their parts in terms of a supposed "purpose for which they were made" is undoubtedly valuable as an heuristic method; and it is difficult to suppose that it does not in some way accord with the facts. But fortunately it is not necessary for our purpose to decide on the legitimacy of such considerations. For the position is this. (*a*) If it be not valid, the argument to show that earwigs are very unlikely to survive falls to the ground; and with it goes the argument from continuity to the probable mortality of human beings. (*b*) If, on the other hand, it be valid, the argument from continuity equally breaks down in another way. For it does seem as if human minds had many powers and faculties which are not merely directed to preserving the life of the individual and the species; and that the continued existence of certain human minds after the death of their bodies would "answer the purpose for which they seem to be made" in a way in which the continued existence of an individual earwig would not. Hence it would be perfectly consistent to hold, on the basis of this argument, that earwigs are most unlikely to be immortal and that men are quite likely to be immortal. As usual, the argument from continuity would raise a doubt only about certain intermediate cases, such as cats and dogs, where the probabilities might be about equally balanced.

To sum up. The argument from continuity makes against the probability of human survival only on two conditions. (1) There must be some reason (and not a mere prejudice) for thinking that the survival of the lower animals is very improbable. And (2) this reason must not be the presence of some characteristic in the lower animals which differentiates them sharply from human beings. For, if our only reason for thinking it very unlikely that earwigs will survive be some characteristic in which earwigs differ profoundly from men, it will be perfectly consistent to think it likely that men will survive and that earwigs will not. The existence of a continuous series of intermediate forms between earwigs and men will prove nothing except that there are certain intermediate cases in which the probabilities for and against survival are about equally balanced. And there would not be the least trace of inconsistency in the position of a man who should be practically certain that earwigs are mortal and human beings immortal but should be quite unable to make up his mind about cats or kangaroos. Now, so far as I can see, these two conditions are never both fulfilled. The alleged reasons for thinking it very unlikely that earwigs are immortal either are no reasons at all or they obviously depend on characteristics in which human beings and earwigs differ profoundly. Hence I doubt whether the argument against the probability of human survival, drawn from the continuous series of living forms between men and the lowest animals, has any logical validity. The world then, as it presents itself to common-sense and everyday experience, offers no positive reasons for and no positive reasons against human survival. The only reason against it is the utter absence of all reasons for it; and we have seen that this is not a strong argument in the present case. Let us now enquire whether the more detailed investigations of science provide us with any grounds for deciding one way or the other.

Science on the whole does not reverse, but merely amplifies and elaborates, the views of common-sense on the connexion of body and mind. We already knew that body and mind were intimately connected, and that injury to the former may gravely modify or to all appearance destroy the latter. The additional information gained from science may be summed up as follows. (i) More detailed knowledge has been got of the correlation between injuries to particular regions of the brain and defects in certain departments of mental life. Connected with this is the knowledge that many mental processes, which seem to common-sense to be almost independent of the body, have bodily correlates. (ii) We have gained the surprising information that, in spite of the apparent interaction of body and mind, the body and its material surroundings form a closed energetic system from the point of view of the Conservation of Energy. (iii) We know more about the detailed structure and general plan of the brain and nervous system. What bearing has all this on the probability of survival? We find bodies without minds; we never find minds without bodies. When we do find minds we always find a close correlation between their processes and those of their bodies. This, it is argued, strongly suggests that minds depend for their *existence* on bodies; in which case, though survival may still be abstractly possible it is to the last degree unlikely. At death there takes place completely and permanently a process of bodily destruction which, when it occurs partially and temporarily, carries with it the destruction of part of our mental life. The inference seems only too obvious. I think it is fair to say that our ordinary scientific knowledge of the relation of body to mind most strongly suggests epiphenomenalism, though it does not necessitate it; and that epiphenomenalism is most unfavourable to the hypothesis of human survival.

F. R. TENNANT

FREDERICK R. TENNANT (1866-1957) was lecturer in theology and philosophy of religion from 1909-1931 at Cambridge University. His concern for a valid rational theology and a broad empirical approach is reflected in his important work, *Philosophical Theology*.

Immortality*

Arguments for and against human immortality, or life after death, may be classified thus:

I. Arguments not presupposing theism.

(1) Empirical.
(2) Metaphysical—i.e. ontological.
(3) Ethical.

II. Arguments presupposing theism, to the effect that immorality is, or is not, a corollary of theism.

I. (1) The form in which the question as to human immortality is usually propounded, viz. has man an immortal soul? tacitly assumes that the man is primarily his body. And there are doubtless reasons why this assumption should be ingrained in common thought leavened with science. Matter seems, to those who have not pursued philosophical inquiries, so much better known than mind or spirit, and mind seems to be so much more dependent upon body than changes in the body are dependent upon mental activities. But while science shews the close connexion between brain and thought it does not warrant the conclusion that the soul and its activities are products of the brain, and that they must vanish when the physical organism dies. The sensation with which we are acquainted is mediated by the body; but it is not a scientifically established fact that the kind of body which we now possess is essential for the soul's life and possession of personality. And there is no scientific reason for believing that the soul shares the change and decay of material things. Their dissolution is generally describable as resolution into parts; but the soul cannot be supposed to consist of separable parts, or to be an aggregate of mind-dust. For all that physiology knows, the soul may at death enter into connexion with another kind of body, about which, how-

* From F. R. Tennant, *Philosophical Theology*, II, 269-272. Published, 1928, Cambridge University Press. Used by permission of Cambridge University Press.

ever, it is futile to speculate. It is possible that while the body that now is determines the nature of the soul's activities, sensations, etc., as we know them, it at the same time imposes limitations upon the potentialities of the soul; and that though the death of the body may put an end to sensation it may be the beginning of a non-sensible experience, or of an experience in which another kind of *rapport* than that which constitutes sensation is substituted for it. Empirical science, therefore, cannot infer, from the fact that the present life of the self is dependent on that of the present body, the impossibility of a future life of the soul. Science here leaves room for faith.

On the other hand, psychical research cannot be said as yet to have established the soul's survival of bodily death. The proofs which have been alleged are based chiefly on facts concerning what is called cross-reference: i.e. two independent mediums may write fragments, both series of which are meaningless by themselves but yield sense when pieced together. But communication from a disembodied spirit is not to be taken to be the only and the certain explanation of the facts until, e.g., telepathy of the living has been shrewn to be inadmissible.

(2) Metaphysical arguments for the immortality of the soul, of several kinds, were put forth by Plato. One of these was based on the fancy that knowledge is reminiscence; others rest on the mistaken notion that knowledge is pure thought about pure essences, or is eternal and implies eternal knowers. Perhaps the most influential of them is that (in the *Phaedo*) which sets out from the assertion that the essence of the soul is life, whence it is concluded that the soul is essentially living. Of course, if the soul be defined as the reified abstraction, life, to speak of a mortal soul involves self-contradiction; but, like all *a priori* proofs, this one assumes that the definition from which the desired consequent is deducible has application to anything that is actual.

Kant brought the same charge, amongst others, against the rational psychology of his day. This, proceeding on lines laid down by Descartes, deduced a *res cogitans* from the empirically given *cogito*, identified this *res* with substance, in the most abstract sense of the term, and asserted it to be imperishable because simple or indiscerptible. Plainly this reasoning is only a linkage of abstract ideas; that the soul, the actuality of which is demanded by the facts of observable human mentality, is a substance as thus conceived, and is consequently imperishable or self-subsistent as well as indiscerptible, is a question of fact, not of ideas, and one which the forthcoming facts do not enable us to answer in the positive.

It may be observed that if the arguments based on definitions of substance, etc., were valid, they would not serve to establish personal immortality: survival of soul-substance is not necessarily continuity of personality. Yet it is immortality in the latter sense that alone is of human interest, of religious worth, and of significance for theistic theology. Some philosophers assert that memory of the previous life, or lives, is essential to personal immortality; others, deeming memory to be conditioned by the body, credit the soul with a power to retain the effects of experiences of the embodied life, e.g. wisdom and love, even if memory be lost. This, however, is dogma concerning the unknowable. And whenever immortality is asserted on metaphysical grounds that are independent of theistic belief or exclusive of such belief, as when souls are identified with self-subsistent differentiations of The Absolute, it would seem that the limits of knowledge are transcended and that definitions of concepts are confounded with matters of fact or actualities.

(3) Moral arguments belonging to class I all rest on ethical postulates which, apart from theism, are uncertain or improbable. Thus, one of Plato's arguments assumes that the soul is made for virtue, i.e. for freeing itself from bodily passions, and concludes that the soul is destined to be separated from the body. Another, resembling Kant's argument which is confessed to rest upon a postulate, assumes the final harmonisation of virtue and happiness: immortality is a condition of the realisation of the highest good. But, apart from theism, there is no ground for reasonable belief as to the realisation of the highest good.

The outcome of the foregoing review of arguments which do not presuppose theism is that a future life is not impossible or inconceivable, but, on the other hand, is not demonstrable.

II. With the presupposition of theism we pass into the sphere of probability and faith. Immortality becomes a matter of more or less reasonable belief, as distinct from deducibility from assured metaphysical principles or from more or less arbitrary postulations concerning the harmonising of moral experience. It is no matter, however, of subjective or personal desires, e.g. for the continuance of life or of love, but rather a demand for coherence in what is, as a matter of fact, a moral universe. The world would not be irrational, in the logical sense, were the present life the only life; but it is a further question whether the world would be reasonable, or rational in the teleological sense: in other words, whether theism does not imply human immortality.

Theists are not altogether agreed on this point. Those who incline toward absolute monism are sometimes disposed to disparage human personality, to regard it as unworthy of survival, and to speak of the conservation of personal values, universalised, in abstraction from the personal bearers of them. But in so far as monism is approached, theism is deserted: wherefore, strictly speaking, these views are irrelevant to the present inquiry. Some theists, however, consider that, before we can assert immortality to be an implication of theism, it is necessary to know more than is known concerning God's purpose for the world. The facts and generalisations which receive an adequate explanation in the postulate of an intelligent and ethical world-ground, it is said, do not of themselves authorise belief in the *perfect* reasonableness of the world, but only in so much of reasonableness as we actually find. It may be the divine purpose in the world to produce moral personalities; but it is a further venture of faith, and a venture which transcends reasonable belief, to assert that the divine purpose includes the perfecting of finite moral persons, or provision for the fulfilment of their aspirations toward holiness and harmony with the will of God.

At first sight this representation, that empirically established theism does not imply immortality, may seem to be more congruent with the inferences reached in this volume than is the opposite view. But, on further examination, the conclusion appears doubtful. The facts, of which theism is the interpretation, may of themselves indicate no more than that the world is a moral order to the extent of producing moral persons and the conditions of rational and moral life. But, just because moral personality is what it is, this interpretation seems to involve more than do the facts themselves. If the *raison d'être* of the world were merely to produce moralised persons and not to provide for their perduringness, the world-purpose could be described as moral, but not in the sense of seeking the highest conceivable good: a Devil might cause moral beings to emerge, in order to tantalise them. A moral odrer, in the latter sense, must not only produce moral beings: it must also respect moral persons and satisfy moral demands. God cannot be an ethically perfect Being and not respect the moral aspirations of the personalities which He has called into existence:

> Thou madest man, he knows not why,
> He thinks he was not made to die;
> And Thou hast made him: Thou art just.

The world, in short, cannot safely be regarded as realising a *divine* purpose unless man's life continues after death. If the world is inexplicable without God, its purpose is immoral without divine righteousness. But righteousness is not merely compensating justice. Just distribution of rewards and punishments is no function of the present dispensation; and if the only reward of virtue be virtue, it is no function of the future dispensation. The righteousness which theism must ascribe to God consists rather in provision of adequate opportunities for the development of all that is potential in God-given personality, conservation of the valuable, and love such as precludes the mockery of scheming that a rational creature's guiding light through life shall be a Will o' the wisp.

IAN T. RAMSEY

IAN T. RAMSEY (1915-   ), Nolloth Professor of the Philosophy of the Christian Religion at Oxford University, is interested in
applying analytical and empirical philosophy
to theological interests. He is also author
of the book *Religious Language*.

Immortality : Persons*

Let us now look at some typical arguments *for* immortality, with the same
purpose in mind; we will divide them into three classes:

(i) arguments from duty;
(ii) arguments based on the results of psychical research;
(iii) other empirical arguments.

(i) Certain duties imply (it is said) immortality. For example (the argument goes) there is no point in devoting our lives to the search for truth, or
exhausting our energies in a moral struggle for perfection, if we are to be
completely snuffed out at three score years and ten, when we shall certainly
not have reached our target. Surely it would be much wiser in such circumstances to concentrate on "immediate pleasure," knowing, if not the world,
at least the shadier part of it. So the fact that we recognise a duty to search
for truth, and a duty to press on morally towards perfection, demands that
we are immortal. If we were not immortal there would be no point in doing
either. The argument thus claims that there are certain "unattainable" duties
to seek perfection of one sort or another which, so to say, make sense, which
we recognise as obligations, and which at the same time we have no chance
here and now to fulfil. Therefore, if we are to take such duties seriously, we
must be immortal.

At this point two difficulties are often raised.

(*a*) Do these duties necessarily demand immortality? We might still wish,
it is argued, to pursue knowledge even if we knew we were mortal, and even
if we recognised that we should never attain perfect knowledge. We might
even defend our pursuit by pointing to its useful social implications for our
contemporaries and successors, or we might be content merely to emphasise

* From Ian T. Ramsey, *Freedom and Immortality*, pp. 70-71, 72-74, 75-89. Copyright,
1960, Student Christian Movement Press, Ltd. Used by permission of Student Christian
Movement Press, Ltd. [Footnotes omitted, Eds.]

509

the joys of the chase itself. Even if we were all mortal, it does not follow that we would wish to make asses of ourselves. Even if "tomorrow we die," it does not follow that we shall wish to spend today eating and drinking. A scientist in Oxford might still wish to spend his last day in the labs. rather than in "The King's Arms."

(b) The other difficulty is this. Do we (it is asked) know any of these duties to be duties at all without having to know first that we are immortal? If so, even if the argument were formally valid, it would be quite worthless. For the argument would then fail in what W. E. Johnson called its "epistemic" conditions: we should have to know the conclusion before we could entertain the premiss, whereas for a satisfactory inference, the original premiss, the ground of the inference, must be *independently* known. . . .

Is it the case, then, that recognition of these "unattainable" duties only follows belief in immortality, or at least is only given along with it? If so, the argument under consideration would be valueless, for we could not know the ground of the inference, viz. that so and so is a duty, before we knew the conclusion of the inference, viz. that we are immortal.

But at this point I think the light begins to break. For the second difficulty emphasises that what is being claimed by the positive argument is that, in some way or another, and at any rate in some cases, our awareness of obligation and our awareness of immortality are given together. Now this reflection enables us, I think, to see the true character of the argument. What it is trying to do is to use an ethical technique, viz. to tell a duty story, in the hope of evoking the kind of situation in which our conviction of immortality is grounded. Let us illustrate this technique in rather more detail before going back to consider the two difficulties we have just formulated. We might picture it as a three-stage technique:

(1) First we call up a behaviour pattern labelled "seeking immediate pleasure," "eating and drinking," where drinking is talked of in terms of throat membranes, stomach capacity and digestive juices. The picture is—quite crudely—of a throat being tickled by half a pint of lemonade or Double Diamond. There is no immortality here: everything is as impersonal as the tongues and the intestines in the jars in the anatomy laboratory.

(2) On this impersonal picture we then superimpose a duty story, and for the moment the mention of any kind of duty will do. The throat is being tickled in the inn when someone runs in:—"A child is drowning outside!" . . . and the whole scene comes to life, takes on "depth." Parallel with the example in Chapter II, we must not now suppose that this is merely a case of efficient reaction to stimuli, but that the people speak of "being compelled" to rush out and with an "inward" compulsion, etc. etc. They would speak of being "obliged" to dive in for the child.

Now the contrast between such a situation and that which occurs at stage (1) may be enough to evoke a situation where we discern and recognise duty. That, in fact, was our hope when we used this sort of story in Chapter II. And it is in so recognising duty as something which transcends the spatio-temporal, that we recognise our own transcendence of the spatio-temporal, our own immortality. On the other hand, the light may not dawn, nor the penny drop.

(3) In such a case a story of so-called unattainable duties comes to its own. For whenever such a duty story as we have outlined at stage (2) does not work, these other stories of unattainable duties enable the technique to be continued and practised for as long as we wish. In the case of unattainable duties, the story can always be pressed further. It can always continue until the light dawns, and it would continue like this.

We could begin, for example, with a scholar who after many years of writing and research, returns to tell us, "At last! I have completed my twentieth volume on the Nagi tribes of India." Has he found the Truth? Has he exhausted an unattainable duty? "No," we say. "What you have done is a magnificent contribution to the search for truth, but the search has scarcely yet begun. Disheartening as it may seem, you have hardly begun to pick up, Newton-like, a pebble on the sea-shore." Our scholar returns years later with yet more volumes. But the answer is the same. No matter when or with what results our imaginary scholar returned, we could still say, "But you have not yet reached the whole truth, *the* Truth." And then the light may dawn: then it may become plain what "*the* Truth" stands for—something which no volumes, however many, can complete, something to which no true story, however long, can do justice. It stands for something which no scholar, however skilled or hardworking, could formulate and describe. In this sense it is unattainable—unattainable in terms of discursive knowledge. Yet in another sense we have recognised it already. For we know what "the Truth" means when the light dawns. It is only its formulation which is a never-ending task. We are reminded of the old Idealist phrase that what is ever "Real" is nevertheless always "waiting to be realised." But the very fact that in this way "the Truth" eludes any discursive enumeration, however long, shows its character, that it is something we understand by reference to a situation which is "objects" and more. In this way never-ending stories about searching after truth become an appropriate technique for evoking a situation which, when it breaks in on us, we shall then call "*the* Truth," and see its challenge as one of Duty. And when that happens, we likewise know ourselves as transcending the spatio-temporal, never exhaustively described by object stories. We are assured of our immorality.

So it is that a description of the never-ending search for knowledge will be a useful technique to evoke a situation which transcends the spatio-temporal while it includes it, a situation which subjectively assures me of my immorality.

So what might be evoked at stage (2), and what stage (3) need never despair of reaching, is a situation never exhaustively treated by "true" propositions about observables, no matter how complex and developed that treatment may be. Here is a situation which subjectively and objectively transcends the spatio-temporal. Subjectively, here is the ground of our immortality, and objectively we have once again what is meant by Duty. . . .

Against the standpoint of this discussion let us now see the significance of the two objections to this argument for immortality which we mentioned above.

(a) The question was: Do any duties demand immortality? Surely we might wish (it was said) to pursue knowledge even if we knew we were mortal. Now when it is said that we might still want to pursue truth, whether we are immortal or not, that we might still wish to devote our last day to some organic synthesis or to the office files rather than having a continuous feast, the point must of course be admitted and agreed. But at the same time it has to be recognised that this *wish* need not arise from a response to anything like Duty. What we did in the lab. or in the office merely to gratify a wish, would not at all be an activity including but transcending the objects it contained. Two people might still elect to do the same organic experiment as a way of passing the last day. But for one it might be no more than gratification of a wish: a matter of mixing the reagents, distillation and the rest, when there would be no response to Duty and no intimation of immortality. For another, however, it could be not only the gratification of a wish, but also a response to Duty, a response to the Truth, a response to a discernment. There would then be a vision made up of reagents *and more*, distillation *and more*; and subjectively there would be a recognition of one's self as more than an organic chemist. The organic synthesis would now do more than exemplify a wish, it would symbolise and portray Duty, as well, and the chemist would have an intimation of immortality.

The contrast is then between, on the one hand, merely eating and drinking, merely spending days in the lab., merely poring over problems, merely writing treatises; and on the other hand doing precisely any or all of these, but within a situation which subjectively and objectively transcends objects while it contains them. To express the contrast as the argument often does, as one between duty and pleasure, is misleading. The contrast is rather between pleasure, and pleasure *plus*.

(b) We can see, too, how the problem of priorities arises. If our account is correct, our sense of duty and our sense of immortality belong together:

to discern our duty is to discern our immortality, and *vice versa*. To recognise our immortality (subjectively) is also to recognise (objectively) a Duty never exhausted in object language, and therefore spoken of as "unattainable," being never adequately portrayed as a pattern in space and time. Again, if once we recognise a Duty, e.g. the pursuit of truth or the search for perfection, whose spatio-temporal translation is never ending, which happens when a Duty situation has been evoked by stories of an "unattainable" duty, the same situation reveals our immortality. In this way, there is no absolute *logical* priority between immortality and unattainable duty, and there is an intimate psychological connection. So we can readily see how it comes to be alleged that we only recognise such and such as a duty when we recognise ourselves as immortal. We can easily see how the argument comes to fail over the epistemic condition. But this does not mean that the argument for immortality from the existence of certain duties is valueless.

Indeed, it may be said that in the very fact that the epistemic conditions cannot be fulfilled lies the possibility of the "argument" being valuable at all. For all the "argument" hopes to do is so to talk about certain duties that there arises a discernment of immortality which for those "with eyes to see" cannot have been there from the start. Even so, talk about epistemic conditions is not without its point. For it properly reminds us that we are not looking on the argument for immortality from duty as taking us on a deductive journey which will at the end lead us to assent to the logical subsequent proposition that we are immortal. We are not led to a proposition which pictures the facts, describing a quality called "immortality" which belongs to some "thing" called a "soul," as longevity may characterise a tortoise. Contrariwise, we take a much looser view of the function of argument and a much different view as to the anchorage of metaphysical words such as "soul" and "immortality." Argument and counter-argument in discussions about immortality are rather stories whose intention is either to evoke or to deny a certain kind of situation. If someone did not recognise as a duty the search for truth and perfection, but knew first that he was immortal, the argument would certainly be useless and unnecessary as an "argument" for immortality. Yet it might now be useful in the opposite direction: to show us that with belief in immortality went necessarily a recognition of duty as something which could "never" (i.e. in terms of spatio-temporal behaviour) be fulfilled. If, however, it be countered that (as a third case) there might be someone who could contemplate and assent to the proposition that if he were immortal it would follow that he had such and such duties, or to the proposition that if he recognised such and such duties it would follow that he were immortal, without believing either that he was immortal or that he had such duties—when the argument would be quite useless all around—

I should doubt it. For I should argue that a recognition of certain duties and a discernment of immortality are only seen to imply one another when each relates to a common situation which subjectively and objectively transcends the spatio-temporal. In short, and without prejudice to any general theory of implication, I am saying that we should not see *this* implication between duty and immortality without recognising certain behaviour as our duty on the one hand, and our immortality on the other. Indeed, the "argument" is but talk to get us to see this implication and the situation in which it is founded.

The next argument, with which we can deal much more briefly, points to the wasted effort, the unrewarded goodness and the frustrations with which human lives abound. We may think of the man who quite devotedly year by year cuts and trims his garden hedge and with the same loving care tends his garden, yet on his death the next occupier neglects hedge and garden alike. Or there are mothers who spend their lives training children who grow up to be utterly thankless. Again, we may think of the kindness and thoughtfulness and generosity which is rejected, spurned, or evil spoken of. What sustains people through all this (the argument runs) is the conviction that some day—though beyond this present life—justice will prevail, that the universe is, on a long-term view, good and fair.

But the objection is then made that while the argument might prove immortality *if* there were also prior belief in God, yet without such a belief or some comparable belief, the argument proves nothing.

How are we to assess such criticisms? First let us reiterate that what the positive argument sets out to do is to evoke a situation which exceeds all the public behaviour it contains. This it does by a technique which concentrates on human struggles and frustrations, the partial character of our lives, our own finitude. All the stories used by the argument are attempts to evoke a situation which is transitory and more, spatio-temporal and more, by pointing to the "unsatisfactoriness" of what is transitory. All the stories are attempts to evoke a sense of the permanent, a sense of what abides, by arousing in us a profound discontent with the changes and chances of a fleeting world.

On this interpretation it is not surprising—and this we would say is the important point behind the criticism just mentioned above—that belief in God has in fact always been closely associated with belief in immortality. For it is the same kind of situation which justifies both reliefs; which reflection leads to a further suggestion. On our view it would be natural to suppose that if either belief was very dominant the other belief might be overlooked and even disappear altogether. This in fact is what has happened. People have often been quite satisfied with what has been given to them either objectively or subjectively in a disclosure situation, and have cared nothing for further complications. The Old Testament, for example, is significant in having from the first a belief in God and only much later (and let us notice it was when personal and responsible decision was more and more emphasised) stirrings of immortality. Before that time the Hebrews thought primarily of God, and of their "solidarity," of their group-life. They were too outward-looking, too little concerned with themselves as "persons" to be concerned about their immortality. The philosopher McTaggart, on the other hand, is an interesting example of a somewhat opposite emphasis. Though he accepted the immortality of persons, he would not agree that such an immortality situation as is specified by his use of the word "love" needed any further reference to the God of traditional belief. Indeed he rather suggested that traditional belief in God compromised and impoverished belief in immortality. McTaggart and the Hebrews were thus alike in seeing one half—though in each case a different half—of the whole truth. For it is one and the same situation which subjectively justifies belief in immortality and objectively justifies belief in God. Belief in God and belief in immortality fit together and find their anchorage in the same kind of situation.

Returning now to our main theme, the suggestion is that the old-fashioned ethical arguments for immortality are best understood (1) as techniques to evoke a particular and distinctive kind of situation, which (2) at the same time claims from the way in which the situation is evoked, that such a situation exceeds the spatio-temporal objects it contains.

(ii) Let us next consider briefly the possible bearing of the results of psychical research on belief in immortality. There have been those who have argued that here we have the best of all empirical arguments for a future life. Even those like C. D. Broad, who have been most cautious about the empirical phenomena, have nevertheless talked of the possible persistence of some "psychogenic factor," of some factor productive of "mental behaviour" at any rate over a limited period of time beyond death. Now I do not propose to examine these various claims in detail. Nor is this the occasion to make a careful and critical assessment of the facts. But suppose it is the case (as seems very likely) that after admitting what may be fraudulent, and what may be given an alternative and not so exciting account, we must nevertheless allow that some of the phenomena of some seances and some accounts of poltergeists are veridical and irreducible. What do we conclude?

The phenomena are significant in two ways.

(a) First, they are important in so far as they recreate for many of our contemporaries a sense of wonder and mystery when so much around us becomes more and more taped and stereotyped; when so much of our behaviour becomes more and more impersonal. The phenomena may be useful in reminding us that the universe is a good deal odder and more mysterious than many would like to think. Not for nothing is the spiritualist Lyceum often to be found in that part of a sprawling city which is most dismal and drab. When as infants we begin by drinking standard orange juice from a disinfected tumbler, and continue by taking up a medically approved straw our prescribed measure of milk from an artificially inseminated cow, thereafter having a full account of the physiology and psychology of sex, until at the end we are moved in composition caskets on ball-bearing rollers through synthetic curtains into electrically-heated furnaces—the movement being synchronized with a pre-recorded hymn—we may think that the time has come to give us all a numinous shudder or two. Let my argument not be mistaken. I am not being so silly and obscurantist as to condemn out of hand all social and scientific development. But I am saying that such developments do not easily provide intimations of immortality, and this fact is something with which empirical arguments for immortality need to reckon, as it is also something to which strange psychical phenomena provide a useful counterbalance.

(b) Secondly, the existence of abnormal psychical phenomena can usefully suggest that there is an element in personal intercourse beyond the observable behaviour with which we normally associate it. Even admitting that some spatio-temporal expression of personal activity is always necessary, abnormal psychical phenomena suggest that this element may in fact on occasion be supplied by someone else's body or (in the case of poltergeists) other physical phenomena altogether. This kind of possibility allows us a useful freedom in thinking about what constitutes, in terms of objects or spatio-temporal phenomena, personal behaviour. Further, this very freedom in relation to observables emphasises the point that characteristically personal behaviour is something which is more than the observables it displays, however diverse these be.

In short, the phenomena revealed and studied by psychical research can provide situations which reveal the transcendence of personal behaviour beyond its public and spatio-temporal manifestations. On the other hand, how this transcendence is best described is left problematical and we need not at all sponsor the kind of language about the "spirit world" which spiritualists traditionally use to map their claims. Here is a point on which I will say something—if not very much—in my next chapter, where we shall be more explicitly concerned with the language in which claims for immortality are expressed.

(iii) We now pass to consider three other empirical arguments for immortality. First there is the argument from universal assent, what is traditionally called the argument *a consensu gentium*, which starts from the widespread popularity of the belief, noting that in various forms it has characterized many religions and many if not most civilisations. A second argument starts from the fact that it is very difficult, if not impossible, to think of our entire cessation. Even if we think of our Wills being read, we think of ourselves hovering round to see the look on old Uncle Sam's face when he hears that we have bequeathed to his reprobate brother that gold cigarette case he has long admired. A third argument tries to develop the alleged analogy between sleep and spring on the one hand, and death on the other: as we wake from sleep, or as spring follows winter, so (it has been argued) we shall survive death.

Once again, to mention such arguments is to provoke counter-arguments. With regard to the first argument, there is the irrefutable fact that even eight million people might be wrong. Why should we perpetuate the Election Fallacy and suppose that what the majority believe, is for that reason necessarily correct? Again, to turn to the second argument, the very act of imagining ourselves present at the reading of our Will, inevitably puts us into the picture. We cannot expect to imagine ourselves present anywhere without having to suppose that we are in some way there, if only peeping from the side-wings. As for the third argument based on the alleged analogy between death and spring or sleep, the analogy, it is said, is quite worthless. It is the obvious differences, not the superficial similarities, between a dead person and someone sleeping, which are significant and important, and there are easy and reliable tests by which to distinguish a dead tree from a tree in winter, despite again their superficial resemblances.

But at this point the pendulum of the argument begins to swing the other way. An error that was committed by (say) eight thousand million people of such diverse creeds and civilisations, would—even as an error—be a curious fact; especially since the existence of the original belief could easily and alternatively be accounted for by supposing that for most people, at one time or another, there occur situations which reveal them, at least to themselves, as more than the public behaviour they display.

Again, with the second argument in mind, it might be said that the important reason why we find it difficult to think of ourselves in the future as "not there" is precisely because we already recognise, as we have said, certain situations which here and now are not exhausted by our present public behaviour. This is the reason, it would be said, why we are not tempted to conclude that the disappearance of our public behaviour tomorrow will mean the end of "us" altogether. For it does not mean the whole of "us" today. We can mutter with Spinoza—even if out of its context—*"sentimus experimurque nos aeternos esse"*: "we discern and discover that we are eternal." We can claim with Butler that to recognise "ourselves" is to recognise "ourselves" as more than "gross bodies."

The argument from considerations about sleeping or winter needs a little more attention. As an argument by analogy, any argument comparing the transition from winter to spring with the transition from death to subsequent life, is plainly weak and confused. It is virtually worthless. But suppose that the argument, the story, the talk, has a different logical point altogether. In the first place, let the argument first suggest to us that we ponder the contrast of winter and spring. What happens? Quite apart from what the botanist or gardener may tell us, we look on a winter's scene and everything is drab, lifeless, bleak and impersonal. We are numb and inactive with cold. We even say our feet are "dead." Then comes spring, and the lifeless begins to show life: buds and blossom appear. Green replaces black. Everywhere the scene changes and in every detail. We even speak of nature "coming alive." At this point let us recall that few circumstances are better than change for reminding us of what abides; witness the easy way by which days registering change, such as New Year's Day, birthdays, anniversary days, and the rest, take on a religious significance. Further, when people are moved by the beauty of blossom and spring flowers, they often talk about "empathy," that curious feeling or sense of kinship with something other than ourselves —that *Einfühlung*—that which (it is said) characterises an aesthetic situation. So to make a contrast between winter and spring is likely to be a successful technique by which to evoke a characteristically religious situation, one in which we discern what abides in what changes, what is seen *and more*.

The second stage of the argument takes this contrast between winter and spring and brings it, as a sort of catalyst, alongside a case of death. Someone is lying dead. Superficially (or so we would say) nothing is left but this dead body. But if we bring alongside the contrast between winter and spring, there is at least enough resemblance (despite major differences) between winter and death for an interlocking of pictures, whereupon a situation is evoked around the dead body as it was earlier evoked by the winter-spring contrast alone. Like manganese dioxide, which as a catalyst assists enormously in the evolution of oxygen from potassium chlorate, without itself being directly involved in the chemical reaction, the winter-spring contrast accelerates and brings off (as we might say) the larger evocation, and without being necessarily involved in the phenomena of death—as it would be if we linked it by the logical relations of an argument from analogy. It is as though (to change the metaphor) having once seen some junior archdeacon "come alive" when he exchanges cassock apron and gaiters for linen apron and dish-cloth, one can then see even the most prelatical-looking bishop as "having a human heart."

Once there has been in this way and around the phenomena of death, a situation not restricted to the dead body and other phenomena which it undoubtedly contains, then we are able to "see" that the physical accompaniments of death, the cessation of a certain kind of objective behaviour, no more exhaust a dead person's existence than the contrast between winter and spring leave us unmoved. Needless to say, if the original contrast *does* leave us unmoved, the "argument" has from the beginning no hope of being successful. Nor is it *bound* to succeed even if the original contrast is in itself evocative. For various reasons, there may be no catalytic interlocking. We may, for instance, as a matter of psychological fact, be so impressed by the differences between winter and death that no similarity whatever is recognised. The prelate may be so prelatical that *all* similarities to the archdeacon disappear.

Take now the story of sleeping. Here, too, the argument cannot start by saying that sleeping is like death. Once again, it is rather that the contrast between ourselves as sleeping and ourselves as waking can be used to evoke a "more than objects" situation which in its turn can be used to assure us that death never exhausts our total existence. Whether with the transition of sleeping-waking, or that of winter-spring, the contrast can be used to evoke and reveal the kind of situation in which immortality is grounded.

In the case of sleeping, however, we may express our point in another way altogether. We may recognise that to make a straight comparison between sleeping and dying can never be the basis of a good argument, because such a comparison ignores obvious and important differences between the two states. Even so, despite these differences, "I am asleep" has certain similarities to "I am dead." Neither can be significantly uttered by the subject of the assertions: though at the same time there is no difficulty about someone else's saying of me either, "He is asleep," or "He is dead." With these last two assertions there is no logical or empirical embarrassment whatever. Now, why is it that one pair of assertions—"I'm asleep" and "I'm dead"—is problematical whereas the other pair—"He's asleep," and "He's dead"—is not? The reason, I suggest, is that "dead" and "asleep" are amongst the very few words in our language whose meaning is inevitably and most plainly given in terms of objects. They therefore attach themselves naturally and appropriately to "He"—a person as objectified for everyone to see. So we have no difficulty over "He is dead" and "He is asleep." Each is logically homogeneous, and none of the words needs relate to more than objects. But the case is different when we introduce the word "I." Here is a word which cannot be wholly "public," which relates to "objects" and more. So it happens that when such words as "dead" and "asleep" are joined with the word "I," logical oddities, hybrids, are produced such as "I am asleep" and "I am dead."

At this point it may be countered that all that is odd about these assertions arises from the fact that people who are dead and people who are asleep do not talk, and that there is no more to the oddness than this. That there *is* this difficulty we need not deny. That one of the problems about asserting "I am dead" is that we do not talk when we are dead, must obviously be granted. But the difficulty isn't merely that I cannot *say*, for example, "I am dead;" it is that, while I cannot say "I am dead," there is no difficulty whatever about someone else saying of me "He is dead." So there is at any rate the possibility that these two sentences do not talk about precisely the same kind of situation.

Let me put my point another way. Normally, we suppose that "I'm eating" describes a situation identical with what an observer describes as "He's eating;" or "I'm running" a situation identical with what is described by "He's running," and so on. And the supposition works normally so well that philosophers such as Hume can be found who have endeavoured to argue logical identity between the two classes of assertion. On this view, "I" and "he" are logically interchangeable, so that "I" relates to no more than "he" legitimately describes, i.e. to a series of "objects" or observables, what the eighteenth century called "ideas," what nowadays would be called my "public behaviour."

But what the puzzle of "I am asleep" and "I am dead" does, I would say, is to cast doubts on the logical assimilation which such a one as Hume would have us make. Instead, those who would say that the difficulty is no more than that dead men and sleeping men do not talk, by saying that, in fact reveal their hand. For they are now saying by implication that in principle "I" am no more than a talker, i.e. no more than my public behaviour. On such a view the *only* difficulty about "I am dead" is that on any occasion when it serves to be said, there is no talker to utter it. Whereas I have suggested that there is a *further* difficulty—the mixed character of what is logically a hybrid.

It follows of course that when I *myself* talk of my "running" or my "eating," these words *for me* mean "more" than what any observer can describe: otherwise we would have countless logical hybrids throughout the whole of our language. But this view—that a first person singular activity word tells of more than "objects"—makes no new claim. It is wholly consistent with what was said in Chapters I and II about free will—that my "free" activity is more than the public behaviour which expresses it.

There is perhaps yet another point worth making. Suppose someone says: "I am asleep" or "I am dead." These are assertions which would be falsified on utterance. We may now remark how similar they therefore are to the *cogito* of Descartes. Here again, the very utterance of the doubt, "I am not existing," is enough to falsify it.

Now, as G. E. Moore pointed out in lectures some twenty-five years ago, the *cogito* of Descartes might be compared with the assertion—"I am not saying the word 'cat.' " This is equally well falsified on utterance. The logical behaviour of all these assertions is therefore (i) quite unlike that of any straightforward empirical assertions, such, for example, as "The elephant is not pink," or "Stanley did not say 'Dr. Livingstone, I presume.' " Nor (ii) are any of the earlier assertions false on inspection, like a formal contradiction such as "p and not-p." They are therefore logical peculiars, and I suggest that their peculiarity arises from the fact that they are special assertions about my own activity whose point is to reveal that I myself and my own activity is something more than the public behaviour I exhibit. Who is to tell whether "I" am "actually" saying the word "cat" or not? Is the occurrence of the noise "cat" from my mouth an infallible clue?

But have these reflections taken us too far? Is it *ever* possible then to give *any* account of "I am dead?" Is there *any* way of understanding such a sentence? Can we, in short, do anything to overcome the difficulties which arise from the fact that while "I" is not exhausted by object words, "dead," as we normally use the word, is? To answer those questions let us return to our starting point, for we have plainly come back very close to it. Let us begin by taking "dead" as no more than a descriptive word equivalent to "mortality." The picture this calls up is of all our public behaviour coming gradually to an end—whether biochemical, psychological, sociological, and the rest. We reflect . . . yes, the day will come when, in my case, there is that final breakdown of organic processes, that permanent failure of appropriate behaviour responses, that ultimate cessation of the social round, that pay-out of premiums, that visit of the undertaker. Suppose in this way we begin to pare off from our existence all the features that the descriptive word "dead" covers, whereupon our lives become empiraclly less and less and less. What is the outcome?

As is well known, some become mad, terror-stricken. They are then said to be "beside themselves" or "out of their mind." Nor is this surprising. Because for them, and in their case, "I" has disappeared. They never were more than could have been known with complete satisfaction by the competent and skilled biologist, psychologist, social worker, economist, and so on. Yet with others the case is utterly different. For these, the same kind of sequence may lead them to talk in terms of such phrases as "peace," "Nirvana," "eternal life in Christ Jesus," and so on. What has happened in this second case? Our suggestion is that these phrases, whatever differences they might have between them, have at any rate this important similarity, that they are all used as appropriate currency when the story we have just told, or some similar one, has led at some point or another to a disclosure, a disclosure of my existence as something more than the most skilled and competent external observer could give an account of. To use such phrases as I have just listed is thus to acknowledge that even stories of death can bring intimations of immortality. Even talk about death may evoke the kind of situation which it has been my purpose throughout this chapter, as well as in other chapters, to emphasise. We may even say, summarily, that whether or not we believe in immortality depends on the meaning which "I am dead" has for us.

In this chapter, then, I have tried to show that the justification of immortality will depend on whether our behaviour can be exhaustively described in spatio-temporal terms or not. If the life of a person is no more than the behaviour pattern he exhibits, there is no sense in talking of immortality; if human "life" is no more than its public expression, there is certainly no meaning in the phrase " 'life' after death." For death brings out publicity to an end, and makes our "mortality" complete. Further, we have seen that the arguments and counter-arguments for immortality are all concerned to substantiate or deny this central claim—that personal behaviour is not exhausted by all that object language talks of. We are immortal in so far as we know a situation which transcends space and time. . . .

NICOLAS BERDYAEV

NICOLAS A. BERDYAEV (1874-1948), émigré Russian philosopher and leading lay-theologian of the Russian Orthodox Church, is well-known for his eschatological philosophy of history, existentialist interpretation of Christian ethics, and penetrating criticisms of extreme rationalism.

Death and Immortality*

Ordinary systems of philosophical ethics do not deal with the problems of eschatology. If they treat of immortality, they do so without going deep into the question of death but discuss it chiefly in connection with man's

* From Nicolas Berdyaev, The Destiny of Man, trans. Natalie Duddington, pp. 249-265. Published, 1937, Geoffrey Bles Ltd. Used by permission of Geoffrey Bles and Harper & Brothers. [Footnotes omitted, Eds.]

moral responsibility, rewards and punishments, or, at best, with the need of satisfying his longing for infinity. The conception of immortality has been defended on the ground of naturalistic metaphysics and the idea of the soul as a substance. It left completely untouched the problem of death, so fundamental for the religious and especially for the Christian consciousness. Death is a problem not only for metaphysics but also for ontological ethics. Thinkers like Kierkegaard and Heidegger recognize this. It also acquires a central significance in Freud. It is the problem of death, inseverably connected with that of time, that has a primary significance; the problem of immortality is secondary, and as a rule it has been wrongly formulated. The very word "immortality" is inexact and implies a rejection of the mysterious fact of death. The question of the immortality of the soul forms part of the metaphysic that is utterly out of date. Death is the most profound and significant fact of life, raising the least of mortals above the mean commonplaces of life. The fact of death alone gives true depth to the question as to the meaning of life. Life in this world has meaning just because there is death; if there were no death in our world, life would be meaningless. The meaning is bound up with the end. If there were no end, i.e. if life in our world continued forever, there would be no meaning in it. Meaning lies beyond the confines of this limited world, and the discovery of meaning presupposes an end here. It is remarkable that although men rightly feel the horror of death and rightly regard it as the supreme evil, they are bound to connect with it the final discovery of meaning. Death—the supreme horror and evil— proves to be the only way out of the "bad time" into eternity; immortal and eternal life prove to be only attainable through death. Man's last hope is connected with death, which manifests so clearly the power of evil in the world. This is the greatest paradox of death. According to the Christian religion death is the result of sin and is the last enemy, the supreme evil which must be conquered. And at the same time in our sinful world death is a blessing and a value. It inspires us with terror not merely because it is an evil, but because the depth and the greatness of it shatter our everyday world and exceed the powers accumulated by us in this life to meet this world's requirements. Spiritual enlightenment and an extraordinary intensity of spiritual life are needed to give us a right attitude towards death. Plato was right in teaching that philosophy was the practice of death. The only trouble is that philosophy as such does not know how one ought to die and how to conquer death. The philosophic doctrine of immortality does not show the way.

It might be said that ethics at its highest is concerned with death rather than with life, for death manifests the depth of life and reveals the end, which alone gives meaning to life. Life is noble only because it contains death, an end which testifies that man is destined to another and a higher life. Life would be low and meaningless if there were no death and no end.

Meaning is never revealed in an endless time; it is to be found in eternity. But there is an abyss between life in time and life in eternity, and it can only be bridged by death and the horror of final severance. When this world is apprehended as self-sufficient, completed and closed in, everything in it appears meaningless because everything is transitory and corruptible—i.e. death and mortality in this world is just what makes it meaningless. This is one-half of the truth seen from a narrow and limited point of view. Heidegger is right in saying that the herd-mentality *(das Man)* is insensitive to the anguish of death. It feels merely a low fear of death as of that which makes life meaningless. But there is another half of the truth, concealed from the ordinary point of view. Death not merely makes life senseless and corruptible: it is also a sign, coming from the depths, of there being a higher meaning in life. Not base fear but horror and anguish which death inspires in us prove that we belong not only to the surface but to the depths as well, not only to temporal life but also to eternity. While we are in time, eternity both attracts and horrifies us. We feel horror and anguish not only because all that we hold dear dies and comes to an end, but still more because we are conscious of a yawning abyss between time and eternity. Horror and anguish at having to cross the abyss contain at the same time a hope that the final meaning shall be revealed and realized. Death holds hope as well as horror for man, though he does not always recognize this or call it by an appropriate name. The meaning that comes from the other world is like a scorching flame to us and demands that we should pass through death. Death is not only a biological and psychological fact but a spiritual fact as well. *The meaning of death is that there can be no eternity in time and that an endless temporal series would be meaningless.*

But death is a manifestation of life, it is found on this side of life and is life's reaction to its own demand for an end in time. Death cannot be understood merely as the last moment of life followed either by non-being or by existence in the world beyond. Death is an event embracing the whole of life. Our existence is full of death and dying. Life is perpetual dying, experiencing the end in everything, a continual judgment passed by eternity upon time. Life is a constant struggle against death and a partial dying of the human body and the human soul. Death within life is due to the impossibility of embracing the fullness of being, either in time or in space. Time and space are death-dealing, they give rise to disruptions which are a partial experience of death. When, in time, human feelings die and disappear, this is an experience of death. When, in space, we part with a person, a house, a town, a garden, an animal, and have the feeling that we may never see them again, this is an experience of death. The anguish of every parting, of every severance in time and space, is the experience of death. I remember what anguish I felt as a boy at every parting. It was so all-embracing that I lived through mortal anguish at the thought of never seeing again the face of a stranger I met, the town I happened to pass through, the room in which I spent a few days, a tree or a dog I saw. This was, of course, an experience of death within life.

Space and time cannot enfold the wholeness of being but condemn us to severances and separations, and death always triumphs in life; it testifies that meaning is to be found in eternity and in fullness of being, that in the life in which meaning will triumph there shall be no parting, no dying, no corruption of human thoughts and feelings. We die not only in our own death but in the death of those we love. We have in life the experience of death, though not the final experience of it. And we cannot be reconciled to death—to the death neither of human beings nor of animals, plants, things or houses. The striving for eternity of all that exists is the essence of life. And yet eternity is reached only by passing through death, and death is the destiny of everything that exists in this world. The higher and more complex a being is, the more it is threatened with death. Mountains live longer than men, although their life is less complex and lower in quality; Mont Blanc appears to be more immortal than a saint or a genius. Things are comparatively more stable than living beings.

Death has a positive significance, but at the same time it is the most terrible and the only evil. Every kind of evil in the last resort means death. Murder, hatred, malice, depravity, envy, vengeance are death and seeds of death. Death is at the bottom of every evil passion. Pride, greed, ambition are deadly in their results. There is no other evil in the world except death and killing. Death is the evil result of sin. A sinless life would be immortal and eternal. Death is a denial of eternity and therein lies its ontological evil, its hostility to existence, its striving to reduce creation to non-being. Death resists God's creation of the world and is a return to the original non-being. Death wants to free the creature by bringing it back to primeval freedom that preceded the creation of the world. There is but one way out for the creature which in its sin resists God's conception of it—death. Death is a negative testimony to God's power and to the Divine meaning manifested in the meaningless world. It might be said that the world would carry out its godless plan of an endless (but not eternal) life if there were no God; but since God exists, that plan is not realizable and ends in death. The Son of God, the Redeemer and Saviour, absolutely sinless and holy, had to accept death, and thereby He sanctified death. Hence the double attitude of Christianity to death. Christ has destroyed death by His death. His voluntary death, due to the evil of the world, is a blessing and a supreme value. In worshipping the cross we worship death which gives us freedom and victory. In order to rise again we must die. Through the cross death is transfigured and leads us to resurrection and to life. The whole of this world must be made to pass through death and crucifixion, else it cannot attain resurrection and eternity.

If death is accepted as a part of the mystery of life, it is not final and has not the last word. Rebellion against death in our world is rebellion against God. But at the same time we must wage a heroic struggle against death, conquer it as the last evil and pluck out its sting. The work of Christ in the world is in the first instance victory over death and preparation for resurrection and eternity. The good is life, power, fullness and eternity of life. Death proves to be the greatest paradox in the world, which cannot be understood rationally. Death is folly that has become commonplace. The consciousness that death is an ordinary everyday occurrence has dulled our sense of its being irrational and paradoxical. The last achievement of the rationalized herd-mind is to try to forget about death altogether, to conceal it, to bury the dead as unobtrusively as possible. It it the very opposite of the spirit expressed in the Christian prayer "ever to remember death." In this respect modern civilized people are incomparably inferior to the ancient Egyptians.

The paradox of death takes an aesthetic as well as a moral form. Death is hideous, the acme of hideousness, it is dissolution, the loss of all image and form, the triumph of the lower elements of the material world. But at the same time death is beautiful, it ennobles the least of mortals and raises him to the level of the greatest, it overcomes the ugliness of the mean and the commonplace. There is a moment when the face of the dead is more beautiful and harmonious than it had been in life. Ugly, evil feelings pass away and disappear in the presence of death. Death, the greatest of evils, is more noble than life in this world. The beauty and charm of the past depends upon the ennobling influence of death. It is death that purifies the past and puts upon it the seal of eternity. Death brings with it not only dissolution but purification as well. Nothing perishable, spoiled and corruptible can stand the test of death—only the eternal can. Terrible as it is to admit it, the significance of life is bound up with death and is only revealed in the face of death. Man's moral worth is manifested in the test of death, which abounds in life itself.

But at the same time struggle with death in the name of eternal life is man's main task. The fundamental principle of ethics may be formulated as follows: act so as to conquer death and affirm everywhere, in everything and in relation to all, eternal and immortal life. It is base to forget the death of a single living being and to be reconciled to it. The death of the least and most miserable creature is unendurable, and if it is irremediable, the world cannot be accepted and justified. All and everything must be raised to eternal life. This means that the principle of eternal being must be affirmed in relation to human beings, animals, plants and even inanimate things. Man must always and in everything be a giver of life and radiate creative vital energy. Love for all that lives, for every creature, rising above the love for abstract ideas, means struggle against death in the name of eternal life. Christ's love for the world and for man is victory over the powers of death and the gift of abundant life.

Asceticism means struggle with death and with the mortal elements within oneself. Struggle with death in the name of eternal life demands such an attitude to oneself and to other people as though both I and they were on the point of death. Such is the moral significance of death in the world. Conquer the low animal fear of death, but always have a spiritual fear of it, a holy terror before its mystery. It was death that first gave man the idea of the supernatural. Enemies of religion such as Epicurus thought they disproved it by showing that it originated in the fear of death. But they will never succeed in disproving the truth that in the fear of death, in the holy terror of it, man comes into touch with the deepest mystery of being and that death contains a revelation. The moral paradox of life and of death can be expressed by a moral imperative: treat the living as though they were dying and the dead as though they were alive, i.e. always remember death as the mystery of life and always affirm eternal life both in life and in death.

Life, not in its weakness but in its strength, intensity and super-abundance, is closely connected with death. This is felt in the Dionysian cults. This is revealed in love which is always connected with death. Passion, i.e. the expression of the highest intensity of life, always holds the menace of death. He who accepts love in its overwhelming power and tragedy, accepts death. He who attaches too much value to life and avoids death, runs away from love and sacrifices it to other tasks of life. In erotic love the intensity of life reaches its highest pitch and leads to destruction and death. The lover is doomed to death and involves the loved one in his doom. In the second act of *Tristan and Isolde* Wagner gives a musical revelation of this. The herd-mind tries to weaken the connection between love and death, to safeguard love and settle it down in this world. But it is not even capable of noticing love. It organizes the life of the race and knows only one remedy against death—birth. Life seems to conquer death through birth. But the victory of birth over death has nothing to do with personality, with its fate and its hopes; it is concerned with life of the race only. The victory over death through birth is an illusion. Nature does not know the mystery of conquering death; the victory can come only from the supernatural world. Throughout

their whole history men have tried to struggle against death, and this gave
rise to various beliefs and theories. Sometimes the struggle took the form of
forgetting about death and sometimes of idealizing it and revelling in the
thought of destruction.

The philosophical idea of the natural immortality of the soul deduced from
its substantiality leads nowhere. It ignores the fact of death and denies the
tragedy of it. From the point of view of such a doctrine there is no need to
struggle against death and corruption for the sake of eternal life. It is
rationalistic metaphysic without any tragic element in it. Scholastic spiritualism is not a solution of the problem of death and immortality, but is a purely
abstract and academic theory. In the same way idealism does not solve the
problem or indeed does not even face it. The idealism of the German metaphysics has no place for personality, regards it merely as a function of the
world-spirit or idea, and therefore the tragedy of death does not exist for it.
Death is a tragedy only when there is an acute awareness of personality. It is
only because personality is experienced as eternal and immortal that death
is felt to be a tragedy. The death of that which is eternal and immortal in its
meaning and destination is alone tragic; there is nothing tragic about the
death of the temporal and the transitory. The death of personality in man is
tragic because personality is God's eternal idea of him. It is unendurable that
a complete personality containing the unity of all human powers and possibilities should die. Personality is not born of the father and the mother, it
is created by God. There is no such thing as immortality of man as a
natural being, born in the generic process; there is no natural immortality of
his soul and body. In this world man is a mortal being. But he is conscious
of the Divine image and likeness in him and feels that he belongs not only
to the natural but to the spiritual world as well. Man regards himself, therefore, as belonging to eternity, and yearns for eternity. What is eternal and
immortal in man is not the psychical or the physical element as such but the
spiritual element which, acting in the other two, constitutes personality and
realizes the image and likeness of God. Man is immortal and eternal as a
spiritual being belonging to the incorruptible world, but his spirituality is not
a naturally given fact; man is a spiritual being in so far as he manifests himself as such, in so far as the spirit in him gains possession of the natural elements. Wholeness and unity may result from the work of the spirit in the
psychic and bodily elements and constitute personality. But the natural individual as such is not yet a personality, and immortality is not characteristic
of him. Natural immortality belongs to the species or to the race but not to
the individual. Immortality has to be won by the person and involves struggle
for personality.

Idealism affirms the immortality of the impersonal or the superpersonal spirit, of the idea and value, but not of the person. Fichte and Hegel have nothing to say about personal human immortality. Human personality and its eternal destiny are sacrificed to the idea, the value, the world-spirit, world-reason, etc. There is an element of truth in this. It is true that it is not the natural, empirical man who is immortal and eternal but the spiritual, ideal, valuable elements in him. The idealists, however, fail to recognize that this spiritual, ideal and valuable element forms an eternal personality and transmutes all man's powers for eternity; they are wrong in separating it out and abstracting it into an ideal heaven as an impersonal and non-human spirit, abandoning the rest of man to death and corruption. A realized and completed personality is immortal. But in the spiritual world there are no self-contained personalities, they are united with God, with other personalities and with the cosmos.

Materialists, positivists and followers of similar theories accept death, legitimize it, and at the same time try to forget about it, building up life on the graves. Their views show a lack of "memory of death" and are therefore shallow and commonplace. The theory of progress is entirely taken up with the future of the species, of the race, of the coming generations, and has no concern with personality and its destiny. Progress, like evolution, is absolutely impersonal. For the progressing species death is an unpleasant fact, but one that has nothing deep or tragic about it. The species has an immortality of its own. It is only for the person and from the personal point of view that death is tragic and significant.

Theories of a nobler variety take up a sad and resigned attitude towards death. They recognize the tragic nature of it, but as conceived by them the human personality, though conscious of itself, has not the spiritual force to struggle with death and conquer it. The Stoic or the Buddhist attitude to death shows impotence in the face of it, but it is nobler than the naturalistic theories which completely ignore death. The emotional as distinct from the spiritual attitude to death is always melancholy and coloured by the sadness of memory which has no power to raise the dead; only the spiritual attitude to death is victorious. The pre-Christian view of it implies resignation to fate. Christianity alone knows victory over death.

The ancient Hebrews were not familiar with the idea of personal immortality. We do not find it in the Bible. Personal self-consciousness had not yet awakened. The Jewish people were conscious of the immortality of their race but not of persons. Only in the book of Job there is awareness of personal destiny and its tragedy. It was not until the Hellenistic era, just before the coming of Christ, that the spiritual element in the Jewish religion came to be to some extent disentangled from the naturalistic, or, in other words, that personality was liberated and no longer dissolved in the collective, racial life. But the idea of immortality was truly revealed in the Greek and not in the Jewish thought. The development of that idea in Greece is very instructive. At first man was recognized as mortal. Gods were immortal, but not men. Immortality was an attribute of the divine and not of the human nature. It came to be ascribed to man in so far as the divine, superhuman element was manifested in him. Not ordinary men but demigods, heroes and demons were immortal. The Greeks knew well the heartrending grief caused by death. Greek tragedy and poetry is full of it. Man was resigned to inevitable death; he was denied immortality which the gods appropriated for themselves alone. The mortal human and the immortal divine principles were dissevered and became united only in heroes and supermen. Man descended into the subterranean realm of shadows and nothing could be sadder than his destiny. The melancholy, characteristic of the Greek and alien in this form to the Hebraic feeling for life, was rooted in the fact that the Greeks were able to reveal the human principle but not to connect it with the divine. It was the humanity of the Greeks that gave rise to the melancholy. And it was from the Greeks we heard the words that it was better for man not to be born. This is not the Indian metaphysical pessimism which denies man and regards the world as an illusion. It is an expression of human sadness for which both man and the world are real. Greeks were realists. But the Greek genius could not endure for ever the hiatus between the divine and the human world that doomed men to death and reserved immortality for the gods. A struggle for human immortality began.

The religious mythological consciousness of Greece recognized that although the divine principle was immortal and the human mortal, man's thought brought him into communion with the divine and enabled him to rise up to it and acquire it. This was the teaching of the Mysteries, of the Orphics and of Plato's philosophy. The human soul contains a divine element, but it must be freed from the power of matter; only then will man become immortal. Immortality means that the divine element of the soul forsakes the lower, material world and does not transfigure it. Immortality is ideal and spiritual. It belongs only to that which is immortal in its metaphysical nature, but is not won for elements that are mortal and corruptible, i.e. death and corruption are not conquered. According to the Orphic myth the soul descends into the sinful material world, but it must be freed from it and return to its spiritual home. That myth had a great influence upon Plato, as can be seen particularly from *Phaedo*, and is one of the most profound human myths. It is connected with the ancient doctrine of reincarnation—one of the few attempts to understand the destiny of the soul in its past and future. And Orphism does contain a certain eternal truth. Christianity teaches of resurrection, of the victory over death for every life, for all the created world, and in this it is infinitely superior to the Greek conception of immortality which dooms a considerable part of the world to death and corruption. But the Christian view does not make clear the mystery of the genesis of the soul. The presence of the eternal element in the soul means eternity not only in the future but in the past as well. That which has an origin in time cannot inherit eternity. If the human soul bears the image and likeness of God, if it is God's idea, it arises in eternity and not in time, in the spiritual and not in the natural world. But Christian consciousness can interpret this dynamically and not statically as Platonism does. In eternity, in the spiritual world, there goes on a struggle for personality, for the realization of God's idea. Our natural earthly life is but a moment in the process which takes place in the spiritual world. This leads to the recognition of pre-existence in the spiritual world, which does not by any means involve reincarnation on earth.

The fact that man belongs to the eternal spiritual world does not imply a natural immortality of the spirit. Our natural world is the arena of the struggle for eternity and immortality, i.e. of the struggle for personality. In this struggle the spirit must gain possession of the natural elements of the soul and body for their eternal life and resurrection. Christianity teaches not so much of natural immortality which does not presuppose any struggle as of resurrection which presupposes the struggle of spiritual gracious forces with the powers of death. Resurrection means spiritual victory over death, it leaves nothing to death and corruption, as abstract spiritualism does. The doctrine of resurrection recognizes the tragic fact of death and means victory over it —which is not to be found in any doctrines of immortality, whether Orphic or Platonic or theosophical. Christianity alone faces death, recognizes both its tragedy and its meaning, but at the same time refuses to reconcile itself to it and conquers it. Eternal and immortal life is possible for man not because it is natural to the human soul, but because Christ rose from the dead and conquered the deadly powers of the world—because in the cosmic miracle of the Resurrection meaning has triumphed over meaninglessness.

The doctrine of the natural immortality of the human soul severs the destiny of the individual soul from the destiny of the cosmos, of the world-whole. It is metaphysical individualism. But the doctrine of the Resurrection links up the destiny of man with world-destiny. The resurrection of my body is at the same time the resurrection of the body of the world. "Body" in this connection means of course "spiritual body" and not the material frame. A complete personality is connected with the body and the eternal form of it and not merely with the soul. If it had not been for the coming of Christ and for His Resurrection, death would have triumphed in the world and in man. The doctrine of immortality is paradoxical: man is both mortal and immortal, he belongs both to the death-dealing time and to eternity, he is both a spiritual and a natural being. Death is a terrible tragedy, and death is conquered by death through Resurrection. It is conquered not by natural but by supernatural forces.

Two Russian religious thinkers have said remarkable things about life and death, from two entirely opposed points of view—V. Rozanov and N. Feodorov. For Rozanov all religions fall into two categories according as to whether they are based on the fact of birth or of death. Birth and death are the most important and significant events in life, and in the experience of them we catch a glimpse of the divine. Judaism and almost all pagan religions are for Rozanov religions of birth, while Christianity is the religion of death. Religions of birth are religions of life, since life springs from birth, i.e. from sex. But Christianity has not blessed birth, has not blessed sex, but enchanted the world with the beauty of death. Rozanov struggles against death in the name of life. In his view death is conquered by birth. Life is for ever triumphant through birth. But then death is conquered by life only for the newly born and not for the dead. To regard birth as victory over death is only possible if one is utterly insensitive to the human personality and its eternal destiny. For Rozanov the primary reality and the bearer of life is the genus and not the individual. In birth the genus triumphs over the personality: the genus lives for ever, the person dies. But the tragic problem of death is the problem of personality and not of the genus, and it is experienced in all its poignancy when personality is conscious of itself as a true reality and the bearer of life. However flourishing the life of the new generations may be, it does not remedy the unendurable tragedy of the death of a single living being. Rozanov knows nothing about eternal life, he knows only the endless life through child-bearing. It is a kind of sexual pantheism. Rozanov forgets that it was not with Christ that death came into the world and that the last word of Christianity is not death, not Calvary, but Resurrection and eternal life. Rozanov seeks escape from the horror of death in the vital intensity of sex. But sex in its fallen state is the very source of death in the world, and it is not for it to conquer death.

For N. Feodorov the problem is quite different. No one in the whole of human history has felt such pain at the thought of death as did Feodorov, nor such a burning desire to restore to life all who died. While Rozanov thinks of the children that are being born and finds comfort in the thoughts of life in the future, Feodorov thinks of the dead ancestors, and finds a source of sorrow in the thought of death in the past. For Feodorov death is the worst and only evil. We must not passively resign ourselves to it; it is the source of all evils. Final victory over death consists, in his view, not in the birth of a new life but in raising up the old, in bestowing resurrection upon the dead ancestors. This feeling for the dead shows how lofty was Feodorov's moral consciousness. Man ought to be a giver of life and affirm life for all eternity. This is the supreme moral truth, whatever we may think of Feodorov's "plan" of raising the dead.

There was a great deal of truth, but also a great deal of error, in Feodorov's attitude to death. He wrongly understood the mystery of it. Feodorov was a believing Christian, but he apparently failed to grasp the mystery of the Cross and to accept the redeeming meaning of death. Death was not for him an inner moment of life, through which every sinful life must inevitably pass. While Rozanov was blind to the Resurrection, Feodorov failed to see the Cross and its redeeming significance. Both wanted to struggle with death in the name of life and to conquer death—one through birth and the other through raising the dead to life. There is more truth in Feodorov's view, but it is a one-sided truth. Death cannot be conquered by denying all meaning to it, i.e. by denying its metaphysical depth. Heidegger rightly says that the source of death is "anxiety," but there is a source visible from our everyday world. Death is also a manifestation of eternity, and in our sinful world eternity means terror and anguish. The paradoxical fact that a man may be afraid of dying in an accident or from a contagious disease, but is not afraid of dying on the battlefield or as a martyr for his faith, shows that eternity is less terrifying when we rise above the level of commonplace everyday existence.

Both individual death and the death of the world inspire horror. There is a personal and a cosmic Apocalypse. Apocalyptic mood is one in which the thought of death reaches its highest intensity, but death is experienced as the way to a new life. The Apocalypse is the revelation about the death of the cosmos, though death is not the last word of it. Not only the individual man is mortal, but also races, civilizations, mankind as a whole and all created things. It is remarkable that the anguish of this thought is even greater than that of the anticipation of personal death. The fate of the individual and of the world are closely interconnected and intertwined by thousands of bonds. Man suffers anguish not only because he is doomed to death but because all the world is doomed to it. During historical epochs which were not marked by apocalyptic moods a man's death was softened by the thought of the race continuing for ever and preserving the results of his life and activity. But Apocalypse is the end of all perspectives of racial or cosmic immortality; in it every creature and all the world is directly faced with the judgment of eternity. There can be no comfort in the thought that we shall be immortal in our children and that our work will last for ever, for the end is coming to all consolations that are in time. Apocalypse is a paradox of time and eternity that cannot be expressed in rational terms. The end of our world will come in time, in time as we know it. But it is also the end of time as we know it and therefore lies beyond its limits. This is an antinomy similar to Kant's antinomies of pure reason. When the end comes there shall be no more time. And therefore we must paradoxically think of the end of the world both as in time and in eternity. The end of the world, like the end of each individual man, is an event both immanent and transcendent. Horror and anguish are caused by this incomprehensible combination of the transcendent and the immanent, the temporal and the eternal. For every one of us and for the world as a whole there comes a catastrophe, a jump across the abyss, a mysterious escape from time which takes place in time. The death of an individual is also a deliverance from time taking place in time. If our sinful temporal world as we know it were endless, this would be an evil nightmare, just like the endless continuation of an individual life. It would be a triumph of the meaningless. And the presentiment of the coming end calls forth, together with horror and anguish, hope and expectancy of the final revelation and triumph of meaning. Judgment and valuation of all that has happened in the world is the final revelation of meaning. The Last Judgment of individuals and of the world, interpreted in an inner sense, is nothing other than the discovery of meaning and the affirmation of qualities and values.

The paradox of time and eternity exists for the destiny both of the world and of the individual. Eternal and immortal life may be objectified and naturalized, and then it is spoken of as life in the world beyond. It appears as a natural realm of being though different from ours. Man enters it after death. But eternal and immortal life regarded from within and not objectified is essentially different in quality from the natural and even the supernatural existence. It is a spiritual life, in which eternity is attained while still in time. If man's existence were wholly taken up into the spirit and transmuted into spiritual life so that the spiritual principle gained final possession of the natural elements of the body and the soul, death as a natural fact would not take place at all. The transition to eternity would be accomplished, without the event which externally appears to us as death. Eternal life is revealed in time, it may unfold itself in every instant as an eternal present. Eternal life is not a future life but life in the present, life in the depths of an instant of time. In those depths time is torn asunder. It is therefore a mistake to expect eternity in the future, in an existence beyond the grave and to look forward to death in time in order to enter in to the divine eternal life. Strictly speaking, eternity will never come in the future—in the future there can only be a bad infinity. Only hell can be thought of in this way. Eternity and eternal life come not in the future but in a moment, i.e. they are a deliverance from time, and mean ceasing to project life into time. In Heidegger's terminology it means the cessation of "anxiety" which gives temporal form to existence.

IMMORTALITY AND ESCHATOLOGY

Death exists externally as a certain natural fact which takes place in the future, and it signifies that existence assumes a temporal form, and life is projected into the future. Inwardly, from the point of view of eternity unfolded in the depths of the moment and not projected into time, death does not exist; it is only an element in the eternal life. Death exists only "on this side of things," in temporal being, in the order of nature. The unfolding of spirituality, the affirmation of the eternal in life and participation in a different order of being mean transcendence of death and victory over it. To transcend death and conquer it is not to forget it or be insensitive to it, but to accept it within one's spirit, so that it ceases to be a natural, temporal fact and becomes a manifestation of meaning which proceeds from eternity.

The personal and the cosmic Apocalypse bring to light our failure to fulfil eternal righteousness in life and are a triumph of righteousness in the dark world of sin. The death of the world and of individuals, of nations, civilizations, customs, historical forms of state and society, is a catastrophic reminder on the part of truth and righteousness of the fact that they have been distorted and not fulfilled. This is the meaning, too, of all great revolutions which indicate an Apocalypse within history, and the meaning of catastrophic events in the individual life. The Revelation about the coming of the antichrist and his kingdom shows that the Christian truth has not been fulfilled and that men are incapable and unwilling to realize it. Such is the law of spiritual life. If men do not freely realize the Kingdom of Christ, the kingdom of the antichrist will be brought about with necessity. Death comes to all life which does not fulfill the divine meaning and the divine truth. The triumph of irrationality is the revelation of meaning in the darkness of sin. Hence death, both cosmic and individual, is not merely a triumph of meaningless dark forces and a result of sin but also a triumph of meaning. It reminds man of the divine truth and does not allow unrighteousness to be eternal.

Theoretically, N. Feodorov was right in saying that the world and man could pass into eternal life without the catastrophe of the end and the Last Judgment, if humanity were fraternally united for the sake of the common task of realizing Christian righteousness and raising the dead. But the world and mankind have gone too far in the path of evil, and judgment has come upon them already. Irrational, meonic freedom prevents the realization of Feodorov's "plan." He was too optimistic and under-valued the forces of evil. But the affirmation of eternity, of eternal life for every being and for all creation, is a moral imperative. Act so that eternal life might be revealed to you and that the energy of eternal life should radiate from you to all creation.

Ethics must be eschatological. The question of death and immortality is fundamental to a personalistic ethics and confronts us in every act and every

expression of life. Insensitiveness to death and forgetfulness of it, so characteristic of the nineteenth and twentieth century ethics, mean insensitiveness
to personality and to its eternal destiny, as well as insensitiveness to the
destiny of the world as a whole. Strictly speaking, a system of ethics which
does not make death its central problem has no value and is lacking in depth
and earnestness. Although it deals with judgments and valuations, it forgets
about the final judgment and valuation, i.e. about the Last Judgment. Ethics
must be framed not with a prospect to happiness in an unending life here,
but in view of an inevitable death and victory over death, of resurrection and
eternal life. Creative ethics calls us not to the creation of temporary, transitory and corruptible goods and values which help us to forget death, the
end, and the Last Judgment, but to the creation of eternal, permanent, immortal goods and values which further the victory of eternity and prepare
man for the end.

Echatological ethics does not by any means imply a passive renunciation
of creative activity. Passive apocalyptic moods are a thing of the past, they
are a sign of decadence and an escape from life. On the contrary, eschatological ethics based upon apocalyptic experience demands an unprecedented
intensity of human creativeness and activity. We must not passively await in
horror and anguish the impending end and the death of human personality
and the world. Man is called actively to struggle with the deadly forces of
evil and creatively to prepare for the coming of the Kingdom of God. Christ's
second coming presupposes intense creative activity on our part, preparing
both mankind and the world for the end. The end itself depends upon man's
creative activity and is determined by the positive results of the cosmic
process. We must not passively wait for the Kingdom of Christ, any more
than for that of antichrist, but must actively and creatively struggle against
the latter and prepare for the Kingdom of God which is taken by force.

To regard apocalyptic prophecies with passive resignation means to interpret them in a naturalistic sense, to rationalize them and deny the mysterious
combination of Divine Providence and human freedom. It is equally wrong
to take up a passive and fatalistic attitude to one's own death, to the death
of personality, and regard it as a predetermined natural fact. We must accept
death freely and with an enlightened mind, and not rebel against it; but this
free and enlightened acceptance of death is a creative activity of the spirit.
There is a false activity which rebels against death and refuses to accept it.
It leads to unendurable suffering. But there is also the true activity which is
the victory of eternity over death. An active spirit does not really fear death
—only a passive spirit does. An active spirit experiences an infinitely greater
fear and terror than that of death—the fear of hell and eternal torments. It
lives through its own eternity; death exists for it not inwardly but merely as

an external fact. It experiences terror at the thought of its eternal destiny and of the judgment which is in eternity.

We come here upon a psychological paradox which to many people is unknown and incomprehensible. An active spirit which has a direct inward experience of being eternal and indestructible may, so far from fearing death, actually desire it and envy those who do not believe in immortality and are convinced that death is the end. It is a mistake to imagine that the so-called faith in immortality is always comforting and that those who have it are in a privileged and enviable position. Faith in immortality is a comfort and makes life less hard, but it is also a source of terror and of an overwhelming responsibility. Those who are convinced that there is no immortality know nothing of this responsibility. It would be more correct to say that the unbelievers rather than the believers make life easy for themselves. Unbelief in immortality is suspicious just because it is so easy and comforting; the unbelievers comfort themselves with the thought that in eternity there will be no judgment of meaning over their meaningless lives. The extreme, unendurable terror is not the terror of death but of judgment and of hell. It does not exist for the unbelievers, only the believers know it. A passive spirit seldom experiences it, but an active one experiences it with particular intensity, because it is apt to connect its destiny, and consequently judgment and the possibility of hell, with its own creative efforts. The problem of death inevitably leads to that of hell. Victory over death is not the last and final victory. Victory over death is too much concerned with time. The last, final and ultimate victory is victory over hell. It is wholly concerned with eternity. Still more fundamental than the task of raising the dead, preached by Feodorov, is the task of conquering hell and freeing from it all who are suffering "eternal" torments. The final task, which ethics is bound to set us in the end, is creative liberation of all beings from the temporal and "eternal" torments of hell. If this task is not realized, the Kingdom of God cannot be realized either.

SUGGESTED ADDITIONAL READINGS

Immortality and Eschatology

Augustine. *Basic Writings of St. Augustine*, 2 volumes. Edited by Whitney Oates. New York: Random House, 1948. See especially volume I, "On the immortality of the Soul." A classic pronouncement by an outstanding philosophical and theological thinker of the early Christian Church.

Baillie, John. *And the Life Everlasting*. New York: Charles Scribner's Sons, 1933. A careful and persuasive work written in the Christian tradition.

Bultmann, Rudolf. *The Presence of Eternity*. New York: Harper & Brothers, 1957. A New Testament theologian discusses the eschatological element in Christian thought.

Ducasse, C. J. *Nature, Mind and Death*. Lasalle, Illinois: Open Court Publishing Company, 1951. An American philosopher who has long been concerned with this problem discusses the meaning of life after death.

Hume, David. *Of the Immortality of the Soul*, Volume 4 of *The Philosophical Works of David Hume*. London: Longmans, 1882. An influential philosopher discusses this topic as it is seen by proponents of empiricism.

Lamont, Corliss. *The Illusion of Immortality*. New York: G. P. Putnam's Sons, 1935. A vigorous attack by a humanist on belief in immortality.

McTaggart, John McT. Ellis. *Some Dogmas of Religion*. London: E. Arnold, 1930. A British idealist philosopher affirms belief in immortality, although he does not admit to being a theist.

Niebuhr, Reinhold. *Faith and History*. New York: Charles Scribner's Sons, 1949. A valuable Christian interpretation of man's destiny by a Protestant theologian.

Plato. *Phaedo*. Trans., R. S. Bluck. New York: Liberal Arts Press, 1955. (This is a paperback edition.) This dialogue is a document basic to the study of writings on immortality.

Santayana, George. *Reason in Religion*. New York: Charles Scribner's Sons, 1905. An American philosopher of note sees immortality as rooted in man's rational nature.

Unamuno, Miguel de. *The Tragic Sense of Life*. Trans., J. E. Crawford Flitch. London: Macmillan & Company, Ltd., 1926. (Also published in paperback by Dover.) One of Spain's best-known philosophers expresses belief that immortality is based on man's capacity for "feeling" or his affective nature.

Whitehead, Alfred North. *Process and Reality*. New York: The Macmillan Company, 1936. Presents a theory of "objective immortality" which is applied to man's everyday experience, rather than to a projected experience after death.

Index of Names